Recht und Verfassung in Afrika – Law and Constitution in Africa

Band/Volume 48

Charles M Fombad | Johannes Socher [Eds.]

Constitutionalisation of Political Parties and the State of Democracy in Sub-Saharan Africa

Nomos

Funded by Deutsche Forschungsgemeinschaft (DFG, German Research Foundation) – project number 533972722 – and Konrad Adenauer Stiftung (KAS, Konrad Adenauer Foundation).

The Deutsche Nationalbibliothek lists this publication in the Deutsche Nationalbibliografie; detailed bibliographic data are available on the Internet at http://dnb.d-nb.de

1st Edition 2025

Published by
Nomos Verlagsgesellschaft mbH & Co. KG
Waldseestraße 3–5 | 76530 Baden-Baden
www.nomos.de

Production of the printed version:
Nomos Verlagsgesellschaft mbH & Co. KG
Waldseestraße 3–5 | 76530 Baden-Baden

ISBN 978-3-7560-3353-9 (Print)
ISBN 978-3-7489-6316-5 (ePDF)
DOI https://doi.org/10.5771/9783748963165

Online Version
Nomos eLibrary

Foreword

Scholars ascribe extensive tasks to political parties in representative democracies that other institutions are unable to fulfil. This description of tasks leads to the realisation that democracies without functioning political parties are inconceivable and, according to the current state of knowledge, also impossible. Institutions such as the Konrad Adenauer Foundation have therefore made co-operation with and support for political parties a focal point of their promotion activities with regard to global democracy. Promotion of and co-operation with political parties is thus first and foremost the promotion of democracy.

Although the theoretical importance of political parties is hardly controversial, their actual performance in representative democracies is often criticised, and not always without justification. The anchoring of parties in society and the population's approval of them vary considerably. Criticism of political parties culminates in the accusation that they are dominated by their own interests in power, posts, and money and that they lack problem-solving competency. For their part, political parties point out that there is insufficient willingness in society to get involved in party politics, that funding for party activities is uncertain or inadequate, and that parties lack adequate legal anchorage, all of which makes their work more difficult.

Germany is a positive example with regard to the framework conditions for party politics. The special importance of political parties to democracy is explicitly recognised, and parties are secured by Article 21 of the German Basic Law as a necessary component of the free democratic order at a constitutional level. Their rights and duties, their funding and their tasks, are described in a separate law, the Political Parties Act. Furthermore, only the Federal Constitutional Court has the power to ban political parties. Nonetheless, there is also so-called party disenchantment in Germany, and willingness to get involved in political parties or become a member of a party is decreasing.

The situation of political parties in Africa appears even more complex. Here, the wave of democratisation in the 1990s has led to a highly dynamic development of the party landscape, which is fundamentally positive but has not always been without risk. Among the extreme examples of these risks was Rwanda in the early 1990s, where the inexperienced handling of political competition in a multiparty system intensified pre-existing ethnic conflict and thus increased the risk of it turning violent.

In many African states, the introduction of multiparty systems led to the exuberant formation of political parties with only a limited capacity for political work. Wherever access to parliament was not restricted by blocking clauses, the large number of small parties was also reflected in the parliaments, where micro-factions emerged that fulfil the requirements of parliamentary work only to a very limited extent.

Among the greatest challenges to effective political-party functioning in Africa are internal party conflicts, which usually arise from a lack of internal democracy. Such conflicts often lead to splitting and further fragmentation of the party system. They also weaken confidence in parties because political parties that are incapable of resolving their own conflicts are not trustworthy in resolving societal conflicts. In extreme cases, such as in Tunisia, this loss of trust in political parties has led to their being regarded as useless by large sections of the population – indeed, a presidential candidate was elected who mobilised against the party system and was himself not supported by a political party.

Not all countries on the continent that consider themselves democracies allow political parties to operate freely. This applies in particular to opposition parties, which are often subject to legal and financial restrictions and also have significantly less access to the media than do ruling parties. Political work in an African opposition party can pose a significant risk for politicians, especially if the judiciary is not independent. Moreover, there seems to be no limit to the inventiveness of authoritarian regimes in developing instruments to suppress opposition forces.

Poor framework conditions for party activity and the suspension of political competition through repression of opposition parties have dramatic consequences for a country's democracy and development. If it is not possible for responsible political parties, representing their respective interests, to negotiate and resolve societal conflicts between themselves, these often remain unresolved or, in the worst case, become violent. Unfortunately, there are all too many examples in Africa of such violent conflicts that could be prevented by a functioning party democracy.

Proceeding on the premise that democracies need functioning political parties, this edited volume deals with the constitutional mandate of political parties in regard to the special role they play in contributing to the functioning of the democratic system. Using 12 case studies reflective of the diversity of the African continent, the volume explores the regional and international context of political-party constitutionalisation and the significance that such constitutionalisation has for the development of multiparty systems, for parties in dominant-party systems, for party funding, and for the work of opposition parties. The case studies make it clear that anchoring parties in constitutions is an essential condition for the success of multiparty democracies.

This publication offers numerous insights, ideas, and arguments that support the development and consolidation of multiparty systems in Africa. The publishers and authors deserve credit for having made an important contribution with this publication to the promotion and consolidation of African democracies.

Holger Dix, Konrad Adenauer Foundation

Preface

The global crisis of democracy deepened in 2024, widely hailed as one of the biggest election years in history, with citizens in more than 65 countries around the world going to the polls. Despite this singular testimony to the routinisation of elections, the existence of constitutional and legal frameworks guaranteeing that political parties can compete freely for power does not appear to have led to genuine multipartyism. This is particularly the case in Africa, which has witnessed a democratic decline in recent years. While there are many reasons for this, at the heart of the problem is a crisis facing political parties in sub-Saharan Africa. Barely three decades after their revival on the sub-continent, systems of multiparty democracy have been captured and manipulated by elites in dominant parties, seemingly reincarnating the one-party institutions of yesteryear and threatening to erode the limited progress made since the 1990s.

This edited volume arises out of concern for the role of political parties in sustaining democracy and constitutionalism in sub-Saharan Africa. Its genesis was also informed by the realisation that there are few theoretical and comparative studies of this critical issue. The objective of the volume is thus to stimulate discussion and understanding of the challenges impeding genuine political-party participation in governance and the adverse impact this is having on democracy and constitutionalism. What has become clear, overall, is that the move from a one-party system to a proliferation of parties overshadowed by a dominant party is unlikely to help the sub-continent's faltering transition to democracy that began in the 1990s.

In concrete terms, this volume originated in a research project designed and coordinated at the Institute for International and Comparative Law in Africa at the Faculty of Law, University of Pretoria, during a Walter Benjamin Fellowship generously funded by the German Research Foundation (DFG). The resultant edited volume is in turn a joint effort by contributors from across sub-Saharan Africa and beyond. Most of the chapters are based on papers presented at an international conference held at the Future Africa Campus of the University of Pretoria in April 2024. We are grateful to the Konrad Adenauer Stiftung (KAS), and in particular Holger Dix, Head of the Regional Programme Political Dialogue Sub-Saharan Africa, for supporting the conference as well as for co-funding the publication together with the DFG. We also wish to thank Sabeeha Majid, Angel Ekata and Nathan Mukoma for helping to organise the event.

Our gratitude goes, furthermore, to Rowland Cole and André Gilles, who provided additional comments on the case studies of Liberia and Germany, respectively. Following an extensive review process, all of the chapters were excellently copy-edited by André Wiesner. At Nomos, we would like to thank Johannes Rux and Josef Herbasch, as well as Oliver C Ruppel, one of the series editors of *Recht und Verfassung in Afrika – Law and Constitution in Africa*. Given that this work is the product of collaboration between a Cameroonian and a German scholar, we could not have found a better home for our co-edited volume than a series dedicated to enhancing academic discourse on comparative law between Africa and Europe.

Charles M Fombad
Johannes Socher
Pretoria 2025

Table of Contents

Chapter 1 Introduction

Charles M Fombad and Johannes Socher

A fundamental requirement for the existence of a modern representative democracy is the presence of political parties that are allowed to compete freely for power. As Elmer Eric Schattschneider famously remarked more than eighty years ago, "modern democracy is unthinkable save in terms of parties".[1] These sentiments were echoed in 1976 by a bi-partisan organisation in the United States, the Committee for Party Renewal, when it declared, "Without parties there can be no organized and coherent politics ... When politics lacks coherence, there can be no accountable democracy."[2]

Accordingly, state institutions, structures, organisations, and constitutional and legal frameworks need to be designed in such a way that they empower political parties to compete freely as well as protect them against partisan manipulation aimed at preventing fair competition. However, although it seems almost impossible to understand the functioning of different institutional arrangements without a proper grasp of the party systems in which they operate, political parties until recently have received little attention in the global discourse on constitutions and constitutionalism.[3] Over the past few years, that has changed, and the field is attracting ever greater interest. This edited volume seeks to contribute to the growing scholarship on political parties and constitutionalism by providing a rich account of the political-party and constitutional experiences of sub-Saharan Africa.[4]

---

1 EE Schattschneider, *Party Government,* London, Routledge (1942), p 1.

2 Cited in JK White, "EE Schattschneider and the Responsible Party Model", 25 (1992) *Political Science and Politics,* pp 167–171, 169.

3 See, for example, R Masterman and R Schütze (eds.), *Cambridge Companion to Comparative Constitutional Law,* Cambridge, Cambridge University Press (2019), which lacks a chapter specifically on political parties and refers to them only in the context of parliaments.

4 See, for example, TG Daly and B Christopher, "Parties Versus Democracy: Addressing Today's Political Party Threats to Democratic Rule", 18 (2020) *International Journal of Constitutional Law,* pp 509–538; T Khaitan, "Political Parties in Constitutional Theory", 73 (2020) *Current Legal Problems,* pp 89–125; and, most recently, the chapters relevant to political parties in T Ginsburg, AZ Huq, and T Khaitan (eds.), *The En-*

Since the reintroduction of multipartyism in Africa in the 1990s, political parties have been the main vehicle of democratisation. This has been underlain by the formal recognition of party pluralism in almost all of Africa's new or substantially revised post-1990 constitutions. Yet while these reforms may have marked the end of the one-party era, their effectiveness in promoting free, fair, and competitive multiparty elections has depended both on the nature and extent of the constitutional entrenchment of parties' rights and obligations and on the manner in which constitutional prescripts are actualised in practice. The critical issue today is whether this combination of entrenchment and implementation has indeed served to foster democracy, good governance, and constitutionalism.

The current global trend in democratic backsliding has seen the use of many novel and sophisticated measures to undermine democracy. This has been particularly acute in Africa, and is a clear indication that the proliferation of political parties and the expansion of political space has not brought about genuine democracy or political stability. In fact, the ominous signs of authoritarian mobilisation and resurgence that has seen several coups in the last few years in countries such as Burkina Faso, Gabon, Guinea, Mali and Niger, the prohibition of political parties and the return to the pre-1990 repressive authoritarian systems, underscore the weak foundations of democracy in Africa.

In spite of some general studies on political parties in Africa,[5] there has been no comprehensive and systematic study of the impact of the post-1990 wave of political party constitutionalisation on the present state of democratisation on the continent. Nevertheless, preliminary research on this suggests that the legal framework that paved the way for democratisation in the early 1990s might not be robust enough to ensure a credible and sustainable system of multiparty democracy in which opposition parties and ruling parties can compete on an equal basis.[6]

---

trenchment of Democracy: The Comparative Constitutional Design of Elections, Parties and Voting, Cambridge, Cambridge University Press (2024).

5 See, for example, M Salih (ed.), *African Political Parties: Evolution, Institutionalisation and Governance*, London, Pluto Press (2003); P Nordlund and M Salih, *Political Parties in Africa: Challenges for Sustained Multiparty Democracy*, Stockholm, International IDEA (2007); M Bogaards, "Political Parties in Sub-Saharan Africa", in N Carter, D Keith, GM Sindre, and S Vasilopoulou (eds.), *The Routledge Handbook of Political Parties*, London, Routledge (2023), pp 392–402.

6 See CM Fombad, "Conceptualising a Framework for Inclusive, Fair and Robust Multiparty Democracy in Africa: The Constitutionalisation of the Right of Political Parties",

Building on such research, this volume expands the understanding of political-party constitutionalisation and its impact on the prospects for constitutionalism in sub-Saharan Africa by situating it in the wider context of international and regional standards and drawing on the constitutional experiences of a number of countries. The 12 countries selected for study reflect the region's diversity in terms of colonial experience, legal and constitutional tradition, and political system, as well as governance ranking and level of respect for civil and political rights according to indicators developed by the Mo Ibrahim Foundation and Freedom House (see Table 1).

Table 1: Comparative diversity indicators of countries covered

Country	Legal tradition	System of government	Level of respect for civil and political rights	Governance ranking (within 54 African countries)
Cameroon	Bi-jural	Presidential	15: Not free	39
Ethiopia	Civil law	Parliamentary	20: Not free	29
Kenya	Common law	Presidential	52: Partly free	10
Liberia	Common law	Presidential	64: Partly free	20
Mauritius	Mixed	Parliamentary	85: Free	2
Mozambique	Civil law	Presidential	44: Partly free	28
Nigeria	Common law	Presidential	44: Partly free	33
Rwanda	Civil law	Presidential	23: Not free	14
Senegal	Civil law	Presidential	67: Partly free	11
South Africa	Mixed	Parliamentary	79: Free	4
Uganda	Common law	Presidential	34: Not free	26
Zimbabwe	Mixed	Presidential	27: Not free	31

Sources: Data on respect for civil and political rights sourced from Freedom House, Freedom in the World 2024*; governance rankings sourced from Mo Ibrahim Foundation,* 2024 Ibrahim Index of African Governance – Index Report[7]

---

48 (2015) *World Comparative Law*, pp 3–27; CM Fombad, "Political Party Constitutionalisation in Africa: Trends and Prospects for Deepening Constitutionalisation", in R Dixon, T Ginsburg, and A Abebe (eds.), *Comparative Constitutional Law in Africa*, Cheltenham, Edward Elgar (2022), pp 109–135.

7 For a detailed explanation of how the Freedom House rankings are determined, see Freedom House, "Freedom in the World Research Methodology", https://freedomhouse.org/sites/default/files/2024-02/FIW_2024_DigitalBooklet.pdf (accessed 1 January 2025). The designations "free", "partly free" and "not free" based on an overall score

From this table, it is clear that, on its own, multipartyism and its constitutional entrenchment is not a guarantee for democracy or constitutionalism, let alone development – it may even operate in a way that counters all three of these objectives. What matters is not just the nature of the constitutional entrenchment, but also how effectively the resultant legal framework is implemented in practice.

This volume is divided into five parts. Part 1 provides an overview of the regional and international instruments that have influenced the approach adopted in entrenching political parties in African constitutions. Parts 2 to 4 contain country case studies that examine various aspects of political-party constitutionalisation:

- the constitutional and statutory regulatory framework in place and whether it provides an impartial and neutral framework for people to freely join or form political parties;
- the extent to which the regulatory framework recognises and protects political parties;
- the evolution of political parties since the reintroduction of multipartyism;
- if a dominant party exists, the extent to which it is able to capture and control state resources;
- whether the regulatory framework ensures internal democracy within political parties;
- whether the main regulatory bodies discharge their functions in an objective and neutral manner;
- the funding of political parties;
- the main challenges that prevent parties from playing an effective role in the governance of the country; and
- the prospects for the future and the wider implications of these aspects for the state of democracy.

Part 1 begins with Chapter 2, where Charles Fombad provides an overview of political-party constitutionalisation under contemporary African constitutions. He starts by indicating that the reintroduction of multipartyism in Africa from the 1990s led many to assume that this would bring an end to

for civil and political rights. Each designation is preceded by a number indicating the country's score out of 100. As regards the Ibrahim Index, it measures governance performance in 54 African countries and ranks them according to their results. See, https://mo.ibrahim.foundation/sites/default/files/2024-10/2024-index-report.pdf (accessed 1 January 2025).

the dark era of one-party dictatorships and pave the way for an ethos of democracy and constitutionalism. Fombad refers to surveys showing that there is strong support by Africans for political parties to compete freely for power. However, the expansion of political space, and the proliferation of political parties that has seen the routinisation of elections, has not led to genuine multipartyism. The signs of global democratic recession seen in the last few years strongly suggest that the routinisation of multiparty elections has not provided the impetus for democratic governance.

Fombad identifies fundamental principles and institutions that have formed the core aspects of political-party constitutionalisation in Africa in the last three decades. He maps out the general trend in the expansion of political space and participation to see how this reflects the present decline in the quality of democracy. Fombad examines the emergence and evolution of African parties, highlighting why the constitutional entrenchment of parties is an imperative in any country that aspires to establish a genuine multiparty democratic system. Next, he considers the nature and extent to which African constitutions have entrenched the type of regulatory environment which is conducive to the effective functioning and consolidation of democracy. After discussing trends and tendencies in political-party constitutionalisation, Fombad concludes that the effectiveness of this constitutionalisation depends not only on its scope and depth but also its full implementation.

Mai Cheng, in Chapter 3, provides a response to the arguments presented by Fombad. In doing so, he highlights the challenges faced by African countries in replicating Western-style political systems which, he argues, often result in dysfunctional governance due to differing socio-economic environments. As Cheng shows, despite the introduction of multiparty politics in the 1990s, African political systems continue to struggle with genuine democratisation. He explores the limitations of externally imposed institutional forms, the high cost of political systems in underdeveloped economies, and the manipulation of political frameworks by self-interested leaders. Cheng argues that the current institutional designs, while theoretically sound, have not fully addressed the underlying socio-economic conditions required for their effective functioning. In discussing potential directions for future reform, he emphasises the importance of decentralised governance and a tailored approach that considers Africa's unique challenges and historical context.

In Chapter 4, Charles Fombad and Johannes Socher examine the regional standards for regulating political parties in Africa. The authors begin by pointing out that parties are essentially national institutions and hence liable to regulation by national constitutions and domestic laws. However, since the end of the Cold War, the capacity of domestic laws to serve as the exclusive framework for self-governing practices within the state has diminished. Globalisation, liberalisation, and regionalism have underscored not only the need for strong linkages between states, regions, and societies, but also the fact that most political and economic crises today have international effects that call for common solutions. This has resulted in the internationalisation of constitutional law through the incorporation of international and regional standards of good governance, democracy, and constitutionalism.

The chapter thus focuses on the African regional and sub-regional standards for regulating political parties, and examines the nature and scope of the regulatory principles that these regional and sub-regional standards have set. It considers the extent to which these have, or could, influence the constitutionalisation of political parties on the continent and whether there is any scope for such standards not only to complement domestic regulations but also compensate for any weaknesses, actual or perceived, in the domestic regulatory framework of political parties. The chapter highlights key features of the African regional and sub-regional normative frameworks and discusses some of the effects of these supranational standards on national practice. It concludes that although some welcome new initiatives are under way, a more proactive approach by the African Union and its regional economic communities could enhance the adoption by African states of constitutional measures to enable political parties play a more effective role in governance.

Part 1 ends with Chapter 5, in which Johannes Socher examines international standards and the experience of continental Europe with the constitutionalisation of political parties. The chapter outlines the relevant international standards emanating above all from human rights instruments, in particular the rights to participate in public affairs and to freedom of association enshrined in the International Covenant on Civil and Political Rights. Other human rights treaties cover specific aspects of the regulation of parties, such as non-discrimination as well as financing and transparency. The chapter shows that the constitutionalisation of these standards in continental Europe occurred in waves and that different models emerged over time. The European experience is illustrated via the case of Germany, which can be seen as a pioneer and model in the constitutionalisation of parties. In concluding, Socher argues that while some principles developed in Europe could offer inspiration for the further constitutionalisation of political parties in Africa, others might be less suitable and should be considered only with caution.

The country case studies start in Part 2, which deals with party constitutionalism and multiparty democracy. The first is by Abdou Khadre Diop, who in Chapter 6, discusses political-party constitutionalisation in Senegal, with the focus on the challenges of majoritarian abuse. Diop examines the constitutional recognition and legal safeguarding of parties in the country against the backdrop of recent political tensions and challenges to democratic processes. He points out that the country, known for its long-standing democracy, has undergone significant constitutional reforms to bolster political pluralism and define the roles and responsibilities of parties. However, despite these advances, practical circumstances reveal instances of majoritarian abuse that undermine the rights of political parties, particularly during Macky Sall's presidency (2012–2024). Diop highlights the gaps in the constitutional and legislative framework, and shows that these have been exploited by the different ruling parties to infringe upon the rights of opposition parties. He concludes by suggesting several ways in which the legal framework should be strengthened in order to protect opposition parties and prevent abuses by ruling parties.

The second case study is by Buluma Bwire, who in Chapter 7 considers intra-party democracy and the chasm between political parties and democratisation in Kenya. Bwire starts by pointing out that the repeal of section 2A of the Kenyan Constitution in 1991 transformed the country from a constitutionalised one-party state into a multiparty democracy. This marked the end of the period in which the Kenya African National Union dominated politics in the authoritarian regimes of Jomo Kenyatta and Daniel arap Moi. Despite this transformation from an authoritarian to a democratic system, Bwire shows that Kenyan parties today are unable to provide democratic space to their members and that the election of party leadership is often undemocratic and lacking in transparency.

According to Bwire, Kenyan parties are ethnic-based alliances formed for the sole purpose of winning elections, after which they disintegrate along ethnic fissures or fall dormant until the next elections. Drawing on the historical development and contemporary characteristics of Kenyan parties' internal structures, Bwire critically analyses their evolution since the reintroduction of multiparty politics in 1992. He concludes that internal democracy within political parties is essential for a country's successful transition to democracy based on the principles of good governance and constitutionalism.

In Chapter 8, Lukman Abdulrauf and Johannes Socher discuss party constitutionalism and political patrimonialism in Nigeria. The authors show how Nigeria's constitutional framework has guaranteed multipartyism since the return to democracy in 1999, with successive legislative reforms aimed at providing a level playing field for political parties to compete for power. However, the manner in which these reforms have been implemented raises doubts about their effectiveness. As Abdulrauf and Socher show, heightened patrimonialism has increasingly encroached upon and narrowed political space. Based on this observation, they argue that political patrimonialism can serve as a lens through which to understand many of the challenges of party constitutionalism in Nigeria. After examining the evolution of party politics and the constitutional framework regulating political parties, the authors analyse the extent to which this framework promotes constitutionalism and democracy. In the light of prevailing practices, they argue that a stronger constitutional and legal framework is needed to further entrench constitutionalism and multipartyism in a meaningful and effective way.

In Chapter 9, Gerald Dan Yeakula discusses the Liberian experience. He starts with the observation that the West African sub-region has been hard hit by military coups and resultant political instability. Nevertheless, Yeakula believes that Liberia remains an example of a country in Africa with good prospects for democracy. An indication of this is the fact that it saw the election of the continent's first female president and has had two democratic transfers of power, the last being one from a defeated incumbent. Yeakula points out that the involvement of political parties has been pronounced, albeit that there is immense room for improvement. With the country's experience of multipartyism having been relatively short, he argues that more reforms are needed to enable pluralism to take root. According to Yeakula, a key change which is necessary is for multipartysim to be more strongly entrenched in Liberia's constitution so that it is insulated from partisan manipulation and abuse.

Neel Purmah ends this part of the volume with a discussion in Chapter 10 of the role of ethnicity in shaping coalition politics in Mauritius. Although a small island state, the country is well known for the political stability and multiparty democracy it has enjoyed since independence in 1968. Purmah explores the intersections between political alliances and ethnic representation in the country's body politic and examines the emergence of major political parties and the influence of ethno-religious dynamics on the political landscape. By examining the constitutional and legal framework applicable to political parties in Mauritius, Purmah reveals the challenges in their governance. He lays particular emphasis on coalitions and ethnicity, showcasing how political alliances shape governance and electoral outcomes in the country. He goes on to analyse the impact on parties of the "best-loser system", a distinctive feature of the country's electoral system that allows for the representation of minorities. By unravelling these complexities with respect to coalition politics, Purmah offers insights into the effectiveness of existing mechanisms and proposes constitutional and other legal reforms to enhance the role that political parties can play in strengthening democratic governance in Mauritius.

Part 3 of the volume examines how political-party constitutionalisation operates in a dominant-party system. This involves three case studies, starting in Chapter 11, where Adriano Nuvunga and José Adalima examine Mozambique's tortuous path to party institutionalisation. The authors show how the country emerged from a protracted civil war in the late 1970s, and how the multiparty system that was introduced in 1990 marked a pivotal moment in the country's trajectory. However, despite initial optimism, Mozambique continues to grapple with myriad challenges hindering effective participation and consolidation of political parties. Nuvunga and Adalima examine the dominance of the former liberation movement, the Mozambique Liberation Front (Frelimo) and its enduring impact on the political landscape. They show how legal and structural constraints thwart meaningful party participation in governance, notably feeble parliamentary oversight and the winner-take-all nature of the electoral system. They also discuss political parties' internal dynamics – characterised by a cult of leadership and the absence of internal democracy, all of which exacerbate challenges to political pluralism and accountability. Nuvunga and Adalima argue that Mozambique desperately needs a legal framework that can promote a more democratic and stable political system; one which is reflective of its diverse populace and responsive to the needs and aspirations of all its citizens.

The second country case study is chapter 12 by Bekezela Gumbo, entitled, "Party constitutionalisation and democracy in securocratic states: Lessons from Rwanda". Gumbo looks at the post-genocide era, scrutinising the constitutional, legal, and institutional frameworks that regulate political parties. He examines the historical context, the legalities of party operations, the institutionalisation of internal governance, funding, accountability, and the broader implications for democracy and human rights in Rwanda. Drawing on an array of sources, he reveals the paradoxical nature of Rwanda's political-party regulatory framework. While it formally recognises democratic structures, it simultaneously imposes stringent conditions that undermine autonomy and fair representation, resulting in what the author refers to as a "guided paper democracy". Gumbo argues that this duality hinders genuine political pluralism and perpetuates the dominance of Paul Kagame's ruling party, the Rwandan Patriotic Front. Gumbo concludes by advocating for policy reforms that respect autonomy, ensure a balanced party system, and maintain a clear distinction between political parties and the state.

In chapter 13, the final case study in this part of the volume, Charles Fombad and Ajereboh Jespa Tichock discuss Cameroon's transition from a monolithic to a multiparty autocracy. When it gained independence in the 1960s, Cameroon had a multiparty system, but this was informally abolished in 1966. Although multipartyism was reintroduced by the present government in the 1990s, the authors show that the government under Paul Biya has since then done everything to ensure that this does not threaten the total dominance by the ruling party, the Cameroon People's Democratic Movement.

The argument of the chapter is that Cameroon has merely transitioned from a monolithic autocratic system to a multiparty one. The framework for the operation of a fully-fledged multiparty system is laid down in the constitution and a series of laws. However, in the last three decades this has been rendered inoperative by the government and ruling party. It has done so through manipulation of electoral laws and electoral district boundaries, restrictions on voter access in opposition strongholds, intimidation and violence against opposition leaders and supporters, the misuse of public resources for partisan purposes, and the co-option of opposition leaders. The situation has been aggravated by divisions within the opposition ranks, the absence of the fundamentals of constitutionalism and the rule of law, and the continual support the regime receives from the international community, particularly France. It is contended that without a new constitutional dispensation based on an inclusive and participatory process that draws lessons from the best processes and best constitutions on the continent, the multiparty autocratic system that is now firmly in place will only be further entrenched regardless of who the president is or which party has a majority in parliament.

Two case studies in Part 4 focus on the plight of opposition parties in Africa's turbulent multiparty environment. This first is Edson Ziso's contribution in Chapter 14, entitled "Exploring the interplay of political-party regulation and the internal contradictions of opposition politics in Zimbabwe: The case of the MDC/CCC". He starts by pointing out that political developments in Zimbabwe involving the hitherto massively popular but now disintegrated opposition party, the Movement for Democratic Change (MDC) (1999–2022), rebranded as the Citizens Coalition for Change (CCC) (2022–2024), provide important insights into the internal regulation of parties in Africa. The MDC/CCC went through turmoil characterised by leadership wrangles, intra-party litigation, abuse of power by the leadership, alleged infiltration, expulsions and counter-expulsions, recalls of members from the legislature, counter-claims to party financing and assets between and among factions, and an unsustainable number of minor and major splits.

Ziso locates the causes of this in the interplay of mutually reinforcing external and internal factors, that is, the political party regulatory framework, on the one hand, and intra-party dynamics, on the other. He analyses the combination of these internal-external dynamics to offer explanations of causality and causation that may help provide a better understanding of party-state relations in Zimbabwe in the context of limited and politicised political party regulation. Ziso's analysis is done within the context of the volatile and authoritarian environment that prevails in Zimbabwe under the Zimbabwe African National Union – Patriotic Front (ZANU-PF). The chapter provides a nuanced understanding of the relationship between the regulation of political parties, and the impact this is having in creating, magnifying, and exploiting complex contradictions in opposition parties.

In Chapter 15, entitled "Swimming against the tide: Militancy and diplomacy as survival mechanisms for opposition parties in Uganda's militarised politics", James Nkuubi argues that despite the much-vaunted re-opening of Uganda's multiparty political space since 2005 after an effective 20-year ban, the dispensation under the National Resistance Movement (NRM) government is besieged by the tripartite challenges of securitisation, militarisation, and a dominant-party system. Amid an environment hostile to multiparty politics, a key question, under-examined in the literature on political parties, arises: How are opposition political parties coping and adapting to ensure their survival? Equally important is the question of the impact of the chosen coping models on the consolidation of constitutionalism and multiparty politics. To answer these questions, the chapter focuses on two political parties in Uganda – the Democratic Party, the oldest opposition party in the country, and the National Unity Platform, the youngest (as at 2023). The chapter interrogates their contrasting coping models: in the case of the former, diplomacy through "working co-operation agreements" with the ruling NRM government, and, in the latter, militancy.

The final part of the volume focuses on political-party financing, illustrated by the two examples of Ethiopia and South Africa. The first example is presented in Chapter 16, written by Heather Thuynsma, uses South Africa's 2024 national and provincial elections to examine the dynamics of party financing in the country. The chapter discusses the influence money has had on politics since the end of apartheid and traces legislative attempts to enhance transparency, reduce corruption, and foster public trust in political institutions. It maintains that to increase trust and transparency within the system, parties must disclose both their funding sources – as argued in *My Vote Counts v President of the Republic of South Africa*[8] – and their expenditure.

As Thuynsma shows, the Political Party Funding Act was a significant step towards these goals, but challenges remain with compliance and the entrenched culture of secrecy in political parties. The chapter uses this context and a "moneyball" framework to assess how political parties have adapted their fundraising strategies in response to regulatory changes.

In Chapter 17, Zelalem Degifie examines the implications of political-party funding in post-2018 Ethiopia for the future of democracy and constitutionalism in the country. He starts by saying that since 2018, Ethiopia has undergone major political reform under the Prosperity Party (PP), with party financing governed by Proclamation No. 1162/2019 and the directives of the National Election Board of Ethiopia (NEBE). Degifie critically examines the legislative framework and practice, and shows that the reforms have not significantly changed the competitiveness of the electoral process: the party finance system unduly benefits the ruling PP, while opposition parties struggle with funding, relying on private funds or diaspora support. Additionally, the public funding scheme not only favours the ruling party, but also results in insufficient resources and delayed disbursements of the limited public funding made available to opposition parties. The absence of donations and expenditure limits and the manipulation of state resources

8 See High Court of South Africa, Western Cape Division, Cape Town, Case No. 1067/24, 27 May 2024, https://www.saflii.org/za/cases/ZAWCHC/2024/137.html (accessed 1 January 2025).

by the PP further skew the political playing field. Degifie shows, too, that political parties often disregard transparency rules, and that enforcement is constrained due to the NEBE's capacity limitations, political reluctance, and weak civic engagement, leading to corruption and finance-driven factionalism. He suggests several measures aimed at reforming the party financing system to ensure a level playing field and institutionalise political parties.

References

Books, articles, chapters in books, and others

Bogaards M, "Political Parties in Sub-Saharan Africa", in N Carter, D Keith, GM Sindre, and S Vasilopoulou (eds.), *The Routledge Handbook of Political Parties*, London, Routledge (2023), pp 392–402

Daly TG and Christopher B, "Parties Versus Democracy: Addressing Today's Political Party Threats to Democratic Rule", 18 (2020) *International Journal of Constitutional Law*, pp 509–538

Fombad CM, "Conceptualising a Framework for Inclusive, Fair and Robust Multiparty Democracy in Africa: The Constitutionalisation of the Right of Political Parties", 18 (2015) *World Comparative Law*, pp 3–27

Fombad CM, "Political Party Constitutionalisation in Africa: Trends and Prospects for Deepening Constitutionalisation", in R Dixon, T Ginsburg and A Abebe (eds.), *Comparative Constitutional Law in Africa*, Cheltenham, Edward Elgar (2022), pp 109–135

Freedom House, "Freedom in the World Research Methodology", *Freedom House*, https://freedomhouse.org/reports/freedom-world/freedom-world-research-methodology (accessed January 2025)

Freedom House, *Freedom in the World 2024: The Mounting Damage of Flawed Elections and Armed Conflict* (2024), https://freedomhouse.org/sites/default/files/2024-02/FIW_2024_DigitalBooklet.pdf (accessed 1 January 2025)

Ginsburg T, Huq AZ, and Khaitan T (eds.), *The Entrenchment of Democracy: The Comparative Constitutional Design of Elections, Parties and Voting*, Cambridge, Cambridge University Press (2024)

Khaitan T, "Political Parties in Constitutional Theory", 73 (2020) *Current Legal Problems*, pp 89–125

Masterman R and Schütze R (eds.), *Cambridge Companion to Comparative Constitutional Law*, Cambridge, Cambridge University Press (2019)

Mo Ibrahim Foundation, *2024 Ibrahim Index of African Governance – Index Report* (2024), https://mo.ibrahim.foundation/sites/default/files/2024-10/2024-index-report.pdf (accessed 1 January 2025)

Nordlund P and Salih M, *Political Parties in Africa: Challenges for Sustained Multiparty Democracy*, Stockholm, International IDEA (2007)

Salih M (ed.), *African Political Parties. Evolution, Institutionalisation and Governance*, London, Pluto Press (2003)

Schattschneider EE, *Party Government*, London, Routledge (1942)

White JK, "E E Schattschneider and the Responsible Party Model", 25 (1992) *Political Science and Politics*, pp 167–171

Table of cases

High Court of South Africa, Western Cape Division, Cape Town, Case No. 1067/24, 27 May 2024, https://www.saflii.org/za/cases/ZAWCHC/2024/137.html (accessed 1 January 2025)

Part 1:
Overview and Regional and International Context

Chapter 2 An Overview of Political Party Constitutionalisation under Contemporary African Constitutions

Charles M Fombad

1. Introduction

Recent years in Africa have been marked by a few democratic gains that have been largely neutralised by huge democratic setbacks. During these years, the continent's most autocratic incumbents appear to have been emboldened after getting away with many anti-democratic measures, such as the removal of presidential term limits and the regular rigging of elections. The reintroduction of multipartyism on the continent during the constitutional reforms that began in the 1990s led many to assume that this would bring an end to the dark era of one-party dictatorships and pave the way for an ethos of democracy and constitutionalism to emerge and be sustained.

In this regard, Afrobarometer data from 36 countries surveyed in 2021/2022 shows that two-thirds (66 per cent) of Africans prefer democracy over any other form of government. It also shows that large majorities reject one-man rule (80 per cent), one-party rule (78 per cent), and military rule (67 per cent), but that only 38 per cent express satisfaction with the way in which democracy functions in their countries.[1]

There is also strong support by Africans for political parties to compete freely for power.[2] In fact, in almost all African countries, the rights and duties of political parties have now been constitutionally entrenched, along with certain fundamental principles and institutions designed to ensure that they can compete freely. The overriding objective has been both to

1 See MAA Twum, "Declining Satisfaction Threatens African Democracy, Afrobarometer CEO Reveals", *Afrobarometer*, 18 July 2023, https://www.afrobarometer.org/articles/declining-satisfaction-threatens-african-democracy-afrobarometer-ceo-reveals/ (accessed April 2024).

2 See Afrobarometer, "PP85: Africans Want More Democracy, But Their Leaders Still Aren't Listening", 19 January 2023, https://www.afrobarometer.org/publication/pp85-africans-want-more-democracy-but-their-leaders-still-arent-listening/ (accessed April 2024).

empower political parties to compete (or what is referred to as positive constitutionalism) as well as to protect them against partisan manipulative measures (negative constitutionalism).[3] As a result of differences in legal traditions, constitutional systems, and political history, the nature, scope, and extent of political-party constitutionalisation varies from country to country.

Today, but for a few aberrations such as Eritrea and Eswatini, multipartyism has become the norm on the continent. The expansion of political space, and the proliferation of political parties that has seen the routinisation of elections, has not, save for a brief interlude in the 1990s, quite led to genuine multipartyism. The ominous signs of authoritarian mobilisation and resurgence, and the growing indications of a global democratic recession in the last five or more years, strongly suggest that the routinisation of multiparty elections has not provided the necessary impetus for democratic governance. This has been particularly the case in Africa, where the promised new dawn of democracy appears to be stalling.[4]

This overview chapter aims mainly to identify the fundamental principles and institutions that have formed the core aspects of political-party constitutionalisation in Africa in the last three decades. It briefly maps out the general trend in the expansion of political space and participation to see how this reflects the present decline in the quality of democracy. The approach adopted is largely theoretical and conceptual; it is the detailed study of how different countries implement them that gives us a practical idea of the impact of these principles.[5]

The discussion continues in section 2 by briefly examining the emergence and evolution of African political parties. Section 3 highlights why the constitutional entrenchment of political parties is an imperative in any country that aspires to establish a genuine multiparty democratic system. This provides the backdrop for an overview of the nature and extent to which African constitutions have entrenched the type of regulatory environment that is conducive to the effective functioning and eventual consolidation of democracy. Section 5 captures the major trends and tendencies in political-party constitutionalisation. In the concluding remarks, it is

3 R Pildes, "Political Parties and Constitutionalism", in T Ginsburg and R Dixon (eds.), *Comparative Constitutional Law*, Cheltenham, Edward Elgar (2011), p 254–264.

4 CM Fombad, "Reversing the Surging Tide Towards Authoritarian Democracy in Africa", in CM Fombad and N Steytler (eds.), *Democracy, Elections, and Constitutionalism in Africa*, Oxford, Oxford University Press (2021), pp 463–517.

5 A matter addressed in the different country case studies in this volume.

noted that the constitutional entrenchment of the basic framework for the functioning of political parties is not an end in itself. The constitutional entrenchment of the framework must be followed by its full implementation.

2. The emergence and evolution of political parties in Africa

It is appropriate to start by saying something about what is meant by "political parties". This is followed by a brief discussion of how they emerged in Africa and evolved prior to 1990.

2.1 Conceptualisation of political parties

Most definitions of political parties have adopted a functional approach that enables us to generalise about some of the universally accepted functions that parties perform whether they operate in Africa or elsewhere. Whilst this functional approach will be our focus, it is important to note that there is also an alternative conceptualisation of political parties that views them as structures and settings in which political activities take place.[6]

Viewed from the functional perspective, political parties, according to Peter Stearns, "are organised groups working to influence public policies and to place their representatives in positions of public authority".[7] He rightly points out that parties are not the only actors that seek to influence public policies in pluralist societies. Others, such as interest groups, political action committees, firms, non-governmental organisations, and civil society organisations also attempt to influence public policies, but only political parties explicitly aim to place their members in public office. As Lowell argues, political parties' essential function and *raison d'être* is bringing public opinion into focus and framing issues for popular verdict.[8] They try to consolidate public opinion in advance of an election and use this to

6 See, for example, WR Schonfe, "Political Parties: The Functional Approach and the Structural Alternative", 15 (1983) *Comparative Politics*, pp 477–499.

7 P Stearns, "Political Parties", in *The Oxford Encyclopaedia of the Modern World*, Oxford, Oxford University Press (2008), https://www.oxfordreference.com/display/10.1093/acref/9780195176322.001.0001/acref-9780195176322-e-1259?rskey=3OblyZ&result=3 (accessed 3 March 2024).

8 L Lowell, *Public Opinion and Popular Government*, New York, Longmans, Green and Company (1913), p 70.

capture power. As LaPalombara puts it, a political party is a formal organisation whose self-conscious, primary purpose is to place and maintain in public office persons who will control, alone or in coalition, the machinery of government.[9]

The ACE Project usefully suggests that political parties perform key tasks in a democratic society, such as:

- soliciting and articulating public policy priorities and civic needs and problems as identified by members and supporters;
- socialising and educating voters and citizens in the functioning of the political and electoral system and the generation of general political values;
- balancing opposing demands and converting them into general policies;
- activating and mobilising citizens into participating in political decisions and transforming their opinions into viable policy options;
- channelling public opinion from citizens to government; and
- recruiting and training candidates for public office.[10]

Although almost all African constitutions refer directly or indirectly to political parties, few actually define them. One example, which provides a detailed definition of parties, is Article 77 of the Burundi Constitution of 2018, which states:

> A political party is defined as an association without a lucrative end and which organizes citizens around a project of democratic society founded on national unity; which has a definite political program of precise objectives; is concerned with serving the general interest; and [seeks] to assure that all citizens thrive.

A number of party types have been discussed in the literature. Stearns, for example, mentions four types, namely, parties grouped according to regime context; parties grouped according to ideology; parties grouped according to voter base; and parties grouped according to whether they are "cadre" or "mass" parties.[11] Only the first two of these distinctions are of some relevance in the African context.

---

9 J LaPalombara, *Politics Within Nations,* Englewood Cliffs, New Jersey, Prentice Hall (1974), p 501.

10 ACE Project, "Roles and Definition of Political Parties", https://aceproject.org/ace-en/topics/pc/pca/pca01/pca01a/mobile_browsing/onePag (accessed 1 March 2024).

11 See, for example, Stearns, *supra* n. 7.

The first are ideological parties. In the Western context, ideological parties range from the left to the centre and the right, and have different names in the different countries in the West. For example, in the United Kingdom, the ideological party on the right is the Conservative Party; in the centre is the Social Democratic Party, and on the left, the Labour Party. Apart from South Africa, where one can clearly identify the ideology of some of the parties, such as the Democratic Alliance, on the right, the African National Congress (ANC) in the centre, and the Economic Freedom Fighters (EFF) on the left, it is difficult to distinguish the political parties in most African countries based on their political ideology. The second category, dictated by the voter base, which may be ethnic, religious or regional, is more significant. Most African political parties usually start with an ethnic and/or religious base, which progressively expands regionally and, eventually, nationally.

What is increasingly common in Africa are cartel parties, a new category of political parties that was introduced in the literature in 1995 through the writings of Richard Katz and Peter Mair.[12] Their cartel-party thesis is that political parties increasingly function like cartels, employing the resources of the state to limit political competition and ensure their own electoral success. The concept applies to a collection of political parties that basically have different ideologies but, for the achievement of the interests of a group of people, they work together at the expense of public interests. They are usually formed based on the needs of the political elite to gain and maintain their power to minimise the differences of opinion among the party elite.[13] In many cases, the coalition of political parties that make up the cartel dominate the government and operate in a manner that strives to eliminate or limit competition and therefore hampers genuine multipartyism and democracy in general.

The most common and prevalent form of these cartel parties in Africa today are the so-called "presidential majority" phenomenon in francophone Africa.[14] This form has been extensively used in these countries as a means

12 R Katz and P Mair, "Changing Models of Party Organisation and Party Democracy: The Emergence of the Cartel Party", 1 (1995) *Party Politics*, pp 5–28; R Katz and P Mair, "The Cartel Party Thesis: A Restatement", 7 (2009) *Perspectives on Politics*, pp 753–766.

13 YS Lestari, "Cartel Party: An Analysis Study", *Atlantis Press*, November 2016, https://www.atlantis-press.com/proceedings/icosop-16/25873519 (accessed 1 March 2024).

14 This refers to a phenomenon in the French system where a group of parties in parliament join the ruling party to support the action of the government. See P

of the ruling party co-opting and neutralising opposition parties that threaten its dominance and thus including them in sharing the spoils of power. In some respects, there is a historical explanation to how these trends developed, a matter to which we will now turn.

2.2 The pre-1990 evolution of African political parties

Unlike in the West, African political parties emerged during the colonial period, in a non-democratic setting, mainly as liberation movements, and this to a large extent influenced the way they operated after independence.[15] On the eve of independence, most of the independence movements declared themselves to be political parties.[16] There was thus a proliferation of parties for a short while after independence. As is shown later, a few of the independence parties have been able to weather the storm of post-independence political instability and are still in power today.

Most of the post-independence constitutions either explicitly or implicitly allowed for multipartyism. In francophone African constitutions, it was often provided thus: "parties and political formations participate in the electoral process; they are created and they exercise their activities in conformity with the law..."[17] The right to form or join political parties could be inferred from the wording of anglophone African constitutions, which explicitly or implicitly allowed citizens to assemble and freely associate with others to form unions and other associations.[18]

After independence, what can be termed the multipartyism honeymoon did not last for long. By 1966, the one-party system had been imposed in most countries. This was either de jure, through an amendment of the constitution or its suspension by the military after a coup d'état, or de

Avril, "Les Chefs de l'État et la Notion de Majorité Présidentielle", 34 (1984) *Revue Française de Science Politique*, pp 752–765.

15 M Salih, "Introduction: The Evolution of African Political Parties", in M Salih (ed.), *African Political Parties: Evolution, Institutionalisation and Governance*, London, Pluto Press (2003), pp 1–33.

16 As Salih, ibid, p 18, rightly points out, the attempts to transform liberation movements and guerrilla forces into mass movements or democratic political parties have proven to be a big challenge in most African countries.

17 See, for example, Article 3 of the Cameroonian Constitution of 1961 and Article 3 of the Senegalese Constitution of 1961.

18 See, for example, section 25(1) of the Nigerian Constitution of 1960 and section 13(1) of the Botswana Constitution of 1966.

facto, through state repression that forced opposition parties to join the ruling party or go underground. Only in Botswana, Mauritius, and, to some extent, Senegal did multipartyism survive. African leaders gave numerous justifications for the imposition of the one-party system.[19] The main argument was that multipartyism promotes division and tribalism and entails a waste of resources needed to focus on enhancing national unity, political stability, and economic development. The argument was also made that the one-party system better reflected African traditional systems of governance than multipartyism.[20]

Needless to say, the one-party system never delivered on any of its promised goals. The corrupt, repressive, and inefficient dictators that it protected instead led to economic stagnation, political instability, poverty, civil conflict, and other problems which the continent is still struggling to recover from. This culminated in the protests of the 1990s that forced African leaders to agree to fairly dramatic constitutional reforms that led to the reintroduction of multipartyism. But as we will see, the return to multipartyism has not quite defied the logic that "winners win twice", in that winning elections affords winners an opportunity to win again. This raises the questions about the regulatory framework, a matter we consider next.

3. Rationalising political-party constitutionalisation

The dire straits of democracy and constitutionalism in Africa today suggest that the advent of multipartyism and the proliferation of political parties has not brought about the genuine democracy and alternation of power that was expected to result from this. As Duverger points out, although political parties originally developed within the framework of liberal democracy in the 19th century, since the 20th century they have been used by

19 K Tuteng, "Towards a Theory of One-party Government in Africa", 13 (1973) *Cahiers d'Etudes Africaines*, pp 649–663; L Zimba, "The Origins and Spread of the One-party States in Commonwealth Africa, Their Impact on Personal Liberties: A Case Study of the Zambian Model", in M Ndulo (ed.), *Law in Zambia,* Lusaka, East Africa Publishing House (1984), pp 113–141; PA Nyong'o, "Africa: The Failure of One Party Rule", 3 (1992) *Journal of Democracy*, pp 90–96.

20 K Robinson, *Autochthony and Transfer of Power,* Oxford, Oxford University Press (1968).

dictators and autocrats for entirely undemocratic purposes.[21] This raises the question of the need for an effective regulatory framework.

It is beyond doubt that in all political systems, whether democratic or not, there is always the risk that without a satisfactory regulatory framework, those in power will try to exploit their incumbency to introduce laws, policies, and other measures designed to keep them in power whilst limiting the prospects of their adversaries winning.[22] To limit the scope for this, since the end of the Second World War many European democracies, with Germany and Italy taking the lead, have progressively entrenched the main principles regulating their political parties in the constitution. It is a regulatory approach with much to offer.

Our main argument here is that the constitutional entrenchment of the framework of political parties would considerably enhance the prospects for genuine, free and fair, competitive multipartyism. "Political-party constitutionalisation" in this context refers to the extent to which the rights and duties of political parties, as well as the basic framework that regulates the relevant institutions and processes needed to ensure that they can discharge their functions efficiently and effectively and compete for power in free and fair elections, is recognised and protected in the constitution itself, and not merely in ordinary legislation.

A number of reasons can be advanced for advocating for constitutionalising the basic framework for regulating political parties.[23] First, a constitutional framework that recognises, promotes, and protects the rights of all political parties will reduce the risk of partisan manipulation of political processes by incumbents. This on its own is no guarantee that there will be no abuses by transient majorities, but it would go some way towards reducing the risk of arbitrary and opportunistic actions, such as changes to electoral laws that violate the principles for free and fair competition laid down in the constitution without amending the constitution itself.

---

21 M Duverger, "Political Party", *Encyclopaedia Britannica*, 14 November 2024, https://www.britannica.com/topic/political-party (accessed 1 March 2024).

22 This is not necessarily limited to ruling parties. For example, one of the new parties contesting the May 2024 parliamentary elections in South Africa has argued that the new Electoral Amendment Act that radically hiked the number of signatures needed to qualify to contest the elections, from 1,000 to 50,000, was passed in Parliament by both the ruling party and the present opposition parties as an act of self-preservation in order to stymie competition and political choice. See "Legal Threat Over Controversial Election Bill", 5845 (8 March 2024) *Legalbrief Today*.

23 See G Borz, "Justifying the Constitutional Regulation of Parties", 38 (2017) *International Political Science Review*, pp 99–113.

Secondly, political-party constitutionalisation, depending on its scope and depth, is a strong indication of a government's commitment to competitive politics. While the same objective or even more could be achieved through the ordinary legislative process, there is no guarantee that this will be so or that, if it happens, it cannot arbitrarily be changed by the ruling party when its position is threatened.

Thirdly, given their nature and status, constitutions are inherently suitable for laying down the basic regulatory framework for political parties. As the constitution is the supreme law of the land and all laws derive their validity from it, any regulatory laws, policies, and practices that are inconsistent with the basic constitutional framework would be declared invalid to the extent of such inconsistency. In view of their special status, constitutions are meant to endure, and are often protected from arbitrary amendments by transient majorities or opportunistic leaders trying to promote a selfish political agenda.[24] From this perspective, the advantage of constitutional entrenchment of political-party regulatory principles is that it provides greater durability, certainty, and predictability than is the case with ordinary legislation.

Fourthly, to the extent to which the critical principles and institutions essential for ensuring a level political playing field are given constitutional status, they impose obligations on both the legislature and executive in a manner that limits their scope of action or inaction. This may be reinforced by a positive obligation to act,[25] one which does not give them the mere discretion to act when it is convenient to them – discretion opens the door for violation of the constitution where the alleged "violation" consists of a failure to fulfil a constitutional obligation. This may result in a declaration of unconstitutionality for the omission to carry out a constitutional obligation.[26] In this way, pressure can be brought to bear on both the legislature

24 CM Fombad, "Some Perspectives on Durability and Change under Modern African Constitutions", 11 (2013) *International Journal of Constitutional Law*, pp 382–413.

25 An example of such an obligation is found in section 2 of the South African Constitution of 1996, which states that "this constitution is the supreme law of the Republic; law or conduct inconsistent with it is invalid, *and the obligations imposed by it must be fulfilled*" (emphasis added).

26 For a discussion of this issue, see G Mendes, "Constitutional Jurisdiction in Brazil: The Problem of Unconstitutional Legislative Omission", *Supremo Tribunal Federal*, 7 October 2008, https://www.stf.jus.br/repositorio/cms/portalStfInternacional/portalStfDiscurso_en_US/anexo/Omisao_Legislativa_v__Ing.pdf (accessed 1 March 2024); P Paczolay, "Experience of the Execution of Constitutional Court's Decisions Declaring Legislative Omission in Hungary", *Council of Europe*, 2 September 2008,

and executive to implement provisions that are designed to promote free and fair political competition, such as a requirement that an independent electoral body should be established to manage elections. It would no longer lie within the exclusive and absolute discretion of these two branches of government to decide when or how to act. The courts would have the power to invalidate any legislation that fails to comply with the obligations imposed by the constitution.

Finally, the significance of constitutional entrenchment will depend on, among other factors, the exact nature, the manner of formulation, and the scope of the rights recognised and incorporated in the constitution. Where these are couched in clear language and in a manner that imposes a legal obligation, this is likely to be more effective than where the constitution merely empowers the legislature to enact laws without providing general principles that limit the propensity for this power to be abused through the making of restrictive laws which protect the incumbent rather than fostering the rights concerned.

However, political-party constitutionalisation certainly has its drawbacks.[27] First, there is the concern that the rigid and inflexible nature of constitutions and the onerous procedures required to amend them do not provide scope for the regulatory changes that are often needed to ensure that political parties respond to fluctuating political needs. Secondly, the unwieldy nature of constitutional regulations may inhibit the vibrant policy debates that usually take place within and between political parties. Finally, there is the concern that legal regulations in general may drag the courts into political disputes that are not necessarily suitable for adjudication.

In spite of the potential problems posed by political-party constitutionalisation, its advantages are undeniable. Yet it is the manner in which the basic framework for political-party constitutionalisation is recognised and protected that matters, as we shall see below.

---

https://www.venice.coe.int/webforms/documents/default.aspx?pdffile=CDL-JU%282008%29029-e (accessed 29 December 2024).

27 Some of them are discussed in K O'Regan, "Political Parties: The Interface between Law and Politics", Keynote address, Cape Town, 27 August 2010, pp 15–16. The pros and cons of political-party constitutionalisation are also discussed in CM Fombad, "Political Party Constitutionalisation in Africa: Trends and Prospects for Deepening Constitutionalism", in R Dixon, T Ginsburg, and AK Abebe (eds.), *Comparative Constitutional Law in Africa*, Cheltenham, Edward Elgar (2022), pp 109–135.

4. Manner and scope of political-party constitutionalisation

As the preceding discussion has shown, the advantages of political-party constitutionalisation surpass its disadvantages. However, capitalising on these advantages depends not only on the manner, depth, and scope of the entrenchment of this basic framework, but also on the implementation mechanism in place for ensuring that the regulatory framework is enforced. The starting-point is the nature of the general regulatory framework.

4.1 General regulatory framework

Even though scholars acknowledge the importance of political-party constitutionalisation, there is no general agreement on the nature, depth, and scope of what this should involve.[28] There are good reasons for this too: it will depend on, and should be influenced by, the history of the country, the challenges it has faced, and its level of constitutional and democratic maturity. It must also be assumed that the designers of African constitutions are mindful of Cass Sunstein's pertinent observation that constitutions should be designed to protect a country "against the most likely problems in the usual political processes", particularly those aspects of the "country's culture and traditions", as well as its history, "that will predictably produce harm through the country's ordinary politics", or its "most threatening tendencies".[29]

Thus, although there is no generally agreed framework of constitutional norms or institutions that need to be entrenched to enhance the prospects for a healthy political-party system, it can be said that, going by the African struggle with effective multipartyism, at least eight principles could provide the foundation for an effective constitutional regulatory framework:

- formal recognition of multipartyism;
- a framework for defining the scope of rights and duties of political parties;
- a framework for free and fair political participation;

28 See, for example, T Khaitan, "Political Parties in Constitutional Theory", in T Ginsburg, A Huq, and T Khaitan (eds.), *The Constitutional Design of Elections and Parties*, Cambridge, Cambridge University Press (2024); Borz, *supra* n. 23, pp 100–102.

29 C Sunstein, "Against Positive Rights", in A Sajó (ed.), *Western Rights? Post-Communist Application*, Netherlands, Kluwer Law International (1996), pp 225–232, 226–227.

- the principle of internal democracy;
- a framework for bans and regulatory restrictions;
- a mechanism for political-party funding;
- the principle of the separation of state and party; and
- ensuring compliance with democratic values and principles.[30]

These principles, if fully entrenched in constitutions, would enhance and deepen democratic governance. There is no African constitution that has fully incorporated all of them. Moreover, it is important to note that there is no rigid separation between the different principles, which in practice often overlap in such a manner that they mutually reinforce each other.

4.2 Formal recognition of multipartyism

Whilst almost all constitutions formally recognise multipartyism, the constitutions of Botswana (1966) and Eswatini (2005) do so only indirectly. The right to form political parties in either of these countries can only be inferred from the constitutional provisions recognising freedom of association.[31] A slightly better approach has been adopted in some constitutions (mainly those of francophone African countries) that have a single provision recognising multipartyism and leave the details as to how this is to be regulated to ordinary legislation.[32]

Both approaches are unsatisfactory. This is because such open-ended legislative powers might, without further constraints on their scope, be taken by a ruling party with a simple parliamentary majority, as a blank cheque to enact laws that will favour it.[33] In other words, the ability of

30 See Fombad, *supra* n. 27.

31 See section 3(b) of the Botswana Constitution and section 25 of the Eswatini Constitution.

32 See, for example, Article 5 and Article 3 of the 1990 and 1996 constitutions of Benin and Cameroon, respectively. Article 19(6) of the 1997 Constitution of Eritrea has a similar effect.

33 For example, in the Democratic Republic of the Congo (DR Congo), former President Joseph Kabila passed a new electoral law in 2017 that introduced electoral thresholds for parties to qualify for parliamentary seats, quadrupled the non-reimbursable deposit for national assembly candidates to USD 1,000, and almost doubled the deposit for presidential candidates to USD 100,000. See International Crisis Group, "Electoral Poker in DR Congo", 4 April 2018, https://www.crisisgroup.org/africa/central-africa/democratic-republic-congo/259-electoral-poker-dr-congo (accessed 1 March 2024).

such laws to promote free and fair competition among the different political parties depends on the goodwill of the ruling party due to the absence of any constitutional constraints that could temper its ability to legislate in a self-interested manner.

Some constitutions go further to protect the principle of multipartyism. The best formulation of this appears in Article 77(a) of the Constitution of Liberia of 1986 which states as follows:

> Since the essence of democracy is free competition of ideas expressed by political parties and political groups as well as by individuals, parties may freely be established to advocate the political opinions of the people. Laws, regulations, decrees or measures which might have the effect of creating a one-party state shall be declared unconstitutional.

In fact, a number of constitutions expressly ban the establishment of the one-party system.[34]

4.3 Framework for defining the scope of parties' rights and duties

Multipartyism has been stifled not simply by banning opposition parties but, in most cases, by treating them in ways that make it impossible for them to operate (with these methods including the persecution of their leaders). For multipartyism to play a role in enhancing democracy, what has to be recognised is the role that the different parties, especially those in the opposition, play in holding the government to account. Although political parties remain associations of private individuals ordinarily subject to private law, the fact that their primary objective is to contest elections and win power makes them quasi-public institutions. To enhance their effectiveness, a number of African constitutions have conferred rights and duties to them, especially so to opposition parties, which are often vulnerable to persecution by the ruling party. In general, whilst about 21 African constitutions explicitly refer to opposition parties, the exact scope of the rights and duties that are recognised varies considerably. A few examples will suffice.

---

34 See similar prohibitions in section 100(2)(a) of the Gambian Constitution of 1996; Article 3(1) of the Ghanaian Constitution of 1992; Article 7 of the Moroccan Constitution of 2011; and Article 75 of the Ugandan Constitution of 1995.

The first, and, in many respects, most important, innovation in constitutional design is the formal recognition and protection of the role of political parties. There are those constitutions which specify parties' rights and duties,[35] and which in some cases explicitly provide that they chair certain parliamentary committees. An elaborate example of this appears in Article 60 of the 2014 Tunisian Constitution:

> The opposition is an essential component of the Assembly of the Representatives of the People. It shall enjoy the rights that enable it to undertake its parliamentary duties and is guaranteed an adequate and effective representation in all bodies of the Assembly, as well as in its internal and external activities. The opposition is assigned the chair of the Finance Committee, and rapporteur of the External Relations Committee. It has the right to establish and head a committee of enquiry annually. The opposition's duties include active and constructive participation in parliamentary work.[36]

Besides recognising opposition parties' roles in parliamentary committees, some constitutions, such as those of Madagascar (2010),[37] Mauritius (1966),[38] South Africa (1996),[39] Seychelles (1993),[40] South Sudan (2011),[41] and Uganda (1995),[42] recognise the status of the leader of the opposition as an official position. Some go further, such as Article 71(2)(a) of the South Sudan Constitution, which ranks the minority leader as the "fourth in protocol after the President, the Vice President and the Speaker". Furthermore, the protection of the opposition is treated as a fundamental principle by certain African constitutions. Thus, the Cape Verde Constitution of 1992 prohibits any amendment to the rights of the opposition, be it through

35 See, for example, Article 58 of Senegal's Constitution of 2019, which states: "The Constitution guarantees to the political parties which are opposed to the policy of the Government the right to oppose it. The Constitution guarantees to the opposition a status that permits it to acquit its missions. The law defines this status and establishes the rights and duties accruing to them as well as to the Head of the opposition." See also Article 14 of the Madagascar Constitution of 2010.

36 See also Article 10 of Morocco's Constitution of 2011 and Article 178 of Burundi's Constitution of 2018.

37 See Article 14 of Senegal's Constitution of 2019.

38 See section 73.

39 See section 57(2)(d).

40 See Article 81.

41 See Article 71.

42 See Article 82A.

popular referendum[43] or revision of the constitution.[44] Another example of this is Article 186(3) of the 2018 Mozambican Constitution, which states that matters relating to the status of the opposition may be changed only by a majority of two-thirds of the votes of the deputies.

Another example comes from constitutions that provide for equality of treatment of all parties, sometimes specifically with respect to matters such as access to public media. For instance, Article 17(4) of the 2010 Constitution of Angola states: "Political parties shall be entitled to equal treatment by entities exercising political power, impartial treatment by the state press and the right to exercise democratic opposition, under the terms of the Constitution and the law".

Finally, a number of constitutions impose certain obligations on political parties. For example, Article 75(3) of the 2010 Constitution of Mozambique requires political parties to "contribute towards peace and stability in the country through the political and civic education of citizens". Article 91(g) of the 2010 Constitution of Ghana requires them to "promote the objects and principles of [the] Constitution and the rule of law". Some constitutions provide for consociational arrangements which require that certain positions must be shared between the different parties, taking due account of their electoral support, and that the leadership of the parties should reflect the national character of the population.[45]

4.4 The framework for free and fair political participation

Ruling parties can hardly resist the temptation to enact laws regulating the electoral process, as well as ones establishing institutions such as the courts, electoral management bodies (EMBs), and election boundaries commissions (EBCs), in a manner that will favour them. The principle of free and fair political participation, or what could also be referred to as the political-process principle, aims to ensure that all such laws are designed in a way that promotes free and fair competition between all the parties and

43 See Article 108(3).
44 See Article 313 (1)(g).
45 See, for example, Article 124 of the Burundi Constitution of 2018. This requires that the President of the Republic and the Vice President belong to different ethnic groups, political parties, and coalitions of political parties, or to be independents of different ethnicities.

which is not biased in favour of the incumbent. Two general observations can be made about how African constitutions incorporate this principle.

First, almost all African constitutions have provisions that provide for a separation of powers and guarantee judicial independence. However, in reality, whilst the constitutions of most anglophone countries have gone to considerable lengths to ensure that their judiciaries are reasonably independent, the scope for judicial independence in francophone, lusophone, and hispanophone Africa is limited. The latter is particularly true when it comes to courts that have been given exclusive rights to deal with electoral disputes.[46]

Secondly, a number of African constitutions entrench EMBs and EBCs. This has, however, not been done in a manner which ensures that they can operate independently without manipulation or interference by the ruling party.[47] So far, only the constitutions of Kenya, South Africa, and Zimbabwe have entrenched these institutions with an explicit mandate to support constitutional democracy and in a way that enhances their prospects for ensuring reasonably free, fair, and competitive elections.[48] Nevertheless, as all the post-2010 elections in Zimbabwe have shown, entrenching such institutions is no guarantee against electoral malpractices under an authoritarian regime with little respect for the rule of law.[49]

What is increasingly clear is that EMBs, EBCs, and "fourth-branch institutions" are now needed to ensure, inter alia, that elections are free and fair, that there is free and fair access to public media, that there is transparency and fairness in determining electoral boundaries, and that public

46 CM Fombad, "A Preliminary Assessment of the Prospects for Judicial Independence in Post-1990 Africa Constitutions", 2 (2007) *Public Law*, pp 233–257; CM Fombad, "The Struggle to Defend the Independence of the Judiciary in Africa", in S Shetreet, H Chodesh, and E Helland (eds.), *Challenged Justice: In Pursuit of Judicial Independence*, Leiden, Brill Nijhoff (2021), pp 223–248.

47 See, for example, CM Fombad, "Election Management Bodies (EMBs) in Eastern and Southern Africa: Some Reflections on their Legal Framework", 15 (2016) *African and Asian Studies*, pp 289–335.

48 CM Fombad, "The Diffusion of South African-Style Institutions? A Study of Comparative Constitutionalism", in R Dixon and T Roux (eds.), *Constitutional Triumphs, Constitutional Disappointments: A Critical Assessment of the 1996 South African Constitution's Local and International Influence*, Cambridge, Cambridge University Press (2018), pp 359–387.

49 G Mwonzora and E Mandikwaza, "The Menu of Electoral Manipulation in Zimbabwe: Food Handouts, Violence, Memory, and Fear – Case of Mwenezi East and Bikita West 2017 By-elections", 54 (2019) *Journal of Asian and African Studies*, pp 1128–1144.

funding is shared amongst political parties in a fair manner. Although the Kenyan, South African, and Zimbabwean entrenchment of a number of fourth-branch institutions is an innovation with strong potential to enhance democracy and constitutionalism, these institutions could do much more with some improvement and political goodwill.[50]

4.5 The principle of internal democracy

At first sight, the principle of internal democracy appears to be in conflict with the private nature of political parties: ideally, the internal functions and processes of political parties should be free from state interference. However, political parties' hybrid, quasi-public nature, which often qualifies them to receive financial support from the government, suggests that they should not be allowed to operate without some restrictions. Perhaps more pertinent is the fact that a party which practices no internal democracy and is controlled by party barons to suit their own selfish interests is unlikely to practice democracy when it comes to power.[51] Furthermore, the internal functioning of political parties may sometimes inevitably be influenced by forces that are external to the party, such as the electoral system, political culture, and legal regulations. Whilst a number of constitutions advocate in one way or another for internal democracy, the most elaborate formulation of this appears in Article 91(1) of the 2010 Kenyan Constitution:

Every political party shall;

50 For ways of enhancing their effectiveness, see Fombad, *supra* n. 48.

51 Whilst undemocratic practices within political parties in Africa are commonplace in countries led by autocrats, the same occurs in some of the continent's best-performing democracies. For example, in South Africa, the two largest party opposition parties, the uMkhonto weSizwe (MK) and the Economic Freedom Fighters (EFF), have on several occasions removed sitting Members of Parliament (MP) without any formal process and replaced them with people who have just recently joined the party. An example is the "appointment" of Busisiwe Mkhwebane, who was impeached as the country's Public Protector (a position in which she was supposed to be apolitical). Shortly after this, she applied to be a member of the EFF and, a week later, an innocent EFF MP was removed for Mkhwebane to be sworn in instead as an MP. She later resigned and joined the MK. For its part, since the May 2024 parliamentary elections in which the MK participated for the first time and won 58 parliamentary seats, more than 20 of its members who were sworn in as MPs have been arbitrarily replaced by others. It is thus the party barons who decide who will be an MP, and not the ordinary members or even the voting public.

a) have a national character as prescribed by an Act of Parliament;
b) have a democratically elected governing body;
c) promote and uphold national unity;
d) abide by the democratic principles of good governance, promote and practise democracy through regular, fair and free elections within the party;
e) respect the right of all persons to participate in the political process, including minorities and marginalised groups;
f) respect and promote human rights and fundamental freedoms, and gender equality and equity;
g) promote the objects and principles of this Constitution and the rule of law; and
h) subscribe to and observe the code of conduct for political parties.[52]

Whilst some legal regulation of internal party processes is necessary, this must be kept to a minimum so that it does not unduly impair parties' autonomy or interfere with their rights as free associations.

4.6 Framework for bans and regulatory restrictions

This regulatory framework strives to balance two considerations. The first is that, without constraints on how governments use bans or other restrictions to regulate political parties, ruling parties can wield this power to frustrate their opponents. The other is that, without some restrictions, political parties can use the freedom to associate to create groups that could sow division or in one way or another threaten the unity and existence of the state. Constraints on the use of bans and other regulatory restrictions therefore aim to reconcile these two risks.

Generally, most constitutions prohibit the establishment of parties that are organised along regional, religious, tribal, ethnic, or racial lines, that incite and practice violence, or that promote tribalism, racism, dictatorship,

52 See also the Constitution of Nigeria of 1999, which in section 223 states: "(1) The constitution and rules of a political party shall – (a) provide for the periodical election on a democratic basis of the principal officers and members of the executive committee or other governing body of the political party; and (b) ensure that the members of the executive committee or other governing body of the political party reflect the federal character of Nigeria."

or xenophobia.[53] Given the challenges posed by the heterogeneous nature of African states, it is no surprise that restrictions are imposed for the sake of promoting diversity and inclusivity.[54] However, democracy thrives on the free exchange of ideas no matter how unfavourable, unpopular, or offensive they may be. It is therefore difficult to justify prohibiting or dissolving a party merely because it is regional, religious, or minority-based as long as it does not use, or call for, violence or threaten civil peace or fundamental democratic principles.[55] At the same time, whilst a one-party system is not good for democracy, the proliferation of parties does no good either. Regulatory constraints must be such that, on the one hand, they do not make the costs of political participation so low that they allow fake or frivolous parties to proliferate, and, on the other hand, make the cost to enter or compete so high that they lock out new or opposition parties.

4.7 Mechanisms for political-party funding

The burden of the economic cost of political participation can be a severe impediment to the right to establish, or become an active member of a political party. Although political parties, as private associations, should in principle depend on membership contributions, the reality is that, given high levels of poverty, ordinary Africans, after struggling to put meat on the table, have hardly anything to spare for contributing in a regular and meaningful way to sustaining the activities of a political party. Without public funding, there is bound to be a problem because most African ruling

53 See, for example, Article 6 of the Djibouti Constitution of 2010, which forbids parties from aligning themselves "to a race, to an ethnicity, to a sex, to a religion, to a language or to a region". Article 79(d) of the Liberian Constitution of 1986 requires that "the name, objective, emblem or motto of the association or of the independent candidate and his organization is free from any religious connotations or divisive ethnic implications ...".

54 See, for example, OT Afisi and AO Oyekan, "Multiculturalism and the Challenges of Heterogeneity in Postcolonial Africa", 8 (2020) *LASU Journal of African Studies*, pp 148–158.

55 A number of cases decided by the European Court of Human Rights take this position. See, for example, *Stankov and the United Macedonian Organisation Ilinden v Bulgaria*, application nos. 29221/95 and 29225/95 [2001], para 89; *United Communist Party of Turkey and Others v. Turkey* [GC], application no. 19392/92 [1998], para 43; *Socialist Party and Others v. Turkey* [GC], application no. 21237/93 [1998], para 45; *Herri Batasuna and Batasuna v. Spain*, application nos. 25803/04 and 25817/04 [2009], para 79.

parties exploit their incumbency and access to state resources to fund their parties. To ensure a level playing field, public funding of political parties is important. A number of constitutions explicitly provide for the funding of political parties, although the details of this are usually left to be determined through legislation.[56]

However, whilst some constitutions are silent on the issue of political-party funding, others, such as the Egyptian Constitution of 2014, actually prohibit it.[57] What is usually prohibited by constitutions, though, is external funding of political parties. There are often good reasons for this: the concern is that external donors may use their funding as a means to influence the agenda of the party once it wins elections. To deal with this, section 225(4) of the 1999 Constitution of Nigeria states that any funds or assets which a political party receives from abroad must be paid to or transferred to the Independent National Electoral Commission within 21 days.

4.8 The principle of separating state and party

The separation of state and party is without a doubt one of the most frequently abused principles in African political life.[58] The mutual absorption of the party by the state, and the state by the party, in the case of many a ruling party means that it is often difficult to distinguish between them.[59] The control by ruling parties of the state not only gives them unhindered access to state resources, but also enables them to manipulate official public media.

A number of constitutions have tried to entrench measures to prevent a conflict of interest between the ruling party and the state and in this way address some of the harmful effects of political-party capture and control of the state apparatus. This calls for a non-partisan public service comprising

56 See, for example, Article 57(a) of the Cape Verde Constitution of 2010; section 40(2) of the Malawi Constitution of 1994; Article 54 of the Constitution of Rwanda of 2015; and section 236 of the Constitution of South Africa of 1996.

57 Article 87 of the 2014 Constitution states, inter alia, that "[t]he use of public funds, government agencies, public facilities, places of worship, business sector establishments and non-governmental organisations and institutions for political purposes and electioneering is forbidden".

58 Fombad, *supra* n. 27, pp 118–119 and 127.

59 R Miller, "The Party-State and Bureaucratic/Political Relations in Africa", 8 (1975) *Comparative Political Studies*, pp 293–317.

the bureaucracy, the judiciary, the prosecution authorities, and any special institutions set up under the constitution, such as the Chapter 9 institutions under the 1996 South African Constitution. Some constitutions go a step further. For example, they expressly prohibit certain public officials from joining parties, or exclude persons who are actively involved in political activities, or have been so involved (for example, for five years preceding an advertised position), from being appointed.[60]

Several other measures also seek to separate the state from the party, but their effectiveness is doubtful. For instance, the constitution of many a francophone African country states that the mandate of the President of the Republic is incompatible with any responsibility within a political party.[61] It is difficult to see how a president who has been elected on a party-political platform can be expected to suddenly distance himself from the party and be apolitical.

4.9 Ensuring compliance with democratic values and principles

A broadly worded constitutional provision which seeks to promote democratic values and principles that enhance free and fair competition can be said to have as its primary objective to internalise democracy as a permanent value in itself and not merely as an instrumental tactic. These democratic values and principles ensure that the broad powers usually given to parliament are constrained. Whilst some constitutions spell out what these principles and values are, certain fundamental rights such as the right to equality of treatment and non-discrimination could be invoked to challenge electoral, media, and broadcasting laws that stifle free and fair competition between political parties.

However, three constitutions entrench robust democratic values and principles that could go a long way to ensure transparency and fairness in elections and electoral practices. The most articulately formulated instance

60 See examples of this in sections 64(4) and (5) and 109 (3) and (4) of the Botswana Constitution of 1966; articles 60, 82, and 250 of the Burundi Constitution of 2015; articles 166(3) and 194 of the Constitution of Ghana of 1992; articles 77(3) and 92(h) of the Constitution of Kenya of 2010; articles 11 and 155 of the Constitution of Morocco of 2011; sections 197(3) and 199(7) of the Constitution of South Africa of 1996; and sections 200(5) and 240 of the Constitution of Zimbabwe of 2011.

61 See Article 96 of the Constitution of DR Congo of 2005; Article 49 of the Madagascar Constitution of 2010; Article 27 of the Constitution of Mauritania of 1991; and Article 65 of the Constitution of Somalia of 2012.

of this is in Article 10 of the 2010 Kenyan Constitution, which deals with "national values and principles of governance." Article 10(1) states as follows:

1. The national values and principles of governance in this Article bind all State organs, State officers, public officers and all persons whenever any of them
   a. *applies or interprets this Constitution;*
   b. *enacts, applies or interprets any law*; or
   c. makes or implements public policy decisions.[62]

Other provisions in the Kenyan Constitution are more specific. For example, Article 92(1), in stating that Parliament shall enact legislation for the allocation of airtime on state-owned and other broadcast media, specifies that this must be "reasonable and equitable". It lays down in Article 81 the general principles for the electoral system.[63] A similar approach is provided for in section 155 of the Constitution of Zimbabwe sets out a number of fundamental principles which are supposed to guide Parliament in enacting electoral laws and any other legislation regulating the electoral process.

Similar provisions that impose a duty on the government, when regulating political parties, to comply with the fundamental principles and values of good governance, transparency, democracy, and fairness can be inferred from the 2013 Constitution of Zimbabwe.[64] Moreover, a law which is biased against opposition parties can be challenged on the grounds that it violates the principle in section 155(1)(d), which requires Parliament to ensure that it does not enact legislation that can provoke "violence and other electoral malpractices". The other equally value-laden constitution is the South African one: the broad manner in which the courts are required to interpret it and the formulation of the equality provisions gives judges considerable leeway to ensure that self-serving legislation and policies are invalidated by the courts.[65]

Apart from a few other anglophone countries, hardly any arabophone, francophone, hispanophone, or lusophone constitutions incorporate a rule

62 Emphasis added.

63 Other provisions that underscore the need for compliance with the values and principles of democracy include articles 20(4) and (5), 56 (a), 232, 234(2)(c), 249(1)(b), and 259(a).

64 See, for example, sections 3(2), 46, and 194(1)(k).

65 See sections 1(d), 7(10), 39(1)(a), 143(2)(a), and 195(1) and (3).

imposing compliance with democratic values and principles.[66] This is a shortcoming on their part, as the significance of such provisions bears underscoring: constitutional entrenchment of such a principle means that all national laws and policies that do not reflect these values and principles will not pass constitutional muster.

5. Post-1990 trends and tendencies in the evolution of political parties

Having constitutions that entrench the basic framework for regulating political parties is one thing; having these constitutions enforced in a manner which ensures parties play their critical role in enhancing constitutional democracy is another. So far, it can be argued that the regular holding of multiparty elections in Africa since 1990 has been the main manifestation of the revival of multipartyism. This raises a number of questions. One concerns the extent to which, if at all, multipartyism has indeed eradicated the cancer of the one-party systems that facilitated the rise of repressive and incompetent dictators. The other is the question whether multipartyism and party constitutionalisation are now ingredients that enable parties to compete for power in an environment where today's losers can become tomorrow's winners.

Two international indicators will be used to see what practical impact multipartyism has had on the evolution of civil and political rights in Africa over the last three decades. The first indicator is from Freedom House's Freedom in the World annual surveys. Since 1973, Freedom House surveys have been used to assess the condition of political rights and civil liberties around the world.[67] Table 1 below captures the trend over the last three decades by using the survey results of 1990 (the beginning of the new wave

66 The few other anglophone constitutions that entrench similar principles include Malawi, in section 11(2)(a) of its Constitution of 1994, and Zambia, in articles 8, 9, and 267(1)(a) of its Constitution of 1991.

67 For information on the methodology and scope of the survey, see Freedom House, "Freedom in the World Research Methodology", https://freedomhouse.org/reports/freedom-world/freedom-world-research-methodology (accessed 1 March 2024). The combination of the overall score awarded for political rights and the overall score awarded for civil liberties is used to determine the status of a country as either Free, Partly Free, or Not Free. An important aspect of the survey on political rights is its focus on political pluralism and participation. In this regard, the survey asks whether people have the right to organise in different political parties or other competitive political groupings of their choice, and the system is free of undue obstacles to the rise and fall of these competing parties or groupings; and also, whether there is a

of multipartyism in Africa) to see how the situation has changed in the course of each decade; the table also shows results from 2023.

Table 1: Evolution of civil and political rights in Africa (1990–2020)

Category	1990 results	2000 results	2010 results	2020 results	2023 results
Free category	3 countries (5.5%	9 countries (16.9%)	10 countries (18.9%)	8 countries (14.9%)	9 countries (17%)
Partly Free category	15 countries (27.8%)	25 countries (47.2%)	23 countries (43.3%)	25 countries (46.2%)	20 countries (37%)
Not Free category	36 countries (66.7%)	19 countries (35.9%)	20 countries (37.8%)	21 countries (38.9%)	25 countries (46%)

Source: Compiled from Freedom House's Freedom in the World reports for 1990,[68] *2000,*[69] *2010,*[70] *2020,*[71] *and 2023*[72]

Two observations can be made about this table. First, the number of "free" states, only three in 1990, had by 2023 increased to nine. What is striking is that the high number of "not free states" (36, or 66.7 per cent, in 1990) dropped dramatically to 19 in 2000, but since then has been on the increase, rising to 25, or 46 per cent, in 2023. In fact, the sharpest increase in the number of "not free" states has been between 2020 and 2023 (an increase of 7.1 per cent).

---

realistic opportunity for the opposition to increase its support or gain power through elections.

68 Freedom House, "Freedom in the World: Political Rights & Civil Liberties 1989–1990", https://freedomhouse.org/sites/default/files/2020-02/Freedom_in_the_World_1989-1990_complete_book.pdf (accessed 1 March 2024).

69 Freedom House, "Freedom in the World: The Annual Survey of Political Rights & Civil Liberties 2000–2001", https://freedomhouse.org/sites/default/files/2020-02/Freedom_in_the_World_2000-2001_complete_book.pdf (accessed 1 March 2024).

70 Freedom House, "Freedom in the World 2010: The Annual Survey of Political Rights & Civil Liberties", https://freedomhouse.org/sites/default/files/2020-03/FIW_2010_Complete_Book_Scan.pdf, (accessed 1 March 2024).

71 Freedom House, "Freedom in the World 2020: The Annual Survey of Political Rights & Civil Liberties", https://freedomhouse.org/sites/default/files/2021-08/FIW2020_book_JUMBO_PDF.pdf (accessed 1 March 2024).

72 Freedom House, "Freedom in the World 2023", https://freedomhouse.org/sites/default/files/2023-03/FIW_World_2023_DigtalPDF.pdf (accessed 1 March 2024).

Secondly, and of particular significance, is that since 1990, 10 countries have been classified continuously as “not free”: Angola, Cameroon, Chad, DR Congo, Equatorial Guinea, Libya, Rwanda, Somalia, South Sudan (since it became independent in 2011), and Sudan. Whilst the general trend confirms the global democratic recession, it is clear that there are countries that have hardly made any progress in spite of professing to be multiparty democracies. This leads to the conclusion that, in spite of the freedom to form political parties today, 46 per cent of Africans live in countries classified as “not free” due to constraints of one form or another on the exercise of these rights.

The second indicator is the Ibrahim Index of African Governance (IIAG), which currently is the most comprehensive dataset on African governance. While the annual survey covers a range of governance issues, we extracted the results that focus on political participation, rights, and inclusion on the continent. Table 2 shows the level of political pluralism, broadly covering the freedom of political parties, overall governance, and participation rights and inclusion in Africa from 2012 to 2021.

Table 2: Political pluralism in Africa (2012–2021)

Form of political participation	**2012**	**2013**	**2014**	**2015**	**2016**	**2017**	**2018**	**2019**	**2020**	**2021**
Freedom of political parties	63.5	63.8	63.8	63.1	62.9	62.6	61.6	61.1	59.6	57.4
Overall governance	47.8	47.8	47.8	48.2	48.3	48.5	48.7	48.9	48.9	48.9
Participation, rights and inclusion	47.5	47.3	47.2	47.5	47.1	47.4	47.4	47.2	47.1	46.7

Source: Compiled from various annual reports of the Ibrahim Index on African Governance

Table 2 indicates that since 2012, participation, rights, and inclusion remain the lowest-scoring IIAG category, with the average rate of decline doubling since 2017.[73] More than 60 per cent of Africa’s citizens, according to the

73 Mo Ibrahim Foundation, “2022 IIAG: Key Findings”, January 2023, https://assets.iiag.online/2022/2022-IIAG-Key-Findings_EN.pdf (accessed 1 March 2024).

reports, live in a country where this category has declined over the past 10 years, and more than one-third live in a country where the decline has accelerated since 2017. In fact, between 2017 and 2021, the deterioration in the participation sub-category has accelerated, driven by further restrictions on freedom of association and assembly, as well as by less free and fair elections.[74] Again, this tells us that, in spite of party pluralism, a majority of Africans still live in countries where effective rights of political participation are being progressively restricted.

Currently, the contracting political space has enabled multipartyism to flourish only in 46 of the 54 countries in Africa (that is, 85 per cent of them). Whilst political parties are banned in Eswatini, where the 2005 Constitution does not even mention them, albeit that it allows for freedom of association, Eritrea is currently the only one-party state on the continent. As a result of the resurgence of coup d'états in the last decade, the suspension of constitutions has also led to bans on political-party activity in Burkina Faso, Guinea, Niger, and Sudan.

It is not easy to present exact figures for the number of parties in the different countries. This is not only because accurate figures are hard to come by, but also because the figures vary from one election year to another. Be that as it may, statistics for a few countries will give us some indication of the number of political parties that are registered in the various African countries.

According to the Independent Electoral Commission of South Africa, in 2022 there were 1,501 registered political parties in the country.[75] With a population of just over 60 million, the latest statistics show that South Africa now has 1,793 registered parties; a further 738 are deregistered, while 94 applications for registration were rejected.[76] By contrast, Ethiopia, with a population of more than 126 million, has only 73 registered political

74 Ibid, p 5, where the report states that, out of all the IIAG's 81 indicators, freedom of association and assembly has deteriorated the most since 2012, with 60 per cent of citizens living in a country where the level is worse than it was in 2012.

75 Africa Check, "How Many Registered Political Parties Are There in South Africa?", *Infofinder*, 31 January 2024, https://africacheck.org/infofinder/explore-facts/how-many-registered-political-parties-are-there-south-africa (accessed 1 March 2024).

76 Independent Electoral Commission of South Africa, "Political Party Statistics", https://www.elections.org.za/pw/StatsData/Political-Parties-Statistics (accessed 1 November 2024).

parties;[77] Nigeria, Africa's most populous country, with a population of almost 224 million, has merely 18.[78] Togo, with a population of 9 million people, has 34 parties. Zambia, with a population of over 20 million, has about 28 parties. Cameroon, with a population of 28.6 million, has 369.

Two overall observations can be made here. The first and fairly obvious point is that party pluralism is very much alive in the countries that have legalised multipartyism; the second is that there is no correlation between population size and the number of political parties.

Perhaps one of the most disappointing features of the last three decades has been the limited scope that the revival of multipartyism has given to the alternation of power. Even on those rare occasions when a new opposition party makes a breakthrough, it starts another endless cycle of winning. In practical terms, the dominant-party system has now emerged as a new form of one-party rule, with the only difference being that it professes to have democratic credentials. There are several manifestations of this.

First, the ruling parties in eight African countries (Angola, Cameroon, Mozambique, Namibia, South Africa,[79] Tanzania, and Zimbabwe) – that is, about 15 per cent – originated in pre-independence liberation movements and have been continuously in power since independence to this day. Ruling-party dominance has occurred not only under manifestly repressive and autocratic regimes, such as those in Angola, Cameroon, and Zimbabwe, but also in countries considered as the most democratic on the continent, such as Botswana (until the 2024 elections) and South Africa. Does this not raise questions about the quality of multiparty democracy in practice on the continent?

Secondly, there are a number of political parties that came to power after the first post-1990 multiparty elections and which have won every election since then. In other words, much like the pre-1990 political parties, they have, whilst allowing space for other parties to participate in elections, used their incumbency to perpetuate their stay in power. In addition to the ruling party in the eight countries indicated above, those in nine other

77 National Election Board of Ethiopia, "Temporary Election Registration", https://nebe.org.et/sites/default/files/Accrediated%20Political%20Party%20Lists.pdf (accessed 1 March 2024).

78 Go Vote, "Political Parties in Nigeria", https://govote.ng/political-parties/ (accessed 1 March 2024).

79 It is worth noting that in the 29 May parliamentary elections, the ruling ANC lost its majority for the first time since 1996 and has been able to hold on to power by forming a government of national unity with several minority parties.

countries (Burundi, DR Congo, Republic of Congo, Djibouti, Equatorial Guinea, Ethiopia, Rwanda, Togo, and Uganda) have won all elections since multipartyism was introduced to date.

This means that in 17 of the 54 countries in Africa (that is, about 31 per cent of them), there has effectively been no alternation of power. If we add the fact that there have been no elections in Eritrea and South Sudan since they gained independence, this means there has been no alternation in 35 per cent of African countries for several decades. It is no coincidence, as we show below, that many of these 19 countries have the longest-serving leaders on the continent and even, in a few cases, the world.

The insidious return of the de jure one-party syndrome through de facto dominant parties has largely been facilitated by leaders who have manipulated their constitutions in one way or another to prolong their stay in power and, in doing so, held their parties in tow. It is no surprise that most of the countries with dominant parties are led by the longest-serving leaders on the continent. These are Teodoro Obiang Nguema Mbasogo of Equatorial Guinea (46 years in power); Paul Biya of Cameroon (43 years); Denis Sassou Nguesso of the Republic of Congo (41 years); Yoweri Museveni of Uganda (39 years); Isaias Afwerki of Eritrea (34 years); Ismail Omar Guelleh of Djibouti (26 years); Paul Kagame of Rwanda (25 years); Faure Gnassingbé of Togo (20 years); and Salva Kiir Mayardit of South Sudan (14 years).

What all of this suggests is that while political-party constitutionalisation and regulation has, on the whole, paved the way for more political elites to sit at the dining table, the substance of governance has remained the same. That is to say, the regulatory framework has changed only the rules of entry, enabling many new parties to emerge and a few alternations of ruling parties to occur, even while the substance of governance and the benefits of democracy remain elusive. In fact, our democracy is becoming a government of politicians, by politicians, for politicians.

6. Conclusion

It is widely accepted that political parties are a key component to entrenching and consolidating democracy and constitutionalism. African constitutions incorporate most of the fundamental principles and institutions needed to facilitate the effective operation of political parties. Whilst the manner, nature, and scope of the incorporation varies from one constitution to the other, none of them fully incorporates all of the eight principles and institutions needed to ensure that parties compete on a level playing field. This is understandable because the exact formulation of these principles will depend on a number of variable factors, such as the country's legal tradition, its electoral system, and the model of democracy.

This overview shows that political-party constitutionalisation is critical to promoting and sustaining the waning momentum towards a culture of genuine democracy, constitutionalism, and respect for the rule of law in Africa. However, the continent's large number of dominant parties at a time of a global democratic recession (particularly severe in Africa) is a clear indication that the constitutional entrenchment of the rights and duties of political parties undertaken has so far not been sufficient to promote political pluralism throughout Africa. The dominant-party system which has emerged is, much like the single-party system, not good for constitutional democracy and constitutionalism, nor is it what one should expect from genuine multipartyism. Instead it has given space to some of the most malevolent authoritarian ruling parties, such as Paul Biya's Cameroon Peoples' Democratic Movement (CPDM), Teodoro Obiang Nguema Mbasogo's Democratic Party of Equatorial Guinea (DPEG), and Emmerson Mnangagwa's Zimbabwe African National Union – Patriotic Front (ZANU-PF).

This raises many questions for which there are no easy answers. Is the problem due to the fact that no constitution fully incorporates all the fundamental principles and institutions needed to ensure free and fair competition among parties? Is it due to the manner of incorporation? Does it have to do with weak enforcement mechanisms? Is it due to lack of political will? One can argue that it is a combination of all these factors.

The evidence is overwhelming that contracting political space is limiting the scope for inclusive participation in governance. Nevertheless, there is no doubt that there has been considerable progress since the pre-1990 era. The foundations for inclusive and competitive multipartyism have been laid; even so, there are enormous challenges due to the resistance of many enemies of democracy posing as democrats. In addition, the history of multipartyism in Africa is short, and traditional African governance practices are not easily reconcilable with contemporary standards of democracy. More fundamentally, perhaps, the foundations for democracy and constitutionalism on the continent are shaky. This underscores the need to deliberately build political-party regulation into our constitutions and thereby nurture a culture of political tolerance, debate, and inclusivity.

There is no denying that political parties are key democratic and constitutional institutions, even if they are not on par with the traditional triad branches of government, but the question after more than three decades of experience is whether they are having the desired impact on the quality of African democracy, constitutionalism, and respect for the rule of law.

References

Books, articles, chapters in books, and others

"Legal Threat Over Controversial Election Bill", 5845 (8 March 2024) *Legalbrief Today*

ACE Project, "Roles and Definition of Political Parties", https://aceproject.org/ace-en/topics/pc/pca/pca01/pca01a/mobile_browsing/onePag (accessed 1 March 2024)

Afisi OT and Oyekan AO, "Multiculturalism and the Challenges of Heterogeneity in Postcolonial Africa", 8 (2020) *LASU Journal of African Studies*, pp 132–142

Africa Check, "How Many Registered Political Parties Are There in South Africa?", *Infofinder*, 31 January 2024, https://africacheck.org/infofinder/explore-facts/how-many-registered-political-parties-are-there-south-africa (accessed 1 March 2024)

Afrobarometer, "PP85: Africans Want More Democracy, But Their Leaders Still Aren't Listening", 19 January 2023, https://www.afrobarometer.org/publication/pp85-africans-want-more-democracy-but-their-leaders-still-arent-listening/ (accessed April 2024)

Avril P, "Les Chefs de l'État et la Notion de Majorité Présidentielle", 34 (1984) *Revue Française de Science Politique*, pp 752–765

Borz G, "Justifying the Constitutional Regulation of Parties", 38 (2017) *International Political Science Review*, pp 99–113

Duverger M, "Political Party", *Encyclopaedia Britannica*, 14 November 2024, https://www.britannica.com/topic/political-party (accessed 1 March 2024)

Fombad CM, "A Preliminary Assessment of the Prospects for Judicial Independence in Post-1990 Africa Constitutions," 2 *Public Law* (2007), pp 233–257

Fombad CM, "Election Management Bodies (EMBs) in Eastern and Southern Africa: Some Reflections on their Legal Framework", 15 *African and Asian Studies* (2016), pp 289–335

Fombad CM, "Political Party Constitutionalisation in Africa: Trends and Prospects for Deepening Constitutionalism", in R Dixon, T Ginsburg, and AK Abebe (eds.), *Comparative Constitutional Law in Africa*, Cheltenham, Edward Elgar (2022), pp 109–135

Fombad CM, "Reversing the Surging Tide Towards Authoritarian Democracy in Africa", in CM Fombad and N Steytler (eds.), *Democracy, Elections, and Constitutionalism in Africa*, Oxford, Oxford University Press (2021), pp 463–517

Fombad CM, "Some Perspectives on Durability and Change under Modern African Constitutions", 11 (2013) *International Journal of Constitutional Law*, pp 282–413

Fombad CM, "The Diffusion of South African-style Institutions? A Study of Comparative Constitutionalism", in R Dixon and T Roux (eds.), *Constitutional Triumphs, Constitutional Disappointments: A Critical Assessment of the 1996 South African Constitution's Local and International Influence,* Cambridge, Cambridge University Press (2018), pp 359–387

Fombad CM, "The Struggle to Defend the Independence of the Judiciary in Africa", in S Shetreet, H Chodesh, and E Helland (eds.), *Challenged Justice: In Pursuit of Judicial Independence*, Leiden, Brill Nijhoff (2021), pp 223–248

Freedom House, "Freedom in the World 2010: The Annual Survey of Political Rights & Civil Liberties", https://freedomhouse.org/sites/default/files/2020-03/FIW_2010_Complete_Book_Scan.pdf, (accessed 1 March 2024)

Freedom House, "Freedom in the World 2020: The Annual Survey of Political Rights & Civil Liberties", https://freedomhouse.org/sites/default/files/2021-08/FIW2020_book_JUMBO_PDF.pdf (accessed 1 March 2024)

Freedom House, "Freedom in the World 2023", https://freedomhouse.org/sites/default/files/2023-03/FIW_World_2023_DigtalPDF.pdf (accessed 1 March 2024)

Freedom House, "Freedom in the World Research Methodology", https://freedomhouse.org/reports/freedom-world/freedom-world-research-methodology (accessed 1 March 2024)

Freedom House, "Freedom in the World: Political Rights & Civil Liberties 1989–1990", https://freedomhouse.org/sites/default/files/2020-02/Freedom_in_the_World_1989-1990_complete_book.pdf (accessed 1 March 2024)

Freedom House, "Freedom in the World: The Annual Survey of Political Rights & Civil Liberties 2000–2001", https://freedomhouse.org/sites/default/files/2020-02/Freedom_in_the_World_2000-2001_complete_book.pdf (accessed 1 March 2024)

Go Vote, "Political Parties in Nigeria", https://govote.ng/political-parties/ (accessed 1 March 2024)

Independent Electoral Commission of South Africa, "Political Party Statistics", https://www.elections.org.za/pw/StatsData/Political-Parties-Statistics (accessed 1 November 2024)

International Crisis Group, "Electoral Poker in DR Congo", 4 April 2018, https://www.crisisgroup.org/africa/central-africa/democratic-republic-congo/259-electoral-poker-dr-congo (accessed 1 March 2024)

Katz R and Mair P, "Changing Models of Party Organisation and Party Democracy: The Emergence of the Cartel Party", 1 (1995) *Party Politics*, pp 5–28

Katz R and Mair P, "The Cartel Party Thesis: A Restatement", 7 (2009) *Perspectives on Politics* , pp 753–766

Khaitan T, "Political Parties in Constitutional Theory," in T Ginsburg, A Huq, and T Khaitan (eds.), *The Constitutional Design of Elections and Parties,* Cambridge, Cambridge University Press (2024)

LaPalombara J, *Politics Within Nations,* Englewood Cliffs, New Jersey, Prentice Hall (1974)

Lestari YS, "Cartel Party: An Analysis Study", *Atlantis Press*, November 2016, https://www.atlantis-press.com/proceedings/icosop-16/25873519 (accessed March 2024)

Lowell L, *Public Opinion and Popular Government*, New York, Longmans, Green and Company (1913)

Mendes G, "Constitutional Jurisdiction in Brazil: The Problem of Unconstitutional Legislative Omission", http://www.stf.jus.br/repositorio/cms/portalStfInternacional/portalStfDiscurso_en_US/anexo/Omisao_Legislativa_v__Ing.pdf (accessed 1 March 2024)

Miller R, "The Party-State and Bureaucratic/Political Relations in Africa", 8 *Comparative Political Studies* (1975), pp 293–317

Mo Ibrahim Foundation, "2022 IIAG: Key Findings", January 2023, https://assets.iiag.online/2022/2022-IIAG-Key-Findings_EN.pdf (accessed March 2024)

Mwonzora G and Mandikwaza E, "The Menu of Electoral Manipulation in Zimbabwe: Food Handouts, Violence, Memory, and Fear – Case of Mwenezi East and Bikita West 2017 By-elections", 54 (2019) *Journal of Asian and African Studies*, pp 1128–1144

National Election Board of Ethiopia, "Temporary Election Registration", https://nebe.org.et/sites/default/files/Accrediated%20Political%20Party%20Lists.pdf (accessed 1 March 2024)

Nyong'o PA, "Africa: The Failure of One Party Rule", 3 *Journal of Democracy* (1992), pp 90–96

O'Regan K, "Political Parties: The Interface between Law and Politics," Keynote address, Cape Town, 27 August 2010

Paczolay P, "Experience of the Execution of Constitutional Court's Decisions Declaring Legislative Omission in Hungary", *Council of Europe*, 2 September 2008, https://www.venice.coe.int/webforms/documents/default.aspx?pdffile=CDL-JU%282008%29029-e (accessed 29 December 2024)

Pildes R, "Political Parties and Constitutionalism", in T Ginsburg and R Dixon (eds.), *Comparative Constitutional Law*, Cheltenham, Edward Elgar (2011), pp 254–264

Robinson K, *Autochthony and Transfer of Power*, Oxford, Oxford University Press (1968)

Salih M, "Introduction: The Evolution of African Political Parties", in M Salih (ed.), *African Political Parties: Evolution, Institutionalisation and Governance,* London, Pluto Press (2003), pp 1–33

Schonfe WR, "Political Parties: The Functional Approach and the Structural Alternative", 15 (1983) *Comparative Politics*, pp 477–499

Stearns P, "Political Parties", in *The Oxford Encyclopaedia of the Modern World*, https://www.oxfordreference.com/display/10.1093/acref/9780195176322.001.0001/acref-9780195176322-e-1259?rskey=3Ob1yZ&result=3 (accessed March 2024)

Sunstein C, "Against Positive Rights," in A Sajó (ed.), *Western Rights? Post-Communist Application*, Netherlands, Kluwer Law International (1996), pp 225–232

Tuteng K, "Towards a Theory of One-party Government in Africa," 13 (1973) *Cahiers d'Etudes Africaines*, pp 649–663

Twum MAA, "Declining Satisfaction Threatens African Democracy, Afrobarometer CEO Reveals", *Afrobarometer*, https://www.afrobarometer.org/articles/declining-satisfaction-threatens-african-democracy-afrobarometer-ceo-reveals/ (accessed in April 2024)

Zimba L, "The Origins and Spread of the One-party States in Commonwealth Africa, Their Impact on Personal Liberties: A Case Study of the Zambian Model", in M Ndulo (ed.), *Law in Zambia,* Lusaka, East Africa Publishing House (1984), pp 113–141

Table of cases

European Court of Human Rights, *Herri Batasuna and Batasuna v Spain,* Application Nos. 25803/04 and 25817/04, Judgement [Section V], 30 June 2009

European Court of Human Rights, *Socialist Party and Others v Turkey* [GC], Application No. 21237/93m, 25 May 1998

European Court of Human Rights, *Stankov and the United Macedonian Organisation Ilinden v Bulgaria,* Application Nos. 29221/95 and 29225/95, 2001

European Court of Human Rights, *United Communist Party of Turkey and Others v Turkey [GC],* Application No. 19392/92, 1998

Table of legislation

National legislation

Benin
 Constitution of 1990: Article 5

Botswana
 Constitution of 1966: sections 3(b), 13(1), 64(4) and (5), 109(3) and (4)

Burundi
 Constitution of 2015: Articles 60, 82, 250
 Constitution of 2018: Articles 124, 178

Cameroon
 Constitution of 1996: Article 3

Cape Verde
 Constitution of 2010: Articles 57(a), 108(3), 313(1)(g)

Djibouti
 Constitution of 2010: Article 6

DR Congo
 Constitution of 2005: Article 96

Egypt
 Constitution of 2014: Article 87

Eritrea
 Constitution of 1997: Article 19(6)

Eswatini
 Constitution of 2005: section 25

Gambia
 Constitution of 1996: section 100(2)(a)

Ghana
Constitution of 1992: Articles 3(1), 166(3), 194

Kenya
Constitution of Kenya of 2010: Articles 20(4) and (5), 56(a), 77(3), 92(h), 232, 234(2)(c), 249(1)(b), 259(a)

Liberia
Constitution of 1986: Article 79(d)

Madagascar
Constitution of 2010: Articles 14, 49

Malawi
Constitution of 1994: sections 11(2)(a), 40(2)

Mauritania
Constitution of 1991: Article 27, section 73

Morocco
Constitution of 2011: Articles 7, 10, 11, 155

Nigeria
Constitution of 1960: section 25(1)
Constitution of 1999: section 223

Rwanda
Constitution of 2015: Article 54

Senegal
Constitution of 1961: Article 3
Constitution of 2019: Article 58

Seychelles
Constitution of 1993: Article 81

Somalia
Constitution of 2012: Article 65

South Africa
Constitution of 996: sections 1(d), 7(10), 39(1)(a), 143(2)(a), 195(1) and (3), sections 57(2)(d), 197(3), 199(7), 236

South Sudan
Constitution of 2011: Article 71

Uganda
Constitution of 1995: Articles 75, 82A

Zambia
Constitution of 1991: Articles 8, 9, 267(1)(a)

Zimbabwe
Constitution of 2011: sections 200(5), 240
Constitution of 2013: sections 3(2), 46, 194(1)(k)

Chapter 3 An Overview of Political-Party Constitutionalisation under Contemporary African Constitutions: A Response

Mai Cheng

1. Introduction

Constitutions and political-party systems in African countries have largely been modeled after those of Western countries. Charles Fombad begins his overview in this volume with a reflection on the conceptualisation of political parties in the Western rather than African context. Such an introduction is good evidence of the Western influence on modern African constitutions and political-party system. While Western systems have achieved significant success and now function with relative stability, observers and researchers should always keep in mind that this success is deeply rooted in unique historical contexts and contemporary conditions.

Nevertheless, African countries face inevitable challenges in replicating this success simply by adopting Western institutional forms. As rightly noted by Fombad, the reintroduction of multipartyism in the 1990s is yet to produce the genuine democracy that has been expected in Africa. Political leaders and governments in Africa, often driven by self-interest, have exploited weaknesses and loopholes in these systems. Sometimes these leaders could indeed be labelled as "enemies of democracy posing as democrats", as Fombad points out. The rise of dominant parties in 18 African countries is vivid evidence of this exploitation. The abuse and manipulation of institutional frameworks and constitutional provisions has, in many cases, led to dysfunctional governance. The two indicators mentioned by Fombad – the annual surveys by Freedom House and the Ibrahim Index of African Governance – both testify to the stagnation, or even regression, of democracy and rule of law on the African continent, especially in the last decade.

Even the effort to constitutionalise political parties, whose potentially positive contribution to democracy in Africa is elaborated on by Fombad, does not seem to change the overall picture in any essential way. Consequently, nearly three decades after the onset of the third wave of democratisation, current institutional practices in Africa, including those in regard to political-party systems, remain far from successful. In the face of this problematical reality, Fombad, at the end of his overview, raises many questions calling for further exploration. Does this reality come into existence because of imperfect system design, or because of inadequate implementation? Fombad leaves the question open, though few would doubt he already has his own firm answer to it. The author of this response, as an outsider of Africa, makes so bold as to offer his own explanation of this reality.

2. Why constitutions and political-party systems in Africa are yet to succeed

2.1 Lack of an enabling environment on the African continent

The development of constitutions and political-party systems in Western countries has been closely synchronised with and supported by these countries' social and economic advancement. As these nations have achieved political stability and the rule of law, their social and economic development has concurrently reached a high level. This historical parallel may have led to an underestimation of the crucial role that a certain level of socio-economic development plays in sustaining the operation of the constitutions and political-party systems of Western countries.

In this regard, Fombad, in his contribution, lays out eight principles as "foundation for an effective constitutional regulatory framework". A "mechanism for political party funding" is among these eight pillars. It is noteworthy that in the constitutions of many Western countries, such as those of the United States of America and France, there is no mention of party funding. In the case of another internationally influential constitution, the German Basic Law, it was not until 2017 that the concept of party funding was constitutionalised after the failed application to ban the National Democratic Party (now known as the Homeland party). This deviation from Western systems reveals the differences in economic background between Africa and the West.

State apparatuses and political-party organisations do not create wealth or provide direct products or services to society; instead, they consume a significant amount of social resources. However, if they function properly, their activities can indirectly contribute to social development. When functioning effectively, they enable the state to better redistribute wealth as well as dismantle obstacles within the existing legal and political system that hinder economic and social progress. While the costs of these institutions are high, the potential benefits they offer may be equally substantial.

However, the high-cost nature of implementing a country's constitution and political-party system can also mean that considerable social resources are consumed without generating direct value for society, potentially acting as an apparent barrier to social progress and development. Unfortunately, this scenario appears to be unfolding in some African countries. For instance, certain African political parties recruit young people as political foot soldiers, diverting a large portion of the country's young labour force without contributing to wealth production. In South Africa, the African National Congress's cadre deployment strategy may decrease the efficiency of state organs and public services, hindering the country's overall development.

These phenomena of institutional inefficiency also occur in Western countries. However, the higher levels of economic and social development in these nations allow the state and society to tolerate and absorb such inefficiencies to some extent, and to implement reforms that minimise waste and attrition. In contrast, African countries, which already suffer from a severe shortage of social resources, face greater challenges. If national constitutions and political-party systems are perceived as contributing to unneglectable waste of resources, it can lead to increased scepticism among ordinary citizens about the legitimacy and effectiveness of these institutions.

Ironically, the high cost of operating these systems could even lead to higher popular expectations for their performance. In the long run, adopting Western constitutional and political-party systems may contribute positively to the formation of open, fair societies and promote innovation and development across Africa, but the current realities are less promising. Operating within institutional frameworks emulating those of the Western world, political leaders in many African countries appear to be more focused on attacking one another and catering to their constituencies than on collaborating with one another to develop long-term strategies that would truly benefit their nations.

Moreover, in response to periodic electoral pressures, political parties and politicians often resort to flashy or short-term campaign promises that in practice will fail to give meaningful impetus to the country's long-term development. In some cases, these strategies may even hinder the nation's proper progress.

In addition, the underdeveloped economic landscape in many African countries has hindered the formation of a decentralised system of resource allocation. As a result, governments often monopolise most of society's resources through their centralised power. The introduction of periodic electoral systems exacerbates this situation by creating insecurity among those in power; the greater the influence of electoral campaigns, the more insecure those in power become. The government's control of resources severely limits the opposition's access to resources, making it difficult for them to mount a significant challenge. When the opposition finally gathers enough resources to contest the ruling parties and politicians, the stakes are extremely high – it is often a win-or-die scenario. If the opposition is defeated, retreating to other areas of social life to regroup is almost impossible, leading to an equally insecure situation for them. When both sides of the political competition are insecure and focused on calculating gains and losses, multiparty politics in African countries often fails to produce policies that address the country's long-term development goals. In this zero-sum game, it becomes more challenging to foster stability and progress in the country with a collaborative, win-win approach to multiparty activities.

In Western countries, the decentralised social and economic structure is complemented by constitutions and political-party systems that lean towards individualism and decentralisation. This is evident in the emphasis these systems place on the right to equality among individual citizens and the secularisation of political life. This tendency towards individualistic and decentralised institutional design stems from the trust that the framers of the constitutions have placed in the rationality of individual citizens. However, the full development of a citizen's capacity for rational judgement is not instantaneous; it requires a long-term educational environment that emphasises tolerance and openness. Through this process of education, citizens, endowed with maximum decision-making freedom, are guided to make political decisions that go beyond their immediate, short-term interest.

The formation of a tolerant and open cultural atmosphere in Western countries is not only the product of purposeful education but also the result of various setbacks and lessons learnt throughout their history. These experiences have been ingrained in the socio-political culture, establishing a collective subconsciousness. As a result, extreme political statements and actions tend to provoke instinctive opposition from society. In societies that have not undergone the same bumpy development, this self-correcting mechanism might not exist, leading to a greater risk of political instability.

In contrast, the education level of most African countries remains relatively underdeveloped. Additionally, the history of democracy and multiparty politics is still quite short, which has hindered the establishment of a well-developed civic culture respecting rational decision-making and tolerance of different opinions. However, in areas where African countries have experienced significant setbacks, there are signs of the emergence of a political culture which is in line with the principles of the constitutions. For instance, in contemporary African countries, few political parties dare to openly incite racial antagonism or national division. Even a populist party like South Africa's Economic Freedom Fighters, which has been known for encouraging black-white tensions, still ground its identity and platform primarily on addressing economic inequality within South African society rather than on open racism.

2.2 Externally driven institutional development can bring only formal changes

To a large extent, the development of political systems in Africa has been driven by external influences. As Fombad points out, the design of the political-party system in African constitutions is basically an unfolding of the principles of Western theories of the expected role and functions of political parties in constitutionalism. While it might not be hard to design a seemingly perfect constitution and political-party system on paper, implementing the values and principles they embody is far more challenging. Experiences in Africa have shown that it is important to have realistic expectations about the impact of formal systems. System design is often the easiest phase. The true measure of success lies in the system's practical effectiveness. When the worst-case scenario emerges, namely that the operation of a system leads to dysfunction in practice or hinders the country's other development goals, then, regardless of the designers' good intentions, the design of the system cannot be considered successful.

From the principles of the constitutions to the institutions ensuring the implementation of the constitution, many African constitutions have a much more detailed design than those of Western countries. The dozens or even hundreds of pages of constitutional texts of many African countries reflect the meticulous consideration given by the framers to all aspects of the new constitutional systems. There are also a number of innovative provisions reflecting local needs in Africa, for example those in regard to specialised constitutional implementation oversight bodies, such as the

South African Human Rights Commission. As for provisions relating to the political-party system, their meticulousness is noteworthy too.

Yet despite the seemingly ideal design of their constitutions and political-party systems, African countries have continued to struggle with persistent underdevelopment. Since gaining independence, many have repeatedly reformed their constitutions – some, like Nigeria, have experimented with various forms of government, including parliamentary and presidential systems, federalism, centralism, multiparty systems, state-run two-party systems, and even military rule, all within just half a century. Regardless of these regime changes, the conditions for the majority of the African population, who endure extreme poverty and lack basic livelihood security, have remained largely unchanged.

The wave of democratisation in African countries during the 1990s was, in many ways, a return to the practice in the 1960s of replicating Western systems. After nearly half a century of experimentation, the most significant outcome may be the recognition of what does not work – unsuccessful institutional designs and the constitutional and political ideas behind these designs. In terms of positive outcomes, there have been few gains. Instead, the fundamental challenge remains that people still lack a clear understanding of which systems can effectively lead African countries toward stable and sustainable development.

Within these limited gains, the experiences of African countries clearly illustrate two key points. First, under external pressure – which can take diverse forms such as financial aid with conditions, diplomatic demands, or threats of sanctions – most countries can rapidly construct various seemingly beautiful systems, including apparently constitutionalist ones. It was no coincidence that the most recent wave of democratisation in Africa began at the end of the Cold War. In the 1990s, against a changed geopolitical backdrop, leaders of most African countries had to reconsider their domestic political system. In the founding era of African countries, the colonial powers as external actors shaped African constitutions, yet even nowadays, those economic and geopolitical factors still carry heavy weight in the development of African constitutionalism. Secondly, the ease and speed of this formal institution-building highlights that a country's constitution and political-party system can function independently of its social and economic development context.

This independence can be advantageous for the constitution and political-party system, as it allows these institutions to develop with relative autonomy. It also enables countries to learn from one another, regardless of their unique social and historical contexts, and even to imitate each other in the design and practice of their constitutions and political systems. By doing so, they can draw on the experiences and lessons of other nations.

However, this independence is not necessarily beneficial for the overall development of the country and society. While the framers invest significant effort in system design, and ordinary people participate in the constitution-drafting process with great enthusiasm and high expectations, they soon discover that this very independence causes the operation of constitutions and political-party systems to become misaligned with the country's development needs and realities. As a result, these systems may fail to deliver the outcomes that people had hoped for, particularly in advancing the country's development or overcoming long-standing challenges the country has been facing. Faced with unmet expectations, ordinary citizens tend to be left confused and disappointed. This disillusionment ultimately undermines the newly established constitutions and political-party systems. Unfortunately, it is the reality that is unfolding in many African countries.

The framers of African constitutions clearly understood the importance of transforming constitutional provisions from mere words on paper into actual rules of conduct. As a result, they placed significant emphasis on building constitutional review systems and creatively established various oversight bodies to promote the implementation of the constitution and a constitutional culture. However, the outcomes of these efforts have been relatively limited. In practice, the implementation of African constitutions has repeatedly exposed the challenges faced by constitutional review and oversight bodies. These challenges often stem from a lack of understanding and support from other state organs, and even from the general public.

It was once anticipated that, as constitutions were implemented, organisations and individuals would gradually adjust their behaviour to align with constitutional requirements. This shift was expected to lead to a transformation in mindset, ultimately fostering a social culture of respect for the constitution.

In the political reality of some African countries, the pattern of political activity does appear to be shifting toward constitutional expectations. For instance, few African nations are currently engaged in civil war, and as Fombad points out, only one African country – Eswatini – continues to reject a multiparty system. More countries are holding regular elections, and while disputes, and even violence, remain common before and after elections, the transfer of power is largely occurring within established institutional frameworks.

A noteworthy example is the 2024 national election of South Africa, where the country avoided political turmoil even though the African National Congress lost its 30-year majority in Parliament. Instead, the ANC formed a government of national unity which includes the main, and predominantly white-led, opposition party, the Democratic Alliance, marking a positive development.

Additionally, constitutional review bodies in some African countries have begun making significant rulings on electoral disputes. A remarkable instance of this occurred in May 2020, when the High Court of Malawi, sitting as the Constitutional Court, for the first time in the country's history nullified the results of a presidential election and ordered that a new one be held.

It is noteworthy, however, that despite gradual improvement in the functioning of constitutions and political-party systems, significant advancements in the economic and social realities of African countries remain elusive. Even within the political landscape of certain African nations, concerning trends are emerging, such as the rise of dominant political parties.

The incompatibility between formal systems and practices in many African countries can be attributed largely to the fact that their transformation has been driven by external factors. From a pessimistic perspective, there is always a risk that local actors – whether politicians, political parties, or even ordinary voters – may continue to adhere to behavioural patterns that are misaligned with the spirit of the new system, making its realisation and localisation even more challenging.

2.3 Why politicians and governments can make systems dysfunctional

It is well known that Africa faces a significant deficit in an indigenous culture of democracy and the rule of law, which negatively impacts the smooth functioning of constitutions and political-party systems. The framers of African constitutions were fully aware of this deficit, which is why these constitutions exhibit a strong value-orientation. In fact, 47 African constitutions include provisions that stipulate the obligations of citizens. Many countries have also established special constitutional bodies tasked with monitoring and promoting the implementation of the constitution, as well as fostering national constitutional awareness.

As regards political parties, the framers of African constitutions also envisioned that they would play a crucial role in cultivating constitutional awareness among the general populace while guiding it in democratic participation. Yet, in addition to these efforts to promote constitutional awareness, the framers of African constitutions recognised that such awareness is still not firmly established. As a result, many political-party systems in African constitutions include numerous provisions that limit the influence of ordinary people. For instance, the right of citizens to stand for election is sometimes restricted on the basis of property status and education. Furthermore, many African constitutions incorporate the concept of militant democracy,[1] such as the ban of amendment of certain constitutional provisions, ban of extremist political parties. offer limited protection for local autonomy, and impose stringent constitutional and legal restrictions on the organisation, programmes, and activities of political parties.

In view of these systemic arrangements, one may reasonably conclude that the framers of African constitutions anticipated that the implementation of these constitutions would gradually strengthen social awareness of constitutional principles. As a result, the reliance on constitutional review and oversight bodies would eventually give way to self-adherence and cooperation from both citizens and political elites. Through the ongoing implementation of these constitutions, the constitutional system would ultimately establish the conducive background conditions necessary for their solid and effective enforcement.

However, the lessons and experiences from African constitutions have shown that it is highly idealistic to expect the promotion of constitutional implementation merely by appealing to the actors involved to embrace constitutional values. Unlike religious beliefs, the values of a constitution are recognised through rational understanding, not faith. This rational recognition is always accompanied by a calculated assessment of interest trade-offs. When constitutional actors "rationally" support the system, it is because they perceive a rational benefit in doing so. Most constitutions adopt the principle of a secular state, and within these frameworks, rational interests are often tied to improved material living conditions. If it serves their interests to disobey or even violate the system, these constitutional actors, from a standpoint of "rational" calculation, lack sufficient incentive

1 On the concept of militant democracy see Johannes Socher, "Constitutionalisation of Political Parties: International Standards and the Experience of Continental Europe", in this volume.

to avoid actions conflicting with the values and spirit of the constitution. In such cases, moral education on constitutional values and spirit proves inadequate for these "rational" actors.

In practice, through the interpretation and balance of the constitutional review bodies, a country always seems to be fortunate to find a solution that can accommodate the interests of all parties. But when a country is not so fortunate, it is left to either compel one of the parties to make compromises, sacrificing its interests, or to introduce a constitutional amendment. When such situations arise, there is a risk that the authority of the constitution can be compromised, making people doubt the actual binding force of constitutional rules.

The framers of Western constitutions attach great value to the electoral system and the important role of multiparty politics in democracy and rule of law. They apparently expect that the process of political competition, organised and guided by political parties, is the most important way to let the ordinary people have a say in the political life of the country.

But behind this expectation, there are two essential assumptions. First, it is assumed that ordinary people already have judgement over policy issues and that the political parties are merely catering to the demands of voters by presenting various implementing plans. Secondly, it is assumed that the competition among political parties is a process of refining and synthesising the will of the voters, and that when the election is over, a political will that represents the majority of the people will automatically emerge.

However, both assumptions will fail in reality; sometimes they can even contradict the political realities of a country. Political parties, in order to demonstrate their distinctiveness to attract followers, may purposely reinforce, or even develop, concepts of difference that might contribute to divisions in the population. Since the goal of party competition is to gain a majority of 50 per cent + 1, it might be not in the interests of the political parties to unite the remaining voters of 50 per cent – 1. In order to attract supporters, parties sometimes intentionally divide voters into different groups. When this occurs, the competitive process of party politics, instead of contributing to synthesising and aggregating public opinion, becomes a process of fragmentation.

These phenomena have, in fact, played out even in Western countries. In recent years, the political atmosphere in Western countries has become increasingly polarised. Taking advantage of the stagnant economy and many social problems, certain extremist political parties that have newly ascended to the political arena have been demagoguing the population. These parties sometimes amplify or exaggerate the current political and social controversies that exist in society. Some voters are easily captured by such inflammatory political propaganda.

As for African countries, the same phenomenon manifests itself in a more blatant manner. Topics related to ethnicity, race, and religion are always divisive elements in the party politics of African countries. Framers of African constitutions clearly realised these risks. As revealed in detail by Fombad, most African constitutions set limitations on the internal organisation and programmes of parties, together with provisions ensuring the parties' compliance with democratic values and principles. But the reality of African countries has revealed the insufficiency of these formal prescriptions.

In the African context, African constitutions have widely adopted the presidential system, with presidents occupying a central leading role in government. As a result, the race for the presidency has become a focal point of rivalry, giving rise to serious polarisation in the politics of African countries. The inability of political parties in African countries, especially opposition parties, to unite and create a strong check on the ruling party – along with the culture of patronage politics that continues to distort party politics – also contributes to this polarisation.

3. The future road of African constitutions and political-party systems

As argued in this chapter, constitutional reforms and democratic transformation in African countries are, to a large extent, the outcome of external dynamics. These are yet to yield the expected positive outcome, even while generating many problems that are difficult to address. In the face of this dilemma, most African countries have to answer the question: What is the next step?

3.1 Starting again from scratch is not a viable option

The history of democracy and the rule of law in African countries, and possibly also other developing countries, shows that, if the existing institutional framework, traditions, and background culture of a country are disregarded and an alien system is imposed top-down, the operation of this system will face huge challenges. No matter how well-intended the system is, it is probable that it will not only fail to realise its goals but also give rise to new problems that are difficult to overcome. Given these lessons of history, an incremental approach to institutional reform, one based on a realistic analysis of the existing institutional and social environment, might be a more viable approach to the further development of African countries.

Judging from African experiences, those countries that have succeeded in development are also those that have adopted an incremental reform strategy, such as South Africa. While some may criticise the incomplete nature of the reforms, for example South Africa's "failure" to completely undo the injustices of the past white apartheid regime, it is very questionable if these countries could have had a better way of transformation. In comparison to these moderate reform measures in other countries, Zimbabwe's ruling party, after the 1990s, gradually abandoned its past policy of compromising and coexisting with the white community and began increasingly to adopt radical reform measures. However, these radical reform measures have not solved the social and political problems that the country has been facing for a long time. What is worse, these measures have dragged the country into political turmoil and international isolation.

Certainly, a country's choice to adopt a gradual or radical reform path depends largely on the severity of the problems it is facing. When the conflicts in a country have intensified to a certain extent, there will be little room for gradual reform. At this point, even if policy-makers clearly realise the risk of radical reform measures, they have little other options in the face of surging public pressure. But if the policy-makers, be they the government or the ruling party, can adopt gradual reform measures before the conflicts have intensified beyond the point of no return, a smooth transition is still feasible.

In many current African countries, the fact that constitutions are not fully implemented seems to pose certain obstacles to the development of the country. However, this obstacle is not as serious as to require that African countries adopt a completely new version of their constitutions. There is still room for African governments, especially the ruling parties, to adopt gradual reform strategies.

Currently, if African countries abandon their established institutions and reconstruct them from the ground up, this option will in fact go back to the old ways before the 1990s: the reintroduction of governmental control over the political and social life of the country; reduction of the space for multiparty politics; or even the abolition of multipartyism itself. History has brought to light the inherent defects of this old strategy, and people can expect that reasonable policy-makers in African countries would not try it again. On the one hand, if history could be repeated and the African people were now to be given the same choice they had in the early 1990s, it is doubtful if they would immediately choose the systems of Western countries as a blueprint for reform. On the other hand, it is clear that they would also not keep their old pre-1990s systems, especially the authoritarian regime, intact.

The new constitutions and political-party systems that arose in Africa in the 1990s have been in place for almost three decades. During this period, some African countries have suffered many setbacks and learnt many a lesson, but on the whole, there has been no significant regression comparable to what obtained before the 1990s. Many African countries, indeed, have even shown notable progress over this 30-year period. Therefore, the current form of the constitutions and political-party systems that exist in African countries are far from being an obstacle to national development; they are more in the nature of an embarrassment, given the reality of their incomplete implementation.

Additionally, after 30 years of experience, many new interest groups have come into being in African countries. In comparison to the era before the 1990s, constitutions and political-party systems in African countries have become much more decentralised, and the number of stakeholders has expanded significantly. For example, although the new constitutions of many African countries have paid little attention to the centrality accorded to the position of the president, or to the protection of local autonomy, other state organs, such as parliament and local government, are still gaining greater influence.

While many countries have witnessed the rise of dominant parties, the framework of multiparty politics continues to provide precious room for opposition parties. In some countries with a dominant party, the hope of the opposition to gain control of the government has become reality, such as in the case of the Democratic Alliance after the elections in South Africa in 2024. Electoral campaigns in African countries are still strongly tinged by patronage politics, with some voters viewing their votes as leverage in exchange for short-term gains, or small gifts, but the status of ordinary voters has nevertheless gained ground compared to the past, when they had little or no say in the political process. If the old trajectory of political development were to return, all parliaments, local governments, political parties, and voters – including political foot soldiers who make a living through campaigns – would lose their vested interests. This possibility would naturally provoke their opposition and lead to political and even social resistance.

In view of these realities, it is fair to say that the problem African countries face is not that a bad system is holding back the progress of the country, but rather that a well-intended system is not functioning as expected.

So far as the political-party system is concerned, the constitutions of African countries, as Fombad explains, have now generally adopted the multiparty system. Some have even elevated multiparty democracy to the level of constitutional principles. In the emerging realities of African countries, a multiparty system is meeting the needs of the people, such as preventing corruption by ruling parties and political elites, or giving more say to the average citizen. The current crucial problem is how to implement these well-intentioned systems in practice.

In regard to preventing corruption by the elites and empowering the ordinary people, in the political arena of multiparty politics parties need to provide the ordinary people with tangible benefits in order to attract supporters and enhance their influence. Such efforts by political parties provide an important institutional channel for the ordinary people to share in the benefits controlled by political elites.

It is evident that political elites in African countries are neither in consensus as to how to advance national development, nor endowed with a tradition of self-discipline and mutual respect for each other. Given this reality, what is needed in order to restrain the elites from their inclination to self-enrichment and provide the ordinary people with a way to exert influence on those elites is an inter-elite competition mechanism. Of all the forms of governments currently conceivable, the multiparty system might be the most desirable option.

3.2 Possible directions for future development

Judging from formal constitutional provisions, the protection of citizen's political rights in the constitutions of African countries is near to adequate. In political reality, additionally election activities are increasingly institutionalised in most countries in Africa. If these developments are taken as indicators of the level to which citizens' rights are being realised, then it might seem that the political rights of African citizens deserve complimentary evaluation.

The fact is, however, as indicated by Fombad, that the vast majority of African countries rank very low on various international indicators of democracy. This discrepancy suggests that, even by the criteria of the Western world, the mere establishment of electoral systems, constitutional review, and institutions overseeing the implementation of constitutions, is not enough to guarantee the attainment of citizens' political rights.

In the context of African countries' development, the most urgent problem might not be the realisation of the political rights of ordinary people, but security of food, clean water, and basic education. Against a backdrop of economic underdevelopment, political rights, which are precious to citizens in the Western world, might merely be ordinary people's leverage in exchange for small gifts in Africa.

In these circumstances, the main goal in further reforming the constitutions and political-party systems of African countries might not be to make the existing systems more seemingly perfect, but rather to ensure these systems genuinely contribute to the economic and social development of the country.

To promote development, continued constitutional reform is needed. This reform needs to start with the structures of government, in particular with further relaxing the control that the government exercises over the allocation of resources. Under conditions of economic underdevelopment, both the people and political parties are dependent on government financial support. The situation will persist for a long time; but it does not mean that all resources should be placed under government control.

In view of the rampant corruption of African elites and the stark influence of patronage politics in Africa, concentrating a large number of resources in the hands of the government will lead not to their effective utilisation but rather to their wastage, due to political corruption and political spoils-sharing. It is testimony to the reality of this risk that international donors are more willing to deal with civil society organisations than with government agencies in Africa.

In order to transfer resources from the government to the society, and to enhance the social momentum driving the national development of the nation, constitutional reform in Africa should continue its decentralisation process. The power centre should be shifted from the executive to the parliament, and from the central government to the local authorities.

After the 1990s, African constitutions largely maintained a strong executive. Some of them even give the central government the authority to intervene in local governments. The motivation of these institutional designs was the concern that African countries would become politically unstable after democratisation and the introduction of multiparty politics. However, subsequent developments have shown that a strong executive and centralised government structure are precisely the source of political turmoil in African countries. When resources and power are concentrated, political competition between politicians and political parties takes on a zero-sum and winner-take-all character. This situation makes it very difficult for the losers in the game to admit or accept their failure, which in turn can easily trigger political unrest.

Within an imbalanced vertical government structure, the central government does not enjoy the respect of the local population, while local governments lack the resources to justify their legitimacy over the local population. Unlike the central government, however, they play an especially important role in promoting social development and improving people's well-being. This disparity between power and resources might also be an obstacle to the development of African countries.

After nearly three decades of implementation of the new constitutions, the cohesiveness of most African countries has increased, and the likelihood of situations such as serious ethnic conflicts, as was the case prior to the 1990s, has been greatly reduced. With the new constitutional systems gradually taking root, relaxing the control of the state and giving society and individual citizens more room might be an appropriate direction for further reform in line with the developmental goals of African countries. Accordingly, reform of constitutions should continue to advance decentralisation and facilitate the transfer of resources to private sectors that can truly drive national development.

In this process of decentralisation and relaxing control, political parties should also be given more room for movement. The constitutions of African countries have a strong value-orientation, and their framers expected parties to act faithfully in accordance with the values and spirit of these constitutions. African constitutions expect parties to play a positive role as political educators of the population. In anticipation of cases where parties fail to adhere to the principles and provisions of the constitutions, the framers of many such constitutions endorsed the concept of militant democracy – for example through the prohibition of amendments of certain constitutional principles, or the banning of parties if they pursue activities that contradict constitutional principles – as constitutional methods to guide party politics.

But within the framework of multiparty politics, the most important consideration for political parties is popular support. Where there are difficulties in fully implementing constitutions, it is inevitable that there will be only limited acceptance of their spirit and values by ordinary people. Insufficiency of popular support for national constitutions will inevitably be transmitted to the organisation and activities of parties, causing them to adopt activities and strategies that may be constitutionally controversial.

In multiparty politics, what parties compete for is popular support. To win the competition, they need to accentuate the differences between themselves to attract the attention of voters. Thus, in their attention-winning endeavours, it becomes unavoidable that parties will make demagogic statements, including ones that are constitutionally controversial. Indeed, demagogic strategies for attracting attention are widespread in Western countries too, but in contexts where party systems have a much longer history than they do in Africa and where constitutional culture is more firmly rooted in society. If it were compulsory for parties in African countries to adhere strictly to the principles and provisions of the constitution and engage "courteously", these are demands that sometimes may well prove difficult to meet.

Even if parties, out of fear of the coercive power of the constitution and state, do not pursue unconstitutional activities openly, this simply means that certain ideas and activities of an unconstitutional tendency slip from the public eye and go underground. Instead of truly eliminating these ideas and activities, prohibition serves only to deprive the constitution-supporting organisation and actors of the chance to engage with such ideas and activities peacefully, as a result of which they miss the opportunity to reflect on whether there are indeed deficiencies in the current constitution.

Therefore, in Western countries, it is noteworthy that there are only few examples where political parties have been banned based on concept of militant democracy. Political practices in these countries involve the use of the political competition to show voters the desirability of the various political ideas and leave it to the voters' decision to accept these ideas or not. Certainly, sometimes this openness might cause temporary setbacks; but these setbacks might be the necessary cost for a robust multiparty politics.

Furthermore, when constitutional provisions are used to regulate political parties, more often than not the ruling party will take advantage of this constitutional powers to restrict the actions of opposition parties. In countries with a mature democratic culture, the ruling party might not pursue these punitive strategies, considering the likelihood of backlash from the electorate and the constraints imposed by other constitutional organs. But on the African continent, constraints from political culture and other constitutional organs tend to be weak. Therefore, in the African context, these powers are bound to be abused by the ruling party, as demonstrated by the political realities of African countries again and again. In view of these realities and risks, deregulating political parties in African countries and granting them more room for their activities might be the direction to take in terms of reforms.

Moreover, the history of party politics in African countries has shown that it does not necessarily exacerbate rivalries and conflicts in the population. The establishment of parties that transcend ethnic boundaries and forge political alliances is perhaps the best evidence of the role they can play in unifying people. If the institutional framework is properly designed, it is possible to enhance the positive role of political parties while contributing to the faithful implementation of the constitution.

Chapter 4 African Regional Standards for Regulating Political Parties

Charles M Fombad and Johannes Socher

1. Introduction

Political parties are essentially national institutions and hence regulated by national constitutions and domestic laws. However, since the end of the Cold War, the capacity of domestic laws to serve as the exclusive framework for self-governing practices within the state has steadily diminished.

The phenomena of globalisation, liberalisation, and regionalism have not only underscored the need for strong linkages between states, regions, and societies, but also underlined the fact that most political and economic crises today have international effects that call for common solutions. This has resulted in the progressive internationalisation of constitutional law through the incorporation of international and regional norms setting standards of good governance, democracy, and constitutionalism.[1]

The focus of this chapter is on African regional and sub-regional standards for regulating political parties.[2] It examines the nature and scope of the regulatory principles that these regional and sub-regional standards have set. It will consider to what extent these have or could influence the constitutionalisation of political parties on the continent. It will also consider whether there is any scope for such standards not only to complement domestic regulations, but also to act as a sort of compensatory backup for any weaknesses, actual or perceived, in the domestic regulatory framework of political parties.

The discussion will proceed in section 2 to highlight some of the key features of the African regional and sub-regional normative frameworks. This will be followed, in section 3, by a discussion of some of the effects of these supranational standards on national practice. In concluding in

1 See generally CM Fombad, "The Internationalisation of Constitutional Law and Constitutionalism in Africa", 60 (2012) *American Journal of Comparative Law*, pp 439–473.

2 On the relevant international standards, see J Socher, "Constitutionalisation of Political Parties: International Strandards and the Experience of Continental Europe", in this volume.

section 4, it is contended that although some welcome new initiatives are currently under way, a more proactive and decisive approach by the African Union (AU) and its regional economic communities (RECs) could enhance the adoption by African states of constitutional measures enabling political parties play a more effective role in governance on the continent.

2. Regional and sub-regional normative frameworks

Although the focus of this chapter is on the regional and sub-regional norms that have influenced the regulation of political parties in Africa, it is apt to at least note that a number of international instruments have also played an important role and often been cited in cases brought before the African Court on Human and Peoples' Rights (ACtHPR) and the African Commission on Human and Peoples' Rights ("the African Commission"). The main international instrument is the International Covenant on Civil and Political Rights (ICCPR), which guarantees not only a number of political rights in relation to elections but also contains specific provisions protecting the right to freedom of association as well as other interconnected fundamental rights, such as freedom of expression and opinion and freedom of assembly.[3] At a regional and sub-regional level, these fundamental rights are entrenched in the normative frameworks of both the AU (section 2.1) as well as the different RECs (section 2.2).

2.1 The AU normative framework for regulating political parties

The AU normative framework relevant for the regulation of political parties consists of two pillars: on the one hand, provisions in the African Charter on Human and Peoples' Rights ("African Charter") and other "classic" human rights instruments; and, on the other, provisions in AU instruments to promote democracy and good governance.

3 Ibid.

2.1.1 The African Charter and other human rights instruments

Although political parties are not explicitly mentioned in the African Charter, the right to form, join, and participate in them is guaranteed as a specific form of freedom of association in its Article 10.[4] Subject to the obligation of solidarity,[5] this includes the negative freedom not to be compelled to join an association.[6] In its 1992 Resolution on the Right to Freedom of Association, the African Commission considered, furthermore, that "in regulating the use of this right, the competent authorities should not enact provisions which would limit the exercise of this freedom" and that "the regulation of the exercise of the right to freedom of association should be consistent with States' obligations [under the African Charter]".[7]

The right to freedom of association guaranteed in the African Charter is complemented by a number of protocols obliging state parties to take positive action to promote participation in the political and decision-making process of specific groups. In particular, Article 9(1) of the Protocol to the African Charter on the Rights of Women in Africa provides that state parties shall enable national legislation and other measures which ensure not only that women participate without any discrimination in all elections but also that they "are represented equally at all levels with men in all electoral processes".[8] Similarly, Article 21 of the Protocol to the African Charter on the Rights of Persons with Disabilities calls for the inclusion of persons with disabilities in public and political life, "including as members of political parties". Although this protocol is not yet in force, it is here that

4 On the right to freedom of association under the African Charter more broadly, see, for example, K Olaniyan, "Civil and Political Rights in the African Charter: Articles 8–14", in MD Evans and R Murray (eds.), *The African Charter on Human and Peoples' Rights: The System in Practice, 1986–2000*, Cambridge, Cambridge University Press, 2nd ed (2008), pp 213–43, 225–30.

5 Article 29 of the African Charter states: "The individual shall also have the duty ... (3) to preserve and strengthen social and national solidarity, particularly when the latter is threatened."

6 Article 10(2) of the African Charter. This aspect was also confirmed by the ACtHPR in *Mtikila & Others v Republic of Tanzania* (see section 3.2.1 below).

7 African Commission, Resolution on the Right to Freedom of Association, ACHPR/Res. 5(XI)92, 9 March 1992.

8 See also African Union Assembly of Heads of State and Government in Addis Ababa, Ethiopia in July 2004, "Solemn Declaration on Gender Equality in Africa", para 5, Assembly/AU, Decl.12 (III) Rev. 1, https://au.int/sites/default/files/documents/38956-doc-assembly_au_decl_12_iii_e.pdf (accessed 20 May 2024).

political parties are explicitly mentioned in an African human rights treaty for the first time.[9] In addition, the African Charter on the Rights and Welfare of the Child should be mentioned, as its Article 8 also guarantees the right to freedom of association. Lastly, the African Youth Charter provides in its Article 11 for a number of ways in which youth may participate in political processes.

Unlike in Europe, for example,[10] no dedicated guidelines have been developed yet for the regulation of political parties in the African region. However, the Guidelines on Freedom of Association and Assembly in Africa ("FoAA Guidelines"), adopted by the African Commission in May 2017, formulate general principles and rules in relation to freedom of association.[11] As the foundational report of the African Commission's Study Group on Freedom of Association and Assembly in Africa makes clear, although political parties were not directly in mind when the FoAA Guidelines were developed, they are of course also covered under them.[12] The Guidelines set standards for national legal frameworks, legal personality, purposes and activities, oversight, internal governance structures, financing, federations and cooperation, and sanctions and remedies for associations. In addition, they formulate 10 fundamental principles. In relation to the regulation of political parties, the following principles[13] are particularly relevant:

---

9 As per the latest available list, only 13 states have signed the Protocol while a mere 10 have ratified it. See African Union, "List of Countries Which Have Signed, Ratified/Acceded to the Protocol to the African Charter on Human and Peoples' Rights on the Rights of Persons with Disabilities in Africa", 19 September 2023, https://au.int/sites/default/files/treaties/36440-sl-PROTOCOL_TO_THE_AFRICAN_CHARTER_ON_HUMAN_AND_PEOPLES_RIGHTS_ON_THE_RIGHTS_OF_PERSONS_WITH_DISABILITIES_IN_AFRICA_0.pdf (accessed 20 May 2024).

10 European Commission for Democracy Through Law (Venice Commission), *Guidelines on Political Party Regulation,* 2nd ed, 14 December 2020, CDL-AD(2020)032.

11 African Commission, *Guidelines on Freedom of Association and Assembly in Africa,* May 2017, https://achpr.au.int/sites/default/files/files/2021-05/guidelinesonfreedomofassociationandassemblyinafricaeng_1.pdf (accessed 22 May 2024).

12 African Commission, *Report of the Study Group on Freedom of Association & Assembly in Africa,* May 2015, p 12, https://www.icnl.org/wp-content/uploads/ACHPR-English-REPORT-21.05.2015.pdf (accessed 15 May 2024).

13 For a proposed list of principles to guide the constitutionalisation of political parties in Africa, see CM Fombad, "Political Party Constitutionalisation in Africa: Trends and Prospects for Deepening Constitutionalism", in R Dixon, T Ginsburg, and AK Abebe (eds.), *Comparative Constitutional Law in Africa,* Cheltenham, Edgar Elgar (2022), pp 109–135.

- there shall be a presumption in favour of the exercise of the right to freedom of association;
- any legal framework put in place to regulate associations shall have the primary purpose of enabling the exercise of that right;
- governance agencies shall conduct their work impartially and fairly;
- procedures relating to the governance of associations shall be clear, simple, and transparent;
- state decisions shall be clearly and transparently laid out, with any adverse decision by written argumentation on the basis of law and challengeable in independent courts of law;
- state sanctions shall be strictly proportionate and applied only as a matter of last resort and to the least extent necessary; and
- the right to a remedy shall be protected in cases of violation of the right to association.[14]

2.1.2 The AU's democracy and good governance agenda

A commitment to multipartyism by member states of regional organisations has now become an established pattern, and, through this, peer pressure can be brought to bear on states to democratise. Hence, one of the major reasons for the establishment of the AU in 2002 was the desire by African leaders to arrest the faltering democratic transitions and rising threats of authoritarian resurgence which had already begun to appear.[15] The AU was given the special mandate to promote democracy and good governance. Of the six main instruments that can be said to comprise the AU's democracy and good governance agenda, three are binding and contain provisions that enjoin states to incorporate, in their constitutional

14 African Commission, *supra* n. 11, pp 10–22.

15 For in-depth discussion of the role of the AU in promoting good governance, constitutionalism, and democracy, see CM Fombad, "The African Union and Democratisation", in J Haynes (ed.), *Routledge Handbook of Democratisation*, London, Routledge (2012), pp 322–336; F Aggad and P Apiko, "Understanding the AU and its Governance Agenda", *European Centre for Development and Policy Management*, March 2017, https://ecdpm.org/wp-content/uploads/African-Union-Governance-Background-Paper-PEDRO-Political-Economy-Dynamics-Regional-Organisations-Africa-ECDPM-2017.pdf (accessed 17 May 2024); J Akokpari, "The OAU, AU, NEPAD and the Promotion of Good Governance in Africa", EISA Occasional Paper No. 14, November 2003, https://www.eisa.org/storage/2023/05/ocassional-paper-2003-oau-au-nepad-promotion-good-governance-africa-eisa.pdf (accessed 17 May 2024).

and legislative frameworks, measures to promote multipartyism and free and fair elections: the Constitutive Act of the AU of 2001; the AU Convention on the Prevention and Combating of Corruption of 2006 (AUCPCC); and the African Charter on Democracy, Elections and Governance of 2012 (ACDEG).

The Constitutive Act of the AU, its founding document, declares in Article 3(g) that one of its objectives is the promotion of "democratic principles and institutions, popular participation and good governance". In addition, its Article 4(m) states that one of its principles is "respect for democratic principles, human rights, the rule of law and good governance". The AUCPCC also contains in its Article 3(1) an undertaking by state parties to abide by various principles, including the "respect for democratic principles and institutions, popular participation, the rule of law and good governance". The AUCPCC's most significant provision in relation to political parties is Article 10, where state parties undertake to introduce measures to combat the use of funds acquired through illegal and corrupt practices whilst incorporating the principle of transparency into funding of political parties.

The furthest-reaching instrument, however, contains elaborate provisions dealing with diverse aspects of democracy, elections, good governance, and constitutionalism within the AU's agenda on democracy and good governance: the ACDEG.[16] Among its objectives is the promotion of regular, free and fair elections as a means to institutionalise and promote best practices in the management of elections for purposes of political stability and good governance.[17] Besides requiring state parties to implement the ACDEG in accordance with a number of principles, which include the holding of regular, transparent, free and fair elections, Article 3(11) specifically requires them to strengthen "political pluralism and recognis[e] the role, rights and responsibilities of legally constituted political parties, including opposition political parties, which should be given a status under national law".

Other sections, such as chapter 6 on democratic institutions, chapter 7 on democratic elections, and chapter 9 on political, economic and social governance, touch on aspects of the regulation of political parties. This is particularly the case with the latter chapter, where, in Article 27(1), state

16 On the ACDEG as an enforceable human rights treaty, see section 3.2.3.
17 See ACDEG, Articles 2(3) and (13).

parties commit themselves to "strengthening the capacity of parliaments and legally recognised political parties to perform their core functions". Equally significant are provisions in the ACDEG that envisage the full and active participation of women in the promotion and exercise of a democratic culture,[18] and which enjoin state parties to institutionalise measures that consolidate "sustainable multiparty political systems".[19]

2.2 The RECs' normative framework for regulating political parties

Unlike the AU, the primary purpose of the RECs is to facilitate the economic integration of AU member states. However, many RECs have broadened their mandate to include governance issues such as the promotion of democracy, the rule of law, and respect for human rights. As far as the regulation of political parties is concerned, only the Economic Community of West African States (ECOWAS) and Southern African Development Community (SADC) have instruments in place that could influence the approach adopted by their member states to regulate parties at the domestic level; other RECs have developed similar instruments but not yet adopted them.

2.2.1. ECOWAS Supplementary Protocol on Democracy and Good Governance

ECOWAS was established in 1975 to facilitate economic integration, trade, and development in the West Africa region. However, it recognised that good governance and respect for the rule of law were essential for achieving these goals, and in 1999 adopted the Protocol on Democracy and Good Governance to promote democracy, constitutionalism, and respect for the rule of law. The 2001 Supplementary Protocol Relating to the Mechanism for Conflict Prevention, Management, Resolution, Peacekeeping and Security has two key provisions relating to the regulation of political parties. The first is contained in Article 1, which sets out a number of constitutional principles "shared by all Member States". Article 1(i) provides as follows:

---

18 See ibid, Article 29.
19 See ibid, Article 32(6) and (7).

> Political parties shall be formed and shall have the right to carry out their activities freely, within the limits of the law.
> Their formation and activities shall not be based on ethnic, religious, regional or racial considerations. They shall participate freely and without hindrance or discrimination in any electoral process. The freedom of the opposition shall be guaranteed.
> Each Member State may adopt a system for financing political parties, in accordance with criteria set under the law.[20]

This provision covers several of the core principles relating to the regulation of parties, such as the freedom to establish parties; the requirement that parties be inclusive; and recognition of the need both for the existence of opposition parties and for funding political parties.

The second relevant provision concerns electoral management bodies (EMBs). Article 3 of the Supplementary Protocol on Democracy states:

> The bodies responsible for organising the elections shall be independent or neutral and shall have the confidence of all the political actors. Where necessary, appropriate national consultations shall be organised to determine the nature and the structure of the bodies.[21]

2.2.2 Other REC instruments on democracy and good governance

Some of the other RECs have also adopted instruments on democracy and good governance that refer to political parties, but none of these are as well established as those adopted by ECOWAS (or the AU itself). Of them, one of the more elaborate frameworks providing guidelines on the regulation of parties appears in the Draft Protocol on Good Governance of the East African Community (EAC), developed in 2012.[22] Thereunder, EAC member states commit to respecting several aspects of good governance, constitutionalism, democracy, and respect for the rule of law.

20 Economic Community of West African States (ECOWAS), Protocol A/SP1/12/01 on Democracy and Good Governance Supplementary to the Protocol relating to the Mechanism for Conflict Prevention, Management, Resolution, Peacekeeping and Security, Dakar, December 2001.

21 Ibid.

22 East African Community, The East African Community Protocol on Good Governance (Draft), https://meaca.gov.ss/wp-content/uploads/2022/08/Pdf-Draft-Protocol-on-Good-Governace.pdf (accessed 13 May 2024).

Apart from requirements in regard to independent EMBs and other election-related standards, the Draft Protocol in its Article 7(3) contains an undertaking by member states to institutionalise democracy, democratisation, and good governance specifically in relation to political parties by doing the following:

(g) Enacting laws that regulate the establishment of political parties that are national in character, internally democratic, with clear ideologies, visions and missions, devoid of all forms of discrimination;
(h) Developing policies and laws that regulate funding of political parties ...
(k) Establishing measures to ensure political parties are accountable through leadership codes, at all levels of governance;
(l) Enacting or reviewing laws and policies that facilitate representation of women, youth, persons with disabilities and other special interest groups to contest electoral and political leadership positions ...

The document remains a draft, though, and its future implementation is very much in doubt. Similarly, three other RECs – the Arab Maghreb Union (AMU), the Intergovernmental Authority on Development (IGAD), and the Community of Sahel-Saharan States (CEN-SAD) – have also developed comparable protocols on democracy and good governance, but none of these has gained any traction so far.[23]

2.2.3 SADC Principles and Guidelines Governing Democratic Elections

Although SADC has not yet developed a comprehensive protocol on good governance, mention should be made of the SADC Principles and Guidelines Governing Democratic Elections (adopted in 2004 and revised in 2015), which are essentially limited to promoting the holding and observa-

23 The only RECs that have not developed comparable protocols are the Common Market for Eastern and Southern Africa (COMESA) and the Economic Community of Central African States (ECCAS). That being said, in its Article 3(d), the treaty establishing COMESA lists good governance as one of this REC's aims and objectives; ECCAS, however, does not so much as even mention governance in its institutional structure.

tion of democratic elections.[24] As a result of this focus, SADC's Principles mention political parties only in this narrow context.

First, the principles for conducting democratic elections require member states to ensure, inter alia, that political parties have equal opportunities to use state media.[25] Secondly, with regard to commitments under the SADC Protocol on Politics, Defence and Security Cooperation, the Principles require member states to provide adequate security for the entirety of the electoral process, including for all political parties participating in elections; furthermore, states have to take reasonable measures to ensure that parties are able to communicate freely with the media and have unhindered access to media organs.[26] Thirdly, the principles prescribe the right of SADC election observers to communicate with all competing parties and candidates, as well as other political associations and organisations.[27]

3. The practical implications of regional standards

Given the existence of the regional and sub-regional frameworks discussed above, the question arises as to whether there is any evidence that they have influenced political-party regulation in practice. This raises two further issues. One relates to the extent of the ratification and domestication of the instruments setting down these standards (section 3.1). The other has to do with the possibility of supranational enforcement of some of the treaty obligations (section 3.2). Against this background, a third avenue – namely, monitoring the compliance of national legislation at a supranational level – will be discussed as well (section 3.3).

3.1 The implications of uneven ratification and domestication

There are several advantages to signing, ratifying, domesticating, and implementing treaties, especially those setting out uniform standards. They not only broaden the rights of citizens and promote best practices, but –

24 Southern African Development Community (SADC), SADC Principles and Guidelines Governing Democratic Elections (Revised, 2015), 20 July 2015, https://www.sadc.int/sites/default/files/2021-08/SADC_PRINCIPLES_AND_GUIDELINES_GOVERNING_DEMOCRATIC_ELECTIONS_REVISED_2015.pdf (accessed 13 May 2024).

25 Ibid, para 4.1.6.

26 Ibid, paras 5.1.6 and 5.1.10.

27 Ibid, para 9.1.8.

perhaps more importantly – serve as an important source of law both for improving national legal frameworks and for affording a benchmark by which to hold member states accountable to their regional and international commitments.

In addition, ratified and/or domesticated treaties provide national courts with a greater panoply of texts with which to inform their jurisdictional decisions. They afford national judges the opportunity as well to proceed by way of a comparative approach when the law being interpreted is similar to that of other member states which are also parties to these treaties. This is particularly so when the constitution provides, expressly or implicitly, for reference to be made to foreign law when courts interpret domestic law.[28] Possibly even more significant is the fact that, in most anglophone African countries, a treaty which has been signed by the government, whether or not it has been ratified and domesticated, can have important legal consequences domestically as an aid to constitutional interpretation.[29]

Despite all of these advantages, the impact that regional standards have had on the regulation of political parties in Africa is not substantial. There are several reasons for this. The first is that the overall record of ratification of regional treaties and protocols among AU member states is poor. A recent study shows that since the creation of the Organisation of African Unity (OAU) in 1963, member states have adopted a total of 57 treaties to advance the overall development of the continent. However, the average percentage of signature and ratification by member states in 2021 (the year

---

28 For example, see section 233 of the South African Constitution of 1996, which states: "When interpreting any legislation, every court must prefer any reasonable interpretation of the legislation that is consistent with international law over any alternative interpretation that is inconsistent with international law."

29 The *locus classicus* for this is the famous case in Botswana, *Attorney General v Unity Dow* [1992] BLR, where at p 154 Amissah J stated: "I bear in mind that signing the [OAU] Convention does not give it the power of law in Botswana but the effect of the adherence by Botswana to the Convention must show that a construction of the section which does not do violence to the language but is consistent with and in harmony with the Convention must be preferable to a 'narrow construction' which results in a finding that section 15 of the Constitution permits discrimination on the basis of sex." The judgement concluded thus: "Botswana is a member of the community of civilised states which has undertaken to abide by certain standards of conduct, and, unless it is impossible to do otherwise, it would be wrong for its courts to interpret legislation in a manner which conflicts with the international obligations Botswana has undertaken."

of the study) was 66 per cent and 42 per cent, respectively.[30] Although this rate is significantly higher for the legally binding instruments relevant for the regulation of political parties (outlined above), far from all member states have signed and ratified them. The African Charter has been ratified by all 55 member states except Morocco, but so far the ACDEG has been signed only by 46 of all such states (84 per cent of them) and ratified by 39 (71 per cent).[31] Moreover, 49 (89 per cent) member states have signed, and 48 (87 per cent), ratified, the AUCPCC.[32]

Secondly, even those AU member states that have signed and ratified or acceded to the instruments have done little to implement them. With the ACDEG, for instance, state parties have committed themselves to pursue the objectives, apply the principles, and respect the commitments enshrined in the Charter,[33] but implementation by many state parties remains incomplete.[34]

A third challenge that impacts on the domestic effectiveness of regional standards is the fact that the public's awareness of the role of the AU and RECs in creating norms and promoting democracy, good governance, and constitutionalism is limited.[35] It is thus a welcome development that the FoAA Guidelines have been drafted with contributions made by a working group that included non-governmental organisations (NGOs) from across the continent. Moreover, the Support Group to the Special Rapporteur on Human Rights Defenders – established to promote and monitor the

30 See UNDP, Accelerating the Ratification, Domestication, and Implementation of African Union Treaties
Project April 2021 – March 2023 (Revised Project Document), https://erc.undp.org/evaluation/managementresponses/keyaction/documents/download/6685 (accessed 16 May 2024).

31 See African Union, "List of Countries Which Have Signed, Ratified/Acceded to the African Charter on Democracy Elections and Governance", 8 July 2024, https://au.int/sites/default/files/treaties/36384-sl-AFRICAN_CHARTER_ON_DEMOCRACY_ELECTIONS_AND_GOVERNANCE.pdf (accessed 25 March 2025).

32 See African Union, "List of Countries Which Have Signed, Ratified/Acceded to the African Union Convention on Preventing and Combating Corruption", 14 February 2023, https://au.int/sites/default/files/treaties/36382-sl-AFRICAN_UNION_CONVENTION_ON_PREVENTING_AND_COMBATING_CORRUPTION.pdf (accessed 15 May 2024).

33 See Article 44(1) of the ACDEG.

34 For an overview of ACDEG implementation, see M Wiebusch, C Aniekwe, L Oette, and S Vandeginste, "The African Charter on Democracy, Elections and Governance: Past, Present and Future", 63 (2019) *Journal of African Law*, pp 9–38.

35 See UNDP, *supra* n. 30.

implementation of the FoAA Guidelines – consists of a dozen NGOs and networks of human rights defenders. As for the ACDEG, it has been noted that civil society does not yet make full use of the Charter.[36] Nevertheless, even though their focus is not on political parties, the launch of civil society initiatives such as the "Charter Africa" project are welcome developments to support state parties to fulfil their commitments outlined in the ACDEG.[37]

3.2 Supranational enforcement

Notwithstanding the incomplete ratification status and lack of implementation of the relevant regional instruments at a national level, a window of opportunity is afforded for supranational enforcement of some of the AU and REC standards by both the African Commission and the ACtHPR and REC courts. Whilst the African Commission makes recommendations,[38] the ACtHPR usually makes binding decisions, although, as is the case with the decisions of many international courts and tribunals, contracting parties often do not comply with these decisions.

The main basis for many of the cases brought before the ACtHPR that raise questions about the conformity of national regulations on political parties is Article 34 of the Protocol to the African Charter on the Establishment of the Court. This article allows member states to sign a declaration that gives individuals and NGOs with observer status before the African Commission the right to institute cases directly before it. Until recently, 12 countries had signed this declaration, though four have withdrawn since then.[39]

---

36 See A Witt, "Whose Charter? How Civil Society Makes (No) Use of the African Democracy Charter", *PRIF Spotlight*, 10 May 2019, https://blog.prif.org/2019/05/10/whose-charter-how-civil-society-makes-no-use-of-the-african-democracy-charter/ (accessed 8 July 2024).

37 Implemented by a consortium of six African and European NGOs, the project supports AU member states to fulfil their commitments under the ACDEG through the use of online citizen consultation. See Charter Africa, "Pan-African Online Citizen Consultation", https://charter.africa/about (accessed 21 May 2024).

38 For an account arguing that the findings of the African Commission are legally binding, see F Viljoen and L Louw, "The Status of the Findings of the African Commission: From Moral Persuasion to Legal Obligation", 48 (2004) *Journal of African Law*, pp 1–22.

39 See African Union, "List of Countries Which Have Signed, Ratified/Acceded to the Protocol to the African Charter on Human and Peoples' Rights on the Establishment

Several cases brought before the ACtHPR and the African Commission concern the obligation of state parties to comply with instruments that have a bearing on the regulation of political parties. Examples of such cases are discussed below. These deal with the freedom of political participation (section 3.2.1); limitations on and dissolution of political parties (section 3.2.2); and various related rights and obligations (section 3.2.3).

3.2.1 Freedom not to belong to a party and the right to political participation

Probably the most prominent case in relation to political parties is *Mtikila & Others v Republic of Tanzania,* brought before the ACtHR.[40] The applicants alleged that Tanzanian election laws prohibiting independent candidates from running for public office were in breach of various articles of the African Charter, Universal Declaration of Human Rights, and ICCPR. In its judgement, the ACtHR held that the freedom of association guaranteed by Article 10(2) of the African Charter "implies freedom to associate and freedom not to associate". Consequently, the Court found "that requiring individuals to belong and to be sponsored by a political party in seeking election ... has violated the right to freedom of association".[41]

In addition to *Mtikila & Others*, a few cases before the African Commission touched on the conception of the right of individuals to establish and join political parties as a form of political participation guaranteed under Article 13(1) of the African Charter. In *Sir Dawda K Jawara v Gambia*, the African Commission found that banning former ministers and members of parliament under the Jammeh regime from taking part in any political activity contravened their right to political participation.[42] Similarly, in *Lawyers for Human Rights v Swaziland*, the African Commission found that

---

of an African Court on Human and Peoples' Rights", 14 February 2023, pp 2–3, https://au.int/sites/default/files/treaties/36393-sl-PROTOCOL_TO_THE_AFRICAN_CHARTER_ON_HUMAN_AND_PEOPLESRIGHTS_ON_THE_ESTABLISHMENT_OF_AN_AFRICAN_COURT_ON_HUMAN_AND_PEOPLES_RIGHTS_0.pdf (accessed 22 May 2024).

40 ACtHR, Application No. 011/2011.

41 Ibid, para 113. See also O Windridge, "A Watershed Moment for African Human Rights: Mtikila & Others v Tanzania at the African Court on Human and Peoples' Rights", 15 (2015) *African Human Rights Law Journal*, pp 299–328, 311–312.

42 African Commission, Communication Nos. 147/95 and 149/96 (2000).

a proclamation in 1973 abolishing and prohibiting political parties restricts citizens' right to participation in governance as guaranteed under Article 13(1) of the African Charter.[43]

3.2.2 Limitations on and dissolution of political parties

In comparison to Article 22 of the ICCPR,[44] Article 10 of the ACHPR in principle provides more room for discretion for member states to limit the right to freedom of association through its clawback clause stating that the right must be exercised "in conformity with the rules laid down by the law". However, in *Mtikila & Others*, the ACtHR was of the view that Article 10 of the African Charter should be interpreted in the light of Article 22 of the ICCPR, to the effect that any limitations that member states put on the right to freedom of association must not only be provided for by law but also be reasonable and legitimate. That is, they must be required to ensure the "respect for the right of others, collective security, morality and common interest".[45]

Limitations to the freedom of association in relation to political parties were also discussed in some cases that came before the African Commission, in particular where political parties had been banned by member states. In the *Sir Dawda Jawara* case, the African Commission found that banning political parties is a violation of the right to freedom of association,[46] a finding which was reiterated in the *Lawyers for Human Rights* case.[47]

A detailed discussion by the African Commission of the dissolution of political parties can be found in *Interights and Others v Mauritania*.[48] Here, the possibilities to ban political parties were discussed in relation not only to freedom of association (under Article 10 of the African Charter) but also to freedom of expression, as guaranteed by the African Charter's Article 9(2). According to the Commission, this interrelatedness is even clearer in the case of political parties, considering their essential role for

43 African Commission, Communication No. 251/02 (2005).
44 On the extent to which the ICCPR allows member states to limit the right to freedom of association, see Socher, *supra* n. 2.
45 ACtHR, *supra* n. 40, paras 29–33. See also Windridge, *supra* n. 41, p 312.
46 African Commission, *supra* n. 42, para 68.
47 African Commission, *supra* n. 43, para 62.
48 African Commission, Communication No. 242/2001 (2004).

the maintenance of pluralism and the proper functioning of democracy. A political group should therefore not be hounded for the simple reason of wanting to hold public debates, with due respect for democratic rules, on a certain number of issues of national interest.[49]

3.2.3 Related rights and obligations

Apart from the cases above relating to political participation and freedom of association, two cases that came before the ACtHR dealt with the representation of political parties in EMBs and how such representation might affect EMBs' independence and impartiality. The first case is *Actions pour la Protection des Droits de l'Homme (APDH) v Côte d'Ivoire*.[50]

In this case, the ACtHR held that Côte d'Ivoire had violated its obligation to establish an independent and impartial electoral body, as provided for under Article 17 of the ACDEG and Article 3 of the ECOWAS Supplementary Protocol on Democracy and Good Governance; thus, the country also violated its obligation to protect the right of citizens to participate freely in the management of public affairs, as guaranteed by Article 13 of the African Charter. In the Court's view, an electoral body can be deemed independent if "it has administrative and financial autonomy; and offers sufficient guarantees of its members' independence and impartiality".[51] In the case at hand, the Court declared that the imbalance in representation in favour of the ruling coalition amounted to a violation of Côte d'Ivoire's obligation to establish an independent and impartial EMB.[52]

The second case is *Suy Bi Gohore Emile & Others v Côte d'Ivoire*.[53] Referring to the *APDH* case, the applicants alleged that, in violation of the Court's previous judgment, Côte d'Ivoire had enacted a new law that recomposed the EMB in such a way that it was still not independent and impartial. The Court held that Côte d'Ivoire had only partially violated its obligations arising from the *APDH* judgement. In particular, the Court found that "having political parties represented in an electoral body does not necessarily exclude the possibility for it to offer sufficient guarantees

49 Ibid, para 80.
50 ACtHR, Application No. 001/2014, Judgement of 18 November 2016.
51 Ibid, para 118.
52 Ibid, para 120–33.
53 ACtHR, Application No. 044/2019, Judgement of 15 July 2020.

of its independence and impartiality" as required by Article 17 of the ACDEG.[54] In addition, the Court provided guidance on the criteria for determining which opposition parties should be invited to propose members for EMBs.[55]

Apart from the direct relevance of these two judgements to the requirement of independence and impartiality of EMBs, their broader significance is that they explicitly confirmed that the ACDEG is a human rights instrument justiciable before the ACtHR.[56]

3.3 Supranational monitoring of national legislative compliance

Given the low level of implementation and limited means of enforcement of the relevant instruments, a third avenue towards increased harmonisation and compliance with the regional standards on the regulation of political parties is supranational monitoring through reporting mechanisms and/or election observation.

3.3.1 Reporting mechanisms and synthesis reports

A first route to increased compliance is offered by the reporting mechanisms envisaged in the different instruments.[57] In the case of the African Charter, however, the reporting mechanism has been characterised by late, vague, *ad hoc*, and limited reporting.[58] It was possibly for this reason that the African Commission recently established a group to support the mandate of the AU Special Rapporteur on Human Rights Defenders for the implementation of the FoAA Guidelines.[59] Moreover, due to concerns

---

54 Ibid, para 171.

55 Ibid, para 176.

56 See B Kioko, "The African Charter on Democracy, Elections and Governance as a Justifiable Instrument', 63 (2019) *Journal of African Law*, pp 39–61.

57 See African Charter, Article 62; ACDEG, Article 49; and AUCPCC, Article 22.

58 See M Evans, T Ige, and R Murray, "The Reporting Mechanism of the African Charter on Human and Peoples' Rights", in MD Evans and R Murray (eds.), *The African Charter on Human and Peoples' Rights: The System in Practice, 1986–2000*, Cambridge, Cambridge University Press, 2nd ed (2008), pp 49–75.

59 African Commission, Res. 406 (LXIII). The support group's mandate was extended in 2020 and again in 2022. See African Commission, Res. 471 (LXII) and Res. 547 (LXIII).

"about the slow implementation and review of laws in line with the Guidelines by State Parties", the Commission has decided to conduct a study to assess the level of compliance of national legislation with the FoAA Guidelines.[60] The study will be undertaken with the AU Special Rapporteur in collaboration with the UN Special Rapporteur on the Rights to Freedom of Peaceful Assembly and of Association under the Addis Ababa Roadmap.[61] Following the adoption of the resolution in 2023, the AU Special Rapporteur invited state parties, national human rights institutions, international organisations, and NGOs, and others to provide input with a view to establishing a consultative process.[62]

As for the ACDEG, state reporting so far is limited to contributions within the African Peer Review Mechanism (APRM).[63] Since the APRM's revitalisation in 2017, its mandate has been expanded to include monitoring and reporting on key aspects of AU governance. Reports prepared within the APRM are reviews that assess performance against objectives set out in the mechanism rather than the implementation of specific ACDEG provisions. Consequently, country review reports regularly contain findings and recommendations in relation to the regulation of political parties as envisaged in the ACDEG.

The 2022 country review report of Namibia, for example, criticises the lack of legislative provisions on the transparency of political-party funding and recommends the adoption of such provisions.[64] It also notes the lack of regulations on the internal operations of political parties, and recommends that national laws be put in place to ensure that parties submit lists which are inclusive and diverse.[65] However, due to the APRM's flexible reporting guidelines, the scope of the sections on political parties varies from country

---

60 African Commission, Res. 571 (LXXVII).

61 Ibid, operational paras 2 and 3.

62 African Commission, "Call for Inputs on the Study to Assess the Level of Compliance of National Legislations with the Guidelines on Freedom of Association and Assembly in Africa", 2 March 2024, https://achpr.au.int/en/news/announcements/2024-03-02/call-inputs-study-assess-level-compliance-national-legislations (accessed 16 May 2024).

63 See ACDEG, Article 36, establishing a link between the ACDEG and the APRM.

64 African Union, *African Peer Review Mechanism: Namibia Country Report*, January 2022, p 19, https://aprm.au.int/doc-viewer/2754 (accessed 21 May 2024).

65 Ibid, pp 22–23.

to country, with the result that the reports sometimes fail to include any critical assessment of the national legal framework in question.[66]

In addition to the country reviews, the APRM, in collaboration with the African Governance Architecture (AGA), published three thematic governance reports, in 2019, 2021, and most recently in 2023. While the 2019 AGA governance report on shared values does not mention political parties at all, the 2021 report on Africa's governance futures highlights their importance to elections and encourages member states "to use available platforms for sharing of best practices on political parties".[67] More importantly, the latest AGA report, on unconstitutional changes of government, makes specific recommendations about the regulation of political parties insofar as they (parties) can potentially contribute to deficits in electoral integrity.[68] In fact, one of the report's key findings is that political-party financing can affect electoral integrity and result in unconstitutional change of government; the report thus recommends developing guidelines and principles in this regard.[69]

More generally, the 2023 governance report suggests that the AU may "establish minimum standards for promoting multipartyism, particularly the recognition and protection of political parties in a way that promotes inclusivity and popular participation in governance".[70]

3.3.2 AU and REC election observation missions

A first route to increased compliance is offered by the findings and recommendations made by election observation missions conducted by the AU

66 For a comprehensive repository of APRM reports, guidelines, and other official documents, see South African Institute of International Affairs, "APRM Toolkit", https://www.aprmtoolkit.saiia.org.za (accessed 22 May 2024).

67 African Union, *Africa Governance Report 2021: Africa's Governance Futures for the Africa We Want*, Johannesburg, African Peer Review Mechanism (2021), p 21, https://au.int/en/documents/20220328/africa-governance-report-2021-africas-governance-futures-africa-we-want (accessed 22 May 2024).

68 African Union, *Africa Governance Report 2023: Unconstitutional Changes of Government in Africa*, Johannesburg, African Peer Review Mechanism (2023), https://aprm.au.int/en/documents/2023-07-12/africa-governance-report-2023-unconstitutional-change-government-africa (accessed 21 May 2024).

69 Ibid, pp 23, 26.

70 Ibid, p 24.

and some of its RECs.[71] In particular, some organisations have developed guidelines which include standards on the regulation of political parties. At the level of the AU, the AU election observation guidelines are relatively vague in that regard.[72] At the level of RECs, the SADC Principles and Guidelines Governing Democratic Elections contain detailed provisions in relation to political parties. In addition to prescribing a number of principles governing democratic elections, section 11 of the Principles set out extensive guidelines for SADC election observation missions (SEOMs). As regards political parties, the Principles prescribe that SEOMs shall observe whether the legal and constitutional framework guarantees freedom of association, including whether any stringent exclusionary elements exist in the regulatory framework for political-party and candidate registration.[73]

Annex 1 to the Principles elaborates on these guidelines, stating that the following factors should be observed in SEOMs in relation to political parties:

(a) Whether criteria for registration of political parties and candidates are explicitly defined in the laws and transparency executed;
(b) The existence of appeal processes and mechanisms upon disqualification of political parties or candidates;
(c) The procedures for nomination and provision of reasonable time frames to allow political parties and candidates to comply with the requirements of the registration process;
(d) The existence of a Code of Conduct governing all political parties and candidates;
(e) The incidence of international interference in the electoral process, through proscribed financial contributions to electoral contestants, or other activities;
(f) Funding to political parties for campaigns, and campaign spending are transparent and oversight of both is in accordance to the laws of the land;

71 See, for example, J Abbink and G Hesseling (eds.), *Election Observation and Democratisation in Africa*, London, Palgrave Macmillan (2000).

72 African Union, *Guidelines for African Union Electoral Observation and Monitoring Missions*, reprinted in African Union Commission, *African Union Election Observation Manual* (2013), Annex 4, https://www.eisa.org/pdf/au2014EOMmanual.pdf (accessed 17 May 2024). On the experience of the AU with election observation, see CC Aniekwe and SM Atuobi, "Two Decades of Election Observation by the African Union: A Review", 15 (2016) *Journal of African Elections*, pp 25–44.

73 SADC, *supra*. n. 24, sections 11.3.2 and 11.3.7.

(g) The use of public assets and funds for electoral campaigns, including impartial application and their improper use for the electoral advantage of particular political parties, candidates or supporters;
(h) The application of anti-corruption laws and other safeguards in the electoral context, including protections for those who expose election related corruption;
(...)
(j) The requirements and practices regarding direct and indirect access to the mass media for political parties, candidates, supporters and the general public;
(k) The requirements and practices concerning reporting by state controlled, public and private media about political parties, candidates and supporters or opponents of referendum initiatives, including quantitative and qualitative coverage of electoral contestants and issues that are pertinent to voter choices in elections or referenda;
(l) The ability of political parties, candidates and supporters and opponents of referendum initiatives to campaign freely for the support of prospective voters.[74]

Looking at some of the election observation reports published in the past, it appears however that SEOMs are not consistently strict with member states' compliance with these guidelines. For example, although the observer mission report by the Electoral Commissions Forum of SADC Countries on the 2023 Eswatini elections repeatedly notes that political parties continue to be banned in the kingdom, it does not condemn the severe restrictions on the right to freedom of association and participation in electoral processes but instead confines itself to noting "the varying views pertaining to the roles political parties can play in the political landscape of the country [are] something which necessitates genuine dialogue and tolerant engagement to promote political inclusion in diversity ..."[75]

Other examples show that SEOM reports can also be critical of the situation in a country. For instance, the SEOM's preliminary statement on the 2018 Madagascar presidential elections notes that "a culture of sustainable

74 Ibid, section 13.2.6.
75 Electoral Commissions Forum of SADC Countries (ECF-SADC), *Observer Mission Report of the Kingdom of Eswatini held on the 29th September 2023*, 6 December 2023, p 15, https://www.ecfsadc.org/observer-mission-report-of-ecfsadc-of-the-kingdom-of-eswatini-2023 (accessed 17 May 2024).

political parties is not apparent", resulting in "a deficit of political institutions and processes with strong and transparent internal democracy".[76]

4. Conclusion

As this chapter has shown, the existing regional and sub-regional normative frameworks provide a broad range of minimum standards on the regulation of political parties in African countries. However, to enable political parties to play a more effective role in governance, the implementation, enforcement, and monitoring of these standards would have to be improved significantly.

At the level of the AU and its RECs, there are in principle two ways of working towards this goal. One approach would look at additional ways for enforcing regional standards. In particular, review of compliance with constitutional amendment requirements laid down in national constitutions could also be performed at the supranational level by the ACtHR and the African Commission. Such supranational review is still possible even where review at the national level is not provided for in the constitution or excluded altogether.[77] Supranational review of the legality of constitutional amendments is also justified at the international level.

In this respect, Article 27 of the 1969 Vienna Convention on the Law of Treaties reaffirms the principle that "a party may not invoke the provisions of its internal law as justification for its failure to perform a treaty". Against the background of rising illiberal regimes on the continent, there is however also a certain risk of backlash in arguing for a more proactive role for supranational institutions in enforcing compliance. Implementation of the ACDEG is more likely in liberal than in authoritarian regimes.[78] It is also contingent on the interests of powerful states. As the editors of a special

76 Southern African Development Community, *Preliminary Statement to the 2018 Presidential Election in the Republic of Madagascar*, 9 November 2018, https://reliefweb.int/attachments/7562f882-996e-3e79-88cd-94575d555f98/Madagascar_SEOM_Preliminary_Statement_English.pdf (accessed 17 May 2024).

77 For a discussion of the possible role of international bodies in offering some protection against abusive constitutional amendments, see G Halmai, "Judicial Review of Constitutional Amendments and New Constitutions in Comparative Perspective", 20 (2016) *Wake Forest Law Review*, pp 101–135.

78 U Engel, "The 2007 African Charter on Democracy, Elections and Governance: Trying to Make Sense of Late Ratification of the African Charter and Non-Implementation of Its Compliance Mechanism", 54 (2019) *Africa Spectrum*, pp 127–146.

issue on the tenth anniversary of the ACDEG's adoption observed, only three of the five AU member states that make the largest contribution to the AU budget have ratified the ACDEG, and none has accepted direct access by individuals and NGOs to the ACtHPR.[79]

Moreover, with non-compliance with the decisions and recommendation already being a problem, if "the ACtHRP's energetic seizure of its mandate (including enforcing the ACDEG) is not matched with a commensurate commitment by states to the idea of human rights and democracy protection, then political backlash against the ACtHPR may follow".[80]

Rather than "hard" enforcement, the other, arguably more promising, approach to reach a higher level of compliance with regional standards would be to look at improving and harmonising existing "soft" mechanisms, that is, undertaking monitoring through reporting and/or election observation. Proposals such as developing guidelines for political parties by the AGA Platform, or the already-initiated process of preparing a study on the implementation of the FoAA Guidelines with the involvement of civil society, are welcome developments in this regard and should be further encouraged. As to the latter initiative, it should be noted that the scope of the study would necessarily be much broader than, and most likely not focus on, political parties as a distinctive subcategory of associations.

Political parties are however different from this broader category in that they aim to express the will of the people by seeking to participate in and influence the governance of the public life of a country, inter alia through the presentation of candidates for public office. While it might not be necessary that political parties are regulated differently than associations, it would be important to have further specific guidance on issues such as political-party funding and oversight to do justice to the unique role that political parties play in a democracy.

Lastly, in relation to election observation, the AU election observation guidelines could be further concretised by taking the guidelines developed by SADC and other international and regional organisations as an inspiration. But above all, just as with any hard approaches to enforcing the regional standards for regulating political parties in Africa, the consistent use of these softer mechanisms across the continent will be crucial to further harmonising and enhancing the implementation of these standards,

79 Wiebusch, et al., *supra* n. 34, p 36.
80 Ibid.

thereby enabling political parties to play a more effective role in African governance.

References

Books, articles, chapters in books, and others

Abbink J and Hesseling G (eds.), *Election Observation and Democratisation in Africa*, London, Palgrave Macmillan (2000)

African Commission on Human and Peoples' Rights, "Call for Inputs on the Study to Assess the Level of Compliance of National Legislations with the Guidelines on Freedom of Association and Assembly in Africa", 2 March 2024, https://achpr.au.int/en/news/announcements/2024-03-02/call-inputs-study-assess-level-compliance-national-legislations (accessed 16 May 2024)

African Commission on Human and Peoples' Rights, *Guidelines on Freedom of Association and Assembly in Africa*, May 2017, https://achpr.au.int/sites/default/files/files/2021-05/guidelinesonfreedomofassociationandassemblyinafricaeng_1.pdf (accessed 10 May 2024)

African Commission on Human and Peoples' Rights, *Report of the Study Group on Freedom of Association & Assembly in Africa*, May 2015, https://www.icnl.org/wp-content/uploads/ACHPR-English-REPORT-21.05.2015.pdf (accessed 15 May 2024)

African Union Assembly of Heads of State and Government in Addis Ababa, Ethiopia in July 2004, "Solemn Declaration on Gender Equality in Africa", Assembly/AU, Decl.12 (III) Rev. 1, https://au.int/sites/default/files/documents/38956-doc-assembly_au_decl_12_iii_e.pdf (accessed 20 May 2024)

African Union, "List of Countries Which Have Signed, Ratified/Acceded to the African Charter on Democracy Elections and Governance", 8 July 2024, https://au.int/sites/default/files/treaties/36384-sl-AFRICAN_CHARTER_ON_DEMOCRACY_ELECTIONS_AND_GOVERNANCE.pdf (accessed 25 March 2025)

African Union, "List of Countries Which Have Signed, Ratified/Acceded to the African Union Convention on Preventing and Combating Corruption", 14 February 2023, https://au.int/sites/default/files/treaties/36382-sl-AFRICAN_UNION_CONVENTION_ON_PREVENTING_AND_COMBATING_CORRUPTION.pdf (accessed 15 May 2024)

African Union, "List of Countries Which Have Signed, Ratified/Acceded to the Protocol to the African Charter on Human and Peoples' Rights on the Establishment of an African Court on Human and Peoples' Rights", 14 February 2023, https://au.int/sites/default/files/treaties/36393-sl-PROTOCOL_TO_THE_AFRICAN_CHARTER_ON_HUMAN_AND_PEOPLESRIGHTS_ON_THE_ESTABLISHMENT_OF_AN_AFRICAN_COURT_ON_HUMAN_AND_PEOPLES_RIGHTS_0.pdf (accessed 22 May 2024)

African Union, "List of Countries Which Have Signed, Ratified/Acceded to the Protocol to the African Charter on Human and Peoples' Rights on the Rights of Persons with Disabilities in Africa", 19 September 2023, https://au.int/sites/default/files/treaties/36440-sl-PROTOCOL_TO_THE_AFRICAN_CHARTER_ON_HUMAN_AND_PEOPLES_RIGHTS_ON_THE_RIGHTS_OF_PERSONS_WITH_DISABILITIES_IN_AFRICA_0.pdf (accessed 20 May 2024)

African Union, *Africa Governance Report 2021: Africa's Governance Futures for the Africa We Want*, Johannesburg, African Peer Review Mechanism (2021), https://au.int/en/documents/20220328/africa-governance-report-2021-africas-governance-futures-africa-we-want (accessed 22 May 2024)

African Union, *Africa Governance Report 2023: Unconstitutional Changes of Government in Africa*, Johannesburg, African Peer Review Mechanism (2023), https://aprm.au.int/en/documents/2023-07-12/africa-governance-report-2023-unconstitutional-change-government-africa (accessed 21 May 2024)

African Union, *African Peer Review Mechanism: Namibia Country Report*, January 2022, https://aprm.au.int/doc-viewer/2754 (accessed 21 May 2024)

African Union, *Guidelines for African Union Electoral Observation and Monitoring Missions*, reprinted in African Union Commission, *African Union Election Observation Manual* (2013), Annex 4, https://www.eisa.org/pdf/au2014EOMmanual.pdf (accessed 17 May 2024)

Aggad F and Apiko P, "Understanding the AU and its Governance Agenda", *European Centre for Development and Policy Management*, March 2017, https://ecdpm.org/wp-content/uploads/African-Union-Governance-Background-Paper-PEDRO-Political-Economy-Dynamics-Regional-Organisations-Africa-ECDPM-2017.pdf (accessed 17 May 2024)

Akokpari J, "The OAU, AU, NEPAD and the Promotion of Good Governance in Africa", EISA Occasional Paper No. 14, November 2003, https://www.eisa.org/storage/2023/05/ocassional-paper-2003-oau-au-nepad-promotion-good-governance-africa-eisa.pdf (accessed 17 May 2024)

Aniekwe CC and Atuobi SM, "Two Decades of Election Observation by the African Union: A Review", 15 (2016) *Journal of African Elections*, pp 25–44

Charter Africa, "Pan-African Online Citizen Consultation", https://charter.africa/about (accessed 21 May 2024)

Electoral Commissions Forum of SADC Countries, *Observer Mission Report of the Kingdom of Eswatini held on the 29th September 2023*, 6 December 2023, accessible at https://www.ecfsadc.org/observer-mission-report-of-ecfsadc-of-the-kingdom-of-eswatini-2023 (accessed 17 May 2024)

Engel U, "The 2007 African Charter on Democracy, Elections and Governance: Trying to Make Sense of Late Ratification of the African Charter and Non-Implementation of Its Compliance Mechanism", 54 (2019) *Africa Spectrum*, pp 127–146

European Commission for Democracy Through Law (Venice Commission), *Guidelines on Political Party Regulation*, 2nd ed, 14 December 2020, CDL-AD(2020)032

Evans M, Ige T, and Murray R, "The Reporting Mechanism of the African Charter on Human and Peoples' Rights", in MD Evans and R Murray (eds.), *The African Charter on Human and Peoples' Rights: The System in Practice, 1986–2006*, Cambridge, Cambridge University Press, 2nd ed (2008), pp 49–75

Fombad CM, "Political Party Constitutionalisation in Africa: Trends and Prospects for Deepening Constitutionalism", in R Dixon, T Ginsburg, and AK Abebe (eds.), *Comparative Constitutional Law in Africa*, Cheltenham, Edgar Elger (2022) pp 109–135

Fombad CM, "The African Union and Democratization", in J Haynes (ed.), *Routledge Handbook of Democratization*, London, Routledge (2012), pp 322–336

Fombad CM, "The Internationalisation of Constitutional Law and Constitutionalism in Africa", 60 (2012) *American Journal of Comparative Law*, pp 439–473

Halmai G, "Judicial Review of Constitutional Amendments and New Constitutions in Comparative Perspective", 20 (2016) *Wake Forest Law Review*, pp 101–135

Kioko B, "The African Charter on Democracy, Elections and Governance as a Justifiable Instrument", 63 (2019) *Journal of African Law*, pp 39–61

Olaniyan K, "Civil and Political Rights in the African Charter: Articles 8–14", in MD Evans and R Murray (eds.), *The African Charter on Human and Peoples' Rights: The System in Practice, 1986–2000*, Cambridge, Cambridge University Press, 2nd ed (2008), pp 213–243

South African Institute of International Affairs, "APRM Toolkit", https://www.aprmtoolkit.saiia.org.za (accessed 22 May 2024)

Southern African Development Community, *Preliminary Statement to the 2018 Presidential Election in the Republic of Madagascar*, 9 November 2018, https://reliefweb.int/attachments/7562f882-996e-3e79-88cd-94575d555f98/Madagascar_SEOM_Preliminary_Statement_English.pdf (accessed 17 May 2024)

Southern African Development Community, *SADC Principles and Guidelines Governing Democratic Elections (Revised, 2015)*, 20 July 2015, https://www.sadc.int/sites/default/files/2021-08/SADC_PRINCIPLES_AND_GUIDELINES_GOVERNING_DEMOCRATIC_ELECTIONS_REVISED_2015.pdf (accessed 13 May 2024)

UNDP, Accelerating the Ratification, Domestication, and Implementation of African Union Treaties Project, April 2021–March 2023 (Revised Project Document), https://erc.undp.org/evaluation/managementresponses/keyaction/documents/download/6685 (accessed 16 May 2024)

Viljoen F and Louw L, "The Status of the Findings of the African Commission: From Moral Persuasion to Legal Obligation", 48 (2004) *Journal of African Law*, pp 1–22

Wiebusch M, Aniekwe C, Oette L, and Vandeginste S, "The African Charter on Democracy, Elections and Governance: Past, Present and Future", 63 (2019) *Journal of African Law*, pp 9–38

Windridge O, "A Watershed Moment for African Human Rights: *Mtikila & Others v Tanzania* at the African Court on Human and Peoples' Rights", 15 (2015) *African Human Rights Law Journal*, pp 299–328

Witt A, "Whose Charter? How Civil Society Makes (No) Use of the African Democracy Charter", *PRIF Spotlight*, 10 May 2019, https://blog.prif.org/2019/05/10/whose-charter-how-civil-society-makes-no-use-of-the-african-democracy-charter/ (accessed 8 July 2024)

Table of cases

Actions pour la Protection des Droits de l'Homme (APDH) v Côte d'Ivoire, Application No. 001/2014, Judgement of 18 November 2016

Interights and Others v Mauritania, Communication No. 242/2001 (2004)

Lawyers for Human Rights v Swaziland, Communication No. 251/02 (2005)

Mtikila v United Republic of Tanzania, Application No. 011/2011, Judgement of 14 June 2013

Sir Dawda K. Jawara v. Gambia (The), Communication Nos. 147/95 and 149/96 (2000)

Suy Bi Gohore Emile & Others v Côte d'Ivoire, Application No. 044/2019, Judgement of 15 July 2020

Table of legislation

Resolutions by the African Commission

Resolution on the Mandate Renewal of the Support Group of the Special Rapporteur on Human Rights Defenders and Focal Point on Reprisals in Africa for the Promotion and Effective Implementation of the Guidelines on Freedom of Association and Assembly in Africa, Res 471 (LXVII), 3 December 2020

Resolution on the Need to Undertake a Study to Assess the Level of Compliance of National Legislations with the Guidelines on Freedom of Association and Assembly in Africa, ACHPR/Res 571 (LXXVII), 9 November 2023

Resolution on the Renewal of the Mandate of the Support Group to the Special Rapporteur on Human Rights Defenders and Focal Point on Human Rights Defenders and Focal Point on Reprisals in Africa for the Promotion and Monitoring, ACHPR/Res 547 (LXVIII), 12 December 2022

Resolution on the Right to Freedom of Association, ACHPR/Res 5(XI), 9 March 1992

Resolution: Establishment of a Group to Support the Mandate of the SRHRD & Focal Point on Reprisals in Africa for the Promotion & Monitoring of the Effective Implementation of the Guidelines on Freedom of Association & Assembly, ACHPR/Res 406 (LXIII), 13 November 2018

Chapter 5 Constitutionalisation of Political Parties: International Standards and the Experience of Continental Europe

Johannes Socher

1. Introduction

This chapter outlines the relevant international standards on the regulation of political parties and analyses the experience of continental Europe in their constitutionalisation, with this experience illustrated via the case of Germany. The discussion is limited in two respects. First, the outline of international standards focuses on state obligations emanating from human rights instruments, and not on obligations of political parties themselves, which have no legal obligations under human rights law.[1] Secondly, the focus is on the entrenchment of the rights and obligations of political parties in constitutions, not on the normative frameworks that regulate parties more broadly.[2]

While international human rights law in relation to political parties has been the subject of extensive research, surprisingly little comparative constitutional scholarship exists on the constitutionalisation of parties.[3] Important exceptions to this relative scarcity are works on the regulation of political parties in continental Europe. In particular, Dimitris Tsatsos published widely in the 1990s on the issue, though mostly in German language, thereby significantly limiting the discourse to a German-speaking

1 But see T Wood, "Reinforcing Participatory Governance Through International Human Rights Obligations of Political Parties" 28 (2015) *Harvard Human Rights Journal*, pp 145–200 for an attempt to construct such obligations.

2 For an overview on the regulation of political parties in Europe in statutory laws, see FC Bértoa, DR Piccio, and ER Rashkova, "Party Laws in Comparative Perspective", in I van Biezen and HM ten Napel (eds.), *Regulating Political Parties: European Democracies in Comparative Perspectives,* Leiden, Leiden University Press (2014), pp 119–148.

3 This may be due at least in part to the dominating influence of American and British constitutional traditions, which tend to have little to say about political parties. See, for example, V Bogdanor (ed.), *The British Constitution in the Twentieth Century,* Oxford, Oxford University Press (2004).

audience.[4] More recently, a group of researchers around Ingrid van Biezen has revitalised the field from a political science perspective.[5]

Revisiting these works, this chapter provides an overview of the different waves of constitutionalising political parties in continental Europe and presents the distinct models that have emerged over time. Following this overview, the continental European experience will be illustrated with the case of Germany, which in many respects can be seen as a pioneer of, and model for, the constitutionalisation of political parties. The conclusion sums up the findings and considers potential lessons for African countries. As will be argued, while some principles developed in Europe could offer inspiration for the further constitutionalisation of political parties in Africa, others might be less suitable and should be considered only with caution.

2. International standards

International standards on the regulation of political parties emanate above all from human rights instruments, interpreted by the United Nations (UN) Human Rights Committee and other human rights monitoring bodies. The main relevant treaty is the International Covenant on Civil and Political Rights (ICCPR), in particular the right to participate in public affairs (section 2.1) and the right to freedom of association (section 2.2). Other human rights treaties cover specific aspects of the regulation of political parties, such as non-discrimination against certain persons and groups (section 2.3) and financing and transparency (section 2.4).

4 See, in particular, DT Tsatsos, D Schefold, and HP Schneider (eds.), *Parteienrecht im europäischen Vergleich: Die Parteien in den demokratischen Ordnungen der Staaten der Europäischen Gemeinschaft*, Baden-Baden, Nomos (1990) DT Tsatsos and Z Kedzia (eds.), *Parteienrecht in mittel- und osteuropäischen Staaten: Entstehungsmomente des Parteienrechts in Bulgarien, Litauen, Polen, Russland, der Slowakei, Tschechien und Ungarn*, Baden-Baden, Nomos (1994).

5 See, in particular, I van Biezen and HM ten Napel (eds.), *Regulating Political Parties: European Democracies in Comparative Perspectives*, Leiden, Leiden University Press (2014); FC Bértoa and I van Biezen (eds.), *The Regulation of Post-Communist Party Politics*, London, Routledge (2017).

2.1. Right to political participation

A first question is whether the right to political participation as guaranteed in Article 25 of the ICCPR includes any obligations for state parties in relation to political parties, in particular whether the right of every citizen to "genuine elections" necessarily requires multipartyism.[6] While it may be argued that Article 25 of the ICCPR, as originally drafted, does not prohibit one-party states if certain criteria are met,[7] the UN Human Rights Committee has consistently argued in favour of multipartyism as a necessary prerequisite for "genuine" elections in the sense of Article 25 of the ICCPR. In the *Bwalya v Zambia* case, the Committee found that preventing an opposition party leader from participating in a general election in the then one-party state of Zambia constituted an unreasonable restriction of his rights guaranteed in Article 25 of the ICCPR.[8] Building on this finding, the Committee expanded and generalised this view in its General Comment No. 25, in which it states that "political parties and membership in parties play a significant role in the conduct of public affairs and the electoral process".[9] More recently, the Committee has found that free and fair elections require the possibility for political parties "to register, contest elections, field candidates or otherwise participate in the formation of a government".[10]

2.2 Freedom of association

Freedom of association, guaranteed in Article 22 of the ICCPR, "enables the very existence of political parties", as a leading commentary on the Covenant highlights, "allowing pluralist expression in a multi-party system,

6 For more on the debate during the drafting of the Covenant, see GH Fox, "The Right to Political Participation in International Law", in GH Fox and BR Roth (eds.), *Democratic Governance and International Law*, Cambridge, Cambridge University Press (2010), pp 48–90, 55–57.
7 Ibid, pp 56–57.
8 UN Human Rights Committee, CCPR/C/48/D/313/1988 (*Bwalya v Zambia*), 14 July 1993, para 6.6.
9 UN Human Rights Committee, General Comment No. 25: Article 25 (Participation in Public Affairs and the Right to Vote), 12 July 1996, CCPR/C/21/Rev.1/Add.7, para 26.
10 UN Human Rights Committee, CCPR/C/SWZ/CO/1 (Swaziland), 23 August 2017, para 52.

and offering choice in popular representation".[11] The general restriction clause in the second paragraph of the article allows, however, for limitations of freedom of association if they are "necessary in a democratic society in the interests of national security or public safety, public order (*ordre public*), the protection of public health or morals or the protection of the right and freedoms of others".

In regard to political parties, the UN Human Rights Committee has discussed limitations in a number of cases. State parties are obliged to "ensure that any limitations on the establishment of a political party are construed narrowly and that the principles of legality, necessity and proportionality are strictly adhered to".[12] Moreover, state parties should not use regulations concerning the registration of political parties "to victimize groups that are considered as holding contrary political views to the ruling party", resulting in major practical obstacles and delays in the registration of opposition parties.[13] Requirements such as high numbers of founders, geographic diversity, and high registration fees may also constitute restrictive and disproportionate rules.[14] In addition, state parties have not only an obligation to respect the exercise of freedom of association but a duty to protect political parties' freedom of association from interference by non-state actors.[15]

In extreme cases, on the other hand, states may enact regulations that allow even the prohibition of political parties. One explicitly envisaged case in a human rights instrument are racist parties, which state parties to the International Convention on the Elimination of all Forms of Racial

11 PM Taylor, *A Commentary on the International Covenant on Civil and Political Rights: The UN Human Rights Committee's Monitoring of ICCPR Rights*, Cambridge, Cambridge University Press (2020), p 610.

12 UN Human Rights Committee, CCPR/C/TKM/CO/2 (Turkmenistan), 20 April 2017, para 49.

13 UN Human Rights Committee, CCPR/C/KAZ/CO/1 (Kazakhstan), 19 August 2011, para 27. See also CCPR/CO/73/AZE (Azerbaijan), 12 November 2001, para 23; CCPR/C/UZB/CO/3 (Uzbekistan), 7 April 2010, para 25.

14 See UN Human Rights Committee, CCPR/C/BLR/CO/5 (Belarus), 22 November 2018, para 54. On the Committee's concerns with respect to the extent of territorial representation, see CCPR/CO/75/MDA (Moldova), 5 August 2002, para 16.

15 See UN Human Rights Committee, General Comment No. 31: The Nature of the General Legal Obligation on State Parties to the Covenant, 26 M2004, CCPR/C/21/Rev.1/Add.13, para 8; UN Human Rights Committee, General Comment No. 28: Article 3 (The Equality of Rights between Men and Women), 29 March 2000, CCPR/C/21/rev.1/Add.10, para 31.

Discrimination (ICERD) are obliged to declare illegal.[16] More generally, political parties may lack protection under the ICCPR in accordance with the latter's Article 5, which prohibits an interpretation of the Covenant "implying for any State, group or person any right to engage in any activity or perform any act aimed at the destruction of the rights and freedoms ... or at their limitation to a greater extent than is provided for [in it]". In an early case, the UN Commission on Human Rights argued that the re-establishment of the dissolved fascist party in Italy was removed from the protection of the Covenant in the sense of this article.[17] Beyond this single instance, however, the exact delimitations and substantial and procedural requirements under which states may prohibit political parties in accordance with Article 5 of the ICCPR remain open to interpretation.[18]

2.3 Equal treatment of and non-discrimination against specific groups

Another standard for the regulation of political parties is the principle of equal treatment before the law. In line with Article 26 ICCPR, regulations on political parties may not discriminate against individuals or groups "on any ground such as race, colour, sex, language, religion, political or other opinion, national or social origin, property, birth or other status". Apart from international standards emanating from the ICCPR, a number of human rights instruments provide for state party obligations in regard to non-discrimination against specific groups, obligations which are also relevant for the regulation of political parties.

A first provision in this regard is Article 7 of the Convention on the Elimination of All Forms of Discrimination against Women (CEDAW), which obliges state parties to take appropriate measures to eliminate discrimination against women in political and public life. In relation to political parties, this includes, first of all, the obligation to ensure to women

16 Article 4(b) of the ICERD. See P Thornberry, *The International Convention on the Elimination of All Forms of Racial Discrimination: A Commentary*, Oxford, Oxford University Press (2016), p 363.

17 UN Commission on Human Rights, *MA v Italy,* Communication No. 117/1981, Supp. No. 40 (A/39/40), para 190.

18 See GH Fox and G Nolte, "Intolerant Democracies", in GH Fox and BR Roth (eds.), *Democratic Governance and International Law*, Cambridge, Cambridge University Press (2010), pp 389–435, 421 et seq.

the right to participate in them.[19] This means that political parties should not be allowed to deny women membership or the possibility to run for elections and that restrictions for women to participate in political parties cannot be justified by religious beliefs or cultural traditions.[20] Furthermore, the obligation in Article 7 of CEDAW requires state parties to identify and implement temporary special measures to ensure the equal representation of women in political parties.[21] In essence, this means that state parties have to "ensure that political parties realize equality by increasing the number of female candidates with realistic chances of being elected".[22] Of the various potential measures to achieve this, the CEDAW Committee views the alternation between men and women for the nomination of candidates in political parties as particularly effective.[23]

Another relevant provision in a human rights instrument that imposes obligations in regard to non-discrimination is Article 29 of the Convention on the Rights of Persons with Disabilities (CPRD).[24] In terms of Article 29(b)(i) of the CPRD, state parties commit to "promote actively an environment in which persons with disabilities can effectively and fully participate in the conduct of public affairs" and to "encourage their participation in public affairs, including ... in the activities and administration of political parties". As the CPRD Committee has noted, this includes the obligation to

19 See Committee on the Elimination of all Forms of Discrimination against Women, General Recommendation No. 23: Political and Public Life, 1997, A/52/38, paras 42–43.

20 S Wittkopp, "Article 7", in P Schulz, R Halperin-Kaddari, B Rudolf, and MA Freeman (eds.), *The UN Convention on the Elimination of All Forms of Discrimination against Women and Its Optional Protocol: A Commentary*, 2nd ed, Oxford, Oxford University Press (2022), p 316.

21 See Committee on the Elimination of all Forms of Discrimination against Women, General Recommendation No. 25: Temporary Special Measures, 18 August 2004, paras 18, 23, 29, 32.

22 Wittkopp, *supra* n. 20, p 316, referring to, inter alia, United Nations Development Programme (UNDP) and National Democratic Institute for International Affairs (NDI), *Empowering Women for Stronger Political Parties: A Guidebook to Promote Women's Political Participation,* New York, UNDP (2012), pp 21–28.

23 See Wittkopp, *supra* n. 20, p 316.

24 See generally I Grobbelaar du Plessis and J Njau, "Article 29: Participation in Political and Public Life", in I Bantekas, MA Stein and D Anastasiou (eds.), *The UN Convention on the Rights of Persons with Disabilities: A Commentary*, Oxford, Oxford University Press (2018), pp 834–862.

ensure that political meetings, as well as materials used and produced by political parties, are accessible.[25]

2.4 Financing and transparency

A third set of international standards on the regulation of political parties relates to financing and transparency. In the above-mentioned General Comment No. 25 on Article 25 of the ICCPR, the Human Rights Committee stated that "reasonable limitations on campaign expenditure may be justified where this is necessary to ensure that the free choice of voters is not undermined or the democratic process distorted by the disproportionate expenditure on behalf of any candidate or party".[26]

In this spirit, Article 7(3) of the United Nations Convention against Corruption (UNCAC) enjoins state parties to take legislative and administrative measures to enhance transparency in the funding of political parties. While the provision is limited to funding, official UN guidance goes beyond that and addresses other political finance issues, such as limitations on private funding, criteria for public funding, spending limits, and abuse of state resources.[27] Moreover, although the provision does not give detail on how to achieve this, Article 7(3) of the UNCAC may be interpreted to mean that disclosure of information has to be adequate, which entails

> that the information provided should allow knowledge of who is providing the funding, including whether this is public or private, and the amount of that funding. This would require disclosing (i) the identity of those providing funding; (ii) the form, whether the funding is provided through direct monetary contributions or through indirect in-kind contributions, for example loans, tax exemptions, time in media outlets, or logistic support; and (iii) the amounts.[28]

25 CPRD Committee, General Comment No. 2: Article 9: Accessibility, 22 May 2014, CPRD/C/GC/2, para 43.

26 UN Human Rights Committee, *supra* n. 9, para 19.

27 See United Nations Office on Drugs and Crime (UNODC), *Technical Guide to the United Nations Convention Against Corruption*, New York, United Nations (2009).

28 J Bacio Terracino, "Article 7: Public Sector", in C Rose, M Kubiciel, and O Landwehr (eds.), *The United Nations Convention against Corruption*, Oxford, Oxford University Press (2019), pp 65–77, 75.

3. The constitutionalisation of political parties in continental Europe

Against the background of the relevant international human rights instruments for the regulation of political parties, this section analyses the experience of their constitutionalisation in continental Europe. Historically, most European constitutions neither mentioned political parties nor said anything about their role in governance.[29] This only changed after World War II with the restoration of democracy in Austria, Germany, and Italy (section 3.1). As will be shown, one can distinguish three distinct models of political-party constitutionalisation that emerged over time (section 3.2). While these three models continue to co-exist, the constitutionalisation of political parties in continental Europe is increasingly shaped by European Court of Human Rights (ECtHR) case law, as well as synthesised and interpreted through guidance issued by the European Commission for Democracy through Law (Venice Commission) and other regional bodies (section 3.3).

3.1 Five waves of party constitutionalisation

According to a periodisation developed by Ingrid van Biezen, one may distinguish five waves of political-party constitutionalisation in post-War Europe (see Figure 1).[30] Beginning in Iceland in 1944, the first wave primarily comprises Austria, Germany, and Italy, where the restoration of democracy following Nazi and fascist rule was not only accompanied by the inclusion of political parties in the respective constitutional frameworks but also symbolised by the adoption of entirely new constitutions (except for Austria, where the constitution of 1920 was merely reinstated). In Iceland's constitution, the first case of party constitutionalisation in Europe, political parties appear only in passing in a provision on proportional representation for parliamentary elections. Similarly, while Austria's constitution makes reference to political parties in a number of provisions,

29 See I van Biezen, "Constitutionalising Party Democracy: The Constitutive Codification of Political Parties in Post-war Europe", 42 (2012) *British Journal of Political Science*, pp 187–212, 191–96.

30 I van Biezen, "The Constitutionalisation of Political Parties in Post-War Europe", in I van Biezen and HM ten Napel (eds.), *Regulating Political Parties: European Democracies in Comparative Perspectives,* Leiden, Leiden University Press (2014), pp 93–118, 94–100.

parties are limited in their significance in that they are referred to simply as parliamentary groups and in regard to their capacity to be elected. By contrast, it is in Italy's new constitution of 1947 and, in much more detail, the German Basic Law of 1949, that political parties are, for the first time, explicitly recognised as relevant subjects for the constitutional order over and above their role in elections.[31]

The second wave of constitutionalisation is linked to decolonisation and begins with the establishment of the French Fifth Republic in 1958; additionally, it includes the constitutions of the newly independent states of Cyprus and Malta, as adopted in 1960 and 1964 respectively. According to van Biezen, unlike in Italy or Germany, political parties in these constitutions appear not as democratically desirable subjects but merely as functional necessities.[32] The French Constitution, for instance, assigns parties a role in contributing to "the exercise of suffrage" and requires them to "respect the principles of national sovereignty and democracy", but otherwise has relatively little to say about them.[33]

This is different again for the third wave, which, according to van Biezen, consists mainly of the comparatively young democracies of Southern Europe – that is, Greece, Portugal, and Spain – which all returned to democracy in the 1970s after periods of military rule.[34] Much as in the case of Germany (see section 4 below) and the overwhelming majority of cases in former socialist countries in Central and Eastern Europe that form the fourth wave of the late 1980s and early 1990s, these constitutions usually recognise

31 The constitutionalisation of political parties in the German Basic Law is analysed further in section 4. For analyses of the regulation of political parties in Italy, see F Lanchester, "Die Institution der politischen Partei in Italien", in DT Tsatsos, D Schefold, and HP Schneider (eds.), *Parteienrecht im europäischen Vergleich: Die Parteien in den demokratischen Ordnungen der Staaten der Europäischen Gemeinschaft*, Baden-Baden, Nomos (1990), pp 367–434; DR Piccio, "A Self-Interested Legislator? Party Regulation in Italy", 19 (2014) *South European Society and Politics*, pp 135–152.

32 Van Biezen, *supra* n. 30, pp 99–100.

33 See M Fromont, "Die Institution der politischen Partei in Frankreich", in DT Tsatsos, D Schefold, and HP Schneider (eds.), *Parteienrecht im europäischen Vergleich: Die Parteien in den demokratischen Ordnungen der Staaten der Europäischen Gemeinschaft*, Baden-Baden, Nomos (1990), pp 219–260.

34 For case studies, see ibid, pp 261–300 (Greece), pp 591–634 (Portugal), and pp 635–694 (Spain). For a comparison of these cases, see I van Biezen and FC Bértoa, "Party Regulation in Post-authoritarian Contexts: Southern Europe in Comparative Perspective", 19 (2014) *South European Society and Politics*, pp 71–87.

parties as direct and desirable subjects.[35] Finally, the fifth wave, starting in the late 1990s, consists of cases, such as Finland and Luxembourg, where the constitutions of older democracies were amended to explicitly regulate political parties for the first time.[36]

Figure 1: Waves of political-party constitutionalisation in post-war Europe[37]

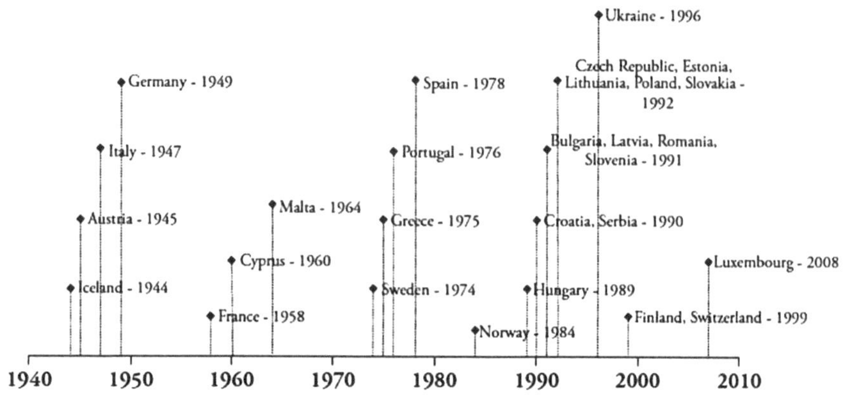

A number of aspects of this evolution are noteworthy. First, the different waves of political-party constitutionalisation in continental Europe by and large correspond to the broader waves of democratisation and constitutional change famously identified by Samuel Huntington.[38] Secondly, as a rule, political-party constitutionalisation seems to have occurred when entirely new constitutions were adopted rather than when existing ones underwent amendment.[39] Thirdly, and perhaps of particular note in regard to lessons for the African context, strong constitutionalisation of political parties has been more likely in young democracies where new constitutions

35 Van Biezen, *supra* n. 30, p 100. For analyses of individual countries, see the case studies in Tsatsos and Kedzia, *supra* n. 4 and Bértoa and Biezen, *supra* n. 5.

36 For the interesting case of Luxembourg, see the brief discussion in the conclusion of this chapter.

37 Ibid, p 95.

38 Van Biezen, *supra* n. 30, p 100, referring to SP Huntington, *The Third Wave: Democratisation in the Late Twentieth Century*, Norman, University of Oklahoma Press (1991) and J Elster, "Forces and Mechanisms in the Constitution-making Process", 45 (1995) *Duke Law Journal*, pp 364–396.

39 Van Biezen, *supra* n. 30, p 100.

were adopted after periods of authoritarian rule.[40] In addition to these observations (also highlighted by van Biezen), one should add that these waves relate only to the *initial* constitutionalisation of political parties. As will be shown further below, the extent to which parties are regulated in a constitution, and the level of detail with which this is accomplished, is of course not set in stone at a single stroke; that is to say, it may well evolve in response to changes in the political landscape and/or in constitutional doctrine.

3.2 Three models of constitutionalisation

Van Biezen (together with Gabriela Borz) also developed another classification which is valuable in the analysis of political-party constitutionalisation in continental Europe: this one identifies three models of such constitutionalisation that have emerged over time.[41]

In the first model, which van Biezen and Borz call "Parties in Public Office", parties act as electoral agents, parliamentary groups, or governmental actors. According to the authors, this model "is illustrative of a more instrumental view of political parties" and is found mainly in the longer-established and continuous liberal democracies of Northern Europe.[42] In these countries, the constitutionalisation of political parties tends to be only indirect in connection with elections, their role as parliamentary groups or in forming government, and no dedicated constitutional provisions regulating political parties exist. In Finland's Constitution, for instance, political parties are mentioned only in the provisions on parliamentary and

40 Ibid.

41 I van Biezen and G Borz, "Models of Party Democracy: Patterns of Party Regulation in Post-war European Constitutions", 42 (2012) *European Political Science Review*, pp 327–359. By contrast, the Venice Commission distinguishes between two models, the "liberal or free market model" (in which political parties are viewed as private associations that should be free from external regulations to the greatest extent possible) and the "egalitarian-democratic model" (in which political parties have a public function and should therefore respect equality and democracy in their internal organisation). See Venice Commission, *Guidelines on Political Party Regulation*, 2nd ed, 14 December 2020, CDL-AD(2020)032, paras 22–31.

42 Van Biezen and Borz, *supra* n. 41, p 349.

presidential elections, which state that the right to nominate candidates is held by registered political parties.[43]

In the second model, "Parties as Public Utilities", political parties are quasi-official agencies for the realisation of democratic values such as participation and representation. This model, which is exemplified by Portugal's constitution, implies a close relation of political parties to the state, one which in turn serves as a justification for support by public means and the granting of special legal status.[44] For instance, while Article 10 of the Portuguese Constitution assigns parties the responsibility to "assist in bringing about the organisation and expression of the will of the people", Article 40 grants them "the right to broadcasting time on publicly owned radio and television".[45]

Lastly, in the third model, "Defending Democracy", parties are permanent extra-parliamentary organisations and their constitutionalisation serves primarily to safeguard the continued existence of democracy. According to an analysis of more than 30 European constitutions conducted by van Biezen and Borz, this model has become the most common and is particularly widespread among the younger democracies in Central and Eastern Europe that were formerly under socialist one-party rule.[46] As will be illustrated with the case of Germany in section 4 below, in this model political parties are strongly protected and enjoy a broad range of constitutional rights, while at the same time their conduct is restricted by the state, requiring that their activities, ideologies and internal organisation are not contrary to fundamental democratic principles.

---

43 Articles 25 and 54 of the Constitution of Finland. Van Biezen and Borz additionally list Austria, Cyprus, Greece, Iceland, Malta, Sweden, and Norway as most closely related to that model. See ibid, p 351 (Table 6).

44 Ibid, pp 349–350.

45 Apart from Portugal, Van Biezen and Borz identify only Luxembourg and Switzerland as most closely related to that model. See ibid, p 351 (Table 6).

46 Ibid, pp 348–49. According to Van Biezen and Borz in ibid, p 351 (Table 6), the following European countries fall under this category: Bulgaria, Croatia, Czech Republic, France, Germany, Estonia, Hungary, Italy, Latvia, Lithuania, Poland, Romania, Serbia, Slovakia, Slovenia, Spain, and Ukraine.

3.3 Harmonisation at the European level

Although different models of political-party constitutionalisation in continental Europe have emerged seemingly of their own accord, many aspects of their regulation have been increasingly shaped by harmonisation efforts at the regional level. Like the ICCPR, Article 11 of the European Convention for the Protection of Human Rights and Fundamental Freedoms (ECHR) guarantees the right to freedom of association for political parties. Moreover, despite a narrower wording, Article 3 of the First Protocol to the ECHR is interpreted by the European Commission and the ECtHR in a way that it guarantees similar rights to political participation as guaranteed by the ICCPR.[47] The ECHR also allows for limitations by way of a restriction clause.[48] In addition, in extreme cases the rights guaranteed in the ECHR may be withheld by its so-called Abuse Clause.[49] Equal treatment is guaranteed by Article 14 of the ECHR and its Protocol No. 12 and a number of other regional human rights instruments guarantee rights for specific groups that are also relevant for the regulation of political parties.[50]

Apart from these regional human rights instruments, participating states of the Organization of Security and Co-operation in Europe (OSCE) have committed themselves to a number of democratic governance principles relevant for the regulation of political parties, most notably through the so-called Copenhagen Document.[51]

Based on these legal obligations and political commitments, and informed by an extensive review of the relevant case law before the ECtHR, as well as international and regional best practice, the Venice Commission, together with the OSCE, has developed detailed guidelines for the regulation of political parties.[52] First published in 2011 and revised in 2020, they set out the following 11 principles:

47 See Fox, *supra* n. 6, pp 59–63.
48 ECHR, Article 11(2).
49 Ibid, Article 17.
50 For example, Article 7 of the Council of Europe Framework Convention for the Protection of National Minorities explicitly guarantees the right to freedom of association for persons belonging to a national minority.
51 Document of the Copenhagen Meeting of the Conference on the Human Dimension of the CSCE, 29 June 1990, www.osce.org/files/f/documents/9/c/14304.pdf (accessed 24 July 2024).
52 Venice Commission (2020), *supra* n. 41.

- The freedom of association of political parties should be granted to the greatest extent possible. This implies a presumption of the lawfulness of parties' establishment, objectives and activities.
- States shall not only respect the exercise of freedom of association of political parties but also actively protect it. In particular, violence and threats of violence are not permissible.
- Political parties shall have the right to freedom of expression and opinion in participating in political and public debate, regardless of whether their views align with government positions.
- States should aim to facilitate political pluralism. Pluralism entails the existence of a genuine choice among political parties.
- Restrictions of any rights in relation to political parties must be in compliance with human rights instruments and be prescribed by precise, certain, and foreseeable laws.
- Restrictions must be necessary in a democratic society, proportionate in nature, and effective in achieving specific purposes.
- States must provide a domestic remedy to enforce rights in relation to political parties. Review of restrictions must be possible before a court, at least in the final instance.
- States shall treat political parties on an equal basis. Regulations on political parties may not discriminate against individuals or specific groups.
- Any differential treatment by and within political parties which is based on personal characteristics or status must be reasonably and objectively justified. At the same time, states may provide for temporary measure aimed at promoting de facto equality within political parties for groups subjected to past discrimination.
- The regulations in relation to political parties shall be implemented by competent and impartial state authorities, including government bodies and courts.
- Privileges such as state funding justify certain obligations on political parties in relation to their accountability, such as reporting requirements and transparency in financing.[53]

In addition to these general guidelines, the Venice Commission has prepared further guidelines and reports addressing specific issues of political-

53 Ibid, paras 32–62.

party regulation, such as the prohibition and dissolution of parties,[54] the method of nomination of candidates,[55] and financing.[56] Furthermore, both the Venice Commission and the OSCE regularly (sometimes jointly) draft opinions on individual countries' laws regulating political parties and assess them against regional standards.[57]

While even a summary of this impressive body of guidance on European minimum standards for the regulation of political parties would go beyond the scope of this chapter, what is noteworthy are the instances in which the level of their regulation of a state's national legal framework is addressed, that is, whether and to what extent constitutionalising political parties is recommended or even required. In this regard, the Venice Commission's general guidelines state only that, apart from freedom of association, other questions, such as the role and functioning of political parties in a democratic system, do not necessarily have to be set out in a country's constitution, even though "the importance of political parties requires that legislation that affects basic rights and obligations of political parties should at least have the status of parliamentary legislation, and not that of regulation issued by an administrative authority".[58]

In its guidelines on the prohibition and dissolution of political parties, the Venice Commission notes that, in their constitutions, most European countries explicitly list the main cases in which restrictions may be placed on political parties.[59] In another report, the Commission argues that the extent to which a state's constitution regulates intra-party democracy has an impact on the possibilities to allow the legislator to establish requirements and proceedings for party candidate nomination:

54 Venice Commission, *Guidelines on Prohibition and Dissolution of Political Parties and Analogous Measures*, 10–11 December 1999, CDL-INF(2000)001.

55 Venice Commission, *Report on the Method of Nomination of Candidates within Political Parties*, Study No. 721/2013, CDL-AD (2015)020.

56 Venice Commission, *Guidelines and Report on the Financing of Political Parties*, 9–10 March 2001, CDL-INF(2001)008.

57 See, for example, Venice Commission, *Opinion on the Draft Amendments to the Law on Political Parties of Bulgaria*, Opinion No. 505/2008, 15 December 2008, CDL-AD(2008)034; Venice Commission, *Opinion on the Constitutional and Legal Provisions Relevant to the Prohibition of Political Parties in Turkey*, Opinion No. 489/2008, 13 March 2009, CDL-AD (2009) 006; OSCE/ODIHR-Venice Commission, *Joint Opinion on the Draft Act to Regulate the Formation, Inner Structures, Functioning and Financing of Political Parties and their Participation in Elections of Malta*, Opinion No. 780/2014, 14 October 2014, CDL-AD(2014)035.

58 Venice Commission (2020), *supra* n. 41, paras 67, 77.

59 Venice Commission (1999), *supra* n. 54, p 13.

> When the constitution only recognises the freedom of political parties, the legislator must be more respectful of the autonomy of parties and the proportionality principle. ... It implies that the requirements for limiting freedom imposed by the proportionality test are more demanding, with the consequence that legislative intervention will, in relative terms, be more difficult to justify.[60]

Alternatively, if a state's constitution makes no reference to political parties at all, the legislator may impose such regulatory requirements and has "greater latitude in this respect than where the constitution explicitly recognises the freedom of political parties".[61] Lastly, in relation to party financing, the Venice Commission notes that in most European countries this area is regulated only by statutory law; while constitutionalising it "offers the advantage of permitting the review of any subsequent law that might have the effect of undermining rights or possibilities granted", it "entails the disadvantage of making it far more difficult to reform the entire body of rules".[62]

4. The German party-state

If one wants an impression of what the constitutionalisation of political parties in continental Europe looks like in concrete terms, the German Basic Law of 1949 offers arguably the best-known example. Germany was one of the first European countries to regulate parties, with its Basic Law containing a dedicated provision that regulates a broad range of issues concerning political parties. Article 21 thereof reads as follows:

(1) Political parties shall participate in the formation of the political will of the people. They may be freely established. Their internal organisation must conform to democratic principles. They must publicly account for their assets and for the sources and use of their funds.
(2) Parties that, by reason of their aims or the behaviour of their adherents, seek to undermine or abolish the free democratic basic order or to endanger the existence of the Federal Republic of Germany shall be unconstitutional.

---

60 Venice Commission (2013), *supra* n. 55, para 15.
61 Ibid, para 16.
62 Venice Commission (1999), *supra* n. 54, p 5.

(3) Parties that, by reason of their aims or the behaviour of their adherents, are oriented towards an undermining or abolition of the free democratic basic order or an endangerment of the existence of the Federal Republic of Germany shall be excluded from state financing. If such exclusion is determined, any favourable fiscal treatment of these parties and of payments made to those parties shall cease.
(4) The Federal Constitutional Court shall rule on the question of unconstitutionality within the meaning of paragraph (2) of this Article and on exclusion from state financing within the meaning of paragraph (3).
(5) Details shall be regulated by federal laws.

Before the adoption of the Basic Law in 1949, political parties were absent in German constitutions. Parties were considered extra-constitutional institutions representing diversity, whereas the German state stood for unity.[63] Consequently, the constitutionalisation of parties in the Basic Law was perceived as "fundamental, almost revolutionary" by German constitutional scholars at the time.[64]

Turning the traditional view on its head, the German Constitutional Court has gradually developed a theory of the country as a "party-state" (*Parteienstaat*). In the case of *Schleswig-Holstein Voters' Association* (1952), the Constitutional Court found that the "incorporation of political parties in Article 21 means that parties are not only political-sociological entities; they are also integral parts of our constitutional structure and our constitutionally ordered political life".[65] Moreover, German political parties hold the rank of constitutional organs and may even defend their constitutionally guaranteed rights in proceedings before the Constitutional Court.[66]

Competing views on what the notion of the party-state means in concrete terms were ventilated in a further set of constitutional court cases

63 For example, the Weimar Constitution of 1919 mentioned political parties only in passing in its Article 130, prescribing that state officials serve the community as a whole and not any particular party.

64 See CJ Schneider, "Political Parties and the German Basic Law of 1949", 10 (1957) *The Western Political Quarterly*, pp 527–540, 527.

65 Federal Constitutional Court of Germany, Judgement, 5 April 1952, 2 BvH 1/52, BVerfGE 208, paras 240–241, English quotation cited from the translation in DP Kommers and RA Miller, *The Constitutional Jurisprudence of the Federal Republic of Germany*, Durham, Duke University Press, 3rd edn (2012), p 271.

66 Federal Constitutional Court of Germany, Judgement, 20 July 1954, 1 PBvU 1/54, BVerfGE 4, 27.

on party financing.[67] Ultimately, the notion was confirmed and laid out in the Political Parties Act, passed in 1967, which explicitly confers a public function to parties, describing them as "integral to the free democratic basic order" and detailing their role "in the formation of the people's political will in all fields of public life".[68]

The detailed constitutionalisation of political parties in the Basic Law and the notion of Germany as a party-state mark a clear break with the country's state tradition, and may be explained largely against the background of the experience with Nazi rule. To illustrate this point, two distinct aspects of German party constitutionalisation will be discussed in more depth: the prohibition of anti-democratic parties (section 4.1), and the intra-party democracy requirement (section 4.2).

4.1 The prohibition of anti-democratic parties

Coined by the German exile Karl Löwenstein during Nazi rule, the concept of "militant democracy" embodies the idea that "pre-emptive, prima facie illiberal measures to prevent those aiming at subverting democracy with democratic means from destroying the democratic regime" can be justified.[69] After World War II, the concept found its way into the German

67 The first case was Federal Constitutional Court of Germany, Judgement, 19 July 1966, 2 BvF 1/65, BVerfGE 20, 56. For a discussion of the subsequent cases, see Kommers and Miller, *supra* n. 65, pp 278–284.

68 Section 1 of the German Political Parties Act, 24 July 1967, last amended on 27 February 2024, Federal Law Gazette I, p 70. The Act explicitly mentions the following functions of political parties: "exerting an influence on the shaping of public opinion; encouraging and enhancing civic education; promoting citizens' active participation in political life; educating citizens capable of assuming public responsibilities; participating in elections at the federal, Land [state] and local levels by nominating candidates; influencing political developments in parliaments and governments; contributing the political aims they have developed to the public decision making and policy formation process; and ensuring a continuing active interrelationship between the people and the state institutions" (cited from the translation available at https://www.bmi.bund.de/SharedDocs/downloads/DE/gesetzestexte/Parteiengesetz_PartG_engl_042009.html, accessed 7 August 2024).

69 For an overview of the concept, see JW Müller, "Militant Democracy", in M Rosenfeld and A Sajó (eds.), *The Oxford Handbook of Comparative Constitutional Law*, Oxford, Oxford University Press (2012), pp 1253–1269.

Basic Law and manifested itself in a number of constitutional provisions.[70] With a view to defending the new democracy against not only the possible threat of a new Nazi party but a similar danger from a German Communist party,[71] Article 21(2) of the German Basic Law prescribes that parties that "seek to impair or destroy the free democratic basic order or to endanger the existence of the Federal Republic of Germany are unconstitutional". Only the Federal Constitutional Court has the authority to decide on a party's unconstitutionality (the so-called party privilege: see Article 21(4) cited above).

Until to date, there have been only two cases in which the Federal Constitutional Court decided to prohibit an anti-democratic political party, namely that of the Socialist Reich Party in 1952 and the German Communist Party in 1956. While in the first case the decision was based exclusively on the party's programme and internal structures,[72] in the second, a higher standard of proof was applied by the Constitutional Court. This requires that, to be declared unconstitutional, a political party has to have a "fixed purpose constantly and resolutely to combat the free democratic basic order" and that the purpose has to manifest itself in "political action according to a fixed plan of action".[73]

A third, and more recent, case – one which did *not* result in a ban in the end – was that of the National Democratic Party (NPD), which since 2023 has been renamed "The Homeland". Following a failed attempt to ban the NPD in the early 2000s (it failed due to procedural reasons), the Constitutional Court found the party to be unconstitutional in second proceedings that ended in 2017, but decided not to ban it because there were no indications that it would succeed in its anti-constitutional aims – that is, there was no imminent threat to the "free basic democratic order".[74]

---

70 For an overview, see M Thiel, "Germany", in M Thiel (ed.), *The Militant Democracy Principle in Modern Democracies*, Farnham, Ashgate (2009), pp 109–146.

71 See P Niesen, "Anti-Extremism, Negative Republicanism, Civic Society: Three Paradigms for Banning Political Parties", 3 (2002) *German Law Journal*, pp 1–32, 5.

72 Federal Constitutional Court of Germany, Judgement, 23 October 1952, 1 BVB 1/51, BVerfGE 2, 1, English translation in Kommers and Miller, *supra* n. 65, pp 286–289.

73 Federal Constitutional Court of Germany, Judgement, 17 August 1956, 1 BvB 2/51, BVerfGE 5, 85, 139, quote cited from the English translation in Kommers and Miller, *supra* n. 65, pp 291.

74 Federal Constitutional Court of Germany, Judgement, 17 January 2017, 2 BvB 1/13, English translation available at https://www.bundesverfassungsgericht.de/SharedDocs/Entscheidungen/EN/2017/01/bs20170117_2bvb000113en.html (accessed 25

The decision triggered a constitutional amendment to Article 21 of the Basic Law, now allowing, as a less severe restriction than a complete party ban, for state funding to be stripped where it cannot be determined conclusively that a political party "seeks to undermine or abolish" Germany's free democratic basic order but is only "oriented" towards it.[75] On the basis of the new provision, the Constitutional Court stripped the NPD of its state funding in January 2024 for a period of six years.[76] The decision was highly anticipated in a context where another far-right party, Alternative for Germany (AfD), has gained increasing popularity, consequently reviving the debate on how best to respond once more to the threat of anti-democratic parties.[77]

Among European constitutions, the German Basic Law is almost unique in providing explicitly for the possibility of prohibiting anti-democratic parties.[78] Only Croatia's constitution has a near-identical provision, whereas Poland's prohibits parties "whose programs are based upon totalitarian methods and the modes of activity of nazism, fascism and communism".[79] Likewise with an eye to the past, Italy's constitution explicitly prohibits the re-establishment of the dissolved Fascist party.[80] Apart from these examples, no other European constitutions have similarly explicit provisions.

So, while it cannot be said that the prohibition of anti-democratic parties is widely constitutionalised in Europe, the Venice Commission is of the view that the concept is indeed reflected in European human rights law.

July 2024). On the potential relevance of the underlying rationale of this decision for ethnic party bans in Africa, see J Socher and CM Fombad, "Prohibitions of Ethnic Political Parties and Constitutionalism in Sub-Saharan Africa", in CM Fombad, N Steytler, and Y Fessha (eds.), *Ethnicity and Constitutionalism in Africa*, Oxford, Oxford University Press, forthcoming.

75 Cf. the wording of the second with that of the third paragraph of Article 21 of the Basic Law, cited above.

76 Federal Constitutional Court of Germany, Judgement, 23 January 2024, 2 BvB 1/19, https://www.bverfg.de/e/bs20240123_2bvb000119.html (accessed 25 July 2024).

77 See, for example, the debate on *Verfassungsblog*, with contributions on party bans in Germany and Europe, https://verfassungsblog.de/category/debates/das-parteiverbot-in-deutschland-und-europa (accessed 13 August 2024).

78 See S Tyulkina, *Militant Democracy: Undemocratic Political Parties and Beyond*, London, Routledge (2015), pp 87–109; AK Bourne and FC Bértoa, "Mapping 'Militant Democracy': Variation in Party Ban Practices in European Democracies (1945–2015)", 13 (2017) *European Constitutional Law Review*, pp 221–247.

79 Article 6(3) of the 1990 Constitution of Croatia; Article 13 of the 1997 Constitution of Poland.

80 Article XII of the 1947 Constitution of Italy.

According to its guidelines on the regulation of political parties, the Abuse Clause in Article 17 of the ECHR, apart from its symbolic value, is a reflection of militant democracy: "The concept as such, that the Convention rights may not be used to destroy democracy and other's Convention rights, forms the backbone of several Court judgements".[81] Taking this view a step further, many commentators even argue that, based on the ECtHR's case law on the prohibition of political parties, militant democracy has become a European constitutional value.[82]

4.2 The requirement of intra-party democracy

A second distinctive feature of German party constitutionalisation – one which, in a way, could be seen as an application of the militant democracy concept to the internal organisation of political parties[83] – is the requirement of intra-party democracy found in the third sentence of Article 21(1) of the German Basic Law ("Their internal organisation must conform to democratic principles").

In the *Socialist Reich Party* case mentioned above, the Federal Constitutional Court decided that in essence the requirement means that a party must be structured from the bottom up; that is, members must not be excluded from decision-making processes, and the basic equality of members as well as the freedom to join or to leave the party must be guaranteed.[84]

Building on this decision, German constitutional doctrine interprets the notion "democratic principles" in Article 21(1) of the Basic Law largely in the same way as the democratic principle enshrined in other constitutional provisions in the constitution. The notion translates, as a result, into four

81 Venice Commission (2020), *supra* n. 41, para 121, citing ECHR, *Refah Partisi (the Welfare Party) and Others v Turkey*, nos. 41340/98, 13 February 2003, paras 98-99 and *Ždanoka v Latvia*, no. 58278/00, 16 March 2006, paras 98–101.

82 See, for example, P Macklem, "Militant Democracy, Legal Pluralism, and the Paradox of Self-Determination", 4 (2006) *International Journal of Constitutional Law*, pp 488–516, 507–508; Tyulkina, *supra* n. 78, p 97; CS Botelho and N Garoupa, "Regulating Parties by Constitutional Rules in Democracies", 24 (2023) *German Law Journal*, pp 1648–1676, 1674.

83 On the nexus between the two aspects, see, for example, Y Mersel, "The Dissolution of Political Parties: The Problem of Internal Democracy", 4 (2006) *International Journal of Constitutional Law*, pp 84–113.

84 Federal Constitutional Court of Germany (1952), *supra* n. 65, para 174, cited from the English translation in Kommers and Miller, *supra* n. 65, p 288.

main principles governing a party's internal organisation: (1) political will has to be formed in a "bottom-up" process; (2) minorities within the party must be protected, in particular through the right to intra-party opposition; (3) party offices are temporary and a real chance for change in leadership must exist; and (4) party members' rights to articulate their political will has to be protected within the framework of internal party rules.[85] Details such as the role of party members in the selection of party representatives, the formulation of policies, or the right to dissent are regulated in Germany's Political Parties Act.[86]

Similar explicit constitutional provisions demanding that political parties be internally democratic exist only in a number of other European countries.[87] As with the prohibition of anti-democratic parties, there is only one other instance close to the German model, namely Croatia's constitution, which in its Article 6 provides that the "internal organisation of political parties shall be in accordance with fundamental constitutional democratic principles". In addition, only Portugal and Spain have explicitly constitutionalised the intra-party democracy requirement.[88]

This aspect of party constitutionalisation is therefore the exception rather than the rule in Europe, even though many constitutions proscribe it implicitly by requiring parties to serve or respect democratic principles or methods[89] and in other cases some countries have introduced the intra-party requirement at a statutory level in their party or election laws.[90] Accordingly, the Venice Commission takes a balanced view on the issue, stating in its guidelines on the regulation of political parties that

---

85 HP Schneider, "Die Institution der politischen Partei in der Bundesrepublik Deutschland", in DT Tsatsos, D Schefold, and HP Schneider (eds.), *Parteienrecht im europäischen Vergleich: Die Parteien in den demokratischen Ordnungen der Staaten der Europäischen Gemeinschaft*, Baden-Baden, Nomos (1990), pp 151–218, 195–200.

86 See R Wolfrum, *Die innerparteiliche demokratische Ordnung nach dem Parteiengesetz*, Berlin, Duncker & Humblot (1974); H Trautmann, *Innerparteiliche Demokratie im Parteienstaat*, Berlin, Duncker & Humblot (1975).

87 See I van Biezen and DR Piccio, "Shaping Intra-Party Democracy: On the Legal Regulation of Internal Party Organisations", in WP Cross and RS Katz (eds.), *The Challenges of Intra-Party Democracy*, Oxford, Oxford University Press (2013), pp 27–48.

88 Article 51(5) of the Constitution of Portugal; Article 6 of the Constitution of Spain.

89 See D Schefold, DT Tsatsos, and M Morlok, "Rechtsvergleichende Ausblicke", in DT Tsatsos, D Schefold, and HP Schneider (eds.), *Parteienrecht im europäischen Vergleich: Die Parteien in den demokratischen Ordnungen der Staaten der Europäischen Gemeinschaft*, Baden-Baden, Nomos (1990), pp 737–853, 809–810.

90 See Van Biezen and Piccio, *supra*, n. 87, p 39 (Table 3.4).

while some kind of state regulation of the inner workings of political parties may be introduced, it is acceptable, in principle, that state interference is limited to requirements for parties to be transparent in their decision-making and to seek input from their membership when determining party constitutions and candidates.[91]

5. Conclusion

International human rights instruments highlight the importance of political parties' engagement in political activity and set binding minimum standards in regard to specific aspects of this activity. As was shown in the first section of this chapter, the ICCPR obliges state parties to allow political parties and to regulate their functioning; at the same time, while guaranteeing freedom of association for political parties, the ICCPR allows for restrictions to be imposed on them under certain conditions. What is more, other international instruments apart from the ICCPR provide for minimum standards in relation to particular aspects of party regulation, such as equal treatment and non-discrimination, as well as financing and transparency. General comments and recommendations, along with communications by international human rights monitoring bodies, provide further guidance on the interpretation of these provisions.

However, as the chapter's second section shows, in spite of increasing regional-level efforts towards harmonisation, Europe's experience with the constitutionalisation of political parties is that many different models in this regard continue to exist. The development of these models came in waves, with the waves by and large corresponding with broader waves of constitution-making and democratisation. Moreover, party constitutionalisation was often a reaction to an authoritarian past, be it to military rule in Southern Europe in the 1970s or to one-party rule in the former socialist countries of Central and Eastern Europe in the late 1980s and early 1990s. This observation is also true of the German party-state, where some of the most distinctive aspects of party constitutionalisation in the Basic Law can be understood (even if not exclusively) as a reaction to Nazi party rule.

Although different models exist, the constitutionalisation of political parties is the norm in Europe, with the most detailed frameworks to be found in the post-War constitutions of Austria, Germany, and Italy, all of which follow (as per van Biezen and Borz) the "Defending Democracy" model.

91 Venice Commission (2020), *supra* n. 41, para 155.

Arguably, this is also the most interesting model to look at when trying to find lessons for the African context, given that the vast majority of African countries have had similar experiences with authoritarian rule prior to democratisation.

Yet, while some of the principles enshrined in these European constitutions could provide inspiration for the further constitutionalisation of political parties in African countries, other concepts may be less suitable, or even prone to abuse. This might be the case especially in regard to the possibility of prohibiting anti-democratic parties. The Venice Commission is, at any event, apt to note in its guidelines on the regulation of political parties that while there is no uniform model on how to regulate the prohibition of parties, "there is a clear European approach as to how these rules are applied in practice: they are not applied".[92]

By contrast, the intra-party democracy requirement may be a more promising aspect of European party constitutionalisation to explore further through comparative research. As has been noted above, more and more European countries follow this approach, if not always explicitly and if not necessarily in their constitutions. However, an important caveat here is that the rules on intra-party democracy as envisaged in Germany, for example, are clearly based on the idea of a mass party.[93] While today's parties in Germany have developed away from that model and it is also arguably the case that democratic theories that justify intra-party democracy should be rethought,[94] they certainly do not fit in with the African context, where political parties may be better described as cartel parties rather than mass parties.[95] Thus, while the general idea of intra-party democracy has grown in popularity and, from the perspective of constitutional theory, has become more justifiable or even desirable, what this would mean in concrete terms is less clear and would need to be carefully considered in the relevant

92 Ibid, para 62.

93 Ibid, pp 44–45.

94 For a discussion of these theories in the German context, see K Detterbeck, "Alte und neue Probleme der innerparteilichen Demokratie", in M Morlok, T Poguntke, and E Sokolov (eds.), *Parteienstaat – Parteiendemokratie*, Baden-Baden, Nomos (2018), pp 123–142.

95 M Boogards, "Political Parties in Sub-Saharan Africa", in N Carter, D Keith, GM Sindre and S Vasilopoulou (eds.), *The Routledge Handbook of Political Parties,* Abingdon, Routledge (2023), pp 392–402.

context.[96] It is in any case important to remember that any requirements as to the internal organisation of political parties are, if adopted, a limitation of the right to freedom of association.

Beyond the two constitutional principles discussed here in more detail for which the German party-state became to be regarded as a pioneer and model, it could be worth analysing in more detail how other aspects of party regulation are dealt with in other European constitutions and how well they have travelled to other contexts. For example, further research could analyse and compare the experiences of other European countries with registration requirements (Latvia), the prohibition of ethnic and religious parties (Bulgaria),[97] or anti-party switching provisions (Portugal).[98]

Lastly, the example of Luxembourg, the most recent example of constitutionalisation of political parties in Europe, highlights the potential role of regional bodies such as the Venice Commission in these processes.[99] In its opinion on the planned reform, the Commission welcomed the constitutionalisation of political parties "in line with modern constitutional developments" and made some concrete recommendations. In particular, it noted the absence of a legal definition of political parties and suggested the development of such a definition.[100] In Africa, equivalent bodies could play a similar role as the Venice Commission in ensuring that international and regional minimum standards for the regulation of political parties are met.

While the case of Luxembourg was an exception and the first constitutionalisation of political parties in Europe was usually accompanied by more fundamental constitutional changes, the example of Germany illustrates that the detail and extent of the regulation of political parties in a constitution is not set in stone and that a changing political landscape and/or evolving constitutional doctrine may trigger adjustments in the constitutional framework. At any rate, it is a truism that different contexts

96 For some of the features proposed as well as the justifications for this, see Mersel, *supra* n. 83, pp 95–98.

97 See Article 11(4) of the 1991 Constitution of Bulgaria: "Political parties on ethnic, racial or religious lines, nor parties which seek the violent seizure of state power may not be formed."

98 See Article 163(3) of the 1976 Constitution of Portugal: "Deputies shall cease to hold office if they ... join a different party from the one that nominates them for election."

99 See G Borz, "Justifying the Constitutional Regulation of Political Parties: A Framework for Analysis", 38 (2017) *International Political Science Review*, pp 99–113.

100 Venice Commission, *Interim Opinion on the Draft Constitutional Amendments of Luxembourg*, Opinion No. 544/2009, 14 December 2009, CDL-AD(2009)57, para 22.

require different design choices at different stages of constitutional development – sometimes resulting even in the deconstitutionalisation of certain aspects while introducing others.[101]

References

Books, articles, chapters in books and others

Bacio Terracino J, "Article 7: Public Sector", in C Rose, M Kubiciel, and O Landwehr (eds.), *The United Nations Convention against Corruption*, Oxford, Oxford University Press (2019), pp 65–77

Bértoa FC and Van Biezen I (eds.), *The Regulation of Post-Communist Party Politics*, London, Routledge (2017)

Bértoa FC, Piccio DR, and Rashkova ER, "Party Laws in Comparative Perspective", in I van Biezen and HM ten Napel (eds.), *Regulating Political Parties: European Democracies in Comparative Perspectives*, Leiden, Leiden University Press (2014), pp 119–148

Bogdanor V (ed.), *The British Constitution in the Twentieth Century*, Oxford, Oxford University Press (2004)

Boogards M, "Political Parties in Sub-Saharan Africa", in N Carter, D Keith, GM Sindre, and S Vasilopoulou (eds.), *The Routledge Handbook of Political Parties*, Abingdon, Routledge (2023), pp 392–402

Borz G, "Justifying the Constitutional Regulation of Political Parties: A Framework for Analysis", 38 (2017) *International Political Science Review*, pp 99–113

Botelho CS and Garoupa N, "Regulating Parties by Constitutional Rules in Democracies", 24 (2023) *German Law Journal*, pp 1648–1676

Bourne AK and Bértoa FC, "Mapping 'Militant Democracy': Variation in Party Ban Practices in European Democracies (1945–2015)", 13 (2017) *European Constitutional Law Review*, pp 221–247

De Sousa MR, "Die Institution der politischen Partei in Portugal", in DT Tsatsos, D Schefold, and HP Schneider (eds.), *Parteienrecht im europäischen Vergleich: Die Parteien in den demokratischen Ordnungen der Staaten der Europäischen Gemeinschaft*, Baden-Baden, Nomos (1990), pp 591–634

Detterbeck K, "Alte und neue Probleme der innerparteilichen Demokratie", in M Morlok, T Poguntke, and E Sokolov (eds.), *Parteienstaat – Parteiendemokratie*, Baden-Baden, Nomos (2018), pp 123–142

101 As happened in Portugal, for example, where several references to political parties were removed by a constitutional amendment in 1982 while simultaneously strengthening their constitutionalisation in other provisions. See MR de Sousa, "Die Institution der politischen Partei in Portugal", in DT Tsatsos, D Schefold, and HP Schneider (eds.), *Parteienrecht im europäischen Vergleich: Die Parteien in den demokratischen Ordnungen der Staaten der Europäischen Gemeinschaft*, Baden-Baden, Nomos (1990), pp 591–634, 603.

Elster J, "Forces and Mechanisms in the Constitution-making Process", 45 (1995) *Duke Law Journal*, pp 364–396

Fox GH and Nolte G, "Intolerant Democracies", in GH Fox and BR Roth (eds.), *Democratic Governance and International Law*, Cambridge, Cambridge University Press (2010), pp 389–435

Fox GH, "The Right to Political Participation in International Law", in GH Fox and BR Roth (eds.), *Democratic Governance and International Law*, Cambridge, Cambridge University Press (2010), pp 48–90

Fromont M, "Die Institution der politischen Partei in Frankreich", in DT Tsatsos, D Schefold, and HP Schneider (eds.), *Parteienrecht im europäischen Vergleich: Die Parteien in den demokratischen Ordnungen der Staaten der Europäischen Gemeinschaft*, Baden-Baden, Nomos (1990), pp 219–260

Grobbelaar du Plessis I and Njau J, "Article 29: Participation in Political and Public Life", in I Bantekas, MA Stein and D Anastasiou (eds.), *The UN Convention on the Rights of Persons with Disabilities: A Commentary*, Oxford, Oxford University Press (2018), pp 834–862

Huntington SP, *The Third Wave: Democratization in the Late Twentieth Century*, Norman, University of Oklahoma Press (1991)

Kommers DP and Miller RA, *The Constitutional Jurisprudence of the Federal Republic of Germany*, Durham, Duke University Press, 3rd edn (2012)

Lanchester F, "Die Institution der politischen Partei in Italien", in DT Tsatsos, D Schefold, and HP Schneider (eds.), *Parteienrecht im europäischen Vergleich: Die Parteien in den demokratischen Ordnungen der Staaten der Europäischen Gemeinschaft*, Baden-Baden, Nomos (1990), pp 367–434

Macklem P, "Militant Democracy, Legal Pluralism, and the Paradox of Self-Determination", 4 (2006) *International Journal of Constitutional Law*, pp 488–516

Mersel Y, "The Dissolution of Political Parties: The Problem of Internal Democracy", 4 (2006) *International Journal of Constitutional Law*, pp 84–113

Müller JW, "Militant Democracy", in M Rosenfeld and A Sajó (eds.), *The Oxford Handbook of Comparative Constitutional Law*, Oxford, Oxford University Press (2012), pp 1253–1269

Niesen P, "Anti-Extremism, Negative Republicanism, Civic Society: Three Paradigms for Banning Political Parties", 3 (2002) *German Law Journal*, pp 1–32

Piccio DR, "A Self-Interested Legislator? Party Regulation in Italy", 19 (2014) *South European Society and Politics*, pp 135–152

Schefold D, Tsatsos DT, and Morlok M, "Rechtsvergleichende Ausblicke", in DT Tsatsos, D Schefold, and HP Schneider (eds.), *Parteienrecht im europäischen Vergleich: Die Parteien in den demokratischen Ordnungen der Staaten der Europäischen Gemeinschaft*, Baden-Baden, Nomos (1990), pp 737–853

Schneider CJ, "Political Parties and the German Basic Law of 1949", 10 (1957) *The Western Political Quarterly*, pp 527–540

Schneider HP, "Die Institution der politischen Partei in der Bundesrepublik Deutschland", in DT Tsatsos, D Schefold, and HP Schneider (eds.), *Parteienrecht im europäischen Vergleich: Die Parteien in den demokratischen Ordnungen der Staaten der Europäischen Gemeinschaft*, Baden-Baden, Nomos (1990), pp 151–218

Socher J and Fombad CM, "Prohibitions of Ethnic Political Parties and Constitutionalism in Sub-Saharan Africa", in C Fombad, N Steytler, and Y Fessha (eds.), *Ethnicity and Constitutionalism in Africa*, Oxford, Oxford University Press, forthcoming

Taylor PM, *A Commentary on the International Covenant on Civil and Political Rights: The UN Human Rights Committee's Monitoring of ICCPR Rights*, Cambridge, Cambridge University Press (2020)

Thiel M, "Germany", in M Thiel (ed.), *The Militant Democracy Principle in Modern Democracies*, Farnham, Ashgate (2009), pp 109–146

Thornberry P, *The International Convention on the Elimination of All Forms of Racial Discrimination: A Commentary*, Oxford, Oxford University Press (2016)

Trautmann H, *Innerparteiliche Demokratie im Parteienstaat*, Berlin, Duncker & Humblot (1975)

Tsatsos DT and Kedzia Z (eds.), *Parteienrecht in mittel- und osteuropäischen Staaten: Entstehungsmomente des Parteienrechts in Bulgarien, Litauen, Polen, Russland, der Slowakei, Tschechien und Ungarn*, Baden-Baden, Nomos (1994)

Tsatsos DT, Schefold D and Schneider HP (eds.), *Parteienrecht im europäischen Vergleich: Die Parteien in den demokratischen Ordnungen der Staaten der Europäischen Gemeinschaft*, Baden-Baden, Nomos (1990)

Tyulkina S, *Militant Democracy: Undemocratic Political Parties and Beyond*, London, Routledge (2015)

United Nations Development Programme (UNDP) and National Democratic Institute for International Affairs, *Empowering Women for Stronger Political Parties: A Guidebook to Promote Women's Political Participation*, New York, UNDP (2012)

United Nations Office on Drugs and Crime (UNODC), *Technical Guide to the United Nations Convention Against Corruption*, New York, United Nations (2009)

Van Biezen I and Bértoa FC, "Party Regulation in Post-authoritarian Contexts: Southern Europe in Comparative Perspective", 19 (2014) *South European Society and Politics*, pp 71–87

Van Biezen I and Borz G, "Models of Party Democracy: Patterns of Party Regulation in Post-war European Constitutions", 42 (2012) *European Political Science Review*, pp 327–359

Van Biezen I and Napel ten HM (eds.), *Regulating Political Parties: European Democracies in Comparative Perspectives*, Leiden, Leiden University Press (2014)

Van Biezen I and Piccio DR, "Shaping Intra-Party Democracy: On the Legal Regulation of Internal Party Organisations", in WP Cross and RS Katz (eds.), *The Challenges of Intra-Party Democracy*, Oxford, Oxford University Press (2013), pp 27–48

Van Biezen I, "Constitutionalising Party Democracy: The Constitutive Codification of Political Parties in Post-war Europe", 42 (2012) *British Journal of Political Science*, pp 187–212

Van Biezen I, "The Constitutionalisation of Political Parties in Post-war Europe", in I van Biezen and HM ten Napel (eds.), *Regulating Political Parties: European Democracies in Comparative Perspectives,* Leiden, Leiden University Press (2014), pp 93–118

Wittkopp S, "Article 7", in P Schulz, R Halperin-Kaddari, B Rudolf, and MA Freeman (eds.), *The UN Convention on the Elimination of All Forms of Discrimination against Women and Its Optional Protocol: A Commentary*, 2nd ed, Oxford, Oxford University Press (2022)

Wolfrum R, *Die innerparteiliche demokratische Ordnung nach dem Parteiengesetz*, Berlin, Duncker & Humblot (1974)

Wood T, "Reinforcing Participatory Governance Through International Human Rights Obligations of Political Parties", 28 (2015) *Harvard Human Rights Journal*, pp 145–200

Table of cases

United Nations Commission on Human Rights communication

MA v Italy, Communication No. 117/1981, Supp. No. 40, A/39/40 (1984)

United Nations Human Rights Committee communications

CCPR/C/48/D/313/1988 (Bwalya v Zambia), 14 July 1993

CCPR/CO/73/AZE (Azerbaijan), 12 November 2001

CCPR/CO/75/MDA (Moldova), 5 August 2002

CCPR/C/UZB/CO/3 (Uzbekistan), 7 April 2010

CCPR/C/KAZ/CO/1 (Kazakhstan), 19 August 2011

CCPR/C/TKM/CO/2 (Turkmenistan), 20 April 2017

CCPR/C/SWZ/CO/1 (Swaziland), 23 August 2017

CEDAW/C/NPL/CO/6 (Nepal), 14 November 2018

CCPR/C/BLR/CO/5 (Belarus), 22 November 2018

CEDAW/C/COL/CO/9 (Colombia), 14 March 2019

CEDAW/C/GUY/CO/9 (Guyana), 30 July 2019

CCPR/CO/72/PRK (Democratic People's Republic of Korea), 27 August 2001

European Court of Human Rights cases

Case of Refah Partisi (the Welfare Party) and Others v Turkey, Application Nos. 41340/98, 41342/98, 41343/98 and 41344/98, 13 February 2003

Ždanoka v Latvia, Application No. 58278/00, 16 March 2006

National court cases

Federal Constitutional Court of Germany, Judgement, 17 August 1956, 1 BvB 2/51, BVerfGE 5, 85

Federal Constitutional Court of Germany, Judgement, 5 April 1952, 2 BvH 1/52, BVerfGE 208

Federal Constitutional Court of Germany, Judgement, 20 July 1954, 1 PBvU 1/54, BVerfGE 4, 27

Federal Constitutional Court of Germany, Judgement, 19 July 1966, 2 BvF 1/65, BVerfGE 20, 56

Federal Constitutional Court of Germany, Judgement, 17 January 2017, 2 BvB 1/13

Federal Constitutional Court of Germany, Judgement, 23 January 2024, 2 BvB 1/19

Federal Constitutional Court of Germany, Judgement, 23 October 1952, 1 BVB 1/51, BVerfGE 2, 1

Table of legislation

National legislation

Constitution of the Federal Republic of Germany, 23 May 1949, last amended on 19 December 2022

German Political Parties Act, 24 July 1967, last amended on 27 February 2024

Comments, guidance, and opinions by international bodies

Committee on the Elimination of all Forms of Discrimination against Women, General Recommendation No. 23: Political and Public Life, 1997, A/52/38

Committee on the Elimination of all Forms of Discrimination against Women, General Recommendation No. 25: Temporary Special Measures, 18 August 2004

Committee on the Rights of Persons with Disabilities, General Comment No. 2: Article 9: Accessibility, 22 May 2014, CPRD/C/GC/2

European Commission for Democracy through Law (Venice Commission), *Guidelines and Explanatory Report on Legislation on Political Parties: Some Specific Issues*, 12–13 March 2004, CDL-AD(2004)007rev

European Commission for Democracy through Law (Venice Commission), *Guidelines and Report* on the Financing of Political Parties, 9–10 March 2001, CDL-INF(2001)008

European Commission for Democracy through Law (Venice Commission), *Guidelines on Prohibition and Dissolution of Political Parties and Analogous Measures*, 10–11 December 1999, CDL-INF(2000)001

European Commission for Democracy through Law (Venice Commission), *Opinion on the Draft Amendments to the Law on Political Parties of Bulgaria*, Opinion No. 505/2008, 15 December 2008, CDL-AD(2008)034.

European Commission for Democracy through Law (Venice Commission), *Opinion on the Constitutional and Legal Provisions Relevant to the Prohibition of Political Parties in Turkey*, Opinion No. 489/2008, 13 March 2009, CDL-AD (2009) 006

European Commission for Democracy through Law (Venice Commission), *Interim Opinion on the Draft Constitutional Amendments of Luxembourg*, Opinion No. 544/2009, 14 December 2009, CDL-AD(2009)57

European Commission for Democracy through Law (Venice Commission), *Report on the Method of Nomination of Candidates within Political Parties*, Study No. 721/2013, CDL-AD(2015)020

European Commission for Democracy through Law (Venice Commission), *Guidelines on Political Party Regulation*, 2nd ed, 14 December 2020, CDL-AD(2020)032

OSCE/ODIHR-Venice Commission, *Joint Opinion on the Draft Act to Regulate the Formation, Inner Structures, Functioning and Financing of Political Parties and their Participation in Elections of Malta*, Opinion No. 780/2014, 14 October 2014, CDL-AD(2014)035

United Nations Human Rights Committee, General Comment No. 25: Article 25 (Participation in Public Affairs and the Right to Vote), 12 July 1996, CCPR/C/21/Rev.1/Add.7

United Nations Human Rights Committee, General Comment No. 28: Article 3 (The Equality of Rights Between Men and Women), 29 March 2000, CCPR/C/21/rev.1/Add.10

United Nations Human Rights Committee, General Comment No. 31: The Nature of the General Legal Obligation on State Parties to the Covenant, 26 May 2004, CCPR/C/21/Rev.1/Add.13

United Nations Human Rights Committee, General Comment No. 32: Article 14 ICCPR: Right to Equality Before Courts and Tribunals and to a Fair Trial, 23 August 2007, CCPR/C/CG/32

Part 2
Party Constitutionalism and Multiparty Democracy

Chapter 6 Political-Party Constitutionalisation in Senegal: The Challenges of Majoritarian Abuse

Abdou Khadre Diop

1. Introduction

Senegal is recognised as a long-standing democratic country in Africa.[1] Political pluralism had been adopted before the country's independence, while the rights of political parties were enshrined in the Constitution as soon as Senegal gained independence in 1960. Political parties were given constitutional status for the first time in Senegal's Constitution of 26 August 1960.[2] After a period of one-party rule from 1966 to 1974, the nation returned to a system of political pluralism, albeit with restrictions on the number of authorised political parties. This limited multiparty system was first codified by Law 76-01 in 1976, which allowed for only three political parties, each representing a specific political current. Subsequent amendments to the constitution gradually expanded the number of authorised parties, with Law 78-60 in 1978 permitting a fourth party, and Law 81-17 (hereafter Law on Political Parties) establishing an unrestricted multiparty system in 1981.

However, despite these legal changes fostering political pluralism, Senegal saw the emergence of dominant parties reminiscent of the one-party systems common in many African countries. For more than 40 years following independence, the *Parti Socialiste* ruled the country. The first significant alternation of power occurred in 2000 when the *Parti Démocratique Sénégalais* (PDS), with Abdoulaye Wade as its leader, peacefully assumed the presidency after disputed elections against the incumbent, Abdou Diouf. In 2012, Macky Sall, leader of *Alliance pour la République* (APR), won the presidential election, thereby putting an end to Wade's

1 See A Stephan, "Stateness, Democracy, and Respect: Senegal in Comparative Perspective", in M Diouf (ed.), *Tolerance, Democracy and Sufis in Senegal*, New York, Columbia University Press (2013), p 205.

2 See AD Kebe, B Ba and SA Ndiaye, *Les Textes Fondamentaux de la République du Sénégal*, Dakar, L'Harmattan (2021).

presidency after 12 years in power and his attempt to run for a third term.[3] Lastly, in 2024, Senegal successfully underwent a third alternation of power with the election of Bassirou Diomaye Faye of the opposition party *Patriotes Africains du Sénégal pour le Travail, l'Ethique et la Fraternité* (PASTEF) as the fifth president of Senegal.

Senegal has progressively undertaken constitutional reforms to reinforce its commitment to democratic principles. The current Constitution, adopted in 2001, acknowledges the vital role of political parties in the democratic process and seeks to clearly define their functions and responsibilities within the framework of the country's governance. It provides in its Article 4 that

> political parties and coalitions of political parties participate in the expression of suffrage within the conditions stipulated by the Constitution and the law. They play a crucial role in educating citizens, promoting their engagement in national affairs, and contributing to the management of public affairs.

Moreover, in 2016, the Constitution was amended by referendum to add a specific provision for opposition parties.[4] According to the new Article 58, the Constitution

> guarantees to the political parties which are opposed to the policy of the Government the right to oppose it. The Constitution guarantees to the opposition a status that permits it to carry out its missions. A law shall define this status and establish the rights and duties accruing to them as well as to the leader of the opposition.[5]

In recent years, there has been a notable surge in nationwide dialogues on the rights and obligations of political parties in Senegal, coinciding with escalating political tensions and social unrest. For instance, in 2019, the Electoral Code was amended to prevent the leader of the PDS from

---

3 AB Fall, "La Démocratie Sénégalaise à l'Épreuve de l'Alternance", 5 (2012) *Afrilex,* https://afrilex.u-bordeaux.fr/wp-content/uploads/2021/03/05dossfall.pdf (accessed 5 February 2023).

4 Constitutional Law No. 2016-10, 5 April 2016, amending the Constitution 2024 of Senegal, https://www.constituteproject.org/constitution/Senegal_2016 (accessed 4 April 2024).

5 For commentary on this provision, see IM Fall, "La Réforme Constitutionnelle de Mars 2016 au Sénégal", in IM Fall and A Sall (eds.), *Actualités de droit Public, Mélanges en l'honneur du Professeur Babacar Kanté*, Dakar, L'Harmattan (2020), p 111.

participating in the presidential elections after having been condemned by a special jurisdiction that did not respect the rights of defence.[6] During the same period, the leader of the *Takhawou Senegal* party[7] also saw its presidential candidate excluded.[8]

More recently, in January 2021, the APR-led government intervened to stop the fundraising activities of the then opposition party PASTEF, asserting that the fundraising strategy violated the Law on Political Parties' provisions on party financing. Additionally, PASTEF's leader, Ousmane Sonko, was arrested and detained on various charges, including incitement to insurrection, endangering state security, and plotting against the authority of the state, only to be released recently following the enactment of an amnesty law.[9] Sonko encountered numerous legal obstacles, including the lifting of his parliamentary immunity and his exclusion from the electoral register, despite a court order to reinstate him on the list. Then, in July 2023, Sonko's party was dissolved by the Minister of the Interior, marking it the first ban of a political party since Senegal embraced party pluralism. According to the minister, the dissolution was rooted in several factors, including allegations of inciting violence, undermining national security, and fostering political instability amidst increasing tensions surrounding the electoral process and political discourse. These developments have triggered a series of legal actions at both national and regional levels focusing on the constitutional rights of political parties, the freedom of expression of citizens, and their right to participate in public affairs.

Against this background, this chapter will examine the constitutional recognition of political pluralism and the legal safeguarding of political parties within institutional, political and democratic frameworks. It contends that although the establishment of political pluralism and the constitutional recognition of political parties are significant advancements, they do not sufficiently guarantee the protection of parties. Using Senegal as a case

---

6 See UN Human Rights Committee, *Karim Meïssa Wade c. Sénégal*, Communication No. 2783/2016, UN Doc CCPR/C/124/D/2783/2016, 22 October 2018.

7 Takhawou Senegal was formed after the breakup of the Parti Socialiste following the decision of the party's leaders to support President Macky Sall's APR in the 2019 presidential elections and not field their own candidate in these elections.

8 See "Opposition Leader Khalifa Sall and Karim Wade Barred from Senegal Presidential Race", *France 24*, 14 January 2019, https://www.france24.com/en/20190114-senegal-opposition-leaders-khalifa-sall-karim-wade-barred-presidential-election (accessed 10 March 2024).

9 Law No. 05-2024, adopted 6 March 2024, relating to general amnesty of the events occurring between March 2021 to February 2024.

study, the chapter argues that practical circumstances often expose how majoritarian abuse can erode the rights of political parties despite the existence of constitutional provisions. The chapter illuminates how actions taken by the APR-led government during Sall's presidency frequently encroached upon the rights of political parties.

The discussion is divided into five sections. After this introduction, section 2 provides an overview of the constitutional recognition of political parties in Senegal and their rights and duties. It examines how the Senegalese Constitution conceptualises the role of political parties in the consolidation of democracy, emphasising the need for protection and the nature of the responsibilities they assume. Section 3 focuses on gaps in the legal framework concerning the protection and regulation of political parties, while section 4 delves into the erosion of parties' rights by majoritarian abuse under Macky Sall's presidency. This section highlights the systematic administrative and parliamentary obstacles that hinder political parties' ability to express themselves freely and conduct their activities. The chapter concludes in section 5 by summarising its findings and offering recommendations for strengthening Senegal's constitutional and legal framework to ensure the protection of political parties. This section emphasises that safeguarding democratic principles and pluralism is essential for the existence of a resilient political landscape.

2. The constitutional recognition of political parties

The political landscape in Senegal is shaped by a complex interplay of rights, duties, and constitutional principles that govern the functioning of political parties. Various provisions enshrined in the Constitution aim to uphold fundamental freedoms such as the freedom of association, assembly, and demonstration, while also delineating the responsibilities incumbent upon political entities.

2.1 The rights of political parties

The foremost right is the freedom to create political parties. According to Article 4 of the Constitution of Senegal, "political parties are created freely". The same formulation is found in most French-speaking African countries.[10] The freedom to create political parties refers to the recognised ability of citizens to establish or join a political party without the authorities impeding their initiative. In concrete terms, the freedom to create political parties gives effect to the freedom of association. The creation of political parties, a driving force behind political pluralism, expresses the right of every citizen to organise, join, and participate in organisations which are intended to seek, exercise, and retain power.[11]

In the democratisation movement, the new constitutions adopted in French-speaking regions of Africa, including Senegal, all recognised the right to freely create political parties. This right has led to an explosion in the number of political parties in Senegal, with more than 300 political formations recorded by the Ministry of the Interior for a population of 17 million inhabitants and an electoral register not exceeding seven million people.[12] During Wade's presidency from 2000 to 2012, there was a significant proliferation of political parties, with 143 parties having been established. This trend continued under President Sall's tenure from 2012 to 2024, with 111 new political parties emerging. The sheer number of parties became a logistical challenge during the 2017 parliamentary elections, when there were 47 different party lists on the ballot. As Senegal does not implement the single ballot system, the abundance of options made voting operations complex and time-consuming. To address this, the Constitutional Council issued Decision No. 5-E-2017, which allowed voters to streamline their options by selecting only five out of the 47 lists before entering the polling booth.[13] This measure aimed to make voting easier and reduce congestion at polling stations.

Finally, during the latest elections, namely the 2024 presidential elections, the Constitutional Council received 93 declarations of candidacy from various political parties or coalitions of parties.[14] Of these 93 candida-

10 For instance, Article 5 of the 1990 Constitution of Benin and Article 3 of the 1996 Constitution of Cameroon.

11 JT Main, *Political Parties before the Constitution*, Chapel Hill, University of North Carolina Press (1973), p 67.

12 A Savana, "Le Sénégal Compte 299 Partis Politiques", *Finanical Afrik*, 6 April 2018, https://www.financialafrik.com/2018/04/06/le-senegal-compte-299-partis-politiques/ (accessed 12 March 2024).

13 Constitutional Council of Senegal, 14 August 2017, Decision 5-E-2017.

14 See Constitutional Council of Senegal, Decision No. 2/E/2024, 20 January 2024.

cies, only 20 were deemed admissible, which is a significant number for a presidential election.[15]

The Constitution of Senegal, like most constitutions in francophone African countries, recognises the freedom of assembly of political parties. According to the Senegalese Supreme Court, assembly is defined as "a temporary grouping of individuals to hear the presentation of ideas or opinions, to consult on the defense of interests".[16] This definition emphasises three points: the gathering is organised, that is, it is not fortuitous but intentional; it remains temporary; and it has a specific purpose, which is the exchange of ideas. This latter element is particularly relevant to the pluralism of political ideas. Any restriction on the freedom of assembly also constitutes a restriction on the possibilities of action of the political party, as the legal regime of assembly applies to gatherings or the exchange of ideas.

Aware of the fundamental nature of this freedom, the Supreme Court has sometimes intervened to act as a guardian of the freedom of assembly of political parties. For example, in the case of *Assane Ba and others v State of Senegal*,[17] the Prefect of the Dakar department banned a sit-in in front of the Ministry of the Interior planned under the banner of the PDS (at the time an opposition party) on the grounds of disturbance to public order. The Court considered that in prohibiting the assembly envisaged by the applicants, the prefect merely invoked threats of disturbance to public order, obstruction of the free movement of persons and goods, and the risk of hindrance to the continuity of public services, without establishing an inadequacy of security forces necessary to maintain order. On this basis, the Court nullified the prohibition of the freedom of demonstration for the PDS, as the justification for such prohibition was deemed insufficient.[18]

15 Ibid.

16 Supreme Court of Senegal, *Assane Ba and 2 others v State of Senegal*, Decision No. 19, 23 May 2019, https://juricaf.org/arret/SENEGAL-COURSUPREME-20190523-19 (accessed 12 March 2024).

17 Ibid.

18 See also the decision of 9 June 2016 of the Administrative Chamber of the Supreme Court, according to which the Prefect is obliged to specify the alleged risk as well as the absence of alternative measures to the ban. The Court found that the only reference to the disturbance of public order was insufficient and inadequate. See Supreme Court of Senegal, *Aa Ab AI v State of Senegal,* Decision No. 37, 9 June 2016, https://juricaf.org/arret/SENEGAL-COURSUPREME-20160609-37 (accessed 12 March 2024). See also Supreme Court of Senegal, *Mamadou Wade v. State of Senegal,* Decision No. 29, 25 April 2024, case N° J/315/RG/23.

The freedom of demonstration, like the freedom of assembly, is also protected in Senegal. It allows citizens to gather publicly to express shared opinions through their presence and voices. This freedom includes the right to organise and participate in demonstrations in public spaces. Article 8 of the Senegalese Constitution guarantees this freedom, with laws detailing the conditions for its exercise. Political parties must declare their intentions to hold demonstrations in public spaces beforehand. Typically, party leaders in a given area submit a declaration to the relevant authority three days before the scheduled demonstration. The competent administrative body can prohibit the demonstration if the venue is unavailable, if there are risks to public order, if there is non-compliance with the law, or if there are other serious reasons. If there is no response or a reasoned refusal within 48 hours before the event, the demonstration is considered authorised.

2.2 The duties of political parties

According to Article 4 of the Senegalese Constitution, "political parties must respect the principles of national sovereignty and democracy". This obligation reflects the intention of the constituent power to impose adherence to the values of the state on political parties. The content of such values is broad. It concerns, first, respect for the characteristics of the state: republican, secular, and democratic. Then, it covers the safeguarding of the republic's institutions: their status, their powers, and their competences. Political parties must also respect national independence, territorial integrity, and the unity of the state, as well as public order and public freedoms.

The obligation to respect democracy raises some questions. First, what is meant by the principle of democracy? Does it cover both external and internal democracy? What makes a party internally democratic? Some scholars have compiled a list of features that characterise internal party democracy and which concern relations between party members and the structure and institutions of the party.[19] These features include the ability of party members to elect the party leadership or recall it, including their ability to elect the party's nominees to public positions; equal and proportional representation of intra-party minorities and majority-rule voting; the

19 See RH Valle, "La Democracia Interna de los Partidos Políticos", in MP Hernandez (ed.), *Partidos Politicos: Democracia Interna y Financiamento de Precampanas*, Doctrina Jurídica, No. 102, p 145.

ability of members to influence the party platform and agenda; the protection of party members' basic rights, including the right not to be expelled without a fair proceeding; the right to information and transparency of party management, especially fiscal accountability; freedom of speech and association within the party, especially with respect to forming factions; and the provision for independent judicial review of internal party democracy.[20]

Senegal offers a demonstration of what Roberto Michels terms the "iron law of oligarchy", a phrase referring to the tendency for excessive power to become concentrated in the hands of party leadership.[21] In terms of this "iron law", the party leadership arrogates ever greater powers to itself, while the power of individual members weakens, with the former becoming more suspicious of change as it concentrates on preserving its control. For example, in most political parties in Senegal, there is a conflation of the party and the figure of its leader, with the most important decisions being made not so much by the party's deliberative bodies as through the unilateral will of the leader.

The most illustrative case is the choice of the candidate for the 2024 presidential elections by the ruling APR. President Sall, the party's leader and unable to run for a third term, chose Amadou Ba as the APR's candidate not through a congress or a deliberative body of the party in accordance with its statutes. This caused frustration among other party leaders, who claimed to have more legitimacy than the chosen candidate, and led to some of them resigning from the party and running for the presidential elections by creating a new political party. The same can be said of the how PASTEF's presidential candidate was determined. Party leader Sonko, having been convicted in court,[22] chose Faye as the party's candidate without this choice being made in accordance with the internal democratic principles of political parties.

As becomes clear from these examples, political parties in Senegal operate on basis of the unilateral will of a party leader, which is contrary to the requirements of democracy that should be observed in the internal gov-

20 Ibid.

21 See also C Grewe and H Ruiz-Fabri, *Droits Constitutionnels Européens*, Presse Universitaire de France (1995), pp 230–231; B Manin, *Principes du Gouvernement Représentatif*, Paris, Calmann-Lévy (1995), pp 279–299; K Lawson, "Partis Politiques et Groupes d'intérêt ", 79 (1996) *Pouvoirs*, pp 37–45.

22 See section 4.2.2 for further discussion.

ernance of political parties. Whereas the Senegalese Constitution mandates that political parties must uphold the principles of national sovereignty and democracy, there is an evident lack of mechanisms for the robust enforcement of intra-party democracy. Currently, the provision largely remains symbolic, as there is no institutionalised oversight body or legal framework tasked with monitoring and ensuring democratic governance within parties.[23] Efforts to address this could involve establishing regulatory guidelines that enforce transparency and participatory decision-making processes within party structures, as demonstrated by the example of Kenya's Political Parties Act of 2011.[24] Additionally, reforms could include the creation of an independent authority to oversee and audit intra-party elections and candidate selection, thereby aligning political-party operations more closely with democratic ideals.

In addition to the obligation to respect national sovereignty and democracy, political parties in Senegal are also prohibited from identifying with "a race, ethnicity, sex, sect, language, or religion" pursuant to Article 4 of the Constitution. Such a prohibition is particularly significant in Africa, where constitutionalism has sought early on to consolidate the idea of the nation and combat national particularisms. The prohibition against identifying with an ethnicity naturally aims to combat the tendency for a political party to anchor itself exclusively in the ethnicity of its leader and to use ethnic particularities as a political platform.[25] However, despite this constitutional prohibition, ethnic voting and discourse have become increasingly prevalent in recent elections in Senegal, largely as a strategy employed by party leaders. This trend began with former President Abdoulaye Wade of the PDS, who leveraged his affiliation with the Mouride brotherhood as a tool for political mobilisation during the 2007 elections. Similarly, President Sall strategically utilised his dual ethnic identity (as a Hal Pular by origin and Serer by adoption) to rally votes. This tactic contributed to significant support for the APR in regions such as Hal Pular-dominated

---

23 Law No. 81-17 of 6 May 1981 on parties reiterates that "in accordance with the Constitution, the statutes of a political party must include a commitment to respect the principles of national sovereignty and democracy", without specifying in concrete terms what the requirements are in terms of democracy within the party.

24 On intra-party democracy in Kenya, see B Bwire, "Intra-Party Democracy and the Chasm between Political Parties and Democratisation in Kenya", in this volume.

25 For a comparative analysis of the widespread prohibition of ethnic parties in African constitutions, see J Socher and CM Fombad, "Prohibition of Ethnic Political Parties and Constitutionalism in Sub-Saharan Africa", in C Fombad, N Steytler and Y Fessha (eds.), *Ethnicity and Constitutionalism in Africa*, forthcoming.

Fouta (93.32 per cent) and Serer-dominated Fatick (80 per cent) during the 2019 presidential elections.

Sonko's emergence as the leader of PASTEF has also intensified debates on ethnicity within Senegal's political landscape. His identity as a politician from the Casamance region attracted significant regional support during the 2019 presidential elections and the 2021 local and legislative elections, where his coalition won multiple polls. His election as mayor of Ziguinchor, a major city in Casamance, underscores this support. However, members of the APR and their allies interpreted Sonko's speeches as promoting ethnic division and potentially exacerbating regional conflict. This reflects ongoing tension around the constitutional prohibition of ethnic parties and the broader issue of ethnicity in Senegal's political dynamics.

The same analysis can be applied to the prohibition against identifying a political party with a religion. Respect for secularism indeed implies the banishment of any political party of religious allegiance. Any political formation that aims to establish a regime based on religion and theocratic in nature, or whose discourse questions the separation between temporal power and spiritual power, should be dissolved or refused legalisation. However, the reality of political life shows a lack of rigour in the enforcement of such prohibition.

As a case in point, two parties in Senegal have been founded by religious leaders without their explicitly affirming the religious character of the parties. These are the *Parti pour la Vérité et la Démocracie* and the *Parti pour l'Unité et le Rassemblement*. The fact that they were created by religious leaders has raised debate about their constitutionality, albeit without the question being brought before the courts. The administration did not refuse to grant registration to these parties because nothing in their statutes suggests that they are parties identifying with a religion. However, it is clear that membership in a religious brotherhood is a criterion for party membership. Furthermore, during the 2000 presidential elections, several candidates openly expressed their desire to implement a political project inspired by Islam – even to place the Muslim religion as a mode of governance in case of victory – without being sanctioned either by the government or by the courts. Thus, even though it is prohibited for a party to identify with a religion, the increasing activism of political leaders in the political field calls for a rethinking of the requirement of the principle of secularism enshrined in the Senegalese Constitution.

3. The gaps in the legal framework

In the realm of Senegalese politics, the issues of political-party financing and the status of the leader of the opposition have emerged as critical points of contention, particularly in the light of recent constitutional reforms and political developments. The intricate relationship between political parties and financial support, both domestically and internationally, underscores the challenges facing democratic processes in Senegal. Additionally, the establishment and delineation of the leader of the opposition's role within the political landscape has sparked debates regarding the most appropriate criteria for selection and representation.

3.1 Political-party financing

If there is a cancer that plagues democracies, it is the issue of political-party financing.[26] In France, the model of inspiration of many African francophone countries, the intertwining of politics and "business" has often been problematic due to meticulous regulation. It is enough to recall the most publicised case of the last decade: the alleged Libyan financing of Nicolas Sarkozy's campaign, which led to his indictment.[27]

Senegal's Law on Political Parties defines the modalities of financing political parties and establishing control of their accounts. Financing may come from the state or the private sector. While state funding, commonly referred to as direct public financing, does not raise particular issues, private sector funding raises several concerns for various reasons. Under

---

26 See I Teguh and AGP Sari, "Political Party Financing Regulation and Gaps for Corporate Donations: Case of the Developing Countries", 13 (2024) *Journal of Governance and Regulation*, p 29.

27 The case involves allegations that Muammar Gaddafi's regime secretly financed Nicolas Sarkozy's 2007 presidential campaign to the amount of about USD 50 million. In the wake of these claims, French authorities launched investigations into potential corruption and foreign influence in politics. In 2021, Sarkozy was indicted on charges of corruption and influence-peddling related to the case, which he denied, asserting that the allegations were politically motivated. The scandal highlights concerns about transparency in political financing in France. See R Dupre, "Sarkozy to Face Trial over Suspected Libyan Financing of 2007 Presidential Campaign", *Le Monde*, 26 August 2023, https://www.lemonde.fr/en/france/article/2023/08/26/sarkozy-to-face-trial-over-suspected-libyan-financing-of-2007-presidential-campaign_6109763_7.html (accessed 4 April 2024).

current Senegalese law, private contributions constitute the main source of financing for political parties. Article 3 of the Law on Political Parties lists the different sources of income for political parties, including membership fees and donations exclusively from national members and supporters.". Article 4(1) prohibits the direct or indirect receipt of subsidies from abroad or foreigners established in Senegal. The prohibition of foreign funding is aimed at ensuring the independence of parties seeking or holding power, and consequently, preserving the sovereignty of states.[28]

However, the existing legislation is insufficiently developed to combat covert financing. Consequently, efforts to combat corruption and promote effective public governance tend to be superficial, as they are often undermined by a system of impunity that safeguards certain special interests. It is therefore necessary to establish a clear and transparent regime for private contributions. Unfortunately, Senegal's current legal framework is characterised by ambiguity. For example, while natural persons or legal entities (whether public or private) of foreign nationality cannot allocate sums of money to political parties, they retain their full legal capacity to make in-kind contributions, such as goods, services, or facilities. For instance, a foreign company might supply campaign materials such as banners and posters, or offer advertising services that enhance a party's visibility. Additionally, foreign individuals could provide logistical support, such as organising rallies or events.

These in-kind contributions can significantly bolster a party's campaign efforts by reducing expenses and enhancing their outreach, ultimately helping to sustain and strengthen their political presence. As noted by Babacar Gueye:

> [P]olitical parties publicly and with impunity receive support from abroad or from foreigners established in Senegal in the form of in-kind donations and the provision of free services. Such practices punctuate Senegal's political life and even intensify as each election approaches.[29]

Furthermore, the prohibition on the direct or indirect receipt of subsidies from abroad remains ambiguous. Are Senegalese citizens residing abroad affected by this prohibition? This is the nub of the issue raised by the so-

---

28 B Gueye, "La Réglementation du Financement des Élections au Sénégal", 25 (1995) *Revue de droit Africain EDJA*, p 50.

29 Ibid.

called "Nemekou tour" on the occasion of the 2024 presidential elections.[30] PASTEF launched a fundraising campaign, called the "Nemekou tour", allowing it to raise FCFA 125 million in just 48 hours, with the majority of contributions coming from the Senegalese diaspora.[31] The Minister of the Interior, through a statement, considered such a campaign to be a violation of Article 4 of the Law on Political Parties prohibiting political-party financing from abroad.[32] PASTEF was therefore ordered to stop the campaign under threat of dissolution.

This reaction from the minister sparked debate on what should be understood by funds coming from abroad. In the minister's interpretation, this also includes Senegalese residents abroad. In other words, the law would allow nationals residing in Senegal to contribute to political-party financing, but such a possibility is prohibited for Senegalese citizens residing abroad. Such an interpretation creates discrimination among Senegalese citizens based on whether they reside in Senegal or abroad. It would have been interesting to bring this question before the Supreme Court to shed light on the interpretation of the prohibition of funding from abroad in the Law on Political Parties. However, in this case, PASTEF stopped its fundraising campaign and did not appeal to the administrative judge for possible clarification.

This case proves that the legal framework on private financing of political parties needs to be reviewed and updated. Overall, it would be necessary to reconsider the absolute nature of the prohibition on contributions from abroad or foreigners living in the countries concerned. In practice, foreign foundations or other institutions are involved in political debates by financially supporting certain political parties. So why not align the law with these realities by allowing and incorporating this type of funding into a framework that combines transparency and equal treatment of political parties? States could then create a fund to assist political parties, which

30 M Soumaré, "Senegal, le Financement des Partis Politiques, un Sujet Tabou", *Jeune Afrique*, 8 January 2021, https://www.jeuneafrique.com/1100750/politique/senegal-le-financement-des-partis-politiques-un-sujet-tabou/ (accessed 4 April 2024).

31 See Sud Quotodien, "Levée de fonds pour le Nemekou Tour: Sonko Mobilise 333 Millions", *Sud Quotodien*, 16 January 2023, https://www.sudquotidien.sn/levee-de-fonds-pour-le-nemekou-tour-sonko-mobilise-333-millions/ (accessed 4 April 2024).

32 Dakaractu, "Levée de Fonds pour le Nemekou Tour: PASTEF menacé de dissolution", *Dakaractu*, https://www.dakaractu.com/Levee-de-fonds-NEMMEEKU-TOUR-Pastef-menace-de-dissolution-par-le-Ministre-de-l-Interieur_a198221.html (accessed 4 April 2024).

would be funded, among other sources, by foreign contributions. Alternatively, they could take into account the freedom of choice of partners by allowing and subjecting foreign individuals or entities' contributions to a cap.[33]

Regarding the public funding of political parties, this is an issue which has been raised repeatedly but never resolved. The Law on Political Parties mentions public financing but provides no indication of its actual implementation. During the 2016 constitutional amendment, the addition "the rules under which political parties operate and benefit from public financing are determined by law" was inserted in Article 4 of the Constitution. However, such a law has not yet been enacted, leaving a sense of incompleteness as regards the issue of public funding of political parties. Currently, no mechanism exists in Senegal to establish a state fund for the financing of political parties, which is unusual in view of the many democracies that provide public financial support. In the absence of government funding, political parties, especially opposition parties, rely primarily on private donations from individuals and businesses, membership fees, and fundraising activities. The law's silence on certain aspects of the modalities of political-party financing leaves the door open to covert financing.[34]

3.2 The Leader of the Opposition

Since the 2016 constitutional amendment, Senegal has opted to recognise the position of the Leader of the Opposition alongside a directly elected executive President.[35] However, the Senegalese Constitution does not provide detailed provisions on this matter; it simply stipulates that an organic law will define the status, rights, and duties of the Leader of the Opposition.[36] To date, no organic law has been adopted concerning this issue. However,

33 El H Mbodji, "Le Financement des Campagnes Électorales et des Partis Politiques dans les États Africains Francophones", in *Les Actes du Symposium International sur les Pratiques de la Démocratie, des Droits et Libertés dans l'espace Francophone,* Bamako, October 2000, 3 ème réunion préparatoire "Les élections – Paris 25–27", April 2000, p 9, www.francophonie.org/bamako (accessed 30 December 2024).

34 Ibid.

35 As is the case in Madagascar, Niger, Burkina Faso, Seychelles, Uganda, Zambia and Zimbabwe.

36 See Article 58 of the Constitution (2001).

through a national dialogue initiated by then President Macky Sall,[37] the topic was raised, and a draft organic law was proposed (though not yet approved by Parliament).

The proposed text specifies that the Leader of the Opposition is the candidate who comes second in the presidential election. Consequently, the status of the Leader of the Opposition would be determined by presidential rather than legislative elections. As a result, the mandate of the Leader of the Opposition aligns with that of the President. The Leader of the Opposition loses this status, apart from electoral defeat, in the event of resignation, permanent impediment, or death. According to the proposed law, the Leader of the Opposition enjoys the following rights: the right to media coverage of events related to the fulfillment of his or her mission; the right to reply to messages and/or other media interventions by the President or the Prime Minister; the right to be invited to all official state ceremonies and to be treated with the respect and honors due to his or her rank; the right to be part of delegations accompanying the President during domestic or international trips; the right to be involved in welcoming distinguished guests of the state; the right to be consulted or received in audience by the head of state whenever necessary on all national or international affairs; the right to be entrusted with specific national or international missions by the President; and the right to be treated as a president of an institution. Moreover, the Leader of the Opposition must refrain from resorting to violence in his or her activities, and is subject to complying with the obligations imposed on political parties by the Constitution.

The decision to appoint the candidate who comes second in presidential elections as the Leader of the Opposition has been contested by PASTEF leaders. They have consistently argued that the Leader of the Opposition should be selected from the most representative opposition parliamentary group in Parliament. In essence, they maintain that the Leader of the Opposition should be chosen by the largest party in Parliament, excluding the President's party. This practice is followed in several countries such as Kenya, Madagascar, or Zambia.[38] Now that PASTEF has come to power, it

---

37 See the conclusions of the national dialogue ("Code électoral, Ousmane Sonko, Troisième Mandat: la Commission du Dialogue National Sénégalais rend ses Conclusions"), *RFI*, 23 June 2023, https://www.rfi.fr/fr/afrique/20230623-code-%C3%A9lectoral-ousmane-sonko-troisi%C3%A8me-mandat-la-commission-du-dialogue-national-s%C3%A9n%C3%A9galais-rend-ses-conclusions (accessed 4 April 2024).

38 E Bulmer, *Opposition and Legislative Minorities: Constitutional Roles, Rights and Recognition*, International IDEA Constitution-Building Primer 22, Stockholm, Inter-

proposes reopening discussions on the organic law concerning the status of the Leader of the Opposition.

4. Majoritarian abuse and the erosion of the rights of political parties

The erosion of the rights of political parties in Senegal is a troubling phenomenon that raises significant concerns about the state of democracy in the country. Majoritarian abuse, characterised by the use of legal and administrative mechanisms to weaken or dissolve opposition parties, threatens political pluralism and the democratic process. This section looks at two critical aspects of this issue: the dissolution of the PASTEF political party, and the violation of the right to participate in elections.

4.1 The dissolution of PASTEF

The Law on Political Parties outlines the circumstances under which political parties may be dissolved. According to Article 4(1), political parties must submit declarations and deposits to the Minister of the Interior, who is obligated to issue a receipt. These declarations involve reporting promptly on any changes to the party's statutes, while financial statements for each year must be deposited by no later than 31 January. These financial statements should demonstrate that the party's resources come exclusively from contributions, donations, bequests from national members and sympathisers, and profits generated from organised events. The failure to comply with these provisions can serve as justification for the dissolution of a political party.

Article 4 of the Law on Political Parties specifies further grounds for dissolution. For instance, a party may face dissolution if it receives subsidies, directly or indirectly, from abroad or from foreign entities within Senegal. Dissolution may also occur if the party, through its actions or public positions, blatantly disregards its constitutional obligations. These obligations include upholding the republican, secular, and democratic nature of the state; respecting the status, powers, and competencies of state institutions; and safeguarding national independence, territorial integrity, and state unity; as well as preserving public order and freedoms. According

national Institute for Democracy and Electoral Assistance (2021) (accessed 4 April 2024).

to the Law, dissolution is officially pronounced by decree following a report from the Minister of the Interior.

The provision was invoked to dissolve PASTEF in 2023.[39] President Macky Sall issued a decree justifying the dissolution on the basis of the party's failure to comply with Article 4 of the Constitution and Article 4 of the Law on Political Parties. According to the Ministry of Interior's report, PASTEF's leader, Sonko, frequently incited his supporters to participate in insurrectionary movements through press statements. These calls were widely heeded, resulting in serious disturbances of public order in March 2021 and again in June 2023, disturbances that led to numerous deaths and injuries, as well as the ransacking and looting of public and private property. According to Human Rights Watch, the government's decision to dissolve PASTEF violates the freedom of expression, association, peaceful assembly, and democratic participation.[40]

Against this background, Sonko, arguing that the decision to dissolve his party was arbitrary and in violation of the freedom of assembly, filed a petition before the ECOWAS Court of Justice.[41] Before the Court, Sonko argued that the dissolution of PASTEF, without a court decision, constituted a violation of the right to a fair trial. However, the ECOWAS Court limited its analysis to Senegalese law concerning political parties, which recognises the authority of the government to dissolve a political party by decree. According to the Court, there is no need for a judicial decision to effect dissolution as long as the law permits the President to take such action, and hence the Court could not supersede national authorities.

This decision was surprising given the regional and universal requirements for democracy and respect for human rights. The decision to dissolve a political party is a serious act with detrimental consequences for democracy and pluralism. Consequently, leaving the power to dissolve a political party in the hands of the President, who is also the leader of a ruling party, raises concerns about potential conflicts of interest. The

39 The last political party to be dissolved in the country was the African Independence Party, in 1960. Since then, even during the Abdou Diouf era (1981–2000) and Abdoulaye Wade (2000–2012), no party has suffered this fate.

40 I Allegrozzi, "Senegalese Government Dissolves Opposition Party", *Human Rights Watch*, 1 August 2023, https://www.hrw.org/news/2023/08/01/senegalese-government-dissolves-opposition-party-cuts-internet (accessed 23 March 2024).

41 ECOWAS Court of Justice, *Ousmane Sonko v Republic of Senegal*, Judgement No. ECW/CCJ/JUD/42/23, 17 November 2023.

intervention of a judge in making such a decision should be established as a procedural rule to avoid the risk of arbitrariness.

The issue of the dissolution of PASTEF subsequently went before the Senegalese Constitutional Council at the time of the publication of the final list of candidates for the presidential election.[42] Faced with manoeuvres by the government aimed at preventing PASTEF from fielding a candidate, the party took the strategy of devising a backup plan in case the candidacy of leader Sonko was rejected. Thus, Sonko designated the secretary-general of his party, Bassirou Diomaye Faye, as the candidate. Before the Constitutional Council, the candidate of the ruling party contested the validity of Faye's candidacy, arguing that he came from a dissolved political entity and therefore could not exercise the rights attached to membership of a political party.[43] The Constitutional Council rejected this request on the grounds that "the investiture of a candidate in the presidential election, even supported by a party or coalition of political parties, is not subject to membership in these entities".[44] Indeed, the candidacy of Faye was supported by a coalition of parties, as allowed by the Constitution,[45] and not formally by the dissolved PASTEF party. Therefore, the freedom to run for office allows a person to be a candidate of a party or coalition of parties without being a member of the party that supports their candidacy. This liberal interpretation by the Constitutional Council echoes the position of the African Court on Human and Peoples' Rights regarding the issue of the prohibition of independent candidates.[46]

The decision to dissolve a political party is a grave and significant action, one often signaling potential democratic backsliding within a nation. While laws providing for dissolution are not inherently undemocratic, the specific grounds for such actions are crucial. When a government resorts to dissolving a political party, it raises concerns about the state of democracy and the protection of fundamental rights and freedoms, particularly if those

42 Constitutional Council, decision 2/E/2024, 20 January 2024, para 77.
43 See paragraph 77.
44 See paragraph 79.
45 The Senegalese political landscape is characterised by major coalitions, especially in electoral cycles, a fact which is true for both the ruling presidential majority as well as the opposition. As a result, political parties that would usually have no prospects of getting a candidate elected often manage to have their candidates elected thanks to coalitions.
46 See African Court on Human and Peoples' Rights, *Tanganyika Law Society v Tanzania*, App. Nos. 9/2011, 11/2011, Judgement, 14 June 2013.

grounds are vague or prone to abuse. Dissolving a party is not merely a matter of administrative procedure; it represents a limitation on political pluralism and the freedom of association, both of which are essential pillars of democracy.[47]

Such actions can be particularly concerning when they are applied inconsistently or seen as targeting specific groups. The dissolution of a party often points to democratic regression, reflecting a weakening of democratic norms, institutions, and principles. Thus, it underscores the need for robust mechanisms to safeguard political freedoms, ensure the rule of law, and uphold democratic principles, including the freedoms of expression, assembly, and association. Balancing the prohibition of potentially divisive ethnic and religious parties with the need to protect political pluralism is essential to maintaining a stable and inclusive democracy. Without such safeguards, the democratic fabric of a society risks being eroded, posing a threat to political stability, social cohesion, and ultimately, the legitimacy of the government itself.[48]

4.2 The violation of the right to participate in elections

Another notable trend observed during President Macky Sall's tenure is the use of the judicial system to restrict political parties and leaders from participating in elections. This was evident in the 2019 presidential elections with the absence of candidates from two significant opposition parties, the PDS, led by Karim Wade, and Takhawu Senegal, represented by Khalifa Sall. Similarly, in the 2024 presidential elections, the PDS candidate was again barred from contesting, as was PASTEF's preferred candidate, Sonko.

4.2.1 The electoral exclusion of PDS and Takhawu Senegal leaders (2019)

The exclusion of Wade as the PDS's presidential candidate was based on a conviction on charges of illicit enrichment and corruption.[49] The charges

47 T Ayres and B Batasuna, "The Dissolution of Political Parties under the European Convention of Human Rights", 27 (2004) *International and Comparative Law Review*, pp 99–113.

48 T Ginsburg and AZ Hu, *How to Save a Constitutional Democracy*, Chicago, University of Chicago Press (2018), p 182.

49 Decision No. 8/CREI, 29 December 2014.

stemmed from his time serving as a minister in the government of his father, former President Abdoulaye Wade. The trial took place before the *Cour de Répression de l'Enrichissement Illicite* (CREI), which had been established in 1981[50] but remained inactive until it was activated for this case.[51] The CREI found Wade guilty of illegally amassing wealth while in office, leading to his conviction and subsequent sentencing to a lengthy prison term.

The legal proceedings were highly contentious, with Wade's supporters alleging political motivations behind the charges and raising concerns about the fairness and impartiality of the trial. His legal saga attracted international attention, with human rights organisations and legal bodies highlighting various irregularities in his trial. Both the ECOWAS Court of Justice[52] and the United Nations Human Rights Committee[53] identified serious violations in these legal proceedings, including infringements of the right to a fair trial, the presumption of innocence, and access to legal representation.[54]

Despite these concerns raised by international bodies, Wade was sentenced to six years in prison, but his conviction was not accompanied by a judicial decision pronouncing the loss of his civil and political rights. However, the Electoral Code stipulates that anyone sentenced to more than five years is not eligible to be registered on the electoral roll and is thus not able to exercise his or her right to vote. In compliance with this provision,

---

50 Law No. 1981/54 of 10 July 1981 establishing the CREI (Cour de Repression de l'Enrichissement Illicite). See International Federation for Human Rights, "Senegal: CREI a Special Court which Does not Guarantee the Right to a Fair Trial", *International Federation for Human Rights*, 25 June 2014, https://www.fidh.org/en/region/Africa/senegal/15634-senegal-crei-a-special-court-which-does-not-guarantee-the-right-to-a-fair (accessed 22 March 2024).

51 The Senegalese parliament recently passed a law abolishing the CREI and replacing it with a financial judicial pool comprising a specialised public prosecutor's office for financial crime, staffed by specialised magistrates. This is Law No. 2023–14 of August 2, 2023, amending Law No. 65–61 of July 21, 1965, concerning the Code of Criminal Procedure, http://news.adakar.com/documents/docs/Journal-Officiel.pdf (accessed 22 March 2024).

52 ECOWAS Court of Justice, *Abdoulye Baldé and others v Senegal* No. ECW/CCJ/JUD/04/13, Judgement, 22 February 2013.

53 Human Right Committee, *Karim Meissa Wade v Senegal* Case No. CCPR/C/124/D/2783/2016.

54 See I Kane, "The Impact of the United Nations Human Rights Treaties on the Domestic Level in Senegal", in C Heyns, F Viljoen, and R Murray (eds.), *The Impact of the United Nations Human Rights Treaties on the Domestic Level: Twenty Years*, Leiden, Boston, Brill Nijhoff (2024), pp 1003–1076.

public authorities refused to register Wade's name on the electoral roll. Yet the law remained silent on his eligibility, specifically his right to stand for elections.

Faced with this ambiguity, the ruling party initiated an amendment to the Electoral Code in 2018,[55] which many viewed as a manoeuvre aimed at excluding the PDS candidate from the presidential elections.[56] This amendment directly linked candidacy eligibility to voter registration status, essentially requiring aspiring candidates to be registered voters. The timing of the legal change, coupled with the APR's legislative majority, raised concerns among opposition parties and civil society about potential changes of electoral laws to disadvantage certain candidates or political groups.

Believing that his right to participate in public affairs had been violated, Wade initiated an action before the ECOWAS Court. The Court issued a decision on 4 March 2019 dismissing Wade's request and deeming the restriction on the right to vote and the right to stand for elections as lawful, legitimate, and necessary.[57] However, this case clearly demonstrates how a ruling party can utilise its majority to enact electoral code reforms aimed at preventing an opposition party from fielding a candidate in presidential elections.

In the case of the exclusion of Takhawu Senegal's presidential candidate, Khalifa Sall, he faced legal challenges stemming from his time as the mayor of Senegal's capital, Dakar. Sall was accused of embezzlement and mismanagement of public funds designated for the city's development projects, and sentenced to five years in prison.[58] Although he was a member of the National Assembly and thus benefited from parliamentary immunity, the presidential majority voted swiftly (it was unprecedented in its speed) to lift this immunity and compel him to face the justice system as the 2019 presidential elections approached. These charges against him resulted in a highly

55 Law No. 2018-22 of 4 July 2018 amending the Law No. 2017-12 of 18 January 2017 concerning the Electoral Code of the Republic of Senegal, https://dge.sn/sites/default/files/2019-01/CODE%20ELECTORAL%202018_0.pdf (accessed 22 March 2024).

56 See M Timeira, M Diongue, and O Thim, "L'election Présidentielle de Février 2019 au Sénégal: Entre Renouveau de l'échiquier Politique et Percée du Vote Régionaliste", *EchoGeo*, 2019, http://journals.openedition.org/echogeo/18183 (accessed 22 March 2024); El HSA Diallo, "L'élection Présidentielle de 2019: le PDS et BBY", in El HSA Diallo (ed.), *Sciences et confréries soufies au Sénégal*, Leiden, Koninklijke Brill NV (2022), https://doi.org/10.1163/9789004503212_008 (accessed 22 March 2024).

57 ECOWAS Court of Justice, *Karim Wade v Republic of Senegal* Judgement No. ECW/CCJ/JUD/13/19, 4 March 2019.

58 Court of Appeal, Judgement No. 168, 16 May 2017.

publicised trial before Senegalese courts, during which Sall consistently asserted his innocence and contended that the accusations were politically motivated.

Despite his defence's efforts, Sall was convicted and handed a prison sentence. Similar to Karim Wade, Sall's conviction led to the loss of his civil rights, including the right to vote and stand for election. Consequently, he was automatically disqualified from participating in the elections as a candidate. Sall's supporters and international observers, as well as the ECOWAS Court, questioned the fairness of the legal proceedings against him, citing allegations of procedural irregularities and political interference in the judicial process.[59] In its ruling, the Court noted that the right to legal representation was not respected at the outset of the proceedings, undermining the integrity of the trial. However, the Senegalese courts upheld the verdict, effectively preventing Sall from running in the elections due to his conviction and loss of civil rights.

The two examples illustrate how a ruling party can use its presidential majority in parliament to prevent an opposition party from fielding a presidential candidate. In the case of Wade, a swift amendment to the Electoral Code prevented the PDS from having a candidate; in Sall's case, an accelerated vote to lift his parliamentary immunity prevented his party from having a candidate.

4.2.2 The electoral exclusion of PDS and PASTEF leaders (2024)

In the 2024 presidential elections, two notable cases raised concerns: the repeated exclusion of Wade of the PDS, and the exclusion of Sonko, the leader of PASTEF. This time around, Wade's exclusion from the presidential elections was based on allegations of dual citizenship, given that Article 28 of the Constitution stipulates that a presidential candidate must exclusively hold Senegalese nationality.[60] Another candidate, Thierno Alassane Sall, filed a petition before the Constitutional Council, arguing that Wade's

59 See ECOWAS Court of Justice, *Khalifa Sall and others v Senegal* No. ECW/CCJ/JUD/17/18, Judgement, 29 June 2018, https://www.eods.eu/elex/uploads/files/5cac54d46382c-K%20Sall%20ECW_CCJ_JUD_17_18.pdf (accessed 22 March 2024).

60 See also Article L.121 of the Electoral Code, which states that "the candidate's declaration must be accompanied by a sworn statement in which the candidate declares that they exclusively hold Senegalese nationality".

candidacy should be declared inadmissible due to the exclusive-nationality requirement.

In his defence, Wade presented a certificate from the Consul at the Embassy of France in Doha, affirming his declaration of loss of French nationality in October 2023. He also provided a copy of a decree indicating the termination of his allegiance to France, which was published in the Official Journal of the French Republic in January 2024. However, in its Decision No. 2/E/2024, the Senegalese Constitutional Council deemed the attestation insufficient to establish the loss of French nationality.[61] The Council emphasised that the decree's effect is not retroactive and that the material date for consideration was 21 December 2023, the date of the candidacy deposit.[62] On that day, Wade made a false sworn statement regarding the loss of French nationality, as the decree's publication in January 2024 marked its effective date.[63]

In response, Wade and other PDS leaders publicly accused two members of the Constitutional Council of corruption and bias in favour of the candidate of the incumbent president's party, Prime Minister Amadou Ba. The PDS, as one of the minority parties in the National Assembly, called for the establishment of a parliamentary commission of inquiry, as provided for by the National Assembly's internal rules,[64] to investigate the corruption allegations against the two judges. Surprisingly, this initiative received support from the ruling party, arguing that it provided an opportunity to clarify the situation and protect its candidate against corruption allegations. However, other opposition parties saw it as a strategy by the APR to support the postponement of what appeared would be a challenging election for it.[65] Consequently, a parliamentary commission of inquiry was established. This action led to the postponement of the presidential elections, initially scheduled for 25 February 2024; the elections were held eventually on 24 March

61 Constitutional Council of Senegal, *List of Candidates for 2024 Presidential Elections*, Decision No. 2/E/2024, 20 January 2024.

62 *Ibid*, paragraph 89.

63 Ibid.

64 Organic Law No. 2002–20 of 15 May 2002 Relating to the Internal Rule of the National Assembly, https://ceracle.com/wp-content/uploads/2020/08/R%C3%A8glement-interieur-de-lAssembl%C3%A9e-nationale-du-S%C3%A9n%C3%A9gal-texte-consolid%C3%A9.pdf (accessed 26 March 2024).

65 AK Diop, "Democratic Backsliding in Senegal: A Legal Analysis of the Postponement of Presidential Elections", *African Network of Constitutional Lawyers*, 9 February 2024, https://ancl-radc.org.za/blog/democratic-backsliding-in-senegal-a-legal-analysis-of-the-postponement-of-presidential-elections (accessed 21 March 2024).

2024 after the Constitutional Council had declared the postponement unconstitutional.[66]

As regards Sonko, his exclusion as the presidential candidate of the dissolved PASTEF arose from a combination of events that demonstrate the practice of majoritarian abuse. Sonko's candidacy faced numerous obstacles, including the mobilisation of the parliamentary majority to amend the electoral code, arguments regarding a criminal conviction, and administrative practices that defy the rule of law. Judicially, too, Sonko encountered a series of legal actions aimed at rendering him ineligible for the presidential elections.

First, he was prosecuted for committing rape in connection with the highly publicised "Sweet Beauty" affair.[67] This case triggered a series of violent protests that resulted in several deaths, with Sonko's supporters alleging that it was a manoeuvre by President Sall to eliminate a political opponent. In addition to this legal procedure, a member of the APR-led government initiated a defamation lawsuit against Sonko. This legal action resulted in Sonko's conviction to six months' suspended imprisonment.[68] Furthermore, another seemingly trivial matter led to Sonko's arrest. In July 2023, five months before the elections, he was arrested for allegedly stealing a mobile phone.

66 Constitution Council of Senegal, Decision No. 1/C/2024, 15 February 2024, https://droit-et-politique-en-afrique.info/la-decision-du-15-fevrier-2024-du-conseil-constitutionnel-la-constitution-rien-que-la-constitution-et-toute-la-constitution (accessed 22 March 2024). See also JL Correa and AK Diop, "La décision 1/C/2024 du Conseil Constitutionnel Sénégalais: Analyse Furtive d'une Décision Attendue ", *African Network of Constitutional Lawyers*, 22 February 2024, https://ancl-radc.org.za/blog/la-decision-1-c-2024-du-conseil-constitutionnel-senegalais-analyse-furtive-dune-decision-attendue (accessed 25 March 2024).

67 The "Sweet Beauty" affair involved allegations made by Adji Sarr, a former employee of a beauty salon, who accused Ousmane Sonko of rape and making death threats against her in early 2021. The case gained significant media attention and quickly escalated into a political controversy, as Sonko, a prominent opposition leader and presidential candidate, claimed that the charges were politically motivated and intended to undermine his candidacy. The accusations led to his prosecution, with Sonko's supporters alleging that the government was using the legal system to eliminate political rivals. The affair sparked widespread protests and public demonstrations in Senegal, highlighting deep divisions within the country regarding political power and judicial independence. See Senegalese Feminist Network, "In Senegal Women's Bodies are Weaponised as Political Objects in Electoral Debate", *Africa is a Country*, 28 June 2023, https://africasacountry.com/2023/06/sweet-beauty (accessed 25 March 2025).

68 Court of Appeal of Dakar, No. 137, Judgement, 8 May 2023.

Subsequently, he was remanded in custody on various charges, including theft with violence, conspiracy to commit a terrorist act, dissemination of false news, endangering the lives of others, financing of terrorism, provocation of armed and unarmed gatherings, complicity in manslaughter, acts likely to compromise public security and cause political unrest, money laundering, attacks on state security, and manslaughter or unintentional injury.[69]

Following these convictions, the government refused to register Sonko on the electoral lists, maintaining that he had lost the rights associated with the status of a voter.[70] Sonko, arguing that the convictions against him were not final and that he had therefore had not lost his status as a voter, decided to challenge the government's refusal before Senegalese courts. An initial action was taken before the Ziguinchor Tribunal, which ruled in his favour, demanding his registration on the electoral lists.[71] The Minister of the Interior refused, however, to execute the decision, arguing that since Sonko's residence is in Dakar (despite his being the mayor of Ziguinchor), it was the Dakar Tribunal that was competent, not that of Ziguinchor. The matter was brought before the Dakar Tribunal, which upheld the decision of the Ziguinchor Tribunal and required the administration to reinstate Sonko on the electoral lists.[72] Once again, the government refused to execute the decision, stating that it had appealed it to the Supreme Court.

Faced with the Interior Ministry's refusal, Sonko requested that the General Directorate of Elections (DGE)[73] provide him with the sponsorship collection forms in accordance with the Constitution and the Electoral

69 See "Au Sénégal l'opposant Ousmane Sonko a été arrêté", *Le Monde Afrique Senegal*, 28 July 2023, https://www.lemonde.fr/afrique/article/2023/07/28/au-senegal-l-opposant-ousmane-sonko-a-ete-arrete-selon-des-membres-de-son-parti_6183778_3212.html (accessed 28 March 2024).

70 In terms of Article L. 30 of the Electoral Code, a candidate who is not registered on the electoral lists cannot be eligible.

71 See T Ollivier, "Au Sénégal la justice relance Ousmane Sonko dans la course à la présidence", *Le Monde Afrique Senegal*, 13 October 2023, https://www.lemonde.fr/afrique/article/2023/10/13/au-senegal-la-justice-relance-ousmane-sonko-dans-la-course-a-la-presidence_6194222_3212.html (accessed 28 March 2024).

72 See DF Roland, "Le Juge de Dakar Confirme le Juge de Ziguinchor", *Enquête Plus*, 19 December 2023, https://www.enqueteplus.com/content/vers-l%E2%80%99independance-de-la-sen-justice-le-juge-de-dakar-confirme-le-juge-de-ziguinchor (accessed 28 March 2024).

73 The Direction Générale des Elections (DGE) is responsible for organising national and local elections as well as referendums. See https://dge.sn/fr (accessed 28 March 2024).

Code. The DGE refused to comply with the request on the grounds that his name was not on the electoral lists, so he could not claim candidate status. Meanwhile, Sonko sent his representatives to the Deposit and Consignment Fund (CDC)[74] to deposit the FCFA 30 million bond required of presidential candidates. The CDC refused to accept the bond deposit, citing the absence of the person's name on the electoral lists despite the court decision in Sonko's favour.[75]

From the above, it is evident that the government refused to execute a judicial decision ordering the reinstatement of Sonko on the electoral lists. Indeed, various administrative structures are controlled by the ruling party. The Constitutional Council, in its decision 2/E/2014, acknowledged that Sonko faced a series of arbitrary administrative obstacles preventing his registration on the electoral lists and provision of sponsorship collection forms and a receipt for depositing the bond.[76] The Council found that these shortcomings were not attributable to Sonko and held the government responsible.[77] However, the Council rejected Sonko's candidacy because his defamation conviction became final with the Supreme Court's ruling a few days before the final publication of the list of presidential candidates.[78] In accordance with the recently amended Electoral Code, a definitive conviction, even with a suspended sentence, of more than six months prevents registration on the electoral lists.[79] The Supreme Court, having confirmed Sonko's conviction to six months suspended for defamation, thereby established Sonko's ineligibility for the presidential elections.

74 The CDC is responsible for managing deposits and safeguarding the assets belonging to organisations and funds held therein or requested to be held therein; for receiving administrative and judicial deposits as well as bonds; and for managing services related to the cash or funds whose management is entrusted to it. See https://cdc.sn/presentation/ (accessed 28 March 2024).

75 See SA Ndiaye and MS Sané, "De la Recevabilité de la Candidature de Monsieur Ousmane Sonko: La Valeur Juridique Superfétatoire de l'attestation de la Caisse de Dépôt et de Consignation", *PressAfrik*, 16 January 2024, https://www.pressafrik.com/De-la-recevabilite-de-la-candidature-de-Monsieur-Ousmane-SONKO-La-valeur-juridique-superfetatoire-de-l-Attestation-de-la_a267309.html (accessed 28 March 2024).

76 Constitutional Council of Senegal, Decision No. 2/E/2024, paragraph 16.

77 Ibid.

78 *Ibid*, paragraph 18.

79 The previous electoral code stipulated that a definitive conviction resulting in a sentence of more than five years could disqualify an individual from being registered on the electoral lists. However, this provision was amended in July 2023, just before the 2024 elections, to reduce the disqualification period to six months for any definitive conviction, even if it included a suspended sentence.

Thus, a series of administrative and politico-judicial obstacles prevented his candidacy in the presidential elections. However, as described earlier, his backup option, Bassirou Diomaye Faye was elected with 54 per cent of the vote, thereby allowing an opposition party, albeit dissolved, to win the presidential elections.[80]

5. Conclusion

The journey to political pluralism in Senegal is a testament to the nation's commitment to democracy, yet it also reveals the challenges inherent in safeguarding the rights of political parties. While the constitutional recognition of political parties has been a crucial step in fostering a democratic environment, legal provisions alone are insufficient to protect these rights in practice. President Sall's government has demonstrated how majoritarian abuse can undermine the democratic process through the strategic use of legal and administrative measures to weaken opposition parties. The dissolution of PASTEF, the exclusion of opposition leaders from elections, and the broader pattern of judicial and legislative obstructions highlight the vulnerabilities within Senegal's political system. Furthermore, the rise of ethnic and religious parties poses additional challenges to political pluralism, often complicating the landscape of governance and representation. In addition, issues of party financing remain a significant concern, as inadequate regulations enable corrupt practices and the undue influence of money in politics. The lack of intra-party democracy fails to prevent the personalisation of party politics, a state of affairs where power becomes concentrated in the hands of a few and undermines broader democratic engagement. As has been shown, the capture of state structures by a ruling party can exacerbate these issues, creating an uneven playing field that threatens fair competition.

To address these issues, it is imperative that Senegal strengthen its legal framework to provide more robust protections for political parties. This includes ensuring fair and transparent electoral processes, safeguarding the rights of opposition parties, and preventing the misuse of legal mechanisms for political gain. Moreover, the role of civil society, international organisations, and regional bodies such as ECOWAS is crucial in holding the government accountable and advocating for reforms that enhance democratic governance. While Senegal has made significant strides in establishing

80 See Constitutional Council of Senegal, Decision No. 7/E/2024, 29 March 2024.

political pluralism, the recent erosion of political-party rights underlines the need for continual vigilance and reform. Protecting the constitutional rights of political parties is essential not only for the health of Senegal's democracy but also for setting a precedent for other countries in the region. The path forward requires a commitment to legal as well as practical measures which ensure that all political parties can operate freely and fairly and thus strengthen the democratic fabric of Senegal.

References

Books, articles, chapters in books, and others

"Au Sénégal l'opposant Ousmane Sonko a été arrété", *Le Monde Afrique Senegal*, 28 July 2023, https://www.lemonde.fr/afrique/article/2023/07/28/au-senegal-l-opposant-ousmane-sonko-a-ete-arrete-selon-des-membres-de-son-parti_6183778_3212.html (accessed 28 March 2024)

"Opposition Leader Khalifa Sall and Karim Wade Barred from Senegal Presidential Race", *France 24*, 14 January 2019, https://www.france24.com/en/20190114-senegal-opposition-leaders-khalifa-sall-karim-wade-barred-presidential-election (accessed 10 March 2024)

Allegrozzi I, "Senegalese Government Dissolves Opposition Party", *Human Rights Watch*, 1 August 2023, https://www.hrw.org/news/2023/08/01/senegalese-government-dissolves-opposition-party-cuts-internet (accessed 23 March 2024)

Ayres T and Batasuna B, "The Dissolution of Political Parties under the European Convention of Human Rights", 27 (2004) *International and Comparative Law Review*, pp 99–113

Ba B, Kebe D, and Ndiaye, SA, *Les Textes Fondamentaux de la République du Sénégal*, Dakar, L'Harmattan (2021)

Bulmer E, *Opposition and Legislative Minorities: Constitutional Roles, Rights and Recognition*, International IDEA Constitution-Building Primer 22, Stockholm, International Institute for Democracy and Electoral Assistance (2021)

Correa JL and Diop AK, "La Décision 1/C/2024 du Conseil Constitutionnel Sénégalais: Analyse Furtive d'une Décision Attendue", *African Network of Consitutional Lawyers*, 22 February 2024, https://ancl-radc.org.za/blog/la-decision-1-c-2024-du-conseil-constitutionnel-senegalais-analyse-furtive-dune-decision-attendue (accessed 30 December 2024)

Dakaractu, "Levée de fonds pour le Nemekou Tour: PASTEF menacé de dissolution", *Dakaractu*, https://www.dakaractu.com/Levee-de-fonds-NEMMEEKU-TOUR-Pastef-menace-de-dissolution-par-le-Ministre-de-l-Interieur_a198221.html (accessed 4 April 2024)

Diallo El HSA, "L'élection Présidentielle de 2019: le PDS et BBY", in Diallo, El HSA (ed.), Sciences et confréries soufies au Sénégal, Leiden, The Netherlands, Koninklijke Brill NV (2022), https://doi.org/10.1163/9789004503212_008 (accessed 22 March 2024)

Diop AK, "Democratic Backsliding in Senegal: A Legal Analysis of the Postponement of Presidential Elections", *African Network of Constitutional Lawyers*, 9 February 2024, https://ancl-radc.org.za/blog/democratic-backsliding-in-senegal-a-legal-analysis-of-the-postponement-of-presidential-elections (accessed 4 April 2024)

Dupre R, "Sarkozy to Face Trial over Suspected Libyan Financing of 2007 Presidential Campaign", *Le Monde*, 26 August 2023, https://www.lemonde.fr/en/france/article/2023/08/26/sarkozy-to-face-trial-over-suspected-libyan-financing-of-2007-presidential-campaign_6109763_7.html (accessed 4 April 2024)

Fall AB, "La Démocratie Sénégalaise à l'Épreuve de l'Alternance", 5 (2012) *Afrilex*, https://afrilex.u-bordeaux.fr/wp-content/uploads/2021/03/05dossfall.pdf (accessed 5 February 2023)

Fall IM, "La réforme Constitutionnelle de mars 2016 au Sénégal", in IM Fall and A Sall (eds.), *Actualités de droit Public, Mélanges en l'honneur du Professeur Babacar Kanté*, Dakar, L'Harmattan (2020), pp 35–62

Fombad C, "Challenges to Constitutionalism and Constitutional Rights in Africa and the Enabling Role of Political Parties: Lessons and Perspectives from Southern Africa", 55 (2007) *American Journal of Comparative Law*, pp 1–45

Ginsburg T and Hu AZ, *How to Save a Constitutional Democracy*, Chicago, University of Chicago Press (2018)

Grewe C and Ruiz-Fabri H, *Droits Constitutionnels Européens*, Presse Universitaire de France (1995), pp 230–231

Gueye B, "La réglementation du financement des élections au Sénégal", 25 (1995) *Revue de droit africain EDJA*, pp 21–50

International Federation for Human Rights, "Senegal: CREI a Special Court which Does not Guarantee the Right to a Fair Trial", *International Federation for Human Rights*, 25 June 2014, https://www.fidh.org/en/region/Africa/senegal/15634-senegal-crei-a-special-court-which-does-not-guarantee-the-right-to-a-fair (accessed 22 March 2024)

Kane I, "The Impact of the United Nations Human Rights Treaties on the Domestic Level in Senegal", in C Heyns, F Viljoen, and R Murray (eds.), *The Impact of the United Nations Human Rights Treaties on the Domestic level: Twenty Years*, Leiden, Boston, Brill Nijhoff (2024), pp 1003–1076

Lawson K, "Partis Politiques et Groupes d'intérêt ", 79 (1996) *Pouvoirs*, pp 37–45

Main JT, *Political Parties before the Constitution*, Chapel Hill, University of North Carolina Press (1973)

Manin B, Principes du Gouvernement Représentatif, Paris, Calmann-Lévy (1995)

Mbodji El H, "Le Financement des Campagnes Électorales et des Partis Politiques dans les États Africains Francophones", in *Les Actes du Symposium International sur les Pratiques de la Démocratie, des Droits et Libertés dans l'espace Francophone*, Bamako, October 2000, 3 ème réunion préparatoire "Les élections – Paris 25–27", April 2000, p 9, www.francophonie.org/bamako (accessed 30 December 2024)

Ndiaye SA and Sané MS, "De la Recevabilité de la Candidature de Monsieur Ousmane Sonko: La Valeur Juridique Superfétatoire de l'attestation de la Caisse de Dépôt et de Consignation", *PressAfrik*, 16 January 2024, https://www.pressafrik.com/De-la-recevabilite-de-la-candidature-de-Monsieur-Ousmane-SONKO-La-valeur-juridique-superfetatoire-de-l-Attestation-de-la_a267309.html (accessed 28 March 2024)

Ollivier T, "Au Sénégal la justice relance Ousmane Sonko dans la course à la présidence", Le Monde Afrique Senegal, 13 October 2023, https://www.lemonde.fr/afrique/article/2023/10/13/au-senegal-la-justice-relance-ousmane-sonko-dans-la-course-a-la-presidence_6194222_3212.html (accessed 28 March 2024)

RFI, "Code électoral, Ousmane Sonko, troisième mandat: la commission du dialogue national sénégalais rend ses conclusions", *RFI*, 23 June 2023, https://www.rfi.fr/fr/afrique/20230623-code-%C3%A9lectoral-ousmane-sonko-troisi%C3%A8me-mandat-la-commission-du-dialogue-national-s%C3%A9n%C3%A9galais-rend-ses-conclusions (accessed on 4 April 2024)

Roland DF, "Le Juge de Dakar Confirme le Juge de Ziguinchor", *Enquête Plus*, 19 December 2023, https://www.enqueteplus.com/content/vers-l%E2%80%99independance-de-la-sen-justice-le-juge-de-dakar-confirme-le-juge-de-ziguinchor (accessed 28 March 2024)

Sari AGP and Teguh I, "Political Party Financing Regulation and Gaps for Corporate Donations: Case of the Developing Countries", 13 (2024) *Journal of Governance and Regulation*

Savana R, "Le Sénégal Compte 299 Partis Politiques", *Finanical Afrik*, 6 April 2018, https://www.financialafrik.com/2018/04/06/le-senegal-compte-299-partis-politiques/ (accessed 12 March 2024)

Senegalese Feminist Network, "In Senegal Women's Bodies are Weaponised as Political Objects in Electoral Debate", *Africa is a Country*, 28 June 2023, https://africasacountry.com/2023/06/sweet-beauty (accessed 25 March 2025)

Soumaré M, "Senegal, le Financement des Partis Politiques, un Sujet Tabou", *Jeune Afrique*, 8 January 2021, https://www.jeuneafrique.com/1100750/politique/senegal-le-financement-des-partis-politiques-un-sujet-tabou/ (accessed 4 April 2024)

Stephan A, "Stateness, Democracy, and Respect: Senegal in Comparative Perspective", in M Diouf (ed.), *Tolerance, Democracy and Sufis in Senegal*, New York, Columbia University Press (2013)

Sud Quotodien, "Levée de fonds pour le nemekou tour: Sonko mobilise 333 millions", *Sud Quotodien*, 16 January 2023, https://www.sudquotidien.sn/levee-de-fonds-pour-le-nemekou-tour-sonko-mobilise-333-millions/ (accessed 4 April 2024)

Timeira MB, Diongue M, and Thim O, "L'election Présidentielle de Février 2019 au Sénégal: Entre Renouveau de l'échiquier Politique et Percée du Vote Régionaliste", *EchoGeo*, 2019, http://journals.openedition.org/echogeo/18183 (accessed 22 March 2024)

Valle RH, "La Democracia Interna de los Partidos Políticos", in MP Hernandez (ed.), *Partidos Politicos: Democracia Interna y Financiamento de Precampanas*, Doctrina Jurídica, No. 102

Table of cases

ECOWAS Court of Justice

Abdoulye Baldé and others v Senegal, No. ECW/CCJ/JUD/04/13, Judgement, 22 February 2013

Karim Wade v Republic of Senegal, No. ECW/CCJ/JUD/13/19, Judgement, 4 March 2019

Khalifa Sall and others v Senegal, No. ECW/CCJ/JUD/17/18, Judgement, 29 June 2018

Ligue Sénégalaise des Droits de l'Homme and Amnesty International v Sénégal, No. ECW/CCJ/JUD/22/22, Judgement, 31 March 2022

Ousmane Sonko v Republic of Senegal, No. ECW/CCJ/JUD/42/23, Judgement, 17 November 2023

USL v Senegal, No. ECW/CCJ/JUD/10/21, Judgement, 28 April 2021

Constitutional Council of Senegal

Decision 5-E-2017, 14 August 2017

Decision No. 1/C/2024, 15 February 2024

Decision No. 7/E/2024, 29 March 2024

List of candidates for 2024 Presidential elections, Decision No. 2/E/2024, 20 January 2024

Supreme Court of Senegal

Aa Ab AI v State of Senegal, Decision No. 37, 9 June 2016, https://juricaf.org/arret/SENEGAL-COURSUPREME-20160609-37

Assane Ba and 2 others v State of Senegal, No. 19, Administrative Chamber Judgement, 23 March 2019

Mamadou Wade v. State of Senegal, Decision No. 29, 25 April 2024, case N° J/315/RG/23.

Court of Appeal and Tribunal

Court of Appeal, No. 168, Judgement,16 May 2017

Court of Appeal of Dakar, No. 137, Judgement, 8 May 2023

Tribunal of Dakar, Ousmane Sonko case, 14 December 2023

Other international bodies

African Court on Human and Peoples' Rights, *Tanganyika Law Society v Tanzania* Application Nos. 9/2011, 11/2011, 14 June 2013

UN Human Rights Committee, *Karim Meïssa Wade c. Sénégal*, Communication No. 2783/2016, U.N. Doc. CCPR/C/124/D/2783/2016, 22 October 2018

Table of legislation

Constitutions

Constitution of Senegal, 22 January 2001

Constitutional Law No. 2016-10 of 5 April 2016 amending the Constitution

Constitutional Law No. 2018-14 of 11 May 2018 amending the Constitution

Organic laws

Law No. 2002-20 of 15 May 2002 relating to the Internal rule of the National Assembly

Law No. 2017-12 of 18 January 2017 concerning the Electoral Code of the Republic of Senegal

Law No. 2018-22 of 4 July 2018 amending the Law No. 2017-12 of 18 January 2017 concerning the Electoral Code of the Republic of Senegal

Ordinary laws

Law No. 81/17 adopted on 6 May 1981 relating to political parties (amended by Law No. 89-36 adopted on 12 October 1989)

Law No. 1981/54 of 10 July 1981 establishing the CREI (Cour de Répression de l'Enrichissement Illicite)

Law No. 2023-14 of August 2, 2023, amending Law No. 65-61 of July 21, 1965, concerning the Code of Criminal Procedure

Law No. 05-2024 adopted on 6 March 2024 relating to general amnesty of the events occurring between March 2021 to February 2024

Chapter 7 Intra-Party Democracy and the Chasm between Political Parties and Democratisation in Kenya

Buluma Bwire

1. Introduction

At independence in 1963, the newly formed Kenyan state had a multiparty devolved system of government. However, its descent into a de facto single-party state began immediately thereafter, starting with a series of constitutional amendments the core objective of which was to centralise power in the executive.[1] The Kenya African National Union (KANU) became the sole political party[2] and only available vehicle for direct political participation in the country's elections.[3] On succeeding President Jomo Kenyatta in 1978, Daniel Moi's government completed Kenya's transformation into a *de jure* single-party state through the insertion of section 2A in the Constitution via the 1982 Constitution of Kenya (Amendment) Act,[4] which

1 D Juma, "The Normative Foundations of Constitution Making in Kenya: The Judiciary Past, Present, and Future", in C Murungi (ed.), *Judiciary Watch Report, Vol. IX: Constitutional Change, Democratic Transition and the Role of the Judiciary in Government Reform: Questions and Lessons for Kenya,* Nairobi, Kenya Section of the International Commission of Jurists (2010), p 220.

2 The only other political parties at independence were the Kenya African Democratic Union (KADU), which was disbanded in 1964 and saw its members integrated in KANU; the African People's Party, which was disbanded in 1963 when its eight Members of Parliament (MPs) crossed the floor to join KANU; the Nyanza Province African Union (NPAU), which held only one Senate seat and became defunct after the Senate was abolished in 1966; the Baluhya Political Union and Coast People's Party, which did not win any seats in the 1963 elections and was deregistered in 1965; and the Kenya People's Union (KPU), which was founded by the founding Vice President, Jaramogi Oginga Odinga, after he fell out with President Kenyatta and resigned in 1966 – thereupon he formed the KPU, but the party was banned in 1969. See SD Mueller, "Government and Opposition in Kenya: 1966–1969", 22 (1984) *Journal of Modern African Studies,* p 399.

3 B Bwire, "Interrogating the Evolution of a Constitutionally-legitimised 'Big Man' Political Culture and its Influence on Political Participation by Kenyan Youth", 23 (2023) *African Human Rights Law Journal,* p 266.

4 Constitution of Kenya (Amendment) Act 7 of 1982.

established KANU as the only political party in Kenya.[5] However, KANU's dominance ended nine years later with the repeal of section 2A via the 1991 Constitution of Kenya (Amendment) Act.[6] This re-transformation was achieved six years later with the 1997 Constitution of Kenya (Amendment) Act's[7] insertion of section 1A in the Constitution, which provided that "[t]he Republic of Kenya shall be a multiparty democratic state".

This constitutional framework marked the establishment of Kenya as a constitutional democracy.[8] A functional constitutional democracy is characterised by two basic elements: regular, free, and fair elections; and respect for basic rights to the freedom of speech, expression, and association.[9] Democracy thus builds upon, and is reinforced by, respect for human rights, particularly civil and political rights, and basic rights to the freedom of speech, expression, and association.[10] Article 25 of the International Covenant on Civil and Political Rights (ICCPR) provides that every citizen has the right to take part in the conduct of public affairs, either directly or through freely chosen representatives; the right to vote and to be elected at genuine periodic elections by universal and equal suffrage; and the right to have access to public service on general terms of equality.[11]

Political parties are private associations whose aim is to be represented in political institutions by fielding their members as candidates to contest elections.[12] They are crucial actors in a democracy because, through their membership and voting, they facilitate the electorate's choices and thus enable citizens to participate in politics, as provided for under Article 25.[13] Given their crucial role, it is therefore desirable that they are also internally democratic institutions that safeguard their members' rights to political participation under Article 25. These rights include the right to vote and to

---

5 Section 2A provided that "[t]here shall be in Kenya only one political party, the Kenya African National Union".

6 Act 12 of 1991.

7 Act 9 of 1997.

8 M Loughlin, "The Contemporary Crisis of Constitutional Democracy", 39 (2019) *Oxford Journal of Legal Studies,* pp 435–454.

9 T Ginsburg and AZ Huq, *How to Save a Constitutional Democracy,* Chicago, University of Chicago Press (2018), p 295.

10 S Lagoutte and MJ Petersen, *Political Parties and Human Rights: An Introduction,* Copenhagen, Danish Institute for Parties and Democracy (2018), p 2.

11 International Covenant on Civil and Political Rights (ICCPR) UN Treaty Series, Vol. 999, I–14668, 179, 19 December 1966.

12 Lagoutte and Petersen, *supra* n. 10, p 4.

13 *Ibid,* p 4.

be elected in regular, free and fair elections, which can be achieved only if political parties also respect and protect their members' basic rights to the freedom of speech, expression, and association.[14]

Intra-party democracy enables party members to participate in the conduct of party affairs, which includes the selection of party leaders and legislative candidates.[15] Moreover, it also enables parties to become vehicles for improved representation by elevating people and policies endorsed by party members.[16] Ignazi argues that a party is considered truly internally democratic when it has "the four knights of intra party democracy": (a) the formal involvement of members in leadership or candidate selection and policy development through votes; (b) a degree of pluralism reflected in internal factions; (c) deliberative processes engaging members in the formulation of party policies; and (d) a diffusion of power through party organs at different levels.[17]

However, despite the existence of a constitutional framework that inherently calls for intra-party democracy, Kenyan political parties seldom practise internal democracy. Prior to the second multiparty elections held in 1997, the International Foundation for Electoral Systems assessed Kenya's electoral system[18] and found that although multiparty politics appeared to be an established fact, the country was not yet a democracy and its democratisation had in fact stalled.[19] The reason for this inference was, among other things, that "political parties in Kenya are severely wanting in respect of the requisite skills and organizational capacity to make them viable political organizations".[20]

Against the backdrop above, this chapter critically analyses the evolution of political parties in Kenya since the restoration of multiparty politics

14 *Ibid*, p 2.

15 SE Scarrow, PD Webb, and T Poguntke, "Intra Party Decision Making in Contemporary Europe: Improving Representation or Ruling with Empty Shells", 37 (2022) *Irish Political Studies*, pp 196–217.

16 *Ibid*, p 6.

17 P Ignazi, "The Four Knights of Intra Party Democracy: A Rescue for Party Delegitimation", 26 (2020) *Party Politics*, pp 9–20.

18 Funded by the United States Agency for International Development (USAID), the study's objectives were to assess the electoral environment, identify constraints to free and fair elections, and recommend steps to eliminate them. See JD Barkan and RE Henderson, "Toward Credible and Legitimate Elections in Kenya: Part II IFES Assessment Report", Nairobi, USAID (May 1997).

19 *Ibid*, p i.

20 *Ibid*, p 27.

in 1992 to the present day, with its focus on their internal organisational structures. The analysis is based on the core thesis that for parties to succeed in facilitating the transition to democracy, they themselves must also be democratic internally. Drawing on the historical development and contemporary characteristics of their internal party structures, the chapter portrays the ineffectiveness and shortcomings of Kenyan political parties in promoting free, fair, and open competition. In so doing, it examines party leadership and candidate selection, while also interrogating the interdependence between political parties and a country's democratic transformation. Ultimately, the chapter argues that internal democracy within political parties is an essential ingredient in a country's transition to democracy based on the principles of good governance and constitutionalism.

2. Internal democracy in Kenya's political parties

2.1 The rise and fall of KANU's strongest opponent

At the advent of multiparty democracy in Kenya in 1992, the Independence Constitution[21] provided a sound constitutional and legal framework on which Kenyan political parties could build their organisational structures to ensure that these were internally democratic. The freedoms of speech, expression, and association were specifically protected under sections 79 and 80 of this constitution. Section 5(3)(a) provided that each political party participating in the general election would nominate one candidate for President, while section 34(d) stipulated that a person qualified to be elected as a member of the National Assembly if he were nominated for election by a political party. The underlying assumption was that party members would be formally involved in the selection of party leaders as well as the candidates which the parties present to contest the elections.

In 1992, the Forum for the Restoration of Democracy (FORD), a movement which led agitation for multiparty democracy in Kenya, was registered as a political party, instantly transforming it into the country's biggest opposition party. [22] It was registered under the Societies Act since at that

21 The Independence Constitution of 1963 was repealed and replaced by the 2010 Constitution. It is this constitution (the former) that was amended several times to transform Kenya into a one-party state. See Juma, *supra*, n. 1.

22 See "Ford Kenya: Our History", *Ford Kenya Party*, https://www.fordkenya.party/our-history/ (accessed 18 February 2024).

time Kenya did not have a Political Parties Act.[23] From the outset, there were tensions between those who had founded the organisation when it was still an opposition movement and those who joined it after it became a political party.[24] FORD's transition to a party raised tensions based primarily on ethnicity, along with generational conflicts, between the six founders, who were veterans of the Kenyan political scene since independence, and the young professionals who joined the party. [25] The latter, known popularly "the Young Turks",[26] also played a vital role in speaking out against the excesses of the Moi regime and agitating for multiparty democracy in Kenya.

FORD was the dominant opposition party in the run-up to the 1992 elections. Consequently, its membership ranks witnessed an increase in numbers, with new members comprising veteran opposition politicians as well as former KANU loyalists who had defected for the sake of their political survival.[27] However, aside from the high-profile recruits who joined of their own volition, the party lacked a structured system for recruiting and registering ordinary citizens as members, a limitation due primarily to its lack of a coherent party structure per se.

FORD had a written constitution which provided for grassroots elections; these were to be followed by an annual delegates conference to elect those who would serve in its national executive council.[28] However, the elections did not take place, owing to persistent squabbles between factions

23 *Ibid.*

24 FORD, an opposition movement, was founded by six people: Oginga Odinga, Masinde Muliro, Martin Shikuku, Philip Gachoka, George Nthenge, and Ahmed Bamahriz.

25 D Throup and C Hornsby, *Multi-Party Politics in Kenya: The Kenyatta & Moi States & the Triumph of the System in the 1992 Election,* Nairobi, East African Educational Publishers (1998), p 92.

26 These were youth leaders who mostly began their political careers fighting against the excesses of the Moi regime as leaders of the Student Organization of Nairobi University and the University Academic Staff Union. They included Paul Muite, Raila Odinga, James Orengo, Anyang Nyong'o, Kiraitu Murungi, and Mukhisa Kituyi. See JM Klopp and JR Orina, "University Crisis, Student Activism, and the Contemporary Struggle for Democracy in Kenya", 45 (2002) *African Studies Review,* pp 43–76.

27 They included two cabinet ministers, Peter Oloo Aringo and Dr Njoroge Mungai, as well as the former vice president, Prof. Josephat Karanja, and the former head of the civil service, Geoffrey Kariithi. See Throup and Hornsby, *supra* n. 25, p 92.

28 *Ibid,* pp 93–94.

in the party;[29] these resulted in a compromise being brokered by the interim chairman, Oginga Odinga, events which saw him establish a 108-member national steering committee and a 14-member interim executive council – structures not provided for in FORD's constitution.[30] Undemocratically, those party members who got to serve in either the steering committee or the council did so on the basis of political patronage rather than through a free and fair electoral process. This political patronage was divided amongst three personalised ethnic-based factions centred around Kenneth Matiba,[31] Martin Shikuku, and Oginga Odinga, who respectively represented Kenya's three largest ethnic groups at the time: Kikuyus, Luos, and Luhyas.[32] As such, these structures were in violation of FORD's own constitution due to the biased selection of their members that denied party members equal voting rights and thereby suppressed their formal participation in party affairs.

There was also disagreement over who should be allowed to join the party, especially when former KANU loyalists began defecting to FORD. However, it soon emerged that such disputes were on account of political machinations to secure leadership of the party, with some amongst the old guard seeing the influx of new members as a threat to their authority in the party.[33] These intrigues gave rise to ethnic-based factions within the party as politicians schemed to position themselves to secure nomination slots to run for office on the party ticket in the upcoming general elections. As a result, FORD neglected to develop a structured system for membership recruitment and registration, as this was abandoned by the party

29 The squabbles resulted in Martin Shikuku, one of the six founding members of FORD, scheming with fellow Luhya lawyers Japheth Shamalla and Benna Lutta to rewrite the party's constitution in a bid to retain and centralise power within FORD's original six founder members. See Throup and Hornsby, *supra* n. 25, pp 93–94.

30 F Holmquist and M Ford, "Kenya: State and Civil Society the First Year after the Election", 41 (1994) *Africa Today*, pp 5–21.

31 Matiba emerged as a dominant force when he declared that he would also be seeking the party's nomination to run for president, becoming the second member to do so after Oginga Odinga. A veteran of the Kenyan political scene since independence, he later became a key agitator for multiparty democracy in Kenya and was jailed by the Moi regime. See Throup and Hornsby, *supra* n. 25, p 106.

32 According to the 1989 census, Kenya's population was 21,443,636, of which the Kikuyu comprised 20.78 per cent, the Luhyas, 14.38 per cent, and the Luos, 12.38 per cent. See Central Bureau of Statistics, "Kenya Population Census, 1989, Volume I" (March 1994), p 390.

33 Throup and Hornsby, *supra* n. 25, p 93.

leadership in favour of schemes to seize overall control of the party. These actions eventually coalesced around two main factions led respectively by the members seeking the party's presidential nomination, namely Oginga Odinga and Kenneth Matiba. The factions subsequently formed parallel party structures that were replicated at all levels of the party, so much so that it was common to find rival formations at the sub-branch and branch level contesting each other's legitimacy while refusing to be merged into a single branch.[34]

Attempts at internal dispute resolution were rendered almost impossible by the contestation of legitimacy among the parallel party structures, as a result of which neither faction was willing to concede to the other's authority. Moreover, the lack of a coherent party structure meant that FORD did not have any suitable internal dispute resolution mechanism in place. Subsequently, when a major dispute arose as to the nomination of the party's presidential candidate, the Matiba faction went to court seeking an injunction to stop the impending elections that were to be held at FORD's first annual delegates conference, called by the Odinga faction.[35] However, the court declined to intervene, with Justice Akiwumi declaring that the court had no authority to intervene in the party's internal affairs.[36]

Ultimately, FORD split into two rival parties, with Odinga's faction transforming into FORD-Kenya and Matiba's faction, into FORD-Asili.[37] This divided KANU's most formidable opponent down the middle, thereby increasing KANU's chances of reclaiming power in Kenya's first multiparty elections and perpetuating the Moi regime in this new political era. FORD's split was a major source of disillusionment for most Kenyans, since at the time it was the only opposition party capable of forming a nationwide multi-ethnic coalition that could win seats in every province and mount a challenge to KANU in forming the next government.[38]

From the foregoing, it is evident that, despite having a written constitution that specified its party structures and provided for elections of office-holders, FORD still failed to achieve the internal organisational coherence required of a national political party and essential for internal democracy to prevail. Consequently, it failed to achieve internal democracy since it was

34 *Ibid*, p 111.
35 *Ibid*, p 131.
36 *Ibid*, p 133.
37 G Muigai, "Kenya's Opposition and the Crisis of Governance" 21 (1993) *Issue*, pp 26–34.
38 Throup and Hornsby, *supra* n. 25, p 109.

unable to hold free and fair elections for internal party positions. Moreover, FORD lacked a credible and verifiable system of membership recruitment and registration, and had a fragmented national presence with parallel party structures, all of which ultimately affected the credibility of its annual delegates conference.

2.2 The fall of KANU and the rise of coalition parties in 2002

Despite the reintroduction of multiparty politics in Kenya, KANU was able to win the first two elections of the multiparty era in 1992 and 1997, thereby prolonging President Moi's reign.[39] Meanwhile, the number of parties continued to increase, such that by 2002 Kenya had 22 registered political parties.[40] Subsequently, in order to strengthen their positions ahead of the impending 2002 elections, most of these parties formed alliances, primarily for the purpose of consolidating their potential vote baskets and increasing their chances of winning more seats, as opposed to forming alliances on the basis of congruence of ideologies. These alliances were based on memoranda of understanding between the parties, and were not specifically provided for under the then constitutional and legal framework of the Independence Constitution.

Ironically, KANU was the first party to enter into a political alliance after the 1997 elections, where it won a pyrrhic victory that left it with a mere four-seat majority in Parliament.[41] Looking ahead to the next elections, to be held in 2002, President Moi foresaw an uphill battle for KANU, and looking to the path immediately ahead, a similarly difficult time for

---

39 Moi won the 1992 elections with 1,927,645 (36.7 per cent) of the votes, while his closest challenger, Kenneth Matiba, had 1,352,856 (26 per cent) of them. Matiba challenged the win in court, but the courts ruled in Moi's favour. See *Kenneth Stanley Njindo Matiba v Daniel Toroitich Arap Moi* (1994) eKLR. Moi later won the 1997 elections with 2,445,801 (40.13 per cent) of the votes against his closest challenger, Mwai Kibaki, with 1,895,527 (31.09 per cent). Kibaki also challenged the win in court but was unsuccessful. See *Kibaki v Moi & 2 others (No.2)* (2008) KLR (EP) 308.

40 Office of the Registrar of Political Parties, "Post-Election Evaluation Report" (May 2023), p 6.

41 KANU emerged on top with 107 elective seats, but the combined opposition captured 103. See "Kenya Parliamentary Election Results 1997", http://archive.ipu.org/parline-e/reports/arc/2167_97.htm (accessed 20 February 2024).

himself, since he was serving his second and final term as President.[42] Consequently, he reached out to Oginga Odinga's son and political heir, Raila Odinga, to form a merger between KANU and Odinga's National Development Party (NDP).[43] The two parties merged on 18 March 2002, albeit for different reasons. Odhiambo-Mbai observes that Moi was focused on his succession plan to hand over power to a proxy who would guarantee his political security, whereas Odinga was intent on seizing total control and becoming the next President.[44]

The two parties began on a solidly democratic footing by deciding that office-bearers to the newly merged KANU-NDP party would be elected at a national delegates conference on 18 March 2002; it was also at this conference that party members would ratify the merger and approve a new constitution for the merged party.[45] Moreover, the NDP would be dissolved and the merged party would be New KANU.[46] However, despite the presence of 6,000 delegates drawn from both parties' nationwide branches, with KANU bringing 4,500 and the NDP, 1,500,[47] it soon emerged that the new party's leadership was predetermined and not subject to any free and fair electoral process. Undemocratically, candidates were elected by acclamation instead of secret ballot; even in instances where delegates jeered to express rejection of a particular candidate,[48] they were simply ignored, with President Moi stating that complaints should be forwarded to party officials overseeing the elections.[49]

42 Section 9(2) of the Independence Constitution specifically stated: "No person shall be elected to hold office for more than two terms."

43 C Odhiambo-Mbai, "The Rise and Fall of the Autocratic State in Kenya", in WO Oyugi, P Wanyande, and C Odhiambo-Mbai (eds.), *The Politics of Transition in Kenya: From Kanu to NARC,* Nairobi, Heinrich Boll Foundation (2003), p 70.

44 *Ibid*, p 71.

45 *Ibid*, p 72.

46 "Merger to Change Kenya Politics", *News24*, 18 March 2002, https://www.news24.com/news24/Africa/Features/Merger-to-change-Kenya-politics-20020318 (accessed 30 December 2024).

47 *Ibid.*

48 Kipngeny Arap Ngeny's election as party treasurer was loudly jeered by the delegates since he had just been charged in court with the embezzlement of millions of shillings during the time he served as the head of the Kenya Posts and Telecommunications Corporation in the early 1990s. See "Kenyan Parties Merge Ahead of Presidential Elections", *Voice of America*, 18 March 2002, https://www.voanews.com/a/a-13-a-2002-03-18-17-kenyan/392132.html (accessed 19 November 2024).

49 *Ibid.*

Ultimately, Moi remained as chair, Odinga was elected as secretary-general, and a newly created four vice-chair positions were shared out between Uhuru Kenyatta, Musalia Mudavadi, Kalonzo Musyoka, and Noah Katana Ngala.[50] Moi came out eventually to declare Uhuru Kenyatta as his preferred successor and choice as New KANU's presidential candidate, doing so without engaging in any free and fair internal electoral process despite vehement reaction from Odinga and the four vice-chairmen, who declared their own interest in running for the party's nomination as New KANU's presidential candidate.[51] Subsequently, a group of 32 KANU Members of Parliament (MPs) called a press conference to announce that while they were not opposed to Moi's choice of Kenyatta as the party's presidential candidate, they believed that the nomination process should be conducted democratically in accordance with the party's constitution.[52] However, Moi pointedly ignored all opposition to his preferred candidate and officially endorsed Kenyatta on 14 October 2002.[53] This marked the end of the coalition experiment that Moi had begun, given that Odinga led the others in abandoning the party to seek viable alternatives ahead of the 2002 elections.

Any chance of resolving the dispute internally was thwarted by the fact that the merger was stillborn and that the proposed New KANU party which would have resulted from the merger between KANU and NDP was never formally established or registered. Additionally, the disgruntled members who wished to contest the presidency in the impending elections were cognizant of the pressure of time, with only two months left before elections were scheduled to be held on 27 December 2002.

Odinga moved quickly to forge another alliance, now with two ex-KANU loyalists, namely the former vice-president, George Saitoti,[54] and the former KANU secretary-general, Joseph Kamotho.[55] However, the Rainbow Alliance, as the new grouping was called, needed to be transformed into

---

50 Odhiambo-Mbai, *supra* n. 43, p 71.

51 *Ibid*, p 75.

52 *Ibid.*

53 *Ibid.*

54 Professor Saitoti was publicly humiliated by President Moi on the day of the merger with the NDP when Moi omitted his name from the list of candidates for vice-chair. On another occasion, Moi told a public crowd, with Saitoti present, that even though Saitoti was his friend, friendship and leadership are two different things. See J Kamau, "Trying Times for George Saitoti under President Moi", *Nation*, 12 March 2020, https://nation.africa/kenya/nation-prime/trying-times-for-george-saitoti-under-president-moi-258962 (accessed 19 November 2024).

55 Odhiambo-Mbai, *supra* n. 43, p 78.

a political party for its members to be able to stand for seats in the upcoming elections, and to this end it usurped a minnow known as the Liberal Democratic Party (LDP).[56] Undoubtedly, the takeover of the LDP by the Rainbow Alliance was anything but democratic since its leadership was simply bought out, thereby setting an enduring trend for Kenyan politicians to buy out the registered leaders of moribund political parties and use these parties as vehicles to contest elections.[57] Kanyinga notes that the vast majority of Kenyan political parties are active only during election years, when they are used as vehicles to maximise votes and win elections;[58] the LDP is a good example of this phenomenon.

Meanwhile, leaders of the main opposition parties – Mwai Kibaki's Democratic Party, Michael Wamalwa's FORD-Kenya, and Charity Ngilu's National Party of Kenya – led 11 other minor parties to form an opposition alliance party, which was dubbed the National Alliance of Kenya (NAK).[59] Ultimately, NAK and the LDP merged to form the opposition super-alliance called the National Rainbow Coalition (NARC).[60]

Unfortunately, even though the NARC's manifesto expressly said that "the NARC leadership will move fast and facilitate the establishment of a firm foundation of a truly democratic and empowered national community",[61] its presidential nominations were not democratically contested. The race for NARC's presidential nomination was prematurely terminated when Odinga, without prior consultation or agreement with other party leaders, proposed Mwai Kibaki's name to the huge crowd gathered for the party's first public rally, held at Uhuru Park on 14 October 2002.[62] Odinga's proclamation of *"Kibaki Tosha!"* ("Kibaki is enough!") was met with loud

---

56 S Karume, "Factional Intrigues and Alliance Politics: The Case of NARC in Kenya's 2002 Elections", 2 (2003) *Journal of African Elections,* pp 1–13.

57 Odhiambo-Mbai, *supra* n. 43, p 83.

58 K Kanyinga, *Kenya: Democracy and Political Participation,* Nairobi, Open Society Initiative for Eastern Africa (2014), p 155.

59 Odhiambo-Mbai, *supra* n. 43, p 83.

60 After its formation on 22 October 2002, it became the biggest opposition party in Kenya. Politicians began to defect to it in droves, as it was almost guaranteed that one would win if one stood on a NARC ticket. See Karume, *supra* n. 56, p 3.

61 National Rainbow Coalition (NARC), "Democracy and Empowerment: Manifesto for the National Rainbow Coalition (NARC)", November 2002, http://libraryir.parliament.go.ke/handle/123456789/15687 (accessed 19 November 2024).

62 Odhiambo-Mbai, *supra* n. 43, p 83.

popular approval from the crowd, and with that Kibaki became NARC's presidential candidate.[63]

After the rally, other party leaders tried to express their disapproval, with the most vocal being Simeon Nyachae,[64] who vigorously protested that the NARC presidential candidate must be democratically nominated by all its constituent parties through a delegates' system.[65] His proposal was rejected by other coalition members on the grounds that NARC could not successfully organise a delegates conference in the one month remaining before the deadline set by the Electoral Commission of Kenya for the national nominations of presidential candidates.[66] Another ground for the rejection of Nyachae's proposal was that some of the constituent parties, particularly Odinga's LDP, did not have verifiable members who could serve as genuine delegates at such a conference.[67]

The subsequent nominations of NARC parliamentary and civic candidates further exposed its complete lack of internal democracy at all levels. The European Union's election observation mission in its final report notes that, in some constituencies, NARC had double nominations, while certain party leaders by-passed party elections to directly give candidates the party's nomination certificates. [68] The nominations were also marred by actual election offences such as rigging, vote-buying, and voter bribery[69], while in other cases some candidates doubled up as returning officers and declared themselves as the sole party nominees.[70] The Carter Center's election observation delegation in its final report notes that NARC's candidate nomination process was marked by "administrative chaos, double

---

63 "The Deal and the Deal Makers in Kibaki's 2002 Victory", *Nation*, 30 August 2008, https://nation.africa/kenya/news/the-deal-and-deal-makers-in-kibaki-s-2002-victory-557104 (accessed 19 November 2024).

64 A veteran in both government and politics since independence. He went on to contest the presidency as the candidate of his Ford-People party, the membership of which was drawn mainly from his Gusii ethnic community. See R Mbula and N Gisesa, "The Life and Times of Political Heavyweight Simeon Nyachae", *Nation*, 2 February 2021, https://nation.africa/kenya/news/-life-times-nyachae-3276590 (accessed 19 November 2024).

65 C Odhiambo-Mbai, *supra* n. 43, p 83.

66 *Ibid*, p 82.

67 *Ibid*, p 83.

68 EU Election Observation Mission, "Kenya General Elections 27 December 2002 Final Report", Nairobi, EU Observation Mission (2002), p 22.

69 At the time they were offences under the Election Offences Act (Cap. 66).

70 Odhiambo-Mbai, *supra* n. 43, p 84.

nominations, and incidents of intraparty violence".[71] The process, overall, was hence not democratic by any measure. Unfortunately, this pattern of undemocratic party nominations endures, and is replicated by virtually all Kenyan political parties, which continue to fall short in their efforts to achieve internal democracy.

Therefore, it is evident that NARC and its constituent parties were in total lack of well-articulated internal structures that could enable them to hold a national delegates conference to democratically elect a presidential candidate or to conduct democratic party elections for parliamentary candidates. Both NARC and its constituent parties thus failed to achieve internal party democracy. Moreover, as with the LDP, most of the smaller constituent parties[72] did not have verifiable members, were dormant prior to the election year, and did not have a national character or presence.

NARC went on to win the 2002 elections resoundingly and form a government with Kibaki as President. However, once in power, it slowly became fragmented owing to disagreements among the leaders of its constituent parties on how to share power.[73] NARC ultimately disintegrated along ethnic fissures,[74] and in the run-up to the 2007 elections was no longer the giant it had been in 2002, with its main factions having splintered into the Kibaki-led Party of National Unity (PNU) and the Odinga-led Orange Democratic Movement (ODM). Just like FORD, New KANU, and NARC, both the PNU and ODM were personalised and ethnic-based parties whose internal organisational structures were dominated by patronage politics. Consequently, they continued to engage in the same undemo-

71 The Carter Center, *Observing the 2002 Kenya Elections: Final Report*, Atlanta, The Carter Center (May 2003), p 10.

72 NARC was a coalition between the NAK and LDP. The NAK itself was a cluster of 12 political parties: the Democratic Party, FORD-Kenya, National Party of Kenya, FORD-Asili, Saba Saba Asili, SPARK, Labour Party of Kenya, United Democratic Movement (UDM), Social Democratic Party, Kenya National Democratic Alliance, Federal Party of Kenya, and Mazingira Green Party.

73 The cause of the disagreement was that Raila accused Kibaki of failing to implement a memorandum of understanding on how to share power that they had signed prior to the elections.

74 Other leaders came to denounce Kibaki for being surrounded only by Kikuyu loyalists (known popularly as "the Mt Kenya Mafia", some of them had also been in Kenyatta's government); a related criticism was that Kikuyus were said to be receiving the lion's share of government appointments. See Bwire, *supra* n. 3, p 269.

cratic practices that they inherited from their leadership's past experiences in both the Moi and Kibaki regimes.[75]

A key trend that emerged during this period and thereafter became a mainstay of Kenya's multiparty politics was the formation of coalitions between different parties. However, this also revealed a lacuna in Kenya's constitutional and legal framework at the time, since the latter did not specifically provide for how coalitions were to be formed or governed. As noted earlier, coalitions were then governed by memoranda of understanding between the constituent parties, and when these were breached, there was no legal recourse for the disaffected parties, as was seen in the cases both of New KANU and NARC. Indeed, NARC became fragmented because one of the key constituent parties, Odinga's LDP, contended that the memorandum of understanding on which the coalition was built was not honoured.[76] Nonetheless, there was no basis in the then prevailing constitutional and legal framework on which to implement it, and some of the positions negotiated in the memorandum were not entrenched in the Constitution.[77]

75 By this point, Kibaki was Kenya's longest-standing politician, having served 10 consecutive terms as an MP before becoming President in 2002, while Odinga had been in opposition politics since the 1980s. See M Mwende, "State Canonizes Kibaki as Kenya's Longest Serving MP", *Pulse*, 27 April 2022, https://www.pulselive.co.ke/news/local/senate-canonises-mwai-kibaki-as-kenyas-longest-serving-mp-for-10-consecutive-terms/gvnvzjp (accessed 19 November 2024).

76 P Wanyande and PO Asingo, "Beyond Election Campaign Rhetoric: Challenges Facing the National Rainbow Coalition (NARC)", 31 (2004) *African Review*, pp 18–38.

77 The NARC memorandum of understanding proposed the creation of the position of an executive prime minister, thereby decentralising power from the executive. It is assumed that Odinga would have occupied this position once created; however, the agreement was never made public. *Ibid*, p 26.

2.3 Political parties in the era of the 2010 Constitution

In the aftermath of the 2007 post-election violence,[78] a coalition government was formed with Kibaki as President and Odinga as Prime Minister.[79] This government later established the Independent Review Commission (IREC) to investigate all aspects of the 2007 elections. In its examination of Kenyan political parties, the IREC found that their internal organisational structures rendered them "incapable of providing democratic space to their membership".[80] It found in this regard that their election of party leaders lacked transparency and was entirely undemocratic, consequently delivering leadership that was inclined to be arbitrary, autocratic, and unaccountable.[81] The IREC thus recommended, amongst other things, a complete overhaul of the Kenyan electoral system so as to change the way in which politics was conducted.[82] In a bid to reform Kenya's political culture and institutionalise political parties, this culminated in the enactment of a revamped Political Parties Act in 2011,[83] which replaced the one which had been enacted just two months before the 2007 elections.[84]

Part IVA of the 2011 Political Parties Act specifically outlines the rules for organising and conducting party nominations. Under section 38B, a political party, when conducting nominations, is obligated to establish structures that provide mechanisms for the resolution of disputes arising from the

78 The dispute over the results of the presidential elections – in which both Kibaki and Odinga claimed victory – degenerated into widespread violence that resulted in the death of 1,133 people. See Commission of Inquiry into Post-Election Violence (CIPEV), *Report of The Commission of Inquiry into Post-Election Violence (CIPEV)*, Nairobi, Government of Kenya (16 October 2008), pp 345–346.

79 The coalition government was the outcome of talks to end the post-election violence; these talks were led by the African Union (AU) Panel of Eminent African Personalities, which was headed by the former United Nations Secretary-General, Kofi Annan, and included the former Tanzanian president, Benjamin Mkapa, and Graca Machel of Mozambique. The Panel was appointed by the AU in January 2008 to mediate in the crisis following the 2007 post-election violence.

80 Independent Review Commission (IREC), *Report of the Independent Review Commission on the General Elections held in Kenya on 27 December 2007*, Nairobi, Government of Kenya (17 September 2008), p 12.

81 *Ibid.*

82 *Ibid*, p 15.

83 No. 11 of 2011 (Cap 7D), http://kenyalaw.org:8181/exist/kenyalex/actview.xql?actid=CAP.%207D (accessed 20 October 2024).

84 The Political Parties Act 10 of 2007 was assented to on 22 October 2007, with a commencement date of 1 July 2008.

nominations, to designate the person to issue nomination certificates, and to prescribe the functions of the internal body responsible for conducting nominations.[85] Moreover, under section 38C(3), a party must apply to the Registrar of Political Parties[86] for a certified copy of the register of members to be used in the party nominations. The Act also provides a Code of Conduct for Political Parties[87] and, among other things, requires every political party to respect, uphold, and promote democratic values and principles as well as the inclusive participation of party members.

The push for reform of Kenya's political culture and the institutionalisation of political parties also found sound footing in the 2010 Constitution. To begin with, Article 4(2) recognises Kenya as a multiparty democratic state founded on national values and principles of governance, which include the rule of law, democracy, and the participation of the people.[88] Article 38 thereafter specifically recognises and protects the political rights of all citizens, including their right to free, fair, and regular elections, based on universal suffrage, in any office of any political party of which the citizen is a member.[89] Moreover, Article 91 outlines the basic requirements for political parties, one of which is that they should have a democratically elected governing body and both promote and practise democracy through regular, free, and fair elections. [90]

However, despite the existence now of a comprehensive constitutional framework for intra-party democracy, Kenyan parties continue to fall short of achieving internal democracy. In 2013, Kenya held its first elections under the 2010 Constitution, with the two main contenders being the Kenyatta[91]-led Jubilee Alliance[92] and Odinga's Coalition for Reform and

85 *Ibid*, section 38B.

86 The Office of the Registrar of Political Parties is established under section 33 of the Political Parties Act. Its mandate is to register, regulate, monitor, investigate, and supervise parties to ensure compliance with the Act.

87 First Schedule of the Political Parties Act.

88 Constitution of Kenya, 2010, Article 10(2)(a).

89 *Ibid,* Article 38(2)(b).

90 *Ibid,* Article 91(1)(b) and (d).

91 The son of Kenya's founding father, Mzee Jomo Kenyatta, he was running for president against Odinga, who in turn was the son of the founding father of Kenya's opposition politics, Mzee Oginga Odinga.

92 Its constituent parties were the National Alliance Party, United Republican Party, Republican Congress, and National Alliance of Rainbow Coalition, which drew the core of their members from the Kikuyu and Kalenjin communities, respectively supporting Uhuru Kenyatta and William Ruto.

Democracy (CORD).[93] However, as with FORD, New KANU, NARC, the PNU, and the ODM before them, CORD and the Jubilee Alliance were formed primarily to serve as vehicles to contest the elections and drew the core of their membership from the ethnic groups of their leaders. Cheeseman, Lynch, and Willis observe that despite the new Constitution's aim to transform Kenyan politics through the institutionalisation of political parties, parties in 2013 were still as organisationally insubstantial and unaccountable as they had been in 2007.[94]

Indeed, the Jubilee Alliance was referred to as the "coalition of the accused"[95] because its two principals, Uhuru Kenyatta and William Ruto, were charged at the International Criminal Court with crimes against humanity committed during the 2007 post-election violence.[96] In keeping with what has been the trend since the reintroduction of multiparty politics in Kenya, both had their own individual parties, parties which relied for their existence on the leaders' personal resources and whose supporters were drawn primarily from their respective ethnic groups. In establishing those parties, they also followed the established trend of taking over dormant parties in an election year and using them as vehicles to contest elections. Subsequently, Kenyatta took over the National Alliance Party of Kenya,[97] while Ruto for his part took over the United Republican Party,[98]

---

93 Its constituent parties were the Orange Democratic Movement, Wiper Democratic Movement, FORD-Kenya, the Kenya Social Congress, KADU-Asili, the People's Democratic Party, the Mkenya Solidarity Movement, Chama Cha Uzalendo, the Muungano Party, the United Democratic Movement, Chama Cha Mwananchi, and the Federal Party. The uniting factor was that Kenya's other 40 tribes coalesced around Raila Odinga (Luo) and Kalonzo Musyoka (Kamba) to overcome the Kikuyu-Kalenjin domination of the Kenyan presidency which had prevailed since independence in 1963.

94 N Cheeseman, G Lynch, and J Willis, "Democracy and its Discontents: Understanding Kenya's 2013 Elections", 8 (2014) *Journal of Eastern African Studies,* p 6.

95 *Ibid,* p 7.

96 Six Kenyans, popularly known as the "Ocampo Six", were charged at the International Criminal Court: William Ruto (Minister of Higher Education); Uhuru Kenyatta (Minister of Finance); Henry Kosgey (Minister of Industrialisation); Francis Muthaura (Head of Civil Service and Secretary to the Cabinet); Major-General Mohammed Hussein Ali (Commissioner of Police); and Joshua Sang (Head of Operations at Kass FM).

97 The party was registered by a wealthy Kikuyu businessman, Nginyo Kariuki, who agreed to hand it over to Uhuru Kenyatta.

98 The party was founded in 2012 by a faction of Ruto-allied politicians in the ODM who left the latter when Ruto fell out with Raila Odinga; they went to form this new party as their own vehicle for running in the 2013 elections.

with these two entities later joining forces as the Jubilee Alliance. As a result, the presidential ticket of the Jubilee Alliance was a foregone conclusion and not open to any democratic contest: Kenyatta was the presidential candidate and Ruto, his running mate. It was in many ways a coronation uniting the two tribes that have dominated the Kenyan presidency since independence, namely the Kikuyu and Kalenjin.[99]

Kenyatta and Ruto's candidacy did not go unchallenged. In keeping with the spirit of the 2010 Constitution, three civil society organisations[100] filed a constitutional petition, *International Centre for Policy and Conflict & 5 others v The Hon. Attorney General & 4 others,*[101] on the grounds, among others, that the "honour, integrity, and confidence bestowed on public office under Chapter Six[102] of the Constitution would be seriously eroded".[103] The petitioners argued that the two candidates did not meet the threshold of the guiding principles of leadership and integrity provided for under Chapter Six and should therefore be barred from holding public office. Ultimately, the High Court held that it did not have the jurisdiction to determine the matter since the Supreme Court possessed exclusive original jurisdiction to hear and determine disputes relating to the elections of the Office of the President under Article 163(3)(a) as read with Article 140 of the Constitution. The court ruling came 15 days[104] before the elections that were due to be held on 4 March 2013, effectively marking the end of any dispute over the Kenyatta-Ruto candidature.

CORD traversed a similar path of ethnic-based calculation to maximise votes. Additionally, CORD's principals, Odinga and Musyoka, signed a memorandum of understanding that Odinga would be President for only one term and then support Musyoka for the presidency in 2017.[105] Consequently, the CORD presidential ticket-holders were arrived at through a negotiated agreement rather than an open, free, and fair democratic contest.

99 All Kenyan presidents since independence have come from one or the other of these two ethnic communities: Jomo Kenyatta (Kikuyu), Daniel arap Moi (Kalenjin), Mwai Kibaki (Kikuyu), Uhuru Kenyatta (Kikuyu), and William Ruto (Kalenjin).

100 The International Centre for Policy and Conflict (ICPC), the Kenya Human Rights Commission (KHRC), and the International Commission of Jurists-Kenya Chapter.

101 [2013] eKLR.

102 It provides the guiding principles of leadership and integrity required for state officers.

103 *Supra* n. 101, paragraph 15.

104 It was delivered on 15 February 2013.

105 Raila Odinga would later renege on the memorandum of understanding in the subsequent elections of 2017.

Kadima and Owuor note that negotiated power-sharing agreements like these, which became common practice in Kenya thereafter, are generally focused on short-term gains, such appointments to lucrative government posts as a reward for party loyalists, and tend to work in favour of only the larger parties in the coalition.[106] In the absence of democratically contested presidential primaries, there is virtually no chance for a candidate from one of the smaller parties in the coalition to be the presidential candidate.

The deficiencies in the internal organisational structures of CORD and the Jubilee Alliance were glaringly exposed during the party primaries. Neither of them was able to hold free, fair, and transparent party nominations. The Kenya National Commission on Human Rights, which monitored the party primaries, notes that the exercise was ruined by sheer lack of preparedness and massive irregularities, while the culture of cronyism and political patronage continued to dominate the nominations.[107] Nevertheless, disaffected candidates had recourse to incremental avenues for dispute resolution, starting with the internal party mechanisms established in line with section 38B of the Political Parties Act.[108] Thereafter, they could pursue the matter at the Independent Electoral and Boundaries Commission (IEBC),[109] the Political Parties Dispute Tribunal,[110] and ultimately the courts.[111] The disputes were raised on the grounds of electoral malpractices such as multiple voting, voter transportation, and voter bribery.[112] Consequently, the IEBC determined 200 nomination disputes,[113] while the

106 D Kadima and F Owuor, "Kenya's Decade of Experiments with Political Party Alliances and Coalitions: Motivations, Impacts and Prospects", 13 (2014) *Journal of African Elections*, p 179.

107 Kenya National Commission on Human Rights (KNCHR), "Break from the Past? A Monitoring Report of the 2013 Political Party Nominations" Nairobi, Kenya National Commission on Human Rights (2013), p vi.

108 *Supra* n. 84.

109 The IEBC has the mandate to settle disputes arising from nominations, as provided for under Article 88(4) of the 2010 Constitution.

110 Established under section 5 of the Political Parties Act.

111 Parties could appeal the decision of the Political Parties Dispute Tribunal to the High Court, and subsequently to the Court of Appeal and the Supreme Court, respectively. However, parties did not pursue the decisions beyond the Tribunal due to the tight deadlines for submission of party candidate lists to the IEBC.

112 KNCHR, *supra* n. 107, p 114.

113 Electoral Institute for Sustainable Democracy in Africa (EISA), *Case Digest: Decisions of the IEBC Dispute Committee*, Nairobi, EISA (2013).

Political Parties Dispute Tribunal determined 60 cases.[114] However, rather than await the outcome of their disputes, most politicians defected to other parties in a rush to secure nomination slots to contest the elections before the IEBC deadline lapsed.[115]

Both of the coalitions tried to establish a nationwide presence by opening up branches in the counties, but the linkages between the branches and the respective coalition headquarters in Nairobi were weak in most cases and entirely lacking in others.[116] Moreover, the branch offices lacked proper facilities while the officials had inadequate knowledge of the rules and regulations governing political parties. Additionally, headquarters did not allocate them the financial resources to enable them to manage the logistics of overseeing the party primaries.[117] Consequently, in most cases it was the candidates who personally facilitated transportation of nomination materials, hence making the entire process susceptible to rigging.[118]

Furthermore, the constituent parties of the two coalitions lacked verifiable membership registers and hence opted to use the IEBC provisional voter register.[119] This opened up the party primaries to people who were not bona fide party members, since all that was required for them to vote was the production of their national identity cards. Consequently, many areas witnessed electoral malpractices such as multiple voting, voter transportation, and voter bribery.[120] Additionally, party officials overseeing the elections were poorly trained, and some also openly engaged in tallying malpractices.[121]

Based on the foregoing, it is evident that both of the coalitions failed to establish intra-party democracy. Nevertheless, some progress was made towards the institutionalisation of Kenyan political parties, given that parties

114 L Awuor and WE Otieno, *Case Digest of the Decisions of the Political Parties Dispute Tribunal,* Nairobi, National Council for Law Reporting (2013).

115 PO Asingo, "Party Strengths, Partisan Identities and Voter Mobilization in the Kenya Elections of 2013", in F Otieno (ed.), *New Constitution, Same Old Challenges: Reflections on Kenya's 2013 General Elections,* Nairobi, Society for International Development and Uraia Trust (2015), p 159.

116 KNCHR, *supra* n. 112, p 12.

117 *Ibid.*

118 *Ibid*, p 11.

119 The IEBC has the constitutional mandate under Article 88 (4) (a) to prepare and maintain a register of voters for each polling station, ward and constituency.

120 KNCHR, *supra* n. 112, p 14.

121 The Carter Center, *Observing Kenya's March 2013 Elections: Final Report*, Atlanta, The Carter Center (2014), p 33.

at least attempted to comply to some degree with the provisions of the 2011 Political Parties Act.

The gains achieved in 2013 include political parties attempting to establish a nationwide presence through membership recruitment and setting up branch offices in the counties. This is in fact a prerequisite for full registration as a political party under section 7 of the Act, which requires that a provisionally registered political party qualifies for full registration only if it has recruited at least 1,000 registered voters from each or more than half of the counties. However, it remains the trend that, once registered, some parties lie dormant and are reactivated, or taken over, by other politicians who were not original members for use as vehicles for contesting the general elections. Another key step forward was that, however deficiently, parties began establishing internal structures – such as election management boards and nomination dispute resolution panels – in order to conduct nominations in keeping with section 38B of the Act.

The party which currently exhibits the longest institutional continuity is the ODM, which was founded in 2005.[122] Unfortunately, however, it exhibits this continuity largely because its party leader, Odinga, has used it as his political vehicle of choice in four presidential bids – in 2007, 2013, 2017, and 2022. Moreover, ODM's core membership is drawn from his near-fanatical following among members of his Luo ethnic group, who are Kenya's fourth-largest tribe.[123] Consequently, as with other Kenyan political parties, the ODM exists in the shadow of being a personalised ethnic-based party.

2.4 A return to single-party dominance cloaked as multipartyism

The Jubilee Alliance went on to win the 2013 elections and dominate the eleventh parliament, commanding 58 per cent of the seats in the National Assembly and 57 per cent in the Senate.[124] It subsequently used its numbers

122 Orange Democratic Movement, "Party Ideology and Our History" https://odm.co.ke/odm-party-ideology-and-our-history/ (accessed 24 February 2024).

123 According to the 2019 census. See Kenya National Bureau of Statistics (KNBS), "2019 Kenya Population and Housing census", Nairobi, KNBS (2019).

124 Inter-Parliamentary Union, "Kenya National Assembly Elections in 2013", http://archive.ipu.org/parline-e/reports/arc/2167_13.htm (accessed 24 February 2024).

to force a majority vote on issues and laws that it wanted passed in what came to be known popularly as the "tyranny of numbers".[125]

In this regard, a clear pattern developed in which the Alliance, at the behest of its party leaders – in this case, then President Kenyatta and Deputy President Ruto – would use its parliamentary majority in attempts to side-step, mutilate, or ignore certain provisions of the Constitution.[126] There was no clear separation between the executive and MPs elected on a Jubilee ticket; as such, these MPs were not in a position to provide effective oversight of the executive, given that their strong allegiance to party politics meant that their decision-making capabilities were dominated by their party leaders.[127]

This dangerous trend began during President Kenyatta's first term and was replicated in his second when he won the 2017 elections. However, as had happened in the case of NARC, at the start of his second term the Alliance fragmented into factions owing to disagreements over power-sharing between Kenyatta and Ruto when Kenyatta chose to call a truce and work with Odinga in what was known as "the handshake".[128] Nevertheless, this truce brought the entire Parliament under Kenyatta's control since Odinga could now be relied upon to marshal those MPs allied to him to support the President's motions in Parliament.[129] In essence, it completed the fusion of

125 W Maina, "What Tyranny of Numbers? Inside Mutahi Ngunyi's Numerology", Nairobi, AfriCOG (2013).

126 G Murunga, D Okello, and A Sjogren, "Preface", in G Murunga, D Okello, and A Sjogren (eds.), *Kenya: The Struggle for a New Constitutional Order*, London, Zed Books (2014), p ix.

127 It also saw Parliament openly ignoring court orders at the instruction of the President, who sought to enact unconstitutional laws in defiance of the doctrine of separation of powers. See B Bwire, "How Far is Too Far? The Separation of Powers Doctrine and Judicial Review of Legislative Action in Kenya", Unpublished PhD Thesis, University of Nairobi (2020), p 227.

128 E Okumu, "How We Got Here: Story of Handshake", *The Standard*, 12 August 2019, https://www.standardmedia.co.ke/politics/article/2001315921/the-story-of-handshake (accessed 19 November 2024).

129 They later launched the Building Bridges Initiative, which was a proposed set of constitutional amendments for bringing about a more inclusive political structure with new positions, such as a prime minister and deputies, introduced in the executive. This was vehemently opposed by President Ruto, whose 2013 agreement with Kenyatta was that after Kenyatta had served his two terms, he would back Ruto for President in 2022. See Building Bridges Taskforce, "Highlights of the Report of the Building Bridges Initiative Taskforce", https://dc.sourceafrica.net/documents/120776-Highlights-of-the-Report-of-the-Building-Bridges.html (accessed 24 February 2024).

the executive and the legislature that began in his first term; henceforth, the country could be said to have reverted to a political structure dominated by a single party, just as KANU had done in the past.

However, in the run-up to the 2022 elections, Ruto finally split with Kenyatta and led his faction out of the Jubilee Alliance to form yet another coalition, the Kenya Kwanza Alliance,[130] which would serve as his instrument for contesting the presidency. In keeping with past practice, ethnic arithmetic was at the core of the coalitions formed to serve as vehicles for the top two presidential contenders in the 2022 elections, Ruto and Odinga. Ruto went on to choose Rigathi Gachagua (Kikuyu) as his running mate as he moved to consolidate the crucial Kikuyu and Kalenjin voting blocs while at the same time seeking to establish alliances with other ethnic groups. For his part, Kenyatta chose to back Odinga's presidential bid and have his Jubilee party join the Odinga-led Azimio La Umoja-One Kenya Party.[131] Odinga selected Martha Karua (Kikuyu) as his running mate; Ruto's Kenya Kwanza Alliance went on to win the elections and form the current government.[132]

President Ruto's Kenya Kwanza government is treading the same path that Kenyatta paved in terms of blurring the separation between the executive and Parliament. This political fusion of the executive and legislature, coupled with strong party politics and ruling-party domination of administrative decision-making, severely limits Parliament's ability to constrain executive power. In turn, this creates opportunities for the re-centralisation

130 Its constituent parties are Ruto's United Democratic Alliance (UDA); the Amani National Congress; FORD-Kenya; Chama Cha Kazi; the Devolution Party of Kenya; Economic Freedom Party; Farmers Party; Service Party; Tujibebe Wakenya Party; Umoja na Maendeleo Party; Democratic Party; Grand Dream Democratic Party; Chama Cha Mashinani; and National Agenda Party of Kenya.

131 Its constituent parties are as follows: the ODM; Jubilee Party; Wiper Democratic Movement; KANU; NARC; NARC-Kenya; Muungano Party; Maendeleo Chap Chap Party; Democratic Action Party-Kenya; United Party of Independent Alliance; United Democratic Movement; United Progressive Alliance; Pamoja African Alliance; Kenya Union Party; Union Democratic Party; Movement for Democracy and Growth; Kenya Reform Party; Chama Cha Uzalendo; Party for Peace and Democracy; National Liberal Party; People's Trust Party; Ubuntu People's Forum; Party of National Unity; and Party for Growth and Prosperity.

132 Ruto won the presidential elections with 50.5 per cent of the vote as against Raila's 48.8 per cent. This was disputed by Raila, however, who filed a petition at the Supreme Court; the Court went on to uphold Ruto's victory. See *Odinga & 16 others v Ruto & 10 others; Law Society of Kenya & 4 others (Amicus Curiae)* [2022] KESC 54 (KLR).

of power in the executive, which was the key deficiency of the structure that bred the dictatorial excesses of the KANU regime. Such a fused structure is a major hindrance to Kenyan democracy since it essentially enables the President to rule by decree – all of which represents a great regression in the progress the country has made since the reintroduction of multiparty politics in 1992.

Nevertheless, the judiciary's invocation of the safeguards in the 2010 Constitution give Kenyans hope. The judiciary is serving as an effective watchdog over democracy, especially in its interpretative role under Article 165(3)(d) of the 2010 Constitution, as is seen in the cases brought before it seeking judicial review of executive or legislative action where such action is deemed unconstitutional.[133] The judiciary has been consistent in issuing orders that invoke constitutional safeguards to prevent excesses in the exercise of either executive or legislative power, which is in keeping with the doctrine of separation of powers. This began during the first term of Kenyatta's presidency and continues to date, with the courts in some instances declaring presidential decrees or laws passed by Parliament as being in contravention of the Constitution. For now, it is the judiciary alone which is fighting to uphold democracy; as for political parties, in their current form they lack the capacity to ensure democracy within their own organisations, let alone at the national level.

2.5 The role of the Office of the Registrar of Political Parties

The Office of the Registrar of Political Parties has a crucial role to play in facilitating intra-party democracy, given that its mandate is to monitor, regulate, and enforce compliance with the Political Parties Act. Under its watch, the financing of political parties has improved greatly thanks to its administration of the Political Parties Fund, which is established under section 28 of the Political Parties Act. This fund gives parties access to 0.3 per cent of national revenue, alongside other revenue sources of their own such as membership fees, contributions, and donations.[134] Stringent administration of the fund by the Registrar, combined with oversight of

133 . See, for example, *Petition No.71 of 2013*; *Petition No. 628 of 2014* (2015) eKLR; *Coalition for Reform and Democracy (CORD) & 2 others v Republic of Kenya & 10 others* (2015) eKLR; *Constitutional Petition E005 and E001(Consolidated) of 2021.*

134 In 2023, the top three recipients of money from the fund were the UDA (KES 577.2 million), ODM (KES 308.3 million), and Jubilee Party (KES 135.1 million). See F

how parties spend the monies received, can help ensure that funding is used to establish and maintain sound internal party structures that enable parties to hold regular, free, and fair party elections. This would promote internal party democracy and support the institutional continuity of Kenyan political parties beyond election years alone; in turn, this could help them wean themselves off their dependency on their founding patrons, evolve organically, and organise themselves on the basis of ideologies that enable them to undertake recruitment and grow their membership bases.

3. The impact of ethnicity on Kenya's democracy

Despite the fact that the reintroduction of multiparty politics in 1992 signalled a major change in Kenya's political direction, "the commitment of Kenya's leadership and its people to the realities of multiparty democracy was always ambiguous".[135] This ambiguity is reflected in the inchoate manner in which opposition parties have been formed, structured, and run. From the outset, they were set up as patronage parties[136] wholly dependent on party leaders, figures whose ascension to leadership was solely on account of their role as the founders of the party. Moreover, ethnicity emerged as a central factor in party mobilisation and sensitisation of members,[137] giving credence to President Moi's ominous warning that the introduction of multiparty politics would divide Kenyans into rival ethnically-based political parties.[138]

Fjelde and Hoglund observe that Kenyan politicians base their mobilisation and sensitisation of voters on ethnicity, which they then use as the

Kagonye, "Full List: Millions of Shillings Your Party has Pocketed from Political Parties Fund", *The Standard*, 2022, https://www.standardmedia.co.ke/article/2001459893/full-list-millions-of-shillings-your-party-has-pocketed-from-political-parties-fund (accessed 25 February 2024).

135 Throup and Hornsby, *supra* n. 25, p 2.

136 Political parties where party leaders use their own private resources to run the party and consolidate support. See P Kopecky, JH Meyer-Sahling, and M Spirova, "(Extreme) Political Polarisation and Party Patronage", 37 (2022) *Irish Political Studies*, pp 218–243.

137 H Fjelde and K Hoglund, "Ethnic Politics and Elite Competition: The Roots of Electoral Violence in Kenya", in MS Kovacs and J Bjarnesen (eds.), *Violence in African Elections: Between Democracy and Big Mana Politics*, London, Zed Books (2018), p 27.

138 D Throup, "Elections and Political Legitimacy in Kenya", 63 (1993) *Africa*, pp 390–394.

conceptual prism through which to explain actual or perceived inequalities in the distribution of national resources.[139] Kenyan political parties are thus a curious amalgam of ethnic alliances; those which are composed of the largest ethnic groups continue to dominate Kenyan politics in much the same way as KANU did, albeit realigning, reinventing, and rebranding themselves as new parties with each passing election.

This echoes Kanyinga's observation that Kenyan parties are poorly organised, lack sufficient financing, are without distinct ideological grounding, and are active only in election years.[140] In addition, the trend since the defeat of the KANU regime in the 2002 elections is for coalitions to be formed for the sole purpose of maximising votes in order to win elections and thereafter exercise power.[141] They are also averse to holding free, fair, and peaceful party elections, and once in power, inevitably splinter into fragments along the ethnic lines represented by their constituent parties.[142]

Although Article 91(2)(a) of the Constitution prohibits the formation of ethnically-based political parties, this prohibition is ineffective in the context of a first-past-the-post (FPTP) electoral system[143] in a non-homogeneous and multi-ethnic society such as Kenya. Political parties follow the trend of forming alliances based on ethnicity – primarily so as to expand their vote baskets and increase their chances of winning more seats – as opposed to forming alliances based on a congruence of ideologies. The FPTP system in the Kenyan context leads to a winner-take-all politics across all arms and at all levels of government and, as a result, to the exclusion of those who do not win elections. This provides a basis for politicians' exclusionary ethnicisation of social, political, and economic spaces, which is potentially a catalyst for violence.[144] It is a state of affairs which stands

139 Fjelde and Hoglund, *supra* n. 137, p 27.

140 Kanyinga, *supra* n. 58, p 155.

141 *Ibid.*

142 *Ibid.*

143 The FPTP system is the simplest form of a plurality or majority electoral system: the winning candidate is the one who gets more votes than any other candidate, even if this is not an absolute majority (that is, more 50 per cent) of valid votes. For the Kenyan context, see B Bwire, "Constitutional Quotas and Women's Political Representation: A Way Out of the Kenyan Dilemma", Unpublished LLM Thesis, University of Nairobi (2012).

144 M Mutua, *Kenya's Quest for Democracy: Taming the Leviathan,* Colorado, Lynee Reiner Publishers (2008).

in direct contrast to the conceptualisation of democracy as a means of containing violence and stabilising political competition.[145]

A possible solution lies in Arend Lijphart's influential model of consociational democracy, which posits that ethnic diversity can be managed by infusing measures that protect the interests of each community into the foundations of the political system.[146] Lijphart identifies executive power-sharing among the representatives of all significant groups as the key pillar of consociationalism,[147] and it is this aspect of consociationalism which is proposed here as a stabiliser of Kenyan politics. Indeed, this has been proposed several times in the past – in 1967, 1970, and 1992; in 2002 in the NARC memorandum of understanding; in 2002–2010 in proposals made during the drafting of the 2010 Constitution; and, recently, in 2019, under the Building Bridges Initiative.[148]

Although these proposals were never permanently integrated in the Kenyan democratic system by way of constitutional amendment, they have prompted different regimes to share power on this basis, albeit temporarily and usually as a reactive measure. This has helped overcome periods of political volatility, and resulted in legislative and policy reforms that strengthened Kenya's democracy. In 1997 when Moi's KANU shared power with Odinga's LDP, it helped move along the Inter-Parliamentary Parties Group reforms, which levelled the political playing field as well as paved the way for constitutional reforms that culminated in the promulgation of the 2010 Constitution.[149] The NARC coalition government, before it dissolved along

145 M Ossome, "States of Violence: Structural Dynamics of Gendered, Ethnicized, and Sexualized Violence in Kenya's Democratic Transitions", Unpublished PhD Thesis, University of Witwatersrand (2015).

146 A Lijphart, *The Politics of Accommodation: Pluralism and Democracy in the Netherlands,* California, University of California Press (1968).

147 According to Lijphart, the four pillars of consociationalism are (a) executive power-sharing among the representatives of all significant groups; (b) a high degree of internal autonomy for groups that wish to have it; (c) proportional representation in civil service positions and public funds; and (d) a minority veto on the most vital issues.

148 The proposals all focused on further decentralising the executive by introducing more executive positions such as a prime minister, more deputy-president slots, and an official leader of the opposition, with all of these positions based on separate mandates derived from executive power.

149 The reforms produced the Constitution of Kenya Review Act of 1997, enabling a comprehensive constitutional review after the elections. Consequently, the Constitution of Kenya Review Commission (CKRC) was established in 2000 under the leadership of the renowned Kenyan constitutional scholar, Yash Pal Ghai. It

ethnic fissures, was able to shepherd the constitutional review process that gave rise to the 2010 Constitution.[150] Power-sharing also saved the country from the brink of the precipice after the 2007 post-election violence,[151] and, more recently, helped calm it after the 2017 elections.[152]

Ultimately, proposals for constitutionally entrenched power-sharing mechanisms merit reconsideration given that whenever the government has entered into informal power-sharing agreements with other parties, it has stabilised Kenyan politics and spurred democratic growth.

4. Conclusion

Kenyan political parties continue to struggle to achieve intra-party democracy despite having a constitutional and legislative framework geared to that end and prescribing key internal infrastructure, such as a written constitution specifying the party's structures and providing for the election of office-holders. This continuing struggle is due primarily to their failure to achieve internal organisational coherence across all organs and levels of the party, as a result of which they are unable to hold free and fair elections for internal positions. The problem is compounded by the enduring trend in which coalitions are formed only to disband in due course because they are unable to achieve internal democracy.

Nevertheless, Kenyan parties can achieve progressive institutionalisation by complying with the mandatory requirements of the 2010 Constitution and the provisions of the 2011 Political Parties Act – which together provide a comprehensive constitutional and legislative framework to facilitate intra-party democracy. Moreover, the growing prominence of the Office of the Registrar of Political Parties in the regulation of the internal affairs of political parties is another bulwark against any regression by the parties. Ultimately, the continued realisation of the requirements of the Constitution and the Political Parties Act, under the oversight of the Office of the

---

was the CKRC which oversaw the consultative process of the drafting of the 2010 Constitution.

150 After the NARC government came to power, it reconvened the National Constitutional Conference under the Constitution of Kenya Review Act, Cap. 3A, to continue the constitution-making process led by the CKRC; the decade-long process of constitutional reform that began in 2000 was concluded in August 2010 with the adoption of the 2010 Constitution.

151 CIPEV, *supra*, n. 78.

152 Okumu, *supra*, n. 128.

Registrar of Political Parties, will steadily build internal democracy within Kenyan political parties and coalitions.

However, there remains the greater challenge of the impact of negative ethnicity on Kenya's democracy as a whole. The positive results of those instances where the government has shared power with other political partics can be studied and used to build a case for the reconsideration of previous proposals to have constitutionally entrenched power-sharing mechanisms. This can help to permanently surmount this recurring challenge that every so often ignites volatility and instability within Kenya's democracy.

References

Books, articles, chapters in books, and others

"Ford Kenya: Our History", *Ford Kenya Party*, https://www.fordkenya.party/our-history/ (accessed 18 February 2024)

"Kenyan Parties Merge Ahead of Presidential Elections", *Voice of America*, 18 March 2002, https://www.voanews.com/a/a-13-a-2002-03-18-17-kenyan/392132.html (accessed 19 November 2024)

"Merger to Change Kenya Politics", *News24*, 18 March 2002, https://www.news24.com/news24/Africa/Features/Merger-to-change-Kenya-politics-20020318 (accessed 30 December 2024)

"The Deal and the Deal Makers in Kibaki's 2002 Victory", *Nation*, 30 August 2008, https://nation.africa/kenya/news/the-deal-and-deal-makers-in-kibaki-s-2002-victory-557104 (accessed 19 November 2024)

Archive.ipu, "Kenya Parliamentary Election Results 1997", http://archive.ipu.org/parline-e/reports/arc/2167_97.htm (accessed 20 February 2024)

Asingo PO, "Party Strengths, Partisan Identities and Voter Mobilization in the Kenya Elections of 2013", in F Otieno (ed.), *New Constitution, Same Old Challenges: Reflections on Kenya's 2013 General Elections,* Nairobi, Society for International Development and Uraia Trust (2015)

Awuor L and Otieno WE, *Case Digest of the Decisions of the Political Parties Dispute Tribunal,* Nairobi, National Council for Law Reporting (2013)

Barkan JD and Henderson RE, "Toward Credible and Legitimate Elections in Kenya: Part II IFES Assessment Report", Nairobi, USAID (May 1997)

Building Bridges Taskforce, "Highlights of the Report of the Building Bridges Initiative Taskforce", https://dc.sourceafrica.net/documents/120776-Highlights-of-the-Report-of-the-Building-Bridges.html (accessed 24 February 2024)

Bwire B, "Constitutional Quotas and Women's Political Representation: A Way Out of the Kenyan Dilemma", Unpublished LLM Thesis, University of Nairobi (2012)

Bwire B, "How Far is Too Far? The Separation of Powers Doctrine and Judicial Review of Legislative Action in Kenya", Unpublished PhD Thesis, University of Nairobi (2021)

Bwire B, "Interrogating the Evolution of a Constitutionally-legitimised 'Big Man' Political Culture and its Influence on Political Participation by Kenyan Youth", 23 (2023) *African Human Rights Law Journal,* pp 256–277

Central Bureau of Statistics, "Kenya Population Census, 1989, Volume I" (March 1994)

Cheeseman N, Lynch G and Willis J, "Democracy and its Discontents: Understanding Kenya's 2013 Elections", 8 (2014) *Journal of Eastern African Studies,* pp 2–24

Commission of Inquiry into Post-Election Violence (CIPEV), *Report of The Commission of Inquiry into Post-Election Violence,* Nairobi, Government of Kenya (16 October 2008)

E Okumu, "How We Got Here: Story of Handshake", *The Standard,* 12 August 2019, https://www.standardmedia.co.ke/politics/article/2001315921/the-story-of-handshake (accessed 19 November 2024)

Electoral Institute for Sustainable Democracy in Africa (EISA), *Case Digest: Decisions of the IEBC Dispute Committee,* Nairobi, EISA (2013)

EU Election Observation Mission, "Kenya General Elections 27 December 2002 Final Report", Nairobi, EU Observation Mission (2002)

Fjelde H and Hoglund K, "Ethnic Politics and Elite Competition: The Roots of Electoral Violence in Kenya", in Kovacs MS and Bjarnesen J (eds.), *Violence in African Elections: Between Democracy and Big Mana Politics,* London, Zed Books, (2018), pp 27–46

Ginsburg T and Huq AZ, *How to Save a Constitutional Democracy,* Chicago, University of Chicago Press (2018)

Holmquist F and Ford M, "Kenya: State and Civil Society the First Year after the Election", 41 (1994) *Africa Today,* pp 5–21

Ignazi P, "The Four Knights of Intra Party Democracy: A Rescue for Party Delegitimation", 26 (2020) *Party Politics,* pp 9–20

Independent Review Commission (IREC), *Report of the Independent Review Commission on the General Elections held in Kenya on 27 December 2007,* Nairobi, Government of Kenya (17 September 2008)

Inter-Parliamentary Union, "Kenya National Assembly Elections in 2013", http://archive.ipu.org/parline-e/reports/arc/2167_13.htm (accessed 24 February 2024)

Juma D, "The Normative Foundations of Constitution Making in Kenya: The Judiciary Past, Present, and Future", in C Murungi (ed.), *Judiciary Watch Report, Vol. IX: Constitutional Change, Democratic Transition and the Role of the Judiciary in Government Reform: Questions and Lessons for Kenya,* Nairobi, Kenya Section of the International Commission of Jurists (2010), pp 215–240

Kadima D and Owuor F, "Kenya's Decade of Experiments with Political Party Alliances and Coalitions: Motivations, Impacts and Prospects", 13 (2014) *Journal of African Elections,* pp 150–180

Kagonye F, "Full List: Millions of Shillings Your Party has Pocketed from Political Parties Fund", *The Standard,* 2022 https://www.standardmedia.co.ke/article/2001459893/full-list-millions-of-shillings-your-party-has-pocketed-from-political-parties-fund (accessed 25 February 2024)

Kamau J, "Trying Times for George Saitoti under President Moi", *Nation,* 12 March 2020, https://nation.africa/kenya/nation-prime/trying-times-for-george-saitoti-under-president-moi-258962 (accessed 19 November 2024)

Kanyinga K, *Kenya: Democracy and Political Participation,* Nairobi, Open Society Initiative for Eastern Africa (2014)

Karume S, "Factional Intrigues and Alliance Politics: The Case of NARC in Kenya's 2002 Elections", 2 (2003) *Journal of African Elections,* pp 1–13

Kenya National Bureau of Statistics (KNBS), "2019 Kenya Population and Housing census", Nairobi, KNBS (2019)

Kenya National Commission on Human Rights (KNCHR), "Break from the Past? A Monitoring Report of the 2013 Political Party Nominations", Nairobi, Kenya National Commission on Human Rights (2013)

Klopp JM and Orina JR, "University Crisis, Student Activism, and the Contemporary Struggle for Democracy in Kenya", 45 (2002) *African Studies Review,* pp 43–76

Kopecky P, Meyer-Sahling JH, and Spirova M, "(Extreme) Political Polarisation and Party Patronage", 37 (2022) *Irish Political Studies,* pp 218–243

Lagoutte S and Petersen MJ, *Political Parties and Human Rights: An Introduction,* Copenhagen, Danish Institute for Parties and Democracy (2018)

Lijphart A, *The Politics of Accommodation: Pluralism and Democracy in the Netherlands,* California, University of California Press (1968)

Loughlin M, "The Contemporary Crisis of Constitutional Democracy", 39 (2019) *Oxford Journal of Legal Studies,* pp 435–454

Maina W, "What Tyranny of Numbers? Inside Mutahi Ngunyi's Numerology", Nairobi, AfriCOG (2013)

Mbula R and Gisesa N, "The Life and Times of Political Heavyweight Simeon Nyachae", *Nation,* 2 February 2021, https://nation.africa/kenya/news/-life-times-nyachae-3276590 (accessed 19 November 2024)

Mueller SD, "Government and Opposition in Kenya: 1966–1969", 22 (1984) *Journal of Modern African Studies,* pp 399–427

Muigai G, "Kenya's Opposition and the Crisis of Governance" 21 (1993) *Issue,* pp 26–34

Murunga G, Okello D, and Sjogren A, "Preface", in Murunga G, Okello D, and Sjogren A (eds.), *Kenya: The Struggle for a New Constitutional Order,* London, Zed Books (2014), pp viii–xi

Mutua M, *Kenya's Quest for Democracy: Taming the Leviathan,* Colorado, Lynee Reiner Publishers (2008)

Mwende M, "State Canonizes Kibaki as Kenya's Longest Serving MP", *Pulse,* 27 April 2022, https://www.pulselive.co.ke/news/local/senate-canonises-mwai-kibaki-as-kenyas-longest-serving-mp-for-10-consecutive-terms/gvnvzjp (accessed 19 November 2024)

National Rainbow Coalition (NARC), "Democracy and Empowerment: Manifesto of the National Rainbow Coalition (NARC)", November 2002, http://libraryir.parliament.go.ke/handle/123456789/15687 (accessed 19 November 2024)

National Rainbow Coalition (NARC), "Democracy and Empowerment: Manifesto for the National Rainbow Coalition (NARC)", November 2002, http://libraryir.parliament.go.ke/handle/123456789/15687 (accessed 19 November 2024)

Odhiambo-Mbai C, "The Rise and Fall of the Autocratic State in Kenya", in WO Oyugi, P Wanyande, and C Odhiambo-Mbai (eds.), *The Politics of Transition in Kenya: From Kanu to NARC,* Nairobi, Heinrich Boll Foundation (2003), pp 51–95

Office of the Registrar of Political Parties, "Post-Election Evaluation Report" (May 2023)

Orange Democratic Movement, "Party Ideology and Our History", https://odm.co.ke/odm-party-ideology-and-our-history/ (accessed 24 February 2024)

Ossome M, "States of Violence: Structural Dynamics of Gendered, Ethnicized, and Sexualized Violence in Kenya's Democratic Transitions", Unpublished PhD Thesis, University of Witwatersrand (2015)

SE Scarrow, PD Webb and T Poguntke, "Intra Party Decision Making in Contemporary Europe: Improving Representation or Ruling with Empty Shells", 37 (2022) *Irish Political Studies*, pp 196–217

The Carter Center, *Observing Kenya's March 2013 Elections: Final Report*, Atlanta, The Carter Center (2014)

The Carter Center, *Observing the 2002 Kenya Elections: Final Report*, Atlanta, The Carter Center (May 2003)

Throup D and Hornsby C, *Multi-Party Politics in Kenya: The Kenyatta & Moi States & the Triumph of the System in the 1992 Election,* Nairobi, East African Educational Publishers (1998)

Throup D, "Elections and Political Legitimacy in Kenya", 63 (1993) *Africa,* pp 390–394

Wanyande P and Asingo PO, "Beyond Election Campaign Rhetoric: Challenges Facing the National Rainbow Coalition (NARC)", 31 (2004) *African Review,* pp 18–38

Table of cases

Court of Appeal of Kenya, *Kenneth Stanley Njindo Matiba v Daniel Toroitich Arap Moi [1994]*, Civil Application NAI 241 of 1993, Electronic Kenya Law Reports (eKLR) https://kenyalaw.org/caselaw/cases/view/73009/ (accessed 19 November 2024)

Court of Appeal of Kenya, *Kibaki v Moi & 2 others (No.2) (2008)*, Election Petitions (EP) 308, Kenya Law Reports (KLR)

High Court of Kenya, *Coalition for Reform and Democracy (CORD) & 2 others v Republic of Kenya & 10 others [2015],* Petition 628, 630 of 2014 & 12 of 2015 (Consolidated), Electronic Kenya Law Reports (eKLR), https://kenyalaw.org/caselaw/cases/view/106083/ (accessed 19 November 2024)

High Court of Kenya, *Coalition for Reform and Democracy (CORD) & 2 others v Republic of Kenya &10; others [2015]*, Petition No. 628, 630 of 2014 and 12 of 2015 (Consolidated) (2015), Electronic Kenya Law Reports (eKLR), https://kenyalaw.org/caselaw/cases/view/106083/ (accessed 19 November 2024)

High Court of Kenya, *Institute of Social Accountability & another v National Assembly & 4 others [2015]*, Petition No.71 of 2013 (2015), Electronic Kenya Law Reports (eKLR), https://kenyalaw.org/caselaw/cases/view/105977/ (accessed 19 November 2024).

High Court of Kenya, *International Centre for Policy and Conflict & 5 others v Attorney General & 5 others [2013]*, Petition Nos 552, 554, 573 & 579 of 2012 (Consolidated), Electronic Kenya Law Reports (eKLR), https://kenyalaw.org/caselaw/cases/view/86293 (accessed 19 November 2024)

High Court of Kenya, *Waweru & 3 others (suing as officials of Kitengela Bar Owners Association) & another v National Assembly & 2 others; Institute of Certified Public Accountants of Kenya (ICPAK) & 2 others (Interested Parties)*, Constitutional Petition E005 and E001(Consolidated) of 2021, Judgement, 20 September 2021, Electronic Kenya Law Reports (eKLR), https://kenyalaw.org/caselaw/cases/view/218609/ (accessed 19 November 2024)

Supreme Court of Kenya, *Odinga & 16 others v Ruto & 10 others; Law Society of Kenya & 4 others (Amicus Curiae)* Presidential Election Petition E005, E001, E002, E003, E004, E007 & E008 of 2022 (Consolidated) [2022] KESC 54 (KLR) (Election Petitions), Judgment, 5 September 2022, Kenya Law Reports (KLR), https://kenyalaw.org/caselaw/cases/view/240578/ (accessed 19 November 2024)

Table of legislation

Constitution of Kenya (Amendment) Act No. 7 of 1982, http://kenyalaw.org/kl/index.php?id=9631 (accessed 8 February 2024)

Constitution of Kenya (Amendment) Act No. 12 of 1991, https://www.kenyalaw.org/kl/index.php?id=9631 (accessed 20 October 2024)

Constitution of Kenya (Amendment) Act No. 9 of 1997, https://www.kenyalaw.org/kl/index.php?id=9631 (accessed 20 October 2024)

Constitution of Kenya 2010, http://kenyalaw.org/kl/index.php?id=398 (accessed 11 February 2024)

Election Offences Act (Cap. 66), http://kenyalaw.org:8181/exist/kenyalex/actview.xql?actid=CAP.%2066 (accessed 20 October 2024)

International Covenant on Civil and Political Rights (ICCPR) UN Treaty Series, Vol 999, I-14668, 179, 19 December 1966, https://treaties.un.org/PAGES/ViewDetails.aspx?chapter=4&clang=_en&mtdsg_no=IV-4&src=TREATY (accessed 16 October 2024)

Political Parties Act, Act No. 10 of 2007, Cap 7A, http://kenyalaw.org/kl/index.php?id=5571 (accessed 11 February 2024)

Political Parties Act, No. 11 of 2011, Cap 7D, http://kenyalaw.org:8181/exist/kenyalex/actview.xql?actid=CAP.%207D (accessed 20 October 2024)

Chapter 8 Party Constitutionalisation and Political Patrimonialism in Nigeria

Lukman Abdulrauf and Johannes Socher

1. Introduction

The biggest challenge to Nigeria's democratic development, it has been argued, is its political party system.[1] While there are different ways of looking at it, the country's party system is perhaps best understood by means of the concept of political patrimonialism. According to Ukana Ikpe, for example, this term describes a system of government based on personal rule in which state officers dispense resources and privileges to subordinates in exchange for loyalty and services. Some of its key features include the control of political power by a godfather or party baron; the practice of treating political offices as personal rewards and benefits for their incumbents; utilising public authority to serve godfathers or party barons; and the deployment of a system of patron-client networks and relationships.[2]

In Nigeria, political patrimonialism is pervasive at both the federal and state levels, where political godfathers or party barons wield significant influence, often leveraging ethno-religious agendas to solidify their dominance within political parties. This raises fundamental questions about the effectiveness of the regulation of political parties and its implications for constitutionalism in Nigeria.

This chapter critically examines the constitutionalisation of political parties and assesses its role in combatting patrimonial politics in Nigeria. It argues that despite constitutional provisions and successive reforms of the regulatory framework governing political parties, undemocratic conduct by political parties is prevalent and often linked to patrimonial politics. Indeed, many of the crises and court cases regarding political parties in

1 See, for example, J Ibrahim, "Democratic Regression, Political Parties, and the Negation of the Popularity Principle", in W Adebanwi (ed.), *Democracy and Nigeria's Fourth Republic: Governance, Political Economy, and Party Politics 1999–2023,* Woodbridge, James Currey (2023), pp 107–128, 107.

2 UB Ikpe, "The Patrimonial State and Inter-Ethnic Conflicts in Nigeria", 32 (2009) *Ethnic and Racial Studies*, pp 679–697.

Nigeria are connected in one way or another to attempts by godfathers or party barons (that is powerful figures who control political parties, influence candidate selection, and shape electoral outcomes, often behind the scenes) to subvert democratic processes for their personal ends and to resist pushback against such actions. This, in turn, has increased inter-party migration, eliminating issue-based politics. Wale Adebanwi aptly notes that "there is little or no ideological implication for victory or success in electoral politics. What is often at stake, particularly for the elite, is access to resources."[3]

The chapter consists of five sections. Section 2 traces the evolution of party politics and multiparty democracy in Nigeria from the period of colonisation until today. Section 3 analyses the nature and scope of political party constitutionalisation in Nigeria, considering the current constitutional and statutory framework regulating political parties. This is followed in section 4 by an analysis of recent trends that significantly undermine political party constitutionalism in Nigeria. Section 5 concludes with a number of critical reflections on the prospects for political party constitutionalism in the country and proposes some ideas for reforms that could enhance the role that Nigerian parties play as essential agents of multiparty democracy.

2. The evolution of political parties in Nigeria: The road to patrimonialism

The historical evolution of Nigerian political parties can be divided into three main periods, each characterised by the prevailing circumstances of the time: the colonial period leading up to independence; military rule; and democratisation and multipartyism.[4]

---

3 W Adebanwi, "Nigeria's Fourth Republic: An Introduction", in W Adebanwi (ed.), *Democracy and Nigeria's Fourth Republic: Governance, Political Economy, and Party Politics 1999–2023,* Woodbridge, James Currey (2023), pp 1–32, 20.

4 Multipartyism was first instituted in 1960 but lasted only until the military took power in 1966. It was reintroduced in 1979, only to be abolished again by the military in 1983. For an alternative periodisation, one distinguishing four periods, see A Agbaje, "A Republic of Dashed Hopes? Party Politics and the Travails of Democracy in Nigeria's Fourth Republic", in W Adebanwi (ed.), *Democracy and Nigeria's Fourth Republic: Governance, Political Economy, and Party Politics 1999–2023,* Woodbridge, James Currey (2023), pp 129–48. See also N Danjibo and K Ashindorbe, "The Evolution and Pattern of Political Party Formation and the Search for National Integration in Nigeria", 5 (2018) *Brazilian Journal of African Studies*, pp 85–100.

2.1 From the colonial period to independence

Although the earliest Nigerian political associations can be traced to the turn of the twentieth century, the first genuine parties were formed only after the British colonial administration adopted a new constitution in 1922 that granted a limited Nigerian electorate the right to elect representatives in the legislative council.[5] The Nigerian National Democratic Party, founded in 1923, is often recognised as the first political party in the country. However, its influence was confined primarily to Lagos, where it focused on local issues and represented the interests of the Lagos elite. The first party with a broader reach was the National Youth Movement, founded in 1934, which established branches in other urban centres across Nigeria. This expansion signalled a shift towards a more inclusive and nationwide form of political organisation, thereby laying the groundwork for future political movements that sought to unify the country across regional and ethnic divides.[6]

From the 1940s onwards, a three-party system gradually emerged, with each party representing a particular region and ethnic group.[7] While the Action Group (AG) represented the interests of the Yoruba in the South, the Northern People's Congress (NPC) represented those of the Hausa and Fulani in the North; as for the National Council of Nigerians and the Cameroons (NCNC), it eventually came to represent the interests of the Igbo and the people of the League of Nations Mandate territories of Southern Cameroons.

Aside from this tripartite ethnic and regional division, what is important to note is that these pre-independence parties were structured around, and dominated by, strong individuals who eventually came to be considered the founding fathers of Nigerian independence: Obafemi Awolowo (AG), Ahmadu Bello and Abubakar Tafawa Balewa (NPC), and Nnamdi Azikiwe (NCNC). Moreover, as will be shown further below, some of the party practices that persist to this day may be traced to this early period. For instance, in 1953, the NCNC, under the leadership of Azikiwe, expelled members of the Eastern regional government from the party and success-

5 For detailed histories, see RL Sklar, *Nigerian Political Parties: Power in an Emergent African Nation*, Princeton, Princeton University Press (1963); U Udoma, *History and the Law of the Constitution of Nigeria*, Lagos, Malthouse Press (1994), pp 111–41.

6 Agbaje, *supra* n. 4, p 135; Sklar, *supra* n. 5, pp 46–7; Udoma, *supra* n. 5, p 111.

7 Sklar, *supra* n. 5, pp 87; Udoma, *supra* n. 5, pp 111.

fully brought a motion of no confidence against them in the regional parliament.[8] Remarkably, the motion against the ministers was not based on accusations of having committed any offence or acted against the NCNC constitution. “The only accusation was that they had refused to toe the party line,” Udo Udoma recalls in *History and Law of the Constitution of Nigeria*, describing Azikiwe’s role as the NCNC leader in this episode as “an extreme kind of dictatorship”.[9]

2.2 Military rule

Only six years following independence in 1960 and three years after the adoption of a republican constitution in 1963, Nigeria’s First Republic came to an abrupt end when a coup d’état ushered in a first period of military rule (1966–1979). For more than a decade, all political parties were banned; new parties were formed only after a transition process was initiated in 1978 by the military regime led by Olusegun Obasanjo (who would eventually return to power as Nigeria’s first president under the 1999 Constitution).

Two important features of political party regulation in Nigeria emerged during this period: the idea that parties should be “Pan-Nigerian”, and strict requirements for their registration to compete in elections.[10] As such, despite the initial announcement that 150 parties intended to compete in the upcoming elections to form the first parliament of Nigeria’s Second Republic (1979–1983), only 18 felt confident that they could meet the registration requirements: in the end, the military government recognised only five.[11] Of these, the National Party of Nigeria (NPN) emerged as predominant. Although it had its roots in the North and comprised many former NPC members, the NPN made efforts to expand beyond its regional base. It is here that the so-called zoning principle for the election of party officials was tested for the first time.[12]

8 *Ibid*, pp 123–28.
9 *Ibid*, pp 126, 128.
10 Ibrahim, *supra* n. 1, pp 108–109.
11 *Ibid*, p 109.
12 See “Zoning” in N Cheeseman, E Bertrand, and S Husaini, *Oxford Dictionary of African Politics*, Oxford, Oxford University Press (2019), https://www.oxfordreference.com/display/10.1093/acref/9780191828836.001.0001/acref-9780191828836-e-367 (accessed 18 June 2024). On the continuing relevance of the principle, see section 4.1 below.

During Nigeria's second period of military rule (1983–1999), political parties were again initially prohibited until the ban was lifted in 1989. New political parties were soon formed, but were banned again by the military when a two-party system was imposed, with the Social Democratic Party "slightly to the left" and the National Republican Convention "slightly to the right".[13] According to Eghosa Osaghae, in hindsight the "manufacturing" of these two parties can be seen as the creation of a new political class consisting of "cronies and protégés of powerful military leaders ... who became the godfathers and strongmen of post-1999 civilian politicians".[14] In contrast, it has also been suggested that the state-dictated creation of this two-party system came the closest to achieving truly national parties in Nigeria because stringent control on registration and funding of parties reduced ethnic and region-based politics.[15]

In any case, following a failed transition to civilian government in 1993, the two parties were banned again, with political pluralism reaching its low point in the ensuing period of military rule under Sani Abacha (1993–1998). The most drastic example is that of KenSaro-Wiwa, the leader of an organisation representing the indigenous Ogoni people, who was tried by a military tribunal and executed for allegedly masterminding the murder of Ogoni traditional leaders in 1995. The execution resulted in Nigeria's suspension from the Commonwealth and led to an important finding by the African Commission of Human and Peoples' Rights, holding that the right to freedom of association guaranteed in the African Charter on Human and Peoples' Rights (ACHPR) protects criticism of state action and that liability shall not be imputed from associations to individuals or vice versa.[16]

2.3 Democratisation and multipartyism

Shortly after Abacha's death in 1998, the current Constitution of 1999 was adopted. Initially, the Independent National Electoral Commission (INEC)

13 Ibrahim, *supra* n. 1, p 110.

14 EE Osaghae, "The Long Shadow of Nigeria's Military Epochs, 1966–79 and 1983–99", in A Carl LeVan and P Ukata (eds.), *The Oxford Handbook of Nigerian Politics*, Oxford, Oxford University Press (2018), pp 171–88, 183–84.

15 Danjibo and Ashindorbe, *supra* n. 4, p 91.

16 African Commission of Human and Peoples' Rights, *International Pen and Others (on behalf of Ken Saro-Wiwa) v Nigeria*, Communication Nos. 137/94, 139/94, 154/96 and 161/97, 1998.

recognised only three parties – the Peoples Democratic Party (PDP), the All-People's Party, and the Alliance for Democracy – with the PDP's candidate, Obasanjo, becoming Nigeria's first president under the new Constitution.[17] However, in the lead-up to the 2003 elections, the Nigerian Supreme Court stepped in and declared the INEC's guidelines for the registration of political parties as unconstitutional insofar as they imposed additional conditions for registration not provided for in the Constitution.[18] The decision removed undue barriers to registration for parties and marked a pivotal moment in broadening Nigeria's political landscape.

Although several further parties emerged thereafter, the PDP continued to dominate Nigerian politics, with Obasanjo (until 2007), Umaru Musa Yar'Adua (2007–2010) and Goodluck Jonathan (2010–2015) as presidents. This only changed in 2013 when several opposition parties merged and formed the All-Progressive Congress (APC),[19] eventually replacing the PDP as the ruling party in the 2015 elections. Although the APC has been in power since then, with Muhammadu Buhari (2015–23) and Bola Tinubu (since 2023) as presidents, the PDP remains highly influential and has provided relatively strong opposition, especially at the state level. In addition, the 2023 elections witnessed the emergence of a third major party, the Labour Party, which also made a good showing at the federal level and in some states.

3. The constitutional and legal framework regulating political parties

Nigeria's constitutional and legal framework regulating political parties is shaped by international, regional, and national instruments. Apart from its obligations under international human rights law guaranteeing the right to freedom of association,[20] Nigeria is one of only two countries in Africa to have domesticated the ACHPR,[21] thereby arguably making the relevant

17 Agbaje, *supra* n. 4, p 139.

18 Supreme Court of Nigeria, *INEC v Musa & Others,* 3 NWLR (Pt. 806), 2003.

19 See Agbaje, *supra* n. 4, p 147.

20 On international standards, see J Socher, "Constitutionalisation of Political Parties: International Standards and the Experience of Continental Europe", in this volume.

21 The other African country to have domesticated the ACHPR is Benin. In Nigeria, it was incorporated in domestic law through the African Charter on Human and Peoples' Rights (Enforcement and Ratification) Act, Ch. A9, Laws of the Federation of Nigeria 1990.

case law in relation to the regulation of political parties binding.[22] Moreover, in *Abacha v Fawehinmi*, the Nigerian Supreme Court made it clear that if there is a conflict between the ACHPR and national legislation, the provisions of the former prevail over domestic statutes.[23] That being said, the following section focuses on the national framework regulating Nigerian political parties – namely, the Constitution as amended in 2023,[24] complemented by the recently revised Electoral Act.[25]

3.1 Scope and limitations of political party regulation

Nigeria's Constitution provides a definition of political parties which is clearly centred around elections. According to section 299, the term "political party" includes "any association whose activities include canvassing for votes in support of a candidate for election to the office of President, Vice-President, Governor, Deputy Governor or membership of a legislative house or of a local government council". The right to form or belong to a political party is guaranteed in section 40 of the Constitution as a particular form of the right to freedom of association. In *Alhaji Abubakar Rimi v Peoples Redemption Party*, the High Court held that section 40 applies to "individuals, corporate and incorporate bodies, and enables them to come together voluntarily under a political banner or leave the association as they please".[26] Therefore, a law that prohibits public or civil service members from being eligible to be registered members of political parties was found to be contrary to the Constitution.[27] Conversely, in *AG Federation v Abubakar*, the Nigerian Supreme Court held that it is unconstitutional to

22 On regional standards for the regulation of political parties in Africa, see CM Fombad and J Socher, "Regional Standards for Regulating Political Parties in Africa", in this volume.

23 Supreme Court of Nigeria, *Abacha v Fawehinmi*, 6 NWLR (Pt. 660) 228, 2000.

24 Constitution of the Federal Republic of Nigeria, 1999, as amended in 2023, https://placng.org/i/wp-content/uploads/2023/05/Constitution-of-the-Federal-Republic-of-Nigeria-2023.pdf (accessed 16 April 2024).

25 Electoral Act 61 of 2022, https://placng.org/i/wp-content/uploads/2022/02/Electoral-Act-2022.pdf (accessed 9 March 2024).

26 High Court of Nigeria, Alhaji Abubakar Rimi v Peoples Redemption Party 2 NCLR 734 HC, 1981.

27 Ibid.

refuse or deny a citizen the right to leave or not to belong to a political party.[28]

The right to form and belong to a political party is not unlimited, however. While individual membership is open to every Nigerian citizen "irrespective of his place of origin, circumstance of birth, sex, religion or ethnic grouping",[29] the Constitution explicitly prohibits ethnic, religious, or regional political parties.[30] Moreover, parties must have their headquarters in Nigeria's capital, Abuja, and members of their governing bodies must "reflect the federal character of Nigeria".[31] The latter requirement is given further detail in a separate provision, which states that political parties fulfil it "only if members thereof belong to different States not being less in number than two-thirds of all the States of the Federation and the Federal Capital Territory, Abuja" (the so-called federal-character principle).[32]

3.2 Intra-Party democracy and promotion of democratic values

Nigeria's Constitution requires political parties to have statutes with rules providing for periodic elections on a democratic basis of the principal officers and members of the executive committee.[33] Elections of these officers and members must take place at regular intervals not exceeding four years.[34] In addition, the Electoral Act sets certain guidelines and rules to

---

28 Supreme Court of Nigeria, *AG Federation v Abubakar* 10 NWLR (Pt 1041), 2007. The case arose when Atiku Abubakar, while serving as Vice President from 1999 until 2007, resigned from the PDP and joined another party, the Action Congress (AC). In response, President Obasanjo declared the Vice President's office vacant. Abubakar challenged this decision, arguing that his term as Vice President was not affected by his decision to leave the PDP and join the AC. The Nigerian Supreme Court agreed, holding that the President did not have the authority to declare the Vice President's office vacant based on a change in party affiliation. The Court emphasised that the Constitution did not grant the President such power and that the Vice President's term of office was protected under the Constitution.

29 Section 222(b) of the Constitution.

30 Section 222(e) of the Constitution. For more detail on this prohibition, see M Bogaards, "Ethnic Party Bans and Institutional Engineering in Nigeria", 17 (2010) *Democratisation*, pp 730–749.

31 Sections 222(f) and 223(b) of the Constitution.

32 Section 223(2)(b) of the Constitution.

33 Section 223(1) of the Constitution.

34 Section 223(2)(a) of the Constitution.

ensure intra-party democracy, in particular by providing procedures for the conduct of party primaries, party congresses, and party conventions.[35]

Political parties, furthermore, shall promote democratic values and principles that enhance free and fair competition. The Constitution explicitly provides that the programmes and the aims and objects of political parties have to conform with the provisions in Chapter II of the Constitution, which contain the so-called fundamental objectives and directive principles of state policy.[36] These include several core democratic values such as social justice, equality, and non-discrimination. Although generally non-justiciable,[37] Chapter II of the Constitution is crucial in defining the basis of democracy in Nigeria.[38] It embodies aspirational values and standards which govern all branches of government entrusted with the exercise of political powers. Therefore, through this explicit link to Chapter II, the Constitution arguably defines Nigerian political parties as public institutions to be guided by these values and standards.[39]

3.3 Party financing

Nigeria's Constitution also regulates certain aspects of party financing.[40] In particular, its section 225 requires political parties to publish their assets and liabilities and submit a detailed annual statement and analysis of their sources of funds and other assets to the INEC, together with a statement of expenditure.[41] Moreover, a political party is constitutionally prohibited

35 See, for example, section 84 of the Electoral Act 2022, outlining detailed provisions for the conduct of party primaries.

36 Section 224 of the Constitution.

37 See section 6(6)(c) of the Constitution.

38 See BO Okere, "Fundamental Objectives and Directive Principles of State Policy under the Nigerian Constitution", 32 (1983) *International and Comparative Law Quarterly*, pp 214–228.

39 ES Nwauche, "Political Parties, the 1999 Constitution and the 2011 General Elections", 46 (2013) *Verfassung und Recht in Übersee/Law and Politics in Africa, Asia and Latin America*, pp 407–429.

40 For more detail on the regulation of party financing in Nigeria, see B Sule, *Political Party Financing and Electoral Politics in Nigeria's Fourth Republic*, Lanham, Lexington Books (2023), pp 145–166.

41 Section 225(1) and (2) of the Constitution.

from holding or possessing funds or assets outside Nigeria, or retaining funds or assets remitted or sent to it from outside the country.[42]

The Electoral Act complements these provisions and establishes electoral offences if political parties fail to comply with them.[43] In addition, the Act sets maximum election expenses, that is, "expenses incurred by a political party within the period from the date notice is given by the Commission to conduct an election up to and including, the polling day in respect of the particular election".[44] Since the adoption of the first Electoral Act in 2010, public funding is not available anymore, and parties finance themselves exclusively through private sources, which contributes to the numerous challenges that are discussed in detail below.

3.4 INEC registration and oversight

The formation of political parties is dependent on formal registration with the INEC.[45] Once registered, they need to continue to comply with all the registration requirements or else risk being de-registered by the INEC. An explicit provision in that regard was constitutionalised in 2017, with section 225A of the Constitution now providing that the INEC has the power to deregister a political party for

(a) breach of any of the requirements for registration;
(b) failure to win at least twenty-five percent of votes cast in (i) one State of the Federation in a Presidential election, or (ii) one Local Government of the State in a Governorship election;
(c) failure to win at least (i) one ward in the Chairmanship election, (ii) one seat in the National or State House of Assembly election, or (iii) one seat in the Councillorship election.

Nigerian political parties are regularly de-registered ahead of elections in high numbers. For example, prior to the 2023 general elections, the INEC de-registered more than 70 parties for not fulfilling the geographical representation requirement.[46]

42 Section 225(3) of the Constitution.
43 Sections 85 and 86 of the Electoral Act 2022.
44 Sections 88 and 89(1) of the Electoral Act 2022.
45 Section 222(a) of the Constitution.
46 See "Supreme Court Upholds INEC's Deregistration of 22 Political Parties", *Premium Times,* 25 March 2022, https://www.premiumtimesng.com/news/headlines/519559-s

Apart from being responsible for registration and de-registration, the INEC has a number of oversight functions in regard to political parties.[47] In particular, it is tasked with monitoring their organisation and operations – including their conventions, congresses and primaries, and political campaigns – and establishing rules and regulations for governing party activities.[48] The INEC also examines and audits the funds and accounts of political parties annually and submits a report on this examination to Parliament.[49] These constitutional provisions are complemented, and elaborated upon, by the Electoral Act. For example, the Act requires that the application for registration as a political party must be submitted to the INEC at least one year before the next general election [50]

4. Party constitutionalism and patrimonialism: Key challenges

As was posited at the outset, the concept of political patrimonialism arguably provides the best means of understanding the Nigerian party system. One of the system's most striking features is the phenomenon of godfathers and party barons controlling political parties.[51] For example, Abubakar Momoh has argued that the "influence and power of godfathers have continued to shape and reshape the nature of internal democracy within political parties and this continues to play a significant role in understanding the crises in political parties in Nigeria".[52] Focusing on developments surrounding the most recent elections in 2023 and also drawing on the experiences of the two preceding elections in 2015 and 2019, this section shows how political patrimonialism has been able to corrupt and

upreme-court-upholds-inecs-deregistration-of-22-political-parties.html (accessed 13 September 2023).

47 See R Suberu, "Nigeria in Search of a Credible Electoral Administration: Recent Reforms and Persistent Challenges", in CM Fombad and N Steytler (eds.), *Democracy, Elections, and Constitutionalism in Africa*, Oxford, Oxford University Press (2021), pp 331–360.

48 Third Schedule, item F, section 15(c) and (f) of the Constitution.

49 Section 226(1) of the Constitution.

50 Section 75(1) of the Electoral Act 2022.

51 See, for example, O Fasan, "Nigeria's Patrimonial Politics and Different Presidents", *Business Day*, 9 March 2015, https://businessday.ng/columnist/article/nigerias-patrimonial-politics-and-diffident-presidents/ (accessed 6 June 2024).

52 A Momoh, "Party System and Democracy in Nigeria", in O Obafemi, S Egwu, O Ibeanu and J Ibrahim (eds.), *Political Parties and Democracy in Nigeria,* Kuru, National Institute of Policy and Strategic Studies (2014), p 91.

compromise the ostensibly robust normative framework governing political parties in Nigeria.

4.1 Undemocratic selection of party candidates

A first issue in which the influence of godfathers and party barons plays a hand concerns the undemocratic processes that are often followed in the selection of candidates for electoral offices. Pursuant to section 84 of the Electoral Act, political parties may determine aspirants and candidates for political offices through direct primaries, indirect primaries, or consensus. While parties are free to choose between these three systems, the Electoral Act sets detailed rules for each of them.[53] In practice, party primaries are seldom conducted in compliance with these provisions, as candidates are usually chosen informally and later endorsed by consensus.[54] Against this background, influential voices, such as the director of the INEC Electoral Institute, have argued that the persistent practice for selecting candidates and party executives "continues to render delegates and party members irrelevant".[55]

The problem is often exacerbated by ethno-religious considerations such as the inconsistently applied rule of "zoning", that is, the largely informal policy in which political parties agree to split their presidential and vice-presidential candidates between the North (predominantly Muslim) and South (predominantly Christian) of the country.[56] For instance, Goodluck Jonathan's presidential candidacy for the PDP in the 2015 elections was criticised as being against zoning, but was eventually confirmed unopposed in the party primaries despite an explicit provision in the PDP party statutes establishing a "policy of rotation and zoning of party and public elective offices".[57] The issue came up again ahead of the 2023 elections, when a major controversy arose over the prospect of another northern Muslim assuming the presidency after Buhari. In the end, however, al-

53 See sections 84(4) (direct primaries), 84(5) (indirect primaries), and 84(5) (consensus) of the Electoral Act 2022.
54 Ibrahim, *supra* n. 1, pp 121–122.
55 Quoted in *ibid.*
56 See Cheeseman, Bertrand, and Husaini, *supra* n. 12.
57 Section 7(3)(c) of the Constitution of the Peoples Democratic Party 2012, as amended, http://www.politicalpartydb.org/wp-content/uploads/2021/01/PDP-CONSTITUTION-2012-AMENDMENT1.pdf (accessed 21 November 2024).

though some PDP candidates opposed Atiku Abubakar's candidacy in the party primaries, citing his northern Muslim background, the PDP's zoning policy was in effect again ignored and Atiku nominated as the PDP's presidential candidate.[58]

By contrast, APC's candidate for the 2023 elections, Bola Tinubu, a Muslim but from the South of Nigeria, insisted that it was his region's turn to field the party's presidential candidate. Using the common Yoruba slogan *awa l'okan* ("it is our turn"), Tinubu was eventually able to secure the APC's ticket. Taking the slogan one step further, he altered it to *emi l'okan* ("it is my turn"), reflecting a sense of personal entitlement to the presidency after having been a political "kingmaker" for many years.[59] Tinubu's usage, and alteration of, the slogan had drawn wide criticism as an open acknowledgement of the institutionalisation of patrimonialism in Nigeria. For example, former president Obasanjo, in an open letter, stated: "Let me say straight away that '*Emi Lokan*' (My turn) and 'I have paid my dues' are one and the same thing and are [a] wrong attitude and mentality for the leadership of Nigeria now."[60]

At the state level, godfathers and party barons often influence selection processes to such an extent that they make nonsense of intra-party democracy. As two recent examples show, this phenomenon is again not limited to a particular party. The first example is from Rivers State, where the previous governor, Nyesom Wike, paid for the PDP party nomination forms of all candidates contesting in the 2023 elections, from the governor candidates and state parliament members to the local government chairpersons.[61] Indeed, Wike boasted about this on various occasions, stating that no candidate in his party themselves paid for the nomination form and

58 See Q Iroanusi, "PDP Dumps Zoning, Throws Presidential Ticket Open", *Premium Times,* 11 May 2022, https://www.premiumtimesng.com/news/headlines/529158-breaking-pdp-dumps-zoning-throws-presidential-ticket-open.html (accessed 18 June 2024).

59 On Tinubu as political kingmaker, see, for example, T Akinboyo, "Bola Tinubu: Kingmaker Who is Now King", *Premium Times,* 2 March 2023, https://www.premiumtimesng.com/features-and-interviews/585655-analysis-bola-tinubu-kingmaker-who-is-now-king.html (accessed 21 November 2024).

60 See T Oke, "Emi L'Okan: Tinubu's Turn to Do What", *Punch,* 13 September 2022, https://punchng.com/emi-lokan-tinubus-turn-to-do-what/ (accessed 3 March 2024).

61 See S Opejobi, "Rivers: No Regrets Making Fubara Governor, I Bought His Nomination Forms – Wike", *Daily Post,* 8 January 2024, https://dailypost.ng/2024/01/08/rivers-no-regrets-making-fubara-governor-i-bought-his-nomination-forms-wike/ (accessed 11 July 2024).

that he had ensured that all his sponsored candidates won the election.[62] The second example occurred in Kogi State, where the previous governor, Yahaya Bello, handpicked his cousin Usman Ododo as his successor from within the APC. Although Ododo was officially elected as the APC's gubernatorial candidate in direct party primaries, his election became a formality after his two main competitors withdrew from the race a day ahead of the primaries following a "stakeholder meeting" hosted by Bello.[63]

The relationship between patrimonial leaders and their chosen successors often becomes fraught with tension and conflict. When successors resist control, political godfathers can mobilise their networks to oust their appointed candidates from office, triggering widespread violence between their supporters and those of the incumbents.[64] In the example of Rivers State, Wike tried to mobilise his supporters to impeach his successor, who sought to resist control after assuming office.[65] This sparked a severe political crisis in the state, culminating in arson against its parliament building. Similarly, in Kogi State, a crisis reportedly emerged between Ododo and his political godfather, Bello.[66]

4.2 Political nomadism

In Nigerian politics, intra-party conflict regularly leads to inter-party migration. This phenomenon underscores the depth of what Wale Adebanwi has described as the "trivialization of party politics", where contestations are predominantly driven by the self-serving interests of elites rather than

62 See D Daniel, "I Bought Nomination Forms – Wike Defends Backing Fubara as Governor", *Politics Nigeria*, 8 January 2024, https://politicsnigeria.com/i-bought-his-nomination-forms-wike-defends-backing-fubara-as-governor/ (accessed 11 July 2024).

63 I Oyewale, "Kogi APC Primary: Onoja, Others Withdraw as Bellow Endorses Ododo", *This Day*, 14 April 2023, https://www.thisdaylive.com/index.php/2023/04/14/kogi-apc-primary-onoja-others-withdraw-as-bello-endorses-ododo/ (accessed 22 November 2024).

64 UB Ikpe, *supra* n. 2, p 692.

65 M Lawal, "Rivers Political Crisis and Unending Debate over Presidential 'Peace' Pact", *Punch*, 20 January 2024, https://punchng.com/rivers-political-crisis-and-unending-debate-over-presidential-peace-pact/ (accessed 4 March 2024).

66 "Crisis Brews Between Kogi Governor Ododo, Predecessor Yahaya Bello over Sacking of Loyalist, Sharing of 1200 Bags of Rice", *Sahara Reporters*, 28 February 2024, https://saharareporters.com/2024/02/28/crisis-brews-between-kogi-governor-ododo-predecessor-yahaya-bello-over-sacking-loyalist (accessed 3 March 2024).

ideological principles.[67] Abubakar Momoh and others have aptly labelled this behaviour as "political nomadism":

> Political nomadism [refers to] the defection(s) or arbitrary movement of politicians from one political party to another, or their formation of completely new party, after dumping their original party of membership. What makes the defection nomadic? This is because first they turn political parties into grazing grounds and second because the rate of defections is so high, arbitrary and sometimes inexplicable ... [As] is the case with any grazing ground, nomads will return to it or abandon it depending on whether the land is vegetated or barren. Hence political nomads do not mind returning to their initial party of origin, if their interest is best served. Interest rather than principle is the driving force.[68]

Political nomadism is legally sanctioned in Nigeria insofar as the Constitution states that Members of Parliament (MPs) have to vacate their seats after migrating from one political party to another if their election was sponsored by that first party.[69] The Constitution provides for an exception, however, if the membership in the new party is "a result of a division in the political party of which he [the MP] was previously a member".[70] As various scholars have noted, this exception has been used by many parliamentarians as a loophole for migrating from one party to another without losing their seats.[71] No similar prohibition exists for other electoral offices such as state governors. Calls for reforms proscribing "party switching" more strictly have not been heeded so far.[72]

Although not limited to election periods, in the past political nomadism on a large scale could be observed in particular ahead of elections. In

67 Adebanwi, *supra*, n. 3, p 20.

68 A Momoh, *supra* n. 52, p 92. See also U Ikechukwu, "Political Nomadism and Its Implications on Political Development in Nigeria: A Critical Analysis", 9 (2015) *International Journal of African and Asian Studies*, pp 75–86.

69 Sections 68(1)(g) and 109(1) of the Constitution.

70 Ibid.

71 V Agboga, "*Waka Waka* Politician: What are the Drivers of Party Switching in Nigeria", 93 (2023) *Africa*, pp 615–633, 623. See also Y Fashagba, "Party Switching in the Senate under Nigeria's Fourth Republic", 20 (2014) *Journal of Legislative Studies*, pp 516–541; Ikechukwu, *supra* n. 68.

72 See, for example, I Oweh, "Proscribe Cross Carpeting Among Candidates if Amendment Must be Effected to 2022 Electoral Act – Jega", *Independent*, 28 November 2023, https://independent.ng/proscribe-cross-carpeting-among-candidates-if-amendment-must-be-effected-to-2022-electoral-act-jega/ (accessed 10 March 2024).

2015, for instance, the newly created APC was able to convince many state governors to abandon the governing PDP and join it instead.[73] Similarly, ahead of the 2019 elections, the tide turned, and many (if not necessarily the same) politicians left the APC, in most cases for the PDP.[74]

4.3 Monetisation of party politics

Another challenge for the prospects of party constitutionalism in Nigeria is the monetisation of party politics. This can be observed in almost every aspect of Nigerian politics, sometimes in addition to the other challenges discussed previously. For example, to regain the allegiance of influential politicians who had left the PDP ahead of the 2015 elections, the party reportedly made "mouth-watering" offers of between one and 10 million US dollars to them if they returned to their former party amid dwindling public support largely attributed to the defection of these same politicians.[75]

Similarly, undemocratic processes for selecting party candidates (discussed above) are further corrupted through their monetisation. For instance, it is common practice for political godfathers and party barons in all major parties to "buy" delegates in party primaries. This is due to the preferred indirect voting system, in which party delegates are responsible for selecting candidates or officials.[76] By bribing delegates, political godfathers and party barons ensure that their preferred candidate is elected or nominated in the primaries. During the PDP's 2023 primaries, for example,

73 I Ekott, "APC Leads House of Reps as 37 PDP Members Defect", *Premium Times*, 18 December 2013, https://www.premiumtimesng.com/news/151695-update-apc-leads-house-reps-37-pdp-members-defect.html (accessed 17 June 2024).

74 N Ayitogo, "37 House of Reps Members Dump APC", *Premium Times*, 24 July 2018, https://www.premiumtimesng.com/news/headlines/277596-breaking-36-house-of-reps-members-dump-apc.html (accessed 17 June 2024).

75 See O Awofeso and P Irabor, "Party Cross-Carpeting in Nigeria's Fourth Republic: Cases and Causes", 6 (2016) *Journal of Public Administration and Governance*, pp 31–41, 37. Awefeso and Irabor comment: "Although this is considered a rumour in some quarters, one cannot completely dispel issues like this in any polity that is not ideologically driven, where possession of political power is viewed directly as economic empowerment."

76 The indirect voting system for primaries is one of three options that the Electoral Act envisages (see section 4.1 above).

more than 3,000 delegates were allegedly each bribed with as much as USD 35,000.[77] Similar allegations were made about the APC's primaries.[78]

While the practice of delegate-buying had been observed already in earlier election cycles,[79] a new phenomenon in the 2023 party primaries was the extreme increase in the costs of nomination forms. Fees for such forms are typically charged by political parties and paid by aspirants as a demonstration of their interest in contesting for a position on the party's platform. Since this practice is not regulated by the Constitution or any statutory law, there is no ceiling to the maximum amount that contestants pay to obtain such forms; as a result, parties can set unlimited fees that are unaffordable to ordinary candidates. Indeed, a recent study has shown that the costs of obtaining party nomination forms have tripled since 2019.[80] In the 2023 elections, presidential aspirants' nomination forms reportedly cost a 100 million naira (roughly USD 240,000 at the time) in the APC and 40 million naira (roughly USD 96,000) in the PDP.[81] Such exorbitant entry costs for candidates make wealthy godfathers indispensable, since they often purchase nomination forms for candidates and then leverage this fact to assert their influence over them and gain greater relevance on the political stage.

The extreme monetisation of Nigerian party politics is well illustrated by the regular increases seen in the maximum amount of election expenses allowed to parties under the Electoral Act; even so, these spending limits are routinely disregarded, resulting in excessive overspending by political

77 Editorial Board, "Monetisation of the Democratic Process", *The Guardian*, 29 June 2022, https://guardian.ng/opinion/monetisation-of-the-democratic-process/ (accessed 3 March 2024).

78 B Majeed, "2023: Delegates Bribed to Vote at APC Presidential Primary, Amaechi Alleges", *Premium Times*, 25 July 2022, https://www.premiumtimesng.com/news/headlines/544781-2023-delegates-bribed-to-vote-at-apc-presidential-primary-amaechi-alleges.html (accessed 13 June 2024).

79 For more on the 2019 primaries, see B Sule, "Effects of Money Politics on Party Primaries in Nigerian 2019 General Election: Reflections on All Progressive Congress (APC) and People's Democratic Party (PDP)", 4 (2022) *Politicon: Jurnal Ilmu Politik*, pp 261–293.

80 U Sambo, B Sule, U Adamu, et al., "Democracy for Sale: Examining the Phenomenon of the Cost of Expression of Interest and Nomination Forms for Major Parties in Nigeria's 2023 General Election", April–June (2024), *SAGE Open*, pp 1–11, 6.

81 "APC, PDP, Oda Political Parties Cost of Nomination Forms for Nigeria 2023 Election and How Pipo See Am", *BBC News Pidgin*, 22 April 2022, https://www.bbc.com/pidgin/tori-61187820 (accessed 3 March 2024).

parties far beyond the maximum amounts.[82] Against the background of the large sums of money used to influence political outcomes, Babayo Sule notes in his comprehensive study of political-party financing in Nigeria that the most recent increase of the election expense limits in the Electoral Act is insufficient and "looks like a joke".[83] He points out too that, apart from the inadequacy of the spending limits, the fines envisaged in the Electoral Act for violations are small and therefore ineffective.[84]

4.4 Judicialisation of party conflicts

Many of the challenges and associated phenomena discussed above increasingly end up in the courts. For example, while nomadism is prevalent across all political parties, the litigation of party defections was until recently not observed to have been initiated by political parties but only by private individuals or civil society organisations (CSOs).[85] However, as Victor Agboga notes, in a few recent cases a political party has sued a former member for migrating to another party, with these actions based on the constitutional provision tying the tenure of MPs to membership of the party that sponsored their election.[86] For instance, in the wake of the 2019 elections, the PDP successfully sued the former speaker of the House of Representatives, Yakubu Dogara, who had joined it before the elections but returned to the APC afterwards.[87]

Intra-party conflicts are also increasingly brought to court. [88] In the build-up to the 2023 elections, the major political parties were all enmeshed in one or another form of intra-party conflict over the conduct of their congresses and conventions, with the result that more than a thousand

82 See B Sule, U Sambo, B Mat, et al., "Issues and Regulations in Party Financing and Electoral Expenses in Nigeria (1999–2020)", 40 (2022) *Journal of Contemporary African Studies*, pp 253–269.

83 Sule, *supra* n. 40, p 146.

84 *Ibid*, pp 149–153.

85 Agboga, *supra* n. 71, p 623.

86 Section 68(1)(g) of the Constitution, discussed in section 4.2 above.

87 Agboga, *supra* n. 71, p 623. The legal dispute did not prevent Dogara from moving back to the PDP again in 2022. See "How Much Value is Dogara Adding to PDP?", *This Day*, 16 December 2022, https://www.thisdaylive.com/index.php/2022/12/16/how-much-value-is-dogara-adding-to-pdp (accessed 22 November 2024).

88 See M Ihembe and C Isike, "Judicialising Party Primaries: Contemporary Developments in Nigeria," 21 (2022) *Journal of African Elections*, pp 24–43.

pre-election matters came before the Federal High Court.[89] Generally, intra-party conflicts are regarded as internal affairs that should not concern the courts.[90] A long line of cases in Nigeria has confirmed this position, especially in regard to questions of party membership.

For example, in *Enang v Asuquo & Others,* the Supreme Court held that "membership of a political party is a matter that is strictly within the domestic affairs of a political party, and the Courts have no jurisdiction to determine who the members of a political party are".[91] Yet while party membership is considered as outside the courts' jurisdiction, the Supreme Court simultaneously emphasised in the same case that this is different where a dissatisfied contestant raises complaints about the conduct of party primaries in order to scrutinise whether the election was conducted in compliance with the party's statutes, as per the Electoral Act.[92] Crucially, as was established in another case, this right of the aggrieved party is not subject to exhaustion of the internal administrative remedy of a political party.[93]

Due to patrimonialism, the resulting conflicts are usually not resolved through internal dispute mechanisms anyway, leaving aggrieved individuals with no recourse for justice within the party itself. The resulting judicialisation of these conflicts can have negative side-effects that extend beyond the parties themselves. For instance, in regard to the 2019 elections, it has been noted that "the prolonged lawsuits arising from disputed primaries brought about delays in the production of ballot papers since most of the contested primaries were still in court".[94] Furthermore, there is often confusion when disputed primaries remain unresolved, elections proceed, and the courts later overturn the unlawful primaries.[95] In the 2019 electoral dispute in Zamfara State, for example, the Nigerian Supreme Court ruled that no valid party primaries were conducted by the APC in the state. Consequently, the

89 J Ojo, "Urgent Need to Reform Nigeria's Politics and Elections", *Punch,* 29 November 2023, https://punchng.com/urgent-need-to-reform-nigerias-politics-and-elections/ (accessed 4 March 2024).

90 See generally FO Ottoh, "Political Question Doctrine and Judicial Attitude to Political Controversies in Nigeria: Implications for Constitutionalism", 9 (2022) *Lentera Hukum*, pp 263–302.

91 Supreme Court of Nigeria, *Enang v Asuquo & Others* (2023) LPELR-60042 (SC).

92 *Ibid*, pp 29–35; section 84(14) of the Electoral Act 2022.

93 Nigeria Court of Appeal, *Odey v APC* & *Others* (2023) LPELR 59695 (CA).

94 *Ibid*, p 30.

95 A popular example is the 2007 Supreme Court case, *Amaechi v INEC & Others* (2008) 5 NWLR (Pt. 1080) 227.

Court ordered that the candidate from the PDP, who received the second highest number of votes, should be declared the winner of the elections.[96]

Another effect of the increasing judicialisation of intra-party conflict is the risk of politicisation of the judiciary. The so-called Yobe North controversy prior to the 2023 elections suffices to illustrate this challenge. Senator Ahmed Lawan, president of the Senate from 2019 until 2023, had decided to stand for the presidency under the APC banner. As a senator representing Yobe North, he withdrew his renewed candidature for the senatorial seat under the APC to contest the presidency. His place was taken by Bashir Machina, who contested the primary elections held in May 2022 and won unopposed. However, after Lawan lost the APC presidential primaries, he wanted to return to his senatorial seat. Owing to Lawan's influence in the APC, Machina was asked to step down but refused, insisting that he was the rightful candidate. After purportedly holding another primary election, the APC submitted Lawan's name to the INEC as the senatorial candidate for Yobe North. But, due to the controversy, the INEC refused to recognise any candidate for the district.[97] In response, Machina filed a lawsuit, with the Federal High Court ordering the APC and INEC to recognise him as the lawfully nominated candidate – a position later affirmed by the Court of Appeal.

Dissatisfied with this judgement, the APC appealed to the Supreme Court. In a surprising turn of events, the Court allowed the appeal, holding that the suit at the trial court was instituted by way of the wrong originating process, and declared Lawan the APC's Yobe North senatorial candidate.[98] Since this apparent procedural flaw had not been raised before in the lower courts, the Supreme Court's decision to allow the appeal and change the outcome of the original judgement raised concerns that the Court had used this as a pretext to prioritise technical over substantive justice. The decision

96 Q Iroanusi, "In APC's Loss of Zamfara, Here's the Man Who Played the Key Role", *Premium Times*, 28 May 2019, https://www.premiumtimesng.com/news/headlines/331794-analysis-in-apcs-loss-of-zamfara-heres-the-man-who-played-lead-role.html (accessed 11 July 2024).

97 See A Ejekwonyilo, "Supreme Court Declares Ahmad Lawan as APC's Yobe North Senatorial Candidate", *Premium Times*, 6 February 2023, https://www.premiumtimesng.com/news/top-news/580227-just-in-supreme-court-declares-ahmad-lawan-as-apcs-yobe-north-senatorial-candidate.html (accessed 6 June 2024).

98 Supreme Court of Nigeria, *All Progressive Congress v Bashir Sheriff & Others* (2022), unreported suit No. SC/CV/1689/2022, https://sabilaw.org/wp-content/uploads/2023/02/MACHINA-1.pdf (accessed 9 March 2023).

in any case subverted the will of the numerous supporters of Machina who had endorsed his candidacy in the APC senatorial primaries.

4.5 Blurring the line between the state and ruling parties

Finally, another issue thwarting the development of party constitutionalism in Nigeria is the persistent blurring of the line between the state and ruling parties. To enforce their separation, the new Electoral Act contains an innovative provision that seeks to reduce the power and influence of government members over party primaries. According to the Act, "no political appointee at any level shall be a voting delegate or be voted for at the convention or congress at any political party for the nomination of the candidate for any election".[99] If a political party fails to comply with this provision in the conduct of its primaries, "its candidate shall not be included in the election for that particular position in issue".[100] In *Peoples Democratic Party v Edede*, however, the Nigeria Court of Appeal ruled that the provision was discriminatory against political office-holders and therefore inconsistent with section 42 of the Constitution.[101]

The blurring of the line between the state and ruling parties is perhaps best demonstrated by the INEC's continual struggle for autonomy. Although its autonomy is constitutionally guaranteed,[102] there are signs that ruling parties over the years have been successful in manipulating the conduct of the electoral commission in their favour in an attempt to remain in power. For example, the INEC has a dubious track record of postponing elections and other statutory deadlines in favour of the ruling party of the day. In the 2015 elections, for instance, extreme pressure was exerted on it in favour of the ruling PDP to postpone the elections by six weeks,

99 Section 84(12) of the Electoral Act 2022.
100 Section 84(13) of the Electoral Act 2022.
101 Nigeria Court of Appeal, *Peoples Democratic Party v Edede* (2022) 11 NWLR (Pt. 1840).
102 See, in particular, section 158 of the Constitution, which states that the INEC "in exercising its power to make appointments or to exercise disciplinary control over persons ... shall not be subject to the direction or control of any other authority or person". For more detail on the INEC's independence, see Suberu, *supra* n. 47.

purportedly for security concerns.[103] However, it was widely believed that the elections were postponed because the PDP feared defeat and needed more time to put its house in order. Similarly, during the 2023 elections, the INEC extended the deadline for party primaries due to internal conflicts within the ruling APC that caused uncertainty about the timing of the latter's presidential primaries.[104] Again, there was widespread speculation that the decision was intended to enable the PDP to select its candidate first, thereby allowing the APC to prepare better and nominate a strong contender.

While extensions of deadlines in favour of ruling parties might be regarded as mere coincidences, a look at some of the more recent appointments at the INEC casts further doubt on the electoral commission's autonomy. According to the Constitution, INEC commissioners shall be "non-partisan" and of "unquestionable integrity".[105] To that end, members of political parties are explicitly disqualified for appointment as members of the INEC,[106] but there are no other explicit limitations on the partisanship of electoral commissioners, thus making questionable appointments possible. For example, then President Buhari appointed his niece as the acting chairperson of the INEC in 2015, sparking criticism in the media that this was a case of nepotism.[107] In addition, the requirement itself that INEC commissioners shall not be party members was possibly violated when, in 2023, Buhari appointed four state commissioners who were reputedly APC loyalists, a decision that came under fire from a coalition of CSOs. The Senate nevertheless confirmed the appointments, resulting in a lawsuit which at the time of writing (March 2025) seemed still to be pending.[108]

---

103 A Oluwafemi, "Four Times INEC has Postponed Elections", *The Cable,* 11 March 2023, https://www.thecable.ng/timeline-four-times-inec-has-postponed-elections (accessed 9 March 2024).

104 A Abubakar, "2023: How Independent is INEC", *The Cable,* 1 June 2022, https://www.thecable.ng/2023-how-independent-is-inec (accessed 8 June 2024).

105 Third Schedule, item F, section 14(2)(a) of the Constitution.

106 Section 156(1)(a) and Third Schedule, item F, sections 14(2) and (3)(b) of the Constitution.

107 See "Why Buhari Should be Grateful to PDP", *Nigerian Tribune*, 27 July 2015, p 22.

108 See "SERAP, BudgIT, 34 Nigerians sue Tinubu 'for appointing APC loyalists as top INEC officials'", *Premium Times,* 19 November 2023, https://www.premiumtimesng.com/news/top-news/644554-serap-budgit-34-nigerians-sue-tinubu-for-appointing-apc-loyalists-as-top-inec-officials.html (accessed 8 March 2024).

5. Conclusion

The disparity between Nigeria's constitutional and statutory framework regulating political parties and its practical implementation is stark. Given that the country is aiming for democratic consolidation, the importance of further entrenching political-party constitutionalism cannot be overstated. As this chapter has shown, the prevalence of patrimonialism in political-party dynamics is a significant threat to this goal, as parties serve as a conduit for politicians to pursue self-serving agendas, thereby undermining the integrity of democracy and constitutionalism. Patrimonialism within political parties has created formidable barriers for ordinary citizens seeking to engage in electoral processes. The dominant influence of godfathers and party barons, which is exacerbated by ethno-religious considerations and the extreme monetisation of party politics, in many instances corrupts or circumvents the constitutional and statutory framework regulating political parties.

If Nigerian politics is to move away from purely transactional thinking, many of these challenges could perhaps only be tackled holistically. Nonetheless, a stronger normative framework regulating political parties might at least contribute to deepening the country's entrenchment of constitutionalism and democracy. In this vein, a number of ideas for reform could be considered.

First, to counter the prevalence of undemocratic practices that enable party godfathers to control internal selection processes, the provisions in the Electoral Act that allow not only for direct primaries but also for an indirect voting system through delegates, as well as the selection of candidates through consensus, should be changed. As has been shown, delegates in indirect primaries are regularly bribed, and the nomination of candidates by consensus encourages informal arrangements brokered by a few influential figures outside of regular party procedures, with ordinary party members having no democratic say in the process. Relatedly, to reduce – or at least channel – ethno-religious considerations, the inconsistently applied policy of zoning could be made mandatory for all parties, or indeed even be constitutionalised, as has been proposed time and again by legal reformers.[109]

109 For more on the most recent attempt, see "Legislators in Nigeria Propose Constitutional Amendments for Presidential Term Limits and Geographical Rotation", *Constitionnet*, 11 June 2024, https://constitutionnet.org/news/legislators-nigeria-pr

Secondly, to reduce the monetisation of party politics, a number of concrete steps should be taken to improve the regulatory framework governing party financing in Nigeria. For instance, the practice among political parties of charging fees for nomination forms in party primaries should be limited, or prohibited altogether, and the buying of such forms by sponsors for others should be sanctioned. In addition, the maximum amounts set for campaign costs should be reduced, not increased, as happened in the latest revision of the Electoral Act.[110] Offering and taking money to migrate from one party to another should also be prohibited so as to reduce the immediate financial benefits resulting from political nomadism.

Thirdly, in general but also for the previous suggestions to have any effect in practice, the existing party oversight mechanisms need to be strengthened significantly. As has become clear, the INEC is often unwilling or unable to fulfil its constitutional and statutory mandate when it comes to monitoring and enforcement in regard to internal party activities. Considering the massive challenges identified in this chapter, the question arises of whether it is realistic to expect the INEC to resolve all or any of them on its own. In addition, the widely shared perception that the electoral commission tends to favour the ruling party has damaged its legitimacy. One way to increase its autonomy would be to change the appointment procedure for INEC commissioners, for example by reducing the influence of the President in the process.

Fourth, to address the challenges of (over)judicialisation of internal party conflicts, it is essential to strengthen internal party dispute-resolution mechanisms. Political parties should be mandated to establish clear, effective, and transparent systems for resolving conflicts and ensure that these mechanisms are fair to all members as well as accessible by them. Members of these internal dispute resolution mechanisms should be able to act independently without fear of reprisal and have no known connection with any party leader. Courts should be given due regard to the outcomes of these internal dispute resolution mechanisms. To ease the burden of the courts tasked with deciding over internal party disputes, parties could be obliged to demonstrate that they have exhausted their internal dispute resolution mechanisms before their cases can be considered on merit in the courts.

---

opose-constitutional-amendments-presidential-term-limits-and (accessed 18 June 2024).

110 In this vein, see also Ibrahim, *supra* n. 1, pp 126–127.

References

Books, articles, chapters in books, and others

"APC, PDP, Oda Political Parties Cost of Nomination Forms for Nigeria 2023 Election and How Pipo See Am", *BBC News Pidgin*, 22 April 2022, https://www.bbc.com/pidgin/tori-61187820 (accessed 3 March 2024)

"Crisis Brews Between Kogi Governor Ododo, Predecessor Yahaya Bello over Sacking of Loyalist, Sharing of 1200 Bags of Rice", *Sahara Reporters*, 28 February 2024, https://saharareporters.com/2024/02/28/crisis-brews-between-kogi-governor-ododo-predecessor-yahaya-bello-over-sacking-loyalist (accessed 3 March 2024)

"How Much Value is Dogara Adding to PDP?", *This Day*, 16 December 2022, https://www.thisdaylive.com/index.php/2022/12/16/how-much-value-is-dogara-adding-to-pdp (accessed 22 November 2024)

"Legislators in Nigeria Propose Constitutional Amendments for Presidential Term Limits and Geographical Rotation", *ConstitionNet*, 11 June 2024, https://constitutionnet.org/news/legislators-nigeria-propose-constitutional-amendments-presidential-term-limits-and (accessed 18 June 2024)

"SERAP, BudgIT, 34 Nigerians sue Tinubu 'for appointing APC loyalists as top INEC officials'", *Premium Times*, 19 November 2023, https://www.premiumtimesng.com/news/top-news/644554-serap-budgit-34-nigerians-sue-tinubu-for-appointing-apc-loyalists-as-top-inec-officials.html (accessed 8 March 2024)

"Supreme Court Upholds INEC's Deregistration of 22 Political Parties", *Premium* Times, 25 March 2022, https://www.premiumtimesng.com/news/headlines/519559-supreme-court-upholds-inecs-deregistration-of-22-political-parties.html (accessed 13 September 2023)

"Why Buhari Should be Grateful to PDP", Nigerian Tribune, 27 July 2015

Abubakar A, "2023: How Independent is INEC", *The Cable*, 1 June 2022, https://www.thecable.ng/2023-how-independent-is-inec (accessed 8 June 2024)

Adebanwi W, "Nigeria's Fourth Republic: An Introduction", in W Adebanwi (ed.), *Democracy and Nigeria's Fourth Republic: Governance, Political Economy, and Party Politics 1999–2023*, Woodbridge, James Currey (2023), pp 1–32

Agbaje A, "A Republic of Dashed Hopes? Party Politics and the Travails of Democracy in Nigeria's Fourth Republic", in W Adebanwi (ed.), *Democracy and Nigeria's Fourth Republic: Governance, Political Economy, and Party Politics 1999–2023*, Woodbridge, James Currey (2023), pp 129–48

Agboga V, "*Waka waka* Politician: What are the Drivers of Party Switching in Nigeria", 93 (2023) *Africa*, pp 615–633

Akinboyo T, "Bola Tinubu: Kingmaker Who is Now King", *Premium Times*, 2 March 2023, https://www.premiumtimesng.com/features-and-interviews/585655-analysis-bola-tinubu-kingmaker-who-is-now-king.html (accessed 21 November 2024)

Awofeso O and Irabor P, "Party Cross-Carpeting in Nigeria's Fourth Republic: Cases and Causes", 6 (2016) *Journal of Public Administration and Governance*, pp 31–41

Ayitogo A, "37 House of Reps Members Dump APC", *Premium Times*, 24 July 2018, https://www.premiumtimesng.com/news/headlines/277596-breaking-36-house-of-reps-members-dump-apc.html (accessed 17 June 2024)

Bogaards M, "Ethnic Party Bans and Institutional Engineering in Nigeria", 17 (2010) *Democratization*, pp 730–749

Cheeseman N, Bertrand E, and Husaini S, *Oxford Dictionary of African Politics*, Oxford, Oxford University Press (2019), "Zoning", https://www.oxfordreference.com/display/10.1093/acref/9780191828836.001.0001/acref-9780191828836-e-367 (accessed 18 June 2024)

Constitution of the Peoples Democratic Party 2012, as amended, accessible at http://www.politicalpartydb.org/wp-content/uploads/2021/01/PDP-CONSTITUTION-2012-AMENDMENT1.pdf (accessed 21 November 2024)

Daniel D, "I Bought Nomination Forms – Wike Defends Backing Fubara as Governor", *Politics Nigeria*, 8 January 2024, https://politicsnigeria.com/i-bought-his-nomination-forms-wike-defends-backing-fubara-as-governor/ (accessed 11 July 2024)

Danjibo N and Ashindorbe K, "The Evolution and Pattern of Political Party Formation and the Search for National Integration in Nigeria", 5 (2018) *Brazilian Journal of African Studies*, pp 85–100

Editorial Board, "Monetisation of the Democratic Process", *The Guardian*, 29 June 2022, https://guardian.ng/opinion/monetisation-of-the-democratic-process/ (accessed 3 March 2024)

Ejekwonyilo A, "Supreme Court Declares Ahmad Lawan as APC's Yobe North Senatorial Candidate", *Premium Times*, 6 February 2023, https://www.premiumtimesng.com/news/top-news/580227-just-in-supreme-court-declares-ahmad-lawan-as-apcs-yobe-north-senatorial-candidate.html (accessed 6 June 2024)

Ekott I, "APC Leads House of Reps as 37 PDP Members Defect", *Premium Times*, 18 December 2013, https://www.premiumtimesng.com/news/151695-update-apc-leads-house-reps-37-pdp-members-defect.html (accessed 17 June 2024)

Fasan O, "Nigeria's Patrimonial Politics and Different Presidents", *Business Day*, 9 March 2015, https://businessday.ng/columnist/article/nigerias-patrimonial-politics-and-diffident-presidents/ (accessed 6 June 2024)

Fashagba Y, "Party Switching in the Senate under Nigeria's Fourth Republic", 20 (2014) *Journal of Legislative Studies*, pp 516–541

Ibrahim J, "Democratic Regression, Political Parties, and the Negation of the Popularity Principle", in W Adebanwi (ed.), *Democracy and Nigeria's Fourth Republic: Governance, Political Economy, and Party Politics 1999–2023*, Woodbridge, James Currey (2023), pp 107–28

Ihembe M and Isike C, "Judicialising Party Primaries: Contemporary Developments in Nigeria," 21 (2022) *Journal of African Elections*, pp 24–43

Ikechukwu U, "Political Nomadism and Its Implications on Political Development in Nigeria: A Critical Analysis", 9 (2015) *International Journal of African and Asian Studies*, pp 75–86

Ikpe UB, "The Patrimonial State and Inter-Ethnic Conflicts in Nigeria", 32 (2009) *Ethnic and Racial Studies*, pp 679–97

Iroanusi Q, "In APC's Loss of Zamfara, Here's the Man Who Played the Key Role", *Premium Times*, 28 May 2019, https://www.premiumtimesng.com/news/headlines/331794-analysis-in-apcs-loss-of-zamfara-heres-the-man-who-played-lead-role.html (accessed 11 July 2024)

Iroanusi Q, "PDP Dumps Zoning, Throws Presidential Ticket Open", *Premium Times,* 11 May 2022, https://www.premiumtimesng.com/news/headlines/529158-breaking-pdp-dumps-zoning-throws-presidential-ticket-open.html (accessed 18 June 2024)

Lawal M, "Rivers Political Crisis and Unending Debate over Presidential 'Peace' Pact", *Punch*, 20 January 2024, https://punchng.com/rivers-political-crisis-and-unending-debate-over-presidential-peace-pact/ (accessed 4 March 2024)

Majeed, B, "2023: Delegates Bribed to Vote at APC Presidential Primary, Amaechi Alleges", *Premium Times*, 25 July 2022, https://www.premiumtimesng.com/news/headlines/544781-2023-delegates-bribed-to-vote-at-apc-presidential-primary-amaechi-alleges.html (accessed 13 June 2024)

Momoh A, "Party System and Democracy in Nigeria", in O Obafemi, S Egwu, O Ibeanu, and J Ibrahim (eds.), *Political Parties and Democracy in Nigeria,* Kuru, National Institute of Policy and Strategic Studies (2014)

Nwauche ES, "Political Parties, the 1999 Nigerian Constitution and the 2011 General Elections", 46 (2013) *Verfassung und Recht in Übersee/Law and Politics in Africa, Asia and Latin America*, pp 407–429

Ojo J, "Urgent Need to Reform Nigeria's Politics and Elections", *Punch*, 29 November 2023, https://punchng.com/urgent-need-to-reform-nigerias-politics-and-elections (accessed 4 March 2024)

Oke T, "Emi L'Okan: Tinubu's Turn to Do What", *Punch,* 13 September 2022, https://punchng.com/emi-lokan-tinubus-turn-to-do-what/ (accessed 3 March 2024)

Okere BO, "Fundamental Objectives and Directive Principles of State Policy under the Nigerian Constitution" 32 (1983) *International and Comparative Law Quarterly*, pp 214–228

Oluwafemi A, "Four Times INEC has Postponed Elections", *The Cable,* 11 March 2023, https://www.thecable.ng/timeline-four-times-inec-has-postponed-elections (accessed 9 March 2024)

Opejobi S, "Rivers: No Regrets Making Fubara Governor, I Bought His Nomination Forms – Wike", *Daily Post,* 8 January 2024, https://dailypost.ng/2024/01/08/rivers-no-regrets-making-fubara-governor-i-bought-his-nomination-forms-wike (accessed 11 July 2024)

Osaghae EE, "The Long Shadow of Nigeria's Military Epochs, 1966-79 and 1983-99", in A Carl LeVan and P Ukata (eds.), *The Oxford Handbook of Nigerian* Politics, Oxford, Oxford University Press (2018), pp 171–88

Ottoh FO, "Political Question Doctrine and Judicial Attitude to Political Controversies in Nigeria: Implications for Constitutionalism", 9 (2022) *Lentera Hukum*, pp 263–302

Oweh I, "Proscribe Cross Carpeting Among Candidates if Amendment Must be Effected to 2022 Electoral Act – Jega", *Independent*, 28 November 2023, https://independent.ng/proscribe-cross-carpeting-among-candidates-if-amendment-must-be-effected-to-2022-electoral-act-jega/ (accessed 10 March 2024)

Oyewale I, "Kogi APC Primary: Onoja, Others Withdraw as Bellow Endorses Ododo", *This Day*, 14 April 2023, https://www.thisdaylive.com/index.php/2023/04/14/kogi-apc-primary-onoja-others-withdraw-as-bello-endorses-ododo/ (accessed 22 November 2024)

Sambo U, Sule B, Adamu U and Septiadi MA, "Democracy for Sale: Examining the Phenomenon of the Cost of Expression of Interest and Nomination Forms for Major Parties in Nigeria's 2023 General Election", April–June (2024) *SAGE Open*, pp 1–11

Sklar RL, Nigerian Political Parties: Power in an Emergent African Nation, Princeton, Princeton University Press (1963)

Suberu R, "Nigeria in Search of a Credible Electoral Administration: Recent Reforms and Persistent Challenges", in CM Fombad and N Steytler (eds), *Democracy, Elections, and Constitutionalism in Africa,* Oxford, Oxford University Press (2021), pp 331–360

Sule B, "Effects of Money Politics on Party Primaries in Nigerian 2019 General Election: Reflections on All Progressive Congress (APC) and People's Democratic Party (PDP)", 4 (2022) *Politicon: Jurnal Ilmu Politik,* pp 261–293

Sule B, Political Party Financing and Electoral Politics in Nigeria's Fourth Republic, Lanham, Lexington Books (2023)

Sule B, Sambu U, Mat B, et al., "Issues and Regulations in Party Financing and Electoral Expenses in Nigeria (1999–2020)", 40 (2022) *Journal of Contemporary African Studies*, pp 253–269

Udoma U, History and the Law of the Constitution of Nigeria, Lagos, Malthouse Press (1994)

Table of cases

African Commission of Human and Peoples' Rights, *International Pen and Others (on behalf of Ken Saro-Wiwa) v Nigeria*, Communication Nos. 137/94, 139/94, 154/96 and 161/97 (1998)

High Court of Nigeria, Alhaji Abubakar Rimi v Peoples Redemption Party (1981) 2 NCLR 734 HC

Nigeria Court of Appeal, *Odey v APC & Others* (2023) LPELR 59695 (CA)

Nigeria Court of Appeal, *Peoples Democratic Party v Edede* (2022) 11 NWLR (Pt. 1840)

Supreme Court of Nigeria, *Abacha v Fawehinmi* (2000) 6 NWLR (Pt. 660)

Supreme Court of Nigeria, *AG Federation v Abubakar* (2007) 10 NWLR (Pt. 1041)

Supreme Court of Nigeria, *All Progressive Congress v Bashir Sheriff & Others* (2022), unreported suit No. SC/CV/1689/2022, https://sabilaw.org/wp-content/uploads/2023/02/MACHINA-1.pdf (accessed 9 March 2023)

Supreme Court of Nigeria, *Amaechi v. INEC & Others* (2008) 5 NWLR (Pt. 1080) 227

Supreme Court of Nigeria, *Enang v Asuquo & Others* (2023) LPELR-60042 (SC)

Supreme Court of Nigeria, *INEC v Musa & Others* (2003) 3 NWLR (Pt. 806)

Table of legislation

African Charter on Human and Peoples' Rights (Enforcement and Ratification) Act, Ch. A9, Laws of the Federation of Nigeria 1990

Constitution of the Federal Republic of Nigeria, 1999, as amended in 2023, https://placng.org/i/wp-content/uploads/2023/05/Constitution-of-the-Federal-Republic-of-Nigeria-2023.pdf (accessed 16 April 2024)

Electoral Act No. 61, 2022, https://placng.org/i/wp-content/uploads/2022/02/Electoral-Act-2022.pdf (accessed 17 June 2024)

Chapter 9 Safeguarding Multiparty Democracy through Constitutional Entrenchment: The Liberian Experience

Gerald Dan Yeakula

1. Introduction

Liberia has a long history of party politics that dates as far back as 1847, the year in which it was founded as a republic. Although the first political parties in Africa emerged in Liberia, it did not take long for the country to become dominated by a single party, the True Whig Party (TWP). By 1980, however, the TWP's rule had come to end, with the prospect of a more participatory democracy beginning to emerge, given that the 1847 Constitution was abrogated by putschists and a commission established to lead the drafting of a new constitution. Yet this constitution-making process (1981–1986) proved to be a missed opportunity to entrench multiparty democracy and limit presidential power. Indeed, the military junta led by Samuel Kanyon Doe undermined the work of the commission, and essential positions suggested by citizens were removed. The first multiparty elections, held in 1985, also fell prey to the machinations of the junta, with the results disputed by many. A few years later, in 1989, the country descended into a horrific civil war that would last 14 years. Liberia's hard-won multiparty democracy was being lost.

In 2005, however, the opportunity arose for the country to revive the democratic experience, and the first post-war elections were held. Although all has not been perfect since then, it is safe to say that Liberia is on the road to democratic consolidation. Here, political parties have played a notable role in this journey. The legal framework has also been a crucial guide to actors in the political space, as has been the overall environment, one which has embraced respect for peace, the rule of law, and political freedom.

Sustaining democracy depends to a large extent on constraints on incumbent power, the vitality of political opposition, and the resilience of civil society. This chapter examines the Liberian experience in order to highlight which legal and political arrangements have worked well and which are in need of attention. Accordingly, section 2 traces the origins of democracy in Liberia with a view to understanding the one-party system that dominated the political system for more than a century. Section 3 in turn explores the making of the 1986 Constitution and the efforts that were taken to entrench political parties, while section 4 discusses how party constitutionalism works in practice, with the focus placed on political parties, electoral processes, and the overall political environment. Section 5 concludes the chapter with a distillation of its key findings.

2. The emergence and dominance of a single party

2.1 Political foundations

With the founding of the Liberian Republic in 1847, the country embraced democracy. The system of government, however, fell far short of an ideal democratic state: inequality, discrimination, and marginalisation were its chief characteristics for well over a century. Liberia's founding settlers hailed from the United States of America (US), yet ironically engineered a system of discrimination similar to what they themselves had been victim to in their former country.[1]

The preamble to the 1847 Constitution declared, "We the people of the Republic of Liberia were originally the inhabitants of the United States of North America",[2] symbolically effacing the country's indigenous inhabitants, who by all accounts were rendered invisible and excluded from participation in governance. For instance, citizenship was granted only to those of settler stock,[3] while exclusionary policies kept the indigenes out of commerce and education.[4] Citizens were, in fact, prohibited by the Constitution from purchasing land directly from indigenes.[5] Nevertheless,

1 BG Dennis and AK Dennis, *Slaves to Racism: An Unbroken Chain from America To Liberia*, New York, Algora Publishing (2008), pp 36–42.

2 Liberian Constitution, 1847.

3 EO Ojo and GA Agbude, "An Exploration of the Historical and the Political Backgrounds of Liberia", 1 (2012) *AFRREV IJAH: An International Journal of Arts and Humanities*, pp 187–200, at p 190.

4 EC Dillon, *The Role of Education in the Rise and Fall of Americo-Liberians in Liberia, West Africa (1980)*, Georgia State University PhD thesis" (2011), p 16, https://scholarworks.gsu.edu/cgi/viewcontent.cgi?params=/context/eps_diss/article/1017/&path_info=The_Role_of_Education_in_the_Rise_and_Fall_of_Americo_Liberians__inforemoved.pdf (accessed 24 March 2025).

5 CJ Stevens, "The Legal History of Public Land in Liberia", 58 (2014) *Journal of African Law*, pp 250-265, at p 251.

Americo-Liberians (that is, the descendants of freed slaves from the US and Caribbean, as well as of slaves rescued before crossing the Atlantic) were but a tiny fraction of the Liberian population and never exceeded 5 per cent of it.[6] As the years passed, the chasm between Americo-Liberians and the indigene population widened, with the prospect of a democracy reflective of the polity growing equally distant.

With democracy came elections, and with elections, partisan politics. At the outset, two groups fielded candidates in the elections, but lacked much in the way of formal organisation. In the country's first elections, held in 1847, Joseph Jenkins Roberts of the Pro-Administration group defeated Samuel Benedict of the Anti-Administration group.[7] In 1850, the Administration group was formally organised as the True Liberian Party, later changing its name to the Republican Party in 1867.[8] The Anti-Administration group in turn became known as the Opposition Party.[9]

However, the notion of organising into political parties was met with scepticism in many circles for its potential to disrupt 'cohesion' in the infant state. Those who instituted and benefited from a divisive system that placed indigenes at the margins of society were afraid of a possible divide based on party politics. Others argued that while party politics had its place, the time was not right. As the *Herald*, Liberia's first newspaper, remarked in its editorial on party politics,

> [W]e anticipate, that the party domination will prevail except the one great party – The Country. We do not intend by this to say that parties when properly, and wisely, organized are not beneficial; we believe that they are; for they mutually probe corruption, vice, and cliques out of each other's ranks, [promote] the general interest, and maintain a political equilibrium among the classes of our great republican family; but we think, there is no necessity for a regular formal organization on those principles now we are confident that any other party ... in whatever

6 Minority Rights Group International, *World Directory of Minorities and Indigenous Peoples – Liberia* (2007), https://www.refworld.org/docid/4954ce5823.html (accessed 24 February 2025).

7 It is unclear if these parties drew their names and inspiration from the Pro-Administration and Anti-Administration parties in the US in the eighteenth century. See CP Burrowes, *Power and Press Freedom in Liberia, 1830–1970: The Impact of Globalization and Civil Society on Media-Government Relations*, Trenton, Africa World Press (2004), p 85.

8 Ibid.

9 Ibid.

> aspect, or disguise it may present itself, would be injurious, and fatal to the best interest of the country; though the time may not be very far distant, when parties, not a party, will exist, growing out of a diffused, general principle of intelligence and education.[10]

At the time, anti-partyism was a phenomenon with deep roots in Europe, where political parties were considered sectarian and divisive.[11] Nonetheless, in Liberia, fears of fragmentation were valid. The Republican Party, on the one hand, consisted of settlers in commercial centres along the coast who originated in the upper US South,[12] and was made up primarily of Americo-Liberians with mixed African and European ancestry (the mulattoes); the Opposition Party, on the other hand, comprised those in outlying agricultural towns who hailed from the lower US South,[13] and consisted mainly of dark-skinned Americo-Liberians.[14] In 1868, recalling the recent assassination of US President Abraham Lincoln as an example of the possible outcome of partisan politics, Liberian President James S Payne warned against the dangers of "ultra party spirit" which had fuelled intense political rivalry, electoral manipulation, and intimidation of opposition in a previous election:

> Let us ask ourselves what effect, what consequences, will probably follow a biennial repetition of the scenes and doings in the last election? Let political parties exist. They are capable of exerting a fine effect upon the country and the government. But they should be restrained from unlawful excesses. The violation of the law to achieve success should be regarded by all good citizens as a dangerous expedient, if not an omen of a future career.[15]

But party politics were here to stay, and no amount of criticism could consign it to oblivion. If anything, it was emboldened and would soon become entrenched – thanks to the prevailing factionalised social order. In 1869, the TWP was formed in the township of Clay-Ashland in response to the

---

10 Ibid.

11 CM Fombad, "Conceptualising a Framework for Inclusive, Fair and Robust Multiparty Democracy in Africa: The Constitutionalisation of the Rights of Political Parties", 48 (2015) *Verfassung in Recht und Übersee,* pp 3–27, at p 6.

12 Burrowes, *supra* n. 7, p 84.

13 Ibid.

14 G Zoegan, "The True Whigs Take Power", *LiberiaInfo,* 26 September 2024, https://liberiainfo.dukaw.com/true-whigs-take-power/ (accessed 16 March 2025).

15 Burrowes, *supra* n. 7, p 85.

dominance of the country's capital, Monrovia, in national and county politics.[16] This coastal-rural dimension fuelled the emergence of a grassroots movement that found expression in the TWP, which in 1870 ascended to power with the election of Edward J Roye. The TWP duly extended the right to vote to the unpropertied as well as to indigenes in contravention of principles in the Constitution.[17] Roye, however, was replaced following a civilian overthrow in 1871 on account of, among other things, his attempts to extend the terms of elective offices and refusal to step down following electoral defeat.[18] The TWP returned to power in 1878 in the wake of the decline of the Republican Party, and from there on dominated the political landscape for more than a century, in the process making Liberia virtually a one-party state. At the same time, skin-colour distinctions had dissipated by the close of the nineteenth century as political actors came to be subsumed within the TWP.[19]

2.2 Century-long rule by a single party

The Americo-Liberian hegemony lasted 133 years (1847–1980), with the period spanning 1878 to 1980 marking uninterrupted rule by the TWP.[20] Indigenes remained consigned to the periphery, given that no major attempts were made to institute pluralism; such tokenistic democratic gestures as there were, served to benefit the ruling class. By 1904, nearly six decades after independence, indigenes became eligible for citizenship;[21] by 1907, the two-year presidential term was extended to four years following several

16 Ibid, p 74.

17 Ibid, p 86. The 1847 Constitution restricted property ownership to citizens; since indigenes were not eligible for citizenship, they therefore could not own property.

18 Ibid, p 89. Roye was arrested on 28 October 1871 by a mob – said to consist mainly of opposition members – and imprisoned. A riot had broken out between his supporters and those of the opposition earlier that month. Roye died a year later under disputed circumstances while attempting to escape from prison. After the civilian overthrow, a junta "executive committee" ruled Liberia until the elections of 1872.

19 "Foreign Relations of the United States, 1951, The Near East and Africa, Vol. 5 (1951)", *Office of the Historian*, n.d., https://history.state.gov/historicaldocuments/frus1951v05/d722 (accessed 28 February 2024).

20 Zoegan, *supra* n. 14.

21 AM Micallef, *Liberia: Development and Resources*, New York, Nova Science Publishers (2011), p 108.

failed efforts in this regard;[22] and by 1912, the government had increased its influence in the interior where the majority of the indigenes lived, even though their assimilation into the democratic project remained superficial at best.[23] Thus, as political parties metamorphosed into a single political entity, the hegemonic order grew ever stronger, much to the detriment of the excluded indigene population.

The collapse of political competition in the 1890s has been ascribed to a number of factors. According to Ellis, it was due in part to the administration's undermining of the opposition through the political preferment of opposition leaders, and in part to the disposition of voters and leaders to be on the winning side.[24] More importantly, Ellis cites economic dependence as the foundation of the one-party system. According to him, decline in the price of coffee – the country's staple industry – pushed formerly self-sustaining planters into abandoning their plantations in favour of politics and office-seeking.[25] In the process, the opposition was weakened to the point of political death.

Three minority parties sprang up between 1923 to 1943 but to no avail.[26] For example, Thomas JR Faulkner founded the Peoples Party, which vainly opposed the TWP in 1923 and 1927. As before, inadequate financial resources were a serious setback. While persons leading organised opposition to the TWP were financially independent of the establishment, their resources could not measure up to those of the TWP, which had acquired a fortune, including by requiring that government employees make their salary checks payable to it at least once a year.[27] Electoral corruption also stifled fair competition. For instance, the election of 1927 gained notoriety in the *Guinness World Book of Records* as the most corrupt and fraudulent in history.[28] Although less than 15,000 persons were registered to votes, the incumbent president, Charles DB King, garnered 243,000 votes while

22 Burrowes, *supra* n. 7, p 84.
23 GW Ellis, "Political Institutions in Liberia", 5 (1911) *The American Political Science Review*, pp 213–223, at p 218.
24 Ibid, p 216.
25 Ibid.
26 "Foreign Relations of the United States", *Supra* n. 19.
27 Ibid.
28 FPM van der Kraaij, "The 1927 Presidential Election:", *Liberia Past and Present*, n.d., https://liberiapastandpresent.org/1927ElectionsMF.htm (accessed 14 March 2025).

his opponent received 9,000.[29] Following King's resignation in disgrace in 1930 over a trade-labour scandal, he founded the Unit Whig Party but was defeated in 1935 by the TWP candidate, Edwin Barclay.[30] Barclay succeeded in amending the Constitution to extend his four-year term to eight years. His successor, William Tubman, was opposed in the 1943 elections by James Cooper of the Democratic Party.[31] Tubman would perpetuate TWP rule for the next 27 years.

2.3 Multipartyism on the horizon

Political conditions began to ripen for inclusivity as the years passed, with the mood of the times demanding the political participation and involvement of all citizens in governance. On the international scene, Liberia was one of four African states to sign the charter establishing the United Nations in 1945, the others being Egypt, South Africa, and Ethiopia.[32] Recognition of civil and political rights expanded as the country endeavoured to improve its image.[33] Although the property ownership requirement for voters was maintained, the right to vote and participate in elections was extended in 1946 to indigenes and women.[34] Regionally, anti-colonial liberation movements began to emerge, aiming to combat oppression akin to that suffered by indigenous Liberians. In 1964, indigenous tribes were accorded representation in the legislature.[35] This built upon efforts by President Edwin J Barclay to integrate the interior, including through effective occupation of the interior by establishing physical presence and control

29 W Osoro, "Most Rigged Elections Ever: He Got 243,000 Votes in Country of Less Than 15,000 Registered Voters!", *The Standard*, n.d., https://www.standardmedia.co.ke/entertainment/africannews/article/2001247031/most-rigged-elections-ever-he-got-243000-votes-in-country-of-less-than-15000-registered-voters (accessed 22 February 2024).

30 "Foreign Relations of the United States", *supra* n. 19.

31 Ibid.

32 F Kuwonu, "Four African Countries at the Founding of the UN in San Francisco in 1945", *Africa Renewal,* 28 October 2020, https://africarenewal.un.org/en/magazine/four-african-countries-founding-un-san-francisco-1945 (accessed 24 March 2025).

33 "About the mission", *Liberia Permanent Mission to the UN, n.d., (accessed 16 March 2025)* https://www.pmun.gov.lr/index.php/about-us.

34 "Constitutional History of Liberia", *ConstitutionNet*, n.d., https://constitutionnet.org/country/liberia (accessed 20 February 2024).

35 CM Waugh, *Charles Taylor and Liberia: Ambition and Atrocity in Africa's Lone Star State*, London, Zed Books (2011), p 40.

through administrative structures and deployment of the Liberia Frontier Force.[36] After William Tolbert succeeded Tubman in 1971 as president, he incorporated indigenes in key positions in government.[37]

These overtures went little further than that, however, as the TWP clung to power and the door to pluralism remained shut. Indeed, grassroots mobilisation that threatened the TWP establishment was quickly suppressed. In 1950, Didwho Twe, an indigenous Liberian who garnered much support from indigenes, formed the United People Party (UPP), but the party's application for certification was rejected on the grounds that its membership did not meet the required number of members.[38] Twe himself was soon arrested on allegations of sedition but later released.[39]

The presidential elections of 1951 marked a new phenomenon, as Tubman ran unopposed. Twe was prevented from participating in the elections on the legal ground that he was not registered more than 60 days prior to the elections as a candidate of the Reformation Party, which had been joined by the UPP. Although these machinations served their purpose, it was not long afterwards that conditions began to change. For instance, Albert Porte, a teacher and pamphleteer, raised the consciousness of society, as he criticised government corruption and the extensive authority of the presidency.[40] At the same time, elements within the establishment were growing desirous of a multiparty or bi-party system of politics. As the Liberian ambassador to the US, Charles, King once stated that "loyal, sincere, constructive, and patriotic opposition must be encouraged".[41] President Tubman unofficially said that there would be two political parties in Liberia before he relinquished power.[42]

In 1970, the Student Unification Party was founded, and soon became active in demanding democratic transformation.[43] Meanwhile, the death of President Tubman in 1971 and the political overtures made by his successor,

36 Ibid, p 44.

37 "President William R. Tolbert, Jr", *Liberia Past and Present*, n.d., https://liberiapastandpresent.org/WilliamTolbert.htm (accessed 19 February 2024).

38 "Foreign Relations of the United States", *supra* n. 19.

39 Ibid.

40 A Toure, "The Role of Civil Society in National Reconciliation and Peacebuilding in Liberia", *International Peace Institute* (April 2002), p 9.

41 "Foreign Relations of the United States", *Supra* n. 19.

42 Ibid.

43 "SUP Celebrates Its Anniversary & Explains Its Struggle History", *Democracy Watch*, n.d., https://democracywatchonline.com/sup-celebrates-its-anniversary-explains-its-struggle-history (accessed 3 March 2024).

William R Tolbert, to indigenous Liberians were critical in paving the way for multipartyism.[44] In 1973, the Movement for Justice in Africa was established by a group of students and professors of the University of Liberia, while the Progressive Alliance of Liberia was founded in the US in the next year.[45] These groups worked together to mobilise grassroots support in agitation for political reform. On 14 April 1979, protests against increases in the price of rice led to the death of 200 protesters and left another 700 injured.[46]

A watershed in the country's politics occurred on 12 April 1980, when 28-year-old Master Sergeant Samuel Doe assumed state power through a military coup d'état that left President Tolbert murdered.[47] Doe became the first head of state of exclusively indigenous heritage, ending 133 years of Americo-Liberian rule.[48] He announced the formation of the Peoples' Redemption Council (PRC) and began to rule the country by military decree.[49] Decree No. 2 of the PRC suspended the Constitution and declared martial law.[50] As Article I of the Constitution, entitled "Declaration of Rights", was thereby also suspended, this affected the exercise and enjoyment of rights by all, including the right of association as a political party.[51]

3. Constitution-making and party constitutionalisation in Liberia

3.1 The 1847 Constitution and later developments

There have been two phases of constitution-making in Liberia's 176-year history, with the constitutions of 1847 and 1986 being their products. Nonetheless, constitution-making predates the Liberian state, given that constitutional politics emerged for the first time in 1839 when settlements,

44 Toure, *supra* n. 40, p 9.
45 Ibid.
46 Waugh, *supra* n. 35, p 63.
47 B Marmon, "25 Years after His Demise, Samuel Doe Continues to Cast a Long Shadow across Liberian Politics", *African Arguments*, 9 September 2015, https://africanarguments.org/2015/09/25-years-after-his-demise-samuel-doe-continues-to-cast-a-long-shadow-across-liberian-politics (accessed 3 March 2024).
48 Ibid.
49 GW Schmidt, "The New Constitutional Developments in the Republic of Liberia", 14 (1981) *Verfassung und Recht in Übersee*, pp 243–268, at p 250.
50 Ibid.
51 Ibid.

governed by the American Colonization Society (ACS), united to form the Commonwealth of Liberia.[52]

Prior to the establishment of the Commonwealth, the 1820 and 1824 constitutions promulgated by the ACS were used in administering the colonies. These constitutions were not the outcome of deliberation by settlers, however, and scarcely reflected their concerns and aspirations. In a bid to defuse rising tensions among settlers about their limited role in administration, the ACS held a convention to allow settlers to propose constitutional amendments. This move in 1839 was the first attempt at participatory constitution-making. Delegates at the convention did not hesitate in crafting a new constitution, known as the Monrovia Draft, which in effect expanded opportunities for self-rule.[53] However, unwilling to grant self-rule, the ACS ignored the Monrovia Draft and turned to Thomas Buchanan, governor of the Bassa Cove settlement, appointed him as governor of Liberia in 1839, and tasked him with drawing up a new constitution.[54] Buchanan's draft was approved by the ACS and became the last colonial constitution.[55] Nearly a decade would pass before another opportunity arose for the settlers to find a voice, summon a renewed spirit of nationalism, design a constitution, and ultimately declare independence.

In July 1847, 12 delegates from the three settlements comprising the Commonwealth gathered at a constitutional convention to write Liberia's first constitution.[56] Details about the convention are scant. Original source materials were never published, and the official minutes and two private

52 Founded in 1816, the ACS led efforts to repatriate freed slaves to present-day Liberia. Persons repatriated lived in settlements governed by the colonial constitutions of 1820 and 1824. When Montserrado, Bassa Cove, and Mississippi in Africa settlements formed the Commonwealth, albeit still under the direction of the ACS, participatory constitution-making emerged. Meanwhile, it is to be noted that Maryland in Africa did not form part of the conglomerate until its annexation by Liberia in 1854.

53 J Cash, "A Purer Form of Government: African American Constitutionalism in the Founding of Liberia", 19 (2021) *Journal of Transatlantic Studies*, pp 408–440, at p 415.

54 The draft retained the ultimate political authority of the ACS and its power to appoint the governor. Nonetheless, it provided that the lieutenant-governor and six councillors would be elected by the settlers. The councillors would also, with the governor, make up the legislative branch. It provided for a separate judiciary, an impeachment process for the governor and other officials, and a list of protections resembling a bill of rights. However, it restricted citizenship of the colony to "coloured persons" and suffrage to citizens who owned property and paid taxes. See Cash *supra*, n. 53, p 415.

55 Ibid, p 416.

56 Ibid, p 418.

diaries have not been found.[57] Additionally, the long-standing assumption that the Constitution was written by Simon Greenleaf, a renowned constitutional lawyer from Harvard, contributed to neglect by scholars of local contributions to the document.[58] Contemporary scholarship, however, suggests that the 1847 Constitution was a product of local design rather than simply a replica of the US Constitution, as had been suggested earlier.[59]

First, the Declaration of Independence produced by the Convention was entirely of local origin, while 34 per cent of the Constitution has not been traced to any existing documents, meaning, as such, that it was probably of local origin.[60] Secondly, although not generally schooled in matters of constitutional law, delegates possessed enough relevant education and expertise to enable them contribute to the making of the 1847 Constitution. All were literate, several were full-time educators, some were newspaper editors, lawyers, and judges,[61] and eight held high church offices.[62] Thus, although Greenleaf drafted the Constitution,[63] delegates made substantial inputs. Even where sections were borrowed from elsewhere, they were appropriated in keeping with local as well as contemporaneous worldviews rooted in three intellectual traditions: Christianity, republicanism, and black nationalism.[64] For instance, one account describes the deliberations on the length of the presidential term in these words: "After a great deal of debating, it was resolved that the President be elected for two years."[65] A unitary republic was preferred over federacy, and the executive, legislative, and judicial branches of government were recognised.[66] Citizenship and property ownership were limited to "persons of colour",[67] while the proper-

57 CP Burrowes, "Black Christian Republicans: Delegates to the 1847 Liberian Constitutional Convention", 14 (1989) *Liberian Studies Journal*, pp 64–89, at p 64.

58 Ibid.

59 AJ Beyan, *The American Colonization Society and the Creation of the Liberian State: A Historical Perspective, 1822–1900*, Michigan, University Press of America (1991), p 95.

60 Burrowes, *supra* n. 57, p 65.

61 Cash, *supra* n. 53, p 418.

62 Burrowes, *supra* n. 57, p 64.

63 Schmidt, *supra* n. 49, p 245.

64 Burrowes, *supra* n. 57, p 66.

65 J Cash, *supra* n. 53, p. 418.

66 Liberia Constitution of 1847, Articles I and II.

67 Liberia Constitution of 1847, Article V, section 13.

ty of a woman before marriage was protected as distinctly hers.[68] Slavery and the trade in slaves were outlawed.[69]

Notwithstanding the outcome of the 1847 Constitution and the many virtues of the constitution-making process, the picture is not unblemished. With only 12 delegates attending the convention, it is safe to conclude that the Constitution did not emerge from widespread public consultation. It appears that settlements were represented in proportion to their populations, with six delegates for Montserrado and its 2,000 inhabitants, four delegates for Bassa's 1,000, and two delegates from Sinoe and its 300 inhabitants.[70] It is unclear, however, whether delegates were elected by inhabitants or selected in any such manner that provides due legitimacy. Assuming the delegates were a true representation of the people of the Commonwealth, indigenes – who constituted the majority in the territory – were left out of the convention. They did not participate despite the fact that, at the time, 500 of them had been recognised officially as citizens forming part of the 3,300-person population of the Commonwealth.[71] Yet the Constitution was binding upon indigenes for the 133 years that followed. Indigenes assimilated into the settler-fold still did not get a chance at the table, as all of the delegates hailed from the settler class. As a result, the language of the Declaration of Independence and the Constitution echoed the harrowing experiences of settlers in the US and advanced their aspirations, whereas the indigenes were "othered".[72]

Political parties were not acknowledged in the 1847 Constitution. The words of Hilary Teage, a delegate to the Convention, condemning the "rage and rancour of party spirit" as "deforming" constitutions, suggest that the country's founders sought to keep the republic free of party politics.[73] Notwithstanding the shortcomings and omissions of the 1847 Constitution, constitutional amendments took place over the course of history to address injustices and other gaps. For instance, as mentioned earlier, amendments

68 Liberia Constitution of 1847, Article V, section 10. This banned coverture – the practice whereby a woman's property became her husband's property upon marriage – and dictated that a married woman would continue to own property in her own name after marriage as well as acquire personal property during the marriage.

69 Liberia Constitution of 1847, Article I, section 4.

70 Burrowes, *supra* n. 57, p 65.

71 Indigenous persons could become citizens only after adopting the "civilised" ways of the settlers. See Burrowes, *supra* n. 57, p 65.

72 See Liberia Constitution of 1847, Article V, sections 14 and 15.

73 Cash, *supra* n. 53, p 428.

to the 1847 Constitution saw the recognition of the citizenship rights of the indigenous population and extensions of the presidential term of office. Meanwhile, other proposals were unsuccessful. For example, a proposal by President Tolbert in 1975 to discard property requirements for suffrage resulted in a bill being passed by the House of Representatives, but it was rejected by the Senate in 1977, thereby preventing a referendum on the issue.[74] During a mayoral election for Monrovia in 1979, there were renewed calls for the Senate to pass the bill.[75] In 1979, Tolbert also proposed an amendment that would grant citizenship to persons of non-Negro descent.[76] The 1980 coup brought discussion of all these amendments to an abrupt end.[77]

3.2 The 1986 Constitution and later developments

In March 1981, Doe, then leader of the PRC, appointed a 25-person national constitutional commission from a cross-section of Liberian society to draft a new constitution.[78] Social conditions ripened in favour of multiparty democracy during this period. Although the citizenry had been unshackled from TWP domination, they remained haunted by the excesses of a military regime with anti-democratic propensities. Hence, there was huge public clamour for a constitution informed and improved through consideration of the shortcomings of the previous 1847 Constitution as well as the excesses of the military junta. The desire by the junta to extend the presidential term, prevent multiparty competition, and enable rule by executive fiat provided impetus for pushback.[79] Conditions under the military regime also fuelled support for provisions in the bill of rights, including the right to due process of law, the writ of *habeas corpus*, freedom of movement, freedom of information and access to state-owned media, and academic freedom.[80] Furthermore, treason was clearly defined, while a claims court

74 Schmidt, *supra* n. 49, p 247.
75 Ibid.
76 Ibid, p 246.
77 Ibid.
78 Ibid, p 265.
79 A Sawyer, "The Making of the 1984 Liberian Constitution: Major Issues and Dynamic Forces", 12 (1987) *Liberian Studies Journal*, pp 1–15 at p 8.
80 Ibid, p 5.

was provided for to enable citizen hold the government liable for damages done by it.[81]

Nonetheless, the constitution-making process did not yield the output anticipated by many. This was due in significant part to the later capture of the process by politicians, including leaders of the military regime who harboured political ambitions.[82] As a result, contrary to the draft prepared by the constitutional commission, the final draft passed in the referendum strengthened presidential authority, eliminated key autonomous commissions, removed provisions barring military personnel from participating in politics, and instituted a six-year tenure for the President.[83] Meanwhile, provisions on political parties appeared in the 1986 Constitution for the first time. An entire chapter – Chapter Eight – is dedicated to matters relating to political parties and elections.

In addition, referendums have been held to amend certain provisions of the new Constitution. A 2011 referendum resulted in a change in the criteria for winning non-presidential elections – namely, from an absolute majority to a simple majority of votes cast.[84] In a referendum held in 2020 and boycotted by the opposition, all eight propositions failed to meet the requirement for amendment.[85] The opposition had suspected that the proposition on reducing the length of a presidential term was a ploy to lengthen then President George Weah's stay in office on the basis that the amendment would have reset his term in office.[86] Notwithstanding efforts

81 Ibid.

82 Most of those elected to the Constitutional Advisory Assembly responsible for reviewing the draft constitution prepared by the constitutional commission were political actors. In 1983, the Commission was dissolved without prior notice. It later became clear that the ambitions of its members dovetailed with those of the military head of state. The final constitution reflected these interests, as key provisions in the draft were removed and others added. See Sawyer, *supra* n. 80, p 15.

83 Ibid, p 15.

84 "Liberia: Supreme Court Ratifies a Constitutional Amendment", *Library of Congress*, 27 September 2011, https://www.loc.gov/item/global-legal-monitor/2011-09-27/liberia-supreme-court-ratifies-a-constitutional-amendment (accessed 3 March 2024).

85 H Karmo, "Liberia: Referendum Fails to Meet Constitutional Requirement for Passage", *FrontPage Africa*, 1 April 2021, https://frontpageafricaonline.com/amp/news/liberia-referendum-fails-to-meet-constitutional-requirement-for-passage (accessed 16 April 2024).

86 F Poquie and K Hoije, "Liberia's George Weah Fails to Win Extra Time in Referendum", *Bloomberg*, 2 April 2021, https://www.bloomberg.com/news/articles/2021-04-02/soccer-star-leader-fails-to-win-extra-time-in-liberia-referendum (accessed 24 March 2025).

aimed at ensuring that the Constitution reflects contemporary realities and aspirations, the place of political parties has attracted little consideration.

But just how entrenched are the rights, roles, and responsibilities of political parties in the new Constitution? Does the latter provide for a free and fair competitive political system? To what extent does it protect the electoral management body from partisan control and manipulation? Such an inquiry is crucial, as the presence of free and vibrant political parties that are allowed to compete openly for political power is fundamental for the existence of a genuine multiparty constitutional democracy.[87] Thus, the argument has been made for a solid constitutional framework that empowers political parties to compete (positive constitutionalism) and protects them against manipulation aimed at preventing fair competition (negative constitutionalism).[88] We will now explore the Liberian case.

3.3 Party constitutionalisation in Liberia

There is no generally agreed framework for analysing constitutions in terms of how political parties' rights are entrenched. However, a threefold classification has been used for examining party constitutionalisation in African constitutions.[89] This approach examines constitutions for their recognition of political pluralism (status provisions), the scope of rights and duties imposed on political parties (ancillary-rights provisions), and the regulation of the various processes in which political parties are involved (political-process provisions).[90]

3.3.1 Status provisions

Article 77 of the Constitution not only recognises political parties but also contains provisions as to their basic regulation. It recognises the importance of political parties in expressing ideas and "advocating the political opinions of the people". In doing so, it provides for the establishment of political parties and outlaws any laws or measures with the "effect of

87 Fombad, *supra* n. 11, p 4.
88 Ibid, p 4. See also CM Fombad, "An Overview of Political Party Constitutionalisation under Contemporary African Constitutions", in this volume.
89 Ibid.
90 Ibid.

creating a one-party state". Thus, although multipartyism is not explicitly provided for, the freedom to establish political parties and the negation of a one-party system implicitly guarantee political pluralism. In addition, Article 78 of the Constitution defines a political party and provides for its qualification, establishment, or dissolution. It defines a "political party" as an association whose activities include "canvassing for votes on any public issue or in support of a candidate for elective public office". To qualify as a political party, an association must meet a required minimum of 500 qualified voters in each of at least six counties.

Articles 79 and 80 of the Constitution include further provisions relevant to political parties such as minimum registration requirements,[91] membership,[92] headquarters location,[93] party elections and notification of amendment to party constitution,[94] the prohibition of ethnic and religious connotations,[95] the denial or revocation of registration for use of force or coercion,[96] or seeking to abolish democracy.[97] While these provisions pay attention to the subject of political parties, some observers hold the view that the Constitution ought to stick to basic requirements and not delve into such details, which could be addressed by a subsidiary legislation such as a law on political parties.[98] Yet these and other provisions set a critical basis for party entrenchment.

3.3.2 Ancillary-rights provisions

The Constitution gives political parties a number of ancillary-rights by virtue of their existence. Parties have legal personality, have the capacity to own property and hold accounts, and can sue and be sued.[99] While similar qualities are bestowed on businesses and non-profit organisations

91 Liberian Constitution of 1986, Article 79(a).
92 Ibid, Article 79(b).
93 Ibid, Article 79(c).
94 Ibid, Article 79(e).
95 Ibid, Article 79(d).
96 Ibid, Article 80(b).
97 Ibid, Article 80(a).
98 See "Briefing Paper on Recommendations for Constitutional Reform", *EC-UNDP Electoral Assistance*, 18 February 2019, https://www.ec-undp-electoralassistance.org/wp-content/uploads/sites/18/2019/02/ec-undp-jtf-liberia-resources-recommendations-for-constitutional-reform-final.pdf (accessed 29 February 2025).
99 Liberian Constitution of 1986, Article 79(b).

by the Associations Law of Liberia, political parties draw their legal capacity directly from the Constitution. In furtherance of a political party's capacity to sue, the Constitution provides that denial of party registration by the National Elections Commission (NEC) can be challenged in the Supreme Court.[100] A political party also has the right to challenge election results at the NEC and up to the Supreme Court.[101] The right of access to state-owned media is guaranteed, although this right applies to the entire citizenry and is not specific to political parties.[102]

A framework for party and campaign financing is also provided in the Constitution. Within this arrangement, public funding of political parties is not provided for. Likewise, parties have the right to receive funds for their activities, but there is an express prohibition against receiving funds from citizens or organisations not of Liberian nationality or origin; the same applies to funding from corporate business organisations and labour unions.[103] Parties, furthermore, are not allowed to hold funds or other assets outside of Liberia, or to retain funds sent from abroad unless by Liberians.[104] Any funds received in contravention of the restriction have to be transferred to the NEC within 21 days of receipt.[105] Parties are required to file a report to the NEC on all funds received from abroad.[106] They are also required to publish and submit to the NEC a detailed statement of assets and liabilities, including funding sources and lists of expenditures, as at 1 September of each year.[107] The NEC in turn is authorised to order certified audits of the financial transactions of political parties.[108] Penalties for violations are not provided in the Constitution, though, but left to legislative enactments and administrative regulations.[109]

100 Ibid.
101 Ibid, Article 83(c).
102 Ibid, Article 15(d).
103 Ibid, Article 82(a).
104 Ibid, Article 82(b).
105 Ibid.
106 Ibid.
107 Ibid, Article 83(d).
108 Ibid, Article 82(c).
109 Ibid, Article 84.

3.3.3 Political-process provisions

A central institution in the electoral process is the NEC, the management body responsible for the organisation of elections. It is, however, not entrenched in the Constitution. The NEC is established by a single line in the Constitution without any provisions as to its governance, which is left to enactment by the legislature.[110] Thus, this body is left vulnerable to political interference owing to the lack of constitutional entrenchment of the following key elements: the qualifications necessary for persons to serve as commissioners; vetting requirements; commissioners' immunity from prosecution related their functions; the protection of their remuneration; their tenure; grounds and processes for removal; operational and financial autonomy; and gender representation.

What the Constitution does refer to is the form and day of voting, electoral constituencies, and criteria for winning elections, as well as procedures for resolving electoral disputes. Elections are held by secret ballot.[111]In regard to electoral constituencies, voters have the right to change constituency and vote by absentee ballot.[112] The Constitution is also specific as to when legislative and presidential elections are to occur, namely the second Tuesday in October of each election year.[113] Article 83(b) – which previously provided that all elections of public officers are determined by an absolute majority of votes cast – has been amended to allow for simple majority in non-presidential elections. In presidential elections, the two candidates with the highest number of votes face-off in a run-off if no absolute majority is attained on the first ballot.[114]

As regards dispute resolution, specific timeframes are stipulated for the announcement of results, as well as submission of complaints or appeals. Results are to be declared no later than 15 days after ballots are cast, and a political party has the right to contest the results no later than seven days after they are announced.[115] The NEC is then required to hear the complaint and render a decision within 30 days. Appeals against the NEC's decisions are made to the Supreme Court no later than seven days after

110 Ibid, Article 89.
111 [118] Ibid, Article 77(b).
112 Ibid, Article 80(c).
113 Ibid, Article 83(a).
114 Ibid, Article 83(b).
115 Ibid, Article 83(c).

they are declared.[116] Thereafter, the NEC is required to forward case documents to the Supreme Court within seven days, and the latter, to hear and decide the matter within seven days.[117]

As seen in this analysis, the Constitution recognises political parties and implicitly guarantees multipartyism; it also grants rights to political parties, and provides the basic framework for electoral processes. Nonetheless, the usefulness of these provisions depends primarily on how they are complied with in practice. In this regard, in view of the role of the legislature in enacting laws that give effect to the Constitution, and the role of the Supreme Court in interpreting the Constitution, understanding multipartyism in Liberia requires further analysis of the legal framework. The section that follows is dedicated to this inquiry.

4. Multiparty democracy in practice

4.1 Overview

Liberia's experience of multiparty democracy is fairly recent. Its first truly multiparty elections were held in 1985, and featured four parties: the National Democratic Party of Liberia (NDPL), Liberia Action Party (LAP), Unity Party (UP), and Liberia Unification Party.[118] This initial brush with multipartyism did not go well, however. A military leader, Samuel Doe of the NDPL, was proclaimed the winner, with 50.9 per cent of votes, even though it was widely held that he had lost.[119] Most observers believed that

116 Ibid.

117 Ibid.

118 Although elections prior to 1985 had featured two or more political parties, most of these parties were not viable and were inconsistent in their participation in elections, in addition to which the TWP dominated the political landscape. See "4 Liberians Run for President in Nation's First Multiparty Election", *New York Times*, 16 October 1985, https://www.nytimes.com/1985/10/16/world/4-liberians-run-for-president-in-nation-s-first-multiparty-election.html (accessed 16 November 2024).

119 B Harden, "Liberia's Incumbent Declared Winner in Disputed Election", *Washington Post*, 29 October 1985, https://www.washingtonpost.com/archive/politics/1985/10/30/liberias-incumbent-declared-winner-in-disputed-election/fd180129-8dc3-4fe6-83ea-599242ceee83 (accessed 5 March 2024).

Doe garnered only half of the votes attributed to him and that Jackson Doe of the LAP was the actual winner.[120]

On 24 December 1989, Charles Taylor launched an invasion of Liberia from the country's border with the Ivory Coast, ostensibly in reaction to corruption, nepotism, tribalism, and a failing democracy.[121] For the next 14 years, the country was afflicted by a civil war that claimed more than 200,000 lives. By the mid-1990s, Taylor's rebel group, the National Patriotic Front of Liberia (NPFL), held more than 95 per cent of Liberia, with Doe and Prince Johnson, a breakaway rebel leader, controlling parts of the capital.[122] Doe was gruesomely murdered by Johnson's forces in 1990 in the presence of a peacekeeping mission from the Economic Community of West African States (ECOWAS) sub-region.[123]

Three interim governments incorporating warring factions were established in the period spanning 1990 to 1997.[124] In August 1996, the fourteenth peace accord was consummated and led to presidential and legislative elections in July 1997.[125] In these elections, Taylor and his National Patriotic Party (NPP), the successor of the NPFL, won with a landslide of 75 per cent of votes,[126] including more than half of the votes in every county.[127] Legislative seats were allocated through proportional representation, with the NPP allocated 49 of 64 seats in the House of Representatives and 21 of 26 seats in the Senate.[128]

---

120 D Harris, "From 'Warlord' to 'Democratic' President: How Charles Taylor Won the 1997 Liberian Elections", 37 (1999) *Journal of Modern African Studies*, pp 431-455, at p 431.

121 S Momodu, "First Liberian Civil War (1989–1996)", *Black Past*, 25 July 2016, https://www.blackpast.org/global-african-history/first-liberian-civil-war-1989-1996 (accessed 16 April 2024).

122 Harris, *supra* n. 127, p 434.

123 "The Death of Samuel Doe", *BBC*, 25 September 2011, https://www.bbc.co.uk/programmes/p00k69lp (accessed 17 November 2024).

124 F Gerdes, *Civil War and State Formation: The Political Economy of War and Peace in Liberia*, Frankfurt am Main, Campus (2013), p 36.

125 Harris, *supra* n. 127, p 431.

126 Ibid.

127 Ibid, p 432.

128 The UP and the All Liberia Coalition Party, which came second and third, respectively, were the only other parties to be represented in both the House and the Senate. In addition, three other parties, the Alliance, the United People's Party, and the Liberian People's Party, gained seats in the House alone. See Harris, *supra* n. 127, p 435.

While most observers reported positively on the elections, the concerns that arose brought into focus the need to reinforce democratic processes. Notably, the playing field was unequal, given the immense resources at Taylor's disposal. The British observer mission, for instance, noted that "most parties attracted attention to their presidential candidates but lacked the finance or organization for effective campaigning";[129] in the Taylor campaign, by contrast, T-shirts and bags of rice flowed freely to voters. Taylor's radio station, Kiss FM, was also a major advantage, as it reached far beyond Monrovia and issued broadcasts throughout the night.[130] Concerns in this regard related to campaign finance controls and the need for state funding of political parties. Other concerns had to do with the lack of voter education, inadequate voter registration, and the disenfranchisement of about 650,000 refugees outside of Liberia.[131] Holding multiparty elections without civic voter education and a process that guarantees the registration of eligible persons calls into question of whether their outcomes could be considered truly democratic.

Taylor did not complete his term in office, as another crisis broke out few years after he took office and pushed him into exile in August 2003, leading to formation of a transitional government called the National Transitional Government of Liberia (NTGL).[132] Liberia's new electoral dispensation thus began in 2005, with the election of Africa's first female president, Ellen Johnson-Sirleaf of the LAP.[133] The success of the 2005 election has been attributed to two main factors: the absence of an incumbent, and the virtual absence of rebel forces from the ballot – the latter was due to the fact that the Comprehensive Peace Accord banned certain individuals in the NTGL from contesting in elections.[134] Despite the lack of an incumbent,

---

129 Ibid, p 438.

130 Harris, *supra* n. 127, p 438.

131 Refugees who were unwilling or unable to return to Liberia were in all likelihood excluded from the elections for reasons related to logistics, costs, the desire to complete an election sooner rather than later, and the reluctance by Guinea and the Ivory Coast to allow voting in refugee camps.

132 K Vick, "Taylor Resigns, Leaves Liberia", *Washington Post*, 27 February 2024, https://www.washingtonpost.com/archive/politics/2003/08/12/taylor-resigns-leaves-liberia/829c9533-e940-480d-a0fd-ec51a5b5ffef (accessed 5 March 2024).

133 T Ford, "Ellen Johnson Sirleaf: The Legacy of Africa's First Elected Female President", *British Broadcasting Corporation*, 21 January 2018, https://www.bbc.com/news/world-africa-42748769 (accessed 5 March 2024).

134 D Harris, "Liberia 2005: An Unusual African Post-Conflict Election", 44 (2006) *Journal of Modern African Studies*, pp 375–395 at p 375. Many rebel leaders pledged

however, the Coalition for the Transformation of Liberia (COTOL) is reported to have received significant government resources, as its leader, Varney Sherman, had been instrumental in the hasty signing of key NTGL deals.[135] Sherman's LAP, the mainstay of COTOL, also enjoyed the NTGL as a member.[136]

Sirleaf won a second presidential term in 2011 but ceded power in 2018 to George Weah of the Congress for Democratic Change (CDC) following the 2017 elections, marking Liberia's first democratic transfer of power in 73 years.[137] The country's most recent elections, in 2023, resulted in a second democratic transfer, this time following a tightly contested election in which Weah lost narrowly to Joseph Boakai of the Unity Party (UP) by a little more than 20,000 votes.[138]

With West Africa having been rocked by military coups and attempts to extend presidential term limits, Liberia hence stands out as a testament to the feasibility of multiparty democracy in the region. Nevertheless, given its not-so-distant history of one-party rule, military dictatorship, and civil war, care must be taken to ensure that the country remains on course. Because political parties are crucial to the democratic process, it is just as crucial that constitutional safeguards be in place to ensure fair and competitive electoral processes.

---

support to other political parties. For example, Sekou Conneh, leader of Liberians United for Reconciliation and Democracy (LURD), contested in the election, but the challenge was ineffectual as his estranged wife and party co-leader, Aisha Konneh, supported Sirleaf.

135 Ibid, p 377.

136 Ibid.

137 "Seven Things to Know About Liberia's First Democratic Handover in 73 years", *TRT World*, 6 October 2017, https://www.trtworld.com/middle-east/seven-things-to-know-about-liberias-first-democratic-handover-in-73-years-13096400 (accessed 5 March 2025).

138 M Garzeawu and F Chothia, "Joseph Boakai: Liberia's New President Takes on Tough Challenge", *British Broadcasting Corporation*, 22 January 2024, https://www.bbc.com/news/world-africa-67995793/ (accessed 5 March 2024).

4.2 Political parties in perspective

Liberia has 46 registered political parties and coalitions.[139] This is reflective of multipartyism, although only to an extent. Of this number, only 20 fielded presidential candidates in the last elections.[140] This raises questions about party proliferation and its propensity to distract from the political process. A key issue is whether inactive political parties are serving the purpose of organising citizens to pursue causes and providing leadership options, or are being used instead by their handlers as means for negotiating patronage. Concerns like these are bolstered by the tendency for such parties to give endorsements during run-off elections and receive rewarding jobs in government thereafter. Indeed, it is evident that a majority of Liberia's parties lack the gravitas, finances, and organisation to be able to function independently, with many of them being little more than cults of personality that fade away when key leaders leave the scene. For example, the NDPL won the first multiparty elections but lost prominence when Samuel Doe passed away in 1990 and is now defunct. Similarly, the NAP declined in relevance with Charles Taylor's exit from power, even though it remains operational and continues to have a support base.

Thus, even though Liberia's framework allows for multiple parties, operational and political exigencies have served to narrow political contests, with fewer and fewer parties appearing on the ballot; conversely, mergers and coalition-building are increasingly becoming an indispensable feature of Liberian politics. The two leading political organisations are a prime example: while the new Unity Party is a product of a merger of the LAP, the Liberia Unification Party, and the UP in 2009,[141] the Coalition for Democratic Change is comprised of the NPP, Liberia People Democratic Party, and the CDC.[142] Furthermore, the absolute-majority standard for

139 National Elections Commission, "Statistics", https://www.necliberia.org/ (accessed 5 March 2025).

140 O Saliu, "Liberia's Political Parties Hold Final Rallies Ahead of Polls", *Xinhua News Agency*, 9 October 2023, https://english.news.cn/20231009/6862d6035f594fe8ba03c3316aafa4f9/c.html (accessed 5 March 2025).

141 C Kelly, "Party Proliferation and Trajectories of Opposition: Comparative Analysis from Senegal", 50 (2018) *Comparative Politics*, pp 209–229.

142 V Kamara, "Liberia: NPP Plans Exit from the Coalition for Democratic Change", *FrontPage Africa*, 19 January 2024, https://frontpageafricaonline.com/news/liberia-npp-plans-exit-from-the-coalition-for-democratic-change (accessed 5 March 2024).

winning presidential elections on the first ballot has incentivised party collaboration. This has prevented a dominant political party from emerging and contributed to power alternation, particularly between the UP and Coalition for Democratic Change. For Boakai, the UP's candidate, to win the 2023 presidential elections, it took the endorsement of key parties that contested in the first round.[143] It is also important to note that in the new dispensation of multipartyism (that is, 2005 to the present), ruling parties have not had a majority of seats in the legislature,[144] a situation that has helped promote collaboration in the legislature across party lines.

While the constitutional entrenchment of political parties is critical to a free and fair political process, the parties themselves must endeavour to be viable if they are truly to benefit from constitutional safeguards. Having strong and enduring political parties depends very much on the institutional framework for party governance. The reason is that parties having, or seeking, state power in a democratic state should aspire to and uphold democratic values: one cannot give what one does not have; hence, intra-party processes prefigure the governance to be offered by political parties. Internal democracy, thus, is a function of the organisation of the party itself and how it interacts with its members, rather than of how it interacts with the state.[145]

As mentioned, the Constitution sets the minimum criteria of party membership at 500 qualified voters in each of at least six counties. However, the new Elections Law as amended 2014 changed this requirement by providing for a minimum of 500 qualified voters in each of at least 12 counties.[146] It is worth noting that the constitutional requirement was set when Liberia had only nine counties and not the 15 of today.[147] Arguably, these provisions aim to ensure that parties' membership spreads across at least two-thirds

143 "Endorsements Epidemic Overwhelms Campaigns -CDC, UP Lobby Political Groups, Other Heavy Weights", *Analyst Liberia*, 3 November 2023, https://analystliberiaonline.com/endorsements-epidemic-overwhelms-campaigns-cdc-up-lobby-political-groups-other-heavy-weights (accessed 5 March 2024).

144 "NEC Policy Paper No. 6", *EC-UNDP Electoral Assistance*, 18 February 2019, https://www.ec-undp-electoralassistance.org/wp-content/uploads/sites/18/2019/02/ec-undp-jtf-liberia-resources-nec-pp-political-party-functioning-31-01-19.pdf (accessed 25 September 2024).

145 Y Mersel, "The Dissolution of Political Parties: The Problem of Internal Democracy", 4 (2006) *International Journal of Constitutional Law*, pp 84-113, at p 86.

146 1986 Elections Law, as amended in 2014, section 1(2)(c).

147 *Supra* n. 105.

of Liberia's counties.[148] Yet, although tending to reflect the spirit of the Constitution in the contemporary era, the new Elections Law contradicts the plain text of the Constitution. As such, there is a need for a constitutional amendment to reflect the new geography. Also, it remains unclear what mechanisms are employed by the NEC to ensure that membership rolls submitted by parties are verified.

There are records indicating that political parties and coalitions hold elections at least once every six years; what is doubted is the extent to which these elections are democratic. For instance, it is unknown whether primary elections were held by all parties or coalitions fielding candidates in the 2023 elections.[149] For example, the UP held endorsement events rather than primary elections, while other parties holding primaries principally used white ballots, as candidates ran unopposed.[150] Furthermore, parties have fallen short in ensuring women's participation in politics. Although parties recently agreed that a minimum of 30 per cent of candidates would be women, women's share of votes amounted only to 15 per cent in the last elections.[151]

Financing is also crucial to party governance. The Constitution, as discussed earlier, does not provide for public funding of political parties, even while it seeks to regulate the sources of party funds. There can be no denying that finances are important in electoral processes; as such, a robust multiparty system should have a place for public funding of political parties if these parties are to be vibrant, competitive, and not beholden to those who finance them. The Constitution prohibits funding from non-Liberian sources, businesses and trade unions, in addition to which campaign finance regulations also spell out what acceptable sources of campaign finance are, but reports show that these provisions are often

148 Ibid.

149 Elections Coordinating Committee Liberia, "Only Six of the 35 Registered Parties and Coalitions' Primaries Were Observed by ECC – 2023 Parties Candidates' List are Generally Based on Consensus", https://eccliberiacom.org/only-six-of-the-35-registered-parties-and-coalitions-primaries-were-observed-by-ecc-2023-parties-candidates-list-are-generally-based-on-consensus/ (accessed 6 March 2024).

150 Ibid.

151 Electoral Institute for Sustainable Democracy, "Liberia's Political Parties Fall Short of Gender Quota Commitment", *Electoral Institute for Sustainable Democracy*, 18 July 2023, https://www.eisa.org/liberias-political-parties-fall-short-of-gender-quota-commitment/ (accessed 7 March 2024).

breached.[152] Levelling the playing field would entail financing from the state. In the absence of state funding, parties remain vulnerable to influence by wealthy donors; at the same time, those unable to find donors soon become irrelevant and virtually collapse. It may also be argued that, given poor compliance with the reporting requirements laid down in the Constitution, state funding of parties would impose a further duty to report on funding received.

4.3 Elections in practice

A key ingredient of a free and fair political process is the operation of the NEC, which sits at the heart of it all. Hence, the need for an independent, competent NEC cannot be emphasised enough. The Constitution establishes the NEC as an autonomous public commission,[153] while the Elections Law goes further to stipulate that it is "independent of any branch of the Government".[154] The reality, however, is that the NEC has been established in such a manner as to render it vulnerable to manipulation by the incumbent government – thanks to the lack of constitutional provisions clearly providing for safeguards.

Although an autonomous commission, the NEC has complained on several occasions about its lack of funds. This is despite the fact that it is meant to receive funding at the beginning of every six months, specifically on 1 January and 1 July.[155] Shortage of funds compromises the independence and autonomy of the NEC, as it has to engage with members of the incumbent government for the allotments due it. Key, too, is the power of President to appoint NEC commissioners, a power often exercised in the absence of vetting procedures involving civil society, political parties, and other actors.[156] For the NEC to be truly independent, it would have to be entrenched more deeply in the Constitution, particularly in regard to questions of

152 GB Quansah, "Integrity Watch Liberia Reports Violation in October 2023 Elections", *Reports 231*, 30 October 2023, https://reports231.com/integrity-watch-liberia-reports-violation-in-october-2023-elections/ (accessed 18 November 2024).

153 Liberian Constitution of 1986, Article 89(b).

154 1986 Elections Law, as amended in 2014, section 2(9).

155 Ibid, section 11(2).

156 "NEC Policy Paper No. 5: Principles for Election Management", EC-UNDP, 31 January 2019, https://www.ec-undp-electoralassistance.org/wp-content/uploads/sites/18/2019/02/ec-undp-jtf-liberia-resources-nec-pp-election-administration-final-31-01-19.pdf (accessed 25 February 2024).

autonomy, vetting, appointment, tenure, and gender – as regards the latter, for example, the Elections Law does not provide benchmarks for gender representation on the seven-person Board of Commissioners.

As matters stand, then, the NEC is vulnerable to manipulation by the legislature and the executive. Given that it is a creature of statute, it is exposed to the possibility that the legislature could decide to amend or repeal the Elections Law that provides its operational framework. It is conceivable, for example, that an amended law could dissolve the NEC's Board of Commissioners; similarly, on the executive front, an incumbent government could use its control of resource allocation and appointments to the NEC to manipulate the latter in a manner prejudicial to the opposition. For instance, there is neither a limit on the number of times commissioners may be reappointed, nor an age limit set for their retirement. Thus, an incumbent government could keep reappointing a commissioner for all eternity as long as he or she works in its interests.

Importantly, the NEC also exercises quasi-judicial powers, albeit that some have questioned the rationale for allowing the NEC to review its own decisions. According to the Elections Coordinating Committee, Article 83(c) of the Constitution "creates conflict of interest and does not reflect transparency and impartiality in adjudicating electoral grievances and petitions in cases wherein [the] NEC is a respondent".[157] Furthermore, a European Union election observer mission stated in its final report on the 2023 elections that " as electoral disputes are handled by the NEC, some stakeholders questioned its capacity to conduct hearings and appeals in an independent manner, as this arrangement can result in adjudications of complaints of the NEC against itself".[158] Nonetheless, the right of appeal to the Supreme Court serves to address concerns about possible missteps by the NEC.

The Commission also plays another important role in elections: constituency demarcation. However, it has been handicapped in performing this task due to the failure of other government functionaries to play their part. Article 80 of the Constitution provides for the conduct of a census, as well as the determination of a population threshold per constituency by the legislature and the reapportionment of constituencies. The Supreme Court

157 European Union Election Observation Mission, *Liberia, 2023: Final Report*, https://www.eods.eu/library/EU%20EOM%20LIB%202023%20FR.pdf (accessed 20 February 2024).

158 Ibid.

of Liberia in the case, *Re: Constitutionality of the National Elections Commission Planned Conduct of Voters Registration without the Demarcation of Constitutional Electoral Constituencies,* held that a census is a precondition for the legislature to set a threshold and that such legislative action is in turn a precondition for boundary demarcation by the NEC.[159] Hence, the Court ruled that the NEC could not be held liable for the failure to demarcate constituencies since, in fact, a final census report had not been submitted to the legislature.[160] As a result, new constituencies were not drawn for the 2023 elections.

Here, it is important to note that a census constitutionally scheduled for 2018 was held only in 2022, but a few months prior to the elections. The decision by the Supreme Court essentially gives a green light to the executive to fail to deliver on preconditions so as to keep the NEC from demarcating boundaries. This has implications for fair representation in a democratic state, as it must necessarily be proportional to population limitations provided for by the Constitution.

As can be gleaned from the above, constitutional review has a crucial role to play in the democratic process. The Supreme Court of Liberia, using its power of judicial review, has reviewed several decisions by the NEC. Also, as a constitutional court, it has handed down rulings interpreting the Constitution, aspects of which border on the rights of political parties. In the case *Unity Party (UP) et al. v Collaborating Political Parties (CPP) et al. (2022),* involving the question of whether an agreement establishing a coalition of political parties can validly prohibit member political parties from disengaging and fielding candidates separately, the Supreme Court held that the right to associate, to dissociate, to refuse to associate, and to contest and participate in elections is fundamentally protected under articles 17 and 19 of the Constitution and cannot be curtailed by an agreement between parties.[161] The Court further asserted that a political party can be denied participation in an election only for a cause under law and not as consented to by the parties.

The Court then elaborated on the role of the NEC in ensuring that agreements or other filings by political parties are not reviewed perfunc-

159 Supreme Court of Liberia, *Re: The Constitutionality of the National Elections Commission Planned Conduct of the Voters Registration,* 3 May 2023.

160 Ibid.

161 Supreme Court of Liberia, *Unity Party (UP) et al. v Collaborating Political Parties (CPP) et al.*, 3 June 2022.

torily but in such a manner as to establish whether any provisions are "manifestly against the letter, intent, and spirit of the Constitution", and if so, deny such filing until said provision is amended or removed. Also, in the case *National Elections Commission et al. v Bility et al.*,[162] the Supreme Court held that where a complaint alleges fraud relating to tampering with legal instruments, or make declarations regarding the illegality of the constitution of a political party, the NEC lacks the power and authority to investigate the complaint – only the courts have such power and authority. Thus, it must be concluded that constitutional courts can exercise checks on election management bodies and political parties.

4.4 The political environment

Credit for the survival of multiparty democracy in Liberia is due in good part to the constitutional, legislative, and regulatory frameworks that address the rights and responsibilities of political parties and define electoral processes. Further credit is due, however, to the determination of the Liberian people, including the military, to sustain the peace by discouraging and disengaging from anti-democratic activities. For instance, campaigning in the 2023 elections was largely peaceful, notwithstanding isolated incidents of violence.[163] The fact that four consecutive presidential elections, and six legislative elections, were held between 2005 to 2023 is testament to the conviction of the Liberian people, government and citizens alike.

Nonetheless, the situation has been less than perfect. This is evident in Freedom House's Freedom in the World report of 2024, which classifies Liberia as "partly free" and assigns it a score of 64 out of 100 points (identical to the global average of 64).[164] Countries in the "partly free" category are regarded as electoral democracies. Liberia saw the largest improvement in score in Africa, having obtained four more points in 2024 over and above the 60 it scored in 2023.[165] According to the report, "political parties

---

162 Supreme Court of Liberia, *National Elections Commission et al. v Bility et al.*, 12 April 2023.

163 European Union Election Observation Mission, *supra* n. 165, p 6.

164 Freedom House, "Freedom in the World 2024: Liberia", *Freedom House*, n.d., https://freedomhouse.org/country/liberia/freedom-world/2024 (accessed 7 March 2024).

165 Freedom House, "New Report: Africa Marks a Decade of Decline in Freedom, with 2023 Being Marred by Electoral Violence and Civil Conflict", *Freedom House*, 29 February 2024, https://freedomhouse.org/article/new-report-africa-marks-decad

generally do not face undue legal or practical obstacles that prevent them from forming or operating".[166] This finding is corroborated by the 2023 election observation report of the European Union, which stated that the political freedoms of candidates and supporters were largely respected.[167]

Despite respect for the political freedoms of political parties, candidates, and their supporter, abuse of incumbency was cited as a problem in the 2023 elections. The NEC's oversight of campaign finance regulation has been non-existent, thus allowing the then ruling coalition (the CDC) to employ state resources and distort the playing field.[168] For example, national and local level government staff campaigned during working hours, and government buildings and vehicles were used for campaign purposes.[169] Also, 84 per cent of time attributed to political contestants by the state-owned broadcaster, Liberia National Television, was allocated to the ruling CDC, while the UP, as the leading opposition party at the time, received under 5 per cent.[170] Similarly, the state-owned station, ELBC, allocated 70 per cent of time attributed to political contestants to the CDC.[171] Public facilities belong to the public, and not an incumbent political party; thus, members of the public, including parties, are entitled to benefit from the services provided.

The incumbent's effective control of state-owned facilities to the exclusion of opposition parties ought to be addressed in order to level the field. Denying opposition parties the use of city halls, stadiums, billboards, and state-owned media is anti-democratic and must not be allowed to continue. For example, in December 2022, the Ministry of Youth and Sports, after receiving payment for use of the facility, denied use of the Samuel Kanyon Doe Sports Complex to the Collaborating Political Parties, ostensibly due to renovation works.[172]

---

e-decline-freedom-2023-being-marred-electoral-violence-and (accessed 7 March 2024).

166 Freedom House, *supra* n. 172.

167 European Union Election Observation Mission, *supra* n.165.

168 Ibid.

169 Ibid, p 6.

170 Ibid.

171 Ibid.

172 "Youth and Sports Minister Says SKD Stadium Will Not Be Used for Any Rally", *Smart News Liberia*, 6 December 2022, https://smartnewsliberia.com/youth-and-sports-minister-says-skd-stadium-will-not-be-used-for-any-rally (accessed 19 November 2024).

One major component of Liberia's political ecosystem is its civil society. There are 647 registered civil society organisations (CSOs), faith-based organisations, and community-based organisations in the country,[173] a number which is likely to be far greater if unregistered and informal grassroots organisations are also considered.[174] CSOs function as "civic intermediaries" between citizens and government because they have earned citizens' trust and possess the networks and skills to mobilise citizens into action.[175] They work on a range of issues, including health, natural resources management, education, governance, and – in particular – elections.

In the 2023 elections, for instance, CSOs such as the Elections Coordinating Committee and the Liberia Elections Observation Network were involved at different stages of the electoral cycle. Observation missions from the African Union, ECOWAS, European Union, and US Agency for International Development also participated in election monitoring. Approximately 8,400 citizens and some 1,500 international observers were accredited to observe the second round of elections in 2023.[176] From voter registration to vote tallying, they identified glitches within the process and raised red flags. Other organisations were involved in civic voter education, raising awareness among citizens of the importance of voting and informing them about how to vote. Others yet, such as Local Voices Liberia, fact-checked campaign messages and messages on electoral fraud and election-related violence.[177] This was key for building voters' trust in the electoral process. When voters are informed about their rights and responsibilities and trust the electoral process, they participate fully, including through poll-watching to protect the democratic process.

173 "2022 Civil Society Organization Sustainability Index", *Fhi 360*, (2023), p 33, https://www.fhi360.org/wp-content/uploads/2024/02/csosi-africa-2022-report.pdf (accessed 2 March 2024).

174 While non-governmental organisations in Liberia may register and operate freely, some of the registration and accreditation requirements are cumbersome, resulting in a large number of such organisations being unregistered.

175 A Ware, "The essential characteristics of Liberian civil society", *Lilly Family School of Philanthropy*, 1 July 2020, https://blog.philanthropy.iupui.edu/2020/07/01/the-essential-characteristics-of-liberian-civil-society (accessed 7 March 2024).

176 European Union Election Observation Mission, *supra* n. 165, p 8.

177 Ibid, p 2.

4.5 The military factor

Although Liberia has felt the debilitating effects of military dictatorships on democracy,[178] the military has, to a large extent, proven to be a transformed "force for good" despite isolated indiscretions. Its non-interference in political and electoral matters sets it apart from many of its counterparts in West Africa.[179] The professionalism of the military may be credited to a reform in 2006 that disbanded the then military and instituted stringent measures for recruitment to a newly constituted army.[180] An important aspect of the reform was the enactment of the National Defense Act, which limits the involvement of the Armed Forces of Liberia (AFL) in civilian affairs by setting out its duties, inter alia, as follows:

> [T]he duties of the AFL in peacetime shall include support to the national law enforcement agencies when such support is requested and approved by the President. Such support shall include the exchange of information, personnel training, and mobilization and deployment of security contingents. At no time during peacetime, however, shall the AFL engage in law enforcement within Liberia, such function being the prerogative of the Liberia National Police and other law enforcement agencies ... The AFL shall intervene only as a last resort when the threat exceeds the capability of the law enforcement agencies to respond.[181]

Importantly, the AFL also has an order of merit that clearly lays out qualifications for military positions, as well as procedures for removal or filling of vacancies.[182] As a result, there is limited political interference in military affairs, with military leaders being required to operate with professionalism and independence.

---

178 C Wratto, "Liberia Transferred Power Peacefully Again: 3 Reasons the Calm is Holding, and One Red Flag", *The Conversation*, 23 January 2024, http://theconversation.com/liberia-transferred-power-peacefully-again-3-reasons-the-calm-is-holding-and-one-red-flag-221656 (accessed 5 March 2024).

179 In Guinea, Mali, Burkina Faso, and Niger, the military has recently toppled constitutionally elected governments. In Nigeria, it has been conspicuous in political processes.

180 M Malan, *Security Sector Reform in Liberia: Mixed Results from Humble Beginnings*, Pennsylvania, US Army War College, Strategic Studies Institute (2008), pp 29–35.

181 2008 National Defense Act, section 2(3)(e).

182 "AFL Administers Officers' Promotion Exam – Exercise Boldstriker 2018", *Ministry of National Defense*, 2018, https://mod.gov.lr/afl-administers-officers-promotion-exam-exercise-boldstriker-2018 (accessed 2 September 2024).

Be that as it may, when Freedom FM, a local media outlet, reported political division in the army during the 2023 elections, the army arrested and interrogated the outlet's owner, Sam Siryon, who was also the Deputy Director of the National Security Agency.[183] Siryon apologised.[184] Meanwhile, others criticised the military's arrest of a civilian as interference in civilian affairs and reminiscent of the dark days of military dictatorship.[185] Others yet argued that the action of the military was important in preventing incitement and polarisation of the army, which could have detrimental effects for the electoral process and the country at large. In any case, through its actions, the military leadership made a strong statement about the importance of its independence and its commitment to remain neutral in the political process.

This commitment was maintained and exhibited in crucial moments. In fact, the military chief, Major-General Prince C Johnson III, was unequivocal in encouraging electoral candidates and their supporters, regardless of status or affiliation, to use the courts in case of disenchantment and to refrain from "taking law into their own hands".[186] He stated that the AFL would intervene in cases the Liberia National Police could not handle, saying, "We will not allow anyone or a group of people to obstruct our hard-earned peace and democracy."[187] He is also on record as saying that the military's loyalty is, first and foremost, to the Liberian state and not to individuals.[188]

183 "Freedom FM Apologizes to AFL for Dangerous Comment, as PUL Rebukes the Pro-Gov't Station", *News Public Trust*, 21 October 2023, https://newspublictrust.com/freedom-fm-apologizes-to-afl-for-dangerous-comment-as-pul-rebukes-the-pro-govt-station (accessed 8 August 2024).

184 Ibid.

185 "Liberia: Military Meddling in Civil Affairs: Condemning the Arrest of Deputy NSA Director Sam Siryon", *FrontPage Africa*, 23 October 2023, https://frontpageafricaonline.com/editorial/liberia-military-meddling-in-civil-affairs-condemning-the-arrest-of-deputy-nsa-director-sam-siryon (accessed 2 September 2024).

186 "Liberian Army Chief of Staff Says Some Citizens Urging Him to Overthrow Pres. Weah", *News Public Trust*, 7 December 2022, https://newspublictrust.com/liberian-army-chief-of-staff-says-some-citizens-urging-him-to-overthrow-pres-weah (accessed 8 August 2024).

187 Ibid.

188 F Sainworla, "At Liberia Media-Security Forum: AFL Chief of Staff Vows to Only 'Obey Legal Orders'", *News Public Trust*, 31 March 2022, https://newspublictrust.com/at-liberia-media-security-forum-afl-chief-of-staff-vows-to-only-obey-legal-orders (accessed 1 September 2024).

This commitment proved to be true even when the 2023 presidential elections became highly contested. Arguably, former President Weah's admission of defeat meant that the army's resilience was not put to the test by a call-up by the President. But it could be argued too that the disposition of the army to take only legal orders and stand by the law dissuaded any attempts by the incumbent to hold on to power. The story of Liberia's progress with multiparty democracy thus cannot be told without recognising the army's role in respecting and promoting democratic space.

5. Conclusion

Liberia is successfully consolidating its democratic gains. This is due not only to its legal framework but to the determination of the Liberian people not return to the dark days of conflict and military rule. The Constitution entrenches political parties through status recognition, grant of ancillary rights, and the stipulation of processes for elections. Yet gaps exist when it comes to party financing and access to state-owned facilities, gaps that serve to hamper competition on an equalised playing field. Providing public funding to political parties would serve three functions. First, it helps reduce dependence on funding by political leaders, thereby strengthening intra-party governance. Secondly, it contributes to the accountability of parties by placing them in the ambit of public-sanctioned audit by virtue of their receipt of public funds; notwithstanding limited compliance with reporting requirements, parties would be obliged to keep proper records and report on finances. Thirdly, the provision of adequate funding to political parties would discourage them from obtaining funds from prohibited sources.

Another key take-away is that participatory democracy in Liberia is undermined by the failure to demarcate electoral boundaries due to a lack of census data. As a result, representation in the national legislature is inconsistent with the population limits set by the Constitution. Furthermore, the abuse of incumbency – including by using state assets for campaign purposes and denying opposition parties access state-owned facilities – is anti-democratic and must be addressed. Dealing with these issues through a constitutional framework would be an appropriate safeguard against abuses that frustrate democratic ends. While subsidiary legislation may help address these issues, it remains subject to change and the whims of legislators, agency officials, and politicians. With the Constitution, there is a greater force of law, and changes in its provisions can occur only by referendum. Furthermore, by enshrining protective provisions in the Constitution, the Supreme Court would be properly vested with the original jurisdiction to regulate political parties.

References

Books, articles, chapters in books, and others

"4 Liberians Run for President in Nation's First Multiparty Election", *New York Times*, 16 October 1985, https://www.nytimes.com/1985/10/16/world/4-liberians-run-for-president-in-nation-s-first-multiparty-election.html (accessed 16 November 2024)

"2022 Civil Society Organization Sustainability Index", *Fhi 360*, (2023), p 33, https://www.fhi360.org/wp-content/uploads/2024/02/csosi-africa-2022-report.pdf (accessed 2 March 2025)

"AFL Administers Officers' Promotion Exam – Exercise Boldstriker 2018", *Ministry of National Defense*, 2018, https://mod.gov.lr/afl-administers-officers-promotion-exam-exercise-boldstriker-2018 (accessed 2 September 2024)

"Briefing Paper on Recommendations for Constitutional Reform", *EC-UNDP Electoral Assistance*, 18 February 2019, https://www.ec-undp-electoralassistance.org/wp-content/uploads/sites/18/2019/02/ec-undp-jtf-liberia-resources-recommendations-for-constitutional-reform-final.pdf (accessed 29 February 2024)

"Constitutional History of Liberia", *ConstitutionNet*, n.d., https://constitutionnet.org/country/liberia (accessed 20 February 2024)

"Endorsements Epidemic Overwhelms Campaigns -CDC, UP Lobby Political Groups, Other Heavy Weights", *Analyst Liberia*, 3 November 2023, https://analystliberiaonline.com/endorsements-epidemic-overwhelms-campaigns-cdc-up-lobby-political-groups-other-heavy-weights (accessed 5 March 2024)

"Foreign Relations of the United States, 1951, The Near East and Africa, Vol. 5 (1951)", Office of the Historian, n.d., https://history.state.gov/historicaldocuments/frus1951v05/d722 (accessed 28 February 2024)

"Freedom FM Apologizes to AFL for Dangerous Comment, as PUL Rebukes the Pro-Gov't Station", *News Public Trust*, 21 October 2023, https://newspublictrust.com/freedom-fm-apologizes-to-afl-for-dangerous-comment-as-pul-rebukes-the-pro-govt-station (accessed 8 August 2024)

"Liberia: Military Meddling in Civil Affairs: Condemning the Arrest of Deputy NSA Director Sam Siryon", *FrontPage Africa*, 23 October 2023, https://frontpageafricaonline.com/editorial/liberia-military-meddling-in-civil-affairs-condemning-the-arrest-of-deputy-nsa-director-sam-siryon (accessed 2 September 2024)

"Liberia: Supreme Court Ratifies a Constitutional Amendment", *Library of Congress*, 27 September 2011, https://www.loc.gov/item/global-legal-monitor/2011-09-27/liberia-supreme-court-ratifies-a-constitutional-amendment (accessed 3 March 2024)

"Liberian Army Chief of Staff Says Some Citizens Urging Him to Overthrow Pres. Weah", *News Public Trust*, 7 December 2022, https://newspublictrust.com/liberian-army-chief-of-staff-says-some-citizens-urging-him-to-overthrow-pres-weah (accessed 8 August 2024)

"President William R. Tolbert, Jr", *Liberia Past and Present*, n.d., https://liberiapastandpresent.org/WilliamTolbert.htm (accessed 19 February 2024)

"Seven Things to Know About Liberia's First Democratic Handover in 73 years", *TRT World*, 6 October 2017, https://www.trtworld.com/middle-east/seven-things-to-know-about-liberias-first-democratic-handover-in-73-years-13096400 (accessed 5 March 2025)

"SUP Celebrates Its Anniversary & Explains Its Struggle History", *Democracy Watch*, n.d., https://democracywatchonline.com/sup-celebrates-its-anniversary-explains-its-struggle-history (accessed 3 March 2024)

"The Death of Samuel Doe", *BBC*, 25 September 2011, https://www.bbc.co.uk/programmes/p00k69lp (accessed 17 November 2024)

"Youth and Sports Minister Says SKD Stadium Will Not Be Used for Any Rally", Smart News Liberia, 6 December 2022, https://smartnewsliberia.com/youth-and-sports-minister-says-skd-stadium-will-not-be-used-for-any-rally (accessed 19 November 2024)

Beyan AJ, *The American Colonization Society and the Creation of the Liberian State: A Historical Perspective*, 1822–1900, Michigan, University Press of America (1991)

Burrowes CP, "Black Christian Republicans: Delegates to the 1847 Liberian Constitutional Convention", 14 (1989) *Liberian Studies Journal,* pp 64-89

Burrowes CP, *Power and Press Freedom in Liberia, 1830–1970: The Impact of Globalization and Civil Society on Media-Government Relations,* Africa World Press (2005)

Cash J, "A Purer Form of Government: African American Constitutionalism in the Founding of Liberia", 19 (2021) *Journal of Transatlantic Studies,* pp 408-440

Dennis BG and Dennis AK, *Slaves to Racism: An Unbroken Chain from America To Liberia,* New York, Algora Publishing (2008)

Dillon EC, *The Role of Education in the Rise and Fall of Americo-Liberians in Liberia, West Africa (1980)*, Georgia State University PhD thesis (2011), https://scholarworks.gsu.edu/cgi/viewcontent.cgi?params=/context/eps_diss/article/1017/&path_info=The_Role_of_Education_in_the_Rise_and_Fall_of_Americo_Liberians__inforemoved.pdf (accessed 24 March 2025)

Elections Coordinating Committee Liberia, "Only Six of the 35 Registered Parties and Coalitions' Primaries Were Observed by ECC – 2023 Parties Candidates' List are Generally Based on Consensus", https://eccliberiacom.org/only-six-of-the-35-registered-parties-and-coalitions-primaries-were-observed-by-ecc-2023-parties-candidates-list-are-generally-based-on-consensus (accessed 6 March 2024)

EC-UNDP Electoral Assistance, "NEC Policy Paper No. 6", EC_UNDP Electoral Assistance, 18 February 2019, https://www.ec-undp-electoralassistance.org/wp-content/uploads/sites/18/2019/02/ec-undp-jtf-liberia-resources-nec-pp-political-party-functioning-31-01-19.pdf (accessed 16 March 2025)

Electoral Institute for Sustainable Democracy, "Liberia's Political Parties Fall Short of Gender Quota Commitment", *Electoral Institute for Sustainable Democracy*, 18 July 2023, https://www.eisa.org/liberias-political-parties-fall-short-of-gender-quota-commitment (accessed 7 March 2024)

European Union Election Observation Mission, *Liberia, 2023: Final Report*, https://www.eods.eu/library/EU%20EOM%20LIB%202023%20FR.pdf (accessed 20 February 2024)

Fombad CM, "Conceptualising a Framework for Inclusive, Fair and Robust Multiparty Democracy in Africa: The Constitutionalisation of the Rights of Political Parties", 48 (2015) *Verfassung in Recht und Übersee*, pp 3–27

Ford T, "Ellen Johnson Sirleaf: The Legacy of Africa's First Elected Female President", *BBC*, 21 January 2018, https://www.bbc.com/news/world-africa-42748769 (accessed 5 March 2024)

Freedom House, "Freedom in the World 2024: Liberia", *Freedom House*, n.d., https://freedomhouse.org/country/liberia/freedom-world/2024 (accessed 7 March 2024)

Freedom House, "New Report: Africa Marks a Decade of Decline in Freedom, with 2023 Being Marred by Electoral Violence and Civil Conflict", *Freedom House*, 29 February 2024, https://freedomhouse.org/article/new-report-africa-marks-decade-decline-freedom-2023-being-marred-electoral-violence-and (accessed 7 March 2024)

Garzeawu M and Chothia F, "Joseph Boakai: Liberia's New President Takes on Tough Challenge", *BBC*, 22 January 2024, https://www.bbc.com/news/world-africa-67995793 (accessed 5 March 2024)

Gerdes F, *Civil War and State Formation: The Political Economy of War and Peace in Liberia*, Frankfurt am Main, Campus (2013)

Harden B, "Liberia's Incumbent Declared Winner in Disputed Election", *Washington Post*, 29 October 1985, https://www.washingtonpost.com/archive/politics/1985/10/30/liberias-incumbent-declared-winner-in-disputed-election/fd180129-8dc3-4fe6-83ea-599242ceee83 (accessed 5 March 2024)

Harris D, "Liberia 2005: An Unusual African Post-Conflict Election", 44 (2006) *Journal of Modern African Studies*, pp 375–395

Harris D, "From 'Warlord' to 'Democratic' President: How Charles Taylor Won the 1997 Liberian Elections", 37 (1999) *Journal of Modern African Studies*, pp 431–455

Harris K, "Liberia's 1927 Presidential Election: The Most Rigged Election Ever", History Daily, https://historydaily.org/liberia-1927-presidential-election-most-rigged-election-ever (accessed 25 February 2024)

Kamara V, "Liberia: NPP Plans Exit from the Coalition for Democratic Change", *FrontPage Africa*, 19 January 2024, https://frontpageafricaonline.com/news/liberia-npp-plans-exit-from-the-coalition-for-democratic-change (accessed 5 March 2024)

Karmo H, "Liberia: Referendum Fails to Meet Constitutional Requirement for Passage", FrontPage Africa, 1 April 2021, https://frontpageafricaonline.com/amp/news/liberia-referendum-fails-to-meet-constitutional-requirement-for-passage (accessed 16 April 2024)

Kelly C, "Party Proliferation and Trajectories of Opposition: Comparative Analysis from Senegal", 50 (2018) *Comparative Politics*, pp 209–229

Kuwonu F, "Four African Countries at the Founding of the UN in San Francisco in 1945", *Africa Renewal,* 28 October 2020, https://africarenewal.un.org/en/magazine/four-african-countries-founding-un-san-francisco-1945 (accessed 24 March 2025)

Malan M, *Security Sector Reform in Liberia: Mixed Results from Humble Beginnings*, Pennsylvania, US Army War College, Strategic Studies Institute (2008)

Marmon B, "25 Years after His Demise, Samuel Doe Continues to Cast a Long Shadow across Liberian Politics", *African Arguments*, 9 September 2015, https://africanarguments.org/2015/09/25-years-after-his-demise-samuel-doe-continues-to-cast-a-long-shadow-across-liberian-politics (accessed 3 March 2024)

Mersel Y, "The Dissolution of Political Parties: The Problem of Internal Democracy", 4 (2006) *International Journal of Constitutional Law,* pp 84–113

Micallef AM, *Liberia: Development and Resources*, New York, Nova Science Publishers (2011)

Minority Rights Group International, *World Directory of Minorities and Indigenous Peoples – Liberia* (2007), https://www.refworld.org/docid/4954ce5823.html (accessed 24 February 2025)

Momodu S, "First Liberian Civil War (1989–1996)", *Black Past*, 25 July 2016, https://www.blackpast.org/global-african-history/first-liberian-civil-war-1989-1996 (accessed 16 April 2024)

Ojo EO and Agbude GA, "An Exploration of the Historical and the Political Backgrounds of Liberia", 1 (2012) *AFRREV IJAH: An International Journal of Arts and Humanities*, pp 187–200

Osoro W, "Most Rigged Elections Ever: He Got 243,000 Votes in Country of Less Than 15,000 Registered Voters!", *The Standard*, n.d., https://www.standardmedia.co.ke/entertainment/african-news/article/2001247031/most-rigged-elections-ever-he-got-243000-votes-in-country-of-less-than-15000-registered-voters (accessed 22 February 2024)

Poquie F and Hoije K, "Liberia's George Weah Fails to Win Extra Time in Referendum", *Bloomberg*, 2 April 2021, https://www.bloomberg.com/news/articles/2021-04-02/soccer-star-leader-fails-to-win-extra-time-in-liberia-referendum (accessed 16 April 2024)

Quansah GB, "Integrity Watch Liberia Reports Violation in October 2023 Elections", *Reports 231*, 30 October 2023, https://reports231.com/integrity-watch-liberia-reports-violation-in-october-2023-elections (accessed 18 November 2024)

Sainworla F, "At Liberia Media-Security Forum: AFL Chief of Staff Vows to Only 'Obey Legal Orders'", *News Public Trust*, 31 March 2022, https://newspublictrust.com/at-liberia-media-security-forum-afl-chief-of-staff-vows-to-only-obey-legal-orders (accessed 1 September 2024)

Sawyer A, "The Making of the 1984 Liberian Constitution: Major Issues and Dynamic Forces", 12 (1987) *Liberian Studies Journal*, pp 1–15

Schmidt GW, "The New Constitutional Developments in the Republic of Liberia", 14 (1981) *Verfassung und Recht in Übersee*, pp 243–268

Stevens CJ, "The Legal History of Public Land in Liberia", 58 (2014) *Journal of African Law*, pp 250–265

Toure A, "The Role of Civil Society in National Reconciliation and Peacebuilding in Liberia" International Peace Institute (2002)

Van Der Kraaij FPM, "The 1927 Presidential Election:", *Liberia Past and Present*, n.d., https://liberiapastandpresent.org/1927ElectionsMF.htm (accessed 14 March 2025)

Vick K, "Taylor Resigns, Leaves Liberia", *Washington Post*, 27 February 2024, https://www.washingtonpost.com/archive/politics/2003/08/12/taylor-resigns-leaves-liberia/829c9533-e940-480d-a0fd-ec51a5b5ffef (accessed 5 March 2024)

Ware A, "The essential characteristics of Liberian civil society", *Lilly Family School of Philanthropy*, 1 July 2020, https://blog.philanthropy.iupui.edu/2020/07/01/the-essential-characteristics-of-liberian-civil-society (accessed 7 March 2024)

Waugh CM, Charles Taylor and Liberia: Ambition and Atrocity in Africa's Lone Star State, London, Zed Books (2011)

Wratto C, "Liberia Transferred Power Peacefully Again: 3 Reasons the Calm is Holding, and One Red Flag", *The Conversation*, 23 January 2024, http://theconversation.com/liberia-transferred-power-peacefully-again-3-reasons-the-calm-is-holding-and-one-red-flag-221656 (accessed 5 March 2024)

Zoegan G, "The True Whigs Take Power", *LiberiaInfo*, 26 September 2024, https://liberiainfo.dukaw.com/true-whigs-take-power (accessed 16 March 2025)

Table of cases

Supreme Court of Liberia, *Re: Constitutionality of the National Elections Commission Planned Conduct of Voters Registration without the demarcation of Constitutional Electoral Constituencies*, 3 May 2023

Supreme Court of Liberia, *National Elections Commission et al. v Bility et al.*, 12 April 2023

Supreme Court of Liberia, *Unity Party (UP) et al. v Collaborating Political Parties (CPP) et al.*, 3 June 2022

Table of legislation

1986 Elections Law Amendment Act, as amended in 2014

Constitution of Liberia, 1847

Constitution of Liberia, 1986

National Defense Act, 2008

Chapter 10 The Role of Ethnicity in Shaping Coalition Politics in Mauritius

Neel R Purmah

1. Introduction

The small island state of Mauritius is one of only a few African countries to have enjoyed sustained political stability through a multiparty democracy since independence. Indeed, over the past decades, it has been hailed as the poster child of democracy and good governance in Africa, with its exceptional governance having been commended by various institutions. For instance, according to the Electoral Integrity Project, which evaluates countries according to expert perception with respect to electoral integrity, Mauritius is ranked 47th globally.[1] Furthermore, it scored 72.8 out of 100 in overall governance in the Ibrahim Index of African Governance in 2023, ranking second out of the 54 African countries.[2]

As is well known, the Ibrahim Index measures the quality of governance in African countries in relation to, among other things, safety and rule of law, participation and human rights, and sustainable economic opportunity and human development. Consistently ranking among the top two countries thus points to Mauritius's relative political stability over the past decades, and cements its position as one of Africa's foremost democratic nations.

Several factors have played a critical role in ensuring the success of the Mauritian democratic model as well as its culture of multipartyism – factors which this chapter sets out to identify and discuss. What will emerge from the discussion are insights into the effectiveness of the framework and mechanisms that foster or constrain the role of political parties in partici-

1 HA Garnett, TS James, M MacGregor and S Caal-Lam, *Year in Elections Global Report 2023*, Ontario and Norfolk, The Electoral Integrity Project (2023), https://static1.squarespace.com/static/58533f31bebafbe99c85dc9b/t/649dee1ee6e6c50219e9fbd9/1688071716978/Electoral+Integrity+Global+Report+2023.pdf (accessed 5 August 2024).

2 Mo Ibrahim Foundation, *2024 Ibrahim Index of African Governance*, October 2024, https://mo.ibrahim.foundation/sites/default/files/2024-10/2024-index-report.pdf (accessed 12 November 2024).

pating in democratic governance. In particular, it seeks to offer a nuanced account of how ethnicity shapes the political landscape in Mauritius.

To this end, section 2 provides an overview on the ethnic make-up of Mauritius; describes the origins and need for the so-called best-loser system (BLS), which caters for adequate representation of all ethnic groups in Parliament; and traces the emergence of the main political parties in Mauritius. Section 3 then examines the constitutional and legal framework regulating political parties and coalitions in Mauritius, while section 4 considers the interplay between ethnicity and the formation of political-party coalitions ahead of general elections. Section 5 proposes various reforms that could address the challenges faced by political parties in Mauritius. A conclusion in section 6 sums up the findings.

2. Background and context

2.1 Ethnic-based political representation

Political parties in Mauritius often align with specific ethnic groups. This can be explained by the colonial influence on the institutionalisation of ethnic identities. The British colonial administration in Mauritius played a significant role in shaping the island's contemporary ethnic-based party structures.[3] During the colonial period between 1810 and 1968, the British implemented policies that in effect categorised the population along ethnic lines in order to maintain control and manage a highly diverse society. This categorisation was reinforced by the introduction of separate educational, religious, and social institutions for different ethnic groups, all of which served to foster a sense of distinct identity among these communities.[4]

The political landscape of Mauritius may thus be traced to the colonial era, when the local population, predominantly comprising indentured labourers, began to engage politically by organising itself in the early 1900s.[5] Indentured labourers were brought principally from India after slavery was abolished, their purpose being to work on the island's sugarcane fields given that the sugar barons could no longer rely on enslaved people.

---

3 MF Nagar, The Road to Democratic Development Statehood in Africa: The Cases of Ethiopia, Mauritius, and Rwanda, 1st ed, Palgrave Macmillan (2021), p 51.

4 TH Eriksen, Common Denominators: Ethnicity, Nation-Building and Compromise in Mauritius, 1st ed., Oxfordshire, Routledge (1998).

5 D Sutton, "The Political Consecration of Community in Mauritius, 1948–68", 35(2) (2007) *Journal of Imperial and Commonwealth History*, pp 239–262.

In this context, the colonial government often favoured certain ethnic groups over others in terms of political representation and economic opportunities. Thus, the Hindus, who eventually became the majority, were initially marginalised by the colonial government in favour of Franco-Mauritians and the Creoles of African or mixed African heritage. Tensions developed between these groups, fomenting ethno-societal divisions that significantly influenced the island's political dynamics. In the course of time, the Hindu community gained political power, leading to the formation of ethnic-based parties that sought to represent their specific interests.[6]

The Mauritian population is composed of five main ethnic communities – Hindus, Sino-Mauritians, Muslims, Creoles, and Franco-Mauritians[7] – though it must be noted that there are other sub-groups which are not mentioned here. Moreover, divisions are evident within each of these main communities.[8] For example, the Sino-Mauritian community exhibits divisions based on religion (Christian or Buddhist), economic status (large business owners or small shopkeepers), and political orientation (communist or nationalist).

Likewise, within the Hindu community, divisions exist along caste, religious and linguistic lines. Various linguistic groups, including Telegu, Marathi, Tamil, and Hindi, coexist alongside distinct castes, such as the Brahmin (high caste), Babouji or Kshatriya (high caste), Vaish (middle caste), and Rajput (low caste).[9] It should be noted that with the sole exception of Paul Bérenger (a Franco-Mauritian), every prime minister of Mauritius since independence has been a Hindu from the Vaish caste, which is the most populous of the Hindu castes in the country.[10] Kasenally has even pointed out that many in the Hindu community take it as an unwritten rule that the Prime Minister should be from this specific caste.[11]

---

6 SR Mehta, "Power Dynamics of Indian Immigrants in Mauritius: A Study in Ethnic Relations", 25(1) (1995) *Indian Anthropologist*, pp 1–11.

7 R Suntoo and HB Chittoo, "Managing Multi-Ethnic Mauritius", 12(3) (2012) *Global Journal of Human Social Science*, pp 33–41.

8 Ibid.

9 O Hollup, "The Disintegration of Caste and Changing Concepts of Indian Ethnic Identity in Mauritius", 33(4) (1994) *Ethnology*, pp 297–316, 301.

10 M Claveyrolas, "Au 'Pays des Vaish' ? Structure et Idéologie de Caste à l'île Maurice", 163 (2013) *Archives de Sciences Sociales des Religions*, pp 191–216.

11 R Kasenally, "Mauritius: Paradise Reconsidered", 22 (2011) *Journal of Democracy*, pp 160–169, 167.

In the face of this diversity, extremist politicians have historically sought to exploit divisions by urging sub-groups to demand parliamentary representation which is proportional to their numerical strength.[12] For example, they have argued that Marathis, Telegus and Tamils should not be classified as Hindu due to their perceived cultural and religious differences.[13]

Similarly, the Muslim community has divisions along caste, linguistic and economic lines, albeit to a lesser extent.[14] However, they have representation in certain constituencies with a huge concentration of the Muslim population, as a result of which political parties always field Muslim candidates in these constituencies.[15]

For election purposes, the Constitution of Mauritius does not take the five ethnic communities above into consideration. Instead, section 3(4) of the First Schedule of the Constitution divides the population into four groups: Hindu, Muslim, Sino-Mauritian, and General Population. As will be discussed later, in order to run as a candidate in the general elections, individuals must declare their affiliation with one of these four constitutionally recognised communities. At this juncture, it should be noted that the General Population is a catch-all category for those who do not believe that they belong to any of the other three recognised groups. This refers chiefly to Creoles and Franco-Mauritians but so too to persons of mixed heritage, such as European-Africans, European-Indians, and African-Indians. This segment of the population may in turn be subdivided further along the lines of skin colour, social standing, and class.

The 1972 census was the last to officially measure ethnicity, but its data continues to influence the distribution of power even if it is patently outdated. This census revealed a diverse population, with Hindus forming the majority (52 per cent), followed by Creoles (27 per cent), Muslims

12 EG Mukonoweshuro, "Containing Political Instability in a Poly-Ethnic Society: The Case of Mauritius", 14(2) (1991) *Ethnic and Racial Studies*, pp 199–224.

13 L Couacaud, SS Sookrajowa, and J Narsoo, "The Vicious Circle that is Mauritian Politics: The Legacy of Mauritius's Electoral Boundaries", 21 (2022) *Ethnopolitics*, pp 48, 61.

14 R Mathur, "Party Cooperation and the Electoral System in Mauritius", in BV Lal and P Larmour (eds.), *Electoral Systems in Divided Societies: The Fiji Constitution*, ANU Press (2012), pp 135–146.

15 S Bunwaree, "Interrogating Liberal Democracy: The Islamic Movement in Mauritius", in MA Mohamed Salih (ed.), *Interpreting Islamic Political Parties*, New York, Palgrave Macmillan (2009), pp 231–248; A Jahangeer-Chojoo, "From Minority to Mainstream Politics: The Case of Mauritian Muslims", 25(1) (2010) *Journal of Social Sciences*, pp 121–133.

(16 per cent), Sino-Mauritians (3 per cent), and Franco-Mauritians (2 per cent).[16] The continued use of this demographic information for parliamentary seat allocation potentially favours certain ethnic groups, particularly those whose population shares may have dropped significantly since 1972.[17] The reliance on outdated data raises questions about the fairness and representativeness of the current political system, insofar as it is unlikely to accurately reflect the evolving ethnic landscape of modern Mauritius.

2.2 Origins and characteristics of the best-loser system

For parliamentary general elections, Mauritius is divided into 21 constituencies, with 20 allocated to mainland Mauritius, and one to Rodrigues (a dependency of the Republic of Mauritius). Each constituency on the mainland elects three representatives, while Rodrigues elects two. This brings the total candidates elected through a first-past-the-post (FPTP) system to 62; these candidates in turn become members of the National Assembly.

Electoral boundaries were demarcated by the British before independence in order to guarantee adequate representation for the two most significant segments of the then Mauritian population, Hindus and Creoles. Traditionally, 10 constituencies have been situated in rural areas where Hindus are predominant, while the remaining 10 are in urban areas. This arrangement ensures that Hindus, comprising more than 50 per cent of the population, receive appropriate representation, as parties typically field Hindu candidates in rural areas. The Creoles, accounting as per the 1972 census for about 30 per cent of the population, hold considerable sway in most urban constituencies and can secure a fair share of seats with the support of other minority groups, thereby ensuring adequate representation for themselves in the National Assembly.

An electoral system that could safeguard adequate representation for minorities in the National Assembly was thus devised in order to mitigate ethnic tensions. Indeed, over the years there has been much discussion

16 R Kasenally, "Mauritius: The Not so Perfect Democracy", (2011) 10(1) *Journal of African Elections*, pp 33–47, 34.

17 SS Sookrajowa, "Legibility and the Politics of Ethnic Classification of the Population in the National Census of Mauritius: A Statist Perspective", 27(2) (2021) *Nationalism and Ethnic Politics*, pp 128–148, 129.

about the best system of minority representation.[18] In the colonial era, the then Parliamentary Under-Secretary for the Colonies, John Stonehouse, proposed an electoral system in which most parliamentary members would be chosen via the FPTP method; however, to address any ethnic imbalances, the system would allocate eight additional seats to the best-performing candidates from under-represented communities who did not win in the initial voting. This came to be termed the "best-loser system".

The BLS operates as follows. To ensure balanced representation of the four constitutionally recognised communities – Hindus, Muslims, Sino-Mauritians, and General Population – up to eight additional seats are allocated by the Electoral Supervisory Commission. The allocation process first determines the most under-represented community by dividing the number of people in each community (as per the 1972 census) by the number of elected members plus one.[19] The community with the highest quota is the most under-represented. The first four additional seats are given to the top candidates from this community who did not win, based on their vote percentage. The next four seats are allocated similarly, but the candidates must belong to the most successful political party or coalition, based on national vote percentage.[20] This ensures that the BLS does not distort the overall election results. If no suitable candidates are found, not all eight seats may be allocated.

Although the BLS is the driver behind the representation of the various ethnic groups in Parliament, there have been calls to reassess its relevance in Mauritius after more than 55 years of independence.[21] The fear is that this system amounts to a perpetuation of institutionalised racism that accords ethnicity and religion a predominant role in shaping the country's socio-political landscape, as opposed to its being a mechanism for building

18 *Ibid*; R Mathur, "The Best Loser System", in S Nirsimloo-Gayan (ed.), *Towards the Making of a Multi-Cultural Society: Conference Papers*, Moka, Mahatma Gandhi Institute Press (2000), pp 203–206.

19 Y Fessha and N Ho Tu Nam, "Is it Time to Let Go? The Best Loser System in Mauritius", 28(1) (2015) *Afrika Focus*, pp 63–79, 66; A Meetoo and C Meetoo, "How Seven Lucky Candidates have been Chosen as Best Loses in 2014 General Elections", *Elections Mauritius*, n.d., https://www.electionsmauritius.com/2014/extra/7/how-seven-lucky-candidates-have-been-chosen-as-best-losers (accessed 5 August 2024).

20 R Mahadew, "The Best Loser System in Mauritius: An Essential Electoral Tool for Representing Political Minorities", in J de Visser, N Steytler, D Powell, and E Durojaye (eds.), *Constitutional Building in Africa*, Nomos, Baden-Baden (2015), pp 135–160.

21 Fessha and Ho Tu Nam, *supra* n. 19.

a nation predicated on a single Mauritian identity. Nonetheless, it should be noted that, to an extent, the BLS caters for the inclusion and representation of the country's full ethnic composition.

Electoral reform – including reform affecting political parties – has been a recurring topic of discussion for various administrations over the past decades. Throughout the 1980s and 1990s, parties advocated for reforms that would introduce an element of proportional representation to address the imbalances inherent in the FPTP system. However, the electoral system in Mauritius has remained largely unchanged since the country gained independence in 1968.

There is nonetheless general consensus among political parties, civil society organisations, and the public that the electoral system needs to be updated to reflect the contemporary realities of Mauritian society.[22] Towards the end of 2018, the government introduced a constitutional amendment bill aimed at overhauling the electoral system, with assurances given that the reforms would enhance the representation of political parties and women in Parliament, as well as promote social cohesion. However, the bill failed to meet the minimum three-quarters majority required for an amendment of the Constitution, as there was insufficient support for it among the opposition.

2.3 Mauritius's main political parties

There are four main political parties in Mauritius: the Mauritius Labour Party (MLP), the Mouvement Socialiste Mauricien (MSM), the Mouvement Militant Mauricien (MMM), and the Parti Mauricien Social Démocrate (PMSD). Both the MLP and PMSD were established in the 1930s and 1940s amidst a socio-political climate in which the two largest ethnic groups – the Hindus and Creoles – were seeking greater political representation and the right to vote. These demands were directed at the then ruling minority, the Franco-Mauritian sugar oligarchs, who dominated the political and economic landscape of the time.

22 A Mahadew, "Reforming Mauritius's Electoral System: More Gender and Less Communal Representation?", ConstitutionNet, 25 February 2019, https://constitutionnet.org/news/reforming-mauritiuss-electoral-system-more-gender-and-less-communal-representation (accessed 5 August 2024).

Each of the four political parties represent specific factions of the different communities. For instance, on the one hand, rural areas – where most of the Hindu population is concentrated – have traditionally been the bastion of the MLP and MSM, whereas urban areas, on the other, have traditionally been represented by the MMM and PMSD. The electoral bases of the main parties have fluctuated over time, though voter allegiance in the rural and urban areas has mostly been constant. All four dominant political parties have an ethnic foundation, but have progressively become multi-ethnic.[23] Even so, since independence the leaders of the MLP and MSM have consistently come from the Hindu Vaish caste, while those of the MMM and PMSD have traditionally been from the General Population. The Mauritian political-party landscape thus encourages bipolarisation in terms of party cooperation and sharing of political power between the Hindus and the General Population (mainly the Creoles).[24] This is also precisely why, before each general election, the MLP and MSM, representing principally the Hindus (in rural areas), have to enter into an alliance or coalition with the MMM or PMSD, the large majority of whose voter base is from the General Population in urban areas.

During the 1963 elections prior to independence, the predominantly Hindu MLP, led by Seewoosagur Ramgoolam, secured just below a majority in the legislative council.[25] Subsequently, it formed a governing coalition with two other political parties, the Muslim Committee of Action, and a smaller Hindu party. However, tensions arose when the PMSD – representing mainly the Creoles – was excluded from the colonial cabinet, a turn of events that led to demonstrations and violence between Hindus and Creoles.[26] In 1964, an attempt was made to establish a grand coalition that included the PMSD, but it collapsed due to disagreements over the issue of independence, which the PMSD opposed. The situation escalated in May 1965, with renewed violence between Creoles and Hindus prompting the intervention of British forces.[27] The elections that followed in 1967, served as a de facto vote on independence for Mauritius. Despite winning 44 per cent of the vote, the PMSD obtained less than 40 per cent of seats, even

23 Sookrajowa, *supra* n. 17, 139.
24 *Ibid*, p 143.
25 ES Poupko, "An Exploratory Study of Constitutional Design in Three Island States: Seychelles, Comoros, and Mauritius", 35(3) (2017) *Journal of Contemporary African Studies*, pp 324–348, 336.
26 Sutton, *supra* n. 5.
27 Ibid.

after having been granted four best-loser seats. When Mauritius gained independence in March 1968, communal violence erupted once more, thus necessitating the intervention of British troops. Simultaneously, there were initial signs of separatist movements forming among the predominantly Creole population of Rodrigues Island.

In response to the turmoil, the MLP (in an alliance with two other smaller parties) and PMSD agreed to establish a coalition under Prime Minister Seewoosagur Ramgoolam, leading to a constitutional amendment that postponed the next elections until 1976. Although the coalition eventually dissolved, there was a period of relative stability during which the process of democratisation was effectively stalled. However, an emerging socialist party, the MMM, led by the Franco-Mauritian Paul Bérenger, began to gain traction by the end of the 1960s, particularly among a more diverse electoral base. The MMM itself was founded as a purely leftist party advocating for the abolition of class struggle and communal divisions. While it began existence as a non-ethnic party, it gradually gave way to ethnicisation. In particular, party candidates are selected on the basis of ethnic profiles, with consideration given to the ethnic configuration of the constituencies where they could be fielded in order to represent their respective ethnicities or castes. This practice has been called "scientific communalism", a term which

> describe[s] the sorts of ethnic calculations that all the major political parties engage in when deciding which candidates to offer a ticket to and how to match their ethnic profile with the constituency they are running for in the run up to general elections.[28]

Seewoosagur Ramgoolam's coalition government faced major challenges in 1971 and 1972, when debilitating general strikes (called by the MMM and General Workers Federation) prompted it to declare a state of emergency. This led the Legislative Assembly to enact the Public Order Act of 1971, which placed restrictions on political parties and union activities. A day after the law's enactment, Bérenger and other members of the MMM were arrested and imprisoned. The state of emergency was lifted eventually in May 1976, as was, in November, the ban on political activities. Elections were finally held in December 1976, but although the MMM won the most seats in the Legislative Assembly, Ramgoolam was able to continue as

28 Couacaud, Sookrajowa, Narsoo, *supra* n. 13, p 51.

Prime Minister thanks to a coalition government made up primarily of the MLP and PMSD.

The 1982 elections saw a landslide victory by the MMM and Mauritian Socialist Party (a now-defunct entity), but this coalition collapsed within a year due to leadership disputes, leading to the formation of the MSM by Anerood Jugnauth. In 1983, the newly created MSM won the elections on the strength of a new alliance with the MLP and PMD, with Anerood Jugnauth again serving as Prime Minister.[29] The MSM emerged as a dominant force primarily within the Hindu community, thus consolidating its support among Hindus who had previously supported the MLP before its decline in 1982. While the MSM positioned itself as a multi-ethnic party, its electoral success often relied on navigating the ethnic dynamics of Mauritius and forming coalition governments affording representation to smaller ethnic groups. This delicate yet essential balancing act highlights the pervasive influence of ethnicity in Mauritian politics, even among parties with ostensibly broad ideological platforms.

The MSM later aligned with the MLP and other parties in various combinations, save for the period in 1995 when a significant coalition between the MLP and MMM won decisively and saw Navinchandra Ramgoolam – the son of Seewoosagur Ramgoolam – becoming Prime Minister 10 years after the demise of his father. The MLP/MMM coalition fell apart in 1997 over policy differences. In 2000, the MSM and MMM formed another coalition, securing a victory but in 2005 this too collapsed.

Subsequent years saw alternating alliances, including the 2014 MSM-led coalition with smaller parties that ousted the MLP, as well as the 2019 MSM-Muvmen Liberater-led alliance under the leadership of Pravind Jugnauth, which retained power. These coalitions, while instrumental in winning elections, have frequently collapsed due to ideological differences, leadership rivalries, or shifting political alliances, thereby clearly demonstrating the fragility of coalition politics in Mauritius. The alternation of power between the MSM and MLP through various coalitions during this period highlights not only electoral competition but also the entrenchment of political families at the helm of these parties.

In this regard, the history of Mauritius has long been marked by the dominance of the Ramgoolams and Jugnauths as political dynasties. Anerood Jugnauth, as indicated above, first rose to power in 1982, leading a coalition of the MMM and his newly formed MSM. His tenure as Prime

29 A Dubey, *Government and Politics in Mauritius*, Delhi, Kalinga Publications (1997).

Minister spanned from 1982 to 1995, barring a brief period of opposition rule in 1983 due to certain political reshuffles. He became Prime Minister again from 2000 to 2003, after a coalition victory with the MSM. Anerood Jugnauth transitioned to the ceremonial role of President from 2003 to 2012, before returning to active politics and winning the 2014 general elections, after which he served as Prime Minister from 2014 to 2017. In 2017, his son Pravind Jugnauth succeeded him as Prime Minister following Anerood Jugnauth's resignation, thereby continuing the family's leadership at the helm of the MSM. As for the MLP, Navin Ramgoolam served as Prime Minister again from 2005 to 2014.

It should be noted, too, that both the MSM and MLP have faced criticism for a lack of internal democracy, as leadership succession has often bypassed broader party consultation in favour of hereditary transition as of right. This dynastic control has limited the emergence of fresh political talent and thus stifled dissent within party ranks.

More recently, Mauritius held its twelfth general elections in November 2024, an occasion that illustrated many of the complexities of political coalition-building in the country; the elections were also marked by significant competition for leadership. Unlike the general elections of 2014 and 2019, in which the MSM emerged as the dominant party, thereby securing consecutive mandates, the 2024 election landscape revealed a highly contested struggle for governance. On the one side, the L'Alliance Lepep – a coalition led by Pravind Jugnauth and comprising the MSM, the PMSD, and a few other small parties – sought to extend its long-standing influence. On the other side, there was the L'Alliance du Changement, an opposition coalition led by Navin Ramgoolam and consisting of the MLP, MMM, and two other small parties. The latter was united by a shared commitment to ousting the current government and advancing reformist policies.

Although Mauritius is known for having one of the most open media landscapes in Africa, during the 2024 campaign, recordings were leaked of private phone conversations among opposition politicians, thus fuelling accusations of wiretapping.[30] In a somewhat misguided response, the MSM-led government under Jugnauth went on to restrict access to social media platforms in the run-up to the election, adding an unexpected layer of tension to the electoral process and hitting the final nail in its own coffin.

30 ENews Channel Africa, "Mauritius Votes in Poll Clouded by Phone Tapping Scandal", 10 November 2024, https://www.enca.com/news/mauritius-votes-poll-clouded-phone-tapping-scandal (accessed 16 November 2024).

The opposition alliance under Ramgoolam won all 60 seats from the 20 constituencies on the mainland. This landslide victory marked only the third occurrence of such a decisive outcome in Mauritius's history since independence.

Earlier, an account was given of the historical context in which Mauritius gained independence in 1968 after years of negotiation between the British colonial authorities and various political parties representing diverse ethnic groups. As this account made clear, a delicate balance was struck between the country's different ethno-religious groups, one that eventually translated into efforts to ensure political representation for all the ethno-religious groups. A core feature of this balance was the establishment of a framework for multiparty politics aimed at fostering political stability, economic diversification, and social cohesion; this multiparty framework in turn facilitated regular alternations of power between parties or coalitions through general elections. However, as mentioned, historically the nation's political leadership has been dominated by a few prominent families (principally the Ramgoolams and Jugnauths), while divisions along ethnic lines have grown increasingly salient.

Indeed, during field work conducted in Mauritius in 1991, researchers were struck by the diversity of ethnic groups and religious associations involved in the country's politics.[31] Many of these organisations were explicitly based on ethnicity, while others consisted primarily of members of a specific ethnic or religious community even if their membership was technically not restricted to those of a particular ethnicity. It seemed evident that the presence of such groups, along with their acknowledgment by the government, played a significant role in legitimising the state and fostering ethnic harmony. The next section will elaborate on the constitutional, legal, and regulatory framework surrounding political parties.

3. Constitutional and legal provisions regulating political parties

The Constitution of Mauritius was adopted on 12 March 1968 when the country attained independence. It has provisions relating to the electoral process, in particular ones setting out the management structure for the organisation and conduct of elections. It also provides for the delimitation

31 BW Carroll and T Carroll, "Accommodating Ethnic Diversity in a Modernizing Democratic State: Theory and Practice in the Case of Mauritius", 23 (2000) *Ethnic and Racial Studies*, pp 120–142.

of constituencies and the review thereof every 10 years or whenever the need arises. Furthermore, section 44 enshrines the right to vote. Universal suffrage was granted in 1959 to people over the age of 18 years. Other relevant provisions in the Constitution cater for the rights of the leader of the opposition (section 73) and articulate the principles of free and fair political participation (sections 38–41).

3.1 Registration and the status of political parties

Section 13 of the Constitution guarantees protection of the freedom of association, in terms of which political parties are allowed to operate freely. However, every party must be registered with the Electoral Supervisory Commission (ESC) at least 14 days prior to the nomination of its candidates in any general election. This is by virtue of paragraph 2(1) of the First Schedule to the Constitution, which requires a political party to be a lawful association and registered with the ESC for the purposes of the general election. It also provides that any two or more political parties may be registered as a party alliance for those purposes. While the roles and responsibilities of the electoral commissioner (section 40), the ESC, and the Electoral Boundary Commission (section 38) are enshrined in the Constitution, "their impact seems to be visible only during the short time preceding, during and after elections".[32]

Although Mauritius has neither an electoral law nor specific legislation on political parties, some of its laws do touch on political parties tangentially. For instance, the National Assembly Act 1968 lays out the process of registration of political parties. Section 7(1) of the latter provides that every political party wishing to be registered under paragraph 2(1) of Schedule 1 to the Constitution shall make an application to the Commission at least 10 days before nomination day. Section 8 of this Act then empowers the ESC to register the name of the party and the names of the person or persons making or authorised to make the application in a register kept for that purpose. More specifically, the National Assembly Elections Regulations 2014 lay out the procedure that political parties or alliances have to follow in order to be registered under paragraph 2(1) of the First Schedule to the Constitution. Every application has to be signed in the presence of

32 S Bunwaree and R Kasenally, *Political Parties and Democracy in Mauritius*, EISA (2005), p 13.

the electoral commissioner and be supported by a certified extract of the minutes of proceedings of the meeting at which the decision to register the application was taken.

These constitutional and legal provisions are applicable during general elections only. In other words, parties are not regulated before or after them. It has even been observed that insofar as political parties in Mauritius have no legal status outside of an electoral campaign, there is no clear process for scrutinising them and keeping them accountable.[33] Indeed, "political parties in Mauritius, outside of an election, are non-registered entities making accountability and transparency around financial activities difficult to monitor even if legislation is in place".[34]

3.2 Intra-party democracy

Although there are no specific laws governing the operation of political parties outside of general elections, each political party has an internal constitution that lays down fundamental political guidelines. However, "the applicability of the party constitution is questionable as members of some political parties have said that they have never been able to access such documents".[35] Political parties nonetheless retain the freedom to choose their structure and operating guidelines. As regards their specific structure and organisation, political parties adhere to internal constitutions that provide operational guidelines and establish sub-structures for the expression and dissemination of views, opinions, and decisions across all levels of the party.[36] Despite minor variations, the four major parties take pride in adopting an inclusive and participatory approach to governance.

These major political parties, along with some of the smaller ones, typically employ a four-tier structure comprising a political bureau responsible for policy formulation, a central committee tasked with decision-making,

33 R Kasenally and R Ramtohul, "The Cost of Parliamentary Politics in Mauritius", *Westminster Foundation for Democracy*, 21 September 2020, p 10, https://www.wfd.org/sites/default/files/2022-01/Cost-of-Parliamentary-Politics-in-MauritiusWEB-FINAL.pdf (accessed 14 January 2024).

34 *Ibid*, p 2.

35 DK Kadima and R Kasenally, "The Formation, Collapse and Revival of Political Party Coalitions in Mauritius: Ethnic Logic and Calculations at Play", 4(1) (2005) *Journal of African Elections*, pp 133–164, 149.

36 Bunwaree and Kasenally, *supra* n. 32, p 12.

a general assembly convening at least annually, and regional branches representing grassroots members.[37] However, despite the appearance of a well-established party framework, closer examination reveals the predominant authority of the party leader. According to Bunwaree and Kasenally, this authority in practice often extends to a veto power in crucial matters such as candidate selection, party financing, and the formation or dissolution of alliances.[38]

Intra-party democracy in Mauritian parties is often limited, with many of them characterised by centralised leadership and personalised control.[39] Party decisions and candidate selections are typically driven by a small group of senior leaders or a single dominant figure, rather than made through broad-based, democratic processes. Bunwaree and Kasenally note that on closer examination; "the actual operative setup of political parties demonstrates the overriding authority of the party leader".[40] This concentration of power can stifle internal debate and reduce accountability, leading to political factionalism and frequent defections as party members seek greater influence or better prospects elsewhere.

Despite these challenges, there are ongoing efforts to enhance democratic practices in parties, the aim being to foster greater transparency, member participation, and responsiveness to the electorate's needs. For example, as noted earlier, successive governments have called for reform of the electoral system – steps in this regard include the promulgation of a law to regulate political parties and clarify their role in democratic governance.

3.3 Oversight of political parties

According to section 41(1) of the Constitution, the ESC has the general responsibility, inter alia, to supervise the conduct of the election of members of the Legislative Assembly. The ESC works in conjunction with the electoral commissioner – a separate constitutional institution under section 41(2) of the Constitution – to oversee elections and ensure that they are free and fair. The ESC comprises a chairperson and between two to seven members. These are appointed by the President following consultation with the Prime Minister, the Leader of the Opposition, and leaders of other parties

37 Ibid.
38 Ibid.
39 Ibid.
40 *Ibid*, p 12.

in the National Assembly. While the Constitution provides safeguards, such as the requirement to consult with particular role-players when appointing ESC members, and guarantees the electoral commissioner's independence from external control, such measures might not insulate these bodies entirely from political influence.

The electoral commissioner is appointed by the Judicial and Legal Service Commission and serves as a public officer. The Constitution ensures the electoral commissioner's independence and impartiality by stipulating that the commissioner shall not be subject to the direction or control of any person or authority in the execution of his or her duties. The commissioner is supported by a team that includes senior officers and other electoral staff. In practice, both the ESC and electoral commissioner have operated with significant autonomy and command respect across the political spectrum.

Moreover, it should be noted that the Judicial Committee of the Privy Council of the United Kingdom – which continues to function as the highest appellate court in Mauritius – had signalled back in 2008 that the ESC should draw up a code of conduct for election periods.[41] The ESC went on to issue its code of conduct for the 2019 National Assembly elections, incorporating, inter alia, rules on campaign and election expenses for political parties.[42] However, parties have not always abided by this code of conduct, and since it was not legally binding, they were not required to follow it to the letter. It is difficult to assess with any precision what impact the failure to abide by this code of conduct had on the behaviour of political parties during the 2019 general elections, but there can be little doubt that it did not help. The code of conduct was eventually ignored as a mere remnant of the past and with no application to the 2024 general elections.

With respect to political financing (discussed further below), parties do not specify in a transparent manner how they finance their campaigns during general elections given that there is a lack of comprehensive regulation.[43] There is, however, outdated legislation regulating electoral expenses. According to the Representation of the People Act 1958, candidates from political parties have a spending limit of MUR 150,000 (USD 3,200), while independent candidates have a limit of MUR 250,000 (USD 5,300).

41 *Jugnauth v Ringadoo* [2008] UKPC 50 at 49.

42 Electoral Supervisory Commission, "Code of Conduct for the National Assembly Elections 2019" https://electoral.govmu.org/oec/wp-admin/admin-ajax.php?juwpfisadmin=false&action=wpfd&task=file.download&wpfd_category_id=8&wpfd_file_id=803 (accessed 5 August 2024).

43 Kasenally and Ramtohul, *supra* n. 33.

These limits have remained unchanged since 1989, even though election campaigns are increasingly expensive and complex. Once election results are declared, candidates are required by this law to swear an affidavit and submit their financial returns to the Electoral Commission within a month. Nevertheless, the latter does not have the authority to verify these declarations or impose sanctions outside of the election period, insofar as political parties are not considered legal entities during that time. This limitation thus undermines the Electoral Commission's effectiveness in monitoring the financing of candidates and parties in the course of the wider political process (that is, outside of election periods).

The discussion above analysed the constitutional and legal framework applicable to elections and political parties in Mauritius; the next section proceeds to examine how ethnicity exerts a gravitational pull on the structure and operation of the country's main political parties.

4. Coalitions and ethnicity

Mauritian politics have been marked by constant shifts in coalitions, seeing as every government since independence has been the result of a coalition, one typically formed before an election.[44] This is so because dominant parties face an ongoing necessity to establish inter-group coalitions in order to achieve a legislative majority; conversely, losing parties seem to have recognised that, in a country where political alliances are fluid, future coalitions are what offer them the opportunity to participate in government. As Poupko observes, this trend would not have arisen if a proportional representation electoral system were in place, as the Hindu majority would probably have been able to gain and maintain power without the inclusion of other groups.[45] The existence of a parliamentary executive system also appears to have played a crucial role, given that a directly elected presidency would likewise have enabled the Hindu majority to govern independently.

When compared with other African countries, Mauritius is unusual for the fact that, ever since independence, it has always had a coalition government of at least two parties, with these coalitions regularly crumbling

44 Kadima and Kasenally, *supra* n. 35.
45 Poupko, *supra* n. 25, p 340.

and then reconstituting themselves in a different guise.[46] Even outside of election periods, this imposes a level of responsibility on governments that surpasses what is typically seen in parliamentary systems with majority governments. In both the 1982 and 1995 elections, opposition party alliances secured all the elected seats in the National Assembly. However, neither coalition government lasted for even half of its five-year term.[47] More recently, the coalition L'Alliance du Changement achieved resounding success by winning every seat in the National Assembly elections of 2024. Whether the MLP and MMM will stick together in government for a five-year term remains to be seen, though, given that coalitions are subject to change in response to internal tensions or evolving public opinion.

4.1 Personalised party factions and temporary alliances

Arguably, the volatility of political alliances is healthy for Mauritian democracy as it serves to remind governments that they are always at risk of losing their legislative power. Yet it also highlights an important flaw in the country's political framework, namely that political parties consist mainly of personalised factions, each led by its own leader who forms a temporary alliance in support of a particular candidate for the prime ministerial position. If a factional leader feels undervalued by the party leader, or sees better prospects in leading a separate party or joining a different coalition, the faction simply leaves the alliance. Indeed, ahead of both the 1991 and 1995 elections, then Prime Minister Aneerood Jugnauth severed ties with junior coalition partners and formed new alliances with what had previously been the main opposition party, partly because he believed it would enhance his chances of re-election.[48]

In election periods, parties typically enter into strategic alliances, marking out constituencies amongst themselves based on ethnic considerations and reaching agreements to prevent vote fragmentation by refraining from contesting against each other; conversely, in non-election periods, these parties often fracture into smaller factions. Party cohesion is thus tenuous, with coalitions and alliances fragmenting regularly. As a recent example,

46 BW Carroll and T Carroll, "The Consolidation of Democracy in Mauritius" 6(1) (1999) *Democratization*, pp 179–197, 180.

47 Ibid.

48 Mathur, *supra* n. 14.

the PMSD left the then main opposition alliance because its leader could not negotiate electoral tickets to field more PMSD candidates as part of the alliance.[49] The PMSD went on to form a coalition with the MSM.

As previously noted, the MLP and MSM represent a significant portion of the Hindu population in rural areas. As such, they always have to enter into alliance with either the MMM or PMSD, which are traditionally seen as representing the other communities, particularly those in urban areas. It comes as no surprise that these political parties often strategically target their specific *bassin électoral* ("electoral pools"), typically defined by ethnic and geographical factors, in order to maximise their vote share. This strategy is crucial in a multiparty system where alliances and coalitions are formed to represent broader, more diverse segments of the population. As William Miles has observed, in the dynamic political landscape of Mauritius, factors such as personality, ideology, and, in particular, ethnicity coalesce unpredictably within a robust democratic framework and result in unexpected electoral outcomes and unconventional alliances.[50] Consequently, coalition governance becomes the norm.

4.2 Consociationalism and its effect on multiparty democracy

While class-based politics is certainly relevant in Mauritius, efforts to supplant communalism with leftist ideologies have had only limited success. This may be attributed directly to the FPTP and BLS, which have been described as "the root cause of the proliferation, creation and ultimately the disbanding of political party alliances ... [that] have created much political instability".[51] It is both interesting and disquieting to see how this electoral system has spurred on an oversimplified ethnic categorisation of political parties, given the need to secure competitive electoral advantage through the formation of party alliances.[52] Mauritius, as noted, has been able to strike a delicate balance in giving adequate representation and protection to its various ethnic groups. As a result, consociationalism – a system

49 S Oodunt, "L'Alliance PTr-MMM-PMSD Vole en éclats", *L'Express*, 15 April 2024, https://lexpress.mu/s/lalliance-ptr-mmm-pmsd-vole-en-%C3%A9clats-533647 (accessed 5 August 2024).

50 WFS Miles, "The Politics of Language Equilibrium in a Multilingual Society: Mauritius", 32 (2000) *Comparative Politics*, pp 215–239, p 220.

51 Bunwaree and Kasenally, *supra* n. 32, p 16.

52 Ibid.

of democracy based on power-sharing between elites from different ethno-religious groups – is deeply entrenched in the country's socio-political landscape.[53] This can be explained by several factors.

First, the FPTP system in itself obliges parties to take ethnic considerations into account in their choice of candidates. Political parties tend to select candidates based on ethnicity and field them in constituencies where the majority population is of the same ethnicity as the candidate. For instance, the big national parties usually field Hindu candidates in rural areas and candidates from other segments of the population in urban areas. Moreover, "in their choice and nomination of candidates in the different constituencies, political parties do not merely look at the ethnic configuration of a constituency".[54] Instead they also have to ensure representation for the different sub-group castes from the Hindu community.

An example of how political parties choose candidates on the basis of ethnic profile is provided by Constituencies 2 and 3, where the majority of the Muslim population is concentrated. The three candidates from these constituencies who have been returned in past elections have consistently self-identifed as "Muslim". There is no doubt, though, that these candidates could determine their community affiliation more freely, which would introduce an element of flexibility in the system. Indeed, in theory this would go some way towards mitigating concerns that the electoral system is perpetuating a form of institutionalised ethnicisation. There may well be expectations on the part of voters about sufficient ethnic representation for their respective communities. It can therefore be observed that the system itself encourages candidates and parties to think and strategise in ethnic terms, in the process maintaining a level of institutionalised ethnic classification.

The second explanation for consociationalism is evident in the persistent coalition politics and the BLS. The necessity for inter-group coalitions to achieve a legislative majority ensures that diverse communities are included in the political process, promoting a sense of shared governance. The BLS reinforces this by correcting ethnic imbalances in parliamentary representation. This framework has prevented any single group from monopolising power, and as such has helped sustain political stability despite the coun-

53 SS Sookrajowa, "The Paradox of Power-Sharing in Mauritius", in EW Aboultaif, S Keil, and A McCulloch (eds.), *Power-Sharing in the Global South: Patterns, Practices and Potentials*, Cham, Springer International Publishing (2024), pp 189–213.

54 Kasenally and Ramtohul, *supra* n. 33, p 5.

try's ethnic diversity. However, the BLS also contributes to the volatility and vulnerability of political alliances, as parties continuously negotiate and reconfigure themselves to maintain political clout.[55] This tentative balance between inclusivity, on the one hand, and political fragmentation, on the other, is a hallmark of consociational democracy, and in the context of Mauritius, both of these strengths and weaknesses are in full view.

4.3 Ethnic representation in political parties

As already noted, the BLS has been criticised for breeding institutionalised racism.[56] It has been claimed that it is an electoral system that "legitimises/institutionalises the process of political ethnicization".[57] Mahadew, though, does not agree with the assessment that it is a system that breeds institutionalised racism, inasmuch as it was introduced in the electoral system to allow for the political representation of minorities.[58] It has, according to him, encouraged political parties to be multi-ethnic in nature and prevented their polarisation on religious or racial grounds.[59] Ethnic representation in political parties does, to a certain extent, prevent polarisation along religious or racial lines.

Be that as it may, the leadership and power structures of the dominant political parties do not always reflect true diversity. All four dominant political parties, as previously discussed, are controlled largely by Hindu or Franco-Mauritian leadership dynasties. The Hindu Ramgoolam family leads the MLP, with Navin Ramgoolam having succeeded his father, Seewoosagur. Similarly, the MSM is dominated by the Jugnauths, also a Hindu family, with Anerood Jugnauth's son, Pravind Jugnauth, as its current leader. The MMM was created and shaped by Paul Bérenger, a Franco-Mauritian, while the PMSD has traditionally been led by the Duval family, which has strong ties to the Franco-Mauritian community notwithstanding that it mostly professes allegiance to the Creole community.

55 Kadima and Kasenally, *supra* n. 35.
56 A Nave, "Nested Identities: Ethnicity, Community and the Nature of Group Conflict in Mauritius", in C Bates (ed.), *Community, Empire and Migration: South Asians in Diaspora*, Basingstoke, Palgrave (2001), pp 87–108.
57 Kadima and Kasenally, *supra* n. 35, p 143.
58 Mahadew, *supra* n. 20.
59 Ibid.

It should be noted, however, that even though the leaders themselves are consistently of a particular ethnicity, their political parties always include candidates from a diversity of ethnic groups in order to appeal to a broader electorate and thus engender a sense of inclusion among the country's multi-ethnic population. This approach most certainly encourages collaboration between communities and prevents the balkanisation of political loyalties along strictly ethnic or religious lines, something which would unravel the fragile democratic fabric of the nation. For instance, there are always attempts to maintain a veneer of ethnic inclusivity through balanced ticket selection and representation in various constituencies. This is to ensure that no group feels entirely excluded from political participation.

5. Suggestions for reform

As previously mentioned, there have been many attempts at reforming the electoral system over the past decades. First, there was the Sachs Commission on Constitutional and Electoral Reform, which was established in 2001 to consider reforms to the Constitution and the electoral system.[60] The Commission recommended that a dose of proportionality should be included to correct any imbalance created by the FPTP system, and that the BLS should be subsumed within this new system. With respect to political parties, it made recommendations on funding and registration (which will be referred to below).

Secondly, the Select Committee on the Funding of Political Parties was instituted to examine the recommendations of the Sachs Commission, further to which it developed additional proposals in the area of public funding of political parties.[61] The Select Committee made a range of recommendations, including providing a model law on the funding of political parties – a law which has never been enacted.

60 Commission on Constitutional and Electoral Reform (Sachs Commission), *Report of the Commission on Constitutional and Electoral Reform 2001/02,* https://mauritiusassembly.govmu.org/mauritiusassembly/wp-content/uploads/2023/03/Report-of-the-Commission-on-Constitutional-and-Electoral-Reform-Volume-I-735.pdf (accessed 19 December 2024).

61 Select Committee on the Funding of Political Parties, "Report of the Select Committee on the Funding of Political Parties" (2004), < https://mauritiusassembly.govmu.org/mauritiusassembly/wp-content/uploads/2023/03/selectCommitteeOnTheFundingOfPoliticalParties.pdf> (accessed 19 December 2024).

There was also the Carcasonne Report, which recommended a radical overhaul of the electoral system by abolishing the FPTP and BL systems. It proposed the creation of new constituencies in which candidates would be elected on the basis of proportional representation. In addition, and fourthly, the Carcassonne Report was followed by the Sithanen Report, which recommended "a mixed electoral system with 62 FPTP [Members of Parliament (MPs)] in three-member constituencies (2 for Rodrigues) and 20 additional [MPs] elected from a closed rank-ordered party list".[62]

Finally, the government adopted a Consultation Paper on Electoral Reform in 2014, which considered all the previous reports and made recommendations geared towards updating and redesigning the electoral framework to better reflect a pluri-ethnic society such as Mauritius.[63] It invited the views of all interested parties before it could draw up legislation on the way forward. The Consultation Paper included recommendations on the following: introducing a dose of proportionality in the current system; anti-defection rules to prevent members elected through the proportional representation system from crossing the floor; subsuming the BLS, as its operationalisation depends on the 1972 census, which should be updated, and discouraging particularistic parties by adopting a formula that does not exacerbate ethnic divisions.

The various reports above focused first and foremost on the electoral system, but also reflected to some extent on the roles and obligations of political parties within the electoral process and beyond. This section sheds light on proposed reforms that relate specifically to political parties.

5.1 Constitutionalisation of political parties

It is beyond doubt that political parties in Mauritius should be recognised and regulated by the Constitution. The constitutional regulation of parties is an "important part of the political and social reality which brings an es-

62 R Sithanen, "Roadmap for a Better Balance Between Stability and Fairness in the Voting Formula" (January 2012), < https://ionnews.mu/wp-content/uploads/2014/03/er-final-report-26-01-2012.docx> (accessed 19 December 2024), 96.

63 Government of Mauritius, "Modernising the Electoral System: Consultation Paper on Electoral Reform", (24 March 2014), https://ionnews.mu/wp-content/uploads/2014/03/document-reforme-electoral.pdf (accessed 19 December 2024).

sential contribution to the functioning of democracy".[64] Given its decisive victory in the 2024 general elections, the newly elected government now has the required majority to amend the Constitution. This presents a golden opportunity for it to solidify the principles outlined by Fombad in the overview chapter of this book[65] by enshrining them in the constitutional framework. For instance, the ESC could be given a clear and independent mandate in the Constitution to oversee political parties, in particular during general elections. The constitutionalisation of parties in Mauritius can secure their long-term existence as well as affirm their place as institutions with a key role in governance and wider democracy.

5.2 Enactment of an electoral law

Another suggestion is to enact an electoral law that regulates political parties. A more widely encompassing law than that which exists at the moment could seek to ensure the impartiality and neutrality of regulatory authorities such as the ESC. This would involve adopting mechanisms for stricter enforcement of the code of conduct during the general elections and making compliance legally binding. Such a law should also address how coalitions are formed and dissolved. The Political Parties Act 2011 of Kenya may be used as a blueprint in regard to the rights and privileges of political parties and coalitions.

Consideration should be given as well to regulating internal party elections by mandating regular leadership contests and establishing clear procedures and criteria for candidate selection. Given that the ethnicity of the candidate is often the determining factor in the selection process, there is a need to regulate such practices at the level of the legal framework. Regarding the problem of anti-defection, reforms should be geared towards refining grounds for disqualification.

64 I van Biezen, "Constitutionalizing Party Democracy: The Constitutive Codification of Political Parties in Post-War Europe' 42(1) (2012) *British Journal of Political Science*, pp 187–212, 190.

65 See CM Fombad, "An Overview of Political Party Constitutionalisation under Contemporary African Constitutions", in this volume.

5.3 Financing political parties

The expenditure caps under the Representation of the People Act 1958 are considered highly unrealistic. As mentioned above, the Sachs Commission was instituted to consider, among other things, the question of public funding of political parties.[66] It noted that these limits are often ignored. Parties raise funds either through directly corrupt tactics throughout their term in power or through what are craftily labelled as "donations", primarily from private sector corporations in ways that are unofficial and undisclosed.[67] The possibly corrupt tactics used by parties to raise funds include taking kickbacks from government contracts, a practice in which a portion of public funds is siphoned off to the party itself in exchange for the contracts it awards.[68] Parties may also misuse state resources, such as public funds or state-owned enterprises, to finance their campaigns or fill their coffers. In addition, they might accept illicit donations in exchange for political favours, in the process using shell companies to launder the money and obscure its origin. The Sachs Commission thus proposed the enactment of legislation which would provide for the establishment of a Fund which will receive funds appropriated by Parliament and such other funds which it may lawfully receive.. Such funds would be controlled by the ESC and allocated to political parties and elected candidates when certain conditions are fulfilled.

Funding for political parties has been a contentious issue in numerous parliamentary debates, but the lack of bipartisan consensus suggests that legislative changes might be challenging to implement. In both 2019 and 2024, the Political Financing Bill did not secure the necessary three-quarters majority in parliament to pass into law.[69] The Political Financing Bill could be enacted only if the Constitution (Amendment) Bill were to be

66 Sachs Commission, *supra* n. 62.

67 AL Darga, "The Electoral Reform Process in Mauritius" 4 (2005) *Journal of African Elections*, pp 117–132, 124.

68 R Sithanen, "Electoral Reform: The Case for Transparent Funding and Better Regulation of Political Parties", *L'Express*, 4 April 2016, https://lexpress.mu/s/idee/279017/electoral-reform-case-transparent-funding-and-better-regulation-political-parties (accessed 16 November 2024).

69 The Political Financing Bill No. XIV of 2019, https://mauritiusassembly.govmu.org/mauritiusassembly/wp-content/uploads/2023/03/bill1419.pdf (accessed 5 August 2024); the Political Financing Bill 2024, https://pmo.govmu.org/Communique/Draft-The_Political_Financing_Bill_29.4.24.pdf, (accessed 5 August 2024).

passed to amend the Constitution and provide additional powers and functions to the ESC and Electoral Commissioner in matters relating to political financing. It thus aimed to expand the roles and authority of both the ESC and the Electoral Commissioner, mandate the registration of political parties with the Electoral Commissioner, enhance transparency in the political donation process, and require political-party accounts to be recorded and audited.[70] Such a law could help to mitigate the influence of private sector donations and promote transparency and accountability in party funding.

6 Conclusion

With its focus placed on coalition politics, this chapter has examined the role of ethnicity in shaping Mauritius's political landscape. The persistence of coalition governments since independence highlights that, in order to secure a majority in the National Assembly, there is a need for forming inter-group coalitions. Coalition politics has in turn led to a sense of shared governance among diverse communities and been integral to the stability and functionality of the Mauritian political system. However, given the presence of an electoral system based on the FPTP and BLS, there is an inherent need for parties to make ethnic calculations in their candidate selections. On the one hand, this practice ensures representation for a variety of ethnic groups, encourages the formation of multi-ethnic political parties, and prevents extreme polarisation along ethnic or religious lines; on the other hand, it also perpetuates a form of institutionalised ethnicisation within the political system.

One is thus left with the impression that ethnicity in coalition politics is a double-edged sword in Mauritius. It tends to promote balanced representation and shared governance, yet at the same time necessitates constant negotiation and recalibration of political alliances. The success of Mauritian democracy, therefore, lies in its ability to maintain this delicate balance of ensuring that all ethnic groups feel adequately represented while navigating the inherent challenges of coalition governance.

More generally, the constitutionalisation of political parties in Mauritius could be a crucial step in promoting internal democracy, ensuring financial transparency, and reducing communal influences. These reforms would not only strengthen the democratic foundations of political parties, but

70 Kasenally and Ramtohul, *supra* n. 33.

also enhance their credibility and accountability to the Mauritian public at large.

References

Books, articles, chapters in books, and others

Bunwaree S and Kasenally R, Political Parties and Democracy in Mauritius, EISA (2005)

Bunwaree S, "Interrogating Liberal Democracy: The Islamic Movement in Mauritius", in MA Mohamed Salih (ed.), *Interpreting Islamic Political Parties*, New York, Palgrave Macmillan (2009), pp 231–248

Carroll BW and Carroll T, "Accommodating Ethnic Diversity in a Modernizing Democratic State: Theory and Practice in the Case of Mauritius", 23 (2000) *Ethnic and Racial Studies*, pp 120–142

Carroll BW and Carroll T, "The Consolidation of Democracy in Mauritius" 6(1) (1999) *Democratization*, pp 179–197

Claveyrolas M, "Au 'Pays des Vaish' ? Structure et Idéologie de Caste à l'île Maurice", 163 (2013) *Archives de Sciences Sociales des Religions*, pp 191–216

Commission on Constitutional and Electoral Reform (Sachs Commission), *Report of the Commission on Constitutional and Electoral Reform 2001/02*, https://mauritiusassembly.govmu.org/mauritiusassembly/wp-content/uploads/2023/03/Report-of-the-Commission-on-Constitutional-and-Electoral-Reform-Volume-I-735.pdf (accessed 19 December 2024)

Couacaud L, Sookrajowa SS, and Narsoo J, "The Vicious Circle that is Mauritian Politics: The Legacy of Mauritius's Electoral Boundaries", 21 (2022) *Ethnopolitics*, pp 48

Darga AL, "The Electoral Reform Process in Mauritius" 4 (2005) *Journal of African Elections*, pp 117–132

Dubey A, Government and Politics in Mauritius, Delhi, Kalinga Publications (1997)

Electoral Supervisory Commission, "Code of Conduct for the National Assembly Elections 2019" https://electoral.govmu.org/oec/wp-admin/admin-ajax.php?juwpfisadmin=false&action=wpfd&task=file.download&wpfd_category_id=8&wpfd_file_id=803 (accessed 5 August 2024)

ENews Channel Africa, "Mauritius Votes in Poll Clouded by Phone Tapping Scandal", 10 November 2024, https://www.enca.com/news/mauritius-votes-poll-clouded-phone-tapping-scandal (accessed 16 November 2024)

Eriksen TH, Common Denominators: Ethnicity, Nation-Building and Compromise in Mauritius, 1st ed., Oxfordshire, Routledge (1998)

Fessha Y and Ho Tu Nam N, "Is it Time to Let Go? The Best Loser System in Mauritius", 28(1) (2015) *Afrika Focus*, pp 63–79

Garnett HA, James TS, MacGregor M, and Caal-Lam S, *Year in Elections Global Report 2023*, Ontario and Norfolk, The Electoral Integrity Project (2023), https://static1.squarespace.com/static/58533f31bebafbe99c85dc9b/t/649dee1ee6e6c50219e9fbd9/1688071716978/Electoral+Integrity+Global+Report+2023.pdf (accessed 5 August 2024)

Hollup O, "The Disintegration of Caste and Changing Concepts of Indian Ethnic Identity in Mauritius", 33(4) (1994) *Ethnology*, pp 297–316

Jahangeer-Chojoo A, "From Minority to Mainstream Politics: The Case of Mauritian Muslims", 25(1) (2010) Journal of Social Sciences, pp 121–133

Kadima DK and Kasenally R, "The Formation, Collapse and Revival of Political Party Coalitions in Mauritius: Ethnic Logic and Calculations at Play", 4(1) (2005) *Journal of African Elections*, pp 133–164

Kasenally R and Ramtohul R, "The Cost of Parliamentary Politics in Mauritius", *Westminster Foundation for Democracy*, 21 September 2020, p 10, https://www.wfd.org/sites/default/files/2022-01/Cost-of-Parliamentary-Politics-in-MauritiusWEB-FINAL.pdf (accessed 14 January 2024)

Kasenally R, "Mauritius: Paradise Reconsidered", 22 (2011) *Journal of Democracy*, pp 160–169

Kasenally R, "Mauritius: The Not so Perfect Democracy", (2011) 10(1) *Journal of African Elections*, pp 33–47

Mahadew A, "Reforming Mauritius's Electoral System: More Gender and Less Communal Representation?", *ConstitutionNet*, 25 February 2019, https://constitutionnet.org/news/reforming-mauritiuss-electoral-system-more-gender-and-less-communal-representation (accessed 5 August 2024)

Mahadew R, "The Best Loser System in Mauritius: An Essential Electoral Tool for Representing Political Minorities", in J de Visser, N Steytler, D Powell, and E Durojaye (eds.), *Constitutional Building in Africa*, Nomos, Baden-Baden (2015), pp 135–160

Mathur R, "Party Cooperation and the Electoral System in Mauritius", in BV Lal and P Larmour (eds.), *Electoral Systems in Divided Societies: The Fiji Constitution*, ANU Press (2012), pp 135–146

Mathur R, "The Best Loser System", in S Nirsimloo-Gayan (ed.), *Towards the Making of a Multi-Cultural Society: Conference Papers*, Moka, Mahatma Gandhi Institute Press (2000), pp 203–206

Meetoo A and Meetoo C, "How Seven Lucky Candidates have been Chosen as Best Loses in 2014 General Elections", *Elections Mauritius*, n.d., https://www.electionsmauritius.com/2014/extra/7/how-seven-lucky-candidates-have-been-chosen-as-best-losers (accessed 5 August 2024)

Mehta SR, "Power Dynamics of Indian Immigrants in Mauritius: A Study in Ethnic Relations", 25(1) (1995) *Indian Anthropologist*, pp 1–11

Miles WFS, "The Politics of Language Equilibrium in a Multilingual Society: Mauritius", 32 (2000) *Comparative Politics*, pp 215–239

Mo Ibrahim Foundation, *2024 Ibrahim Index of African Governance*, October 2024, https://mo.ibrahim.foundation/sites/default/files/2024-10/2024-index-report.pdf (accessed 12 November 2024)

Mukonoweshuro EG, "Containing Political Instability in a Poly-Ethnic Society: The Case of Mauritius", 14(2) (1991) *Ethnic and Racial Studies*, pp 199–224

Nagar MF, The Road to Democratic Development Statehood in Africa: The Cases of Ethiopia, Mauritius, and Rwanda, 1st ed, Palgrave Macmillan (2021)

Nave A, "Nested Identities: Ethnicity, Community and the Nature of Group Conflict in Mauritius", in C Bates (ed.), *Community, Empire and Migration: South Asians in Diaspora*, Basingstoke, Palgrave (2001), pp 87–108

Oodunt S, "L'Alliance PTr-MMM-PMSD Vole en éclats", *L'Express*, 15 April 2024, https://lexpress.mu/s/lalliance-ptr-mmm-pmsd-vole-en-%C3%A9clats-533647 (accessed 5 August 2024)

Poupko ES, "An Exploratory Study of Constitutional Design in Three Island States: Seychelles, Comoros, and Mauritius", 35(3) (2017) *Journal of Contemporary African Studies*, pp 324–348

Sithanen R, "Electoral Reform: The Case for Transparent Funding and Better Regulation of Political Parties", *L'Express*, 4 April 2016, https://lexpress.mu/s/idee/279017/electoral-reform-case-transparent-funding-and-better-regulation-political-parties (accessed 16 November 2024)

Sookrajowa SS, "Legibility and the Politics of Ethnic Classification of the Population in the National Census of Mauritius: A Statist Perspective", 27(2) (2021) *Nationalism and Ethnic Politics*, pp 128–148

Sookrajowa SS, "The Paradox of Power-Sharing in Mauritius", in EW Aboultaif, S Keil, and A McCulloch (eds.), *Power-Sharing in the Global South: Patterns, Practices and Potentials*, Cham, Springer International Publishing (2024), pp 189–213

Suntoo R and Chittoo HB, "Managing Multi-Ethnic Mauritius", 12(3) (2012) *Global Journal of Human Social Science*, pp 33–41

Sutton D, "The Political Consecration of Community in Mauritius, 1948–68", 35(2) (2007) *Journal of Imperial and Commonwealth History*, pp 239–262

Table of cases

Jugnauth v Ringadoo [2008] UKPC 50

Jhuboo v Ganoo [2021] SCJ 284

Table of legislation

African Charter on Democracy, Elections and Governance 2007

African Union Declaration on the Principles Governing Democratic Elections in Africa 2002

Code of Conduct for the National Assembly Elections 2019

Constitution of Mauritius, 1968

National Assembly Act, 1968

Political Financing Bill No. XIV of 2019

Political Financing Bill, 2024

Representation of the People Act, 1958

Part 3
Constitutionalism and Dominant Party Systems

Chapter 11 The Tortuous Path to Party Institutionalisation in Mozambique

Adriano Nuvunga and José Adalima

1. Introduction

The political landscape in Mozambique has been characterised by a complex and often contentious process of party institutionalisation. Since the end of the civil war, the adoption of the General Peace Agreement (GPA) in 1992, and the inception of multiparty democracy in the years thereafter, the country has struggled with the establishment of stable and enduring political parties other than the dominant Mozambique Liberation Front (Frelimo), which has held power since independence.

In the course of three decades of multipartyism, Mozambique has shifted from a two-party system, dominated by the Frelimo and Mozambican National Resistance (Renamo), to a single-dominant-party system controlled by Frelimo. To consider Renamo first, it suffered from two breakaways – initially in 2001, with the establishment of the Peace and Development Party (PDD), and again in 2008, with the creation of the Democratic Movement of Mozambique (MDM).[1] In 2024, Venâncio Mondlane, a Member of Parliament (MP) and former advisor to Renamo's president, left Renamo following tensions with its leader. Running as an independent in the presidential election with the backing of the Optimist Party for the Development of Mozambique (PODEMOS), Mondlane emerged as the second most-voted candidate, according to preliminary results from the electoral commission. Taking Renamo's performance in this election into consideration, it is clear that Mondlane drew considerable support from its traditional base, marking what could be regarded as the third major breakaway from the party.

1 A Nuvunga and J Adalima, *Mozambique Democratic Movement: An Analysis of a New Opposition Party in Mozambique*, Studies on Political Parties and Democracy Edition, Mozambique, Friedrich Ebert Stiftung (2011), http://library.fes.de/pdf-files/bueros/mosambik/09174.pdf (accessed 30 December 2024).

Secondly, as regards Frelimo, its consolidation as the sole dominant party stemmed in good part from its use of state resources for its benefit, which in turn contributed to the erosion of opposition parties, notably Renamo. Amidst this bipartisanship, smaller parties and coalitions struggled to gain traction, facing numerous obstacles to their establishment.[2] As a result, the involvement of political parties in governance besides Frelimo encountered significant constraints, primarily of a legal nature. These challenges arose from the architecture of the Mozambican electoral system, which despite its provision in theory for proportional representation, operates in effect on a winner-take-all basis.

Based on a desktop review and the authors' first-hand research on party politics, this chapter explores Mozambique's tortuous path towards political party development by examining the challenges that party structures face, the influence of historical legacies, and the impact of current electoral dynamics. Through this analysis, we aim to shed light on the broader implications of party institutionalisation for democratic governance in Mozambique.

After this introduction, section 2 delves into the evolution of the party system since the start of Mozambique's democratisation. The section highlights how the two main political parties, Frelimo and Renamo, have marginalised small parties due to these parties' limited role in the peace process. Section 3 considers the legal framework for political parties' institutionalism from a historical perspective by foregrounding, on the one hand, the tension between the provisions of the law and how political parties function in practice, and, on the other, the dominance of Frelimo, which makes it difficult to implement meaningful reforms. Thereafter, the chapter assesses how political parties are nurturing the state of democracy in the country. The conclusions in section 5 underscore that party institutionalisation has been heavily skewed towards a winner-takes-all model. This works primarily to the benefit of Frelimo, and raises the need for reforms that ensure a more inclusive and democratic political framework.

2 A Nuvunga, "From the Two-Party to the Dominant-Party System in Mozambique, 1994–2012: Framing Frelimo Party Dominance in Context," Erasmus University Rotterdam, Unpublished PhD Thesis (2014); A Nuvunga and M Salih, "Mozambique's 2009 Elections: Framing Democratic Consolidation in Context", 9 (2010) *Journal of African Elections,* pp 34–54; E Sitoe, Z Matsimbe, and A Pereira, *Parties and Political Development in Mozambique*, Johannesburg, EISA Research Report 22 (2005); A Nuvunga and M Salih, "Party Dominance and Electoral Institutions: Framing Frelimo's Dominance in the Context of an Electoral Governance Deficit", 5 (2013) *Africa Review*, pp 23–42.

2. The evolution of the party system since 1991

Following a prolonged civil war that spanned 16 years,[3] Mozambique underwent a political transformation when it adopted a new constitution in 1990 and lifted the ban on political parties imposed by the Frelimo government in 1977. The 1990 Constitution provided, inter alia, for freedom of expression and the press (Article 48), freedom of assembly (Article 52), political participation (Article 53), and the right to private property (Article 82). Chapter 1(3) declares that "[t]he Republic of Mozambique is a State of law, founded on pluralism of expression, democratic political organisations, and the respect and guarantee of fundamental human rights and freedoms". Consequently, the prohibition of political parties was lifted, inaugurating a multiparty system in Mozambique through Law No. 7/91 on Political Parties, enacted on 23 January 1991.

Over the past more than three decades of Mozambican democracy, the political-party landscape has undergone significant transformation in two distinct phases – the first saw two-party domination by Frelimo and Renamo, and the second, the growing dominance of Frelimo and the decline of Renamo

2.1 1994–2004: Two-party domination by Frelimo and Renamo

The first phase spanned the ten years between the inaugural democratic elections in 1994 and 2004. During this period, Frelimo emphasised its identity as a former liberation movement, drawing on its historical role in leading the country's struggle for independence from Portugal and securing peace after the conflict with Renamo. Conversely, Renamo positioned itself as the "mother of democracy", claiming credit for having forced Frelimo to shift from a socialist regime to a liberal democratic system.

In the inaugural multiparty democratic elections of 1994, Frelimo and its presidential candidate, Joaquim Chissano, won with 44.33 per cent and 53.30 per cent of the votes, respectively, while Renamo and its presidential

3 The armed conflict between the Frelimo government and Renamo began in 1976 and lasted until 1992. For detailed insight into this conflict, see M Hall, "The Mozambican National Resistance Movement (Renamo): A Study in the Destruction of an African Country", 60 (1990) *Africa*, pp 39–68; A Vines, "The Business of Peace: 'Tiny' Rowland, Financial Incentives and the Mozambican Settlement", 3 (1998) *Accord*, pp 66–74; A Vines, *Renamo: Terrorism in Mozambique*, London, James Currey (1991).

candidate, Afonso Dhlakama, followed with 37.78 per cent and 33.73 per cent.[4] Ideally, a coalition government between the two parties would have been beneficial, as Renamo lacked experience in operating outside the context of armed conflict. The absence of a coalition government after the 1994 elections marginalised Renamo from post-election discussions about resource allocation. Meanwhile, Frelimo capitalised on its governmental authority to endorse decentralisation policies and strategies, bolstering its political stronghold while eroding Renamo's influence. The governance strategy adopted by state institutions consistently aimed at marginalising and weakening the opposition, particularly Renamo. Consequently, two additional peace agreements were necessitated after the GPA was signed in 1992. Under Dhlakama's leadership, Renamo used the threat of renewed conflict as leverage to pressure Frelimo into addressing key issues, including systemic electoral irregularities.

Despite strong electoral competition, Frelimo emerged victorious once again in the 1999 elections. Under the majority-based electoral system, Renamo's success in key constituencies such as Nampula, Zambézia, Tete, Manica, and Sofala – which together account for nearly two-thirds of the Mozambican population – did not translate into an overall victory. Moreover, Frelimo's narrow victory in 1999 raised suspicions of electoral fraud.[5] The official results reportedly gave Chissano a contentious win, with 2,338,333 votes (52.3 per cent) compared to Dhlakama's 2,133,655 votes (47.7 per cent) – a slim margin of 205,000 votes.[6] In subsequent elections, however, Renamo's performance declined for various reasons, as discussed in the following sections.

---

4 National Elections Commission (CNE), "Official Map of the Results of the Elections of the President of the Republic", I Series, No. 47, 23 November 1994, https://archive.gazettes.africa/archive/mz/1994/mz-government-gazette-series-i-supplement-dated-1994-11-23-no-47.pdf (accessed 31 October 2024).

5 J Hanlon, *25 Anos de Fraude Eleitoral Protegida Pelo Secretismo*, Maputo, Centro de Integridade Pública (CIP) (2024), https://www.cipmoz.org/wp-content/uploads/2024/02/25-anos-de-fraude-eleitoral-protegida-pelo-secretismo.pdf (accessed 18 November 2024).

6 A Van Dokkum, "Moçambique-Eleição Presidencial de 1999, Vitória Infundada" (July 2021), https://www.researchgate.net/publication/352902547_MOCAMBIQUE-ELEICAO_PRESIDENCIAL_DE_1999_vitoria_infundada (accessed 28 July 2024).

2.2 Since 2004: Growing dominance of Frelimo and decline of Renamo

Electoral competition remained strong until 2004, the year of the third presidential and parliamentary elections. The latter marked a further decline in voter turnout: whereas voter participation in the inaugural 1994 elections was high at 89 per cent, it dropped to 79 per cent in 1999 and fell sharply to less than 50 per cent in 2004, reaching just 35 per cent. The decline favoured Frelimo by allowing it to win easily in presidential and legislative elections. Two main factors contributed to this trend.

First, Frelimo changed its presidential candidate, replacing Chissano with Armando Guebuza. Serving as Frelimo's secretary-general from 2002 to 2004, Guebuza leveraged state resources for a two-year election campaign and re-established Frelimo's influence across all provinces and districts, which delivered electoral gains for the party. The second factor relates to Renamo's position. Although Mozambique has a proportional-representation electoral system, the representation it affords does not translate into effective governance, as the President serves as the central authority while Parliament wields only limited influence. This dynamic is due largely to the executive branch's control of both the judiciary and Parliament, which diminishes the effectiveness of opposition parties with seats in Parliament. Additionally, political parties receive little to no funding, with only those represented in Parliament receiving minimal budget allocations to support their operations.

Despite enjoying substantial support, particularly in the central and northern regions, and its significant presence in the National Parliament, Renamo faced challenges in providing resources to its members and supporters.[7] Consequently, disillusioned with the situation, many of them began to abstain from voting, which presented a significant setback for Renamo. At the same time, Renamo suffered from two breakaways due to tensions within its leadership. In 2001 Raul Domingos established the PDD after being expelled from Renamo following the 1999 elections. Domingos had previously served as Renamo's chief negotiator in the 1992 GPA with the Frelimo government and was appointed head of the Renamo parliamentary group after the 1994 elections.

Seven years later, tensions mounted with another important figure in the party, Davis Simango. Simango served as Renamo's mayor of Beira

7 A Nuvunga, "Mozambique's 2014 Elections: A Repeat of Misconduct, Political Tension and Frelimo Dominance", 16 (2017) *Journal of African Elections*, pp 71–93.

(Mozambique's second-largest and most significant city), delivering a strong performance. However, he faced a surprise replacement by another candidate and eventual expulsion from the party after opposing this decision. Subsequently, in 2009 he ran again for mayor of Beira, this time as an independent candidate, securing victory with 62 per cent of the votes – by contrast, Frelimo's candidate obtained 32 per cent and Renamo's, 3 per cent.

During this period, Frelimo solidified its status as the dominant party in the political landscape, while Renamo's performance faltered.[8] Following the 2009 election, Renamo's president alleged fraud and chose to retreat to the bush to mobilise his forces against Frelimo's ongoing violations of the GPA. This escalated tensions, resulting in localised confrontations between government forces and Renamo's soldiers. Following negotiations (supported by Mozambique's development partners), a second peace agreement was signed in 2014 between Dhlakama and then President Guebuza. The agreement marked the end of the military hostilities which had persisted since 2012,[9] paving the way for elections that led to Frelimo's new leader Filipe Nyusi's rise to power in 2014.

2.3. Since 2018: The consolidation of Frelimo's dominance

The death of Afonso Dhlakama in 2018 further weakened Renamo's position. Ossufo Momade succeeded him, but his ascent was not the result of internal democracy and caused discomfort within the party ranks. Momade's leadership has been widely criticised as lacking charisma and marked by perceived weakness. Having served as an MP for 20 years following the 1994 elections, he had lost touch with the grassroots and become accustomed to the comforts of urban life in Maputo. Renamo,

8 Bertelsmann Stiftung, BTI 2020 Country Report – Mozambique, Gütersloh, Bertelsmann Stiftung (2020), https://bti-project.org/fileadmin/api/content/en/downloads/reports/country_report_2020_MOZ.pdf (accessed 30 December 2024); CanalMoz, "Ultrapassado Obstáculo Guebuza/Paúnde: Antigos Combatentes Abrem Espaço Para Outros Pré-Candidatos", *Facebook*, 24 February 2014, www.facebook.com/CanalMoz/posts/607318489337252/ (accessed 22 February 2024).

9 Voice of America (VOA), "Governo e Renamo Assinam Acordo para o Fim das Hostilidades", *VOA Português*, 24 August 2014, https://www.voaportugues.com/a/governo e-renamo-assinam-acordo-para-o-fim-das-hostilidades/2426618.html (accessed 18 November 2024).

under Momade's leadership, has not effectively challenged the government since Dhlakama's death. Consequently, it lost its ability to pose a credible threat to Frelimo, particularly after Nyusi and Momade signed another peace agreement in 2019.[10]

Following this agreement, the rapid dismantling of the remaining Renamo military bases sparked speculation that Momade had been influenced by Frelimo to sever ties with these bases, lead the party from Maputo, and embrace its status as the second-largest party in parliament. Contrary to his predecessor, Momade accepted the Special Status of Leader of the Second-largest Party in Parliament,[11] which grants him funds from the state budget amounting to nearly USD 1 million per year – these are allocated to his office without any requirement of accountability.[12]

The 2023 local elections revealed Momade's apparent lack of drive to secure political power. After initially calling for nationwide protests over alleged electoral fraud, he directed leaders to halt the demonstrations despite Renamo's refusal to recognise the results. When they refused to comply with Momade's instructions, they faced legal charges. The police accused them of inciting public disobedience, which led to their house arrest until the end of their terms as mayors of Nacala Porto and Nampula municipalities. In Maputo, Mondlane (at the time an MP for Renamo) had police encircling his residence.[13] Once again, Renamo's top leadership, notably Momade, remained conspicuously silent on these developments, a silence that persists to this day. The sections below highlight the challenges of implementing the country's legal framework on political parties.

---

10 A Sebastião, "Moçambique: Nyusi e Momade Assinam Acordo de Paz", *Deutsche Welle*, 1 August 2019, https://www.dw.com/pt-002/moçambique-nyusi-e-momade-assinam-acordo-de-paz-na-gorongosa/a-49845768 (accessed 22 February 2024).

11 See Law No. 33/2014 of 30 December 2014. Dhlakama did not accept the privileges associated with that role, such as a government-provided residence, state security, or state budgetary support. He chose instead to rely on resources he could mobilise independently, which enabled him to retreat to the bush and rally his soldiers in response to government actions that undermined Renamo.

12 E de Salema, "Estatuto Especial do Líder do Segundo Partido com Assento Parlamentar", *Carta de Moçambique*, 10 June 2020, https://cartamz.com/index.php/opiniao/carta-de-opiniao/item/5341-estatuto-especial-do-lider-do-segundo-partido-com-assento-parlamentar (accessed 22 February 2024).

13 Centro Para Democracia e Direitos Humanos (CDD), "Frelimo Está a Usar a Justiça Como Arma de Arremesso Contra Opositores Politicos", 20 December 2023, https://cddmoz.org/wp-content/uploads/2020/07/Frelimo-esta-a-usar-a-Justica-como-arma-de-arremesso-contra-opositores-politicos.pdf (accessed 22 February 2024).

3. The legal framework regulating political parties

Law No. 7/91 on Political Parties sets the legal parameters governing the formation of political parties and delineates their operational guidelines. It is regarded as one of Mozambique's progressive statutes, given that it provides ample room for citizens to establish political parties and engage in political-party activities irrespective of ethnicity, race, or religion. Despite criticisms that it is deficient when it comes to addressing illicit political financing, its fundamental principles uphold fairness and inclusivity in the political domain.[14]

The legal framework acknowledges and safeguards political parties as the rightful institutions for organising the country's political landscape. Consequently, parties have a central role in the electoral process as entities that shape and guide democratic exercise. However, the Constitution does impose limitations: Article 76 states that party names containing expressions directly related to any religious confessions or churches are prohibited, as is the use of emblems that can be confused with national or religious symbols. Additionally, since 2018, it is up to the Constitutional Council to decide on the legality of the statutes of political parties and coalitions, as well as the legality of actions challenging elections and deliberations by political-party bodies.[15]

3.1 Parliamentary thresholds for political parties

The foremost challenge to multipartyism in Mozambique lies in the historical and political trajectory the country has followed since the GPA was signed in 1992, a trajectory that perpetuates the marginalisation of parties other than Frelimo and Renamo. Concerning power-sharing, the two parties agreed that a threshold of 5 per cent of the national vote is necessary to secure seats and form a parliamentary group. As a result, in 1994, none of the smaller parties could form parliamentary groups save for the coalition known as the Democratic Union, which obtained 5.2 per cent.

14 E Cortez, A Orre, B Fael, et al., *Costs and Consequences of the Hidden Debt Scandal of Mozambique*, Moçambique, Centro de Integridade Pública (CIP) and Norway, Chr. Michelsen Institute (2021), https://www.cmi.no/publications/file/7841-costs-and-consequences-of-the-hidden-debt-scandal-of-mozambique.pdf (accessed 27 February 2024).

15 Article 243(2)(e) and (f) of the Constitution, as amended in 2018.

Moreover, under the proportional representation system, the size of a parliamentary group determines the number of its members who are eligible to sit on Parliament's Permanent Committee (CPAR) and its sub-committees. Generally, the heads of each parliamentary group sit on the CPAR, which is responsible for coordinating the activities of the plenary, sub-committees, and national groups. For sub-committees, members are nominated by the groups and then elected by the plenary. Vote declarations are made in person, and are exclusive to each parliamentary group. Each group nominates a member to be elected as the Speaker. Parliamentary groups can propose laws.[16] Parties with parliamentary seats are also entitled to have representatives in all other state bodies, based on proportional representation in Parliament. This mechanism allows political parties with seats in Parliament to have representatives in electoral bodies and the Constitutional Council.

In 2004, the 5 per cent electoral threshold was abolished after extensive debate about its impact on smaller parties' ability to enter Parliament. However, this change did not increase smaller parties' presence in Parliament. Parliamentary rules introduced in 2009 stipulated that a political party needed at least nine elected MPs to form a parliamentary group. In that year's election, the newly formed MDM won only eight seats, falling short of the requirements to establish a parliamentary group under existing rules. However, a later revision of the parliamentary regulations lowered the threshold to eight MPs, allowing the MDM to establish a parliamentary group. This change solidified its position as the third-largest party in Parliament, where it remains represented to date. This arrangement aimed to break the two-party system by introducing a third party. However, in practice, it remains largely a two-party system, given that the MDM is not regarded as influential enough to shift the political landscape and that its presence in Parliament is seen as purely symbolic.

3.2 The status of political parties in the electoral system

Unlike the previous constitution that was adopted in 1990, the current Constitution, adopted in 2004, includes a section outlining the general principles of the electoral system. Its Article 135(1) states that "universal, direct, equal, secret, personal and periodic suffrage constitutes the gener-

16 Articles 183(1)(b) and 196 of the Constitution.

al rule for designating the holders of the elective bodies of sovereignty, provinces and local power". In the same vein, Article 135(3) provides that

> the supervision of elections registration and all electoral acts are the responsibility of the National Elections Commission (CNE), an independent and impartial body, whose composition, organisation and functioning and powers are established by electoral law and regulated by law.

In 2018, a constitutional amendment introduced provincial assemblies. In addition, independent candidates are now allowed for the presidential position, while all other positions – such as those for the National Parliament, provincial assemblies, provincial governors, and local authorities – are still limited to candidates nominated by political parties.

Since the advent of multiparty elections in 1994, political parties have been represented in electoral bodies such as the CNE and the Technical Secretariat for Electoral Administration (STAE). This arrangement, facilitated by then UN Secretary-General, Boutros Boutros-Ghali, was designed to build trust between Frelimo and Renamo. At the time, Renamo saw participation in these electoral bodies as essential for monitoring the electoral process and influencing it in its favour. However, this was far from the case because the proportional representation system favoured Frelimo, with its majority in Parliament allowing it to exert influence on the composition of these bodies from the national to district level.

Despite recent changes permitting the inclusion of members of civil society organisations, Frelimo's dominance remains unchallenged. This is because such organisations must still submit their candidates' names for approval via political-party representatives within these institutions. Additionally, the government has the prerogative to appoint an extra member. As a result, the governing party controls the CNE through its parliamentary majority and the government appointee. As for STAE, the general director is appointed by the government and is a public official, whereas the two deputies are chosen by the majority parties in Parliament (Frelimo and Renamo). This structure is mirrored at the national, provincial, and district levels.

This partisan arrangement is also evident in the Constitutional Council, the institution responsible for ruling on electoral disputes and validating election results produced by electoral bodies. Five of the seven Constitutional Council judges are appointed by Parliament according to proportional representation. The other two are appointed separately: one by the

President, who also serves as the President of the Constitutional Council, and the other by the Superior Council of the Judiciary.[17]

This underscores Frelimo's significant influence on electoral governance, which undermines the independence of electoral bodies and contributes to the "Frelimisation" of public institutions. Moreover, the electoral system, based on closed lists, not only grants the mandate solely to the political party, which retains the prerogative to recall elected MPs but, crucially, also makes re-election contingent on the favour of the party leadership rather than the popularity or performance of the individual MP.

Implementing meaningful reforms is challenging because the state is controlled entirely by Frelimo by its majority parliamentary representation. Additionally, nominated members often lack the necessary technical capacity. Therefore, under the dominant-party system currently prevailing in Mozambique, the independence of electoral administration bodies increasingly appears to be a mirage.

3.3 Intra-party democracy

Article 74(2) of the Constitution states that political parties' internal structure and functioning must be democratic. However, internal democracy in Mozambique's political parties remains notably limited, despite what their statutes may claim. Apart from Frelimo, most parties do not hold regular elections, and when elections do occur, they are often marred by exclusion, manipulation, and corruption. In some cases, candidates are physically barred from running, as in the case of Renamo in 2024, while others face internal mechanisms or directives that are designed to exclude them, such as Frelimo's process for nominating presidential candidates for 2024. Exacerbating this problem is the lack of institutions for overseeing and regulating internal democracy within political parties. This gap in oversight is a significant weakness in upholding standards of internal democracy. The discussion below takes up this theme by examining the state of internal democracy in Mozambique's major political parties in greater detail.

17 Article 241(1) of the Constitution, as amended in 2018.

3.3.1 Frelimo

As mentioned, Frelimo is the only political party in Mozambique that consistently holds internal elective conferences from the local to the national level. This is facilitated by the overlap between the party and the state, given that Frelimo's leaders often hold key government positions and leverage state resources for political activities, especially during election periods.

While Frelimo may project an image of having a relatively democratic culture, particularly in internal election processes, there are indications of authoritarian tendencies among the party's leadership. For instance, during the succession process following Guebuza's tenure in 2014, an attempt was made to limit the pool of presidential candidates.[18] However, internal pressure, especially from the Association of Combatants of the National Liberation Struggle,[19] forced the party to expand the candidate pool and include two additional names.[20]

A similar situation unfolded during the selection of Frelimo's presidential candidates in 2024. The party's central committee initially shortlisted three candidates, but further names were proposed during the plenary, ultimately leading to the election of Daniel Chapo as Frelimo's presidential candidate. Provincial leadership elections in Gaza and Zambézia were also marred by interference. In Zambézia, when the candidate favoured by the Maputo leadership was not elected, the results were nullified and the provincial committee leadership was disbanded for failing to secure the national leadership's preferred candidate.

3.3.2 Renamo

Despite branding itself as a champion of democracy, Renamo exhibits significant deficiencies in its democratic culture. Although the party has been

---

18 CanalMoz, "Nervosismo na Frelimo. Paúnde Diz Que Não Há Espaço Para Mais Candidatos", *Facebook*, 13 December 2013, https://www.facebook.com/140291742706598/posts/580570602012041/?locale2=es_LA&paipv=0&eav=AfZLrlWW-Wb_vwrDgzPWPESgRylokaQCvs7R1tkBMfc97Oh7oSv4fNhTSIqtnF1_lNg&_rdc=1&_rdr (accessed 27 February 2024).

19 CanalMoz, *supra* n. 8.

20 L Matias, "Luísa Diogo e Aires Aly Adicionados à Lista de Pré-Candidatos da Frelimo", *Deutsche Welle*, 27 February 2014), https://www.dw.com/pt-002/luísa-diogo-e-aires-aly-adicionados-à-lista-de-pré-candidatos-da-frelimo/a-17463936 (accessed 27 February 2024).

represented in the National Parliament and some municipalities, it has not transformed itself internally from a guerrilla movement to a conventional political party. Until Dhlakama's passing away, Renamo operated both as a political party and a military organisation.

During periods of tension with the government, Renamo's generals who were not MPs often claimed to be the "owners" of the party, a move designed to legitimise decisions that benefit the leadership. However, there have been two notable instances of a lack of internal democracy in Renamo: the selection of Momade to succeed Dhlakama as the leader of the party,[21] and Momade's response to Mondlane's scrutiny of his leadership following the 2023 local elections.

Momade's term as party president expired in January 2024, prompting Mondlane to file a precautionary measure with the Judicial Court of Maputo City demanding the scheduling of a party congress and the annulment of dismissals by Momade that were allegedly beyond his mandate. Mondlane argued that this would "restore democracy" within the party. The court ruled in his favour, requiring Renamo's president to call an elective congress in which Mondlane was a candidate.[22] However, on the day of the congress, he was barred from entering the venue by security despite his being a legitimate delegate, causing him to miss the election. Momade was re-elected with 57 per cent of the vote.[23] Three months later, Mondlane, who had been a member of Renamo for six years, renounced his party membership.[24]

---

21 Throughout its more than 30 years of existence, Renamo has had only two presidents.

22 Alto Molocue Court, Precautionary Notice No. 8/2024, pp 34–36. See Carta de Mocambique, "Sucessao na Reanamo: Tribunal ordena Renamo a Admitir Venâncio Mondlane no Congresso", 15 May 2024, https://www.cartamz.com/~cartamzc/index.php/politica/item/16601-sucessao-na-renamo-tribunal-ordena-renamo-a-admitir-venancio-mondlane-no-congresso (accessed 1 November 2024).

23 "Ossufo Momade reeleito para a presidência da Renamo", *Ikweli*, 17 May 2024, https://ikweli.co.mz/2024/05/17/ossufo-momade-reeleito-para-a-presidencia-da-renamo/ (accessed 29 October 2024).

24 N Mboane, "Venâncio Mondlane já não é Membro da Renamo nem Deputado do Parlamento", *O País*, 3 June 2024, https://opais.co.mz/venancio-mondlane-ja-nao-membro-da-renamo/ (accessed 29 October 2024).

3.3.3 The MDM, other parties, and extra-parliamentary groups

When the MDM was formed in 2009, it appealed to many as an alternative to the two-party system, but disillusionment was soon to come. The party has been criticised for its alleged lack of internal democracy, particularly during the tenure of its founder, Daviz Simango.

According to the MDM's statutes, the authority to create and dissolve its political committee rests with the party's congress. However, in violation of these statutes, Simango dissolved the political committee just 10 months after the party's founding, citing the need to introduce a new dynamic in its operations. This sparked an internal power struggle between the party's office in Maputo – home to the general secretariat and other governing bodies – and Beira, where the office of the party president was located. In 2010, Simango appointed his elder brother, Lutero, as head of the MDM parliamentary group, a decision widely seen as the peak of Simango's practice of allocating senior party positions to family members.[25] Simango's leadership became a point of contention within the party, with figures such as the mayor of Nampula, Mahamudo Amurane, accusing him of disregarding democratic principles, resisting power alternation, and unilaterally selecting party members for the National Assembly.[26]

When Simango passed away in 2021, his succession was contentious due to his centralised management style. As the elective congress approached, none of the succession candidates were publicly known except for Lutero Simango. This posed a dilemma: choose an unknown candidate, or support Lutero Simango, which would reinforce the perception that the MDM was in effect a Simango family enterprise.[27] Ultimately, Lutero Simango was elected party president, securing 87.9 per cent of the vote.[28]

The situation among extra-parliamentary parties is even more challenging, as they lack the resources to function effectively as institutions. Only

25 Nuvunga and Adalima, *supra* n. 1, p 28.

26 "Amurane diz que MDM e Daviz não são alternativa para Moçambique", *Moçambique Terra Queimada*, 30 May 2017, https://ambicanos.blogspot.com/2017/05/amurane-diz-que-mdm-e-daviz-nao-sao.html (accessed 27 February 2024).

27 VOA, "Analista Fernando Lima alerta para o colapso do MDM na eleição de um líder anónimo", *VOA Português*, 8 June 2021, https://www.voaportugues.com/a/analista-fernando-lima-alerta-para-o-colapso-do-mdm-na-elei%C3%A7%C3%A3o-de-um-l%C3%ADder-an%C3%B3nimo/5921156.html (accessed 29 October 2024).

28 "Mozambique: Lutero Simango Elected President of the MDM", *Club of Mozambique*, 6 December 2021, https://clubofmozambique.com/news/mozambique-lutero-simango-elected-president-of-the-mdm-206196/ (accessed 29 October 2024).

the president is widely known in most small parties, and the party headquarters often operate as the president's domain. In such circumstances, internal democracy is essentially non-existent.

3.3.4 Conclusions on intra-party democracy

The absence of internal democracy in parties, coupled with opaque political and electoral financing practices, not only fosters vote-buying within party ranks but also leaves parties susceptible to illicit funding and money laundering. This undermines the institutionalisation of political parties on two fronts. First, it sustains Frelimo's political dominance at the expense of other viable parties, a trend that in turn erodes the overall quality of governance in the country; and, secondly, it diminishes the ability of political parties to aggregate and articulate societal interests, thus curtailing their role in fostering democracy, development, and peace.[29]

Internal democracy in Mozambique's parties is notably feeble. In all parties, especially those with representation in Parliament – Frelimo, Renamo, and MDM – the cult of party leadership is prevalent. It is a state of affairs reinforced by the organisational structures and operational dynamics of these parties, as well as the design of the electoral system itself. This has resulted in a decline in parties' popular legitimacy, as evidenced by increasing electoral abstention and diminishing vote shares in successive elections.

3.4 Financing of political parties

Mozambique lacks a dedicated law regulating the financing of political parties. Instead, the issue is addressed inadequately by three separate laws that focus on funds from the state budget while neglecting private financing. This omission creates an avenue for parties to finance themselves through funds of dubious provenance, such as the proceeds of corruption, kidnappings, drug trafficking, and money laundering.

Apart from Law No. 7/91 on Political Parties, the relevant laws regulating party finance are Law No. 2/2019 (enacted on 31 May 2019), which delin-

29 A Nuvunga, *supra* n. 2; A Nuvunga and E Sitoe, "Party Institutionalisation in Mozambique: 'The Party of the State' vs the Opposition", 12 (2012) *Journal of African Elections,* pp 109–142.

eates the legal procedures for the election of the President of the Republic and MPs; and Law No. 3/2019 (also issued on 31 May 2019), which set out the legal framework for the election of members of provincial assemblies and provincial governments. According to Article 17 of the Law on Political Parties, financing may be sourced from (a) contributions from party members; (b) donations and legacies; (c) funds allocated in the general state budget; and (d) other forms of financing. There is no explicit mention of private financing, which creates a potential gap in funding under Article 17(d). This omission, coupled with the absence of a regulatory mechanism, might be facilitating the exploitation of illicit financing channels.

Frelimo enjoys access to state resources, which gives it a significant advantage over the opposition in several ways. First, Frelimo affiliates hold positions in public entities ranging from state corporations to government agencies and diplomatic missions, allowing it to command an extensive patronage network. For instance, within Frelimo's Political Commission, the party's highest governing body, key ministers are appointed to lead internal working commissions aimed at channelling funds to the party. For the 2024 elections, for example, the Prime Minister and the Minister of Finance headed a working group on Finance and Logistics. This practice came to light during a scandal in which the former Minister of Finance had been crucial in securing an illegal loan for the country without parliamentary approval.

According to Article 178(2)(p) of the Constitution, it is the responsibility of Parliament to authorise the government to contract loans that extend beyond a fiscal year and set the limits for guarantees to be issued by the state. It is alleged that large bribes were paid to secure contracts to supply boats and equipment to state-owned companies in Mozambique. The deal was funded by USD 2 billion in loans by the London branches of Credit Suisse and VTB Capital. Bankers working for Credit Suisse have admitted to receiving millions of dollars in kickbacks to arrange the deal.[30] Recently, the issue was brought before a New York court in a case implicating Frelimo's leadership. Documents revealed that bank transfers totalling about USD 10 million were used to finance the party's campaign.[31]

30 D Namburete, "How Public Interest Litigation Led to Invalidation of Illegal Mozambican Debt", *Afronomics Law*, 4 August 2020, https://www.afronomicslaw.org/2020/08/04/how-public-interest-litigation-led-to-invalidation-of-illegal-mozambican-debt (accessed 11 November 2024).

31 Cortez et al., *supra* n. 14, p 11.

Another party-funding irregularity surfaced in 2021, when it emerged that, between 2012 and 2021, the Tax Authority, headed by a member of the Frelimo Political Commission, had allowed the Frelimo party to import goods valued at about USD 7.6 million while evading approximately USD 3 million in taxes through customs exemptions.[32]

Moreover, Frelimo's campaign funding often stems from public entities, with the State Participation Management Institute being one avenue through which such financing occurs.[33] Additionally, Frelimo operates a holding company, SPI-Gestão e Investimentos SARL, which secures profitable contracts with the state and strengthens its financial resources.[34] In contrast, the opposition lacks similar avenues for accessing resources, resulting in a heavily skewed and unequal playing field as regards financial backing.

In the absence of specific legislation governing private financing, the prevailing trend is for entities to seek to finance Frelimo in exchange for lucrative contracts with the state. This pattern benefits the ruling party significantly, enabling it to solidify its power base and prolong its term in office.

4. Political parties, organised crime, and the state of democracy

Numerous studies highlight that Mozambique is a significant transit and consumption hub for drugs, with the indications being that the drug trade thrives under the protection provided by Frelimo.[35] For example, Mohamed Bachir Suleman, named a drug baron by the United States government in

32 B Nhamirre, *Financiamento Político Ilícito em Moçambique: da Manipulação do Procurement Público à Venda de Isenções Aduaneiras*, Maputo, CIP (2022), https://www.cipmoz.org/wp-content/uploads/2022/05/Financiamento-poli%CC%81tico-ili%CC%81cito-em-Moc%CC%A7ambique-1.pdf (accessed 26 February 2024).

33 Evidências, "Saque às Empresas Públicas: As Boladas do Fim de Mandato", 25 March 2021, *Evidências*, https://evidencias.co.mz/2021/03/25/saque-as-empresas-po sisublicas-as-boladas-do-fim-de-mandato/ (accessed 27 February 2024).

34 "Moçambique para todos", *Macua*, 17 November 2010, https://macua.blogs.com/moambique_para_todos/2010/11/spi-o-bra%C3%A7o-financeiro-da-frelimo.html (accessed 27 February 2024).

35 CDD, "Beatriz Buchili Deve parar de se Lamentar e Atacar os Grandes 'Barões' da Droga Dentro da Frelimo Porque tem Mecanismos para o Fazer", 4 February 2024, https://cddmoz.org/wp-content/uploads/2020/07/Beatriz-Buchili-deve-parar-de-se-lamentar-e-atacar-os-grandes-baroes-da-droga-dentro-da-Frelimo-porque-tem-mecanismos-para-o-fazer.pdf (accessed 27 February 2024).

2010, has been a major financier of Frelimo's campaigns for many years. His support dates back to the Chissano era in the 1990s and continued until recent years. In May 2007, Chissano presided over the inauguration of the Maputo Shopping Center – then the largest in Mozambique and owned by Suleman. Suleman frequently donated to Frelimo as well as senior officials in the police and tax authorities. In 2009, *Savana*, a weekly newspaper, reported that Suleman contributed USD 1 million to President Guebuza's election campaign. He was also invited to a fundraising dinner for Frelimo's 2014 presidential candidate, Nyusi. However, Suleman does not appear to be well-regarded within Nyusi's inner circle. [36]

Collusion between political parties – particularly Frelimo – and drug networks has fuelled rampant organised crime in Mozambique. Kidnappings, for example, have become increasingly common over the past decade. It is estimated that nearly 150 businesspeople have been kidnapped over the last 12 years, with 100 others reportedly leaving the country out of fear for their safety· [37] The outlook therefore appears bleak, given the significant challenges facing the institutional development of political parties. Frelimo, in particular, is marred by internal factional conflicts that extend to the functioning of the state. These intense struggles within the party, driven by opportunism, hinder its political evolution, transforming it into a battleground for individuals lacking a national developmental agenda.

There have been allegations of politicians involved in organised crime, as evidenced by numerous incidents. In November 2022, a Frelimo MP representing the Zambézia constituency was allegedly linked to drug trafficking by the National Criminal Investigation Service of Zambézia.[38] Renamo brought this issue to Parliament, prompting the creation of a parliamentary

36 J Hanlon, *Heroína continua sendo uma das maiores exportações*, Maputo, Centro de Integridade Publica (CIP) (2018), https://www5.open.ac.uk/technology/mozambique/sites/www.open.ac.uk.technology.mozambique/files/files/Heroina%20continua%20sendo%20uma%20das%20maiores%20exportac%CC%A7o%CC%83es.pdf (accessed 1 November 2024).

37 Agencia Lusa, "Mozambique: Almost 150 Business People Kidnapped, 100 Left the Country over 12 years – CTA", *Club of Mozambique*, 25 July 2024, https://clubofmozambique.com/news/mozambique-almost-150-business-people-kidnapped-100-left-the-country-over-12-years-cta-262758/ (accessed 1 November 2024).

38 CDD, "CPI vai Concentrar-se na Informação de Venâncio Mondlane e não no Crime de Tráfico de drogas Envolvendo um Deputado", 23 December 2022, https://cddmoz.org/wp-content/uploads/2020/07/CPI-vai-concentrar-se-na-informacao-de-Venancio-Mondlane-e-nao-no-crime-de-trafico-de-drogas-envolvendo-um-deputado-1.pdf (accessed 11 November 2024).

commission of inquiry to investigate allegations of a drug kingpin among the MPs. The commission consisted of seven members: four from Frelimo, two from Renamo, and one from the MDM.[39] In the end, it found no evidence implicating any MP in the drug trafficking case that arose in Zambézia province.[40]

These dynamics unfold against a backdrop where the youth feel unrepresented by Frelimo or any other party. However, the entrenched political culture within these parties stifles the emergence of alternative political forces capable of championing youth interests and mobilising those who feel disconnected from the electoral system, thus perpetuating their marginalisation.

Hence, political parties are failing to fulfil their role, leading to repercussions that undermine both the present and future state of democracy in Mozambique. Despite three decades of democratic journey, the people have not reaped its benefits. There has been a notable absence of democratic dividends, resulting in stagnant living conditions for many. While democracy remains valued by Mozambican citizens, the latest Afrobarometer results suggest growing scepticism towards democracy as mediated through political parties.[41] Additionally, political instability, including the conflict in Cabo Delgado's northern region, may also stem from the lack of democratic dividends over the past 30 years. The prospect ahead is thus one fraught with continued challenges in the foreseeable future.

5. Conclusion

Political-party development in Mozambique has been characterised by significant challenges and dynamic shifts, all of which shape the current

39 Orfeu Lisboa, "Moçambique: Deputado Suspeito de Envolvimento em Tráfico de Droga", *Radio France Internationale (RFI)*, 29 December 2022, https://www.rfi.fr/pt/%C3%A1frica/20221229-mo%C3%A7ambique-deputado-suspeito-de-envolvimento-em-tr%C3%A1fico-de-droga (accessed 11 November 2024).

40 Folha de Maputo, "'Não há envolvimento de deputado no caso de tráfico de drogas', avança a AR", *Folha de Maputo*, 2 March 2023, https://www.folhademaputo.co.mz/pt/noticias/nacional/nao-ha-envolvimento-de-deputado-no-caso-de-trafico-de-drogas-avanca-a-ar/ (accessed 22 November 2024).

41 Afrobarometer, "Fewer than Half of Mozambicans Feel 'Completely Free' at the Ballot Box, Afrobarometer Survey Shows", *Afrobarometer*, 24 October 2023, https://www.afrobarometer.org/wp-content/uploads/2023/10/News-release-Fewer-than-half-of-Mozambicans-feel-%E2%80%98completely-free-in-voting-Afrobarometer-24oct23.pdf (accessed 1 November 2024).

political landscape. The entrenched dominance of Frelimo, coupled with internal divisions in Renamo and the marginalisation of smaller parties, points to a complex pattern of party institutionalisation, one with profound implications for democratic governance.

This chapter has underscored the fact that while Mozambique theoretically operates under a proportional representation system, political practice leans heavily towards a winner-take-all model that disproportionately favours Frelimo. This imbalance weakens parliamentary oversight, reducing the legislature to a body that largely rubber-stamps the dominant party's agenda. Consequently, the popular legitimacy of parties has waned through rising electoral abstention and diminishing vote shares in successive elections. Furthermore, the persistent use of state resources by the ruling party to consolidate power, alongside legal and institutional barriers faced by emerging parties, highlights a democracy still in its nascent stages and struggling to ensure a level playing field for all political actors. This environment has also provided fertile ground for criminal syndicates to operate within political parties and exert influence on the political system. Coupled with historical legacies and evolving electoral dynamics, these factors present formidable obstacles to the growth of a robust democracy.

Mozambique must hence undertake comprehensive electoral and political reforms and bolster institutional mechanisms that foster a more equitable and representative political landscape. This entails revising electoral laws, building the capacity and independence of electoral institutions, and cultivating a political climate conducive to diverse participation and genuine competition. The Constitutional Council should be transformed into a Constitutional Court, with members elected through the same process as other judges rather than being appointed by Parliament, which risks politicisation. The Constitutional Court must have a clear mandate to decide on electoral matters. Additionally, the CNE and STAE should be depoliticised and restructured into technical and independent institutions with appointments made through a public selection process. STAE should be legally and administratively subordinate to the CNE. Moreover, a robust political-party financing law is essential, alongside an independent institution to oversee party expenses. This institution should monitor sources of funding and expenditures during election campaigns.

A more inclusive and democratic political framework in Mozambique demands sustained efforts from all stakeholders, including political parties, civil society, and international partners. By addressing the entrenched challenges outlined in this chapter, Mozambique can chart a course towards a more democratic and stable political future, one reflective of its diverse populace and responsive to the needs and aspirations of all its citizens.

References

Books, articles, chapters in books, and others

"Amurane diz que MDM e Daviz não são alternativa para Moçambique", *Moçambique Terra Queimada*, 30 May 2017, https://ambicanos.blogspot.com/2017/05/amurane-diz-que-mdm-e-daviz-nao-sao.html (accessed 27 February 2024)

"Moçambique para todos", Macua, 17 November 2010, https://macua.blogs.com/moambique_para_todos/2010/11/spi-o-bra%C3%A7o-financeiro-da-frelimo.html (accessed 27 February 2024)

"Mozambique: Lutero Simango elected president of the MDM", *Club of Mozambique*, 6 December 2021, https://clubofmozambique.com/news/mozambique-lutero-simango-elected-president-of-the-mdm-206196/ (accessed 29 October 2024)

"Ossufo Momade Reeleito para a Presidência da Renamo", *Ikweli*, 17 May 2024, https://ikweli.co.mz/2024/05/17/ossufo-momade-reeleito-para-a-presidencia-da-renamo/ (accessed 29 October 2024)

Afrobarometer, "Fewer Than Half of Mozambicans Feel 'Completely Free' at The Ballot Box, Afrobarometer Survey Shows", *Afrobarometer*, 24 October 2023, https://www.afrobarometer.org/wp-content/uploads/2023/10/News-release-Fewer-than-half-of-Mozambicans-feel-%E2%80%98completely-free-in-voting-Afrobarometer-24oct23.pdf (accessed 1 November 2024)

Agencia Lusa, "Mozambique: Almost 150 Business People Kidnapped, 100 Left the Country over 12 years – CTA", *Club of Mozambique*, 25 July 2024, https://clubofmozambique.com/news/mozambique-almost-150-business-people-kidnapped-100-left-the-country-over-12-years-cta-262758/ (accessed 1 November 2024)

Bertelsmann Stiftung, *BTI 2020 Country Report – Mozambique*, Gütersloh, Bertelsmann Stiftung (2020), https://bti-project.org/fileadmin/api/content/en/downloads/reports/country_report_2020_MOZ.pdf (accessed 30 December 2024)

CanalMoz, "Nervosismo na Frelimo. Paúnde Diz Que Não Há Espaço Para Mais Candidatos", *Facebook*, 13 December 2013, https://www.facebook.com/140291742706598/posts/580570602012041/?locale2=es_LA&paipv=0&eav=AfZLrlWW-Wb_vwrDgzPWPESgRylokaQCvs7R1tkBMfc97Oh7oSv4fNhTSIqtnF1_lNg&_rdc=1&_rdr (accessed 27 February 2024)

CanalMoz, "Ultrapassado Obstáculo Guebuza/Paúnde: Antigos Combatentes Abrem Espaço Para Outros Pré-Candidatos", *Facebook,* 24 February 2014, www.facebook.com/CanalMoz/posts/607318489337252/ (accessed 22 February 2024)

Carta de Mocambique, "Sucessao na Reanamo: Tribunal ordena Renamo a Admitir Venâncio Mondlane no Congresso", 15 May 2024, https://www.cartamz.com/~cartamzc/index.php/politica/item/16601-sucessao-na-renamo-tribunal-ordena-renamo-a-admitir-venancio-mondlane-no-congresso (accessed 1 November 2024)

CDD, "CPI vai Concentrar-se na Informação de Venâncio Mondlane e não no Crime de Tráfico de drogas Envolvendo um Deputado", 23 December 2022, https://cddmoz.org/wp-content/uploads/2020/07/CPI-vai-concentrar-se-na-informacao-de-Venancio-Mondlane-e-nao-no-crime-de-trafico-de-drogas-envolvendo-um-deputado-1.pdf (accessed 11 November 2024)

CDD, "Frelimo Está a Usar a Justiça Como Arma de Arremesso Contra Opositores Politicos", 20 December 2023, https://cddmoz.org/wp-content/uploads/2020/07/Frelimo-esta-a-usar-a-Justica-como-arma-de-arremesso-contra-opositores-politicos.pdf (accessed 22 February 2024)

Centro Para Democracia e Direitos Humanos (CDD), "Beatriz Buchili Deve parar de se Lamentar e Atacar os Grandes 'Barões' da Droga Dentro da Frelimo Porque tem Mecanismos para o Fazer, 4 February 2024, https://cddmoz.org/wp-content/uploads/2020/07/Beatriz-Buchili-deve-parar-de-se-lamentar-e-atacar-os-grandes-baroes-da-droga-dentro-da-Frelimo-porque-tem-mecanismos-para-o-fazer.pdf (accessed 30 December 2024)

Cortez E, Orre A, Fael B, et al., *Costs and Consequences of the Hidden Debt Scandal of Mozambique*, Moçambique, Centro de Integridade Pública (CIP) and Norway, Chr. Michelsen Institute (2021), https://www.cmi.no/publications/file/7841-costs-and-consequences-of-the-hidden-debt-scandal-of-mozambique.pdf (accessed 27 February 2024)

De Salema E, "Estatuto Especial do Líder do Segundo Partido com Assento Parlamentar", *Carta de Moçambique*, 10 June 2020, https://cartamz.com/index.php/opiniao/carta-de-opiniao/item/5341-estatuto-especial-do-lider-do-segundo-partido-com-assento-parlamentar (accessed 22 February 2024)

Evidências, "Adriano Nuvunga Denuncia a Existência de um Deputado "Barão de Drogas" da Frelimo na AR", *Evidências*, 29 August 2023, https://evidencias.co.mz/2023/08/29/adriano-nuvunga-denuncia-a-existencia-de-um-deputado-barao-de-drogas-da-frelimo-na-ar/ (accessed 27 February 2024)

Evidências, "Saque às Empresas Públicas: As Boladas do Fim de Mandato", *Evidências*, 25 March 2021, https://evidencias.co.mz/2021/03/25/saque-as-empresas-publicas-as-boladas-do-fim-de-mandato/ (accessed 27 February 2024)

Folha de Maputo, "'Não há envolvimento de deputado no caso de tráfico de drogas', avança a AR", *Folha de Maputo*, 2 March 2023, https://www.folhademaputo.co.mz/pt/noticias/nacional/nao-ha-envolvimento-de-deputado-no-caso-de-trafico-de-drogas-avanca-a-ar/ (accessed 22 November 2024)

Frelimo, *Estatutos do Partido*, Maputo, Coleccçao 12 Congresso (2023), https://www.frelimo.org.mz/wp-content/uploads/2023/10/estatudo_do_partido_06_02_23.pdf (accessed 30 December 2024)

Hall M, "The Mozambican National Resistance Movement (Renamo): A Study in the Destruction of an African Country", 60 (1990) *Africa*, pp 39–68

Hanlon J, *25 Anos de Fraude Eleitoral Protegida Pelo Secretismo*, Maputo, Centro de Integridade Pública (CIP) (2024), https://www.cipmoz.org/wp-content/uploads/2024/02/25-anos-de-fraude-eleitoral-protegida-pelo-secretismo.pdf (accessed 30 December 2024)

Hanlon J, *Heroína continua sendo uma das maiores exportações*, Maputo, Centro de Integridade Pública (CIP) (2018), https://www5.open.ac.uk/technology/mozambique/sites/www.open.ac.uk.technology.mozambique/files/files/Heroina%20continua%20sendo%20uma%20das%20maiores%20exportac%CC%A7o%CC%83es.pdf (accessed 30 December 2024)

Matias L, "Luísa Diogo e Aires Aly Adicionados à Lista de Pré-Candidatos da Frelimo", *Deutsche Welle*, 27 February 2014, https://www.dw.com/pt-002/luísa-diogo-e-aires-aly-adicionados-à-lista-de-pré-candidatos-da-frelimo/a-17463936 (accessed 27 February 2024)

Mboane N, "Venâncio Mondlane já não é Membro da Renamo nem Deputado do Parlamento", *O Pais*, 3 June 2024, https://opais.co.mz/venancio-mondlane-ja-nao-membro-da-renamo/ (accessed 29 October 2024)

Namburete D, "How Public Interest Litigation Led to Invalidation of Illegal Mozambican Debt", *Afronomics Law*, 4 August 2020, https://www.afronomicslaw.org/2020/08/04/how-public-interest-litigation-led-to-invalidation-of-illegal-mozambican-debt (accessed 11 November 2024)

National Elections Commission (CNE), "Official Map of the Results of the Elections of the President of the Republic", I Series, No. 47, 23 November 1994, https://archive.gazettes.africa/archive/mz/1994/mz-government-gazette-series-i-supplement-dated-1994-11-23-no-47.pdf (accessed 31 October 2024)

Nhamirre B, "Financiamento Político Ilícito em Moçambique: da Manipulação do Procurement Público à Venda de Isenções Aduaneiras", Maputo, CIP (2022). .https://www.cipmoz.org/wp-content/uploads/2022/05/Financiamento-poli%CC%81tico-ili%CC%81cito-em-Moc%CC%A7ambique-1.pdf (accessed 26 February 2024)

Nuvunga A and Adalima J, *Mozambique Democratic Movement: An Analysis of a New Opposition Party in Mozambique*, Studies on Political Parties and Democracy Edition, Mozambique, Friedrich Ebert Stiftung (2011), http://library.fes.de/pdf-files/bueros/mosambik/09174.pdf (accessed 30 December 2024)

Nuvunga A and Salih M, "Mozambique's 2009 Elections: Framing Democratic Consolidation in Context", 9 (2010) *Journal of African Elections*, pp 34–54

Nuvunga A and Sitoe E, "Party Institutionalisation in Mozambique: 'The Party of the State' vs the Opposition", 12 (2012) *Journal of African Elections*, pp 109–142

Nuvunga A, "From the Two-Party to the Dominant-Party System in Mozambique, 1994–2012: Framing Frelimo Party Dominance in Context," Erasmus University Rotterdam, Unpublished PhD Thesis (2014)

Nuvunga A, "Mozambique's 2014 Elections: A Repeat of Misconduct, Political Tension and Frelimo Dominance", 16 (2017) *Journal of African Elections*, pp 71–93

Nuvunga, A and Salih, M "Party Dominance and Electoral Institutions: Framing Frelimo's Dominance in the Context of an Electoral Governance Deficit", 5 (2013) *Africa Review*, pp 23–42

Orfeu Lisboa, "Moçambique: Deputado Suspeito de Envolvimento em Tráfico de Droga", *Radio France Internationale (RFI)*, 29 December 2022, https://www.rfi.fr/pt/%C3%A1frica/20221229-mo%C3%A7ambique-deputado-suspeito-de-envolvimento-em-tr%C3%A1fico-de-droga (accessed 11 November 2024)

Sebastião A, "Moçambique: Nyusi e Momade Assinam Acordo de Paz", *Deutsche Welle*, 1 August 2019, https://www.dw.com/pt-002/moçambique-nyusi-e-momade-assinam-acordo-de-paz-na-gorongosa/a-49845768 (accessed 22 February 2024)

Sitoe E, Matsimbe Z, and Pereira A, *Parties and Political Development in Mozambique*, Johannesburg, EISA Research Report 22 (2005)

Van Dokkum A, "Moçambique-Eleição Presidencial de 1999, Vitória Infundada" (July 2021), https://www.researchgate.net/publication/352902547_MOCAMBIQUE-ELEICAO_PRESIDENCIAL_DE_1999_vitoria_infundada (accessed 28 July 2024)

Vines A, "The Business of Peace: 'Tiny' Rowland, Financial Incentives and the Mozambican Settlement, 3 (1998) *Accord*, pp 66–74

Vines A, *Renamo: Terrorism in Mozambique*, London, James Currey (1991)

Voice of America (VOA), "Analista Fernando Lima alerta para o colapso do MDM na eleição de um líder anónimo", *VOA Português*, 8 June 2021, https://www.voaportugues.com/a/analista-fernando-lima-alerta-para-o-colapso-do-mdm-na-elei%C3%A7%C3%A3o-de-um-l%C3%ADder-an%C3%B3nimo/5921156.html (accessed 29 October 2024)

Voice of America (VOA), "Governo e Renamo Assinam Acordo para o Fim das Hostilidades", *VOA Português*, 24 August 2014, https://www.voaportugues.com/a/governo-e-renamo-assinam-acordo-para-o-fim-das-hostilidades/2426618.html (accessed 18 November 2024)

Table of legislation

Constitution of the Republic of Mozambique, I Series, No. 104, Law No. 33/2014, 30 December 2014

Constitution of the Republic of Mozambique, I Series, No. 105, Law No. 2/2019, 31 May 2019

Constitution of the Republic of Mozambique, I Series, No. 105, Law No. 3/2019, 31 May 2019

Constitution of the Republic of Mozambique, I Series, No. 44, 2 November 1990

Constitution of the Republic of Mozambique, I Series, No. 51, 22 December 2004

Law No. 7/91, 23 January 1991

Chapter 12 Party Constitutionalisation and Democracy in Securocratic States: Lessons from Rwanda

Bekezela Gumbo

1. Introduction

Political parties are essential to the functioning of representative democracy, as they facilitate political participation, representation, competition, and accountability.[1]

However, the quality and sustainability of democracy depends on the constitutional and legal frameworks that regulate and protect political parties, as well as on the behaviour and performance of parties themselves.

In some sub-Saharan African countries (Egypt, Zimbabwe, and Rwanda, for example), parties operate under a securocratic state framework, where ruling elites prioritise security over liberty and use coercion and repression to maintain their power and legitimacy.[2] This chapter examines how the constitutionalisation of political parties has shaped the nature and quality of democracy in Rwanda – a paradigmatic case of a securocratic state that has undergone party constitutionalisation, in its case since the end of the genocide in 1994.[3]

---

1 See UN Human Rights Committee, General Comment No. 25: Article 25 (Participation in Public Affairs and the Right to Vote), 12 July 1996, CCPR/C/21/Rev.1/Add.7, paragraph 26. See also Venice Commission, *Guidelines on Political Party Regulation*, 2nd ed, 14 December 2020, CDL-AD(2020)032, paragraphs 17–18, www.eods.eu/library/VeniceCommission_OSCE_2020_PartyRegulation.pdf (accessed 16 April 2024).

2 OS McDoom, "Securocratic State-Building: The Rationales, Rebuttals, and Risks Behind the Extraordinary Rise of Rwanda after the Genocide", 121 (2022) *African Affairs*, pp 535–567. For a case study on Zimbabwe, see E Ziso, "Exploring the Interplay of Political Party Regulation and Internal Contradictions of Opposition Politics in Zimbabwe: The Case of the MDC/CCC", in this volume.

3 M Bogaards, "Counting Parties and Identifying Dominant Party Systems in Africa", 43 (2004) *European Journal of Political Research*, pp 173–197. See also G Borz, "Justifying the Constitutional Regulation of Political Parties: A Framework for Analysis", 38 (2017) *International Political Science Review/Revue Internationale de Science Politique*, pp 99–113.

The chapter adopts a single-case-study approach in examining the constitutionalisation of political parties in Rwanda. This allows for an in-depth analysis of the complex and dynamic phenomenon of party constitutionalisation and its implications for democracy and human rights.[4] The chapter seeks to uncover causal mechanisms that link party constitutionalisation to the nature and quality of democracy in Rwanda.[5] It also situates the Rwandan case within the broader literature and its debates on democracy and securitisation in sub-Saharan Africa (and beyond).[6] The chapter draws on primary and secondary data sources – including the Constitution,[7] legal texts, laws, court judgements, academic literature, and media reports – and seeks to answer the following questions: (1) How and why did party constitutionalisation take place in Rwanda; (2) what are the main features of and challenges to party constitutionalisation; (3) how does party constitutionalisation affect the state of democracy and human rights; and (4) what can be learnt from the Rwandan case in the interests of promoting democracy and constitutionalism in sub-Saharan Africa?

The chapter is structured as follows. After this introduction, section 2 presents the historical and political context of party constitutionalisation in Rwanda, and explains the objectives that the ruling party and opposition parties have had in engaging in party constitutionalisation. Section 3 examines the legal framework for party constitutionalisation, and assesses its impact on the formation, operation, and inclusivity of political parties. In so doing, the section highlights the implications that party constitutionalisation has for the state of democracy and human rights in Rwanda. It also examines the limits and achievements of constitutionalisation in promoting democratic values and institutions in the context of a securocratic state. Section 4 presents the conclusions of the study and identifies key lessons

4 For more on the case-study approach, see J Gerring, *Case Study Research: Principles and Practices*, Cambridge, Cambridge University Press (2007). See also P Baxter and S Jack, "Qualitative Case Study Methodology: Study Design and Implementation for Novice Researchers", 13 (2008) *The Qualitative Report*, pp 544–559; RK Yin, *Case Study Research Design and Methods*, 5th ed, Thousand Oaks, Sage (2014).

5 Specifically, the study utilises process-tracing. See D Beach and RB Pedersen, *Process-tracing Methods: Foundations and Guidelines*, 2nd ed, Michigan, University of Michigan Press (2019); A Bennett and JT Checkel (eds.), *Process Tracing: From Metaphor to Analytic Tool*, Cambridge, Cambridge University Press (2015).

6 G Erdmann and M Basedau, "Problems of Categorising and Explaining Party Systems in Africa", 4 (2007) *GIGA Working Papers* 40 (2007), ssrn.com/abstract=978166 or dx.doi.org/10.2139/ssrn.978166 (accessed 16 July 2024).

7 Constitution of the Republic of Rwanda of 2003, amended in 2015 and 2023.

and recommendations that can be derived from the Rwandan case in terms advancing democracy in sub-Saharan Africa.

2. Historical and political context

Composed as it is of three main ethnic groups – the Hutu (about 85 per cent), the Tutsi (about 14 per cent), and the Twa (about 1 per cent) – Rwanda has a long and turbulent history of ethnic conflict which, culminating in the 1994 genocide, has shaped its political and social landscape.[8] These same ethnic dynamics were decisive for the outcomes of the independence elections and subsequent post-independence subjugation of minority groups. Party constitutionalisation in Rwanda has thus been shaped by the country's historical political experiences of colonialism, ethnic division, civil war, and genocide.[9] Specifically, two main factors undergird party constitutionalisation in Rwanda: the legacy of the genocide and civil war, and the international legal justice pressure of the regional and international community.[10]

In 1884, Rwanda was established as a German protectorate and, in 1890, incorporated into German East Africa as Ruanda-Urundi.[11] After World War I, and under the terms of the Versailles Treaty, it fell under Belgian administration under a League of Nations mandate; after World War II, it became a United Nations trust territory, with Belgium as the administra-

8 For information on population estimates, ethnic divisions, and the ethnicisation of Rwandan society by Belgian administration, see United Nations, "Outreach Programme on the 1994 Genocide against the Tutsi in Rwanda and the United Nations", n.d., paragraphs 1–3, http://www.un.org/en/preventgenocide/rwanda/historical-background.shtml#prior-to-colonial-era (accessed 23 October 2024). For a historical account of Rwanda's political parties and the origins of ethnic conflict, the exclusionary state, and genocide, see M Mamdani, *When Victims Become Killers: Colonialism, Nativism, and the Genocide in Rwanda*, Princeton, Princeton University Press (2001), p 70. See also F Golooba-Mutebi, "Collapse, War and Reconstruction in Rwanda: An Analytical Narrative on State-Making", Crisis States Research Centre (2008), pp 3–12, www.lse.ac.uk/international-development/Assets/Documents/PDFs/csrc-working-papers-phase-two/wp28.2-collapse-war-and-reconstruction-in-rwanda.pdf (accessed 25 March 2024).

9 Golooba-Mutebi, *supra* n. 8, pp 3–12.

10 *Ibid*, p 6.

11 See Commonwealth Election Observer Mission, "Chapter 2 Political Background", 2013, p 3, https://www.thecommonwealth-ilibrary.org/index.php/comsec/catalog/download/288/285/2283?inline=1 (accessed 26 October 2024).

tive authority.[12] During this period of Belgian administration, Rwandans were subjected to an exclusionary "divide-and-rule" political system. This initially favoured the Tutsi minority over the Hutu majority, and citizens were required to carry identity cards marking their ethnic identity. Later, the Belgians supported Hutu insurgence, including violence against, and ultimately the replacement of, the Tutsi monarch's authorities.[13] The colonial legacy was profound. It thoroughly ethnicised Rwandan politics, and allowed inter-ethnic violence to be engaged in with impunity. This led ultimately to the mutually antagonistic ethnic parties that were to have grave implications for the future of Rwandan politics.

Thus, the two most prominent parties that emerged in the late 1950s to contest in the elections marking Rwanda's independence were the Party of the Movement for Hutu Emancipation (Parmehutu) and the Rwandan National Union. While the former advocated for Hutu supremacy and independence from Belgium, the latter supported the Tutsi monarchy and independence.[14] The two parties each provoked inter-ethnic violence for political gain and mobilised party membership and structures along ethnic lines. Parmehutu – having now become Mouvement Démocratique Republicain-Parmehutu (MDR-Parmehutu) – won the first elections in 1961. It established a one-party dictatorship under President Gregoire Kayibanda, who conducted an onslaught against the Tutsis in the immediate post-independence period (1962–1973), one that included a series of massacres, as well as the general persecution, marginalisation, and exiling of Tutsis. The MDR-Parmehutu was established as the only legal party and Kayibanda was re-elected unopposed in 1965 and 1969.[15]

However, on 5 July 1973, Kayibanda was overthrown in a military coup led by his defence minister, Juvénal Habyarimana. Habyarimana, in turn,

12 Ibid.

13 See C Newbury, "Background to Genocide: Rwanda", 23 (1995) *Issue: A Journal of Opinion*, pp 12–17; "Divided by Ethnicity", *United States Holocaust Memorial Museum*, September 2021, https://www.ushmm.org/genocide-prevention/countries/rwanda/divided-by-ethnicity (accessed 23 March 2024). See also S Strauss, *The Order of Genocide: Race, Power, and War in Rwanda*, Ithaca and London, Cornell University Press (2006), pp 181–182.

14 Parti du Mouvement de l'Emancipation Hutu later became the Republican Democratic Movement – Party of the Movement for Hutu Emancipation (MDR-PARMEHUTU). See Golooba-Mutebi, *supra* n. 8, pp 4–5.

15 D Zuber, "Gregoire Kayibanda (1924–1976)", *Black Past*, 23 March 2022, https:www.blackpast.org/global-african-history/people-global-african-history/gregoire-kayibanda-1924-1976 (accessed 23 October 2024).

established a Hutu-dominated one-party state under his Mouvement Révolutionnaire National pour le Développement (MRND) party.[16] According to Article 7 of the 1978 Constitution of Rwanda, the "National Revolutionary Movement for Development constitutes the unique political framework outside which no political activity [can] be exercised". The 1978 constitution granted Habyarimana extensive powers as President of the republic, as well as, according to Nkunzumwami, "Prime Minister, Army Chief of Staff, Minister of Defence, President of the MRND's Central Committee, and President of the High Judicial Council".[17] Not surprisingly, he was re-elected with overwhelming majorities in 1978, 1983, and 1988: the regime's one-party state forced every Rwandan to become a member of the ruling party by law.[18]

The period 1990–1994 is referred to as a transition period, and sowed the seeds of the instability which is still current today. 1990 saw the outbreak of the civil war as the Rwandan Patriotic Front (RPF), a rebel group composed of predominantly Tutsi refugees, invaded Rwanda from Uganda and challenged the MRND regime.[19] The RPF demanded a wide range of political reforms, including power-sharing, and the return of refugees. The civil war prompted international mediation, and a peace agreement, the Arusha Accords, was signed in 1993.

The Arusha Accords provided for a multiparty system; a transitional government; a new constitution; and the integration of the RPF in the national army. Implementation was obstructed by the hardliners in the MRND and its allied parties, who opposed the concessions to the RPF made in the Accords.[20] The situation deteriorated sharply in 1994 when Habyarimana was assassinated by unknown assailants. This triggered a nation-wide genocide in which Hutu extremists killed an estimated 800,000 Tutsis and moderate Hutus in 100 days. The genocide was stopped in its tracks by the military victory of the RPF, led by Paul Kagame. The

---

16 Rwanda Parliament and the Senate, *Political Pluralism and Power Sharing*, Kigali, Rwanda, Parliament and the Senate (2010), p 94, https://www.parliament.gov.rw/fileadmin/user_upload/Parliament/Research/Political_Plurarisme_and_Power_sharing_in_Rwanda.pdf (accessed 7 November 2024).

17 E Nkunzumwami, *La Tragédie Rwandaise: Historique et Perspectives*, Paris, L'Harmattan (1996), p 74. See also Rwanda Parliament and the Senate, *ibid*, p 94.

18 FX Munyarugerero, Réseaux, Pouvoirs, Oppositions: La Compétition Politique au Rwanda, Paris, Editions l'Harmattan (2003), pp 213–225.

19 Golooba-Mutebi, *supra* n. 8, pp 22–23.

20 *Ibid*, p 23.

RPF took control of the country and established a government of national unity.[21]

Even a minimal survey of the historical data suggests the existence of three major fault lines in Rwandan political culture. First, the establishment of a politics of ethnic hegemony made it difficult if not impossible for parties to create the common ground necessary for a sustainable nation-building project: the resulting ethnic animosity and mutual sense of grievance between the Hutu and Tutsi tribes undermined the legitimacy of the state.

Secondly, the political organisation which resulted from the primacy of ethnicity meant that the smaller ethnic groups perceived zero chance of ever winning any elections. Given such a divided political culture, the perception that only a military coup might allow minorities inclusion in the governance and distribution of state resources becomes powerful.

Thirdly, the creation of a clientelist and exclusionary state meant elections were undemocratic: it was practically impossible for the opposition to defeat the ruling party, and this entailed a failure to bring key stakeholders to the governing table to ensure that the socio-economic demands of all key segments of the state are addressed equitably. Under these circumstances, a military coup d'état or armed rebellion is seen as the only means of alternating power.[22]

The post-genocide period (1994 to the present) has been characterised as one of political transition, reconstruction, and reconciliation in Rwanda. Under the leadership of the RPF and its president, Paul Kagame, the country aims to prevent the resurgence of political instability.[23] This transition has taken the form of a securocratic state-building model. In this model, military elites infiltrate and capture the key state institutions responsible for ensuring political transition through democratic elections; these are then used to ensure that the ruling party wins elections.[24] The securocratic state

21 *Ibid*, pp 23–24.

22 Previous studies in Africa have shown that monopolies of power and exclusionary political systems lead rival elites to choose a military option to gain power. See DM Tull and A Mehler, "The Hidden Costs of Power Sharing: Reproducing Insurgent Violence in Africa", 104 (2005) *African Affairs*, pp 375–398.

23 Paul Kagame became President of Rwanda in 2000. For more on the Rwandan transition, see B Ingelaere, M Verpoorten, ME Desrosiers, and F Reyntjens, *Genocide, Ideology and Politics in Rwanda*, London, Routledge (2018); B Chemouni, "The Political Path to Universal Health Coverage: Power, Ideas and Community-based Health Insurance in Rwanda", 106 (2018) *World Development*, pp 87–98.

24 For a detailed account of the securocratic state, see P Ruhanya and B Gumbo, "The Securocratic State: Conceptualising the Transition Problem in Zimbabwe", 8

exhibits all the characteristics of a competitive authoritarian regime, including the capture of the legislature, judiciary, the media and the electoral arena, as well as the use of these institutions to manipulate and control the electoral environment so as to ensure that the opposition always loses.[25] Elections are held, but are lacking in the fundamentals of democracy: they work only to keep the ruling party in power and make sure that the opposition loses, even before the ballots are counted.[26] Competition between parties exists, but the outcome is rigged and blatantly unfair.[27]

Securocratic state-building in Rwanda, which is intended to further Rwanda's developmental aims following the genocide, involves a strategic contradiction between the state's aspiration for unity and its preoccupation with security.[28] The RPF has often cited the need to prevent the recurrence of genocide and the need to ensure national unity and security as the rationale for its tight control of the political sphere.[29] It is in this policy context that the RPF government has pursued a form of party constitutionalisation that aims to regulate the formation, functioning, and financing of political parties while at the same time promoting national unity, democracy, and human rights in the new political order.

Indeed, scrutiny of Rwanda's provisions on party constitutionalisation reveals an attempt to prevent the ethnic hegemony and exclusionary, tribally-based party politics that were responsible for the country's previous instability. These have important implications for the development of party systems, the nature and quality of party competition, the internal democracy and organisation of parties, their funding and accountability, and the

(2023) *Third World Thematics: A TWQ Journal*, pp 219–237. The term "military elites" refers to serving and retired members of the uniformed forces who occupy high-level decision-making posts in the country.

25 For an in-depth study of competitive authoritarian regimes, see C Carothers, "The Surprising Instability of Competitive Authoritarianism", 29 (2018) *Journal of Democracy*, pp 129–135. See also S Levitsky and LA Way, "The Rise of Competitive Authoritarianism", 13 (2002) *Journal of Democracy*, pp 51–65.

26 See L Diamond, "Elections without Democracy: Thinking about Hybrid Regimes", 13 (2002) *Journal of Democracy*, pp 21–35.

27 S Mainwaring, "From Representative Democracy to Participatory Competitive Authoritarianism: Hugo Chávez and Venezuelan Politics", 10 (2012) *Perspectives on Politics*, pp 955–967.

28 McDoom, *supra* n. 2, p 539.

29 For a detailed examination of authoritarian rule in Rwanda, see F Reyntjens, "Rwanda, Ten Years on: From Genocide to Dictatorship", 103 (2004) *African Affairs*, pp 177–210.

relationship between parties and institutions of governance. However, the regulation of parties in Rwanda is a disputed and constrained process, as the RPF and government have used various legal and extra-legal means to limit their autonomy, diversity, and competitiveness, as well as to co-opt or repress those who challenge the RPF's dominance and ideology.[30]

3. The state of party constitutionalisation in Rwanda

As a multidimensional phenomenon, party constitutionalisation is measured by a variety of indicators. These include the constitutional status of parties; the legal framework for party registration; organisation, funding, and accountability; internal democracy and representation within parties; and the degree of party competition and pluralism.[31]

The regulation of political parties also has both an international and regional dimension as well as a domestic one. As for regional and international frameworks in this regard, they are covered in detail in preceding chapters.[32] One of the central features of securocratic regimes is that they have little or no regard for international norms once the security and longevity of the regime is seen as under threat. Here, the Rwandan government's response to the ruling issued by the African Court on Human and Peoples' Rights (ACtHPR) for violating rights provided in international covenants is instructive: it responded by withdrawing its Article 34(6) "Additional Declaration" to the ACtHPR Protocol.[33] This declaration had allowed individuals to bring cases directly to the ACtHPR, and its removal

30 See S Strauss and L Waldorf (eds.), *Remaking Rwanda: State Building and Human Rights after Mass Violence*, Madison, University of Wisconsin Press (2011), p 4.

31 Z Nwokora and R Pelizzo, "Measuring Party Constitutionalisation: A Comparative Study of 144 Parties from 20 African Countries", 22 (2016) *Party Politics*, pp 521–533.

32 See J Socher, "Constitutionalisation of Political Parties: International Standards and the Experience of Continental Europe", in this volume. For discussion of African regional standards, see C Fombad and J Socher, "Regional Standards for Regulating Political Parties in Africa", in this volume.

33 ACtHPR, *Ingabire Victoire Umuhoza v The Republic of Rwanda*, App. No. 003/2014, Judgement of 24 November 2017. Similarly, in 2017 the Zimbabwean securocratic regime went ahead with a militarily assisted overthrow of then President Mugabe despite constitutional, regional and international law outlawing unconstitutional change of government, and no harm or sanction befell them.

was thus intended to suspend all the cases against Rwanda before the court.[34]

This chapter focuses instead on Rwanda's domestic legal framework for party regulation and constitutionalisation. It asks how this framework promotes or shrinks the democratic space, looking at questions of freedom of association, expression, and protest for political parties and assessing the implications of these for democracy. As will be shown below, in the absence of supportive political institutions, political will, and a citizen-centred (rather than state-centred) legal system, party constitutionalisation can easily become little more than a tool in lawfare targeting the defenders of democracy and political opponents.

Two key legal instruments come under the spotlight in this chapter. The first is the Constitution of the Republic of Rwanda, as adopted in 2003 and last amended in 2023.[35] The second is the 2013 Organic Law Governing Political Organisations and Politicians (as amended in 2018 and referred to hereinafter as the Law Governing Political Organisations).[36] Together, these legal instruments regulate the formation, registration, operation, and inclusivity of political parties in Rwanda. They also strive to ensure the stability and security of the country, and to prevent the recurrence of ethnic divisions and conflicts.

At the outset, it is to be noted that the Constitution and Law Governing Political Organisations use the term "political organisations" rather than "political parties". This choice is designed to ensure inclusivity and flexibility, as "political organisations" is broader than "political parties" in that it encompasses a wide range of entities (including movements, coalitions, and other forms of political association) that might not fit the traditional definition of a party. Although using "political organisation" rather than just "political party" is a nice, inclusive thing to do as it covers associations

34 This attempt was not entirely successful. Although the ACtHPR ruled in the *Ingabire Victoire Umuhoza Case* on 5 September 2016, that Rwanda's withdrawal of its Article 34(6) declaration was legal, the Court also determined that the withdrawal did not affect cases that were already pending before it, including the *Ingabire* case.

35 Constitution of the Republic of Rwanda of 2003, amended in 2015 and 2023, Official Gazette No. Special, 4 August 2023, Chapter vi, https://ihl-databases.icrc.org/en/national-practice/constitution-republic-rwanda-2003-revised-2015-and-2023 (accessed 5 March 2024).

36 Organic Law No. 005/2018.Ol of 30 August 2018 Modifying the Organic Law No. 10/2013/Ol of 11 July 2013 Governing Political Organisations and Politicians, Official Gazette No. 37 of 10 September 2018, https://archive.gazettes.africa/archive/rw/2018/rw-government-gazette-dated-2018-09-10-no-37.pdf (accessed 5 March 2024).

over and beyond conventional parliamentary parties - but by the same token, and a twist of the knife, it dramatically expands the scope of entities to which the state's repressive control applies to cover essentially any form of organised political activity imaginable.

The political organisations and politicians affected by these regulations are defined in Article 2(6) and (7) of the Law Governing Political Organisations as follows:

(6) political organisation: an association of citizens sharing the same thinking and views on the development of social welfare of all the population and the development of the country, with the objective to accede to power through democratic and peaceful ways, to be able to put them in action;
(7) politician: any person carrying out political activities as provided for in item six (6) of this Article, be it individually or through a political organisation.

To understand the broader democratic implications, the analysis in this chapter focuses on the implications of this regulatory framework for four critical conditions that significantly impact the quality of political-parties' participation in democratic contestation: autonomous formation of political parties, their recognition and protection, their inclusion and participation in electoral affairs, and their internal democracy.[37]

Evidence shows that Rwanda's political-party regulatory framework is typical of securocratic states: while it formally acknowledges democratic structures, it constrains party operations.[38] The framework's dual nature is evident in the fact that, while permitting multiple parties, it imposes stringent conditions that erode their autonomy and fair representation of varied political views. This results in a "guided paper democracy", where the appearance of multiparty democracy is belied by regulations that limit true pluralism and allow the ruling party to retain substantial control of the political landscape.[39]

37 I van Biezen, "Constitutionalising Party Democracy: The Constitutive Codification of Political Parties in Post-war Europe", 42 (2012) *British Journal of Political Science*, pp 187–212.

38 P Niesen, "Political Party Bans in Rwanda 1994–2003: Three Narratives of Justification", 17 (2010) *Democratization*, pp 709–729.

39 On the notion of a "guided democracy" that exists on paper but not in practice, see, for example, L Palmier, "Review of Guided Democracy, by TK Tan and Hong Lee Oey", 7 (1973) *Modern Asian Studies*, pp 296–305.

3.1 The right to existence: limited multipartyism?

In Rwanda, registered political parties are constitutionally recognised, albeit that the right to form political parties is a privilege restricted to adult citizens domiciled within the country. The aim appears to be, on the one hand, to recognise the right of political parties to exist but, on the other, to limit this right in restrictive ways and dictate their internal democracy. These tensions are evident in articles 54 and 55 of the Constitution read together with article 13 of the Law Governing Political Organisations. Article 54 of the Constitution states:

1) A multiparty system is recognised.
2) Political organisations fulfilling the conditions required by law may be formed and operate freely.
3) Duly registered political organisations receive State grants.
4) An organic law determines the modalities for the establishment and functioning of political organisations, the conduct of their leaders, and the process of receiving State grants.

Article 54 is supported by the East African Community's regional framework for the regulation of political parties, in particular Article 7(3) of the Draft Protocol on Good Governance, developed in 2012.[40] In addition, the African Charter on Democracy, Elections and Governance (ACDEG) of 2012[41] requires state parties to strengthen "political pluralism and recognis[e] the role, rights and responsibilities of legally constituted political parties, including opposition political parties, which should be given a status under national law"; they are also called on to institutionalise measures that consolidate "sustainable multiparty political systems".[42]

The recognition of multipartyism and the provision of financial support to "duly registered political organisations" sought to limit the possibility of a return to a one-party state and the attendant exclusionary politics that led to genocide and civil war. During the Habyarimana era, all citizens were

40 East African Community, The East African Community Protocol on Good Governance (Draft), https://meaca.gov.ss/wp-content/uploads/2022/08/Pdf-Draft-Protocol-on-Good-Governace.pdf (accessed 22 October 2024).

41 For a detailed analysis of the regional frameworks for political party regulation, see Fombad and Socher, *supra* n. 32.

42 See articles 3(11) and 32(6) and (7) of the ACDEG, https://au.int/sites/default/files/treaties/36384-treaty-african-charter-on-democracy-and-governance.pdf (accessed 23 March 2024).

required to join the ruling party, an arrangement that violated the freedom of association undergirding multipartyism, leaving minority Tutsi groups with the sole recourse of political participation or mobilisation through external and violent insurgent organisations. To alleviate this, Article 55 of the Constitution states:

1) Every Rwandan has a right to join a political organisation of his or her choice, or not to join any.
2) No Rwandan shall be subject to discrimination on grounds of membership in a given political organisation, or non-membership in a political organisation.

This echoes Article 10(2) of the African Charter on Human and Peoples' Rights (ACHPR) (alongside other regional and international covenants), which extends freedom of association by including the negative freedom of not being compelled to join an association.[43]

Article 54 of the Constitution sets limits on the right to form political parties and mandates legislation to set those conditions and limitations.[44] Some of these conditions and limitations are stipulated in article 13 of the Law Governing Political Organisations:

> For anyone to be in the management of a political organisation he/she shall fulfil the following:
>
> 1) to be of Rwandan nationality;
> 2) to be at least twenty-one (21) years old;
> 3) not to have been deprived of his/her civil or political rights by court;
> 4) to have his/her domicile in Rwanda;
> 5) not to have been sentenced to an imprisonment equal to or exceeding six (6) months ...

The requirements seek to ensure that individuals in these positions are qualified and have an unblemished legal and civic record, thereby preventing the formation of fraudulent or extremist groups. However, the emphasis on citizenship and Rwandan residence also reflects the government's desire

43 African Charter on Human and Peoples' Rights (1981), https://achpr.au.int/en/charter/african-charter-human-and-peoples-rights (accessed 23 October 2024). This was also reiterated by the ACtHPR in *Mtikila and Others v Republic of Tanzania*.

44 In addition, Article 29(3) of the ACHPR imposes the duty on individuals "to preserve and strengthen social and national solidarity, particularly when the latter is threatened".

to monitor politicians while excluding Rwandan refugees and members of the diaspora from political participation. Article 13 in fact suffers from four major flaws.

First, the requirement that only Rwandan nationals can be in the management of a political organisation ignores the fact that non-citizens may offer significant expertise and experience and bring valuable contributions. This can marginalise individuals who, despite their long-term residence and contribution to the country, are not granted citizenship.

Secondly, setting the minimum age at 21 excludes younger individuals who are politically active and already making meaningful contributions to political organisations. This can be seen as a way for the older generation to maintain control and limit the influence of younger (and potentially more progressive) voices.

Thirdly, when a judicial system is not fully independent, the clause disqualifying someone from office on the grounds of being deprived of civil or political rights by a court can be problematic. When judiciaries in securocratic states are captured by the ruling elite, the courts can be used to target political opponents unfairly and strip them of their rights through biased legal proceedings, thus preventing them from participating in political management.

Additionally, requiring individuals to be domiciled in Rwanda excludes Rwandan citizens living abroad who might wish to make a contribution to political life in their country of origin. This measure is used to limit the influence of the diaspora, the members of which may well have different perspectives and promote ideas that challenge the status quo.

Finally, the restriction imposed on those sentenced to imprisonment of six months or more is overly broad and does not take into account the nature of the offence or the context in which it occurred. It could thus be used to disqualify individuals who have been politically persecuted or imprisoned for minor offences, thereby reducing political diversity and opposition.

In practice, all the terms above have been devised to maintain the power of the RPF political elite and actively suppress dissenting voices.[45] So, all in

45 For instance, Rwandan courts rejected appeals by two prominent opposition leaders, Bernard Ntaganda and Victoire Ingabire, to remove previous convictions that effectively barred them from contesting the July 2024 elections. Ingabire, the leader of Dalfa Umurinzi ("Development and Liberty for All"), saw her application to the Kigali High Court for reinstatement of her right to contest the 2024 polls rejected,

all, the elements of article 13 entail that, in Rwanda, the right to freedom of association is limited, vulnerable, and exclusionary. By employing the term "political organization" rather than just "political party," the scope of entities subject to state control is dramatically expanded. This inclusive terminology, while seemingly positive, actually broadens the state's repressive reach to encompass virtually any form of organized political activity, thus reinforcing the limitations on freedom of association. This is contrary to the position taken by the African Commission that "in regulating the use of this right, the competent authorities should not enact provisions which would limit the exercise of this freedom" and that "the regulation of the exercise of the right to freedom of association should be consistent with States' obligations" under the ACHPR.[46]

To ensure a fair multiparty system and help create a more inclusive political environment, it would thus be necessary to reconsider the age and nationality restrictions and allow for the diaspora's inclusion in political-party formation.

3.2 Establishing a political organisation

The Constitution grants operational rights exclusively to political organisations that are duly registered in accordance with the Law Governing Political Organisations.[47] However, this law requires that before applying to register a political party, the political party in question must first be properly established.[48] There are four preconditions for satisfying the "proper establishment" clause, and these are discussed below.

---

on the grounds that she had applied before completing all the conditions set by the presidential pardon order and therefore a reinstatement of her rights could not be considered. See "Rwanda Court Upholds Election Ban on Opposition Leader", *The Guardian*, 13 March 2024, https://www.theguardian.com/world/2024/mar/13/rwanda-victoire-ingabire-barred-election (accessed 7 November 2024).

46 African Commission, Resolution on the Right to Freedom of Association, ACHPR/Res. 5(XI)92, 9 March 1992. For detailed discussion, see Fombad and Socher, *supra* n. 32.

47 Law Governing Political Organisations.

48 As of 14 July 2024, there were 11 registered political parties in Rwanda, but only two of them fielded candidates in the 2024 presidential election.

3.2.1 Founded by statute in accordance with the law

The law states that

> [a] political organisation shall be established upon the decision of the first general assembly of its members in which they approve its statutes and internal rules and regulations. Meetings preparing or deciding on the establishment of a political organisation shall comply with the laws governing public gatherings.[49]

The "legislation governing public gatherings" referred to is Article 19 of the Law Governing Political Organisations. This reads: "A political organisation that wishes to hold a public meeting of its members shall inform the relevant administrative authorities at least five (5) working days before the meeting. Notification modalities must conform to the relevant laws."

The requirement that the establishment of a political organisation needs the approval of the first general assembly of its members, with representation from across the nation, including of women, aims – on the face of it – to foster national unity and enhance representativeness, promote transparency and accountability, and establish a democratic foundation for political organisations. However, the requirement for inception meetings to comply with laws governing public gatherings has been used to delay or obstruct the formation of new organisations seen as a threat to the ruling RPF, mainly because the laws governing public gatherings are stringent and selectively enforced.

More specifically, conducting the first general assembly meeting to ratify a founding statute – required before a party can register – has been classified by the Rwandan authorities as an illegal activity if done by unregistered entities, with this leading to persecution and disruption. The law is a contradictory Catch-22 and fails to provide legal certainty: How can a political party that has not registered hold its founding meeting when authorisation for public meetings is granted only to registered legal entities?

Just note how the Democratic Green Party's efforts to register and nominate its leader, Frank Habineza, for the presidency were hindered for years.[50] Key issues included a lack of signed documents, disruptions al-

49 *Supra* n. 47.

50 The party failed more than 10 times to get the Gasabo district mayor's permission to hold the founding congress needed to register the party. See F Habineza, "Opposition Party Registration is Impossible in Rwanda Said Green Party Boss", *The Rwandan*, 20

legedly by RPF supporters, local authorities' denial of meeting permissions without police clearance, and unfulfilled promises of follow-up meetings by ministry officials before the final official recognition in 2013, but this coming just a few days before elections.[51] The alternative attempt at private inaugural meetings simply resulted in the disqualification of registration on the grounds of the illegal adoption of founding statutes or the imposition of punitive measures as stipulated in Article 46 of the Law Governing Political Organisations.

Similarly, the notification requirement for public meetings entails that political organisations have to inform administrative authorities at least five working days prior to any meeting. While the requirement is understandable as part of an effort to maintain public order, here by giving authorities the time to prepare for and manage public gatherings effectively, it has also been exploited to block political activities. In addition, public notification of a first general assembly compromises the privacy and confidentiality of members, exposing them to state-sponsored harassment and disruption. Freedom of assembly is curtailed by an enforced apathy.

Note, for example, the cases of Sylvain Sibomana and Anselme Mutuyimana. Sibomana, the former secretary-general of United Democratic Forces-Inkingi (FDU-Inkingi), was arrested in 2012 alongside party member Anselme Mutuyimana for an unauthorised meeting in a public bar. Mutuyimana was released in 2018 but died under mysterious circumstances in 2019, while Sibomana was released only in 2021.[52]

All in all, when handling party registration and regulation, the Rwandan authorities have adopted a presumption of guilt and unlawfulness that paves the way for excessive interference by them. By contrast, international standards on political-party registration emphasise that authorities should adhere to "a presumption in favour of the lawfulness of their establishment, objectives and activities, regardless of the formalities applicable for establishment or official recognition"; they also stress that "limitations must be prescribed by law, pursue a legitimate aim recognised by international stan-

May 2013, https://www.therwandan.com/opposition-party-registration-is-impossible-in-rwanda-said-green-party-boss/ (accessed 23 April 2024).

51 Commonwealth Election Observer Mission, "Chapter 4 Election Campaign and the Media", 2013, p 15, https://www.thecommonwealth-ilibrary.org/index.php/comsec/catalog/download/288/285/2285?inline=1 (accessed 23 March 2024).

52 Human Rights Watch, "Rwanda: Crackdown on Opposition, Media Intensifies", *Human Rights Watch*, 19 October 2021, https://www.hrw.org/news/2021/10/19/rwanda-crackdown-opposition-media-intensifies (accessed 23 March 2024).

dards, necessary in a democratic society, and proportionate in measure and duration".[53] Balancing the need for public order with the right to political participation and expression remains a critical challenge in Rwanda.

3.2.2 Nationwide mobilisation and presence in the capital

Pursuant to Article 11 of the Law Governing Political Organisations, political parties are required to fulfil certain criteria. The provision reads as follows:

1) Founders of political organisations shall submit to the authority in charge of the registration of political organisations a letter requesting for their organisation to be registered with an acknowledgement for receipt.
2) The number of members who signed the statutes governing the political organisation shall be at least two hundred (200) in the whole country, with at least five (5) people having their domicile in each district.
3) Paragraphs 1 and 2 of this Article shall not apply to political organisations officially recognised in Rwanda that were established before the publication of this Organic Law in the Official Gazette of the Republic of Rwanda.

First, the requirement for founders to submit a registration request with an acknowledgement of receipt aims to ensure a formal, verifiable procedure for the establishment of political organisations, something which promotes transparency and accountability. However, the need for formal acknowledgment can lead to bureaucratic delays, especially when the process is not managed efficiently. The exemption of political organisations recognised before the publication of the Organic Law seeks to provide continuity for existing parties and ensure they are not unduly burdened by new regulations. This is beneficial for maintaining political stability; however, it also creates an uneven playing field where established parties have an advantage over new entrants, thus stifling political competition and innovation.

The requirement for at least 200 members to sign the statutes, with at least five members being from each district, seeks to ensure that political organisations have broad-based, geographically widespread support as well

53 Venice Commission, *supra* n. 1, paragraph 36.

as a centralised administrative hub. Moreover, it strives to foster inter-ethnic cooperation, recognising that this is essential for national unity since it tempers the ethnic politicking that led historically to exclusion, civil war, and genocide. However, these requirements present significant obstacles for nascent or smaller parties. They may well find the conditions hard to fulfil, as was evident in the difficulties (cited above) faced by the Democratic Green Party and Dalfa-Umurinzi.[54] The requirement can also work to unduly diminish competitive dynamics and the plurality of political representation. The formation of political parties becomes an arduous, expensive, elitist, and exclusionary process, in effect precluding small parties or individuals with limited resources from mobilising on a national scale and potentially marginalising regional, ethnic, or ideological groups.

3.2.3 Commitment to the nation-building agenda

The law insists that those wishing to establish political organisations must first conduct themselves in a manner that proves their commitment to "nation-building". This can be shown through conduct that desists from genocide, minimising past genocide history, and fanning divisiveness. The Constitution declares as follows:

> The State of Rwanda commits itself to upholding and ensuring respect for the following fundamental principles:
>
> (a) prevention and punishment of the crime of genocide, fight[ing] against denial and revisionism of genocide as well as eradication of genocide ideology and all its manifestations;
> (b) eradication of discrimination and divisionism based on ethnicity, region or any other ground, as well as promotion of national unity ...[55]

With reference specifically to political parties, Article 57 states that "[p]olitical organisations are prohibited from basing themselves on race, ethnic group, tribe, lineage, ancestry, region, sex, religion or any other division which may lead to discrimination".

---

54 J Clover, "Rwandan Opposition Party Registers Days before September Vote Deadline", *Reuters*, 10 August 2013, https://www.reuters.com/article/us-rwanda-politics-idUSBRE97903B20130810/ (accessed 10 May 2024).

55 Article 10 of the Constitution.

The principle of commitment to nation-building is reiterated in Article 7 of the Law Governing Political Organisations, which emphasises national unity and prohibits the establishment of political parties on divisive grounds such as race or ethnicity. Clauses 2 to 4 of the same article also provide as follows:

(2) Political organisation must constantly reflect the unity of the people of Rwanda, gender equality and complementarity, whether in the recruitment of members, putting in place organs of leadership and in their operations and activities.
(3) Each political organisation shall have at least thirty percent (30%) of posts in decision-making organs awarded to women.
(4) Management positions in all organs of a political organisation must be elected for.

Additionally, Article 34 of the same law states that "the conduct of political organisations and politicians shall not undermine the public order or the rights and freedoms of the individual in particular and of the people in general". Article 37 stipulates, furthermore, that during elections, politicians and political organisation must "avoid any speeches, writings and actions based or leading to discrimination or divisionism ... [and must] respect their opponents and avoid disparaging or defaming them". They must also "inform Rwandans of the objectives and program of the political organisation aiming at building the nation".

These requirements are designed to ensure that political organisations adhere to legal boundaries and contribute to national cohesion. The Law Governing Political Organisations contains three particularly noteworthy points in its promotion of the nation-building agenda. Article 10(a) concerns the prevention and punishment of genocide and the eradication of genocidal ideology; Articles 10(b) and 57 promote the eradication of discrimination and divisionism and prohibit political organisations based on divisive grounds, doing so as a way of fostering national unity and social cohesion; and Article 7 calls for political organisations to reflect unity and gender equality – a progressive step designed to ensure inclusivity and the representation of women in decision-making positions. Read together, these clauses are meant to promote a culture of remembrance and justice in Rwanda, and to ensure that the horrors of the genocidal past, caused by the exclusionary ethnic political parties, are not repeated.

The nation-building clauses do have several loopholes, however, and these have been exploited by the ruling elite to undermine their political opponents and shrink democratic space. Notably, the overly broad scope of "genocide ideology" has at times been exploited to suppress legitimate dissent and political opposition, thus stifling free speech and political pluralism.

Take Victoire Ingabire Umuhoza, for instance. Umuhoza, the leader of the unregistered FDU-Inkingi party, was sentenced to 15 years in prison for conspiracy and genocide denial for publicly advocating for the rights of Hutu refugees and criticising the state's own genocidal ideology.[56] In the *Ingabire Victoire Umuhoza* case, the ACtHPR found that this sentence was a violation of the International Covenant on Civil and Political Rights (ICCPR).[57] Umuhoza, through this case, sought to challenge the Rwandan government for violation of her rights protected under the ACHPR.[58] The court, in its ruling, reiterated that states have the right to enact laws that restrict freedom of expression but only if the restrictions meet four conditions: they are provided by law; serve a legitimate purpose; are necessary in a democratic society; and are proportionate to the achievement of a legitimate aim.[59]

In this case, the ACtHPR found that the Rwandan law meets the first two conditions but fails to satisfy the other two. It accepted that, given Rwanda's history of genocide, the law served the legitimate interest of national security and public order.[60] However, the ACtHPR held that political speech aimed at the government or officials, or speech that comes from public figures, "deserve[s] a higher degree of tolerance than others", and found that the restrictions imposed on Ingabire fell short of the other two conditions in that they were neither necessary in a democratic society nor proportional to the aims sought.[61]

56 Although she received a presidential pardon in 2018 and formed the Development and Liberty for All (DALFA-Umurinzi) party in 2019, at the time of this writing (2024) her party had not yet been granted registration. See VU Ingabire, "Rwanda's Consensual Democracy Needs a Reset", *Al Jazeera*, 15 September 2022, https://www.aljazeera.com/opinions/2022/9/15/rwandas-consensual-democracy-needs-a-reset (accessed 24 March 2024). See also ACtHPR, *supra* n. 33, paragraphs 5–8, 32.

57 ACtHPR, *supra* n. 33, paragraph 173(viii)–(ix).

58 *Ibid*, paragraphs 77–78.

59 *Ibid*, paragraph 133.

60 *Ibid*, paragraphs 135–138, 139–141.

61 *Ibid*, paragraphs 141–142, 160–163, 173(viii)-(ix). See also ACtHPR, *Lohe Issa Konate v Burkina Faso*, App. No. 004/2013, Judgement, 5 December 2014, paragraph 155, which ruled that the right to freedom of expression protects opinions that "offend, shock or disturb".

Additionally, political leaders who deviate from the ideology of the ruling RPF government have been barred from running for presidential office. For example, Theoneste Niyitegeka, recognised for aiding genocide victims, was barred from the 2003 presidential election and later himself imprisoned for genocide in 2008.[62] Another example is Yvonne Idamange, a Tutsi genocide survivor, who was convicted in 2021 for inciting unrest and other offences after accusing the Rwandan government of exploiting the genocide and criticising the RPF's post-genocide actions in her YouTube videos.[63]

A second loophole is found in the imposition of a national identity on all political organisations in Rwanda. This creates a situation in which the law could be weaponised to arbitrarily deny the existence of minority groups and obstruct the formation of political parties that represent specific community interests: according to Rwandan law, associations or political parties based on self-identification by minority groups may not be established. Such a prohibition of regional or ethnic organisations based on minority or communal identities deviates from the best democratic practices to be found in international law, where the emphasis is on the right of minority groups to the freedom of association and self-identification necessary for aggregating their interests.[64] The quest for national unity and the prevention of genocide caused by ethnic mobilisation needs to be balanced with the need to protect the rights of minority groups. To curtail the erosion of minority groups' freedom of association, self-determination, and self-identification is to lay the basis for future political instability. The law needs to find a way to make the use of seemingly ethnically divisive language grounds for the rejection of the registration of minority political parties while not necessarily outlawing them from the outset.

---

62 US Department of State, "Rwanda 2013 Human Rights Report", Washington, United States Department of State, Bureau of Democracy, Human Rights and Labor (2013), p 13, https://2009-2017.state.gov/documents/organisation/220359.pdf (accessed 23 March 2024).

63 Human Rights Watch, "Rwanda: Alleged Genocide Mastermind Arrested: Fulgence Kayishema Caught after Two Decades; Should Face Swift, Fair Trial", *Human Rights Watch*, 2 June 2023, https://www.hrw.org/news/2023/06/02/rwanda-alleged-genocide-mastermind-arrested (accessed 23 March 2024).

64 See, for example, OSCE High Commissioner on National Minorities, *Handbook on Observing and Promoting the Participation of National Minorities in Electoral Processes*, Warsaw, OSCE Office for Democratic Institutions and Human Rights (2014), pp 29–32, which points out that party regulations which prohibit minority organisations violate international law. For an analysis of applicable international law, see Socher, *supra* n. 32.

The third loophole lies in the vagueness of highly abstract concepts such as sovereignty, unity, and division. Where the interpretation of such terms is left entirely to the discretion of officials appointed by the ruling party to the Rwanda Governance Board (RGB), these officials are in effect endowed with unchecked authority. In practice, the application and enforcement of principles of national unity and the like has been manipulated to exclude specific groups and ideologies from the political arena. Two examples highlight the dangers of this practice.

In 2001, Pasteur Bizimungu, Rwanda's first post-genocide president, was barred from registering his party to challenge the RPF. In 2004, he was arrested and imprisoned after being accused of inciting civil disobedience, associating with criminals, and embezzlement (though he was later granted a presidential pardon and released in 2007).[65] Another example is the case of Théophile Ntirutwa, a member of the Dalfa-Umurinzi opposition party, who in 2022 was sentenced by the High Court's Rwamagana chamber to seven years in prison. The accusation against him was of spreading false information or harmful propaganda with the intent to foment international opinion hostile to the Rwandan government.[66]

Such contentious prosecutions work to undermine pluralism, diminish the representativeness of the political system, and tarnish democratic quality as they have the effect of restricting political discourse to government-sanctioned interpretations of unity and division.

3.3 Party registration: Transparency or vulnerability?

The registration of political parties in Rwanda is a laborious process. This sub-section focuses on the requirement that a party's founding statutes and accompanying paperwork must be provided prior to registration.

---

65 Amnesty International, "Elections in Rwanda: Rwanda's Repressive Tactics Silence Dissent before Elections", *Amnesty International,* 5 September 2017, https://www.amnesty.org/en/latest/campaigns/2017/09/rwandas-repressive-tactics-silence-dissent-before-elections/ (accessed 23 March 2024).

66 Human Rights Watch, "Politician Convicted for Harming Rwanda's Image", *Human Rights Watch*, 18 January 2023, https://www.hrw.org/news/2023/01/18/politician-convicted-harming-rwandas-image (accessed 23 March 2024).

3.3.1 Detailed design of founding statutes

Article 14 of the Law Governing Political Organisations lays down the following guidelines for the submission of the paperwork necessary for a party's legal registration:

> The statutes governing a political organisation must especially indicate the following:
>
> 1. its full name;
> 2. its objectives;
> 3. its insignia;
> 4. its organs and their structure including the organ in charge of discipline and settlement of disputes and the organ in charge of audit;
> 5. its head office which must be in Rwanda;
> 6. members of its organs, modalities for their election and replacement, their term of office and their responsibilities;
> 7. requirements for membership, procedures for resignation and reasons for dismissal of members;
> 8. the legal representatives of a political organisation;
> 9. provisions related to the property;
> 10. provisions relating to the amendments of its statutes or its dissolution;
> 11. allocation of its assets in case of its dissolution.

Four of these registration conditions impact on the quality of democracy in ways that reveal both their intended benefits as well as their potential drawbacks. The first is the requirement for a political organisation to have its head office in Rwanda.

This measure seeks to ensure that the organisation's leadership is physically present in the country, an arrangement that stands to facilitate better coordination of party affairs, closer attention to local issues, and liability for, and control of, the actions, of party members. At the same time, the measure restricts the ability of those living abroad to participate in domestic political activities; put differently, it centralises control within the country and reduces the scope for external influences to challenge the givens of the current political landscape. Indeed, this stringent requirement for political-party formation is designed to serve as a deterrent against unauthorised political action, thereby allowing the ruling elite to enforce the law selectively and so suppress opposition and limit political pluralism.

This was evident in the way the National Electoral Commission prevented Diane Rwigara's participation in the 2017 elections, citing invalid signatures as well as the harassment and imprisonment of her supporters. Opposition figures thus face clear challenges in Rwanda, and such challenges are likely to lead to a culture of self-censorship in public life as citizens grow wary of legal harassment.[67]

Moreover, in the guidelines above, note the detailed requirements as regards the structure and functioning of political organisations, including their organs for discipline, dispute settlement, and auditing. These aim, at face value, to ensure transparency and accountability and prevent abuse of power and resources; such detailed statutory requirements promote the operational transparency of political parties, which in turn can enhance public trust in political processes. However, the measures also leave the door open for excessive bureaucratic control that stifles the independence of political parties and heightens their susceptibility to state interference. What is more, the guidelines impose administrative burdens that may discourage the formation and operation of smaller or emerging parties, thus impairing the overall inclusivity of the political landscape and the possibilities for the representation of diverse political voices.

A further stipulation in the guidelines is that members of the organs, their election modalities, terms of office, and responsibilities must be clearly defined. On the one hand, this aims to promote clarity, democracy, and order, by ensuring that everyone understands their roles and the rules governing their actions; on the other, it can lead to the creation of rigid structures that are difficult to change, that entrench existing power dynamics, and that pose significant challenges to any attempt to introduce necessary reforms or adapt to new political realities.

Similarly, the requirement for legal representatives and detailed provisions related to property and amendments to statutes or dissolution seeks to engender legal and financial accountability, thereby aiming to prevent misuse of resources and ensure that political organisations operate within the law. These provisions, however, can easily be exploited to exert control over political organisations, particularly if the processes for amendment or dissolution are cumbersome or subject to state approval, thus delaying or blocking changes that might threaten the current power structure.

---

67 Freedom House, "Freedom in the World 2018 – Rwanda", *UNHCR Refworld*, 1 August 2018, https://www.refworld.org/reference/annualreport/freehou/2018/en/121588 (accessed 17 March 2024).

Additionally, the allocation of assets in case of dissolution is necessary to prevent misuse of resources and ensure instead that the assets of a dissolved organisation are handled responsibly. Nonetheless, this can dissuade political organisations from dissolving, even when it might be in their best interests, due to the complexity and potential loss involved. In practice, these detailed statutory requirements can be manipulated to maintain the power of the current political elite and suppress dissenting voices. Ensuring a fair and transparent legal framework, with provisions that balance accountability with flexibility, could help address some of these flaws and create a more inclusive political environment.

3.3.2 Documentation accompanying registration applications

Pursuant to articles 10 and 12 of the Law Governing Political Organisations, political organisations are required to submit a formal registration request to the RGB accompanied by certified copies of their statutes, as well as by their addresses, insignia, programme information, and the names, identities, and criminal records of their representatives. The central role the RGB plays in registering political organisations helps to ensure consistency and oversight by maintaining a standardised approach to the registration and monitoring of political organisations. Nonetheless, centralisation can also lead to bureaucratic delays and raise the question of potential bias, particularly where the RGB is not perceived as an impartial actor.

To delve into the particulars, the requirement for political organisations to inform the RGB of their head office locations and representatives promotes transparency and accountability and enables authorities and the public to be aware of the structure and leadership of political parties. At the same time, this requirement can be seen as intrusive, especially when there are concerns about the misuse of such information for the purposes of control or harassment. Indeed, the registration requirements are comprehensive, and entail, among other things, the submission of the criminal records of representatives, certified copies of statutes, minutes of constituent assembly meetings, rules of procedure, and the certificates of legal representatives.

All of this serves to enhance transparency and accountability in political organisations by ensuring that they are well-structured and legally compliant, characteristics that testify to their legitimacy and seriousness. However, the demand for such extensive documentation is burdensome, particularly for new or smaller organisations, and also stands to discourage political participation. Both the administrative load placed on the RGB and the discretionary power vested in it to approve registrations could be exploited to hinder the establishment of new parties and disqualify existing ones, hence jeopardising the democratic process.[68] Detailed documentation, furthermore, can be used to identify the politically active and target them for harassment and persecution.

Several well-known cases underline the reality of these dangers in Rwanda. In 2019, Syldio Dusabumuremyi, the co-ordinator of the United Democratic Forces (FDU-Inkingi) party, was murdered, while, in 2016, his fellow activist, Illuminée Iragena, went missing in a suspected forced disappearance. Similarly, 13 October 2021 (a day prior to Ingabire Day, an annual event raising awareness about repression in the country) saw the arrest of several Dalfa-Umurinzi party members, including Victoire Ingabire's assistant, Joyeuse Uwatuje.[69]

Turning to Article 12(c) of the Law Governing Political Organisations (requiring any criminal records for public office candidates), it aims to deter criminals from taking influential roles in political life and prevent negative role-modelling. However, this requirement can also suppress opposition by disqualifying potential candidates whose only criminal records result from politically motivated charges, thereby hindering party-formation and election participation.

Once approved, political parties must publish – at their own expense – their founding statutes in the Official Gazette of the Republic of Rwanda. The Law Governing Political Organisations states in Article 17 that

1) [t]he statutes of a political organisation are published in the Official Gazette of the Republic of Rwanda and the related fees are paid by the concerned political organisation.
2) When a political organisation is approved, it can start to run its activities while waiting for the publication of its statutes in the Official Gazette of the Republic of Rwanda. The publication of its statutes in the Official Gazette of the Republic of Rwanda does not exceed three (3) months.

---

68 International watchdogs allege that the RGB, a government-controlled entity, has denied the registration of opposition parties at its discretion and without giving proper justification. See Freedom House, *ibid.*

69 Human Rights Watch, *supra* n. 52.

Publishing the statutes of a political organisation in the Official Gazette ensures transparency and public accessibility: it allows the public and other stakeholders to be informed about the foundational rules and regulations governing political organisations. However, the cost of publication, which must be borne by the political organisation, could be a financial burden, especially for smaller or newly established parties, in the context of what is one of the poorest and most poverty-afflicted countries in the world.

Allowing political organisations to start their activities upon approval (rather than after the actual publication of their statutes) is practical. This enables organisations to begin their operations without unnecessary delays, fostering political engagement and activity. On the downside, there could be some risk involved in their operating without full public scrutiny during this interim period, leading to legal challenges if the statutes are later found to be problematic. The obligation to publish statutes in the Official Gazette, coupled with potential delays, can obstruct a party's prompt and efficient operationalisation.

The three-month deadline for publication helps prevent indefinite delays and ensures that the public can access this information in a timely manner. However, if the process of approval and publication is not efficiently managed, this could result in delays that hinder the transparency and accountability of political organisations.

3.4 Regulation of political-party financing

Political plurality entails that political parties need financial autonomy and protection from the influence of powerful individuals to operate freely and maintain political independence. The Law Governing Political Organisations creates a complex financial landscape for political parties. It combines the prohibition of foreign and independent funding with restrictive conditions for state funding. These are discussed in this sub-section.

3.4.1 Fundraising and financial transparency

Article 24 of the Law Governing Political Organisations states as follows:

> A political organisation or a politician may receive donations and bequests. When the donations and bequests have the value of at least one million Rwandan francs (FRW 1,000,000), a political organisation or a

politician informs in writing the authority in charge of registration of political organisations within thirty (30) days from the date of reception, indicating the donor, the type and value of donations, with a copy to the Office of the Ombudsman.

(2) A political organisation or a politician are not allowed to receive donations and bequests granted by:
1. foreigners;
2. foreign States;
3. non-governmental organisations;
4. faith-based organisations;
5. foreign business companies or industries, and organisations owned by foreigners or in which foreigners are shareholders.

The requirement to report donations and bequests valued at one million Rwandan francs or more ensures transparency and accountability in political financing. Corruption watchdogs point out that “unregulated or poorly managed money in politics is often considered as one of the biggest threats to democracy worldwide and means that the political playing field is not level”.[70] The provision in Article 24 thus helps prevent corruption and the exertion of undue influence by making the sources of significant funds public knowledge. However, the administrative burden of reporting might discourage some donors, especially if the process is perceived as cumbersome or if there are concerns about privacy and political repercussions. The requirement to report private donors to the government deters donors due to the potential for government monitoring and the consequent risk of targeted harassment and persecution.

As regards the prohibition on receiving donations from foreigners, foreign states, non-governmental organisations, faith-based organisations, and foreign businesses, its aim is to protect the political independence and integrity of Rwanda. Yet while this measure prevents external entities from exerting undue influence on domestic politics, it limits the financial resources available to political organisations, particularly those that might rely on international support for their activities. As a result, they are cut off from the support of the international allies and partners who had previously fi-

70 U4 Anti-Corruption Helpdesk, “The Role of Political Party Finance Reform in the Transition from Dominant to Competitive Party Systems”, *Transparency International*, 2019, p 2, https://www.u4.no/publications/the-role-of-political-party-finance-reform-in-the-transition-from-dominant-to-competitive-party-systems.pdf (accessed 11 November 2024).

nanced political parties in Rwanda (including the RPF) as well as elsewhere in Africa.

The following example illustrates some of the issues at stake. The main opposition candidate in the 2003 presidential election was Faustin Twagiramungu, the first post-genocide prime minister. He was supported in his campaign by the Alliance for Democracy, Equity and Progress (ADEP-Mizero), but this was denied legal status on the grounds that it received foreign funding.[71] In addition, individuals who had added their names to the official list of people endorsing his candidacy were subjected to harassment.[72] Forced to contest as an independent candidate, Twagiramungu lost the presidential bid.

It is also to be noted that the operational capacity of emergent political parties is undermined, since the law requires them to mobilise across the country as a precondition for registration despite limiting their sources of funding. This makes it challenging for opposition parties to sustain activities and compete effectively.

Lastly, the requirement to inform the Office of the Ombudsman adds a further layer of oversight to help detect and prevent corruption. This is beneficial for maintaining the integrity of political processes. However, the effectiveness of this measure depends on the impartiality and efficiency of the Office of the Ombudsman. If the office is not perceived as independent, this requirement could be seen as a tool for political control rather than genuine oversight.

3.4.2 Government financial support to political parties

Article 28 of the Law Governing Political Organisations sets out the state's role in providing financial support to political parties and guarantees equal grants to all registered political organisations as well as additional campaign support. It reads:

> State assets cannot be used in the activities or interest of a political organisation. However, the State provides grant as follows:

71 Amnesty International, *Rwanda: Setting the Scene for Elections: Two Decades of Silencing Dissent in Rwanda*, London, Amnesty International (2017), p 12, https://www.amnesty.org/en/wp-content/uploads/2023/06/AFR4765852017ENGLISH.pdf (accessed 11 November 2024).

72 *Ibid*, p 12.

1. each financial year, the Government equally provides registered political organisations with grants through the authority in charge of registration of political organisations, according to the State's financial resources;
2. the Government provides in the budget grants for political organisations and independent candidates to support campaign activities.

The State's grant provided for in item 2 of paragraph 2 of this Article is given to a political organisation or an independent candidate that has scored at least five per cent (5%) of the votes cast.

The prohibition on using state assets for political activities is designed to prevent the abuse of public resources for partisan purposes. This can help maintain a level playing field for parties and prevent the abuse of state power for political gain. However, the effectiveness of this provision depends on strict enforcement and monitoring. A lack of proper enforcement means that state resources can still be used, albeit indirectly, to benefit certain political groups. Such abuse undermines the democratic process by giving undue advantage to the incumbent.[73]

However, it should be noted that the impact of such abuse on the probability of change through elections should not be exaggerated. Historical examples from countries such as Benin, Cape Verde, Ghana, Kenya, Madagascar, Malawi, Mali, São Tomé and Príncipe, Senegal, and Zambia show that incumbency alone does not guarantee a continued hold on power.[74] If access to state funds guaranteed electoral success, one would not have seen changes of power through elections in countries like Ghana, Kenya, Malawi, Senegal, and Zambia in 2021, or the loss of the 2024 presidential elections in Botswana by former president Masisi.

Despite this, the abuse of state resources remains a significant problem in Africa. Legislative provisions against it, such as requirements for civil servants to be neutral or bans on the use of public resources for campaign purposes, are not particularly effective. Tellingly, in Rwanda, the Office of the Ombudsman conducted investigations into political finance during the

73 M Ohman, "The State of Political Finance Regulations in Africa", 14 (2016) *International IDEA Discussion Paper,* p 7, https://www.idea.int/sites/default/files/publications/the-state-of-political-finance-regulations-in-africa.pdf (accessed 10 November 2024).

74 M Ohman, The Heart and Soul of the Party: Candidate Selection in Ghana and Africa, Uppsala, Uppsala University (2004), pp 70–71.

2010 and 2013 elections but released no information about the results.[75] The political finance regulatory framework in Rwanda is weak, with few laws addressing the issue and practical enforcement being limited.

Although there is a lack of concrete information about political finance in Rwanda that goes beyond detail on formal regulation, the dataset developed by the Money, Politics and Transparency (MPT) project provides some vital insights.[76] The dataset includes a Political Finance Index with scores between 0 (the worst score) and 100 in different categories (see the table below). For example, Kenya scores highest overall with 42, reflecting strong regulations and enforcement, while Malawi scores lowest with 5, indicating significant gaps in its political financing system. The data indicates that Rwanda has a composite score of 30, reflecting a mixed performance in political financing regulations. While Rwanda excels in providing direct and indirect public funding (score of 59), it faces significant challenges in monitoring and enforcement (score of 65). Compared to other African countries, Rwanda's regulatory framework shows both strengths and areas needing improvement, particularly in ensuring effective oversight and transparency.

Table 1: Political finance scores for selected African countries in the MPT dataset[77]

	Composite score	In law/ practice	Direct and indirect public funding	Contribution and expenditure restrictions	Reporting and public disclosure	Third-party actors	Monitoring and enforcement
Botswana	18	23/13	18	30	8	0	35
Ghana	26	36/22	21	23	28	0	58
Kenya	42	67/18	43	72	31	16	46
Malawi	5	6/2	25	0	0	0	0
Nigeria	29	45/17	31	43	28	0	42
Rwanda	30	28/41	59	5	24	0	65
South Africa	36	36/47	81	0	17	0	82

75 *Ibid*, p 10.
76 *Ibid*, p 3.
77 *Ibid*, p 4.

As indicated above, reporting on political finance and expenditure during campaigns does not take place in Rwanda: candidates have no reporting obligations. This means that very little meaningful political finance data is reported, and even less is readily accessible to the public. The public can only access submitted reports upon request, which limits transparency and accountability in political financing.[78] Arguably, this low level of compliance is due to the fear among opposition parties that revealing their sources of income would lead to a loss of such income and reprisals against their donors. In addition, many political parties simply lack the administrative capacity to track their own finances effectively.[79]

The provision of equal grants to registered political organisations each financial year aims to promote fairness and support the functioning of political parties. In other words, it seeks to ensure that all registered parties have some level of financial support (crucial for their operations and activities). However, the amount of the grant is dependent on the state's financial resources. In practice, this means that there can be insufficient funding available for political organisations, especially the smaller or newly established ones.

That the power to allot such support is in the hands of the government gives the ruling RPF unchecked power to control the opposition through financial sanctions and conditionalities. The dominance of the ruling party can be consolidated by rewarding compliant parties and withholding funds from the opposition. As the MTP survey shows, the RPF government has adopted a granting approach in which political parties do not have full control of these resources. Instead of receiving subsidies in cash, they are reimbursed for the activities they organise.[80] This system imposes limits on the direct financial autonomy of political parties.

Finally, it is worth considering the allocation of budget grants for campaign activities to parties and independent candidates that secure at least 5 per cent of votes cast. This undoubtedly encourages political participation

78 Ibid.

79 M Ohman, "Africa", in E Falguera, S Jones, and M Ohman (eds.), *Funding of Political Parties and Election Campaigns: A Handbook on Political Finance*, Stockholm, International IDEA (2014), p 59.

80 CB Camargo and T Gatwa, *Informal Governance and Corruption – Transcending the Principal Agent and Collective Action Paradigms: Rwanda Country Report*, Basel, Basel Institute on Governance (2019), p 13 https://baselgovernance.org/sites/default/files/2019-04/rwanda.informalgovernance.country_report.pdf (accessed 11 November 2024).

and competition and supports candidates who have demonstrated a minimum level of public support, helping them to campaign more effectively. However, the 5 per cent threshold excludes new candidates or previously smaller parties that have grown bigger after the last elections. The 5 per cent criterion inadvertently favours established parties with a history of electoral success, thereby reinforcing their dominance.

In other words, by basing finance allocations on previous election performance, the system fails to account for shifts in public support that may have occurred since the elections. This means that, even if a party's popularity has waned significantly over the past five to seven years, it will still receive state funding, giving it an unfair advantage over newer or smaller parties that may have gained traction in the meantime. Established parties with their record of electoral participation are guaranteed funding, regardless of their current levels of support. An electoral contest between an older party with state funding and a newer party without it cannot pass the level-playing-field test which is necessary to meet in order to satisfy the criterion of "fairness" in democratic elections.

3.5 Dialogue and consensus-building provisions

At the heart of the Rwandan political system are the principles of power-sharing and decision-making by consensus. These principles are enshrined in Article 62 of the 2003 Constitution. Thus, for example, Article 62 states that the President cannot belong to the same party as the Speaker of Parliament, while no single party is allowed to have more than 50 per cent of total membership in the cabinet.

The principle of power-sharing is reinforced by the electoral system, where elections to the lower house are based on proportional representation. In addition, Article 59 of the Constitution and articles 49–50 of the Law Governing Political Organisations provide for the establishment of a National Consultative Forum of Political Organisations (NCFPO). This is intended to promote power-sharing and consensual decision-making, with long-term outcomes to include moderating inter-party hostilities, fostering cooperative behaviour, and cultivating a culture of elite compromise and political accommodation, with the ultimate aim of achieving a consociational democracy.

Consociational democracy is praised for its inclusiveness, pluralism, moderation, and stability.[81] This system fosters inter-group cooperation and representation, and the participation of diverse interests. By encouraging multiparty consensus and compromise, it reduces the potential for violence and instability. This is achieved through mechanisms such as power-sharing arrangements, proportional representation, and mutual vetoes. Together, they ensure that all significant groups have a stake in governance and decision-making processes. These mechanisms help to build trust among different political factions, mitigate conflicts, and create a stable political environment where diverse groups can coexist peacefully.

Differing from the strict Lijphartan model, however, Rwanda's emphasis on cooperation between parties with cross-country mobilisation and membership aligns with an alternative model of consociational democracy. This is one that aims at centripetalism by transcending group divisions and encouraging inter-group integration and competition.[82] As operationalised in Rwanda, centripetalism entails the adoption of a deliberate policy to promote multi-ethnic political parties and create electoral incentives that encourage politicians to seek support from a broad spectrum of the population rather than only their own ethnic or regional groups. This approach includes mechanisms such as cross-cutting electoral districts (which require candidates to appeal to voters from diverse backgrounds) and policies that incentivise coalition-building across ethnic lines. By fostering inter-group cooperation and competition, centripetalism aims to integrate different segments of society, reduce ethnic tensions, and create a more stable and inclusive political environment.

The Rwandan experience shows that in practice this works to reduce the opposition's role to a merely consultative one, where it is overshadowed by the ruling party's agenda and its ideology of "consensus politics" and "Rwandaness". It is seen as a strategic move to co-opt opposition voices, effectively making them extensions of the ruling party and weakening their ability to hold the government accountable and present alternative policy

81 This is emphasised in A Lijphart, "Consociational Democracy", 21 (1969) *World Politics*, pp 207–225. See also B Barry, "Political Accommodation and Consociational Democracy", 5 (1975) *British Journal of Political Science*, pp 477–505; J McGarry and B O'Leary, "Consociational Theory, Northern Ireland's Conflict, and its Agreement. Part 1: What Consociationalists can Learn from Northern Ireland", 41 (2006) *Government and Opposition*, pp 43–63.

82 For more detail, see D Horowitz, "Electoral systems: A Primer for Decision Makers", 14 (2003) *Journal of Democracy*, pp 115–127.

options. In this way, parties that participated in the consultative forum (such as the Republican Democratic Movement, the Social Democratic Party, the Liberal Party, and the Centrist Democratic Party) and which were initially active post-genocide, are now perceived as mere satellites of the ruling RPF.[83] Conspicuously, these parties did not field candidates in the 2003 presidential elections but came together to endorse and support the RPF's Paul Kagame. Indeed, in 2003, Parliament voted to dissolve Rwanda's second largest political party, the Mouvement Démocratique Republicain (MDR), following a parliamentary commission report that accused the party of propagating a "divisive" ideology.[84] A critical examination of these examples of co-optation reveals the RPF government's effort to maintain control under the pretext of legal and democratic governance. This raises considerable concerns about the nation's democratic health and true level of pluralism.

As for the NCFPO, it is plagued by opacity, elitist aloofness, and capture by ruling-party interests. This assertion is supported by several findings. For example, a 2010 survey by the Senate of Rwanda shows limited citizens' awareness of the NCFPO: only 63 per cent of respondents were aware of its existence, while 34 per cent said they had no knowledge of it.[85] Notably, 68 per cent of the respondents were members of political parties and thus comprised politically active citizens, yet only 22 per cent expressed satisfaction with the NCFPO. Comparing the 63 per cent who knew about the NCFPO with the 22 per cent who are satisfied with its conduct, it becomes evident that the NCFPO has ceased to serve the interests of the Rwandan people. Crucially, in the 2001 district elections, only councillors and district executives who endorsed the policy of national unity and reconciliation were elected.[86]

83 See National Democratic Institute, *NDI Assessment of Rwanda's Pre-Election Political Environment and the Role of Political Parties*, Washington DC, National Democratic Institute (2003), p 6, https://www.ndi.org/sites/default/files/1642_rw_assessment_092203_0.pdf (accessed 13 March 2024).

84 Human Rights Watch, "Rwanda Preparing for Elections: Tightening Control in the Name of Unity", *Human Rights Watch Backgrounder*, 8 May 2003, https://www.hrw.org/legacy/backgrounder/africa/rwanda0503bck.htm (accessed 11 November 2024). See also "Parliament Upholds Ban on Bizimungu's Party", *The New Humanitarian*, 28 June 2001, https://www.thenewhumanitarian.org/fr/node/191824 (accessed 10 November 2024).

85 See the results in Rwanda Parliament and the Senate, *supra* n. 16, pp 248, 250–251.

86 Camargo and Gatwa, *supra* n. 80, p 13.

3.6 Punitive measures on politicians

Article 42 of the Law on Political Organisations stipulates that politicians who violate certain articles (discussed above) may receive a formal warning or be removed from their political positions, though they retain the right to defend themselves against accusations. This provision ensures that politicians have a chance to challenge accusations in court, something crucial to the protection of their freedoms as well as the integrity of the political parties themselves.

Article 46 of the Law Governing Political Organisations specifies the following offences and penalties:

I. Illegally forming or leading a political organisation, or falsely claiming membership, results in imprisonment (1–2 years) and/or a fine (FRW 1,000,000 – FRW 2,000,000).
II. Leading or claiming membership in an organisation that operates post-registration cancellation incurs imprisonment (3–5 years) and/or a fine (FRW 3,000,000 – FRW 5,000,000).

From a positive perspective, these stipulations can be read as a safeguard against the misuse of political entities for unlawful purposes and as helping to ensure that political organisations operate within the bounds of the law. As such, they potentially enhance the integrity of political processes and institutions. However, the stringent penalties attached to them can also be viewed as detrimental to political party viability, inclusion, autonomy, and capacity. They may deter individuals from engaging in political activities for fear of the severe repercussions that can follow any misstep, whether intentional or accidental. This leads to a chilling effect on political participation and a reduction in the diversity of political discourse – both essential components of a vibrant democracy.

The quality of democracy is inherently linked to the freedom and capacity of political parties to operate without undue restrictions. The ACDEG, as well as international protocols such as the ICCPR, emphasise the importance of inclusive participation and the autonomy of political parties as fundamentals of democratic governance.[87] Restrictions that excessively penalise political participation can undermine these principles, potentially affecting the quality of democracy by limiting the spectrum of political

87 See articles 3(11), 32(6) and (7) of the ACDEG in African Union, *supra* n. 42, and Article 25 of the ICCP.

ideas and the ability of citizens to freely associate and express their political preferences.

Article 46 of the Law Governing Political Organisations details sanctions against political organisations that fail to comply with specific provisions on financial accountability and transparency. These range from a formal warning to the invalidation of their registration certificate, while organisations that accept illegal contributions may be suspended for up to five years, with all such contributions eligible for confiscation by the government. The sanctions, especially when applied during elections, significantly restrict the operational freedom of political parties. They potentially consolidate the ruling party's dominance through their imposition of financial penalties on opposition groups. The requirement for an investigation by the Senate prior to the imposition of certain sanctions introduces a layer of legislative oversight, while the publication of the final decision in the Official Gazette ensures transparency. However, these measures can also be seen as a means for the government to exert control over political organisations, thereby affecting their autonomy and ability to function effectively within the political landscape of Rwanda.

4. Conclusion

Rwanda is arguably one of the few African countries which enjoy comprehensive constitutional provisions for recognising and guaranteeing the rights and obligations of political parties as stipulated in regional laws and international standards. The Constitution provides for legislation that regulates political organisations and specifies the extent of their rights and obligations. However, the constitutionalisation of the rights and duties of parties in Rwanda presents a paradoxical situation, one in which democratic promise is always overshadowed by securocratic control.

After the 1994 genocide, the historical and political evolution of party constitutionalisation produced a legal and institutional framework that, while ostensibly supporting multiparty democracy, simultaneously imposes constraints that undermine the autonomy and diversity of political representation. This duality results in a "guided paper democracy", where the semblance of pluralism is undercut by regulations that favour the ruling party's dominance. This yields the bitter lesson that inserting clauses that recognise and guarantee the existence, rights, and obligations of political parties in the constitution of a country is not a strategy that, at a stroke, can resolve authoritarian hegemony of one-party dominant regimes. Indeed, such provisions can, paradoxically, serve as an enabler of authoritarian control.

In the face of the weaponisation of the Constitution against political opponents by the ruling party, and to safeguard the future of democracy and human rights, policy reforms are necessary. These should work to reconcile the dual objectives of security and liberty, ensuring that the regulatory framework for political parties not only formally acknowledges democratic structures but also fosters genuine political pluralism. Such reforms should seek to instantiate the principles of autonomy, a balanced party system, and clear separation of state and party.

The Rwandan case holds valuable lessons for anyone interested in sub-Saharan Africa's democratic and constitutional development. It highlights the importance of a constitutional framework that protects the rights and functions of political parties while promoting an inclusive and competitive political environment. Addressing the challenges identified in this study could pave the way for a more robust and sustainable democracy, one in which human rights and political participation are not mere formal abstractions but lived realities. By drawing on Rwanda's experience, this chapter contributes to the broader discourse on democracy and constitutionalism in Sub-Saharan Africa. It calls for a nuanced understanding of party constitutionalisation, one that recognises its potential to both support and suppress democratic ideals. The future of democracy in securocratic states hinges on the delicate balance between security imperatives and the fundamental tenets of liberty and political diversity.

References

Books, articles, chapters in books, and others

"Divided by Ethnicity", *United States Holocaust Memorial Museum*, September 2021, https://www.ushmm.org/genocide-prevention/countries/rwanda/divided-by-ethnicity (accessed 23 March 2024)

"Parliament Upholds Ban on Bizimungu's Party", *The New Humanitarian*, 28 June 2001, https://www.thenewhumanitarian.org/fr/node/191824 (accessed 10 November 2024)

AFP, "Rwanda Court Upholds Election Ban on Opposition Leader", *The Guardian*, 13 March 2024, https://www.theguardian.com/world/2024/mar/13/rwanda-victoire-ingabire-barred-election (accessed 7 November 2024)

Amnesty International, "Elections in Rwanda: Rwanda's Repressive Tactics Silence Dissent Before Elections." *Amnesty International*, 5 September 2017, www.amnesty.org/en/latest/campaigns/2017/09/rwandas-repressive-tactics-silence-dissent-before-elections/ (accessed 23 March 2024)

Amnesty International, *Rwanda: Setting the Scene for Elections: Two Decades of Silencing Dissent in Rwanda*, London, Amnesty International (2017), https://www.amnesty.org/en/wp-content/uploads/2023/06/AFR4765852017ENGLISH.pdf (accessed 11 November 2024)

Barry B, "Political Accommodation and Consociational Democracy", 5 (1975) *British Journal of Political Science*, pp 477–505

Baxter P and Jack S, "Qualitative Case Study Methodology: Study Design and Implementation for Novice Researchers", 13 (2008) *The Qualitative Report*, pp 544–559

Beach D and Pedersen RB, *Process-tracing Methods: Foundations and Guidelines*, 2nd ed, Michigan, University of Michigan Press (2019)

Bennett A and Checkel JT (eds.), *Process Tracing: From Metaphor to Analytic Tool*, Cambridge, Cambridge University Press (2015)

Bogaards M, "Counting Parties and Identifying Dominant Party Systems in Africa", 43 (2004) *European Journal of Political Research*, pp 173–197

Borz G, "Justifying the Constitutional Regulation of Political Parties: A Framework for Analysis", 38 (2017) *International Political Science Review/Revue internationale de Science Politique*, pp 99–113

Camargo CB and Gatwa T, *Informal Governance and Corruption – Transcending the Principal Agent and Collective Action Paradigms: Rwanda Country Report*, Basel, Basel Institute on Governance (2019), https://baselgovernance.org/sites/default/files/2019-04/rwanda.informalgovernance.country_report.pdf (accessed 11 November 2024)

Carothers C, "The Surprising Instability of Competitive Authoritarianism", 29 (2018) *Journal of Democracy*, pp 129–135

Chemouni B, "The Political Path to Universal Health Coverage: Power, Ideas and Community-based Health Insurance in Rwanda", 106 (2018) *World Development*, pp 87–98

Clover J, "Rwandan Opposition Party Registers Days before September Vote Deadline", *Reuters*, 10 August 2013, https://www.reuters.com/article/us-rwanda-politics-idUSBRE97903B20130810/ (accessed 10 May 2024)

Commonwealth Election Observer Mission, "Chapter 2 Political Background", Commonwealth, (2013), https://www.thecommonwealth-ilibrary.org/index.php/comsec/catalog/download/288/285/2283?inline=1 (accessed 26 October 2024)

Commonwealth Election Observer Mission, "Chapter 4 Election Campaign and the Media", 2013, https://www.thecommonwealth-ilibrary.org/index.php/comsec/catalog/download/288/285/2285?inline=1 (accessed 23 March 2024)

Diamond L, "Elections without Democracy: Thinking about Hybrid Regimes", (13) (2002) *Journal of Democracy*, pp 21–35

Erdmann G and Basedau M, "Problems of Categorising and Explaining Party Systems in Africa", *GIGA Working Papers*, 40 (2007), ssrn.com/abstract=978166 or dx.doi.org/10.2139/ssrn.978166 (accessed 16 July 2024)

Freedom House, "Freedom in the World 2018 – Rwanda", *UNHCR Refworld*, 1 August 2018, www.refworld.org/reference/annualreport/freehou/2018/en/121588 (accessed 17 March 2024)

Gerring J, *Case Study Research: Principles and Practices*, Cambridge, Cambridge University Press (2007)

Golooba-Mutebi, F, "Collapse, War and Reconstruction in Rwanda: An Analytical Narrative on State-Making." *Crisis States Research Centre* (2008), www.lse.ac.uk/international-development/Assets/Documents/PDFs/csrc-working-papers-phase-two/wp28.2-collapse-war-and-reconstruction-in-rwanda.pdf (accessed 25 March 2024)

Habineza F, "Opposition Party Registration is Impossible in Rwanda Said Green Party Boss", *The Rwandan,* 20 May (2013), www.therwandan.com/opposition-party-registration-is-impossible-in-rwanda-said-green-party-boss/ (accessed, 23 April 2024)

Horowitz D, "Electoral Systems: A Primer for Decision Makers", 14 (2003) *Journal of Democracy*, pp 115–127

Human Rights Watch, "Politician Convicted for Harming Rwanda's Image", *Human Rights Watch*, 18 January 2023, www.hrw.org/news/2023/01/18/politician-convicted-harming-rwandas-image (accessed 23 March 2024)

Human Rights Watch, "Rwanda Preparing for Elections: Tightening Control in the Name of Unity", *Human Rights Watch Backgrounder*, 8 May 2003, https://www.hrw.org/legacy/backgrounder/africa/rwanda0503bck.htm (accessed 11 November 2024)

Human Rights Watch, "Rwanda: Alleged Genocide Mastermind Arrested: Fulgence Kayishema Caught after Two Decades; Should Face Swift, Fair Trial", *Human Rights Watch,* 06 June (2022), www.hrw.org/news/2023/06/02/rwanda-alleged-genocide-mastermind-arrested (accessed 23 March 2024)

Human Rights Watch, "Rwanda: Crackdown on Opposition, Media Intensifies", *Human Rights Watch*, 19 October 2021, https://www.hrw.org/news/2021/10/19/rwanda-crackdown-opposition-media-intensifies (accessed 23 March 2024)

Ingabire UV, "Rwanda's Consensual Democracy Needs a Reset", *Al Jazeera*, 15 September 2022, www.aljazeera.com/opinions/2022/9/15/rwandas-consensual-democracy-needs-a-reset (accessed 24 March 2024)

Ingelaere B, Verpoorten M, Desrosiers ME, and Reyntjens F, *Genocide, Ideology and Politics in Rwanda,* New York, Routledge (2018)

Levitsky S and Way LA, "The Rise of Competitive Authoritarianism", 13 (2002) *Journal of Democracy*, pp 51–65

Lijphart A, "Consociational Democracy", 21 (1969) *World Politics*, pp 207–225

Mainwaring S, "From Representative Democracy to Participatory Competitive Authoritarianism: Hugo Chávez and Venezuelan Politics", 10 (2012) *Perspectives on Politics*, pp 955–967

Mamdani M, When Victims Become Killers: Colonialism, Nativism and the Genocide in Rwanda, Princeton, NJ, Princeton University Press (2001)

McDoom OS, "Securocratic State-building: The Rationales, Rebuttals, and Risks Behind the Extraordinary Rise of Rwanda After the Genocide", 121 (2022) *African Affairs*, pp 535–567

McGarry J, O'Leary B, "Consociational Theory, Northern Ireland's Conflict, and Its Agreement. Part 1: What Consociationalists Can Learn from Northern Ireland", 41 (2006) *Government and Opposition*, pp 43–63

Munyarugerero F-X, Reseaux, Pouvoirs, Oppositions: La Compétition Politique au Rwanda, Paris, Editions l'Harmattan (2003)

National Democratic Institute, *NDI Assessment of Rwanda's Pre-Election Political Environment and the Role of Political Parties*, Washington DC, National Democratic Institute (2003), https://www.ndi.org/sites/default/files/1642_rw_assessment_092203_0.pdf (accessed 13 March 2024)

Newbury C, "Background to Genocide: Rwanda", 23 (1995) *Issue: A Journal of Opinion*, pp 12–17

Niesen P, "Political Party Bans in Rwanda 1994–2003: Three Narratives of Justification", 17 (2010) *Democratization*, pp 709–729

Nkunzumwami E, La Tragédie Rwandaise: Historique et Perspectives, Paris, L'Harmattan (1996)

Nwokora Z and Pelizzo R, "Measuring Party Constitutionalisation: A Comparative Study of 144 Parties from 20 African Countries", 22 (2016) *Party Politics*, pp 521–533

Ohman M, "Africa", in E Falguera, S Jones, and M Ohman (eds.), *Funding of Political Parties and Election Campaigns: A Handbook on Political Finance*, Stockholm, International IDEA (2014), p 59

Ohman M, "The State of Political Finance Regulations in Africa", 14 (2016) *International IDEA Discussion Paper*, p 7, https://www.idea.int/sites/default/files/publications/the-state-of-political-finance-regulations-in-africa.pdf (accessed 10 November 2024)

Ohman M, The Heart and Soul of the Party: Candidate Selection in Ghana and Africa. Uppsala, Uppsala University (2004)

OSCE High Commissioner on National Minorities, *Handbook on Observing and Promoting the Participation of National Minorities in Electoral Processes* Warsaw, OSCE Office for Democratic Institutions and Human Rights (2014)

Palmier L "Review of Guided Democracy, by TK Tan and Hong Lee Oey", 7 (1973) *Modern Asian Studies*, pp 296–305

Reyntjens F, "Rwanda, Ten Years On: From Genocide to Dictatorship", 103 (2004) *African Affairs*, pp 177–210

Ruhanya P and Gumbo B, "The Securocratic State: Conceptualising the Transition Problem in Zimbabwe", 8 (2023) *Third World Thematics: A TWQ Journal*, pp 219–237

Rwanda Parliament and the Senate, *Political Pluralism and Power Sharing*, Kigali, Rwanda, Parliament and the Senate (2010), https://www.parliament.gov.rw/fileadmin/user_upload/Parliament/Research/Political_Plurarisme_and_Power_sharing_in_Rwanda.pdf (accessed 7 November 2024)

Strauss S and Waldorf L (eds.), *Remaking Rwanda: State Building and Human Rights after Mass Violence*, Madison, University of Wisconsin Press (2011)

Strauss S, *The Order of Genocide: Race, Power, and War in Rwanda*, Ithaca and London, Cornell University Press (2006)

Tull DM and Mehler A, "The Hidden Costs of Power Sharing: Reproducing Insurgent Violence in Africa", 104 (2005) *African Affairs*, pp 375–398

U4 Anti-Corruption Helpdesk, "The Role of Political Party Finance Reform in the Transition from Dominant to Competitive Party Systems", *Transparency International,* 2019, https://www.u4.no/publications/the-role-of-political-party-finance-reform-in-the-transition-from-dominant-to-competitive-party-systems.pdf (accessed 11 November 2024)

United Nations, "Outreach Programme on the 1994 Genocide against the Tutsi in Rwanda and the United Nations", n.d., http://www.un.org/en/preventgenocide/rwanda/historical-background.shtml#prior-to-colonial-era (accessed 23 October 2024)

US Department of State, Bureau of Democracy, Human Rights and Labor, "Country Reports on Human Rights Practices for 2013", United States Department of State (2013), state.gov/documents/organisation/220359.pdf (accessed 23 March 2023)

Van Biezen I, "Constitutionalising Party Democracy: The Constitutive Codification of Political Parties in Post-war Europe", 42 (2012) *British Journal of Political Science*, pp 187–212

Yin RK, *Case Study Research Design and Methods*, 5th ed, Thousand Oaks, Sage (2014)

Zuber D, "Gregoire Kayibanda (1924–1976)", *Black Past*, 23 March 2022, https:www.blackpast.org/global-african-history/people-global-african-history/gregoire-kayibanda-1924-1976/ (accessed 23 October 2024)

Table of cases

African Court on Human and Peoples' Rights cases

Lohe Issa Konate v Burkina Faso, Application No. 004/2013, Judgement, 5 December 2014

Mtikila v United Republic of Tanzania, Application No. 011/2011, Judgement, 14 June 2013

Ingabire Victoire Umuhoza v The Republic of Rwanda, ruling on Jurisdiction, 5 September 2016

Ingabire Victoire Umuhoza v The Republic of Rwanda, App. No. 003/2014, Judgement, 24 November 2017

Table of legislation

National legislation: Rwanda

Constitution of the Republic of Rwanda 2003, amended in 2015 and 2023

Government of Rwanda, Organic Law No. 005/2018.Ol of 30/08/2018 Modifying the Organic Law No. 10/2013/Ol Of 11/07/2013 Governing Political Organisations and Politicians, Official Gazette No. 37, 10 September 2018

International covenants and resolutions

African Commission on Human and Peoples' Rights, African Charter on Human and Peoples' Rights, adopted 27 June 1981, entry into force 21 October 1986

African Commission on Human and Peoples' Rights, Resolution on the Right to Freedom of Association, ACHPR/Res. 5(XI)92, 9 March 1992

African Union, African Charter on Democracy, Elections and Governance

East African Community, The East African Community Protocol on Good Governance (Draft)

United Nations General Assembly, International Covenant on Civil and Political Rights, United Nations General Assembly

Comments, guidance and opinions by international bodies

UN Human Rights Committee, General Comment No. 25: Article 25 (Participation in Public Affairs and the Right to Vote), 12 July 1996, CCPR/C/21/Rev.1/Add.7

Venice Commission, *Guidelines on Political Party Regulation*, 2nd ed, 14 December 2020, CDL-AD(2020)032

Chapter 13 Cameroon and the Transition from a Monolithic to a Multiparty Autocracy

Charles M Fombad and Ajereboh J Tichock

1. Introduction

Between the late 1950s and early 1960s, the period when most African countries gained their independence, multipartyism was widely practised across the continent. However, it proved to be poorly rooted, and it was not long before it was abandoned.[1] In Cameroon, prior to the union that led to the country's establishment as a federal republic in 1961,[2] both the former French Cameroon and the British Southern Cameroons were home to fledgling multiparty systems, but these were informally abolished by the country's first independence president, Ahmadou Ahidjo. On 1 September 1966, he replaced multipartyism with a single party, the Cameroon National Union (CNU), which he maintained, was created to facilitate nation-building and national unity. This one party – renamed in 1985 as the Cameroon People's Democratic Movement (CPDM) – was to dominate the country's political landscape not only from 1966 to 1990, when multipartyism was reintroduced, but throughout the entire period of multipartyism in Cameroon to this day.

---

1 CM Giovanni, "Political Parties and Party Systems in Africa: Themes and Research Perspectives", 3(3) (2007) *World Political Science*, pp 1–29.

2 Present-day Cameroon was one of the creations of the infamous Berlin Conference of 1884, where it was declared a German colony by the name of Kamerun. It remained a German colony until a British and French expeditionary force defeated the German army there in 1916 during the First World War and partitioned the territory into two regions. The British took control of two small, disconnected portions, known as Northern and Southern Cameroons, while the French took a larger portion amounting to about four-fifths of the territory. This arbitrary division was later ratified by the League of Nations and its successor, the United Nations. After a United Nations-organised plebiscite on 11 February 1961, Southern Cameroons voted in favour of reuniting with the former French Cameroon, which had gained independence as the Republic of Cameroon on 1 January 1960. Northern Cameroons, for its part, opted to remain within the Federation of Nigeria.

The reintroduction of multipartyism in Cameroon was initially resisted by the ruling political elites. In fact, six young people were killed by the security forces during the launch of the first opposition party, the Social Democratic Front (SDF), in Bamenda in the North-West Region on 26 May 1990. After intense local and international pressure on the government, Law No. 90/056 of 19 December 1990 on Political Parties was enacted, and it was through this that multipartyism was formally reintroduced and institutionalised, though not constitutionalised. Political parties were later constitutionalised in the 1996 Constitution. Although there are now more than 367 registered parties in Cameroon,[3] there is hardly any evidence in what has happened since 1990 to show that the country's monolithic one-party culture has changed. This chapter will critically examine why this has been so.

Accordingly, section 2 presents an overview of the formal return to multipartyism in Cameroon. Section 3 discusses the constitutional and regulatory framework for political parties. This is followed in section 4, by an account of what can only be described as the country's farcical descent into multiparty autocracy. In section 5, some reasons will be advanced to suggest that the future for multipartyism in Cameroon is bleak. The chapter concludes that there is an urgent need for inclusive, people-centred, and people-driven constitutional and institutional reforms capable of redirecting the country on the path towards genuine multiparty democracy. The way in which multipartyism was revived in Cameroon in the 1990s, a matter to which we now turn, tells us much about what has happened since then.

2. The revival of multipartyism

After close to three decades under a one-party autocratic system, Cameroon, like most of its African counterparts, came under the influence of the winds of change brought about by the fall of the Berlin Wall. Early attempts, pre- and post-independence, at multiparty politics in Cameroon were halted by President Ahidjo in 1966 when he imposed a

3 The number of parties is constantly increasing. For example, on 9 November 2023, the Minister of Territorial Administration signed an order recognising 40 new political parties. See PR Wandji, "Cameroon: 40 New Political Parties Receive Approval", *Journal du Cameroun.com* 13 November 2023, https://www.en.journalducameroun.com/cameroon-40-new-political-parties-receive-approval/ (accessed 1 May 2024).

single party, the CNU. However, multipartyism was never formally banned in Cameroon. When Ahidjo created the CNU, supposedly composed of representatives of all existing parties, those who resisted joining the party were harassed, persecuted, and sometimes imprisoned. With the change of guard at the presidency in 1982 when Ahidjo resigned and handed over power to his constitutional heir, Paul Biya, the new dispensation was marked by little more than a simple change in the party's name from the CNU to CPDM, made in 1985 at the party's congress in Bamenda in the North-West Region.

This section of the chapter describes the events surrounding the reintroduction of multipartyism and the first multiparty elections in 1992 – elections that were to be instrumental in shaping the trajectory of multipartyism in Cameroon.

2.1 The bloody path to the reintroduction of multipartyism in 1990

From the beginning of his political career, Ahidjo made national unity a prerequisite for maintaining peace and advancing development. To this end, he dismantled any remnants of decentralised power stemming from the 1961 Federal Constitution and steadily created a highly centralised authoritarian system. Ahidjo used the resources of the state to build a coalition of supporters across the country by creating an elaborate system of patronage to reward his allies and their clients. He kept potential rivals at bay by regularly appointing academics and bureaucrats, such as his successor, Biya, to positions of power, while many of his adversaries, especially after the imposition of the one-party rule in 1966, were bought off by appointments to positions where they could share in the spoils of power. Through the creation of an effective and much-feared repressive machinery, threats to his authority were virtually eliminated during his reign until his voluntary resignation in 1982.

For all his authoritarianism, Ahidjo is considered by many analysts to have been a shrewd pragmatist who managed not only to maintain peace but to ensure a measure of prosperity and stability that made Cameroon the envy of its neighbours. Le Vine, one of the pre-eminent scholars on Cameroon, said of him:

> [I]t was Ahidjo's tactics that made the difference in the final analysis. He treated his opponents firmly, sometimes harshly, but made sure that

> even his bitterest enemies had both the chance of joining his side and actively sharing in the perquisites of power. That he was never vindictive is to his credit. The style of the regime appears to have been actively reconciliationist, pragmatic and tactically consistent.[4]

Biya came to power in 1982 on a wave of popular support and did not disappoint with his initial promises of more democracy, "rigour and moralisation"; he affirmed his commitment to stability and national unity, which he described as a "cardinal historic task of highest priority".[5] Declaring the "consolidation of national unity ... the indispensable foundation [of nation-building]," he rejected the "collection and juxtaposition of our diversities" and pronounced himself "firmly convinced that we should move on a higher level of unification, which is that of national integration".[6]

After a false dawn of promised relaxation of restrictions imposed by his predecessor, an attempted coup d' état in 1984 was suppressed, giving Biya the pretext to reassert the full repressive machinery he had inherited. This included transforming an already centralised bureaucracy into one of the most sclerotic and corrupt of its kind in Africa.[7] Unlike that of his predecessor, Biya's approach to the spoils system allowed little room for participation by anyone other than close affiliates and members of his own Beti ethnic group from the Centre, South and East regions – though it made up less than 10 per cent of the population, this group controlled most of the senior positions in the administration, military, and parastatals. Although Biya adopted much the same methods and policies as his predecessor – centralisation, co-option, coalition-building, and repression – he lacked Ahidjo's political savvy. The corruption that began in the Ahidjo era became endemic under Biya. As the consequent economic crisis deepened, frustration mounted at the defects of the country's authoritarian system.

It was a bold move by John Fru Ndi – who, in March 1990, exploited widespread feelings of alienation, especially among the anglophones, by launching his SDF party – that set in motion the process of democratisation

4 See V le Vine, *The Cameroon Federal Republic*, Ithaca, Cornell University Press (1971), p 230.

5 See P Biya, *Communal Liberalism*, London, Macmillan (1987), pp 24–26.

6 Ibid. See also MJ Azevedo (ed.), *Cameroon and Chad in Historical Contemporary Perspectives*, Lewiston, Edwin Mellen Press (1988), pp 178–185.

7 See CM Fombad, "Endemic Corruption in Cameroon: Insights on Consequences and Control", in R Hope and B Chikulo (eds.), *Corruption and Development in Africa. Lessons from Country Case – Studies,* Hampshire, Macmillan (2000), pp 234–260.

still falteringly at work in Cameroon today. [8] The events of this period have brought forth a voluminous literature.[9] The demand for a change to multipartyism, despite growing national and international pressures, was initially resisted – vehemently – by the CPDM one-party regime. This was unsurprising because Biya, in his book, *Communal Liberalism*, had stated that "the present phase of the history of Cameroon does not permit the institution of a multiparty system". [10]

It was on this basis that the first attempt by some Cameroonians in late 1989 to form an opposition party was dealt with decisively by the regime. Those who were involved in this attempt, including a Douala-based lawyer, Yondo Black, were arrested and charged with subversion and tried by a military tribunal.[11] This was followed by a crackdown on pro-democracy activists, supporters, and politicians. None of this, however, deterred Fru Ndi from launching, on 26 May 1990, the first opposition party since 1966, the SDF, even though six people were killed by government security forces during their attempts to halt the launch. Ndi, in his short speech, declared:

> Today is the most significant day in the struggle for democracy in Cameroon .... Democracy has never been handed down to a people on a platter of gold ... We have set as one of our goals to rid the Cameroonian society of a system that deprives people from being free men or other-

8 Most of the ruling elites, particularly those in the CPDM, condemned the SDF – and anglophones in general – for what they considered a "treacherous act" and the premature birth of multipartyism. In many respects, the plight of the country's anglophones today is linked to their bold decision to challenge the ruling group.

9 See, for example, CM Fombad and J Fonyam, "The Social Democratic Front, the Opposition, and Political Transition in Cameroon", in JM Mbaku and J Takougang (eds.), *The Leadership Challenge in Africa: Cameroon Under Paul Biya,* Africa World Press, Trenton NJ (2004), pp 453–488; D Eyoh, "Conflicting Narratives of Anglophone Protest and the Politics of Identify in Cameroon", 16(2) (1988) *Journal of Contemporary African Studies*, pp 249–276; PJJ Konings, "Opposition and Social-Democratic Change in Africa: The Social Democratic Front in Cameroon", 42(3) (2004) *Commonwealth and Comparative Politics*, pp 289–311; M Krieger, "Cameroon's Democratic Crossroads, 1990–4", 32(4) (1984) *Journal of Modern African Studies*, pp 605–628; J Takougang, "The 1992 Multiparty Elections in Cameroon: Prospects for Democracy and Democratisation", 31(1–2) (1996) *Journal of Asian and African Studies*, pp 52–65.

10 See Biya, *supra* n. 5, pp 24–26.

11 A Mehler, "Cameroun: Une Transition Qui n'a pas eu Lieu", in JP Daloz and P Quantin (eds.), *Transitions Démocratiques Africaines*, Paris, Karthala (1997), pp 217–241; E Nikolas, "'With a Friend Like This ...': Shielding Cameroon from Democratization", 48(2) (2013) *Journal of Asian and African Studies*, pp 145–160.

> wise punishing them for daring to think freely, associate freely, assemble peacefully and freely ... We call upon you to stand up and be counted amongst those who share our democratic ideal. You have nothing to lose but the straitjacket in which freeborn citizens have been cast.[12]

The occasion marked a turning-point in the country's political history. Other events rapidly ensued, among them the France-Africa Summit in La Baule, France, in June 1990, where, with Biya in attendance, French president Francois Mitterrand announced that France's aid to Africa would henceforth be conditional on democratisation. Biya, in a *volte-face,* spoke at a CPDM congress in Yaoundé on 28 June 1990 where he called on his party members to prepare for multipartyism.[13] This was followed by the enactment in December 1990 of a series of laws formally reintroducing multipartyism in Cameroon. Several new parties, including the SDF, were immediately legalised and registered.

Cameroonians welcomed this development with euphoria and hopes for a better future, with demands being made for a sovereign national conference like those that had been held, for example, in Benin, Congo Brazzaville, Mali, and Zaire (the present-day Democratic Republic of the Congo). The regime's refusal to allow this led to the emergence of so-called "ghost towns" throughout most of the country, with the exception of CPDM strongholds in the Centre, South and East regions.[14] Ghost towns were marked by stay-aways, street blockades, the refusal to pay bills and taxes, and boycotts of market and offices. The regime's response to protests in support of opposition-party demands for a sovereign national conference was violent, but eventually it convened a "tripartite meeting" involving the government, opposition leaders, and well-known public figures.

This was followed in November 1991 by the signing by some of the legalised opposition parties of the so-called Yaoundé Declaration, in terms of which the ghost-town campaign was called off pending elections and a promise by the government to hold discussions on electoral and constitutional reforms thereafter. The SDF, the then leading opposition party, refused to sign the declaration or cooperate with the government. Hence, the

12 Quoted in JF Gwellem, *Fru Ndi and the SDF Revolution,* Bamenda, Unique Press (1996), p 12.

13 J Derick, "Political Economy: Cameroon: One Party, Many Parties and the State", 22(3) (1992) *Africa Insight*, pp 165–177.

14 See generally ANT Mbu, "Civil Disobedience in Cameroon Bamenda", Douala, Imprimerie Georges Freres (1993).

first multiparty elections were held against a background of agitation for a fair and transparent electoral system as well as a regulatory framework for political parties. This framework was profoundly shaped by what happened in those first post-one-party-system elections, events to which we now turn.

2.2 The twin elections of 1992 and the trajectory of multipartyism

Without meeting any of the demands made by the opposition parties, especially the SDF's demands for an independent electoral commission, Biya went ahead and planned parliamentary and presidential elections for 1 March and 11 October 1992, respectively. The SDF (by then the largest and most popular opposition party) and a number of other parties decided to boycott the parliamentary elections. The ruling CPDM, for the first and only time since its formation, lost its parliamentary majority, winning only 88 of the 180 seats. The rest went to three opposition parties: the National Union for Democracy and Progress (UNDP), with 68 seats; the Union of the People of Cameroon (UPC), with 18 seats; and the Movement for the Defence of the Republic (MDR), with six seats.

It has been debated since then whether it had been an act of wisdom or folly for the SDF to have boycotted this first founding parliamentary elections.[15] Our view is that, had the SDF, at that stage widely supported throughout the country, participated and won, the CPDM would still have been declared the winner. This view is reinforced not only by what happened when its leader, Fru Ndi, contested in the 11 October 1992 presidential elections (discussed below) but also by declarations made by French officials before and after the presidential election.[16]

After the 1992 presidential election, the incumbent, Biya, was declared the winner, with 40 per cent of the total votes cast, while Fru Ndi of the SDF gained 36 per cent; Bello Bouba of the UNDP, 19 per cent; and Adamu Ndam Njoya of the Cameroon Democratic Union (UDC), 4 per cent. The results were widely condemned by local and international observers. The Washington-based National Democratic Institute for International Affairs (NDI), which had been invited to observe the elections, noted "widespread irregularities" that called the results into question and maintained that the "election system was designed to fail", with the "overwhelming weight

15 See, for example, Konings, *supra* n. 9, p 8.

16 See section 5.8.

of responsibility for this failed process [lying] with the government and President Biya". The Cameroonian government, it said, had taken "unusually extreme and illegitimate actions to ensure the president's victory".[17] Dissatisfaction with the election results led to rioting and the destruction of property in parts of the country; violent state suppression and associated human rights violations in turn saw sanctions being imposed on the government by many Western powers, including the United States (US), Britain, and the European Union.

For all that, these twin elections came the closest ever to reflecting the general will of the people, given that subsequent elections have been marred by massive fraud and vote-rigging, as well as various schemes to disenfranchise voters in opposition strongholds. Indeed, the regime's near-defeat and removal from power served to awake its elites to the reality of multiparty democracy. The government quickly recovered from its embarrassment and used the opportunity it had to fulfil its promises to the opposition to carry out constitutional and electoral reforms, the objective being, however, to tighten its grip on power. In short, the 1992 twin elections set the trajectory for multipartyism in Cameroon, in particular for the nature of the country's constitutional and regulatory framework for governing political parties.

3. The constitutional and regulatory framework for political parties

Multipartyism, as noted, was never formally banned in Cameroon. On the contrary – using similar language – Article 3 of the Federal Constitution of 1961, Article 3 of the 1972 Constitution of the United Republic of Cameroon, and Article 3 of the present 1996 Constitution have all recognised the right to establish political parties. Article 3 of the 1996 Constitution puts it thus:

> Political parties and groups shall help the electorate in the making of voting decisions. They shall be bound to respect the principles of democracy, national sovereignty and unity. They shall be formed and shall exercise their activities in accordance with the law.

---

17 National Democratic Institute for International Affairs, *Assessment of the October 11, 1992 Elections in Cameroon* (1993), p 19, http://www.electionpassport.com/files/1992-NDI-Cameroon-Election-Report.pdf (accessed 1 May 2024).

The de facto ban on multipartyism came to an end when Fru Ndi launched the SDF on 26 May 1990. However, it took six months after the launch of this first post-1966 opposition party for a law on political parties (Law No. 90/056 of 19 December 1990) to be enacted and thereby pave the way for their formal legalisation and registration.

All that the various constitutions have done has been to recognise a right to form political parties in obscure terms; the exact nature, scope and limits of the right was left to be determined by legislation at the absolute discretion of the legislator and with no obligation on it to act. It is thus no surprise that, until 1990, the failure of the legislature to enact an implementing law amounted to an indirect ban on the formation of political parties, especially since no one had the authority to compel the legislature to enact such legislation. The major change in 1990, therefore, was that pressure was brought to bear on the legislator to enact the necessary law.

In addition to the 1990 law on political parties (Political Parties Law), a flurry of legislation, referred to as the "liberty laws", was enacted in December 1990 to regulate the newly reintroduced multiparty system. It included Law No. 90/053 of 19 December 1990 on Freedom of Associations; Law No. 90/052 of 19 December 1990 on Freedom of Mass Communications; Law No. 90/054 of 19 December 1990 on the Maintenance of Law and Order; and Law No. 90/055 of 19 December 1990 to Lay Down Regulations Governing Public Meetings and Processions. Subsequently, after sustained pressure from opposition parties and other stakeholders, further pieces of legislation relating to multiparty politics were enacted.[18] Some of them were later repealed and replaced by a so-called harmonised law, Law No. 2012/001 of 19 April 2012 Relating to the Electoral Code (as Amended). The next section examines aspects of the different laws, such as the freedom to form and/or join political parties; the registration of parties; the protection afforded to them; the main regulatory bodies; and issues of funding and internal democracy.

18 They include Law No. 2019/024 of 24 December 2019 to Institute the General Code of Regional and Local Authorities ("the General Code"); Law No. 91/20 of 16 December 1991 to lay down conditions governing the election of Members of Parliament; Law No. 92/10 of 17 September 1992 to lay down conditions governing the vacancy of and election to the Presidency of the Republic; Law No. 97/6 of 10 January 1997 to determine the period for the revision and recompilation of registers of electors; Law No. 2000/15 of 19 December 2000 relating to the funding of political parties and election campaigns; Law No. 2006/11 of 29 December 2006 to set up and lay down the organization and functioning of Elections Cameroon (ELECAM).

3.1 Key aspects of the regulatory framework

One of the first issues that the Political Parties Law deals with is that of actualising the freedom to form and/or join political parties. It makes it clear that no one can be compelled to join a political party or harassed for being a member of a particular party.[19] However, the law precludes armed forces and police personnel in active service from joining any political party. Any qualified Cameroonian who satisfies the conditions laid down in Article 5(1) of this law is free to form a political party. Even so, a party may be refused registration if:

- it undermines territorial integrity, national unity, the republican form of the state, the national sovereignty and national integration, including through all kinds of discrimination;
- it is based on tribes, provinces, language groups or religious denominations;
- it advocates the use of violence or contemplates the establishment of a military or paramilitary organisation;
- it receives subsidies from abroad or one of its statutory directors resides abroad; or
- it promotes belligerence between components of the nation or between countries.[20]

The application to register a political party must be addressed to the Minister of Territorial Administration through the governor of a region and accompanied by documents specified in Article 5(1) of the Political Parties Law. The law provides that the decision to authorise the legal existence of a party depends on the Minister of Territorial Administration, but where there is silence on the application for three months from the date of application, the party is deemed to exist legally.[21] There is also a provision that in the event of a refusal to authorise the party, the applicant may appeal to the President of the Administrative Court.[22]

In practice, most applications for registration of political parties in Cameroon post-1990 are approved. No fee is required for registering a party. If, as some have suggested, the idea behind making the formation

19 See Article 3(1) and (2) of the Political Parties' Law, 1990.
20 Ibid, Article 9.
21 Ibid, Article 7.
22 Ibid, Article 8.

of parties so easy was to enable their proliferation and thereby fragment the opposition, the existence today, often only on paper, of more than 367 parties is evidence that the government has succeeded in this beyond its wildest dreams. Indeed, many of these entities, which only become active during elections, are alleged to have been deliberately created by the CPDM itself and for the same reason, that is, dividing the opposition.[23]

There are no provisions in the relevant laws protecting the rights of political parties. In fact, by placing them under the Ministry of Territorial Administration (MINAT), the 1990 law exposes parties to the whims and caprices of the ruling party. For example, a group of opposition parties were vilified when, in anticipation of the 2025 elections, they started discussions in March 2024 aimed at forming an Alliance for Political Change as well as an Alliance for Political Transition. The Minister of Territorial Administration, on 12 March 2024, held a press conference at which he threatened action against the parties concerned for trying to form what he described as an illegal or clandestine alliance.[24] It is business as usual in any normal democracy for opposition parties to hold meetings to coordinate activities and form alliances, but in Cameroon this is seen as enemy action even though no law prohibits it. The Political Parties Law of 1990 confers on MINAT the sole powers to regulate the activities of political parties. Thus, unlike other African countries where independent regulatory authorities are responsible for parties – such as Nigeria, with its Inter-Party Advisory Council, Sierra Leone, with its Political Parties Registration Commission, or Kenya and its Office of the Registrar of Political Parties – Cameroon has no equivalent such body.

MINAT has also been involved in the management of multiparty elections since the reintroduction of multipartyism in 1990. In this regard, section 43 of the Electoral Code states:

23 See D Tande, "Why So Many Political Parties?" *Scribbles from the Den*, 17 June 2007, https://www.dibussi.com/2007/06/cameroon_why_so.html (accessed 1 May 2024); D Kiwuwa, "Paul Biya has been Cameroon's President for 40 Years – and He Might Win Office Again", *The Conversation*, 28 November 2022 https://theconversation.com/paul-biya-has-been-cameroons-president-for-40-years-and-he-might-win-office-yet-again-194856 (accessed 1 May 2024).

24 See press release by the Minister of Territorial Administration, 12 March 2024; *The Guardian Post Newspaper* No. 3056, 14 March 2024; *Horizon Newspaper* No. 302, 13 March 2024; *Mutations Newspaper* No. 6027, 13 March 2024; "Cameroon Government Warns Two Opposition Groups Are Illegal", *Voice of America*, 13 March 2024, https://www.voaafrica.com/a/cameroon-government-warns-two-political-groups-are-illegal/7526515.html (accessed 1 May 2024).

1) Government services shall collaborate with and support Elections Cameroon in the performance of its statutory duties.
2) The Minister in charge of territorial administration shall ensure permanent liaison between Government and Elections Cameroon. In this respect, the latter shall submit copies of minutes and progress reports to him.[25]

Since the dawn of multipartyism in Cameroon, MINAT's role has been criticised, given that the vague wording of section 43 endows it with almost absolute powers to micromanage ELECAM, the country's electoral management body. For instance, the Commonwealth Report on the 2004 presidential election in Cameroon held that MINAT was the main obstacle to holding genuine democratic elections.[26] It is, after all, MINAT, and not ELECAM, that accredits national election observers[27] and international election observers after consultation with the minister in charge of external relations.[28] In the 2018 presidential election, it accredited fake international election observers, supposedly from Transparency International (TI), who pronounced the electoral process free and fair.[29] For its part, TI issued a press release on 9 October 2018 making it plain that it had never sent any such election observer mission to Cameroon.[30] This, clearly, was a desperate attempt by the government to give a modicum of international credibility to a manifestly flawed election.[31] MINAT and ELECAM have thus in essence been serving the interests of the ruling party, rather than

25 Emphasis added.
26 See Commonwealth Secretariat, *Cameroon Presidential Election 11 October 2004: Report of the Commonwealth Observer Group* (16 October 2004), https://aceproject.org/ero-en/regions/africa/CM/cameroon-final-report-presidential-elections/view (accessed 1 May 2024).
27 See Electoral Code, section 296(2).
28 See ibid, section 296(3).
29 See "Cameroon 'Fake' Election Observers Mask the Truth about Reality of Presidential Polls", *RFI*, 11 October 2018, https://www.rfi.fr/en/africa/20181011-cameroon-fake-election-observers-mask-truth-about-reality-presidential-polls (accessed 1 May 2024).
30 See D Mumbere, "We Have No Observers in Cameroon, Transparency International", *Africa News*, 9 October 2018, https://www.africanews.com/2018/10/09/we-have-no-observers-in-cameroon-transparency-international// (accessed 1 May 2024); F Nikolas, "Trends in Electoral Fraud: The Usage of Fake Election Monitors in Cameroon and Beyond", 7 (2022) *African Humanities*, pp 6–20.
31 See T Sama, "Cameroon: 'Zombie Observers' Confuse Narrative of Dubious Elections", *Democracy in Africa*, 2018, https://democracyinafrica.org/cameroon-zombie-observers-confuse-narrative-dubious-elections/ (accessed 1 May 2024).

providing any neutral and independent platform for the management of all political parties.

As regards funding, parties in Cameroon are funded under the Electoral Code of 2012, which provides for two types of public funding. The first is a yearly subsidy provided to legally recognised political parties for recurrent administrative expenses, the dissemination of political programmes, the co-ordination of activities by party members, and preparation for elections.[32] The second type is provided in every election year for parties to prepare for election or referendum campaigns.[33] The yearly subsidy is not provided to all the legally recognised political parties but divided into two equal parts for the following categories of parties:

- the first part is allocated to political parties represented in the National Assembly, the Senate, the regional councils and/or the municipal councils; and
- the second part is allocated to political parties in accordance with the results of the last election of Members of Parliament (MPs), senators, and/or regional and municipal councillors.[34]

However, the second part of the subsidy is paid only to parties which obtained at least 5 per cent of the votes cast in at least one constituency in the last elections, and the distribution is in proportion to the results obtained. Meanwhile, the funds for election and referendum campaigns are provided in two parts:

- the first part is paid after publication of the lists of candidates to all parties, depending on the lists submitted, and endorsed in the various constituencies; and
- the second part is paid after the proclamation of results to parties proportionately to the number of seats obtained.

Section 278(1) of the Electoral Code forbids all political parties from receiving subsidies or funding from abroad, as well as from foreign persons, organisations, powers or states. The second subsection declares that "the private funding of political parties and election and referendum campaigns shall be fixed by a special instrument". This is an obscure provision whose exact purport is unclear, and the hope that this will be clarified when the

32 See Electoral Code, sections 279–280.
33 See ibid, section 284.
34 See ibid, section 281.

"special instrument" is enacted is yet to be fulfilled, as no such instrument has been enacted. Besides this, it needs to be noted that, in spite of these provisions regulating public funding of political parties, the exact amount of funds available, as well as exactly how and when they are distributed, is determined by the government through the controversial MINAT.

Finally, neither the Constitution nor any law regulating political parties says anything about internal democracy. As we will see below in section 5, the absence of a formal requirement of internal democracy has helped the ruling party strengthen its hegemony, and, conversely, been a permanent source of internal strife within opposition parties, one that has sapped their ability to compete with the one-man-dominated and deeply entrenched CPDM.

4 The multiparty farce and descent into multiparty autocracy

The trajectory of elections since the twin elections of 1992, and in particular the performance of the ruling party vis-à-vis opposition parties, well illustrates the farce that is Cameroonian multipartyism. As Table 1 shows, the enormous public support which the opposition, especially the SDF, once enjoyed has all but disappeared. Biya has not only steadily neutralised a once-vibrant opposition polity that nearly removed him from power but, under the cloak of democracy, returned the country to its pre-1990 status as a repressive, one-party dictatorship.

Having begun with the 48.9 per cent of 180 seats that it won in the 1992 parliamentary elections, the CPDM is now in complete control of Parliament, gaining 60.6 per cent in 1997, 82.8 per cent in 2002, 85 per cent in 2007, 82.2 per cent in 2011, and 84.2 per cent in 2020. For their part, all opposition parties combined have seen a decline from the 51.1 per cent majority they enjoyed in 1992 and the 39.4 per cent share they had in 1997 to a merely token presence, with 17.2 per cent of seats in 2002, 15 per cent in 2007, 17.8 per cent in 2011, and 15.8 per cent in 2020.

Perhaps the biggest loser has been the once-formidable SDF. After boycotting the 1992 election, it won 43 seats (23.9 per cent) in the 1997 election, dropped to 22 seats (12.2 per cent) in 2002 and went further down to 16 seats (8.9 per cent) in 2007, after which it had a slight increase to 18 seats (10.0 per cent) in 2013. In the current parliament following the 2020 election, its fortunes plummeted, winning only five seats (2.8 per cent).

Table 1: Party-political shares in Cameroon's 180-seat parliament (1992–2020)

Political parties[35]	1992		1997		2002		2007		2013		2020	
	No. MPs	%	No. MPs	%	No. MPs	%	No. MPs	%	No. MPs	%	No. MPs	%
CPDM	88	48.9	116	60.6	149	82.8	153	85.0	148	82.2	152	84.4
SDF	Boycotted		43	23.9	22	12.2	16	8.9	18	10.0	5	2.8
UNDP	68	37.8	13	7.2	1	0.6	6	3.3	5	2.8	7	3.8
UPC	18	10.0	1	0.6	3	1.7	-	-	3	1.7	-	-
MDR	6	3.3	1	0.6	-	-	-	-	1	0.6	2	1.1
UDC	Boycotted		5	2.8	5	2.8	4	2.2	4	2.2	4	2.4
MP	-	-	-	-	-	-	1	0.6	-	-	-	-
MLJC	-	-	1	0.6	-	-	-	-	-	-	-	-
MRC	-	-			-	-	-	-	1	0.6	-	-
PCRN	-	-	-	-	-	-	-	-	-	-	5	2.8
USM	-	-	-	-	-	-	-	-	-	-	2	1.1
FSNC	-	-	-	-	-	-	-	-	--		3	1.7

What could explain the catastrophic performance of opposition parties in Cameroon and the steep decline in their support?

5. Reasons for multiparty democracy's bleak prospects

One basic answer is that the government was quick to grab the tiger of multiparty democracy by the tail and tame it before Cameroonians could realise what genuine multipartyism is about; or, to put it differently, the seed of multiparty democracy that the SDF planted in 1990 was destroyed before it could germinate. The result is that the system which the government has entrenched for the past 30 years makes it extremely unlikely that any opposition party could ever win elections. The more detailed reasons may be summarised under eight heads:

- continual manipulation of electoral laws and electoral district boundaries (section 5.1);
- restrictions on voting access in opposition strongholds (section 5.2);

35 MP is the French acronym for the Progressive Party; MLJC, for the Movement for the Liberation of Cameroonian Youths; MRC, for the Cameroon Renaissance Movement; PCRN, for the Cameroon Party for National Reconciliation; USM, for the Union of Socialists Movement; and FSNC, for the Front for the National Salvation of Cameroon.

- intimidation and violence against opposition leaders and supporters (section 5.3);
- co-option and neutralisation of opposition leaders (section 5.4);
- division amongst opposition parties (section 5.5);
- misuse of public funds for political parties (section 5.6);
- absence of constitutionalism and respect for the rule of law (section 5.7); and
- continued international support for the incumbent regime (section 5.8).

5.1 Manipulation of electoral laws and electoral districts

In spite of demands by opposition parties since 1990, the government has refused to have an open discussion with them and other stakeholders aimed at reforming the electoral laws by consensus. It has instead regularly used its parliamentary majority to revise these laws in a manner that favours the ruling party. Two examples of this will suffice.

Basing her arguments on empirical research in urban centres in Cameroon, Albaugh describes three strategies the government has used not only to entrench autocracy but emasculate the opposition.[36] One of these has been the manipulation of electoral district boundaries. Using geographic information system (GIS) software to map Cameroon's electoral constituencies for 1992, 1997, 2002 and 2007, she undertook an analysis of changes to electoral boundaries between 1992 and 2010. Since 1992, Albaugh finds, gerrymandering of electoral districts has occurred in several ways.

The basis for this manipulation is contained in the 2012 Electoral Code, which repeats similar provisions in earlier laws. It states in section 149 that the division shall constitute an electoral constituency, but adds: "However, certain electoral constituencies could be warded on the grounds of their peculiar situation by a decree of the President of the Republic." Section 150(2) also states: "A decree by the President of the Republic shall fix the number of members representing each constituency." What this means is that the President has absolute power to carve out electoral constituencies by decree, as well as determine the number of members that will represent a

36 For a detailed discussion, see EA Albaugh, "An Autocrat's Toolkit: Adaptation and Manipulation in 'Democratic' Cameroon", in G Crawford and G Lynch (eds.), *Democratization in Africa: Challenges and Prospects*, London, Routledge (2012), pp 388–414.

constituency, with no provision made for objective criteria that could guide the process. This has a number of implications.

The first is reflected in the distribution of population per parliamentary seat. For example, in the opposition strongholds of the Littoral and North regions, there were 138,000 persons and 121,000 persons per parliamentary seat, respectively, whereas in the ruling party's stronghold of the South region, there were only 58,000 persons per seat in the 2007 parliamentary elections.[37] In other words, the allocation of seats has no bearing on population size.

Secondly, these irregularities were pronounced in anglophone regions, particularly so in the home ground of the SDF. For example, in the South region, voters in Dja et Lobo Division – Biya's home region, with 121,000 inhabitants – elected five MPs, which is the same number of MPs obtained by voters in Mezam Division (the SDF's home region), with a population of 313,000 – that is, about 2.5 times as large as the one in Dja et Lobo. In this instance, it "cost" the CPDM 24,200 votes to get one seat, while the same thing would have cost the SDF the considerably higher price of 62,600 votes.

Thirdly, the allocation of seats within districts in each region is even more arbitrary: with each election, this has been redrawn in a manner that increasingly favours the ruling party. As a result, urban centres, where opposition parties have strong support, have been allocated fewer seats in municipal elections than are allocated to rural areas, where the ruling party has its main support base. Perhaps the most profound distortion in this regard was effected through a series of presidential decrees made after the 1997 elections.[38]

Cameroon has a mixed electoral system combining multi-member districts and single-member districts.[39] In the case of the former, the party with the absolute majority of votes takes all the seats, and if no party has such a majority, the seats are split proportionately. By contrast, in the single-member district, the party with the highest number of votes takes the seat. Because the seats in a single-member district can be won by a simple majority, this lowers the threshold for the strongest party. Mindful of the

37 Ibid, p 121 and footnote 54.

38 As previously indicated, the basis for these frequent distortions of electoral constituencies is section 150(2) of the Electoral Code, which gives the President the right to set by decree the number of members representing each constituency.

39 See Electoral Code, sections 152 and 172.

divisions within opposition parties, the government after 1992 strategically redrew electoral districts by changing numerous multi-member districts into single-member districts, as well as creating many more single-member districts. The effect was that the CPDM won most of the seats in single-member districts. As Albaugh shows, while the ruling party in 1992 won 88 parliamentary seats (that is, 49 per cent of the legislature) on a 38.9 per cent share of the vote, in 1997 – as a result of the manipulation – it won 116 seats (that is, 64 per cent of the legislature) with a lower voting share of 37 per cent.[40]

The manipulation of electoral districts in Cameroon has gone hand in hand with other equally dubious constitutional and legislative changes. These have been designed to perpetuate the ruling party's control of regional and local authorities, especially in any opposition strongholds that it loses in elections. It has effected this through a medley of vague and undefined concepts, introduced in the 1996 Constitution, which purport to apply a decentralised system of governance through regional and local authorities.[41]

The preamble to the Constitution and Article 57(2) in particular provide, inter alia, that the regional council shall reflect the various sociological components of the region.[42] The Electoral Code – in addition to imposing a questionable residency requirement of six months[43] – similarly requires that candidates and electoral lists reflect the sociological components of their constituencies.[44] The stated objective is to "protect" marginalised or autochthonous ethnic groups in urban centres where they have become a minority. However, neither the Constitution nor any of the several pieces of legislation adopted to implement this provides any indication of who these minorities or indigenous populations are or what is meant by the "sociological components" of a region. Since 1996, the government has regularly used the pretext of protecting minorities after regional and local council elections to appoint ruling-party loyalists to head local authorities in areas

40 See generally Albaugh, *supra* n. 40.

41 See articles 55–62 of the Constitution. Law No. 2019/024 of 24 December 2019 contains several provisions for instituting the General Code of Regional and Local Authorities ("the General Code").

42 Article 57(3) of the Constitution also provides that "the regional council shall be headed by an indigene of the region elected from among its members for the life of the council".

43 See Electoral Code, section 175(1) and (2). (See also section 5.2 of this chapter.).

44 See ibid, sections 151 (3), 151 (4)(e) and 171(3).

won by opposition parties. In other words, it has exploited the politics of indigeneity in order to neutralise unfavourable electoral outcomes in most major urban centres by usurping control of local authorities which it lost in elections.

Indeed, the General Code allows the government to go even further than this and in effect reverse unfavourable electoral outcomes. The most strategic administrative positions in all local authorities are reserved for people appointed mostly by the President or, in a few instances, his ministers in charge of local authorities or finance. These include the head of the local authority's administration (the Secretary General),[45] the Public Independent Conciliator (provided for only in the North-West and South-West regions),[46] the Finance Controller, and the regional and council treasurers as well as other officials in the regional accounting office.[47] Thus, regardless of the political party that has a majority and is hence supposed to run the local authority, all of those who hold key administrative and financial positions are appointed by the central government and accountable to it – and, for political reasons, may not want to cooperate with a local authority controlled by an opposition party.

Over and above this, the so-called decentralisation provided for in the General Code (which in practice is nothing more than an attempt at deconcentration of powers) has provided an opportunity for the ruling party to distribute rewards to those regions and local authorities that vote for it, to attract new supporters, and to sanction those areas that vote for opposition parties. The government has since 1992 ensured that there is little development funding for projects in opposition strongholds, thus making the economic cost of voting for the opposition high. As a result, many opposition areas are compelled out of desperation to vote for the ruling party so as to attract government development assistance.[48]

45 See General Code, sections 214(1), 323(1), 324(1), and 366.

46 See ibid, section 368(1).

47 See ibid, sections 436(1), 439(1), 439(2), and 439(3).

48 For further discussion, see CM Fombad, "Cameroon and the Anomalies of Decentralisation with a Centralist Mindset", in CM Fombad and N Steytler (eds.), *Decentralisation and Constitutionalism in Africa*, Oxford, OUP (2019), pp 326–364.

5.2 Restrictions on voting access in opposition strongholds

Numerous tactics are used to make registration and voting difficult in opposition strongholds. In a post-2007 election survey of voter-registration experiences in four urban locations, each in four different regions (Yaoundé in the Centre region, Ebolowa in the South region, Douala in the Littoral region, and Buea in the South-West region), Albaugh arrived at findings that confirm the widespread reports of targeted disenfranchisement in opposition strongholds.[49]

She found that nearly 90 per cent of Bulu and Ewondo speakers (from Biya's Centre and South regions' stronghold) were able to obtain their voting cards; this contrasts sharply with only 30 per cent of respondents in the English-speaking North-West regions. The latter region has consistently had the lowest rate of registration per population. More generally, registration figures from 2002 to 2007 show that there was a decrease in the number of registered voters in the two largest cities in the country, Douala and Yaoundé – by 18 per cent and 25 per cent, respectively – which is less than population growth would have predicted.

In most opposition areas, voting cards are available either at the mayor's office or in the palaces of traditional rulers. Whilst the former makes registration processes so needlessly complicated that it discourages many potential voters, the latter (traditional rulers), many of whom depend on government largesse, are open supporters of the ruling party and do not hesitate to register, and issue cards to, only people whom they are certain will vote for the ruling party.

Perhaps the most serious problem of all (briefly mentioned earlier) has been the abuse of the six-months' residency requirement. This has been applied arbitrarily, particularly in the South-West region, to bar pro-SDF supporters from registering to vote in their area of residence; when they then try to do so in their area of origin instead, they are referred back to their area of residence and asked to apply for a certificate of residency, which in most cases is never issued. All of these registration restrictions are applied so as to favour the ruling party.[50]

---

49 See Albaugh, *supra* n. 40, pp 125–128.

50 Ibid.

5.3 Intimidation and violence against opposition leaders and supporters

Opposition parties are considered an essential feature of modern liberal democracy. They are supposed to challenge the ruling party on issues of governance and propose alternatives to extant policies. Yet ever since the Biya government bowed to pressure to accept multipartyism, it has failed to come to terms with the idea that opposition parties are fellow interlocutors deserving respect rather than enemies warranting demonisation. The mould was cast long ago in the 1990s when Biya would show his contempt for opposition parties by routinely castigating them as "thugs", "outlaws", "hooligans", "merchants of illusion", and unpatriotic "self-seeking political opportunists" with nothing to offer Cameroonians.[51]

One may argue that over the last 30 years the government has taken as its guiding principle the Machiavellian notion that enemies must either be lured by co-option into sharing the spoils of power (as we will see in the next section) or systematically annihilated. Indeed, since 1990, the political environment has been extremely hostile to opposition leaders and their supporters. There have been innumerable accounts, particularly in the media, detailing various forms of harassment and intimidation, ranging from arbitrary arrest and torture to imprisonment and death at the hands of security forces. Opposition rallies are regularly banned or, when sometimes authorised, violently broken up if the authorities perceive a threat to law and order.

Perhaps a few incidents in the last few years will serve to illustrate the extremes to which the government is prepared to go in order to make it life-threatening to become an opposition leader or be seen to be one of such a leader's prominent supporter. One of the most recent waves of repression occurred after the October 2018 presidential elections, which ended with Biya being declared the winner. When the results were announced, Maurice Kamto, the leader of the MRC, who had been declared the runner-up after Biya, claimed that he was the actual winner and called for nationwide protests.[52] The government responded with a crackdown and use of excessive force by the police, army, and gendarmes.

51 See Fombad and Fonyam, *supra* n. 9, p 473.

52 See "Cameroon: Government Bans Opposition Coalitions Solidifies Crackdown on Free Association, Expression Ahead of 2025 Vote", *Human Rights Watch*, 21 March 2024, https://www.hrw.org/news/2024/03/21/cameroon-government-bans-opposition-coalitions (accessed 1 May 2024); Amsterdam & Partners LLP, "One Minute to

In January 2019, Kamto, along with more than 200 of his supporters, was arrested and detained on charges of insurrection, inciting insurrection, hostility against the homeland, criminal association, threats to public order and rebellion – crimes that can carry the death penalty. He was freed on 5 October 2019, and the charges dropped, after the intervention of the French president, Emmanuel Macron, although the crackdown on the opposition continued.[53] At present, 41 opposition members, including Olivier Bibou Nissack and Alain Fogue Tedom, two of the MRC's leaders, remain behind bars after having been sentenced to seven years.

In September 2020, Cameroonian authorities banned demonstrations across the country after Kamto's MRC exhorted people to take to the streets over the government's decision to hold regional elections in December 2020. Opposition parties had expressed concerns that the elections could not be conducted freely and fairly without reforming the electoral code and addressing the lack of security in the country's minority anglophone regions, where separatist groups and security forces have repeatedly clashed. When the protests went ahead, security forces fired water cannons and teargas and arrested more than 550 people, mainly opposition-party members and supporters. Many peaceful protesters were beaten and mistreated while being arrested and kept in detention. Kamto himself was rearrested on 20 September 2020 and held under de facto house arrest until 8 December, with a heavy security presence outside his residence. The authorities never charged him or gave an explanation for his house arrest.[54]

In this vein, it is to be recorded that, at the time of this writing, the countdown to the 2025 presidential and parliamentary elections has begun, as has the usual clampdown on opposition parties. For example, as mentioned, two parties that were discussing the possibility of forming an alliance to contest the 2025 elections were threatened with a ban by the Minister of Territorial Administration. It is also true, nonetheless, that the use of intimidation and violence is not necessarily the government's

---

Midnight: The Cameroon Crisis", White Paper, April 2021, https://robertamsterdam.com/wp-content/uploads/2021/04/One-Minute-to-Midnight-The-Cameroon-Crisis-Amsterdam-and-Partners-LLP.pdf (accessed 1 May 2024).

53 See F Foute, "Emmanuel Macron Remarks Spark Public Outcry in Cameroon", *The Africa Report*, 26 February 2020, https://www.theafricareport.com/23912/emmanuel-macron-remarks-spark-public-outcry-in-cameroon/ (accessed 1 May 2024).

54 See "Cameroon: Repression Marks Crackdown Anniversary", *Amnesty International*, 22 September 2021, https://www.amnesty.org/en/latest/news/2021/09/cameroon-repression-marks-crackdown-anniversary/ (accessed 1 May 2024).

first recourse in every instance; often it resorts to these measures only after opposition parties and leaders have resisted nullification by other, less heavy-handed means – namely, seduction into co-option by the ruling party.

5.4 Co-option and the neutralisation of opposition leaders

There is no doubt that one of Biya's most successful strategies for countering meaningful and effective multipartyism and any potential threat from opposition parties and their leaders is co-opting and neutralising the most threatening of them. This has been combined with a policy of divide-and-rule. In fact, this has been one of the government's strategies right from the outset in the 1990s, as is evident in its policy of trying to drive a wedge between the two anglophone North-West and South-West regions – this was something that weakened the foundations of the SDF, even if the latter's eventual collapse was caused by other factors.[55] Biya has survived for so long due in good part to his successful capture, early in the multiparty era, of key opposition leaders when it mattered most, taming them and moving them away from confrontation to collaboration. It has resulted in what may be termed a pacified democracy with a "domesticated opposition".[56]

One of the hallmarks of the Biya era has been the entrenchment of a nationwide system of patronage networks in which core elites are allowed to amass wealth by looting the government treasury, albeit not as a right but as a privilege.[57] Corruption is the oil that greases the wheels of the ruling party. Ministries and posts are created to accommodate party loyalists, but

55 For more on this "divide-and-rule" strategy and its impact on the SDF, see Konings, *supra* n. 9 , pp 11–16; F Nyamnjoh and M Rowlands, "Elite Associations and the Politics of Belonging in Cameroon", 68(3) (1998) *Africa: Journal of the International African Institute*, pp 320–337.

56 See B Ndjio, "Millennial Democracy and Spectral Reality in Post-colonial Africa", 11(2) (2008) *African Journal of International Affairs*, pp 142–147.

57 Under this dispensation, you are free to use your position to enrich yourself as long as you do not become too ambitious and try to use your ill-gotten gains to threaten Biya's position: the price for this is heavy indeed. See generally CM Fombad, "The Dynamics of Record-breaking Endemic Corruption and Corruption and Political Opportunism in Cameroon", in JM Mbaku and J Takougang (eds.), *The Leadership Challenge in Africa: Cameroon Under Paul Biya,* Africa World Press, Trenton NJ (2004), pp 357–394; S Kamga and CM Fombad, "The Cameroonian Special Criminal Court: The Futility of Combating Corruption Where the Basics of Constitutionalism

what has been a key factor in the regime's survival is that this is also used to woo and absorb leaders of opposition parties and other defectors in their ranks. Thus, a once-vibrant opposition has been reduced to a group of lethargic, self-seeking opportunists, each aspiring to become sufficiently threatening to be invited to join Biya's patronage network.

Table 2 below illustrates these points by presenting a selection of leaders of political parties who have been co-opted and rewarded with government ministerial appointments, even when it was clear that the parties they were supposed to lead enjoyed little popular support.

Table 2: Co-option of selected opposition parties and leaders into governments of national unity since 1992

Political leaders co-opted	Political parties	Periods of appointments and portfolios	No. of seats in Parliament
1. Issa Tchiroma Bakary	UNDP	Served from 1992 to 1996 as minister of transport. He was one of the first opposition leaders to be co-opted.	68
	FSNC	Left the UNDP and formed the FSNC. Appointed and served from 2009 to 2019 as minister of communication.	No seat
		Serving since 2019 as minister of employment and vocational training.	3
2. Hamadou Moustapha	UNDP	Served as deputy prime minister for urban planning and housing from 1992 to 1997.	68
	ANDP[58]	Left the UNDP and formed the ANDP. Appointed as minister in charge of special duties at the presidency, where he has served since 2004 up to the present.	No seat
3. Dakole Daissala	MDR	Minister of state for post and telecommunication from 1992 to 1997, together with four others from MDR. His party formed a coalition with the CPDM that enabled the latter to have an absolute majority in the 1992 parliament.	6
		Served as minister of transport from 2004 to 2007.	No seat
		In 2013 Biya appointed him as one of 30 appointed senators.	1
4. Augustin Frédéric Kodock	UPC	Served as minister of state for planning and regional development from 1992 to 1994.	18
		Served as minister of state for agriculture from 1994 to 1997. He was dropped in 1997 and his party's faction leader, Henri Hogbe Nlend, was co-opted.	18
		Served as minister of state for agriculture from 2002 to 2004.	3

are Absent", in CM Fombad and N Steytler (eds.), *Corruption and Constitutionalism in Africa: Revisiting Control Measures and Strategies* Oxford, OUP (2020), pp 417–435.

58 ANDP is the French acronym for the National Alliance for Democracy and Progress.

Political leaders co-opted	Political parties	Periods of appointments and portfolios	No. of seats in Parliament
		Served as minister of state for planning from 2004 to 2007	3
5. Bello Bouba Maigari	UNDP	Served as minister of industrial development from 1997 to 2004. He initially condemned members of his party (Issa Tchiroma and Hamadou Moustapha) who had been co-opted before him in 1992.	13
		Served as minister of state for post and telecommunications from 2004 to 2009.	1
		Served as minister of state for transport from 2009 to 2011.	6
		Served as minister of state for tourism and leisure from 2011 to 2019.	5
		Serving since 2019 as minister of state for tourism and leisure.	7
6. Henri Hogbe Nlend	UPC	Served as minister of scientific and technical research from 1997 to 2002. He was appointed when his party's faction leader, Augustin Frédéric Kodock, was dropped from government.	1
7. Hele Piere	UNDP	Serving as minister of environment, nature, and sustainable development since 2004. A close ally of Bello Bouba Maigari.	See UNDP seats from 2004 to the present.
8. Momo Jean de Dieu	PADDEC	Serving since 2019 as minister delegate to the minister of justice, keeper of the seals; he turned from a vocal critic of the regime to make a U-turn prior to the 2018 presidential elections and support Biya.	No seat

The list above is by no means a comprehensive record of the opponents of the government who have been co-opted over the years. For example, Biya's most vocal opponent today, Maurice Kamto, had been co-opted and appointed minister delegate to the Minister of Justice and keeper of the seals from 2004 to 2011, after which he resigned to form his own party, the MRC; before then, he had been, as he is now again, an outspoken critic of the regime. With that being noted, several observations can be made to show how Biya's strategy of co-option has been designed not with a view to a more inclusive system of governance but rather (as pointed out above) to neutralise the opposition and thwart any genuine multipartyism.

First, the loss of the CPDM's parliamentary majority in 1992 certainly meant that the ruling party needed to form a coalition in order to have a parliamentary majority, but the CPDM did more than form a governing coalition. It brought in the UNDP with its 68 seats, the UPC with its 18 seats, and the MDR with its six seats, with their leaders being given fairly important ministerial positions. The effect was that, right at the outset of the first supposedly multiparty parliament, there was no real opposition to the government: in other words, the only opposition parties were promptly captured and tamed by virtue of being part of the government coalition.

This coincided with Biya's declaring himself winner of the 1992 presidential election, one which most objective commentators and election observers said he had lost.

Secondly, from 1992 until the last parliamentary elections in 2020, as a result of the co-option of the leaders of the UNDP, UPC, MDR, ANDP and FSNC, the effective share of parliamentary opposition parties in Cameroon's Parliament was as follows:

- 0 per cent from 1992 to 1997;
- 26.7 per cent from 1997 to 2002 (consisting of the SDF with 43 MPs and the UDC with five);
- 11.7 per cent from 2002 to 2007 (consisting of the SDF with 16 MPs, UDC with four, and MP with one);
- 12.8 per cent from 2007 to 2013 (consisting of the SDF with 18 MPs, UDC with four, and MRC with one); and
- 9.1 per cent from 2013 to 2020 (consisting of the SDF with five MPs, the UDC with four, PCRN with five, and USM with two).

This means that, since 1992, the effective political-party representation in Cameroon's National Assembly by opposition parties that were not part of the ruling parliamentary majority was on average made up of only 15 per cent of the 180 MPs in Parliament. With such a token genuine opposition presence in Parliament, the opposition parties that joined the ruling party have served only to give the regime a veneer of democratic legitimacy that helps it disguise what is in effect a continuation of the illegitimate and repressive pre-1990 autocratic system.

Thirdly, certain categories of civil servants – namely, the security forces who are responsible for law and order (most of whose service heads are people from Biya's ethnic group), the members of the judiciary who act as election supervisors, and the senior administrative officials who also act as election supervisors – are placed on much higher salaries than the rest of the civil servants. As a result, they have a stake in the survival of the regime and will do everything necessary to keep it in power. The same is true of the administrators who are appointed by the President to the various electoral commissions at local, regional and national level.[59]

Finally, it is clear that the level of support for the ruling party has progressively increased over the years whilst that for opposition parties has been decreasing. The most dramatic drop is in the support for the once

59 See Electoral Code, sections 64, 68 and 191.

most popular opposition party, which took considerable risks in the 1990s to force a return to political pluralism. In the first parliamentary election that it contested, it was able, in spite of the rigging machinery used by the regime, to win 43 parliamentary seats, with 23.9 per cent of the popular vote. This declined, and in the 2020 parliamentary elections, it won only five seats (with 2.8 per cent of the popular vote) and also lost its position as the main opposition party, a position now occupied by the UNDP, with seven seats, but which is part of the government. The government has indeed been resoundingly successful in its co-option of those critical to its survival – and divisions within the ranks of the genuine opposition have not helped the latter's cause either.

5.5 Divisions within opposition ranks

Since much has been written about how opposition parties in Cameroon have contributed to their present predicament,[60] we will simply highlight some of the main problems they created for themselves. In many respects, opposition parties have been their own worst enemies and made it easy for the ruling party to cling to power in spite of its record of corruption, gross mismanagement of the economy, and overall incompetence.

The proliferation of opposition parties (367 at the last count) – parties with little ideological content, no clearly constructed alternative programmes, and no agenda to cultivate and nurture – has not helped. A mushrooming of political parties has never on its own produced democracy. This is particularly so in Cameroon, where it hardly costs anything to form a party and where many of the parties exist in name only. In fact, at a time of economic crisis in the early 1990s, the Biya government encouraged the formation of parties by rewarding any party that participated in the ill-conceived parliamentary elections of 1992 with CFA 500 million.[61]

In the 1990s the government sponsored a number of "mushroom parties" run by individuals whose mission was to sow discord within the ranks of

60 See, for example, Fombad and Fonyam, supra, n. 9; J Takougang, "The 2002 Legislative Election in Cameroon: A Retrospective on Cameroon's Stalled Democracy Movement", 41(3) (2003) *Journal of Modern African Studies*, pp 421–435; Konings *supra* n. 9, pp 16–20; G Ngwane, "The Opposition and their Performance of Electoral Power in Cameroon (1992–2007)", *gngwane.com*, n.d., https://www.gngwane.com/files/cameroon_opposition_and_electoral_performance.pdf (accessed 1 May 2024).

61 See Konings, *supra* n. 9, p 8.

the opposition parties that had been struggling to form a united front. It has now become clear that many so-called opposition parties, such as the UNDP, UPC, MDR, and FSNC (parties whose leaders in some cases have been in government continuously since 1992), were formed strategically not to promote a policy agenda but to provide an opportunity for them to negotiate with Biya to share in the spoils of power. It was these leaders that in the early 1990s not only betrayed the cause of the opposition parties but sowed the seeds of the discord and division that persist today.

The divisions and ultimate betrayal within the ranks of the opposition started at the very early stages of the reintroduction of multipartyism. At the time when the SDF and its leader enjoyed nationwide popularity that not only threatened the survival of the CPDM but far surpassed that of the other newly formed parties, the most prominent being Bello Bouba Maigari of the UNDP and Ndam Njoya of the UDC, these parties and a host of others met to discuss the possibility of putting forward a single candidate to contest the presidential elections of 1992. What emerged then, and has been the pattern since, was that none of the francophone opposition leaders were ready to support a coalition led by Fru Ndi or any anglophone leader. This became apparent in the muted reaction of Ndam Njoya and Bello Bouba Maigari to the serious election irregularities and human rights violations in the North-West region when the people protested against what was widely regarded as Fru Ndi's "stolen victory".

The fragmentation of the opposition was aggravated by contradictions. As noted above, neither the Constitution nor any of the laws regulating political parties says anything about internal democracy. As a result, the leadership of opposition parties has displayed all the authoritarian tendencies, intolerance of dissenting views, and personality-cult dynamics of which they accuse Biya and his government. This, more than anything else, explains why the once-dominant SDF, which started as a national party set to replace the CPDM, degenerated into an anglophone, a regional, an ethnic, and, finally, a personal party.

Fru Ndi led the party from 1990 until his death on 12 June 2023 when a new party chairman, Joshua Osih, the former deputy chairman, was elected on 28 October 2023. Before his death, anybody who dared challenge Fru Ndi's leadership was demonised and purged from the party. The increasing perception over the years that it was an anglophone party cost it the broad support it once enjoyed in the francophone regions. It was finally Fru Ndi's intolerance and elimination of all potential leaders who disagreed with him or threatened his position that resulted in many senior officials leaving the party.

What happened within the SDF has happened to almost all other opposition parties. Those who created these parties have remained leaders and, in most cases, those members who threatened their positions were also, as in the case of the SDF, purged and, like Hamadou Moustapha and Issa Tchiroma Bakary of the UNDP (see Table 2), who left and formed their own parties.

5.6 Political-party funding and abuse of incumbency

Substantial sums of public funds are set aside for the funding of political parties. The manner in which this is distributed is heavily skewed in favour of the ruling party, as its historical domination of the National Assembly, along with its 100 per cent control of the Senate after the 2023 elections, has meant that most of the funding goes to itself. Even when the government allocates money, there is no guarantee that it will be paid as promised. For example, during the campaign for the presidential elections of 2004, the SDF was promised CFA 400 million but allegedly received only CFA 46 million.[62]

Besides the limited public funding which is made available to the opposition, there are several other obstacles to the effective operation of opposition parties. They have very limited access to state-owned media, comprising radio and television channels as well as a newspaper (the *Cameroon Tribune*); the latter are all controlled by the government and openly serve as the semi-official propaganda mouthpiece of the ruling party. In addition, as mentioned, the officials of the main bodies responsible for elections, MINAT and ELECAM, are appointed, controlled, and answerable to the government.[63] Finally, because all senior officials are appointed by the government, they are required, especially during election periods, to go out to their regions of origin to campaign for the ruling party. Some of these abuses of incumbency by the ruling party could have been checked in a

62 See D Tande, "State Funding of Political Parties: A Democratic Imperative or Hush Money for the Opposition?" *Scribbles from the Den*, 18 July 2007, https://www.dibussi.com/2007/07/state-funding-o.html (accessed 1 May 2024).

63 For the appointment of the senior officials of ELECAM, see sections 12 and 24 of the Electoral Code. Although the President is required to consult opposition parties and other stakeholders, this is a mere ritual.

system where the rule of law is in force, but as we will see, this is not the case in Cameroon.

5.7 The absence of the fundamentals of constitutionalism and the rule of law

After Eritrea, Cameroon has the weakest constitution in Africa. It lacks all the fundamentals of constitutionalism, in the sense that the constitutional protection of human rights is very weak.[64] Equally weak is the system of separation of powers, which allows considerable scope for arbitrary changes to the Constitution at the whim of the President. Yet perhaps the biggest challenges to constitutionalism and effective operation of the rule of law lie in two basic flaws of the Constitution.

First, the system of constitutional review, in which reviews are carried out exclusively by the Constitutional Council (a body that also has exclusive powers to resolve electoral disputes), is deeply flawed. All the members of this council are appointed directly or indirectly by the President, and their appointment does not depend on any objectively stated criteria other than loyalty to the government. The chances of their ruling against the government are thus remote, to say the least. Indeed, the furthest they have come to being objective was when the Supreme Court deliberated on the controversial presidential elections in 1992 and, much like Pontius Pilate, made the flabbergasting declaration that although there were discomfiting irregularities, its duty was only to declare the results, and not to investigate electoral irregularities.[65] Since then, the Constitutional Council has indeed applied itself to investigating such irregularities, albeit in a manner that serves the government's interest.

The second flaw is especially troubling: the country lacks an independent judiciary. Judges are all appointed by the President and virtually serve at his pleasure.[66] The net effect of this is that Cameroon is a classic example of a state governed according to the personal rule of one man, its president,

---

64 For a discussion of the fundamentals of constitutionalism, see CM Fombad, "Challenges to Constitutionalism and Constitutional Rights in Africa and the Enabling Role of Political Parties: Lessons and Perspectives from Southern Africa", 55 (2007) *American Journal of Comparative Law*, pp 1–46.

65 See Fombad and Fonyam, *supra* n. 9, pp 480–481.

66 See CM Fombad, "Judicial Power in Cameroon's Amended Constitution of 18 January 1996", 9 (1996) *Lesotho Law Journal*, pp 1–11.

where elections are a ritual and constitutionalism and the rule of law are a forlorn hope. Moreover, as we will now see, the ruling elite and its patronage network of colluding "opposition" parties have nothing to fear from external pressure and criticism.

5.8 Continued international support for the Biya government

The first and probably only elections that the Biya regime allowed national and international election observers to observe freely were the twin 1992 elections. After the presidential elections of that year drew heavy criticism, particularly in the report of the NDI in 1992 and that of the Commonwealth in 2007, the regime took to being highly selective in deciding which election observers to allow entry to. For the 2020 elections, it all but kept them out and instead created its own fictitious international election observer team from TI, which as we saw earlier, quickly disassociated itself from this claim.

In the aftermath of the 1992 presidential elections and the repressive state of emergency declared in the North-West region for three months, most Western governments, except France, not only condemned the Biya government but also imposed various sanctions or suspended loans to it. This aggravated an economy that was already under strain from previous nationwide strikes, and a collapse was averted only due to financial support provided by France.

In fact, French influence has had, and continues to have, a negative impact on the operation of multipartyism in Cameroon. After the controversial 1992 presidential elections, the French minister of interior justified France's support for the government by declaring that "an Anglophone cannot be president of Cameroon".[67] The French did everything they could to counter the threat posed by the SDF and its charismatic leader, Fru Ndi. Not only did they fabricate stories claiming that Fru Ndi was involved in illegal arms imports, but the French Ambassador in Cameroon, Gilles Vidal, and other French embassy officials undertook missions to the strongholds of the SDF in the francophone regions to persuade them to abandon the party.[68]

---

67 See TN Fonchingong, "Multipartyism and Democratization in Cameroon", 15(2) (1998) *Journal of Third World Studies*, pp 119–136, 130.

68 Ibid, pp 130–131.

Continuous French support over the years has not only contributed to the demise of the SDF and other parties that could threaten the Biya government but in fact is behind the present military operations which the government is conducting in the two anglophone regions.[69] In some cases, the French have gone to absurd lengths. For example, in the 2004 presidential elections, the French president, Jacques Chirac, embarrassed even the francophone election observer mission when he sent a message of congratulations to President Biya commending him for his "brilliant" re-election even though the results had not yet all come in and the vote counting commission had barely begun to work.[70]

Given that France has made francophone Africa its fiefdom through its *francafrique* policies,[71] most Western countries have left it to manage these countries as it wishes. In fact, the attitude of many of them, particularly the United Kingdom, Canada, Germany, and the US, is increasingly ambivalent. Their criticism of the situation in Cameroon has become muted. This is so because, on the one hand, they prefer to support the devil they know who can maintain peace and stability, regardless of the implications for democracy; on the other hand, their indifference to the abuses of democratic process is dictated by the objective of promoting their national economic interests and that of their companies, many of which have lucrative contracts in Cameroon's huge natural and mineral resources sector.

It is not clear whether France in particular and the West at large have learnt from the French debacles in Burkina Faso, Mali, and Niger, which led not only to coups d'état in these countries but the replacement of the French by the Russians, with the Chinese waiting in the wings. At present, it could be argued that China and Russia have joined the French in supporting the Biya government and ensuring its survival as the best way to promote their own economic interests.

---

69 After President Macron's visit to Cameroon in July 2022, he appointed General Thierry Marchand, head of the Directorate of Security and Defence Cooperation and a person with extensive experience in military training and operations across Africa, as France's new ambassador to Cameroon.

70 See B Adams, "SDF Protests Chirac's Congratulations to Biya", *PostNewsLine*, 18 October 2004, https://www.postnewsline.com/2004/10/strongsdf_prote.html (accessed 1 May 2024). The SDF protested "vehemently" at this interference by the French government.

71 See T Korkmaz, '"La Françafrique": The Special Relationship between France and Its Former Colonies in Africa', *Insamer*, 2 August 2019, https://en.insamer.com/la-francafrique-the-special-relationship-between-france-and-its-former-colonies-in-africa_2307.html (accessed 1 May 2024).

6. Conclusion

President Biya reluctantly revived multipartyism in Cameroon in the 1990s. Whilst he weathered the early storm that came with the transition from a one-party repressive autocracy, he has done no more than transform the country into a repressive multiparty democratic autocracy in which elections are the same symbolic rituals they were before the 1990s. Unlike in the past, there is, in addition to a constitutional framework, an elaborate set of laws that regulates the operation of political parties, but this is merely part of the sophisticated autocratic toolkit put in place to keep the ruling party in power. As we have seen in the preceding discussion, the nature of the legal framework and the manner of its implementation is such that the prospects of an opposition party or opposition leader winning elections have progressively diminished. The reality is that the chances of an opposition leader winning a presidential election, or an opposition party winning an absolute majority in Parliament, are as good as one's winning of the South Africa's Powerball jackpot, that is, near to zero.[72] In short, all the stops have been pulled to rule out any prospect of an opposition party victory through the ballot box in Cameroon. We can summarise the reasons for this bleak state of affairs under three points.

First, elections in Cameroon are won by the ruling party long before the first votes are cast. Electoral districts have been manipulated in advance to favour it; voting access is restricted in those areas that are likely to vote for the opposition; and opposition leaders and supporters are harassed, beaten, locked up, and sometimes killed. Even in those few urban cities that opposition parties win, the law allows the President to appoint senior officials such as chief administrative and finance officers.

What is more, the funding of political parties is skewed in favour of the ruling party, which takes advantage of its incumbency to control the state-owned media. The bodies responsible for managing elections – chiefly ELECAM and MINAT – are controlled by the government. Ever since the reintroduction of multipartyism, opposition party leaders have been neutralised by being co-opted to share in the spoils of power. Similarly, top government officials who nominally have a role in the proper functioning

72 See B Coetzer, "South Africa's R120 Million Powerball Jackpot", *BusinessTech*, 24 January 2024, https://businesstech.co.za/news/wealth/744917/south-africas-r120-million-powerball-jackpot-here-are-your-actual-odds-of-winning/ (accessed 1 May 2024). Putting this differently, the odds of one's joining the list of jackpot winners are infinitesimally small – 1 in 20,358,520, to be precise.

of the political system, such as top security officials, senior administrative officials at the local, regional and national level, and the judiciary, have been given financial inducements and other privileges that lead them to identify themselves with the survival of the regime.

At the same time, greed, lack of a clear alternative vision for the country, factionalism and division, and the failure to unite in presenting a common front, have contributed to the undoing of opposition parties. It is a weakness that has been exploited by the regime, which is aided and abetted by the international community, especially France. With their national economic interests bound up in deals with the Cameroonian government, most foreign countries and financial institutions have moderated their criticism of its abuse of democratic processes.

Secondly, the prospect of there being credible, responsible, and effective opposition parties that could threaten the hegemony of the CPDM has been further compromised by the absence of the core elements of constitutionalism and respect for the rule of law in Cameroon. Particular manifestations of this are the absence of full recognition and protection of fundamental human rights, the lack of an effective separation of powers, the lack of an independent judiciary, and the lack of a credible system of judicial review. Ultimately, the combination of a weak system of respect for the rule of law and a weak foundation for constitutionalism has led to a system where Biya is above, rather than subject to, the Constitution. He makes and unmakes laws, often with a complicit Parliament, as it suits his selfish wishes and those of the ruling clique.

Thirdly, the negative impacts of French policies on Cameroon's political developments are not likely to end soon, especially when dealing with a wily, ruthless autocrat and an entrenched corrupt elite determined to hang on to power at all costs. Their survival game now is to play the French and the West against the Chinese and Russians. The latter have no qualms whatsoever in supporting dictators like Biya and, moreover, will be only too happy to perfect his syllabus in authoritarian democracy.

In many respects, the multiparty aeroplane in Cameroon stalled before it could even taxi to the end of the runway. There is little to suggest that anything will change with or without the architect of this autocratic multiparty farce, Biya. Indeed, the main concern for the future is that any new leader or party that might displace the present leadership or party will only start another cycle of autocratic renewal disguised in new promises of change. The culture of "it's our turn to eat" is heavily ingrained in the mindset of Cameroonian political elites, and the present repressive outdated constitutional framework is too attractive to be changed.

The constitutional entrenchment of multipartyism and the elaborate legislative framework adopted to implement it has failed to provide a foundation for a genuine multiparty democratic culture to emerge in the country. What is required is a new constitution based on the fundamental elements of constitutionalism and the rule of law. This can come about only if opposition parties put aside their differences and campaign vigorously for a new constitutional dispensation. It would never be handed down on a platter; hence, the people must revive the spirit of the SDF of the early 1990s that forced the regime to reintroduce the multiparty system. Without a new constitutional dispensation, one based on an inclusive and broadly participatory process that draws lessons from the best processes and best constitutions on the continent, such as the Kenyan and South African constitutions, the multiparty autocratic system which is now in place will only become more deeply entrenched regardless of who the President is or which party happens to have a majority in Parliament.

References

Books, articles, chapters in books, and others

"Cameroon 'Fake' Election Observers Mask the Truth about Reality of Presidential Polls", *RFI*, 11 October 2018, https://www.rfi.fr/en/africa/20181011-cameroon-fake-election-observers-mask-truth-about-reality-presidential-polls (accessed 1 May 2024)

"Cameroon Government Warns Two Opposition Groups Are Illegal", *Voice of America*, 13 March 2024, https://www.voaafrica.com/a/cameroon-government-warns-two-political-groups-are-illegal/7526515.html (accessed 1 May 2024)

"Cameroon: Government Bans Opposition Coalitions Solidifies Crackdown on Free Association, Expression Ahead of 2025 Vote", *Human Rights Watch*, 21 March 2024, https://www.hrw.org/news/2024/03/21/cameroon-government-bans-opposition-coalitions (accessed 1 May 2024)

"Cameroon: Repression Marks Crackdown Anniversary", *Amnesty International*, 22 September 2021, https://www.amnesty.org/en/latest/news/2021/09/cameroon-repression-marks-crackdown-anniversary/ (accessed 1 May 2024)

Adams B, "SDF Protests Chirac's Congratulations to Biya", *PostNewsLine*, 18 October 2004, https://www.postnewsline.com/2004/10/strongsdf_prote.html (accessed 1 May 2024)

Albaugh EA, "An Autocrat's Toolkit: Adaptation and Manipulation in 'Democratic' Cameroon", in G Crawford and G Lynch (eds.), *Democratization in Africa: Challenges and Prospects*, London, Routledge (2012), pp 388–414

Amsterdam & Partners LLP, "One Minute to Midnight: The Cameroon Crisis", White Paper, April 2021, https://robertamsterdam.com/wp-content/uploads/2021/04/One-Minute-to-Midnight-The-Cameroon-Crisis-Amsterdam-and-Partners-LLP.pdf (accessed 1 May 2024)

Azevedo MJ (ed.), Cameroon and Chad in Historical Contemporary Perspectives, Lewiston, Edwin Mellen Press (1988)

Biya P, *Communal Liberalism*, London, Macmillan (1987)

Coetzer B, "South Africa's R120 Million Powerball Jackpot", *BusinessTech*, 24 January 2024, https://businesstech.co.za/news/wealth/744917/south-africas-r120-million-powerball-jackpot-here-are-your-actual-odds-of-winning/ (accessed 1 May 2024)

Commonwealth Secretariat, *Cameroon Presidential Election 11 October 2004: Report of the Commonwealth Observer Group* (16 October 2004), https://aceproject.org/ero-en/regions/africa/CM/cameroon-final-report-presidential-elections/view (accessed 1 May 2024)

Derick J, "Political Economy: Cameroon: One Party, Many Parties and the State", 22(3) (1992) *Africa Insight*, pp 165–177

Eyoh D, "Conflicting Narratives of Anglophone Protest and the Politics of Identify in Cameroon", 16(2) (1988) *Journal of Contemporary African Studies*, pp 249–276

Fombad CM and Fonyam J, "The Social Democratic Front, the Opposition, and Political Transition in Cameroon", in JM Mbaku and J Takougang (eds.), *The Leadership Challenge in Africa: Cameroon Under Paul Biya,* Africa World Press, Trenton NJ (2004), pp 453–488

Fombad CM, "Cameroon and the Anomalies of Decentralisation with a Centralist Mindset", in CM Fombad and N Steytler (eds.), *Decentralisation and Constitutionalism in Africa*, Oxford, OUP (2019), pp 326–364

Fombad CM, "Challenges to Constitutionalism and Constitutional Rights in Africa and the Enabling Role of Political Parties: Lessons and Perspectives from Southern Africa", 55 (2007) *American Journal of Comparative Law*, pp 1–46

Fombad CM, "Endemic Corruption in Cameroon: Insights on Consequences and Control", in R Hope and B Chikulo (eds.), *Corruption and Development in Africa. Lessons from Country Case – Studies,* Hampshire, Macmillan (2000), pp 234–260

Fombad CM, "Judicial Power in Cameroon's Amended Constitution of 18 January 1996", 9 (1996) *Lesotho Law Journal*, pp 1–11

Fombad CM, "The Dynamics of Record-breaking Endemic Corruption and Corruption and Political Opportunism in Cameroon", in JM Mbaku and J Takougang (eds.), *The Leadership Challenge in Africa: Cameroon Under Paul Biya,* Africa World Press, Trenton NJ (2004), pp 357–394

Fonchingong TN, "Multipartyism and Democratization in Cameroon", 15(2) (1998) *Journal of Third World Studies*, pp 119–136

Foute F, "Emmanuel Macron Remarks Spark Public Outcry in Cameroon", *The Africa Report*, 26 February 2020, https://www.theafricareport.com/23912/emmanuel-macron-remarks-spark-public-outcry-in-cameroon/ (accessed 1 May 2024)

Giovanni CM, "Political Parties and Party Systems in Africa: Themes and Research Perspectives", 3(3) (2007) *World Political Science*, pp 1–29

Gwellem JF, *Fru Ndi and the SDF Revolution,* Bamenda, Unique Press (1996)

Horizon Newspaper No. 302, 13 March 2024

Kamga S and Fombad CM, "The Cameroonian Special Criminal Court: The Futility of Combating Corruption Where the Basics of Constitutionalism are Absent", in CM Fombad and N Steytler (eds.), *Corruption and Constitutionalism in Africa: Revisiting Control Measures and Strategies* Oxford, OUP (2020), pp 417–435

Kiwuwa D, "Paul Biya has been Cameroon's President for 40 Years – and He Might Win Office Again", *The Conversation*, 28 November 2022 https://theconversation.com/paul-biya-has-been-cameroons-president-for-40-years-and-he-might-win-office-yet-again-194856 (accessed 1 May 2024)

Konings PJJ, "Opposition and Social-Democratic Change in Africa: The Social Democratic Front in Cameroon", 42(3) (2004) *Commonwealth and Comparative Politics*, pp 289–311

Korkmaz T, '"La Françafrique": The Special Relationship between France and Its Former Colonies in Africa', *Insamer*, 2 August 2019, https://en.insamer.com/la-francafrique-the-special-relationship-between-france-and-its-former-colonies-in-africa_2307.html (accessed 1 May 2024)

Krieger M, "Cameroon's Democratic Crossroads, 1990–4", 32(4) (1984) *Journal of Modern African Studies*, pp 605–628

Le Vine V, *The Cameroon Federal Republic*, Ithaca, Cornell University Press (1971)

Mbu ANT, "Civil Disobedience in Cameroon Bamenda", Douala, Imprimerie Georges Freres (1993)

Mehler A, "Cameroun: Une Transition Qui n'a pas eu Lieu", in JP Daloz and P Quantin (eds.), *Transitions Démocratiques Africaines*, Paris, Karthala (1997), pp 217–241

Minister of Territorial Administration, Press Release, 12 March 2024

Mumbere D, "We Have No Observers in Cameroon, Transparency International", *Africa News*, 9 October 2018, https://www.africanews.com/2018/10/09/we-have-no-observers-in-cameroon-transparency-international// (accessed 1 May 2024)

Mutations Newspaper No. 6027, 13 March 2024

National Democratic Institute for International Affairs, *Assessment of the October 11, 1992 Elections in Cameroon* (1993), p 19, http://www.electionpassport.com/files/1992-NDI-Cameroon-Election-Report.pdf (accessed 1 May 2024)

Ndjio B, "Millennial Democracy and Spectral Reality in Post-colonial Africa", 11(2) (2008) *African Journal of International Affairs*, pp 142–147

Ngwane G, "The Opposition and their Performance of Electoral Power in Cameroon (1992–2007)", *gngwane.com*, n.d., https://www.gngwane.com/files/cameroon_opposition_and_electoral_performance.pdf (accessed 1 May 2024)

Nikolas E, "'With a Friend Like This ...': Shielding Cameroon from Democratization", 48(2) (2013) *Journal of Asian and African Studies*, pp 145–160

Nikolas E, "Trends in Electoral Fraud: The Usage of Fake Election Monitors in Cameroon and Beyond", 7 (2022) *African Humanities*, pp 6–20

Nyamnjoh F and Rowlands M, "Elite Associations and the Politics of Belonging in Cameroon", 68(3) (1998) *Africa: Journal of the International African Institute*, pp 320–337

Sama T, "Cameroon: 'Zombie Observers' Confuse Narrative of Dubious Elections", *Democracy in Africa*, 2018, https://democracyinafrica.org/cameroon-zombie-observers-confuse-narrative-dubious-elections/ (accessed 1 May 2024)

Takougang J, "The 1992 Multiparty Elections in Cameroon: Prospects for Democracy and Democratisation", 31(1–2) (1996) *Journal of Asian and African Studies*, pp 52–65

Takougang J, "The 2002 Legislative Election in Cameroon: A Retrospective on Cameroon's Stalled Democracy Movement", 41(3) (2003) *Journal of Modern African Studies*, pp 421–435

Tande D, "State Funding of Political Parties: A Democratic Imperative or Hush Money for the Opposition?" *Scribbles from the Den*, 18 July 2007, https://www.dibussi.com/2007/07/state-funding-o.html (accessed 1 May 2024)

Tande D, "Why So Many Political Parties?" *Scribbles from the Den*, 17 June 2007, https://www.dibussi.com/2007/06/cameroon_why_so.html (accessed 1 May 2024)

The Guardian Post Newspaper No. 3056, 14 March 2024

Wandji PR, "Cameroon: 40 New Political Parties Receive Approval", *Journal du Cameroun.com* 13 November 2023, https://www.en.journalducameroun.com/cameroon-40-new-political-parties-receive-approval/ (accessed 1 May 2024)

Table of legislation

Constitution of Cameroon, 1996

Electoral Code of 2012

Law No. 2000/15 of 19 December 2000 relating to the funding of political parties and election campaigns

Law No. 2006/11 of 29 December 2006 to set up and lay down the organization and functioning of Elections Cameroon (ELECAM)

Law No. 2019/024 of 24 December 2019 to Institute the General Code of Regional and Local Authorities ("the General Code")

Law No. 91/20 of 16 December 1991 to lay down conditions governing the election of Members of Parliament

Law No. 92/10 of 17 September 1992 to lay down conditions governing the vacancy of and election to the Presidency of the Republic

Law No. 97/6 of 10 January 1997 to determine the period for the revision and recompilation of registers of electors

Part 4
Constitutionalism and Opposition Parties

Chapter 14 External Regulation and Internal Contradiction in Zimbabwean Opposition Politics: The Case of the MDC/CCC

Edson Ziso

1. Introduction

Save for the brief period from 2009 to 2013, when a government of national unity brokered by the Southern African Development Community (SADC) was in place, Zimbabwe has, since independence in 1980, been ruled by a single party: the Zimbabwe African National Union – Patriotic Front (ZANU-PF). This does not mean that ZANU-PF's dominance has not been seriously challenged; indeed, it has faced opposition since the very first elections in 1980. Though it proved victorious in the subsequent elections of 1985, 1990 and 1995, it has always faced opposition, albeit with the election results increasingly undermined by allegations of violence, vote-rigging, and widespread intimidation of opposition supporters.

For the first two decades of independence, ZANU-PF consistently and emphatically claimed the lion's share of the votes in both parliamentary and presidential elections. In the Parliamentary elections, for example, it claimed 62.99 per cent of the vote in 1980,[1] 80.55 per cent in 1990,[2] and 77.2 per cent in 1995.[3] Robert Mugabe's victories in the accompanying presidential elections were equally resounding. From 2000 on, however, ZANU-PF faced a serious and consistent threat to its political dominance and retention of power.

1 M Gregory, "Zimbabwe 1980: Politicisation through Armed Struggle and Electoral Mobilisation", 19 (1981), *Journal of Commonwealth & Comparative Politics*, pp 63–94.

2 VC Kwashirai, "The New Enemy in the 1990 General Elections Was Zum", in VC Kwashirai, *Election Violence in Zimbabwe: Human Rights, Politics and Power*, Cambridge, Cambridge University Press (2023), pp 65–93.

3 L Laakso, "Relationship between the State and Civil Society in the Zimbabwean Elections 1995", 34 (1996), *Journal of Commonwealth & Comparative Politics*, pp 218–234.

1999 saw the launch of the Movement for Democratic Change (MDC).[4] The new party was immediately well received by many Zimbabweans, who were disillusioned with the direction the country was taking economically and politically. One of the MDC's objectives was captured in the party's constitution: "The MDC shall pursue social liberation policies aimed at completing the unfinished business of the national liberation movement and in particular shall strive for the democratic structural economic liberation, empowerment and transformation of Zimbabwe."[5] In 2000, the barely one-year-old party garnered 45.6 per cent of the vote in the parliamentary elections against ZANU-PF's 47.23 per cent.[6] This performance was matched in the presidential election of March 2002, when the MDC candidate, Morgan Tsvangirai, won 42 per cent of the vote compared to Mugabe's 56 per cent, and this despite the allegations of vote-rigging, intimidation, and violence made against the MDC.[7]

Since then, elections in Zimbabwe have essentially been a fierce two-horse race between the ruling ZANU-PF and opposition MDC and, after 2022, the Citizens Coalition for Change (CCC). Although ZANU-PF had already demonstrated its authoritarian character in the 1980s and 1990s, the new MDC threat after 2000 saw it rise to the occasion with a new level of viciousness. It became an even more lethal organisation, one determined to maintain its power and dominance in Zimbabwe by any means necessary, with the MDC/CCC being the target of its gloves-off approach to politics. ZANU-PF justified its actions by characterising the MDC as a British-sponsored party, one created to fight on behalf of the minority com

4 A note on terminology: in this chapter, the Movement of Democratic Change (MDC) refers to the party as it was before the split in 2005. Thereafter, it became the MDC-T, led by Morgan Tsvangirai, and later yet the MDC Alliance, before transforming into a new party called the Citizens Coalition for Change (CCC), led by Nelson Chamisa. The breakaways are here not considered as the MDC. Any reference to them – including the MDC-Mutambara, MDC Renewal, MDC-99, MDC-N, or MDC-T (Khupe) – is for the purpose of amplifying some of the arguments in the chapter in regard, for example, to the intra-party upheavals that characterised the MDC until its demise. Where the two parties the MDC and CCC are treated separately, it is only to highlight the fact that the CCC was a reorganisation of the former but without the burden of the old name.

5 Constitution of the Movement for Democratic Change, Article 3(2), January 2000, https://www.veritaszim.net/sites/veritas_d/files/THE%20FINAL%20CONSTITUTIO N.pdf (accessed 13 October 2024).

6 D Pottie, "Parliamentary elections in Zimbabwe, 2000", 1 (2001) *Journal of African Elections*, pp 61–70.

7 Kwashirai, *supra* n. 2, p 77.

mercial white farmers against the government's land reforms. The party used wartime rhetoric and declared the MDC/CCC an enemy of the state and a security threat.[8]

Nonetheless, despite these external pressures, the MDC continued to perform well electorally, though it was increasingly also undermined by a number of challenges arising from within. While it had survived several internal, as well as externally induced, upheavals since its formation, the MDC suffered a deadly blow with the split of January 2022, which effectively ended it. Nelson Chamisa later revived the MDC, but only by forming a new party, the CCC. This too faced numerous problems and met its demise in January 2024.

What were the determining factors in the demise of the two parties? Tsvangirai, who had led the party since its formation, died at the helm in 2018. Due to the mishandling of his succession, Chamisa (then the party spokesperson and Tsvangirai's preferred successor) and Thokozani Khuphe (Tsvangirai's deputy, elected at a 2014 party congress) both laid claim to the presidency of the party. Shortly before his death, apparently, Tsvangirai had unilaterally appointed Chamisa and Elias Mudzuri as the second and third vice presidents of the party to serve alongside Khuphe.[9] The confusion culminated in Khuphe and her allies splitting from the party to head what became known as the MDC-T, (the "T" being a reference to the now deceased Tsvangirai). Khuphe argued that her party was the only *bona fide* movement following in the footsteps of the departed founding president. In 2019, the High Court of Zimbabwe ruled that the decision by the late Morgan Tsvangirai to handpick two additional vice presidents was illegal.[10] In spite of the ruling, Chamisa used his charisma, eloquence, and popularity among the party faithful to lay claim to the MDC leadership, and he prevailed.

The 2018 elections were unique in Zimbabwean history as this was the first time that Robert Mugabe was not on the ballot paper. In 2017, just a year earlier at the age of 93, Mugabe had been unceremoniously

8 T Zindoga and F Machivenyika, "MDC–T Sanctions Call Rapped", *The Herald*, 20 August 2015, https://www.herald.co.zw/mdc-t-sanctions-call-rapped/ (accessed 22 November 2024).

9 Khuphe had been procedurally elected as vice president at the 2014 congress in accordance with the party's constitution.

10 F Munyoro and V Maphosa, "Chamisa, Mudzuri Appointments Illegal – Court", *The Herald*, 9 May 2019, https://www.herald.co.zw/chamisa-mudzuri-appointments-illegal-court/ (accessed 18 October 2024).

removed from power through a military coup engineered by his long-time right-hand man, Emmerson Mnangagwa, who was immediately instated as the republic's President. Chamisa went on to contest the 2018 elections as the head of a coalition, the MDC-Alliance, which brought together several opposition groups (including the MDC-T). Chamisa narrowly lost the hotly disputed election to Mnangagwa.

The ZANU-PF victory in the 2018 elections was followed by serious disputes over the leadership of the MDC Alliance. In March 2020, Thokozani Khuphe won a Supreme Court judgement which confirmed that Chamisa was not the legitimate MDC leader on the grounds that his appointment as vice president by the late Tsvangirai was illegal.[11] Khuphe then became the official leader of the MDC Alliance. But in December 2020, Khupe herself was displaced at a chaotic extraordinary congress of the party, in a move engineered by Douglas Mwonzora.[12] As the new MDC Alliance leader, Mwonzora immediately went after Chamisa, who still held onto the party name and assets. In September 2021, Mwonzora took control of the MDC and all its assets, including the party headquarters. Chamisa tried to continue his political career under the name of the MDC Alliance, but had to stop using it after Mwonzora threatened him with legal action.

After losing the battle over the control of the MDC, Chamisa established a new political body, the CCC, in January 2022. The CCC sought to distance itself from the MDC-T structures, while claiming to represent the original MDC essence in terms of grassroots membership, vision, and legacy. To visibly distinguish itself from the Mwonzora-led MDC-T, it adopted yellow as its official colour (in place of the traditional red); changed the party symbol from the open palm to a pointing finger; and introduced new songs and party slogans (as discussed below). Moreover, it sought to introduce a new way of doing politics, one which included the abandonment of traditional party structures.

The party instantly proved to be extremely popular across the country and immediately prepared to contest the 2023 elections. Chamisa narrowly lost the 2023 presidential election with 44 per cent of the vote compared

11 Supreme Court of Zimbabwe, *Movement for Democratic Change & Anor v Mashavira & 3 Others* (Civil Appeal SC 289 of 2019; SC 56 of 2020) [2020], ZWSC 56, 31 March 2020.

12 ZimLive, "Mwonzora Wins Chaotic MDC-T Congress, Khupe Claims Voter Fraud", *ZimLive*, 28 December 2020, https://www.zimlive.com/mwonzora-wins-chaotic-congress-abandoned-by-khupe-and-others-over-voter-fraud-violence/ (accessed 11 October 2024).

to Zanu-PF's Mnangagwa (52.6 per cent), according to the official results. By contrast, Mwonzora did poorly, with only 0.65 per cent of the vote. He later claimed that he had pulled out of the election in advance, but that the Zimbabwe Electoral Commission (ZEC) had refused to remove his name from the ballot because he missed the 21-day notice period.[13] He also conspicuously failed to field candidates in all constituencies.[14] The CCC performed reasonably well in the parliamentary elections, denying ZANU-PF the two-thirds majority necessary to effect any amendments to the Constitution. This promising start for the CCC came to a sticky end, however. Just five months after the election, Chamisa quit the party. We shall discuss below (section 4.2) how a shadowy figure, Sengezo Tshabangu, engineered the takeover of the party that resulted in Chamisa's resignation.

Whilst this introduction has focused on the splits within the opposition, it should be noted that many other factors were involved. These included expulsions and counter-expulsions, suspensions, and intra-party violence; counterclaims to the party and its assets (including offices, symbols, and insignia); recalls from local, parliamentary, and senate seats; and clashes between rival supporters. This chapter argues that the external regulation of political parties played a key role in fostering the contradictions that bedeviled the opposition party. In making its case, it draws on the troubled 25-year lifespan of the opposition party in the context of Zimbabwe's political environment. Put simply, the ineffective constitutional and legal but also heavily politicised framework regulating political parties is hostile to the envisaged development of oppositional politics in Zimbabwe. The chapter thus contributes to recent discussions of the efficacy of political-party regulation in Africa, doing so through an analysis of the challenges opposition parties face in authoritarian contexts and of the wider implications this holds for the state and future of democracy in the region.

To be clear, this chapter is not intended to be an explanation of the opposition's failure to gain political power in Zimbabwe (even though some inferences might be drawn in that regard). Rather, the main aim

---

13 Business Times, "Douglas Mwonzora Pulls out of August 23 Presidential Race", *Business Times*, 8 August 2023, https://businesstimes.co.zw/douglas-mwonzora-pulls-out-of-august-23-presidential-race/ (accessed 1 October 2024).

14 N Guma, "Mwonzora Kills MDC as it Awaits its Burial during General Elections", *The NewsHawks*, 26 June 2023, https://thenewshawks.com/mwonzora-kills-mdc-as-it-awaits-its-burial-during-general-elections/ (accessed on 17 June 2024).

is to place opposition parties (rather than ruling parties) at the centre of debates around democratisation in Africa. Opposition parties in Africa are under-researched, but they are important because their appeal lies in the nature of the democratic promise they maintain against the practice of incumbents. Opposition parties are the lifeblood of a vibrant democracy. It is important here to remember the simple fact that both the MDC and CCC campaigned on a platform to deliver Zimbabwe from authoritarianism and ZANU-PF's "tired rhetoric of nationalism".[15] Their promise was to usher in a democratic dispensation underpinned by the rule of law, constitutionalism, and respect for human and property rights. The necessary implication is that the opposition party itself must practice, internally, the democratic constitutionalism that it preaches if it is to be seen as a genuine political alternative. The chapter will discuss both how Zimbabwe's opposition is caught up in internal problems in ways that undermine its envisaged democratic role, and also how these internal problems are heightened by the external regulatory and legal environment in which it operates.

The chapter draws on a rich tradition of African scholarship on political parties in general and their constitutional regulation in particular. According to Tsholo, the transformation of liberation movements into political parties was meant to see democracy prevail.[16] Sachikonye adds that political parties are an important medium for citizens' participation in the political process both during and between elections.[17] Closer to home, this rhymes with Selolwane and Shale's argument that

> the existence and increased number of political parties in Zimbabwe, like elsewhere on the continent, is a manifestation of the colonial legacy and victory over colonialism at the same time. This is because political parties were formed as the vehicles through which power would be transferred to Africans.[18]

---

15 C Sabao, "'Sanctions Are the Source of Our Suffering': Of ZANU-PF's 'Exhausted' Rhetoric and Blame-Gaming Tactics as Hegemonic Preservation", in E Mavengano and I Mhute (eds.), *Sub-Saharan Political Cultures of Deceit in Language, Literature, and the Media*, Vol. I, Switzerland, Cham, Springer Nature (2023), pp 343–365.

16 K Tsholo, "Do Transitions from Liberation Movements to Political Parties Guarantee Good Governance? The Case of ZANU-PF and the ANC", 43 (Nov/Dec 2021) *Strategic Review for Southern Africa*, pp 11–39.

17 LM Sachikonye, "Political Parties and the 2005 Elections in Zimbabwe", 4 (2005) *Journal of African Elections*, pp 63–73.

18 O Selolwane and V Shale, "Inter-Party Relations and Democracy in Botswana", *Electoral Institute for Sustainable Democracy in Africa*, 2008, https://policycommon

The chapter thus concurs with Lawson "that constitutional opposition is the *sine qua non* of contemporary democracy in mass polities ... its institutionalization in some form or another is required before a regime can be called 'democratic' with any real meaning".[19] Crucially, however, it is Fombad who offers the cautionary note that "political-party constitutionalisation is not a magic wand that can solve all challenges to free and fair political-party competition. Nevertheless, it is an important starting-point."[20] This chapter seeks to build on this inspiring work by contributing to a better understanding of the challenges faced by opposition parties in poorly regulated contexts under very illiberal regimes and what this portends for democracy on the continent. Opposition parties, as noted previously, are the lifeblood of a democracy, and without their proper and democratic regulation there is little hope of establishing real democracy in Africa.

Section 2 provides a brief overview of the Zimbabwean political context. It shows how the incumbent regime's desire for a one-party state has worked to create Zimbabwe's treacherous political landscape. Section 3 offers an overview of the constitutional and regulatory framework which governs political parties in Zimbabwe and also presents an analysis of how this framework impacted on both the MDC and the CCC. Section 4 shows the politicisation of the regulatory framework in favor of the ruling party, while section 5 shows the effects of all this on the internal contradictions in the opposition party. Section 6 concludes the chapter.

2. ZANU-PF and the desire for a one-party state

By far the most significant factors to consider when analysing Zimbabwe's political landscape is ZANU-PF's declared desire for a one-party state system. The one-party state plan was explicitly promoted by Robert Mugabe

s.net/artifacts/1448811/inter-party-relations-and-democracy-in-botswana/2080589/ (accessed 23 February 2024).

19 S Lawson, "Conceptual Issues in the Comparative Study of Regime Change and Democratisation", 25 (1993), *Comparative Politics*, pp 183–205.

20 C Fombad, "Political Party Constitutionalisation in Africa: Trends and Prospects for Deepening Constitutionalism", in R Dixon, T Ginsburg and A Abebe (eds.), *Comparative Constitutional Law in Africa,* Cheltenham, Edward Elgar Publishing (2022), pp 109–135.

and ZANU both before[21] and after[22] independence. Even the 1987 Unity Accord agreement that merged ZANU and ZAPU specified that the unified "party shall seek to establish a one-party state in Zimbabwe and establish a socialist state along Marxist-Leninist principles".[23]

In the post-Mugabe era, Emmerson Mnangagwa has maintained this same vision. ZANU-PF has managed for 45 years to maintain and develop a de facto one-party state structure, and this despite the fact that Zimbabwe officially exists as a multiparty democracy in what Dawson describes as a "representative one-party state".[24] ZANU-PF sees itself as the permanent and sole guardian of the liberation war legacy, ethos, and its promise, as well as the sovereignty of Zimbabwe and the safeguarding of its interests through its espousal and rhetoric of nationalist politics. For ZANU-PF, opposition parties are not seen as political contestants: they are annoyances that must be silenced. Not surprisingly, ZANU-PF thus has a conflicted but strong interest in the formal regulation of political parties in the country.

It is almost impossible to establish and maintain a one-party state without heightened degrees of coercion and repression, including limiting the political competitiveness of rival political forces as far as possible. According to Sachikonye, ZANU-PF brings a zero-sum game mindset to politics: it must always prevail, and its opponents must be crushed rather than accommodated. While opposition parties exist, they have never been allowed to win an election.[25] Sylvester's observation in 1995 that "Zimbabwe is a textbook case of a country where opposition is provided for constitutionally as a right of political dissent" remains true.[26] ZANU-PF's one-party state system rests on ever-deepening practices of exclusionary politics, includ-

21 RH Shaw, "Towards the One-Party State in Zimbabwe: A Study in African Political Thought", 24 (1986), *Journal of Modern African Studies*, pp 373–394.

22 TIME, "Zimbabwe: One-Party State", *TIME*, 20 August 1984, https://content.time.com/time/subscriber/article/0,33009,954344,00.html (accessed 13 June 2024).

23 The Herald, "Two Parties Merge as ZANU (PF)", *The Herald,* 23 December 2021, https://www.herald.co.zw/two-parties-merge-as-zanu-pf/ (accessed 21 August 2024).

24 RW Dawson, "The Representative One-party State: Mugabe's Search for Political Control in Zimbabwe", Unpublished PhD Thesis, University of British Columbia (1989).

25 L Sachikonye, "Between Authoritarianism and Democratisation: The Challenges of a Transition Process in Zimbabwe", Occasional Paper 2 (July 2009), *Institute for Development Studies*, Paper presented at Centre of Political and Historical Studies on Africa and the Middle East, Bologna.

26 C Sylvester, "Whither Opposition in Zimbabwe?" 33 (1995), *Journal of Modern African Studies*, pp 403–423.

ing patronage; the capture of key state institutions; and the use and/or abuse of the constitution to destroy potential opposition, both internal and external. According to Ndlovu-Gatsheni, a political philosophy based on the annihilation of the enemy underpinned ZANU-PF's attitude to state power not only during the liberation struggle and the 1980 election, but was also in every subsequent election as the ethic for dealing with political opposition.[27] The ruling party's politicisation of political-party regulation is a key manifestation of this philosophy.

This brief account of the political environment in which the MDC and CCC operate is crucial for understanding what can be called the "political economy" of the regulatory framework. However, the chapter is not devoted to ZANU-PF. Rather, its focus is on the opposition and its often unacknowledged centrality to the understanding of democracy, governance, and political debates in Zimbabwe. How has working in this political environment affected opposition parties like the MDC and the CCC? The analysis shows that the MDC and CCC not only abandoned some of their defining democratic principles (such as constitutionalism, democratically elected leadership, consensus-based decision-making, and transparency) but also slowly began to become a mirror image of ZANU-PF. This contradiction is firmly linked to the constitutional and legal framework that regulates political parties in Zimbabwe. The following section provides an overview of this framework.

3. The constitutional and legal framework for political parties

The constitutional and legal framework for the regulation of political parties is an essential component of democracy and has significant implications for the integrity of the whole political process. Political-party regulation sets the rules of the game: it establishes the minimum requirements for political-party organisation and how parties conduct their business.[28] In democratic societies, party regulation is used as a mechanism to promote

27 SJ Ndlovu-Gatsheni, *Elections in Zimbabwe: A Recipe for Tension or a Remedy for Reconciliation*, Wynberg, Institute for Justice and Reconciliation (2012), https://paren.org.za/site/wp-content/uploads/2016/07/IJR-Zimbabwe-Elections-OP-WEB.pdf (accessed 3 September 2024).

28 C Chibango, "The Registration and Regulation of Political Parties in Zimbabwe: A Key Pillar in Prospects for Free and Fair Election", 1 (2022) *Journal on Governance, Human Rights and Democracy in Zimbabwe*.

and guarantee citizens' rights to political participation. Regulation also seeks to ensure that political parties' activities and behaviour comply with the goals and practices of modern democracies.[29]

It is useful to consider, for instance, the role of a political party as this is conceived in Article 21 of the German Constitution, the Basic Law.[30] Several questions emerge regarding political-party regulation in Zimbabwe. According to Wulf, the Zimbabwean Constitution of 2013 expressly affirms a multiparty system but no further regulations exist regarding the nature, rights, and functions of political parties.[31] Chibango suggests that in Zimbabwe, only the financing of parties is regulated, while other factors – such as registration, de-registration, ideology, internal democracy, accountability, and campaign financing – escape regulation.[32]

In fact, regulation does extend to several other areas. Section 129(1)(k) of the Constitution, for example, gives political parties the power to recall their Members of Parliament (MPs) if they abandon its cause. In addition, all political parties sign a code of conduct which covers their behaviour during election periods. This code is to be found in the Fourth Schedule of the Electoral Act.[33] Moreover, section 160 of the Act compels political parties to participate in multiparty liaison committees chaired by the ZEC. In short, political-party regulation in Zimbabwe does exist. The main problem is that regulation is only visibly at work in some areas (such as the financing of parties and electoral conduct) while in others it is invisible. This chapter focuses on these gaps in regulatory practice.

Masunungure puts matters well: "When done in good faith i.e., without ulterior and sinister motives, party regulation promotes transparency and democratic accountability to the public, curbs corrupt practices and provides for penalties for breach of the regulations." However, he adds: "[W]hen the impulse to control drives the introduction of party regulation,

29 S Vohito-Anyanwu, "Promoting Constitutional Democracy: Regulating Political Parties in the Central African Republic and Senegal", 23 (2020) *Potchefstroom Electronic Law Journal*, pp 1–34.

30 A Wulff (ed.), *Legal Framework for Political Parties in Selected Countries of Sub-Saharan Africa*, Nairobi, Konrad-Adenauer-Stiftung Rule of Law Program for Sub-Saharan Africa (2017), p 15, https://www.kas.de/c/document_library/get_file?uuid=735c449b-fd52-c43f-6f58-403a818d3be9&groupId=252038 (accessed 12 September 2024). In the case of Germany, see also J Socher, "International Standards on the Regulation of Political Parties and the Experience of Continental Europe", in this volume.

31 Wulff, *supra* n. 30, p 15.

32 Chibango, *supra* n. 28, p 13.

33 Electoral Act No. 25 of 2004, Chapter 2:13.

then the move can be a recipe for mutual suspicion and distrust which can further poison the political atmosphere."[34]

This chapter argues that there are two key challenges regarding party regulation in Zimbabwe. The first is that political-party regulation is not sufficiently comprehensive (regulation exists in some areas but not in others); the second is related to Masunungure's main point: constitutional party regulation in Zimbabwe is too politicised. It is therefore infected by what Roux terms "authoritarian legalism", [35] namely a situation in which the law is used for authoritarian ends. As this chapter will show, this created unending problems for the MDC/CCC in terms of intra-party relations; party-society relations (with members and stakeholders); and government-party relations.

4. The regulatory framework and its impact on the MDC/CCC

4.1 Formation and registration of political parties

The consistently high number of political parties that take part in Zimbabwe gives an impression of competitive elections; but there is considerable debate as to whether Zimbabwe enjoys a multiparty democracy or only the façade of one. The Electoral Act does not provide the chief elections body (the ZEC) with the authority to set registration requirements for political parties or essential provisions for party constitutions (such as gender parity).[36] Forming a political party is guaranteed as a right in section 67(2)(a) of the Constitution but is not further detailed by any law. A political party simply needs to notify the ZEC of its existence and intention to participate in an election any time before the sitting of the nomination court: it is then automatically qualified to participate.[37] The absence of a comprehensive

---

34 E Masunungure, *Regulation of Political Parties in Zimbabwe: Registration, Finance, and other Support*, Zimbabwe Elections Support Network (ZESN), August 2006, https://www.zesn.org.zw/wp-content/_protected/publications/publication_113.pdf (accessed 18 August 2024).

35 T Roux, "The Postcolonial Adaptation of Authoritarian Legalism in Zimbabwe", in T Roux (ed.), *The Politico-Legal Dynamics of Judicial Review: A Comparative Analysis*, Cambridge, Cambridge University Press (2018), pp 193–241.

36 USAID, *An Analysis of the Legal Framework Governing Elections in Zimbabwe, USAID*, 1 September 2019, https://pdf.usaid.gov/pdf_docs/PA00W598.pdf (accessed 14 February 2024).

37 Chibango, *supra* n. 28, p 16.

and depoliticised regulation of political-party registration created severe problems for the MDC and CCC. For instance, in the absence of a law that creates a central registry in which all parties can depose their names, symbols, colors and logos, it is possible for more than one party to use a similar name, as well as similar symbols, logos and colours, causing potential confusion among voters.[38] Bitter disputes over party names are obvious examples of this failure.

In his study of the significance of party names in the Irish political system, Coakley explains that "in most political systems, party names serve a crude – but by no means unambiguous – indicator of the positions of parties in the ideological spectrum".[39] Names play a similar role in corporate business strategies. Meanwhile, anthropologists and linguists alert us to the criticality of names as core to identity, especially in politics. For Jarvis, names are dynamic entities for political organisations, ones that can be either positioned successfully and adorned with positive characteristics or repositioned by opponents or the media and charged with negative connotations.[40]

From its inception in 1999, the MDC carried all the weight and symbolism of being Zimbabwe's main opposition party. Its name came to represent both the being and the legacy of the party and embodied all its history, struggle, and aspirations. Not surprisingly, the fact of the vicious and repeated struggles between factions over the ownership of the name, assets, and elected representatives of the party, over the years, weighed heavily on the opposition, distracting it from its core business and leaving both voters and members disillusioned. At times, the struggle degenerated into a circus as rival leaders went all-out to get even. All too often, rival factions ended up contesting elections under the same name. The absence of a regulatory provision for protecting political parties from such unending disputes negatively affected the opposition in both more and less visible ways.

For example, the 2013 split in the MDC resulted in the two factions contesting the 2013 election as MDC-T (Tsvangirai) and MDC-N (Ncube). In 2018, the ballot had MDC-Alliance and MDC-T (now led by Khuphe), causing a lot of unnecessary confusion for voters who struggled to differen-

38 Chibango, *supra* n. 28, p 17.

39 J Coakley, "The Significance of Names: The Evolution of Irish Party Labels", 5 (1980) *Études irlandaises*, pp 171–182.

40 SE Jarvis, *The Talk of the Party: Political Labels, Symbolic Capital, and American Life*, Maryland, Rowman and Littlefield Publishers (2005).

tiate the parties. Over the years, this situation invariably resulted in spoiled ballot papers as confused voters ended up voting for multiple candidates. This was rife among the elderly as well as the uneducated and any other voter unfamiliar with the fast-moving events, or without updated information on the never-ending splits in the opposition. The overall effect was to split the opposition vote to the advantage of ZANU-PF. Simultaneously, disappointed voters grew tired of the opposition's unending divisions and often chose to stay at home rather than go out to vote, worsening voter apathy and polarisation, and fueling disinterest in politics in general.

The battle over the identity and brand of the opposition parties also became a huge opportunity for the ruling government. Through its control of a thoroughly compromised judiciary, ZANU-PF was able to bring its influence to bear on the adjudication of such intra-party disputes in ways which always worked to destabilise the opposition and promote its one-party-state agenda. ZANU-PF strategically intervened in the sensitive MDC name-dispute in ways that disadvantaged and weakened its real opponents among and within the feuding factions.

When Mwonzora (and not Chamisa) won the dispute over the name, symbol, and assets of MDC, most critics viewed the judgement as a ZANU-PF inside job to cripple Chamisa, their real nemesis. There was also an inordinate and unexplained delay in the delivery of the judgement that held up some important party operations. As the then MDC-Alliance Secretary for Legal Affairs, Innocent Gonese, put it, "[T]he judgment delivered by Justice Patel on the 31st of March 2020 will be rightly or wrongly seen as a political judgment."[41] In addition, in 2021, the state distributed the funds under the Political Parties (Finance) Act despite a High Court order that no funds were to be distributed until the dispute over the ownership had been fully settled. It was also inexplicable that the funds were allocated to MDC-T despite its failure to reach the necessary 5 per cent of votes stipulated by law as a threshold. As the human rights activist Pedzisayi Ruhanya summed it up on Twitter: "Thokozani's MDC-T, according to ZEC results, got 0.96% of votes in 2018 elections. On what account does it get the political-party finances money of ZW60 million that is meant for

41 Zimeye, "Gonese Analyses Supreme Court Judgement On MDC Leadership Battle", 9 April 2020, https://www.zimeye.net/2020/04/09/gonese-analyses-supreme-court-judgement-on-mdc-leadership-battle (accessed 7 March 2025).

MDC Alliance Nelson Chamisa?"[42] The controversy of party financing is discussed in more detail in Section 4.4.

The absence of more detailed regulation regarding the formation, registration, and internal operation of political parties has proved fatal for the operation of internal democracy inside the opposition. Vote-rigging, imposition of candidates, multiple or duplicate nominations, and violence (both physical and structural) became rife in the MDC and CCC, especially in their intra-party primary elections. In the 2018 general elections, the MDC-Alliance was a grand coalition of eight parties. This alliance sought to use its economies of scale to challenge ZANU-PF's continued rule. Despite agreement among the coalition members on a pre-electoral pact, the absence of a relevant regulatory statute meant that several of these prior agreements could easily be dishonoured. For example, an agreed seat-sharing formula was opposed by some MDC-T officials, who fielded their own candidates in constituencies reserved for smaller coalition partners. The EU Election Observation Mission concluded that "this led to a split of the MDC-Alliance vote and the possible loss of at least two seats".[43]

4.2 Use and abuse of the power to recall MPs

By far one of the most controversial constitutional provisions in party regulation in Zimbabwe is section 129(1)(k) of the Constitution. This gives political parties the power to recall MPs if they cease to belong to the party. It states:

> The seat of a Member of Parliament becomes vacant –
> (k) if the Member has ceased to belong to the political party of which he or she was a member when elected to Parliament and the political party concerned, by written notice to the Speaker or the President of the Senate, as the case may be, has declared that the Member has ceased to belong to it.

42 Voice of America, "MDC Alliance Fuming over Govt's Disbursement of Almost $60 Million in State Funds to Mwonzora's MDC-T", *Voice of America*, 29 August 2021, https://www.voazimbabwe.com/a/mdc-alliance-state-disbursement-funds/6078040.html (accessed 22 November 2024).

43 European Union Election Observation Mission, *Final Report Republic of Zimbabwe: Harmonised Elections 2018*, Veritas (2018), https://www.veritaszim.net/sites/veritas_d/files/EU%20Election%20Observers%20Final%20Report%20Zimbabwe%202018-.pdf (accessed 2 October 2024).

The objective of the provision is apparently to protect political parties from defections; in practice, though, it has become the most abused provision in the regulatory framework. It has resulted in the winners of elections becoming losers (and losers becoming winners) overnight. Following the 2014 split of the MDC, for example, 21 opposition MPs were expelled from Zimbabwe's parliament after they broke away to form a new party, MDC Renewal. The group had contested the 2013 elections under the banner of Tsvangirai's MDC but then left the party to form MDC Renewal after rejecting his leadership.[44] Similarly in 2020, Mwonzora, having gained control of the MDC-Alliance, recalled dozens of elected MPs, accusing them of supporting Chamisa. This left the electorate disenfranchised and underrepresented when the government failed to hold by-elections within the constitutionally mandated 90-day timeframe (citing the Covid-19 lockdown order as grounds). The by-elections were held only in March 2022 and later that year.[45]

A third instance in which the abuse of the recall provision is evident took place when Tshabangu assumed the role of the Secretary-General of the CCC, instigating the fatal blow that effectively killed the nascent party. Chamisa eventually abandoned the CCC, alleging that it had "been contaminated, bastardized, hijacked by ZANU PF through the abuse of State institutions."[46] The significance of this recent split cannot be overemphasised.

Tshabangu, who suddenly and unceremoniously announced on 4 October 2023 that he was the Secretary-General of the CCC led by Nelson Chamisa, caused a political thunderstorm that most observers and opposition supporters are still grappling with at the time of this writing. His self-imposed position empowered him to recall elected CCC members from the Senate, Parliament and local government. Despite Chamisa's claim that he did not recognise him, Tshabangu invoked section 129(1)(k) of the Constitution, writing a notification to the Speaker of Parliament, Jacob

44 T Chiripasi, "Tsvangirai MDC-T Recalls Biti, 17 Lawmakers from Parliament", *Voice of America*, 6 November 2014, https://www.voazimbabwe.com/a/zimbabwe-mdc-t-recalls-biti-17-lawmakers-from-parliament/2510826.html (accessed 30 December 2024).

45 LB Harris, "Swift Recall of CCC MPs Shows ZANU-PF's Meddling, Analysts Say", *CITE*, 10 October 2023, https://cite.org.zw/swift-recall-of-ccc-mps-shows-zanu-pfs-meddling-analysts-say/ (accessed 12 October 2024).

46 BBC, "Nelson Chamisa: Zimbabwe Opposition CCC Leader Quits 'Contaminated' Party", *BBC*, 26 January 2024, https://www.bbc.com/news/world-africa-68095685 (accessed 30 December 2024).

Mudenda, and Minister of Local Government and Public Works, Winston Chitando, to recall several CCC MPs and councillors.[47] Traditionally, the authority in the MDC to recall a member of the party from the legislation had resided constitutionally in the office of the Secretary-General. Chamisa made representations through his then spokesman, Promise Mkhwananzi, instructing the Speaker not to act on Tshabangu's instruction, arguing that Tshabangu was not even a member of the CCC. However, the Speaker determined that Tshabangu was acting procedurally and legally. Six days later, the Speaker notified the ZEC that there were now 15 vacant seats in the legislative body.[48] Further recalls were instituted in a calculated, staggered manner until all Chamisa loyalists were expelled. To seal their fate, Tshabangu also secured a legal victory when the courts ruled in his favour that recalled CCC MPs, Senators and Councillors could not contest in subsequent by-elections under the party.[49] This was controversial because, at this stage, the position of Secretary-General did not exist in the "structureless" CCC. On 11 October 2024, Tshabangu went for the jugular and fired Chamisa himself from the party.[50]

The consequence of all this was that, within days of the swearing in of new MPS after the 2023 election in which Chamisa's CCC had claimed an impressive 100 seats (and denying ZANU-PF a two-thirds majority), Tshabangu spectacularly flipped the script. He used the power of recall to remove those aligned to Chamisa from the party, and also prevented them from contesting the resulting by-elections under the CCC banner. At the end of this bloodletting, ZANU-PF emerged as the overall winner and now commands 190 seats in the 280-member Parliament. This is entirely due to the fact that the recalls necessitated a series of by-elections which were comfortably won by ZANU-PF, allowing it the two-thirds majority it needed to effect constitutional changes. Constitutionally, Mnangagwa

47 G Dube, "CCC 'Interim Secretary General' Recalls Dozens of Party Lawmakers, Councilors", *Voice of America*, 4 October 2023, https://www.voazimbabwe.com/a/7296398.html/ (accessed 20 November 2024).

48 I Mafundikwa, "Zimbabwe's CCC Crisis: Farce Turning to Tragedy for the Opposition", *BBC*, 8 December 2023, https://www.bbc.com/news/world-africa-67647449 (accessed 19 November 2024).

49 New Zimbabwe, "Recalled CCC MPs, Councillors barred from contesting in February 3 by-elections" https://www.newzimbabwe.com/recalled-ccc-mps-councillors-barred-from-contesting-in-february-3-by-elections/ (accessed 17 July 2025).

50 I Zhakata, "Chamisa Kicked out of CCC", *The Herald*, 11 October 2023, https://www.herald.co.zw/chamisa-kicked-out-from-ccc/ (accessed 17 November 2024).

is currently serving his second and final presidential term. However, he is widely suspected to be harbouring plans to extend his term of office, an extension made possible only by amending the Constitution, and this in turn possible only by a two-thirds parliamentary majority vote. As explained by the prominent human rights lawyer Musa Kika, a "two-thirds majority in parliament is enough to change anything in the Constitution except Chapter 4 (Declaration of Rights), Chapter 16 (Agricultural Land) and Section 328 (Amendment of the Constitution). These three require a referendum."[51]

4.3 Regulating political parties in the electoral space

The situation in Zimbabwe, according to Mude, is one in which, to the detriment of democratic values, election management institutions, procedures, regulations, and personnel all serve as agents representing the interests of the ruling party.[52] Indeed, the history of elections in Zimbabwe is one best understood not only in terms of the frequent contestation of election results, but also with regard to the ways in which elections are conducted and organised throughout the entire electoral cycle.

From the very first "democratic" elections in 1980, Zimbabwe's opposition parties have alleged that elections are deliberately manipulated at every stage of the process (including voter registration, delimitation of electoral boundaries, and the counting of votes) to the benefit of ZANU-PF. These allegations have been backed up both by hard evidence and by independent observers and institutions. In its 2017 report on Zimbabwe's preparedness for free and fair elections, the Zimbabwe Democracy Institute (ZDI) pointed out that key state institutions which should act in a non-partisan manner (including the media, the legislature, the judiciary, and the electoral system) have in fact suffered state capture.[53]

---

51 FS Matiashe, "Zimbabwe: With Its Two-Thirds Majority, How Far will ZANU-PF Go?", *The Africa Report*, 15 February 2024, https://www.theafricareport.com/336371/zimbabwe-with-its-two-thirds-majority-how-far-will-zanu-pf-go/ (accessed 18 October 2024).

52 T Mude, "Digital Technologies and Election Management in Zimbabwe: Pseudo-democratic Transition and Contorted Delirium?", 47 Special Issue (2022) *Africa Development*, pp 179–198.

53 Zimbabwe Democracy Institute, "Zimbabwe Transition in a Muddy Terrain: Political Economy under Military Capture", *Kubatana*, 14 December 2017, https://kubatana.n

Involving political parties is critical for the preservation and integrity of the electoral process. Political parties' participation should not be restricted to just the election day. Rather, they ought to be involved in election matters through election management bodies. According to Rusinga, who served as an election observer in the 2018 elections, the ZEC "tried to engage stakeholders, particularly political parties, through Multi-Party Liaison Committees" in an attempt to minimise the perception that the election had been biased.[54] These committees were established under section 160 of the Electoral Act. They are charged to work in the common pursuit of electoral justice, including conflict management on contentious issues such as political violence among supporters of various parties. They consist of representatives of all the political parties contesting the election, as well as the representatives of independent candidates, the ZEC, and, where necessary, the government, the security forces, and other stakeholders. All representatives are meant to see that elections are conducted in a free and fair manner.[55] To this end, their main aim is to set up structures that prevent or resolve conflicts and ensure observance of the Code of Conduct for Political Parties and Candidates. However, this has proved ineffective in democratising the electoral space or improving its governance.

Decision-making by consensus has been a weak point in the effectiveness of these committees, particularly when considering the fact that elections in Zimbabwe are a matter of life and death and always take place in an environment of extreme polarisation and violence. They are hotly contested, with state security agents often implicated in electoral malpractice and even violence (security forces backed by ZANU-PF have long engaged with impunity in acts of extra-legal violence). As Chikohora and Chokutamba argue, the problem is deeply rooted:

> [T]he current military-political alliance between ZANU-PF and the security sector has its roots in the liberation struggle, when the Zimbabwe African National Liberation Army (ZANLA) and the Zimbabwe People's Revolutionary Army (ZIPRA), the military wings of ZANU and the

---

et/2017/12/14/zimbabwe-transition-muddy-terrain-political-economy-military-capture/ (accessed February 2024).

54 R Rusinga, "Zimbabwe's 2018 Harmonised Elections: An Assessment of Credibility", 20 (2021), *Journal of African Elections*, pp 90–114.

55 S Vengesai, "A Critical Examination of the Effectiveness of the Zimbabwean Multi-party Liaison Committee", 1 (2022), *Journal on Governance, Human Rights and Democracy in Zimbabwe.*

Zimbabwe African People's Union (ZAPU) respectively, formed close bonds with their respective parties.[56]

Opposition party members, detainees, and protesters often face police brutality, at times resulting in death.[57] These practices were particularly evident during the 2008 elections when the army played a major role in supporting widespread and systematic abuse, leading to the killing of up to 200 people; the beating and torture of some 5,000 more; and the displacement of around 36,000.[58] Since the state refuses to prosecute any of its agents, no progress has been made in curbing such abuse.[59]

By the time of the 2018 elections, the multiparty liaison committees were reported to have failed because

> [the] ZEC did not present a clear direction for redressing concerns, resulting in redundancies in the plenary at successive [commission] meetings. In addition, it was unclear whether the issues raised at the local level were shared with higher levels of the ZEC.[60]

Commissions met only infrequently at national level and did not serve as a forum where decisions were made, undermining their effectiveness.

4.4 The politics of party-funding regulations

Another controversial feature of Zimbabwe's regulatory framework is to be found in the funding of political parties from private and public

56 E Chikohora and L Chokutamba, "Governing Security Sector Reform in Zimbabwe and the Prospects of Positive Peace in a Polarised Polity", 10 (2022), *Global Scientific Journals*, pp 961–988.

57 Freedom House, "Freedom in the World 2024: Zimbabwe", *Freedom House*, n.d., https://freedomhouse.org/country/zimbabwe/freedom-world/2024 (accessed 31 October 2024).

58 Human Rights Watch, "The Elephant in the Room: Reforming Zimbabwe's Security Sector Ahead of Elections", *Human Rights Watch*, 4 June 2013, https://www.hrw.org/report/2013/06/04/elephant-room/reforming-zimbabwes-security-sector-ahead-elections (accessed 16 November 2024).

59 For example, Freedom House's *Freedom in the World* report states that "pressure on the courts to endorse executive actions and protect ZANU-PF's interests has eroded the judiciary's independence. Judges occasionally rule against the government in sensitive cases, and such rulings are not always respected." Freedom in the World 2024, *supra* n. 56.

60 International Republican Institute and National Democratic Institute, *IRI/NDI Zimbabwe International Election Observation Mission Final Report*, Washington DC, International Republican Institute (2018), https://www.ndi.org/sites/default/files/2018-10-29%20Final%20ZIEOM%20Report%20%288MB%29.pdf (accessed 16 October 2024).

sources. Indeed, this funding is precisely the most regulated aspect of the Political Parties (Finance) Act 2001.[61] It is a flashpoint in Zimbabwe's politics and a key indicator of the manipulation of a regulatory framework to the incumbent party's benefit. As an instrument of party regulation, it was strategically deployed against the MDC and CCC by the state to devastating effect.

One of the Act's key objectives is the prevention of foreign interference in the internal affairs of Zimbabwe through the funding of political parties. Section 6(1) states that "no political party, member of a political party or candidate shall accept any foreign donation, whether directly from the donor or indirectly through a third person". Section 6(2) states further that

> any donation accepted by a member of a political party shall be deemed to have been accepted by the political party, unless the member willfully fails to disclose such donation to the political party, in which case the candidate shall be liable for any [solicitation of donations by foreigners].

With this regulation in place, opposition parties that receive any foreign funding are liable to prosecution – the security establishment pays keen attention to any infringement of this rule by the opposition. At the same time, the Act has been brazenly ignored by ZANU-PF without its suffering legal consequences. Thus, for example, when it emerged that the party received various forms of electoral support from the Chinese Communist Party (CCP) in the 2013 elections, the party spokesperson simply commented:

> When we get money from the Chinese, what is wrong with that? That did not in any way affect the election results, so where is all this noise coming from? ... We have every right to get funding for our political programming, no matter where that comes from. Why should they [MDC-T] make noise about us getting funding from the Chinese when they go to the British and Americans to ask for money to sponsor their activities?[62]

The ruling party has never faced legal consequences for this violation (Moore explores this blatant admission of guilt in some depth).[63] Opposition politics, however, is crippled when political-party regulation is en-

61 Political Parties (Finance) Act No. 4 of 2001, Chapter 2:11.

62 "Zanu (PF) Admits Breaking Law", *The Zimbabwean*, 18 September 2013, https://www.thezimbabwean.co/2013/09/zanu-pf-admits-breaking-law/ (accessed 4 April 2024).

63 D Moore, "ZANU-PF and the Ghosts of Foreign Funding", 32 (2005) *Review of African Political Economy*, pp 156–162.

forced only on one side and the incumbent party can disobey the rules at will. This is particularly so in an environment like Zimbabwe's, where the domestic resources for political financing are extremely limited. The legal position – that political parties should rely on the funding provided for them by the law – should be enforced, precisely according to the provisions of the Political Parties (Finances) Act.

Section 3(1) of the Act states that "every political party shall be entitled in each Parliamentary year to receive from the State the sums of money that are payable to it in terms of this Act". Nonetheless, a party has to meet certain criteria to be eligible for funding. Section 3(3) of the Act provides that

> each political party whose candidates received at least five per centum of the total number of votes cast in the most recent general election shall be entitled to the same proportion of the total money appropriated as the total number of votes cast for its candidates in the election bears to the total number of votes cast for all its candidates in that election.

Despite the spirit of this provision, when it comes to actual practice, the state has potently weaponised it as an instrument for controlling the opposition.

The constant splits in the MDC and CCC were always followed by claims and counter-claims by rival factions for access to this legislated political funding. Indeed, Chamisa never benefitted from the provisions promised by the Act. This is so in spite of the fact that his former political party, the MDC Alliance, and the CCC after it, each won more than 5 per cent of the total votes in the 2018 and in 2023 elections, respectively (as prescribed as necessary for funding by the Act).[64] Instead – and despite the obvious conflicts involved – the state apparatus consistently manipulated these intra-party disputes in ways that benefitted its preferred opposition candidate.

Ahead of the 2023 elections, for example, Mwonzora was awarded the funds allocated to the opposition.[65] By virtue of winning the Supreme

64 V Langa, "Zimbabwe's Ruling Party is Squeezing the Opposition's Finances", *The Africa Report*, 20 September 2024, https://www.theafricareport.com/362149/zimbabwe-how-political-parties-finance-act-is-weaponised-to-annihilate-the-opposition/ (accessed 28 October 2024).

65 N Ndoro, "Zanu-PF, Mwonzora Share US$1,5 Million Ahead of 2023 Elections", *Nehanda Radio*, 21 March 2023, https://nehandaradio.com/2023/03/21/zanu-pf-mwonzora-share-us15-million-ahead-of-2023-elections/ (accessed 20 November 2024).

Court judgement (as previously discussed) that gave him control of the party, the distribution of the funds became a *fait accompli*. It is widely suspected that Mwonzora is a Trojan horse for ZANU-PF in its endeavor to undermine the *bona fide* opposition. Analysts say that the financial regulation of parties in Zimbabwe is an ongoing scandal: the government has a consistent record of choosing to allocate political leaders to faction leaders that it has itself sponsored in order to divide the main opposition parties.[66] The CCC did not receive any funding because by the time the funds were allocated, the party (MDC-Alliance) that had qualified to get the funds under the Act was now in the hands of Mwonzora, technically making his party the legal recipient of the funding.

5. The impact of limited and politicised party regulation

The limited and politicised regulatory framework in Zimbabwe has left the opposition exposed and vulnerable. The previous section discussed the treacherous political terrain that the opposition MDC and CCC had to navigate over the years. In the absence of a properly and fairly administered constitutional framework, especially in the context of a country like Zimbabwe where a de facto one-party system is firmly in place, opposition parties face unique challenges, including attempts to extirpate them from the political space altogether. In the case of the MDC and CCC, this led to serious levels of destabilisation. The parties faced severe internal contradictions, including high levels of mistrust amongst themselves (as well as towards the political system itself). Paranoia and fear resulted in the adoption of a general siege mentality and defensive posture. In a bid to counteract or minimise its exposure, the opposition parties resorted to a new praxis in its politics, with this having a negative impact on internal democracy. A few examples are discussed below.

5.1 Strategic ambiguity: the CCC goes "structureless"

In response to the onslaught on the party after the 2018 elections and the suspicion that ZANU-PF had already compromised some of the top leadership of the party, Chamisa pursued a new, and controversial, political

66 Langa, *supra* n. 64.

strategy. Prior to its announcement, the party had functioned as a unit with collective decision-making as per its constitution.[67] Acting unilaterally, however, Chamisa surprised many observers (but excited his millions of supporters) by announcing that in the run-up to the 2023 elections, the CCC would operate without its structures (including the party's hitherto crucial women and youth assemblies). It would also operate without a constitution (even though one was in the process of being put together). Referring to the need for "strategic ambiguity", the party would, also for the first time, not be holding an elective congress: he, Chamisa, would be the sole, uncontested candidate for the presidential election. The brave new era of "strategic ambiguity" demanded changes.

Chamisa's rationale for the new strategy was to provide protection for the party in anticipation of further interference from the government. It was widely reported that for the 2023 elections, ZANU-PF, through a state-security-aligned organisation, Forever Associates of Zimbabwe (FAZ), had devised a grand plan to deploy its own agents to contest the CCC's primary parliamentary elections. Such a move would facilitate a smooth capture of the party and lead to the creation of a loyal opposition in parliament and in national politics, thus furthering the one-party-state agenda.

Despite the CCC's efforts to resist this attempt, the FAZ still managed to interfere with the initial candidate-selection process. Such interference resulted in double candidates appearing as contestants for the CCC in parliament as well as local government.[68] Consequently, this blatant exposure forced the CCC to find ways of circumventing this blind spot, but it only created further problems.

In addition, Chamisa focused all power on himself, in the process barring any official from speaking to the media (with the exceptions of CCC spokesperson Fadzayi Mahere and her deputy, Gift Ostalos Siziba). He also side-lined some of the key leaders who had been founding members of the party in 1999 and wielded substantial influence in the party, such as Welshman Ncube and Tendai Biti. In this way, he entered new and uncharted waters. These moves proved to be immensely popular among grassroots supporters and went either unquestioned or endorsed by them. Among the

67 Article 6(1) of the MDC constitution outlines the party's 15 organs, starting with the congress, national conference, national council, and national executive committee, and extending to ward- and branch-level.

68 P Masau, "CCC Double Candidates 'Sponsor' Exposed", *Newsday*, 20 July 2023, https://www.newsday.co.zw/local-news/article/200014206/ccc-double-candidates-sponsor-exposed (accessed 19 November 2024).

former leadership, it generated a great deal of animosity. In particular, Biti and Ncube proved to be so disillusioned by Chamisa's unilateral action that – feeling disrespected – they began to work behind the scenes to undermine Chamisa.

To further ring-fence the party from infiltration, Chamisa outlined what he called "citizenocratic" candidate selection. This was to be a process which would involve wide consultation with stakeholders in particular constituencies or wards, while the traditional party structures of the party that had previously done this work were to be done away with completely.[69] This proved difficult to implement in practice, with some members of the party claiming that the process lacked transparency and in fact even left the party more vulnerable to infiltration and manipulation by external forces (anyone could claim to be a CCC member for voting purposes or to seek nomination).

5.2 Abandonment of the party constitution

Another drastic measure was Chamisa's decision to operate without a party constitution, something which severely undermined the CCC's internal democracy. Previously, the MDC had always been guided and constrained by its constitution. Article 3(1) of the MDC constitution envisaged "a Social Democratic Party whose core values shall be solidarity, justice, equality, liberty, freedom, transparency, humble and obedient leadership and accountability".[70] Chamisa's move was therefore highly unexpected. Even though it could be understood as an exercise in realism in response to the existential threat to the party posed by ZANU-PF's unrelenting efforts to infiltrate it, this represented a huge contradiction and was a major gamble on Chamisa's part.

In fact, Chamisa's initiative would contribute to the subsequent demise of the party as top officials like Ncube and Biti not only dumped him but began working with Tshabangu behind the scenes to undermine him. It led, finally, to Chamisa's voluntarily walking away from the party he had fought

69 A Vinga, "Zimbabwe: Chamisa Outlines 'Citizenocratic' Candidate Selection – Says Nomination Process Kicks off This Week", *AllAfrica*, 3 April 2023, https://allafrica.com/stories/202304030114.html (accessed 30 December 2024).

70 Constitution of the Movement for Democratic Change, Article 3(1), January 2000, https://www.veritaszim.net/sites/veritas_d/files/THE%20FINAL%20CONSTITUTION.pdf (accessed 30 October 2024).

so hard to rebuild from the ashes of the MDC. Ncube's recent remarks in that context are worth quoting at length since they bring out the deep resentment that led to Chamisa's ousting:

> When you are in the struggle for democracy, when you say you are a democratic alternative that you will govern democratically, that means that you must be organised democratically yourselves. When you say you are the only leader with authority over everything, you become the dear leader. You are the president and chief spokesperson. You are the secretary-general. You are the treasurer-general. You direct the closure of all party accounts. You operate without any known party accounts. There are no financial oversight procedures mechanisms.[71]

Chamisa may have felt justified to act in the manner he did as a response to the challenges the party faced in a chaotic political landscape. This chapter suggests that he might not have been compelled to take this unprecedent route had a proper regulatory framework been in place, one that ring-fences political parties from illegalities and state-sanctioned attacks.

6. Conclusion

This chapter has explored the toxic political environment in Zimbabwe and how the formal regulation of political practice in this environment has impacted on opposition parties. It has shown that the MDC and CCC were forced to abandon some of their key principles as democratic alternatives in an attempt to survive in this harsh environment. Where regulation did exist, its intention, efficiency, and effectiveness are matters of dispute. In providing only limited regulation, political parties are faced with numerous, devastating, and often decisive challenges. It is trite to mention that the opposition faces a difficult conundrum: the very principles of openness, constitutionalism and internal democracy that make the opposition so valuable render it, at the same time, extremely vulnerable to state-sponsored destabilisation. But it cannot abandon these same principles without opening itself up to the problems and vulnerabilities discussed above. Despite the reality of the fears that Chamisa had regarding state-orchestrated

71 D Gatsi, "Welshman Ncube Tears into 'Completely Autocratic' Chamisa – Says He Led Opposition through 'Runners'", *New Zimbabwe*, 25 June 2004, https://www.newzimbabwe.com/welshman-ncube-tears-into-completely-autocratic-chamisa-says-he-led-opposition-through-runners/ (accessed 3 February 2024).

infiltration, his principle of "strategic ambiguity" seems only to have further weakened his party. (For example, when the CCC began to operate without any structures or a constitution, this created much confusion, as anyone could claim to be a member.) This has led some analysts (such as Ibbo Mandaza) to conclude that Chamisa's "gamble of having a structureless party failed".[72]

Political-party regulation is vulnerable to abuse because it does not operate in a political vacuum. Whilst section 129(1)(k) of the Constitution exists to protect political parties against members who use it as a vehicle to get elected and then abandon it, it is clear that this aspect of political-party regulation regarding recalling elected representatives is highly problematic. The relevant law is vulnerable to abuse as the vagueness following the split of a party creates difficulty if, for example, a member is purportedly expelled without a procedural disciplinary hearing. Furthermore, when abused, this law does the electorate a great injustice if it is assumed that voting is based solely on the candidate's membership of a political party. In fact, a significant number of voters do not belong to a political party, or if they do, may vote for a member of a different political party based on the candidate's individual traits and qualities. The recalls are done summarily without any consultation with the electorate. To compound everything, in a political context like Zimbabwe's, where the ruling party is avowedly focused on maintaining a one-party state, the law is weaponised to meet this ultimate objective.

There are dire implications to having a poorly regulated framework for political parties in Africa. It makes good leaders bad and bad leaders worse in their search for survival at all costs. As this chapter has shown, it also stifles opposition parties and political competition. As the political history of Zimbabwe shows, extreme actions are all too easily undertaken once political leaders feel they can justify undemocratic actions as responses to the urgency of political demands. The rule of Mugabe exemplified this. Mugabe made full use of the emergency powers provided by the Constitution to crush dissent in the early 1980s under the cover of restoring law and order. On the apparent justification that a security response to so-called dissidents

72 I Mafundikwa, "'Structureless Party': Has Chamisa Led Zimbabwe's Main Opposition Astray?", *Al Jazeera*, 12 February 2024, https://www.aljazeera.com/features/2024/2/12/structureless-party-how-chamisa-led-zimbabwes-main-opposition-astray (accessed 30 December 2024).

was necessary, more than 20,000 ethnic Ndebeles were killed in just over five years.[73]

Without suggesting in any way that Chamisa is equivalent to Mugabe, the argument here is that Chamisa, who presents himself as an avowed democrat, appears to have adopted ZANU-PF methods despite having fought against ZANU-PF throughout his life. In his attempt to save his party, he abandoned consensus-based leadership, sacrificing his party's prime commitments to constitutionalism and accountability. This chapter argues, moreover, that the subsequent contradictions in the CCC were the result of its attempt to deal with the challenges posed by the difficult political environment and, in particular, the weaponised regulatory and legislative framework it operated within. Many of these contradictions were so severe that they could not be reconciled with the identity of the party and what it stood for.

The question is not whether Tsvangirai and Chamisa were motivated by genuine concerns to protect the party, or whether they were acting in the personal pursuit of political power; it is impossible to know as only they can answer that. Rather, the analysis is interested in the fact that this mutilation of party processes and procedures becomes the unintentional result of vulnerability arising from the lack of the protection that a proper regulatory framework would otherwise normally provide.

References

Books, articles, chapters in books, and others

BBC, "Nelson Chamisa: Zimbabwe Opposition CCC Leader Quits 'Contaminated' Party", *BBC*, 26 January 2024, https://www.bbc.com/news/world-africa-68095685 (accessed 30 December 2024)

Catholic Commission for Justice and Peace in Zimbabwe and the Legal Resources Foundation, *Breaking the Silence: A Report into the Disturbances in Matabeleland and the Midlands 1980–1988*, Harare, Legal Resources Foundation, CCJPZ (1997), https://davidcoltart.com/wp-content/uploads/2006/10/breakingthesilence.pdf (accessed 30 December 2024)

73 Catholic Commission for Justice and Peace in Zimbabwe and the Legal Resources Foundation, *Breaking the Silence: A Report into the Disturbances in Matabeleland and the Midlands 1980–1988*, Harare, Legal Resources Foundation, CCJPZ (1997), pp 1–36, https://davidcoltart.com/wp-content/uploads/2006/10/breakingthesilence.pdf (accessed 30 December 2024).

Chibango C, "The Registration and Regulation of Political Parties in Zimbabwe: A Key Pillar in Prospects for Free and Fair Election", 1 (2022) *Journal on Governance, Human Rights and Democracy in Zimbabwe*

Chiripasi T, "Tsvangirai MDC-T Recalls Biti, 17 Lawmakers from Parliament", *Voice of America*, 6 November 2014, https://www.voazimbabwe.com/a/zimbabwe-mdc-t-recalls-biti-17-lawmakers-from-parliament/2510826.html (accessed 30 December 2024)

Coakley J, "The Significance of Names: The Evolution of Irish Party Labels", 5 (1980) *Études irlandaises*, pp 171–182

Constitution of the Movement for Democratic Change, as amended and adopted at the 4th Congress of the Party at the City Sports Centre Harare from 31st of October to the 1st of November 2014

Dawson RW, "The Representative One-party State: Mugabe's Search for Political Control in Zimbabwe", (1989), Unpublished PhD Thesis, University of British Columbia

Dube G, "CCC 'Interim Secretary General' Recalls Dozens of Party Lawmakers, Councilors", *Voice of America*, 4 October 2023, https://www.voazimbabwe.com/a/7296398.html/ (accessed 20 November 2024)

USAID, *An Analysis of the Legal Framework Governing Elections in Zimbabwe, USAID*, 1 September 2019, https://pdf.usaid.gov/pdf_docs/PA00W598.pdf (accessed 14 February 2024)

European Union Election Observation Mission, *Final Report Republic of Zimbabwe: Harmonised Elections 2018*, Veritas (2018), https://www.veritaszim.net/sites/veritas_d/files/EU%20Election%20Observers%20Final%20Report%20Zimbabwe%202018-.pdf (accessed 2 October 2024)

Fombad C, "Political Party Constitutionalisation in Africa: Trends and Prospects for Deepening Constitutionalism", in R Dixon, T Ginsburg and A Abebe (eds.), *Comparative Constitutional Law in Africa*, Cheltenham, Edward Elgar Publishing (2022), pp 109–135

Freedom House, "Freedom in the World 2024: Zimbabwe", *Freedom House*, n.d., https://freedomhouse.org/country/zimbabwe/freedom-world/2024 (accessed 31 October 2024)

Gatsi D, "Welshman Ncube Tears into 'Completely Autocratic' Chamisa – Says He Led Opposition through 'Runners", *New Zimbabwe*, 25 June 2004, https://www.newzimbabwe.com/welshman-ncube-tears-into-completely-autocratic-chamisa-says-he-led-opposition-through-runners/ (accessed 3 February 2024)

Guma N, "Mwonzora Kills MDC as it Awaits its Burial during General Elections", *The NewsHawks*, 26 June 2023, https://thenewshawks.com/mwonzora-kills-mdc-as-it-awaits-its-burial-during-general-elections/ (accessed on 17 June 2024)

Gregory M, "Zimbabwe 1980: Politicisation through Armed Struggle and Electoral Mobilisation", 19 (1981), *The Journal of Commonwealth & Comparative Politics*, pp 63–94

Harris LB, "Swift Recall of CCC MPs Shows ZANU-PF's Meddling, Analysts Say", *CITE*, 10 October 2023, https://cite.org.zw/swift-recall-of-ccc-mps-shows-zanu-pfs-meddling-analysts-say/ (accessed 12 October 2024)

Human Rights Watch, "The Elephant in the Room: Reforming Zimbabwe's Security Sector Ahead of Elections", *Human Rights Watch*, 4 June 2013, https://www.hrw.org/report/2013/06/04/elephant-room/reforming-zimbabwes-security-sector-ahead-elections (accessed 16 November 2024)

International Republican Institute and National Democratic Institute, *IRI/NDI Zimbabwe International Election Observation Mission Final Report*, Washington DC, International Republican Institute (2018), https://www.ndi.org/sites/default/files/2018-10-29%20Final%20ZIEOM%20Report%20%288MB%29.pdf (accessed 16 October 2024)

Jarvis SE, *The Talk of the Party: Political Labels, Symbolic Capital, and American Life*, Maryland, Rowman and Littlefield (2005)

Kwashirai VC, "The New Enemy in the 1990 General Elections Was Zum", in VC Kwashirai, *Election Violence in Zimbabwe: Human Rights, Politics and Power*, Cambridge, Cambridge University Press (2023), pp 65–93

Langa V, "Zimbabwe's Ruling Party is Squeezing the Opposition's Finances", *The Africa Report*, 20 September 2024, https://www.theafricareport.com/362149/zimbabwe-how-political-parties-finance-act-is-weaponised-to-annihilate-the-opposition/, (accessed 28 October 2024)

Laakso, "Relationship between the State and Civil Society in the Zimbabwean Elections 1995", 34 (1996), *Journal of Commonwealth & Comparative Politics*, pp 218–234

Lawson S, "Conceptual Issues in the Comparative Study of Regime Change and Democratisation", 25 (1993), *Comparative Politics*, pp 183–205

Mafundikwa I, "Zimbabwe's CCC Crisis: Farce Turning to Tragedy for the Opposition", *BBC*, 8 December 2023, https://www.bbc.com/news/world-africa-67647449 (accessed 19 November 2024)

Mafundikwa I, "'Structureless Party': Has Chamisa Led Zimbabwe's Main Opposition Astray?", *Al Jazeera*, 12 February 2024, https://www.aljazeera.com/features/2024/2/12/structureless-party-how-chamisa-led-zimbabwes-main-opposition-astray (accessed 30 December 2024)

Masau P, "CCC Double Candidates 'Sponsor' Exposed", *Newsday*, 20 July 2023, https://www.newsday.co.zw/local-news/article/200014206/ccc-double-candidates-sponsor-exposed (accessed 19 November 2024)

Matiashe FS, "Zimbabwe: With Its Two-Thirds Majority, How Far will ZANU-PF Go?", *The Africa Report*, 15 February 2024, https://www.theafricareport.com/336371/zimbabwe-with-its-two-thirds-majority-how-far-will-zanu-pf-go/ (accessed 18 October 2024)

Masunungure E, *Regulation of Political Parties in Zimbabwe: Registration, Finance, and other Support*, Zimbabwe Elections Support Network (ZESN), August 2006, https://www.zesn.org.zw/wp-content/_protected/publications/publication_113.pdf (accessed 18 August 2024)

Mude T, "Digital Technologies and Election Management in Zimbabwe: Pseudo-democratic Transition and Contorted Delirium?", 47 Special Issue (2022) *Africa Development*, pp 179–198

Munyoro F and Maphosa V, "Chamisa, Mudzuri Appointments Illegal – Court", *The Herald*, 9 May 2019, https://www.herald.co.zw/chamisa-mudzuri-appointments-illegal-court/ (accessed 18 October 2024)

New Zimbabwe, "Recalled CCC MPs, Councillors barred from contesting in February 3 by-elections", New Zimbabwe, 19 January 2024, https://www.newzimbabwe.com/recalled-ccc-mps-councillors-barred-from-contesting-in-february-3-by-elections/ (accessed 17 July 2025).

Ndlovu-Gatsheni SJ, *Elections in Zimbabwe: A Recipe for Tension or a Remedy for Reconciliation*, Wynberg, Institute for Justice and Reconciliation (2012), https://paren.org.za/site/wp-content/uploads/2016/07/IJR-Zimbabwe-Elections-OP-WEB.pdf (accessed 3 September 2024)

Pottie D, "Parliamentary elections in Zimbabwe, 2000", 1 (2001) *Journal of African Elections*, pp 61–70

Roux T, "The Postcolonial Adaptation of Authoritarian Legalism in Zimbabwe", in T Roux (ed.), *The Politico-Legal Dynamics of Judicial Review: A Comparative Analysis*, Cambridge, Cambridge University Press, (2018), pp 193–241

Rusinga R, "Zimbabwe's 2018 Harmonised Elections: An Assessment of Credibility," 20, *Journal of African Elections*, pp 90–114

Sabao C, "'Sanctions Are the Source of Our Suffering': Of ZANU-PF's 'Exhausted' Rhetoric and Blame-Gaming Tactics as Hegemonic Preservation", in E Mavengano and I Mhute (eds.), *Sub-Saharan Political Cultures of Deceit in Language, Literature, and the Media*, Vol. I, Switzerland, Cham, Springer Nature (2023), pp 343–365

Sachikonye LM, "Between Authoritarianism and Democratisation: The Challenges of a Transition Process in Zimbabwe", Occasional Paper 2 (July 2009), *Institute for Development Studies*, Paper presented at Centre of Political and Historical Studies on Africa and the Middle East, Bologna

Sachikonye, LM, "Political Parties and the 2005 Elections in Zimbabwe", 4 (2005), *Journal of African Elections*, pp 63–73

Shaw RH, "Towards the One-Party State in Zimbabwe: A Study in African Political Thought", 24 (1986) *Journal of Modern African Studies*, pp 373–394

Selolwane O and Shale V, "Inter-Party Relations and Democracy in Botswana", *Electoral Institute for Sustainable Democracy in Africa*, 2008, https://policycommons.net/artifacts/1448811/inter-party-relations-and-democracy-in-botswana/2080589/ (accessed 23 February 2024)

Sylvester C, "Whither Opposition in Zimbabwe?" 33 (1995), *Journal of Modern African Studies*, pp 403–423

The Herald, "Two Parties Merge as ZANU (PF)", *The Herald*, 23 December 2021, https://www.herald.co.zw/two-parties-merge-as-zanu-pf/ (accessed 21 August 2024)

Tsholo K, "Do Transitions from Liberation Movements to Political Parties Guarantee Good Governance? The Case of ZANU-PF and the ANC", 43 (Nov/Dec 2021) *Strategic Review for Southern Africa*, pp 11–39

Vengesai S, "A Critical Examination of the Effectiveness of the Zimbabwean Multi-party Liaison Committee", 1 (2022) *Journal on Governance, Human Rights and Democracy in Zimbabwe*

Vinga A, "Zimbabwe: Chamisa Outlines 'Citizenocratic' Candidate Selection – Says Nomination Process Kicks off This Week", *AllAfrica*, 3 April 2023, https://allafrica.com/stories/202304030114.html (accessed 30 December 2024)

Vohito-Anyanwu S, "Promoting Constitutional Democracy: Regulating Political Parties in the Central African Republic and Senegal", 23 (2020) *Potchefstroom Electronic Law Journal*, pp 1–34

Voice of America, "MDC Alliance Fuming over Govt's Disbursement of Almost $60 Million in State Funds to Mwonzora's MDC-T", *Voice of America*, 29 August 2021, https://www.voazimbabwe.com/a/mdc-alliance-state-disbursement-funds/6078040.html (accessed 22 November 2024)

Wulff A (ed.), *Legal Framework for Political Parties in Selected Countries of Sub-Saharan Africa*, Nairobi, Konrad-Adenauer-Stiftung Rule of Law Program for Sub-Saharan Africa (2017), https://www.kas.de/c/document_library/get_file?uuid=735c449b-fd52-c43f-6f58-403a818d3be9&groupId=252038 (accessed 12 September 2024)

Zimbabwe Democracy Institute, "Zimbabwe Transition in a Muddy Terrain: Political Economy under Military Capture", *Kubatana*, 14 December 2017, https://kubatana.net/wp-content/uploads/2017/12/Zimbabwe-Transition-in-A-Muddy-Terrain-Political-Economy-Under-MilitaryCapture-Terrain (accessed 17 November 2024)

Zimeye, "Gonese Analyses Supreme Court Judgement on MDC Leadership Battle", 9 April 2020, https://www.zimeye.net/2020/04/09/gonese-analyses-supreme-court-judgement-on-mdc-leadership-battle (accessed 7 March 2025)

ZimLive, "Mwonzora Wins Chaotic MDC-T Congress, Khupe Claims Voter Fraud", *ZimLive*, 28 December 2020, https://www.zimlive.com/mwonzora-wins-chaotic-congress-abandoned-by-khupe-and-others-over-voter-fraud-violence/ (accessed 11 October 2024)

Zindoga T and Machivenyika F, "MDC–T Sanctions Call Rapped", *The Herald*, 20 August 2015, https://www.herald.co.zw/mdc-t-sanctions-call-rapped/ (accessed 22 November 2024)

Chikohora E and Chokutamba L, "Governing Security Sector Reform in Zimbabwe and the Prospects of Positive Peace in a Polarised Polity", 10 (2022), *Global Scientific Journals*, pp 961–988

Moore D, "ZANU-PF and the Ghosts of Foreign Funding", 32 (2005) *Review of African Political Economy*, pp 156–162

"Zanu (PF) Admits Breaking Law", *The Zimbabwean*, 18 September 2013, https://www.thezimbabwean.co/2013/09/zanu-pf-admits-breaking-law/ (accessed 4 April 2024)

TIME, "Zimbabwe: One-Party State", *TIME*, 20 August 1984, https://content.time.com/time/subscriber/article/0,33009,954344,00.html (accessed 13 June 2024)

Zhakata I, "Chamisa Kicked out of CCC", *The Herald*, 11 October 2023, https://www.herald.co.zw/chamisa-kicked-out-from-ccc/ (accessed 17 November 2024)

Ndoro N, "Zanu-PF, Mwonzora Share US$1,5 Million Ahead of 2023 Elections", *Nehanda Radio*, 21 March 2023, https://nehandaradio.com/2023/03/21/zanu-pf-mwonzora-share-us15-million-ahead-of-2023-elections/ (accessed 20 November 2024)

Business Times, “Douglas Mwonzora Pulls out of August 23 Presidential Race”, *Business Times*, 8 August 2023, https://businesstimes.co.zw/douglas-mwonzora-pulls-out-of-august-23-presidential-race/ (accessed 1 October 2024)

Table of cases

Supreme Court of Zimbabwe, *Movement for Democratic Change & Anor v Mashavira & 3 Others (Civil Appeal SC 289 of 2019; SC 56 of 2020)* [2020], ZWSC 56, 31 March 2020

Table of legislation

Political Parties (Finance) Act No. 4 of 2001, Chapter 2:11

Electoral Act No. 25 of 2004, Chapter 2:13

Constitution of Zimbabwe 2013

Chapter 15 Swimming against the Tide: Militancy and Diplomacy as Survival Mechanisms for Opposition Parties in Uganda's Militarised Politics

James Nkuubi

1. Introduction

2005 saw the much-vaunted re-opening of multiparty political space in Uganda after 20 years of closure. This chapter argues that since 2005, this "open" space has in fact shrunk with every passing year. Despite the formal fact of the support for a multiparty system in Uganda in the 1995 Constitution, attempts to stifle oppositional political parties continue. To this end, the National Resistance Movement (NRM) government has deployed various means: coercive force; a restrictive legal framework; patronage; state capture; a highly securitised and militarised social fabric; and a dominant-party system.

Despite manifest evidence of hostility to multiparty democracy, many have been deceived by the existence of what on the surface appears to be a fairly comprehensive and seemingly facilitative legal framework for multiparty democracy. This framework formally guarantees the protection of civil liberties, including the freedoms of assembly, association, and political participation. However, oppositional political parties are coming to realise that they need to reflect on how best to survive in what is a hostile political space. Given the fact of NRM dominance (enforced as it is by open military support and a general militarisation of society), questions of how to promote the necessary adaptation, coping, collaboration, and resilience of opposition political parties are becoming ever more pressing.

This chapter examines the effectiveness of the survival mechanisms that political parties adopt in response to militarised politics. Can these strategies enable parties to survive, grow, and maintain oversight and accountability against the ruling government, or if they inadvertently weaken the parties and make them easier targets for government repression? Do these survival mechanisms provoke retaliation from the state, or are they regarded with indifference?

The chapter takes a new perspective (adapted from the thinking of the opposition parties themselves) to rejuvenate the discourse on the evolution of multiparty politics in Uganda. It examines how (with some parties at least) their resilience and adaptation of "non-conventional" methods of coping with state-led militarised politics come to border on "criminal militancy". It also examines another model of survival adopted by parties under siege, one that ordinary citizens refer to as "sell-out diplomacy". The upshot is that each opposition party retreats and re-emerges with unpredictable and innovative strategies for coping with state restrictions that redefine what is "acceptable" and "rightful".

The chapter examines the factors that inform and motivate these strategies, the links between them, and how effective (if at all) they have been in helping opposition political parties to survive the effects of the militarisation of the state. It argues that the modes of survival and resistance adopted by opposition parties in their struggle to survive have both short- and long-term ramifications, both positive and negative, for multiparty politics in Uganda, and particularly so for the quest for constitutionalism. It also notes how these survival mechanisms themselves attract the attention of the state, resulting in reactions which have diverse implications for the political landscape of the country.

The chapter examines the evolution of multiparty resilience in Uganda by examining the experience of two opposition parties: the National Unity Platform (NUP), formerly the People Power Movement (PPM) and the youngest opposition political party in Uganda as of October 2024; and the oldest opposition party, the Democratic Party (DP). It looks at a new trend in Ugandan opposition politics, that of forming "working co-operation agreements" with the ruling NRM government (which means effectively being subsumed in the NRM government in contrast to widely known coalition government politics). The chapter uses the case of the DP, which concluded such an agreement in 2022, to show how this works in practice and what it is likely to mean for Uganda's multiparty dispensation.

In contrast to previous discussions, this chapter examines how certain parties (such as the NUP) are employing militant yet legal forms of opposition and how this has led to the rise of militancy and counter-militancy in Ugandan politics.[1] It argues that the more militant models of political

1 Y Kiranda and M Kamp (eds.), *Reality Check: The State of Multiparty Democracy in Uganda*, Kampala, Uganda, Konrad-Adenauer-Stiftung (2010), https://www.kas.de/c/document_library/get_file?uuid=3deffb14-7b9c-9a87-cad8-33ddc54e26d5&groupId

opposition are under-explored within the scholarship on multiparty politics in Uganda. Ultimately, the chapter asserts that the approaches these opposition parties take, whether diplomatic or militant, will significantly influence the future of multiparty democracy and the consolidation of constitutionalism in Uganda. It concludes that the chosen method of coping can either empower or undermine a party's viability.

This chapter is divided into four sections. Section 1 (namely, this brief introduction) lays the groundwork for the central argument and outlines the evolution of Uganda's multiparty system up until October 2024. Section 2 provides an overview of the current state of multiparty politics in militarised Uganda, detailing how this militarisation has subtly transformed the state over the past 20 years (2004–2024). Additionally, this section provides an overview of the inner state of health of political parties, and particularly of the opposition political parties. Section 3 delves into case studies of two parties, the NUP and the DP, highlighting the strategies they employ to navigate the challenges of militarised politics in contemporary Uganda. The chapter concludes in section 4 with a summary of the main findings and a number of recommendations aimed at promoting the de-militarisation of politics.

2. The state of multiparty politics in militarised Uganda

2.1 The evolution of multipartyism in post-independence Uganda (1962–1995)

Uganda's journey to independence was significantly shaped by a variety of political parties that emerged during the pre-independence period, and especially in the 1950s. Each party reflected different interests, produced different ideologies, and targeted different constituencies, contributing to the complex political landscape of the time. The three main parties formed in this period were the Uganda National Congress (UPC) (1952); the DP (1954); and the Progress Party (established in 1955).[2] In addition, the United Congress Party began in 1957; the Uganda People's Union in 1958; the

=252038 (accessed 18 November 2024); JO Onyango and J Ahikire (eds.), *Controlling Consent: Uganda's 2016 Elections*, Trenton, New Jersey, Africa World Press (2017).

2 Tumushabe G, Rwakakamba M, and Makhone B, "Hard Choices or No Choice at All: Questions for Uganda's Political Parties", 1 (2015) *The Situation Room Uganda Debates Papers*, pp 7–8.

Uganda National Movement (1959); and the UNC in 1960.[3] Finally, the Kabaka Yekka (KY) (loosely interpreted as "King Alone") was established in 1962 (with its roots in the Buganda Kingdom, it arguably aligned with the interests and identities of the Baganda ethnic group located in central Uganda).[4]

Of these, the two parties most influential in shaping Uganda's multiparty democracy were the DP (often seen as a voice for the Catholic community and a strong advocate for democratic principles), and the UPC, which aimed to creating a broader nationalist agenda. The rivalry and interaction between the two not only provided the electorate with political choices but also contributed to shaping Uganda's ideas about multiparty governance, coming to a sudden halt with what was effectively a total ban on political parties in 1971.[5]

Prior to this, the two parties were major players in the 1962 general elections, with the DP's popular support reflected in the majority it gained in Parliament. However, the UPC sought to enhance its influence by forming a controversial alliance with the KY. This was described by many observers as "artificial": it represented a strategic political manoeuvre rather than a genuine unification of ideologies brought about through grassroots support.[6] Nonetheless, this alliance enabled the UPC to establish Uganda's first post-independence government, with Milton Obote as Prime Minister and Sir Edward Muteesa II as the ceremonial President (and also the "king" of Buganda).[7] Obote's administration faced the daunting task of addressing the country's ethnic and political divisions while seeking to create a cohesive national identity and a framework for multiparty governance that could successfully respond to the aspirations of the people.

The quest for multiparty politics was severely undermined by various measures taken by the governments of the time, including banning political parties or crippling them with restrictions on recruitment and mobilisa-

3 *Ibid*, p 8.

4 *Ibid*.

5 L Wild and F Golooba-Mutebi, "Review of International Assistance to Political Party and Party System Development, Case Study Report: Uganda", London, Overseas Development Institute (August 2010), p 2.

6 *Ibid*.

7 F Musisi, RO Herbst, and A Mahajubu, "Unlocking the Mysteries of the Origins of the 1966 Ugandan Constitutional Crisis Global", 6 (2018) *Journal of Arts, Humanities and Social Sciences*, pp 14–25, 19.

tion.[8] On 20 December 1969, President Obote, in an effort to counter the momentum that the opposition was gaining, and as a response to an assassination attempt, declared a state of emergency and banned opposition political parties.[9] This action was a significant setback to the young nation, as Obote had in effect created a path to a one-party authoritarian state. Ironically enough, Uganda had won independence in the first place partly as a result of the organised demands made by nationalist-based parties and social movements formed during the colonial era between 1920 and 1956 – parties and movements whose political descendants were now banned.[10]

The attack on opposition political parties continued apace during General Idi Amin's "reign of terror" (1971–1979). In this period, the rule of military officers and martial law prevailed, with no signs of democracy or any form of citizen involvement in governance.[11] Amin was overthrown on 11 April 1979 by armed dissidents from the Uganda National Liberation Front acting together with the Tanzanian Defence Forces. A civil war ensued, with no prospect of multipartyism.[12] The 1980 attempt of holding multiparty elections – which enjoyed the limited participation of the two older political parties, the UPC and DP, along with a sprinkling of smaller parties – ended in a shambles, with widespread vote-rigging and intimidation.[13]

Despite its promises of political reform after gaining power in 1986, the National Resistance Army/Movement (NRA/M) maintained the ban on political-party activities. Legal Notice 1 of 1986 effectively banned parties by prohibiting them from holding conferences; opening branches; sponsoring candidates; recruiting members; or displaying party colours. At the same

8 GM Carbone, "Political Parties In A 'No-Party Democracy': Hegemony and Opposition Under 'Movement Democracy' in Uganda", 9 (2003) *Party Politics*, pp 485–501, 486.

9 *Ibid.*

10 C Summers, and A Sikainga, "Ugandan Politics World War II (1939–1949)", in JA Byfield, CA Brown, and T Parsons (eds.), *Africa and World War II*, Cambridge, Cambridge University Press (2015), pp 480–498.

11 S Makara, "The Challenge of Building Strong Political Parties for Democratic Governance in Uganda: Does Multiparty Politics Have a Future?", 41 (2009) *East African Review*, p 10.

12 G Roberts , "The Uganda-Tanzania War, the Fall of Idi Amin, and the Failure of African Diplomacy, 1978–1979", 8 (2014) *Journal of Eastern African Studies*, pp 692–709, 700.

13 Makara, *supra* n. 11, p 10.

time, the NRA/M actively recruited citizens into its movement.[14] Beginning with Obote in 1969, intensified by Amin from 1971 to 1979, and maintained by the NRA/M after 1986, the ban on political parties significantly altered Uganda's political landscape. It restricted political pluralism, hindered organised political participation, and ushered in an era of repression that would have lasting repercussions for the country's political environment.

Various justifications have been provided by post-independence Ugandan leaders for the bans on political parties. One explanation predominates: this is that political parties contribute to ethnic and religious division within the country, given that the politicisation of ethnicity has played a significant role in party-formation.[15] Makara has summed up how leaders from Obote onwards made their case, noting that "for the sake of national unity, the fight against poverty, disease and ignorance, it was necessary to establish a one-party system instead of the factional and tribal groupings that characterized political parties".[16] Against this background, Makara maintains that there was tangible progress in the country in the immediate post-independence era (1962–1966) when Uganda was functional under multiparty dispensation. The real issue is not parties but their vulgarisation through ethnicisation.[17] All in all, the first 30 years of Uganda's independence were characterised by a deep disdain for political parties. Only in 1995, with the advent of a new constitution, did this change.

2.2 Elusive multipartyism in the post-1995 dispensation

The 1995 Constitution aimed to usher in a new era focused on human rights, the rule of law, and enhanced efforts at democratisation. Notably robust, the 1995 Constitution includes a dedicated chapter on rights and establishes a framework for a multiparty governance system. It has eight key provisions that support the development of such a system. This section examines these foundational provisions and their implications for multiparty politics.

---

14 JA Okuku J, "Beyond 'Third Term' Politics: Constitutional Reform and Democratic Governance in Uganda", 11 (2005) *East African Journal of Peace and Human Rights*, pp 182–219.

15 J Okuku, "Ethnicity, State Power and the Democratization Process in Uganda", Discussion Paper No. 17, The Nordic Africa Institute (2002), pp 7–8.

16 Makara, *supra*, n. 11, p 10.

17 *Ibid.*

The first such provisions are found in the Constitution's National Objectives and Directive Principles of State Policy. These serve as the guiding framework for all state organs, citizens, organisations, and individuals in applying or interpreting the Constitution and laws, as well as in making and implementing policy decisions.[18] According to the framework, the Ugandan state shall be based on "democratic principles which empower and encourage the active participation of all citizens at all levels in their own governance".[19] It further provides that "all political and civic associations aspiring to manage and direct public affairs shall conform to democratic principles in their internal organizations and practice".[20] The principle also calls for the independence of civic organisations in "pursuit of their declared objectives".[21]

The second provision, Article 38 of the Constitution, highlights the importance of participatory democracy, which empowers citizens to engage actively in the political process. It guarantees every Ugandan citizen the right to "participate in the affairs of government, individually or through his or her representatives in accordance with law".[22] This dual approach allows citizens to voice their opinions and concerns directly, while also enabling them to elect or appoint representatives who can advocate for their interests in government. The second arm of the provision guarantees every Ugandan "a right to participate in peaceful activities to influence the policies of government through civic organizations".[23] By acknowledging the role of civic organisations, this article fosters participatory democracy and establishes a basis for the formation of political organisations and parties.

Thirdly, Article 29 of the Constitution strengthens multiparty politics by guaranteeing every individual the right to peacefully assemble, demonstrate, and petition, as well as the freedom of association. This includes the right to form and join groups such as trade unions, political parties, and other civic organisations.[24] It also guarantees individuals the "freedom of thought, conscience, and belief", something which implicitly allows them to create and join political parties that are aligned with their values and

18 National objective I(i), of the Constitution of Uganda, 1995, as amended.
19 *Ibid*, National objective II(i).
20 *Ibid*, National objective II(v).
21 *Ibid*, National objective II(vi).
22 *Ibid*, Article 38(1).
23 *Ibid*, Article 38(2).
24 *Ibid*, Article 29(1)(d) and (e).

aspirations. Together, these provisions form a crucial foundation for the establishment and growth of political parties.[25]

The fourth is Article 72 of the Constitution. This is essential to the definition of the multiparty-political landscape because it guarantees the right to form political organisations, including political parties (a right augmented by the Constitution (Amendment) Act, 2015). However, this right is not unconditional. The Constitution stipulates that such organisations must operate within specific guidelines (such as the requirement for registration) before they can begin to function. Additionally, it mandates Parliament to establish laws to regulate their financing and operations.[26] By requiring adherence to constitutional principles, registration, and regulatory oversight of financing, the article aims to promote a healthy environment in which diverse views coexist and democracy and the rights of citizens are safeguarded.

The fifth provision is Article 69. This is perhaps the most fundamental, as it expressly establishes the constitutionalisation of political parties. It sets forth a foundational principle for democratic governance in Uganda, entitling the populace to select and evolve their political systems according to their preferences. It underscores the significance of democratic processes, the importance of political pluralism, and the need for governance structures that reflect the will and interests of the people. The article explicitly states that the people of Uganda have the right to choose a political system that aligns with their "preferences through free and fair elections or referenda".[27] It further recognises multiple types of political systems through which Ugandans can exercise preference (indicating a commitment to political diversity). The systems mentioned are: (1) the so-called movement system, a broad-based political structure developed and promoted during the tenure of the NRA/M based on inclusivity and non-partisanship; (2) the multiparty political system, which allows multiple political parties to compete for power and promote democratic pluralism; and (3) any other democratic and representative political system, which leaves room for new

25 *Ibid*, Article 29(1)(d) and (e).

26 *Ibid*, Article 72(2) and (3). Article 72's headnote was amended in 2015, via the Constitution (Amendment) Act 12 of 2015. Section 2 of Act 12 of 2015 states: "Article 72 of the Constitution is amended by substituting for the headnote the following – 'Right to form political parties or political organisations'". In the previous provision, this right had been restricted solely to the "right to form political organisations".

27 Article 69(1) of the Constitution of Uganda, 1995, as amended.

political systems to emerge in the future in reflection of changes in society, governance needs, or popular preferences.[28]

The sixth provision is Article 70. This provides for the movement political system, which is described as broad-based, inclusive and nonpartisan and conforming to a diversity of principles.[29] These include participatory democracy; accountability and transparency; and accessibility to all positions of leadership by all citizens. The most significant of these principles concerns individual merit as a basis for election to political offices rather than affiliation to political parties.[30]

The seventh provision is Article 71. This establishes the framework for a multiparty political system in Uganda and outlines several critical principles that political parties must adhere to (in their formation, membership, organisation, and operations) in order to ensure a democratic and inclusive political environment.[31] Among things, the political party must have a national character;[32] show inclusivity in membership; demonstrate a democratic internal organisation (conforming to democratic principles as stipulated in the Constitution); ensure gender equality and representation; hold regular elections for national organs of the party; and demonstrate financial accountability. By establishing a framework for a multiparty political system that emphasises the above principles, Article 71 was intended not only to shape the political landscape and political parties generally, but also to enhance social cohesion and foster a more robust and participatory multiparty democracy. Of course, the realisation of these principles is contingent on effective implementation and a commitment to them by all stakeholders, including the government, political parties, civil society, and citizens themselves.

Equally important is Article 75. This, in the attempt to mark a fundamental departure from Uganda's turbulent past, prohibits Parliament from

28 *Ibid*, Article 69(2)(a)–(c).

29 *Ibid*, Article 70(1).

30 *Ibid*, Article 70(1)(d).

31 *Ibid*, Article 71. This article was amended in 2005 under section 15(b) of the Constitution (Amendment) Act 11 of 2005 by way of insertion. This particular provision allowed for the insertion of a new clause (2) stating as follows: "Parliament shall by law prescribe a code of conduct for political organisations and political parties and provide for the establishment of a national consultative forum for political parties and organisations with such functions as Parliament may prescribe." Section 15(a) of the Constitution (Amendment) Act affected only the numbering of clauses and had no substantive effect on the content of the provisions.

32 Article 71(a) –(f) of the Constitution of Uganda, 1995, as amended.

enacting a law to establish a one-party state. Here we find the endorsement of the multiparty-political system writ large.

2.3 Claw-back clauses in the Constitution

Although the Constitution includes measures aimed at constitutionalising political parties, their effectiveness is diminished by a number of restrictive clauses. Indeed, the very ban on political gatherings, association, and assembly that had characterised Uganda's turbulent past was carried forward in the 1995 Constitution. This prepared the ground for a one party-state by presenting "the movement" as the only viable alternative system of political governance for Ugandans. Consequently, while the Constitution ostensibly recognised multiparty politics, practical implementation remained constrained, eviscerating the promise of a diverse and functional political environment.

This retrogressive provision was embedded jointly in articles 271 and 270 of the Constitution. Article 271 recognised the political parties or organisations that were in existence immediately before the coming into force of the 1995 Constitution, extending their lease of life and allowing them to "continue to exist and operate [but only] in conformity with the provisions of the Constitution until Parliament was to enact laws relating to registration of political parties and organizations".[33] Similarly, Article 270 put a hold on the full functioning of political parties "until Parliament makes laws regulating the activities of political organizations in accordance with Article 73 of the Constitution". It provided for the continuance of political activities except in regard to the following:

> (a) opening and operating branch offices; (b) holding delegates' conferences; (c) holding public rallies; (d) sponsoring or offering a platform to or in any way campaigning for or against a candidate for any public elections; [and] (e) carrying on any activities that may interfere with the movement political system for the time being in force.[34]

The irony is that the activities restricted by these provisions were fundamental to the existence, functionality, identity, operation, survival, efficacy, and viability of political parties. They were crucial to the ability of political

33 *Ibid*, Article 271.
34 *Ibid*, Article 270 (a)–(e).

parties to establish the local presence essential to grassroots mobilisation and to develop their internal democratic processes and governance. In short, the prohibitions hollowed out the substance of what it is to be a political party. Parties hence remained side-lined and constrained under a de facto one-party system dominated by the NRA/M. This consolidation of power allowed the NRA/M to utilise its resources, state apparatus, and influence to make itself the only significant player in the political arena.

2.4 Enabling unfettered multipartyism: The 2000 and 2005 referendums

Political parties were legally recognised under the 1995 Constitution. However, while this legal framework was ostensibly there to support political pluralism, in reality it created an environment in which parties were unable to translate their legal status into any meaningful practice. They operated under a framework of legally enforced restrictions that stifled their development and rendered them largely insignificant in the country's political arena.

As a result, Uganda remained under the influence of an NRM political framework, one predicated on the concept of "individual merit" as the entry-card for anyone intending to engage in elective politics. The emphasis on individual merit remained a double-edged sword. On the one hand, it allowed for a broad range of candidates to participate in politics based on their qualifications and abilities; on the other, it reinforced the idea that political affiliation is secondary to personal credibility and accomplishments. Consequently, political parties could not gain any traction as collective entities representing diverse interests, ideologies, and constituencies.

But the winds of change were gathering momentum and clamouring for a full, unfettered return to a multiparty political system. The first window of opportunity came in June 2000 when a historical referendum asked voters: "Which political system do you wish to adopt, Movement or Multiparty?"[35] The results proved disappointing to advocates of the multiparty system. The referendum saw 91 per cent of voters in favour of continuing with the movement system. However, the low turnout (of about 47 per cent) and the lack of adequate campaigning opportunities for the pro-multiparty side raised questions about the legitimacy of the outcome.

35 M Bratton and G Lambright, "Uganda's Referendum 2000: The Silent Boycott", 100 (2001) *African Affairs*, pp 429–452, 435.

The environment during the referendum was marked by restrictions on opposition groups, leading to allegations of unfair practices.[36] Nonetheless, the movement system (the de facto one-party state of the NRA/M) was given another lease of life.

The turning-point for Uganda's political system came with the constitutional referendum of July 2005. Here, the people voted to lift the existing restrictions on the political space and re-introduce multipartyism.[37] The subsequent transition to an effective multiparty political system was codified by the passing of the Political Parties and Organizations Act (2005), which laid down the framework for the operation of political parties in Uganda. This legislation contains several key elements: a framework for the registration of political parties and political organization;[38] rules for the internal conduct of political parties, focusing on financial audits, mergers and alliances with other political parties, and membership (among other things);[39] a code of conduct for political parties;[40] and provision for a national consultative forum for political parties and political organisations.[41]

With the opening up of the new political space, political parties appeared to flourish. By the end of December 2023, 26 political parties were certified by the Uganda Electoral Commission.[42] However, these numbers alone may paint a falsely rosy picture. Only eight of the newly registered parties are fully operational and with the substantial presence across the nation necessary to challenge the current NRM government. These include the DP; UPC; National Unity Platform; Conservative Party; and four other smaller parties (the Forum for Democratic Change (FDC); NUP; Social Democratic Party (SDP); Justice Forum (JEEMA); and Alliance for National Transformation (ANT)). Of these eight, only the NRM, UPC, NUP,

---

36 O Therkildsen, "Uganda's Referendum 2000: The Silent Boycott: A Comment", 101 (2002) *African Affairs*, pp 231–241.

37 A Meldrum, "Ugandans Vote for Multi-party State", *The Guardian*, 30 July 2005, https://www.theguardian.com/world/2005/jul/30/andrewmeldrum (accessed 19 November 2024); M Khisa, "How Museveni Has Twisted Uganda's Constitution to Cling to Power", *The Conversation*, 20 June 2019, https://theconversation.com/how-museveni-has-twisted-ugandas-constitution-to-cling-to-power-118933 (accessed 13 November 2024).

38 Political Parties and Organizations Act (2005), sections 3–8.

39 *Ibid*, sections 9–18.

40 *Ibid*, section 19.

41 *Ibid*, section 20.

42 Electoral Commission, "Political Parties", https://www.ec.or.ug/political-parties (accessed 24 February 2024).

DP and FDC may be regarded as fully active in elections, and even then, active in a highly restrictive environment.

2.5 Uganda at 62: Between militarisation and democratisation

On 9 October 2024, Uganda celebrated 62 years of independence. A notable pattern has emerged from this history: usually, the presidency has been held by individuals with military backgrounds or by leaders with strong military support. The militarisation of political power has been a key factor in how presidential authority is obtained, maintained, and consolidated in Uganda. This intertwining of military influence with political leadership indicates that political power not only belongs to politics and politicians but is also deeply embedded in the military's role in society. This dominance of the military poses serious challenges to multiparty democracy and civilian governance (evident in allegations as to the partisanship of the Uganda Peoples' Defence Forces). This section explores how militarisation manifests itself in Uganda and the effects it has on political-party development and the overall political landscape.

In this discussion, we adopt Enloe's definition of militarisation as a "a step-by-step process by which a person or a thing gradually comes to be controlled by the military or comes to depend for its well-being on militaristic ideas".[43] Enloe adds that "the more militarization transforms an individual or a society, the more that individual or society comes to imagine military needs and militaristic presumptions to be not only valuable but also normal".[44] Similarly, Adelman notes that militarism "blurs the boundaries between what can be defined as military and what can be viewed as part of civilian life".[45] Consequently, "militarism demands that an entire society become permeated with and built according to military values and priorities."[46]

What Enloe and Adelman describe is a lived reality in contemporary Uganda. It comes through at different levels of society, in varying degrees of severity, and as the common denominator of the different regimes that

43 C Enloe, *Maneuvers: The International Politics of Militarising Women's Lives*, Oakland, California, California University Press (2000), p 3.

44 *Ibid.*

45 M Adelman, "The Military, Militarism, and the Militarisation of Domestic Violence", 9 (2003) *Violence Against Women*, pp 1118–1152.

46 *Ibid.*

have ruled the country. There is consensus among scholars and political commentators that the militarisation of the Uganda state has been and remains important in Ugandan political life.

Militarisation became particularly pronounced in 2001 with the appointment of a serving senior military officer, Major-General Katumba Wamala, as the inspector general of the civilian-oriented Uganda police force.[47] This decision not only signalled a significant militarisation of the police but also facilitated the infiltration of military influence into other aspects of Ugandan society. Since then, the presence and impact of the military has expanded. It has become increasingly intertwined with many dimensions of the nation's social framework, and has taken over spaces and spheres hitherto reserved for civilians. It is important to highlight key manifestations of this militarisation, as they illustrate the challenging operational landscape that opposition political parties face.

Militarism has permeated Uganda's economy and public service delivery through the agency of the Uganda Peoples' Defence Forces (UPDF). In 1994, the Uganda Air Cargo Corporation was established as a government-owned entity to provide efficient and coordinated air transport services.[48] By the end of 2023, five of its eleven board of directors' positions were occupied by senior military personnel, while the general manager was a lieutenant-general.[49] This reflects the extent of military involvement at the highest levels of the organisation.[50]

In addition, the significant military presence in Uganda's fisheries sector became apparent in 2017 when the fisheries protection unit was established in the UPDF by a presidential directive. This unit was tasked with combatting harmful fishing practices that were believed to be causing fish-stock

---

47 "Profile: Gen. Edward Katumba Wamala", *The Independent*, 7 February 7 2017, https://www.independent.co.ug/gen-edward-katumba-wamala/ (accessed 24 October 2024).

48 Section 4 of the Uganda Air Cargo Corporation Act, 15 December 1994, https://ulii.org/akn/ug/act/statute/1994/18/eng@2000-12-31 (accessed 17 November 2024).

49 K Kazibwe, "Uganda Air Cargo Boss Fired as Museveni Continues Purge," *Nile Post*, 15 June 2020, https://nilepost.co.ug/2020/06/15/uganda-air-cargo-boss-fired-as-museveni-continues-purge/ (accessed 23 October 2024).

50 D Lumu and C Kiwawulo, "Museveni Appoints Lt. Gen. Lakara as Uganda Air Cargo Boss", *The New Vision*, 15 June 2020, https://www.newvision.co.ug/news/1520888/museveni-appoints-lt-gen-lakara-uganda-air-cargo-boss (accessed 23 October 2024).

depletion in the country's lakes.[51] However, its operations were marred by human rights abuses, including extra-judicial killings, the torture of fishermen, and the destruction of fishing equipment, all conducted under the guise of enforcing better fishing practices.[52]

Militarisation has also been visible in the construction sector. In 1 July 2021, the President issued an executive directive to both the ministers of health and of education (at the time, the Minister of Education was the President's wife, Janet Museveni). They were to cede all current and future government construction projects of hospitals, health centres,[53] and schools to the UPDF Engineering Brigade.[54] The directive commenced in the financial year of 2021/2022. The President argued the need for this on the grounds that the UPDF was not corrupt and was also more efficient than red-tape civilian public servants.[55]

The increasing militarisation of public security and law enforcement in Uganda represents a critical shift away from traditional governance of internal affairs by civilian authorities. This is particularly the case with the Uganda Police Force.[56] Here, senior military officers (from the rank of colonel and above) have been placed in high ranking positions that determine policy directions.[57] These include the position of the deputy

51 J Nalwooga, "UPDF Soldier Shoots Fisherman Dead on Lake Kyoga", *The Daily Monitor*, 2 May 2024, https://www.monitor.co.ug/uganda/news/national/updf-soldier-shoots-fisherman-dead-on-lake-kyoga-4610230 (accessed 23 October 2024).

52 "UPDF Fisheries Protection Unit to be Deployed on Lake Albert", *The Independent*, 18 June 2020, https://www.independent.co.ug/updf-fisheries-protection-unit-to-be-deployed-on-lake-albert/ (accessed 18 October 2024).

53 K Kazibwe, "Museveni Directs all Gov't School, Hospital Construction Projects to be Handled by UPDF", *Nile Post*, 9 July 2021, https://nilepost.co.ug/2021/10/06/updf-takes-over-construction-of-all-hospitals/ (accessed 19 October 2024).

54 K Kazibwe, "UPDF Takes over Construction of all Hospitals", *Nile Post*, 6 October 2021, https://nilepost.co.ug/2021/10/06/updf-takes-over-construction-of-all-hospitals/(accessed 15 October 2024).

55 A Bagala, "Museveni Orders Army to Build Schools, Health Centres", *The Daily Monitor*, 9 July 2021, https://www.monitor.co.ug/uganda/news/national/museveni-orders-army-to-build-schools-health-centres-3466800 (accessed 15 October 2024).

56 R Tapscott, *Arbitrary State: Social Control and Modern Authoritarianism in Museveni's Uganda*, Oxford, Oxford University Press (2021), pp 79–80; A Mubiru, "The Rise and Fall of Gen. Kayihura," *The New Vision*, 14 June 2018, https://www.newvision.co.ug/new_vision/news/1479729/rise (accessed 15 October 2024).

57 "Army Command, Power in Uganda Police Widens", *Africa Press*, 11 February 2022, https://www.africa-press.net/uganda/all-news/army-command-power-in-uganda-police-widens (accessed 19 October 2024).

inspector general, as well as posts in the directorates of human resources[58] and criminal investigations,[59] among others. Militarisation is also evident at the top of the Ministry of Internal Affairs which is entirely led by high-ranking military officials, including the minister and the permanent secretary.[60]

All in all, there are substantial questions around "the independence of the police and the application of military law in a domestic setting".[61] Thus, it is not surprising that the militarised police institution in Uganda is described "as the main state agency at the center of securing the NRM regime".[62]

The implications of militarisation are profound, and particularly so for the multiparty-political landscape in Uganda. Opposition political parties face significant challenges, as their legitimate mobilisation efforts and other party activities are not only monitored but actively suppressed by a militarised police force. The militarised approach to internal security fosters a climate of fear and repression that poses significant risks to the prospects of realising the foundational ideals of multiparty democracy and human rights in Uganda.[63]

Militarisation has also swallowed the National Identification and Registration Authority (NIRA). This is the national agency mandated to "create, manage, maintain and operationalize the National Identification Register

58 I Mubiru, "Museveni Appoints Four UPDF Officers as Police Directors", *Watchdog Uganda*, 3 July 2019, https://www.watchdoguganda.com/news/20190703/71522/museveni-appoints-four-updf-officers-as-police-directors.html (accessed 19 October 2024).

59 *Ibid.*

60 S Namwase and J Nkuubi, *Guns, Bread and Butter: Militarisation of Economic Sectors and Public Institutions in Uganda: A Socio-Legal Analysis,* Kampala, Human Rights and Peace Centre, Makerere University (2024), pp 167–173.

61 CE Bailey, "Meeting the Needs of the State: Intelligence, Security and Police Legal Frameworks in East Africa", in Ryan Shaffer (ed.), *African Intelligence Services: Early Postcolonial and Contemporary Challenges*, Maryland, Rowman and Littlefield (2021), pp 257–280, 266.

62 J Kagoro, *Inside an African Police Force: The Ugandan Police Examined*, Geneva, Springer (2022), pp 26. See also "What You Should Know about New Deputy IGP Maj Gen Paul Lokech", *The Independent*, 16 December 2020, https://www.independent.co.ug/what-you-should-know-about-new-deputy-igp-maj-gen-paul-lokech/ (accessed 17 October 2024); C Etukuri, "Parliament Clears Lokech's Appointment as Deputy IGP," *The New Vision*, 19 December 2020, https://www.newvision.co.ug/news/1535695/parliament-clears-lokech-appointment-deputy-igp (accessed 19 October 2024).

63 Namwase and Nkuubi, *supra* n. 60, p 173.

by registering all citizens of Uganda".[64] From the board of directors of the NIRA through to its mid-level portfolios, senior military officers maintain a controlling hand in what was initially a civilian-administered institution.[65] The involvement of senior military officials in the civilian agency responsible for citizen registration threatens the democratically crucial process of creating and maintaining an accurate electoral roll. There are many allegations regarding military officers' interference. In 2014, opposition political parties protested the issuance of new identity cards just before the 2016 general elections, fearing that military influence might allow for partisan control of voter registration and disenfranchise voters supporting opposition parties to the advantage of the ruling party.[66]

Uganda is alone in Africa (and perhaps the world) in allocating 10 seats in Parliament to the military. UPDF MPS are there to act as "listening posts" and provide guidance for the country.[67] This is allowed for by Article 78 of the Constitution, which prescribes that the composition of Parliament includes "representatives of the army" as well as other special interest groups.[68] In a healthy democracy, elected representatives are supposed to reflect the interests of their constituents rather than serve as proxies for mil itary interests.[69] This dual role blurs the lines between civilian governance and military authority. The measure contributes to weakening the foundations of the multiparty system. Additionally, the military's representation in Parliament contributes to the concentration of power within the NRA/M ruling party, thereby undermining the potential for competitive politics.

64 See National Identification and Registration Authority, https://www.nira.go.ug/home (accessed 30 December 2024).

65 M Karugaba, "NIRA in ID Cards Printing Crisis", *The New Vision*, 14 October 2021, https://www.newvision.co.ug/category/news/nira-in-id-cards-printing-crisis-117255 (accessed 18 October 2024).

66 "Government Rejects Opposition Demands to Stop ID Registration", *The Daily Monitor*, 24 April 2014, https://www.monitor.co.ug/uganda/news/national/government-rejects-opposition-demands-to-stop-id-registration-1570676 (accessed 25 October 2024).

67 Namwase and Nkuubi, *supra* n. 60, p 179.

68 "UPDF MPS Defend Role in Parliament", *The Independent*, 20 May 2021, https://www.independent.co.ug/updf-mps-defend-role-in-parliament/ (accessed 25 October 2024).

69 Namwase and Nkuubi, *supra* n. 60, p. 180.

3. Ways of coping with militarised politics: Options for the opposition

3.1 "Sell-out diplomacy": The case of the Democratic Party

On 21 July 2022, the NRM signed what was publicised as a "working cooperation agreement" with the DP. This agreement was signed by the leaders of the two parties, President Museveni (NRM) and Norbert Mao (DP).[70] Central to this was the pledge "to share political power and also to foster constitutionalism and the respect of human rights", both of which are somewhat plausible undertakings.[71] Not unexpectedly, however, and of critical importance to this chapter, the two signatories made several interesting remarks after the signing.

Museveni's comments worked to undermine any sense that the agreement had been signed between equals. He noted that it should have happened earlier and boasted, with condescension, "You know the history. I keep telling you that DP without Museveni is not a serious group because I was a very active member of DP."[72] Museveni was also reported as saying that although the DP was "supporting opposition, they have been friendly and not destructive".[73] For his part, Mao said the DP-NRM agreement was "a living document" and would "continue growing"; it had been signed in "good faith", and marked the resolution of a number of differences that the DP apparently had had with the NRM.[74]

One day after the signing of the cooperation agreement, Museveni appointed Mao as Minister of Justice and Constitutional Affairs as a part of the agreement. In addition, the DP was also allowed to appoint someone to a junior minister portfolio,[75] to select four of its members for other appointments to "government departments, statutory bodies and government agencies";[76] in turn, the NRM would support the election of the

70 "Mao Signs Cooperation Agreement with Museveni", *The Independent*, 21 July 2022, https://www.independent.co.ug/mao-signs-cooperation-agreement-with-museveni/ (accessed 18 September 2024).

71 URN, "Details of Museveni, Mao 42-clause Agreement", *The Observer*, 22 July 2022, https://observer.ug/news/headlines/74458-details-of-museveni-mao-42-clause-agreement (accessed 18 September 2024).

72 *Ibid.*

73 *Ibid.*

74 *Ibid.*

75 *Ibid.*

76 *Ibid.*

secretary-general of the DP to the East African Legislative Assembly.[77] The agreement also provided that the ministerial positions above were to be held by the appointed ministers for "the full term of the 11th Parliament or for the duration of this agreement, whichever comes first".[78] Further spoils of victory extended to Parliament. In this regard, the agreement stipulated that

> the National Resistance Movement will support the nomination of a Democratic Party member of parliament to be the chair of a standing committee, as well as a democratic party member of parliament in the role of deputy chair of an additional committee.[79]

It is important to note that the cooperative agreement also bound those DP members who were given cabinet positions to accept the notion of collective responsibility. To this effect, the agreement stipulated that the "Democratic Party ministers agree to be bound by the cabinet rules in the exercise of ministerial responsibilities, and in particular, agree to be bound by the provisions on conduct, public duty, and personal interests of ministers".[80] In other words, the DP president general could neither express nor maintain any views which diverged from those of the NRM. The possibility of the DP's opposition to any government programmes was now effectively ruled out in advance.

To compound this silencing, DP cabinet ministers were bound by the confidentiality rules that govern the executive.[81] The agreement stipulated that where "cabinet papers or other briefings are provided to the Democratic Party, or where the Democratic Party is involved in consultation on legislation, policy or budgetary matters, all such material and discussions shall be confidential unless otherwise agreed".[82]

Perhaps as a means of evaluating the success of this cooperation, meetings between Museveni and Mao were to be held every three months. At this writing (March 2025), it was too early to assess the functionality of this agreement and what would happen if any of its fundamental terms are breached. However, some of the consequences of the agreement were already becoming apparent, as we shall see below.

---

77 *Ibid.*
78 *Ibid.*
79 *Ibid.*
80 *Ibid.*
81 *Ibid.*
82 *Ibid.*

3.2 The impact of "sell-out diplomacy" on multiparty politics

This alliance has important implications for the DP's internal dynamics, its relationship with the public, and the fostering of multiparty politics in the country. Many members of the public viewed the agreement as primarily a means for ensuring individual political survival and self-promotion, rather than as an effort to serve the needs of ordinary citizens. The commentator Michael Mutyaba suggested that such cooperation, which extends to joining the government, is a strategy that "relies on identifying frustrated opposition leaders whose careers face some sort of crisis and who are eager to rekindle their political fortunes"; though seemingly far-fetched, the argument is plausible and not easy to dismiss.[83]

Indeed, an examination of various political entities that chose to ally themselves with the NRM reveals two common concerns: the fear of political irrelevance, and anxiety over decline of financial support for their parties (sentiments also to be found in the current DP leader Mao).[84] Mutyaba argues that "Mao – frustrated by a waning career, internal factionalism, and displacement by more popular opposition rivals – was a prime candidate for co-option".[85] When the agreement was reached, the DP had only nine members in a 529-seat parliament, a modest representation compared to that of the NRM, with its 343 members.

Whereas public communications on the new partnership emphasised the attempt at "ensuring collaboration on matters of constitutional importance", ordinary people were not convinced and expressed both nostalgia for the old arrangements and pessimism for the new.[86] The agreement did mark a new strategy by Museveni and the NRM for dealing with the opposition, one which moved away the old tactics of coercion and intimidation. Mutyaba refers to it simply as an example of "Museveni's long-established pattern of co-opting opposition figures into government".[87] However, this went beyond the co-opting of individuals; it effectively involved handing over control of an oppositional political party and its leaders to the NRM.

83 M Mutyaba, "Is Co-opting the Opposition Shrewd Politics or a Desperate Ploy?", *African Arguments,* 10 August 2022, https://africanarguments.org/2022/08/uganda-museveni-mao-is-co-opting-the-opposition-shrewd-politics-or-a-desperate-ploy/ (accessed 19 October 2024).

84 *Ibid.*

85 *Ibid.*

86 *Ibid.*

87 *Ibid.*

As a result, the agreement lacked legitimacy in the eyes of the public, prompting scepticism about the NRM-DP alliance. The agreement never had a strong social foundation and promised only a precarious future due to prevalent distrust of the DP. Indeed, following the agreement, a large number of DP members moved to other parties, and particularly to the NUP, while a court case was filed against the president-general and secretary-general of the DP seeking to annul the agreement on the grounds that there had been no effective consultation with, nor consent from, actual party members. At the time of writing, the case has still to be decided.[88]

A second consequence of the agreement centres on the sense of betrayal felt by DP members after it was signed. Many viewed it as a betrayal of the core values of truth and justice which the party had championed for more than 60 years in Ugandan politics. Given the widespread perception of the lack of precisely these values in the NRM government, there was little belief that the DP could continue to uphold them in this new and compromised arrangement. Thanks to its apparent abandonment of its own core values, the DP lost a great deal of popular support.

Perhaps even more disturbing was that the DP had abandoned the most important roles that opposition parties can play in a country like Uganda. They are that a party not only acts a platform that enables citizens to "participate in the governance process (political participation), but also structure[s] the political landscape to enable competition between varying interests and policy objectives (political competition)".[89] For now, it is impossible to claim that the DP works as a party in competition with the NRM, seeking to elicit accountability and ensure oversight and so propel democratisation forward; instead it has consigned itself to the abyss. It is now referred to as conquered territory, condescendingly spoken of as a mere footnote to the broader narrative in which the NRM represents itself as the land's great mother and liberator.

For the co-opted DP members, there is also the further danger of being discarded once their purpose has been served. The NRM government,

88 "Court Issues Timelines in Mao-NRM Deal Case", *The Independent*, 27 February 2024, https://www.independent.co.ug/court-issues-timelines-in-mao-nrm-deal-case/ (accessed 28 February 2024). See also *Michael Phillip Lulume Bayigga, John Paul Lukwago Mpalanyi, Fortunate Rode Nantongo, Richard Sebamala and Fred Kayondo v Gerald Siranda, Mao and the Attorney General, Constitutional Petition, 2023.*

89 J Maiyo, "Political Parties and Intra-Party Democracy in Uganda: Challenges and Opportunities for Democratic Consolidation", *SSRN*, 13 May 2020, p 14, https://ssrn.com/abstract=3600470 (accessed 24 October 2024).

particularly under President Museveni, has a history of drawing opponents into the cabinet with promises of ministerial roles or similar positions. Initially, these individuals may indeed receive public praise from the President for their cooperation and patriotism. However, after about two years (typically coinciding with cabinet reshuffles), they are often dropped without warning. They are then left completely stranded, having lost all credibility and public support for having been seen to compromise their principles for the sake of personal gain. Many who are recruited in this manner find that their political careers end when they lose their positions, as they no longer have favour with the electorate.

At the time of writing, there were concerns that this fate might be in store for the DP and those of its members in government positions. This is what Mtyaba calls the "all-too-common risk of being dumped by Museveni once the defector has served their purpose".[90] Collectively, these sentiments from everyday citizens portray opposition figures and parties as merely serving the interests of the NRM government. This perception is echoed by Mutyaba:

> While defectors may enjoy various financial benefits, they are also typically tasked with doing the NRM's dirty work. Mao, for instance, will likely become the face of further proposed constitutional amendments that would entrench Museveni's rule or ease his son Muhoozi Kainerugaba's ascendance to power. The NRM likely hopes the new justice minister will act as a shock-absorber, diverting public criticism from the regime and preventing anti-Museveni sentiments from crystallizing. To the public and many in the opposition, however, Mao's departure is both evidence that he was a secret NRM agent all along and a reason to stop infighting and develop greater clarity of vision.[91]

In a country as deeply polarised as Uganda, such cooperation is often represented as prompted by the need for national reconciliation. While there may be some theoretical validity to this claim, the reality suggests an entirely different agenda, one focused on suppressing opposition parties and undermining the multiparty system in Uganda. Furthermore, this approach has negatively impacted future collaboration among political parties, as the DP has become deeply isolated from other opposition groups. Indeed, Lewis Rubongoya, the secretary-general of the NUP, has branded the DP

90 Mutyaba, *supra* n. 83.

91 *Ibid.*

leader, Mao, a "self-seeker", noting that "the pretence is over. [It] explains the attacks on NUP. Hope this clears the air for those who always ask about 'opposition unity' in Uganda."[92]

All in all, this development has deepened discontent among Uganda's opposition parties and resulted in historically low levels of trust among the key opposition players. Accusations of being "moles" for the NRM and claims that certain members have been "bought" by the ruling party have intensified. The DP's coping strategies have fostered further mistrust within the opposition and among the public, and resulted in a significant loss of legitimacy. The agreement emerged amid the promising discussions within the opposition to unite and field a single presidential candidate against the NRM in the 2026 elections; that goal now appears highly uncertain. Diplomacy as a coping mechanism thus seems shaky compared to the militancy model, something we shall now examine in relation to the experience of the NUP.

3.3 The rise of militancy in Uganda's opposition politics

The People Power Movement (PPM) emerged under the leadership of the music icon Kyagulanyi Ssentamu, known popularly by his stage name, Bobi Wine. Its message was simple: after nearly four decades of the NRM, it was time for it to give up power as it was no longer in touch with the contemporary aspirations of the youthful population. Ssentamu accused the government of multiple sins: authoritarianism, poverty, corruption, and nepotism and sectarianism in the distribution of government services and employment opportunities; he decried the dwindling trust in elections as conduits for the peaceful transfer of power and the representation of the will of the people. Ssentamu presented the PPM as the formation needed

> [to] spearhead the first-ever inclusive, non-violent transition of political power in Uganda ... from the 35-year long dictatorial regime to a people's choice government through free and fair elections ... compelled by Arti-

92 J Kamoga, "Uganda's Oldest Opposition Party Agrees to a New Deal Ruling NRM", *The East African* (Nairobi), 23 July 2022, https://www.theeastafrican.co.ke/tea/news/east-africa/uganda-oldest-opposition-party-agrees-new-deal-ruling-nrm-3889630 (accessed 18 September 2024).

cle 1 of the Constitution of Uganda 1995, which grants all power to the people of Uganda.[93]

In order to reach its goals, the PPM social movement had to acquire the formal legal standing necessary to access the relevant rights and privileges of a registered party, including of course, the right to participate in the national elections. Hence the birth of the NUP.

The establishment of the NUP in July 2020 was a significant development in Ugandan politics, and particularly for opposition politics given the government's attempts restrict the growth of opposition parties. Prior to the formation of the NUP, the PPM had raised concerns about the potential obstruction it faced from the Uganda Electoral Commission in any attempt to register as a formal political party. The NUP was created to provide a legitimate platform for the PPM to contest the 2021 general elections.

The NUP was marketed as a new political entity, one which brought forward fresh ideas and a acted as a new platform for the voices of ordinary Ugandans. The reality was a little more complex. Essentially, the NUP was simply a rebranding of the existing National Unity, Reconciliation and Development Party (NURP), first registered as a political party in 2004.[94] This pre-existing status allowed the NUP to circumvent some of the more significant barriers to registration that would have otherwise confronted them.[95] The strategic transformation of NURP into NUP allowed the easy inclusion of prominent figures from the PPM, and especially Bobi Wine as the party president, while maintaining a sense of continuity. The new party sought to translate the energy and enthusiasm of the PPM into a political structure that could effectively challenge the ruling regime.[96]

In the 2021 elections, the political landscape suddenly looked very different. Now, for the first time, a 36-year-old musician standing for a fully established party was in a position to challenge the 74-year-old veteran of

93 National Unity Platform, *People Power Movement Manifesto, 2021–2026: A New Uganda*, p 1, https://nupuganda.org/wp-content/uploads/2021/12/NUP-MANIFESTO.pdf (accessed 18 November 2024).

94 I Katusiime and D Wandera, "Bobi Wine Finds Party Shelter with Eyes on 2021 Presidential Election", *The East African*, 23 July 2020, https://www.theeastafrican.co.ke/tea/news/east-africa/bobi-wine-party-shelter-eyes-2021-presidential-election-1904780 (accessed 26 October 2024).

95 *Ibid.*

96 "How Bobi Wine, NUP deal was negotiated", *The Daily Monitor*, 23 July 2020, https://www.monitor.co.ug/uganda/news/national/how-bobi-wine-nup-deal-was-negotiated-1908714 (accessed 26 October 2024).

the NRM – Museveni – who had been in power for over 30 years and knew every trick in the book.[97] At long last, the liberation party electoral dividend which had been a constant of President Museveni's long rule looked as though it might not hold against new generation of youthful and energetic politicians. This is a generation that the state prefers to refer to, in derogatory terms, as "militant", refusing to recognise that any such militancy is a necessary survival mechanism in a situation where state resources are used to undermine – often with force – any political opposition.[98]

From the very beginning, the NUP/PPM showed itself willing to put into action what has been described as "a highly resistant, assertive, aggressive and militant model of politics".[99] In response to the increasing levels of state militarism, the new party adopted forms of language, conduct, and dress (military-style fatigues) that show that NUP members are ready and willing to challenge the state. Musinguzi has described well the growing militancy within the lowest ranks of the NUP structure, writing of how Kyagulanyi Ssentamu (aka Bobi Wine)

> uses foot soldiers for his National Unity Platform (NUP) party, running a group imitating a military structure ... Foot soldiers hold ranks, wear red berets and red overalls complete with pips, and organize themselves into military-like structures. They participate in parades and salute whenever Bobi Wine arrives at events. Additionally, they serve as his security detail during travels to places with large crowds ... The preference for red berets and overalls is inspired by Bobi Wine, and the foot soldiers take pride in dressing like and protecting their leader.[100]

Especially revealing is the fact that the pips on these civilian overalls imitate those of military ranks, as do the structure of authority within the party: its generals and colonels must be obeyed with appropriate deference. The fact that the party president, Bobi Wine, is referred to as the commander-in-chief has not gone unnoticed. One commentator notes the following:

97 AM Tripp, *Museveni's Uganda: Paradoxes of Power in a Hybrid Regime*, Boulder, Colorado, Lynne Rienner Publishers (2010), pp 4–5.

98 H Athumani, "Uganda's People Power Movement Registers a Political Wing Ahead of 2021 General Elections", *Voice of America News*, 22 July 2020, https://www.voanews.com/a/africa_ugandas-people-power-movement-registers-political-wing-ahead-2021-general-elections/6193238.html (accessed 20 October 2024).

99 *Ibid.*

100 B Musinguzi, "Uganda: Bobi Wine Foot Soldiers, a Symbol of Pride, Defiance," *The Africa Report*, 8 October 2024, https://www.theafricareport.com/363788/uganda-bobi-wine-foot-soldiers-a-symbol-of-pride-defiance/ (accessed 25 March 2025).

> These NUP uniforms being used at their offices, functions, political meetings and on daily public display as already noticed have no standardization except the swastika armband worn on the left. Like Hitler's youth brigades, NUP activists share the same agenda in the belief and identity by costumes, intimidation, intolerance, violence, bigotry and other fascist tendencies. In so doing, NUP supporters imitate military formations including burly bodyguards for no other useful purpose than to spread intimidation, harassment and fear.[101]

The NUP argues that it is the harsh restrictions and violence visited on opposition parties that have encouraged them to mirror the militant stance and tactics used by the ruling NRM: a government's actions and character often shape and define the nature of its opposition. The more militant approach of the NUP can best be understood as an inevitable response to the NRM's own aggressive tactics. At the same time, this new politically aggressive stance can be attributed to a lack of viable options, particularly when the public is expressing increasing disapproval of the "diplomatic" politicians who have failed to provide any effective challenge the NRM. All of this is reinforced by the current political climate which offers few (if any) opportunities for peaceful and non-violent political engagement.

3.4 NUP Militancy and Multiparty politics

Understanding the implications of the emergence of a militant oppositional politics provides valuable insight into the ongoing struggle for democratic participation and the future of multiparty governance in Uganda. This is particularly important with regard to four distinct but related areas: political engagement, public perception, state repression, and societal dynamics.

The NRM government's initial response to the new militancy of the PPM/NUP has been to try and suppress it. Faced with a challenge to its power, the rattled NRM – particularly President Museveni, who is prone to favour strong-arm approaches – has resorted to methods akin to bush war-guerrilla tactics and the extensive militarisation of the political milieu.

---

101 O Opondo, "The NUP Politics of Bullying and Insolence Must be Tackled", *Watchdog Uganda*, 19 September 2023, https://www.watchdoguganda.com/op-ed/20230919/159837/ofwono-opondo-the-nup-politics-of-bullying-and-insolence-must-be-tackled.html (accessed 17 November 2024).

The government's first instinct has been to confront perceived threats with force rather than dialogue.

In 2019, the Ugandan army designated the red beret, typically worn by military police, as part of its official uniform, and hence forbidden to the non-military. Despite this ruling, Bobi Wine and his supporters persisted in wearing the berets, leading to widespread arrests by security forces. A legal challenge against the ban on red berets was never addressed in court, as a hearing on the matter was never scheduled. During the 2021 presidential election, more than 400 people were arrested for wearing red berets, with total arrests in the aftermath possibly numbering in the thousands.[102] For now (as at October 2024), over 20 NUP party supporters arrested in December 2020 remain in military custody. While the NUP contends that the pretext for their arrest was purely sartorial, the charges facing them include possession of explosives.[103]

The supporters of the NUP have been systematically stripped of all constitutionally guaranteed procedural rights, and notably of the right to bail, which so crucial for any suspect in the criminal justice system. The implications of the denial of rights extend far beyond the individual cases of these supporters. It has adverse effects on all opposition political parties, creating an environment of fear and repression that stifles political dissent in Uganda. By undermining the legal rights of those associated with opposition movements, the government sends a clear message: dissent will not be tolerated, and those who challenge the status quo risk facing severe legal repercussions.

The general conduct, dress code, and militant words of NUP supporters and leaders has also provided the NRM government with useful political ammunition: it has enabled the government to depict the opposition party as violent and unfit to govern. Many NRM party functionaries have been deployed to attack the NUP on every front, but attention is always focused on the party's militant stance.

---

102 "NUP Supporters Protest Continued Detention as Army Court Denies Them Bail Again", *The Observer* (Uganda), 16 April 2024, https://observer.ug/index.php/news/headlines/81066-nup-supporters-protest-continued-detention-as-army-court-denies-them-bail-again (accessed 25 October 2024).

103 "Military Police Called into Action as Court Martial Denies NUP Supporters Bail", *The Independent* (Uganda), 16 April 2024, https://www.independent.co.ug/military-police-called-into-action-as-court-martial-denies-nup-supporters-bail/ (accessed 25 October 2024).

Take, for instance, the Government Media Centre. This is the official public relations department, under the Ministry of Information and Communications Technology and National Guidance. It is mandated to "facilitate communication of government policies, programmes and projects to the public through the media".[104] In practice, the Government Media Centre does not function as a neutral governmental body; it is better understood as an extension of the NRM party's apparatus.[105] As such, it works to disseminate to the public only the information that is consistent with NRM party narratives and political strategies. The synergy between the NRM and the Government Media Centre plays a pivotal role in framing public discourse. It influences media portrayals of political events and bolsters the ruling party's position in the face of opposition. By leveraging such state resources for party objectives, the NRM effectively consolidates its control over public communications in Uganda, reinforcing its governance agenda while marginalising dissenting voices.

It is in light of the above that the attacks of Government Media Centre on the NUP are to be read: the Centre is a de facto agent of the NRM party. Its director began the attack on the NUP by describing it as a "rogue tribal sectarian outfit whose impudence, bullying, mob mentality and crude arrogance at the national level must be knocked down if Uganda is to maintain stability and social cohesion".[106] NUP members were also represented as a militant gang that harbours a belief that it "can overrun Uganda with mob mentality and disrupt the hard-won democratization and progress that Uganda is today".[107]

In 2024, the Inspector-General of Police (appointed directly from the military) announced a ban on the NUP's nationwide mobilisation tour on the grounds that its members "incite violence, promote sectarianism, make illegitimate calls for the removal of an elected government, and issuance of defamatory statements against the person of President Museveni".[108] As a result, the "activities of the NUP were immediately suspended ... until such

104 Uganda Media Centre, https://www.mediacentre.go.ug/about-us (accessed 18 November 2024).

105 "Museveni Reappoints Ofwono Opondo as Media Centre Boss", *The Kampala Post*, August 30 2022, https://kampalapost.com/content/museveni-reappoints-ofwono-opondo-media-centre-boss (accessed 18 November 2024).

106 The Independent, *supra* n. 103.

107 *Ibid.*

108 "Uganda Police Ban Bobi Wine Rallies over 'Sectarian' Comments", *The East African*, 14 September 2023, https://www.theeastafrican.co.ke/tea/news/east-afr

a time that they are ready to comply with the guidelines and rule of law".[109] Later, the police head further denounced NUP militancy in the following terms:

> We are sending this strong message, that our country, Uganda, will not wait for its villages, towns, urban centers and cities to burn, before taking action to protect its citizens and property. We are going to put an end to the mob mentality, bullying and intimidating tactics of NUP radicals, against innocent civilians and law enforcers. Uganda is one of the safest countries in the region and across the globe and we plan for it to remain that way. This directive stands until such a time when the NUP is compliant and law-abiding.[110]

This framing helps to promote public support for the government even as it actively suppresses political dissent by appealing to all those who fear instability and disorder. The rhetoric works to frame the government as a protector of the peace, with the NUP as the party responsible for conflict and violence.

Such portrayals work to delegitimise NUP political activities by portraying them as threats to national security and stability, partly because of their militantly aggressive political activism. By employing strong language and framing the situation as a battle against violence and lawlessness, the government can justify its actions against the NUP while reinforcing its strong-man image. This not only targets the NUP directly but also sends a message to other opposition groups about the potential repercussions of any challenge to the established order. This all works to stifle democratic engagement and participation in Uganda.

It appears that this characterisation of the NUP is a response to the "credible threat" theory. This is built on the narrative that opposition political parties must have the capability to pose a perceived or real "credible threat" to the incumbent government for them to be taken seriously. In Uganda's case, this was and remains urgent, considering that the populace believes that only a militant opposition or an opposition leader with a

---

ica/uganda-police-ban-bobi-wine-mobilisation-activities-4368488 (accessed 25 October 2024).

109 K Kazibwe, "Police Bans Bobi Wine Mobilisation Tours", *Nile Post*, 13 September 2023, https://nilepost.co.ug/news/171404/police-bans-bobi-wine-mobilization-tours (accessed 25 October 2024).

110 *Ibid.*

military history has the capacity to counter the NRM government. As Benjamin Acosta usefully explains: "In attempts to get their adversaries to 'take them seriously', organizations rely on violent tactics for coercive political strategies ... In this sense, the allure of gaining the 'credible threat" instigates oppositions to use violence."[111]

There is something tragic about this militancy of opposition politics. It has undermined the credibility of the party as a potentially all-encompassing transition vehicle from the 40-year rule of the NRM. By adopting a militant posture, the party has probably alienated as many potential supporters as it attracted. Abrahms refers to this as

> "the credibility paradox" – when oppositions employ violence, they create a new challenge as the very escalatory acts that add credibility to a [militant organisation's] threat can subtract credibility from [its pledge to end the threatening act if the target makes institutional changes or grants concessions].[112]

Given the repression that NUP supporters face, it is understandable that the party adopted a more aggressive approach to political activism. This can be understood as a reaction to the systemic suppression of dissent in Uganda and the repeated failure to gain political traction through peaceful means. When traditional channels for activism – such as rallies, campaigns, and public discourse – are heavily monitored and curtailed, political parties such as the NUP are likely to feel compelled to escalate their tactics in order to draw attention to their cause and rally support from their base. The NUP's argument is that diplomatic politicking with a highly militarised government and a former liberation movement has proven to afford little scope for advancing collective goals and the quest for political transformation.

The perception that a government is unwilling to engage constructively with opposition voices can incentivise militancy. As frustration grows among supporters who feel marginalised, the adoption of more aggressive strategies can appear to be the only viable option for effecting political change. A political culture which is characterised by aggression and retaliation can easily become self-perpetuating. If the NUP's militants are met

111 B Acosta, "From Bombs to Ballots: When Militant Organisations Transition to Political Parties", 76 (2014) *Journal of Politics*, pp 666–683.

112 M Abrahms, "The Credibility Paradox: Violence as a Double-Edged Sword in International Politics", 57 (2013) *International Studies Quarterly*, pp 660–671.

with increased repression, this can start a cycle which may lead to further radicalisation of both the party and its supporters. Ultimately, this would entrench a political climate defined by divisiveness, making it increasingly challenging for Uganda to cultivate a robust and pluralistic multiparty system that works to the benefit of all citizens.

However, the use of militant tactics can be counterproductive. It may alienate moderate supporters and reinforce a government narrative that opposition parties are threats to national stability. This model for coping is inherently geared towards replicating a cancer that needs to be eradicated from Uganda's political culture. This is the cancer of a militant populace that can easily slide into violence should the social triggers of marginalisation and frustration be set off.

4. Conclusion

Ugandan opposition parties face significant pressure from the NRM government's coercive measures. Whereas the existing scholarship has focused on their legal repression, this chapter has interrogated different survival strategies of opposition parties. It has demonstrated that these survival mechanisms against state-led militarisation impacts their evolution and has broader implications for the citizens of Uganda.

The examination of NUP's militancy as one strategy against a repressive government has illustrated how such an approach can escalate violence and frame the opposition as a threat to national peace and stability. Such a framing risks alienating the public, raising doubts about the party's suitability for governance, and undermines the opposition's democratisation aspirations. The NUP case also reveals how militant attitudes among the youth can extend beyond party control, contradicting values of non-violence and breeding further conflict. Ultimately, this strategy exposes the party and its supporters to heightened state repression from a government itself born of militancy and composed of hardened guerrilla war veterans.

The chapter has also illustrated how opposition parties can use diplomacy as another survival mechanism, but this must be balanced with the need to maintain political independence. The example of the DP highlights that this strategy risks losing legitimacy and can be perceived as engaging in "sell-out" diplomacy. Once subsumed by the dominant party, these opposition parties are no longer trusted to represent and fulfil the electorate's aspirations. Cooperation agreements like those of the DP, intended to navigate a hostile and militarised environment, can inadvertently lead to co-option rather than true coalition, further entrenching dominant party politics and jeopardising the opposition party's existence.

As a result, this chapter recommends that opposition parties should rather cope with a hostile political climate by undertaking joint political and legal initiatives to challenge militarisation and champion discourse on the de-militarisation of the country. Examples of this include but are not limited to public interest litigation to challenge the appointment of military personnel to civilian positions, as such appointments are inimical to building a democratic country based on constitutional order and constitutionalism.

References

Books, articles, chapters in books, and others

"Army Command, Power in Uganda Police Widens", *Africa Press*, 11 February 2022, https://www.africa-press.net/uganda/all-news/army-command-power-in-uganda-police-widens (accessed 19 October 2024)

"Court Issues Timelines in Mao-NRM Deal Case", *The Independent,* 27 February 2024, https://www.independent.co.ug/court-issues-timelines-in-mao-nrm-deal-case/ (accessed 28 February 2024)

"Government Rejects Opposition Demands to Stop ID Registration", *The Daily Monitor,* 24 April 2014, https://www.monitor.co.ug/uganda/news/national/government-rejects-opposition-demands-to-stop-id-registration-1570676 (accessed 25 October 2024)

"How Bobi Wine, NUP deal was negotiated", *The Daily Monitor,* 23 July 2020, https://www.monitor.co.ug/uganda/news/national/how-bobi-wine-nup-deal-was-negotiated-1908714 (accessed 26 October 2024)

"Mao Signs Cooperation Agreement with Museveni", *The Independent,* 21 July 2022, https://www.independent.co.ug/mao-signs-cooperation-agreement-with-museveni/ (accessed 18 September 2024)

"Military Police Called into Action as Court Martial Denies NUP Supporters Bail", *The Independent* (Uganda), 16 April 2024, https://www.independent.co.ug/military-police-called-into-action-as-court-martial-denies-nup-supporters-bail/ (accessed 25 October 2024)

"Museveni Reappoints Ofwono Opondo as Media Centre Boss", *The Kampala Post,* August 30 2022, https://kampalapost.com/content/museveni-reappoints-ofwono-opondo-media-centre-boss (accessed 18 November 2024)

"NUP Supporters Protest Continued Detention as Army Court Denies Them Bail Again", *The Observer* (Uganda), 16 April 2024, https://observer.ug/index.php/news/headlines/81066-nup-supporters-protest-continued-detention-as-army-court-denies-them-bail-again (accessed 25 October 2024)

"Profile: Gen. Edward Katumba Wamala", *The Independent*, 7 February 2017, https://www.independent.co.ug/gen-edward-katumba-wamala/ (accessed 22 February 2024)

"Uganda Police Ban Bobi Wine Rallies over 'Sectarian' Comments", *The East African*, 14 September 2023, https://www.theeastafrican.co.ke/tea/news/east-africa/uganda-police-ban-bobi-wine-mobilisation-activities-4368488 (accessed 25 October 2024)

"UPDF Fisheries Protection Unit to be Deployed on Lake Albert", *The Independent*, 18 June 2020, https://www.independent.co.ug/updf-fisheries-protection-unit-to-be-deployed-on-lake-albert/ (accessed 23 February 2024)

"UPDF MPS Defend Role in Parliament", *The Independent*, 20 May 2021, https://www.independent.co.ug/updf-mps-defend-role-in-parliament/ (accessed 25 October 2024)

"What You Should Know about New Deputy IGP Maj Gen Paul Lokech", *The Independent*, 16 December 2020, https://www.independent.co.ug/what-you-should-know-about-new-deputy-igp-maj-gen-paul-lokech/ (accessed 17 October 2024)

Abrahms M, "The Credibility Paradox: Violence as a Double-Edged Sword in International Politics", 57 (2013) *International Studies Quarterly*, pp 660–671

Acosta B, "From Bombs to Ballots: When Militant Organisations Transition to Political Parties," 76 (2014) *Journal of Politics*, pp 666–683

Adelman M, "The Military, Militarism, and the Militarisation of Domestic Violence", 9 (2003) *Violence Against Women*, pp 1118–1152

Athumani H, "Uganda's People Power Movement Registers a Political Wing Ahead of 2021 General Elections", *Voice of America News*, 22 July 2020, https://www.voanews.com/a/africa_ugandas-people-power-movement-registers-political-wing-ahead-2021-general-elections/6193238.html (accessed 20 October 2024)

Bagala A, "Museveni Orders Army to Build Schools, Health Centres", *The Daily Monitor*, 9 July 2021, https://www.monitor.co.ug/uganda/news/national/museveni-orders-army-to-build-schools-health-centres-3466800 (accessed 23 February 2024)

Bailey CE, "Meeting the Needs of the State: Intelligence, Security and Police Legal Frameworks in East Africa", in R Shaffer (ed.), *African Intelligence Services: Early Postcolonial and Contemporary Challenges,* Maryland, Rowman and Littlefield (2021), pp 257–280

Bratton M and Lambright G, "Uganda's Referendum 2000: The Silent Boycott", 100 (2001) *African Affairs*, pp 429–452

Carbone GM, "Political Parties in A 'No-Party Democracy': Hegemony and Opposition Under 'Movement Democracy' in Uganda", 9 (2003) *Party Politics*, pp 485–501

Electoral Commission, "Political Parties", https://www.ec.or.ug/political-parties (accessed 24 February 2024)

Enloe C, *Maneuvers: The International Politics of Militarizing Women's Lives*, Oakland, California, California University Press (2000)

Etukuri C, "Parliament Clears Lokech's Appointment as Deputy IGP", *The New Vision*, 19 December 2020, https://www.newvision.co.ug/news/1535695/parliament-clears-lokech-appointment-deputy-igp (accessed 19 February 2024)

Kagoro J, *Inside an African Police Force: The Ugandan Police Examined,* Geneva, Springer (2022)

Kamoga J, "Uganda's Oldest Opposition Party Agrees to a New Deal ruling NRM", *The East African*, 23 July 2022 https://www.theeastafrican.co.ke/tea/news/east-africa/uganda-oldest-opposition-party-agrees-new-deal-ruling-nrm-3889630 (accessed 18 February 2024)

Karugaba M, "NIRA in ID Cards Printing Crisis", *The New Vision*, 14 October 2021, https://www.newvision.co.ug/category/news/nira-in-id-cards-printing-crisis-117255 (accessed 18 October 2024)

Katusiime I and Wandera D, "Bobi Wine Finds Party Shelter with Eyes on 2021 Presidential Election", *The East African*, 23 July 2020, https://www.theeastafrican.co.ke/tea/news/east-africa/bobi-wine-party-shelter-eyes-2021-presidential-election-1904780 (accessed 26 October 2024)

Kazibwe K, "Museveni Directs All Gov't School, Hospital Construction Projects to be Handled by UPDF", *Nile Post*, 9 July 2021, https://nilepost.co.ug/2021/10/06/updf-takes-over-construction-of-all-hospitals/ (accessed 23 February 2024)

Kazibwe K, "Police Bans Bobi Wine Mobilisation Tours", *Nile Post*, 13 September 2023, https://nilepost.co.ug/news/171404/police-bans-bobi-wine-mobilization-tours (accessed 25 October 2024)

Kazibwe K, "Uganda Air Cargo Boss Fired as Museveni Continues Purge", *Nile Post*, 15 June 2020, https://nilepost.co.ug/2020/06/15/uganda-air-cargo-boss-fired-as-museveni-continues-purge/ (accessed 23 February 2024)

Kazibwe K, "UPDF Takes over Construction of all Hospitals", *Nile Post*, 6 October 2021, https://nilepost.co.ug/2021/10/06/updf-takes-over-construction-of-all-hospitals/(accessed 15 October 2024)

Khisa M, "How Museveni Has Twisted Uganda's Constitution to Cling to Power", *The Conversation*, 20 June 2019, https://theconversation.com/how-museveni-has-twisted-ugandas-constitution-to-cling-to-power-118933 (accessed 13 November 2024)

Kiranda Y and Kamp M (eds.), *Reality Check: the State of Multiparty Democracy in Uganda*, Konrad-Adenauer-Stiftung (2010) https://www.kas.de/c/document_library/get_file?uuid=3deffb14-7b9c-9a87-cad8-33ddc54e26d5&groupId=252038 (accessed 18 November 2024)

L Wild and F Golooba-Mutebi, "Review of International Assistance to Political Party and Party System Development, Case Study Report: Uganda", London, Overseas Development Institute (August 2010)

Lumu D and Kiwawulo C, "Museveni Appoints Lt. Gen. Lakara as Uganda Air Cargo Boss," *The New Vision*, 15 June 2020, https://www.newvision.co.ug/news/1520888/museveni-appoints-lt-gen-lakara-uganda-air-cargo-boss (accessed 23 February 2024)

Maiyo J, "Political Parties and Intra-Party Democracy in Uganda: Challenges and Opportunities for Democratic Consolidation", *SSRN*, 13 May 2020, https://ssrn.com/abstract=3600470 (accessed 24 October 2024)

Makara S, "The Challenge of Building Strong Political Parties for Democratic Governance in Uganda: Does Multiparty Politics Have a Future?", 41 (2009) *East African Review*

Meldrum A, "Ugandans Vote for Multi-party State", *The Guardian*, 30 July 2005, https://www.theguardian.com/world/2005/jul/30/andrewmeldrum (accessed 19 November 2024)

Mubiru A, "The Rise and Fall of Gen. Kayihura," *The New Vision*, 14 June 2018, https://www.newvision.co.ug/new_vision/news/1479729/rise (accessed 21 February 2024)

Mubiru I, "Museveni Appoints Four UPDF Officers as Police Directors", *Watchdog Uganda*, https://www.watchdoguganda.com/news/20190703/71522/museveni-appoints-four-updf-officers-as-police-directors.html (accessed 18 February 2024)

Musinguzi B, "Uganda: Bobi Wine Foot Soldiers, a Symbol of Pride, Defiance," *The Africa Report*, 8 October 2024, https://www.theafricareport.com/363788/uganda-bobi-wine-foot-soldiers-a-symbol-of-pride-defiance/ (accessed 25 March 2025)

Musisi F, Herbst RO, and Mahajubu A, "Unlocking the Mysteries of The Origins of the 1966 Ugandan Constitutional Crisis Global," 6 (2018) *Journal of Arts, Humanities and Social Sciences*, pp 14–25

Mutyaba M, "Is Co-opting the Opposition Shrewd Politics or a Desperate Ploy?", *African Arguments*, 10 August 2022, https://africanarguments.org/2022/08/uganda-museveni-mao-is-co-opting-the-opposition-shrewd-politics-or-a-desperate-ploy/ (accessed 19 October 2024)

Nalwooga J, "UPDF Soldier Shoots Fisherman Dead on Lake Kyoga", *The Daily Monitor*, 2 May 2021, https://www.monitor.co.ug/uganda/news/national/updf-soldier-shoots-fisherman-dead-on-lake-kyoga-4610230 (accessed 23 October 2024)

Namwase S and Nkuubi J, *Guns, Bread and Butter: Militarisation of Economic Sectors and Public Institutions in Uganda: A Socio-Legal Analysis*, Kampala, Human Rights and Peace Centre, Makerere University (2024)

National Unity Platform, *People Power Movement Manifesto, 2021–2026: A New Uganda*, p 1, https://nupuganda.org/wp-content/uploads/2021/12/NUP-MANIFESTO.pdf (accessed 18 November 2024)

Okuku J, "Beyond 'Third Term' Politics: Constitutional Reform and Democratic Governance in Uganda", 11 (2005) *East African Journal of Peace and Human Rights*, pp 182–219

Okuku J, "Ethnicity, State Power and the Democratisation Process in Uganda", Discussion Paper No. 17, The Nordic Africa Institute (2002)

Onyango JO and Ahikire J (eds.), *Controlling Consent: Uganda's 2016 Elections*, Trenton, New Jersey, Africa World Press (2017)

Opondo O, "The NUP Politics of Bullying and Insolence Must be Tackled", *Uganda Media Centre,* 16 September 2023, https://www.mediacentre.go.ug/Opinion/nup-politics-bullying-and-insolence-must-be-tackled (accessed 4 November 2024)

Roberts G, "The Uganda-Tanzania War, the Fall of Idi Amin, and the Failure of African Diplomacy, 1978–1979", 8 (2014) *Journal of Eastern African Studies*, pp 692–709

Summers C and Sikainga AA, "Ugandan Politics World War II (1939–1949)", in JA Byfield, CA Brown, and T Parsons (eds.), *Africa and World War II*, Cambridge, Cambridge University Press (2015), pp 480–498

Tapscott R, *Arbitrary State: Social Control and Modern Authoritarianism in Museveni's Uganda*, Oxford, Oxford University Press (2021)

Therkildsen O, "Uganda's Referendum 2000: The Silent Boycott: A Comment," 101 (2002) *African Affairs*, pp 231–241

Tripp AM, *Museveni's Uganda: Paradoxes of Power in a Hybrid Regime*, Boulder, Colorado, Lynne Rienner Publishers (2010)

Tumushabe G, Rwakakamba M, and Makhone B, "Hard Choices or No Choice at All: Questions for Uganda's Political Parties", 1 (2015) *The Situation Room Uganda Debates Papers*

URN, "Details of Museveni, Mao 42-clause Agreement", *The Observer*, 22 July 2022, https://observer.ug/news/headlines/74458-details-of-museveni-mao-42-clause-agreement (accessed 18 September 2024)

Table of legislation

Constitution of the Republic of Uganda, 1995

Political Parties and Organisations Act, 2005

Uganda Air Cargo Corporation Act, 1994

Part 5
Constitutionalism and Party Financing

Chapter 16 Political Moneyball: Mapping South Africa's Party-Financing Ecosystem

Heather A Thuynsma

1. Introduction

There is growing scepticism about the role that money, particularly when it involves political parties, plays in shaping a country's politics.[1] In South Africa, money has had a corruptive influence within the broader political system and regulating its flow has become the focus of both legislative agendas and academic studies. The purpose of the legislation is to foster a more transparent political environment, build public trust, reduce corruption, ensure fair competition, and ultimately strengthen democracy by improving the responsiveness of political parties and the policy system. Since 1994, there have been a number of moves to encourage greater transparency in the country's political system. For instance, electoral and party finance legislation was enacted to help parties and the broader public hold elected leaders to account.

This chapter argues that there is a complex interrelationship between party financing and expenditure and how responsive parties are to voters and their concerns. It further maintains that to increase trust and transparency within the system, parties must disclose both their funding sources and their expenditure. It uses South Africa ahead of the 2024 national and

1 D Kotze, "Political Party Funding in the 2004 Election", 3 (2004) *Journal of African Elections*, pp 27–46; M Pinto-Duschinsky, "Financing Politics: A Global View", 13 (2002) *Journal of Democracy*, pp 69–86; DM Primo, "Information at the Margin: Campaign Finance Disclosure Laws, Ballot Issues, and Voter Knowledge", 12 (2013) *Election Law Journal*, pp 114–129; V Robinson and S Brummer, "SA Democracy Incorporated: Corporate Fronts and Political Party Funding", 129 (2006) *Institute for Security Studies Papers*, pp 1–129, 38; A Butler (ed.), *Paying for Politics: Party Funding and Political Change in South Africa and the Global South,* Johannesburg, Jacana Media (2010); G Pienaar, "Addressing the Implications of Political Party Funding for Democratic Governance: A South African Case Study", 58 (2014) *Journal of African Law*, pp 259–287; A Venter, "The Need to Reform the Electoral System in South Africa", in H Thuynsma (ed.), *Political Parties in South Africa: Do They Undermine or Underpin Democracy?* Pretoria, Africa Institute of South Africa (2017), pp 23–46.

provincial election cycle as a case study to show how money shaped party decision-making in terms of donor-targeting and soliciting. The chapter engages with the main scholarly debates about the financing of political parties, highlights the junction between finance, politics and law, and explores how these intersect to effect transparency, electoral fairness, and public trust in the political system.[2] It traces the need for party-finance reform in South Africa; the sources of funding that exist within the system; and the legislation that has been enacted to promote greater transparency.

As a conceptual framework, the chapter uses a "moneyball" approach (explained later in more detail) to assess how parties have adapted their fundraising strategies in response to finance regulations. In doing so, it relies on secondary sources such as academic articles; funding disclosure reports by the Independent Electoral Commission (IEC); and various media sources, policy reports, and legal cases to explain the positive and negative consequences for party responsiveness and transparency.

2. The evolution of party finance regulation in South Africa

South Africa has a long history of questioning the transparency of party financing. During the apartheid era, many of the regime's financiers, such as Barlow Rand (now trading as the conglomerate Barloworld), "preferred to keep their support confidential".[3] This inability to conclusively finger the bankrollers certainly helped to prolong the apartheid regime's tenure. But it can also be argued that this secrecy protected those supporting the struggle against apartheid from local and international retribution.[4]

In 1996, when the new Constitution was signed into law, citizens were guaranteed certain rights, including:

> [the] free[dom] to make political choices, which includes the right – (a) to form a political party; (b) to participate in the activities of, or recruit

---

2 M Bailey, "The Two Sides of Money in Politics: A Synthesis and Framework", 3 (2004) *Election Law Journal*, pp 653–669; S Power, *Party Funding and Corruption*, Berlin, Springer Nature (2020).

3 Open Secrets, "Declassified: Apartheid Profits – Who Funded the National Party?", *News24*, 14 August 2017, https://www.news24.com/News24/declassified-apartheid-profits-who-funded-the-national-party-20170814 (accessed 30 December 2024) ; H van Vuuren, *Apartheid Guns and Money: A Tale of Profit*, Johannesburg, Jacana Media (2017).

4 Ibid.

members for, a political party; and (c) to campaign for a political party or cause.[5]

Such participation, although not specifically identified, includes being able to make financial or in-kind donations to a party. These private donations, which supplement a modest amount of public funding,[6] should fund party activities such as providing information to help citizens make informed choices about participating in elections and the broader political system. But they also fund a party's ability to contest elections which is also supported by the IEC, a Chapter 9 institution[7] under Section 190 of the Constitution. Besides managing the flow of public funds to parties, the IEC

> manage[s] elections of national, provincial and municipal legislative bodies; ensure[s] that those elections are free and fair; [and] declare[s] the results of those elections within a period that must be prescribed by national legislation ...[8]

In the years that followed, the country evolved into a dominant-party system with largely free and fair elections repeatedly returning the former liberation movement, the African National Congress (ANC), to power. The ANC abused this dominance, according to Pienaar,[9] and used it to frustrate the efforts by opposition parties to keep the government in check.[10] For instance, prior to 2018, political parties were not required to disclose the donations or the amounts they received, creating the perception that there was limited democratic accountability in the political system. Robinson and Brummer found, for instance, that this lack of transparency undermined the national government's good governance initiatives.[11] They argued for

5 Section 19 of the Constitution of the Republic of South Africa 1996.

6 Sources of public funding include the Represented Political Parties Fund and the Multiparty Democracy Fund, which are managed by the IEC (and discussed in detail later in this chapter).

7 Chapter 9 of the South African Constitution mandates the creation of institutions to protect and support democracy. They include the Public Protector; the South African Human Rights Commission; the Commission for the Promotion and Protection of the Rights of Cultural, Religious and Linguistic Communities; the Commission for Gender Equality; the Auditor-General; the Independent Authority to Regulate Broadcasting; and the IEC. These institutions are meant to be independent from the government, political parties, and interest groups.

8 Section 190 of the Constitution of the Republic of South Africa 1996.

9 Pienaar, *supra* n. 1, p 263.

10 Venter, *supra* n. 1.

11 Robinson and Brummer, *supra* n. 1.

all public organisations, including political parties, to be subject to public scrutiny. Rowbottom's subsequent investigation into corruption, transparency, and reputation also uncovered a growing apprehension about the potential for donors to exert undue influence.[12] In this context, calls for greater transparency within the political system have persisted but, as Kotze[13] and Pinto-Duschinsky[14] have noted, such calls tend to fall outside the purview of existing regulatory frameworks. Moreover, since exposing their funding sources could jeopardise the credibility of both the party and specific politicians,[15] political parties were understandably hesitant to agree to being regulated.[16]

This reticence was clear in 2005, when the civil society organisation, the Institute for Democracy in South Africa (IDASA), tried to use the Promotion of Access to Information Act (PAIA)[17] to compel parties to disclose their funding sources. It launched a High Court application, *Institute for Democracy in South Africa & Others v African National Congress & Others*,[18] against the ANC, the Democratic Alliance (DA), the Inkatha Freedom Party (IFP), and the New National Party, which were then all political parties registered under the Electoral Commission Act.[19] The Court, however, denied the IDASA application, holding that political parties were "private bodies" and therefore revealing their funding sources did not fall within the public's interest.

---

12 J Rowbottom, "Corruption, Transparency, and Reputation: The Role of Publicity in Regulating Political Donations", 75 (2016) *Cambridge Law Journal*, pp 398–425.

13 Kotze, *supra* n. 1.

14 Pinto-Duschinsky, *supra* n. 1.

15 MD Gilbert, "Disclosure, Credibility, and Speech", 27 (2012) *Journal of Law & Politics*, pp 627–683.

16 MD Gilbert and BF Aiken, "Disclosure and Corruption", 14 (2015) *Election Law Journal*, pp 148–164.

17 Promotion of Access to Information Act 2 of 2000 (Vol. 416, No. 20852, Cape Town, 3 February 2000), https://www.gov.za/sites/default/files/gcis_document/201409/a2-000.pdf (accessed 17 September 2024).

18 High Court of South Africa – Western Cape Division, *Institute for Democracy in South Africa and Others v African National Congress and Others* (9828/03), ZAWCHC 30; (5) SA 39 (C); 3 All SA 45 (C); (10) BCLR 995 (C), Judgement, 20 April 2005, https://www.saflii.org/za/cases/ZAWCHC/2005/30.html (accessed 30 December 2024).

19 Electoral Commission Act 51 of 1996, section 15 (Vol. 376, No. 17478, Cape Town, 4 October 1996), https://www.gov.za/sites/default/files/gcis_document/201409/act51of1996.pdf (accessed 15 September 2024).

A second source of frustration is evident in relation to the dramatic increase in party spending. This has raised red flags across the political spectrum.[20] In particular, the campaign for senior leadership positions within the ANC's National Executive Committee proved to be an expensive and hotly contested affair. Since the 2009 national elective conference that saw Jacob Zuma elected as party president, campaigns such as this have provoked allegations of vote-buying.[21] The same concern was raised about Cyril Ramaphosa's roughly ZAR 300 million (the amount is disputed) ANC presidential bid in 2017, nicknamed "CR17".[22] The questionable origins of money used to fund the ANC's internal party campaigns (which were then unregulated) reinforced the impression that corruption exists and that it was crippling the noble intentions of the former liberation movement. There were also concerns that "[w]hen political parties come to rely on the financial support of a few – not just the votes of a majority – to win and maintain power, public accountability and internal party democracy are undermined".[23]

Finally, there is an observable trend of decreasing public participation in elections and trust in the broader political system.[24] A resulting lack of transparency and responsiveness has become deeply embedded in the political culture of South Africa's political parties, and this (in part at least) helps to explain why a culture of secrecy and mistrust exists amongst political actors in post-apartheid South Africa.

There have been attempts to redefine the political landscape and make the funding of political parties both more transparent and more responsive.

---

20 Corruption Watch, "Political Parties: The Missing Link in Our Constitution?", *Corruption Watch*, 28 August 2015, https://www.corruptionwatch.org.za/political-parties-the-missing-link-in-our-constitution/ (accessed 12 December 2016); Corruption Watch, "Cleaning up Political Party Funding", *Corruption Watch*, 15 June 2016, https://www.corruptionwatch.org.za/cleaning-political-party-funding/ (accessed 12 December 2016).

21 M Makhanya, "The Horse Has Bolted", *City Press*, 6 November 2022; N Njilo, "Zuma Rips into Ramaphosa's 'Vote-Buying' to Secure ANC Top Job", *Daily Maverick*, 7 November 2022; S Payne, "ANC NEC Candidates Ordered to Divulge All Election Campaign Financial Details", *Daily Maverick*, 3 November 2022.

22 C du Plessis, "Cyril Ramaphosa to Zondo Commission: My CR17 Campaign Did Not Cost a Billion Rand", *News24*, 29 April 2021.

23 Pienaar, *supra* n. 1, p 263.

24 Human Sciences Research Council (HSRC), *Assessing Progress after the First Year of Implementation of the Political Party Funding Act (PPFA) in South Africa.* Report prepared for the Electoral Commission of South Africa (IEC), Pretoria, HSRC (2023), p 1.

As Booysen[25] pointed out, initial proposals in this regard were timid. They set minimum disclosure requirements but did little to dislodge the embedded financing tactics (which relied on a mix of public and private funding).[26] The apparent objective was to fulfil the spirit of the Constitution and to "enhance multi-party democracy [by enacting] national legislation ... [that] ... provide[s] for the funding of political parties participating in national and provincial legislatures on an equitable and proportional basis".[27] Opposition parties complained that the ultimate effect was in reality to further entrench incumbent parties and fill their party coffers rather than promote new voices that could respond to changes in voter preferences.

The Public Funding of Represented Political Parties Act[28] (also known as the Public Funding Act) was the first serious foray into party-finance regulation. It established that political parties represented in Parliament and provincial legislatures would share monies from a public fund (also referred to as the Multiparty Democracy Fund – MDF) managed by the IEC.

In the 2012/2013 financial year alone, this public funding amounted to ZAR 110 million. It was divided proportionally among the represented parties. Parties who received funds were obliged to report on how these monies were spent, but a distinct lack of internal financial management capacity meant that many parties commingled the funds along with their other monies (such as membership fees) and were unable to provide the required reports.

In 2005, the Public Funding Act was amended to promote greater transparency in how political parties operated their constituency offices. It also sought to

> provide for the re-allocation of moneys from the Represented Political Parties' Fund and to regulate the repayment of unspent balances of all moneys allocated to political parties participating in Parliament and provincial legislatures where a member of a legislature becomes a member of another party whilst retaining membership of that legislature

25 S Booysen, "Money, Politics and Power: Impacts of Party Financing in South Africa", 50 (2012) *Journal of Modern African Studies*, pp 221–248.

26 Ibid.

27 Section 236 of the Constitution of the Republic of South Africa.

28 Public Funding of Represented Political Parties Act 103 of 1997 (Vol. 390, No. 18517, Cape Town, 19 December 1997), https://www.gov.za/sites/default/files/gcis_document/201409/a103-97.pdf (accessed 17 September 2024).

> or where an existing party merges with another party, subdivides into more than one party or subdivides and any one subdivision merges with another party ...[29]

In addition, the amended Act amended the Determination of Delegates (National Council of Provinces) Act[30] to account for potential changes in party membership at the provincial level. Reporting once again proved to be inconsistent, with funding to some parties suspended until they could demonstrate compliance.[31] A key omission, though, was that the amended Public Funding Act concentrated entirely on regulating state funding but did not require that private donations be disclosed. In effect, the Act created conditions where financial influence could go unchecked, leading to an erosion of public trust in political processes.

Calls for greater financial transparency within the political system have persisted. The most recent was made by Raymond Zondo, former Chief Justice of the Constitutional Court and Chairman of the Commission of Inquiry into State Capture of State-Owned Enterprises. His reports from the inquiry blamed the level of corruption, and the broader systemic failures it produced, on politicians who were either unable or unwilling to hold officials accountable because their livelihoods depended on their loyalty to the party and its narrow (donor) interests.[32] However, almost two years after the Commission's conclusion and despite the evidence gathered during this inquiry, the country's National Prosecuting Authority has yet to bring a successful prosecution against anyone identified in the hearings. As a result, and because there is seemingly no legal recourse on the cards, voters ahead of the 2024 national and provincial election cycle felt that

29 Constitutional Matters Amendment Act 15 of 2005.

30 Determination of Delegates (National Council of Provinces) Act of 1998 (B 56B–98), https://www.gov.za/sites/default/files/gcis_document/201409/b56b-98.pdf (accessed 17 September 2024).

31 Pienaar, *supra* n. 1, p 266.

32 RM Zondo, *Judicial Commission of Inquiry into State Capture Report: Parts I–VI* (2022); E Ferreira, "National Assembly Passes Controversial Electoral Amendment Bill amid Protests from Opposition Parties", *Mail & Guardian*, 20 October 2022, https://mg.co.za/politics/2022-10-20-national-assembly-passes-controversial-electoral-amendment-bill-amid-protests-from-opposition-parties/ (accessed 22 April 2023).

senior ruling party officials were acting with impunity. This belief affected how, and indeed if, they chose to participate.[33]

Furthermore, successive ANC administrations have had to address the wealth, housing, education, and health-care imbalances that they inherited from the apartheid state. After three decades, the continued failure to provide essential infrastructure and the inability to enforce accountability on those in office have stoked national frustrations, with these now posing as perhaps the most significant threat to the country's democracy.[34]

2.1 Building transparency by disclosing donations

The importance of financial transparency and responsiveness to political life cannot be overstated. These principles uphold the constitutional right of citizens to access information regarding political funding which is crucial for informed political participation.[35] To its credit, South Africa's Constitutional Court has played a pivotal role in shaping the discourse around party-finance restrictions.[36] Its decisions reflect a commitment to ensuring that political parties operate within a framework that promotes democratic values. It has emphasised the need for transparency in political funding to combat corruption and improve public trust in political institutions.

For instance, the case of *One Movement South Africa NPC v President of the Republic of South Africa*[37] saw the court address the unconstitutionality of certain provisions in the Electoral Act that limited access to political office solely through membership in a political party. The judgement underscored the importance of transparency and inclusivity in political participation, deeming it integral to mitigating corruption. *My Vote Counts*

33 L Patel, Y Sadie, M Bryer, and J de Klerk, *Factors Determining Voter Choice between 2017 and 2021*, Johannesburg, Centre for Social Development in Africa, University of Johannesburg (2021); HSRC, *supra* n. 24.

34 Thuynsma, *supra* n. 1.

35 N Netshakhuma, "The Implications of Political Party Funding Act, No. 6 of 2018 in South Africa on Records Management", 70 (2020) *Global Knowledge Memory and Communication*, pp 293–303.

36 K Maphunye and K Motubatse, "Consequences of (Un)Regulated Party Funding in South Africa between 1994 and 2017", 15 (2019) *The Journal for Transdisciplinary Research in Southern Africa*, pp 1–10.

37 *One Movement South Africa NPC v President of the Republic of South Africa and Others* (CCT 158/23), Judgement, 4 December 2023; ZACC 42; 2024 (3) BCLR 364 (CC); 2024 (2) SA 148 (CC), Judgement, 4 December 2023.

v President of the Republic of South Africa[38] is another landmark ruling that required political parties to disclose their sources of funding. In this case, the court recognised that political parties needed to be more transparent to ensure that they are more responsive to voters' needs and, ultimately, to promote integrity within the electoral process. This judicial approach underlines the need to maintain the integrity of the political process.

The efforts to regulate political-party funding have been influenced by international norms and practices. Analyses by Rashkova and Biezen[39] indicate that many European democracies have instituted similar regulations to mitigate the risks associated with unregulated political financing. The South African context, however, is different from many European countries due to its historical background and the specific challenges faced by smaller political parties in a predominantly ANC-dominated political environment.[40] The legal framework, therefore, seeks to regulate funding but also aims to level the playing field for all political entities in the general attempt to create a more equitable political landscape.

The next firm attempt to embed a degree of transparency and responsiveness into the system was the enactment of the Political Party Funding Act (PPFA) in 2018.[41] The Act mandates that political parties disclose their sources of funding and expenditure in an effort to promote ethical conduct in political financing.[42] Figure 1 illustrates how the PPFA was supposed to change the political culture of both leaders and individual voters.

38 Constitutional Court of South Africa, *My Vote Counts NPC v Minister of Justice and Correctional Services and Others* (CCT249/17), ZACC 17, Judgement, 21 June 2018, http://hdl.handle.net/20.500.12144/34577 (accessed 30 December 2024); (8) BCLR 905 (CC); (5) SA 1 (CC), 21 June 2018.

39 E Rashkova and I van Biezen, "The Legal Regulation of Political Parties: Contesting or Promoting Legitimacy?", 35 *International Political Science Review* (2014), pp 265–274.

40 K Maphunye, "Politics-Law Convergence or Divergence? 'Small' Political Parties, Realpolitik and South Africa's 20 Years of Democracy", 2 (2015) *Journal of Law Society and Development*, pp 66–92.

41 Political Party Funding Act 6 of 2018.

42 Netshakhuma, *supra* n. 35.

Figure 1: Flowchart illustrating the intended effect of the Political Party Funding Act 2018.

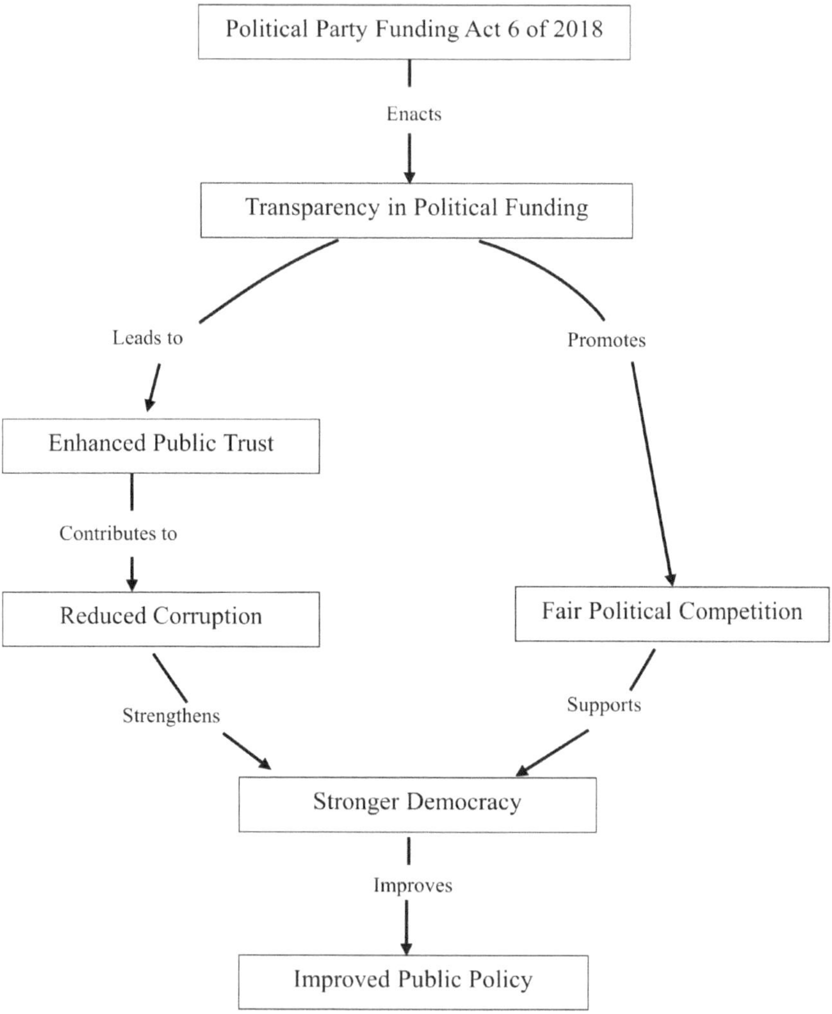

There was real hope for substantive change when the PPFA was passed. For the first time, the law required that political parties disclose those who contributed above a certain threshold and also limited the amount of money that both individuals and corporate bodies could give. To reduce the possibility of external influence on national politics, the Act excluded foreign funding in certain contexts. By forcing parties to disclose their funders and to quantify the sum of their support, the law was supposed to open up what was traditionally a closed financing system. Indeed, studies such as that published by Crepaz and Arikan,[43] suggest that an open system increases public trust because it exposes potential conflicts of interest and reduces perceptions of corruption.

In turn, publicising these disclosure reports was supposed to encourage an environment of greater responsiveness, one in which fair competition between political parties could exist. This law also sought to promote a political culture in which voters would be able to make more informed decisions about political parties, with this shift contributing to a more robust and democratic political system.

The key question remains, however, as to how well the PPFA was able to achieve this goal ahead of the 2024 national and provincial election cycle.

2.2 The operation of the PPFA

The PPFA was seen as both an incentive for those stakeholders (that is, businesses, investors, civil society, and voters) pushing for a more responsive system as well as a way of creating greater transparency because it requires political parties to disclose donors that give money and in-kind gifts of ZAR 100,000 or more.[44] The Act also retains the Represented Political Parties Fund (RPPF), which was originally established under the Public Funding Act and enables the IEC to disburse an annual amount of public money to political parties. The DA, however, argued that the amount of public funding it received was inadequate and that its distribution was not equitable given a party's size or electoral performance.[45] It argued that, in effect, the largest party in Parliament, the ANC, was also the largest beneficiary of state funding.

---

43 M Crepaz and G Arikan, "The Effects of Transparency Regulation on Political Trust and Perceived Corruption: Evidence from a Survey Experiment", September (2023), *Regulation and Governance.*

44 E Stoltz, "'All Systems Go' for IEC's Political Party Funding Act", *Mail & Guardian*, 1 April 2021, https://mg.co.za/politics/2021-04-01-all-systems-go-for-iecs-political-party-funding-act/ (accessed 30 March 2023).

45 Ibid.

The MDF was also retained to encourage corporates, individuals, and foundations to support the country's nascent democracy by funding non-partisan activity such as issue advocacy and civic education training sessions. In line with its code of ethics, both funds prohibit money from being used to "defray any costs or expenses incurred directly or indirectly, arising from and pursuant to inter-political party disputes", remunerate individuals employed by the state including members of national, provincial and local legislatures, defray legal expenses, or establish a business.[46] According to the Act's provisions, the IEC is charged with publicising the disclosures on a quarterly basis to ensure transparency in the political system. That said, there have been challenges to ensuring that parties comply with these new legal requirements, especially in providing full and timely disclosures of their funders and expenditure.

For instance, receiving money through the MDF is in itself not controversial, but reporting on how the funds are spent can be a challenge. This is because, as mentioned earlier, most parties are unable to afford the cost of setting up a separate bank account and auditing structure to comply with the mandatory reporting requirements. As a result, most parties accept such grants into their central bank account, in effect commingling these funds with other party resources and thus making it difficult to report on the grant's specific expenditure.

In addition, the marked rise in campaign spending and the questionable nature of private donor funding, forced legislative amendments to the Executive Members' Ethics Act[47] in an attempt to monitor the ethical conduct of cabinet members, deputy ministers and members of provincial executive councils. Under this Act, an executive member must disclose all gifts, sponsorships and other benefits received in his or her private capacity. This was thought to exclude donations to an internal party campaign that is established as an independent legal entity and separate from the individual member seeking election.[48] The AmaBhungane Centre for Investigative

46 Section 7 No. 2(d) of the Political Party Funding Act 6 of 2018.

47 Executive Members' Ethics Act 82 of 1998 (Vol. 400, No. 19406, Cape Town, 28 October 1998), https://www.gov.za/sites/default/files/gcis_document/201409/a82-98.pdf (accessed 4 July 2024).

48 D Milo and L Pillay, "Donations to Political Party Candidates Must Now See the Light of Day after Successful Court Challenge by Amabhungane", *Daily Maverick*, 6 December 2021, https://www.dailymaverick.co.za/article/2021-12-06-donations-to-political-party-candidates-must-now-see-the-light-of-day-after-successful-court-challenge-by-amabhungane/ (accessed 30 March 2023).

Journalism (in *Amabhungane Centre for Investigative Journalism NPC v President of the Republic of South Africa (2022)*)[49] successfully challenged this latter point in the High Court, stating that section 96 of the Constitution protects against a potential conflict between the official responsibilities and private interests of a member. Accordingly, members of the executive must now disclose all donations to their political campaigns.[50]

3. Conceptual framework: The moneyball approach

Most post-election reports issued by political parties in South Africa (as across the world) cite lack of resources as the primary reason for not achieving a particular goal. In fact no political party has ever had enough time, people or money to contest an election, which is why most parties spend the time between elections raising funds from a variety of sources.

This endless fundraising cycle has the obvious benefit of raising a party's stature and outreach capacity, but there are also several disadvantages to this, notably its effects on voters and their freedom to choose. For instance, Overton's article on the donor class in the United States (US) discusses how the unequal distribution of wealth has enabled a small number of wealthy individuals and organisations to exert an outsized influence on the political process, potentially undermining the principle of political equality.[51] Thomsen's valuable study on competition in US Congressional elections suggests that the need for campaign dollars has influenced candidates to focus more on fundraising than garnering votes, which can certainly compromise the quality of electoral competition.[52]

As already mentioned, in the South African context, although public financing exists for political parties, it is not nearly enough, and its reporting requirements are too restrictive for parties to implement or the IEC, the primary management body, to enforce. Considering this context, this chapter explores the costs and benefits of private party financing and considers

49 Constitutional Court of South Africa, *Amabhungane Centre for Investigative Journalism v President of the Republic of South Africa, CCT 385/21*, Judgement, 20 September 2022, https://www.concourt.org.za/index.php/judgement/483-amabhungane-centre-for-investigative-journalism-npc-v-president-of-the-republic-of-south-africa-cct385-21 (accessed 30 December 2024).

50 Milo and Pillay, *supra* n. 48; Payne, *supra* n. 21.

51 S Overton, "The Donor Class: Campaign Finance, Democracy, and Participation", 153 (2004) *University of Pennsylvania Law Review*, p 73.

52 DM Thomsen, "Competition in Congressional Elections: Money versus Votes", 117 (2022) *American Political Science Review*, pp 675–691.

the implications this money has on party responsiveness and transparency which includes the issues that parties champion as well as the campaigns they are able to afford.

The moneyball approach adopted in this chapter shows how legislation has influenced party fundraising strategies. The term "moneyball" is taken from Michael Lewis's book.[53] Lewis details how Billy Beane, the general manager of the US baseball team the Oakland Athletics, used statistical analysis to build a highly competitive team on a very limited budget. By focusing on metrics rather than on traditional scouting methods, Beane identified undervalued players and so was able to optimise the team's performance. This approach has since been adopted in various fields, including government and politics, to enhance decision-making processes. It is used here to explain how political-party financing strategies work to maximise their gains within the PPFA's regulations.

4. Moneyball strategies for political parties

Political parties in South Africa have increasingly adopted a moneyball approach to fundraising, particularly when considering the PPFA's regulatory framework. This approach emphasises data-driven strategies to optimise fundraising efforts while ensuring compliance with campaign finance legislation.

4.1 Data-driven donor targeting

The primary strategic priority under a moneyball approach is to use data on historical giving patterns as well as demographic information to identify high-potential donors. In this way, parties tailor their messaging and solicitation strategies to target individuals and organisations that are most likely to contribute to their cause. Targeting donors in this manner maximises the efficiency of the fundraising operation and ensures that all efforts are legally compliant.

It should be noted that, while voicing their general support for the PPFA, South African political parties consider the legislation something of

53 M Lewis, *Moneyball: The Art of Winning an Unfair Game*, New York, WW Norton & Company (2004).

a disincentive. First, the disclosure requirements mean that parties need to be more open about from whom they receive their money, information they are neither accustomed nor equipped to provide. Parties, including the ANC, have also complained that the new legislation makes it difficult for them to raise money. Donors, they argue, are reluctant to link their names to a specific political party. This may also be an issue for the other political parties, but it is difficult to compare since the reporting requirement has only been implemented since 2021. However, opposition parties such as Abantu Integrity Movement, the African Christian Democratic Party, the Patriotic Alliance, and the GOOD Party all declared donations of more than ZAR 100,000 between 2021 and 2023.[54]

In addition, the law restricts parties from accepting donations of more than ZAR 15 million from a single source and also prohibits foreign governments, their agencies and citizens, and their state departments and state-owned enterprises, from making donations. Essentially the Act imposes controls on the amount and sources of party funding in the hopes of restricting the potential political influence that external actors might exert. The IEC reports, however, reveal that the Economic Freedom Fighters (EFF) received donations from South African billionaire Patrice Motsepe's African Rainbow Minerals (Motsepe's sister is married to President Cyril Ramaphosa), Harmony Gold Mining, 3Sixty Health, South African Breweries, and SN Maseko.[55] Interestingly, according to IEC reports[56] African Rainbow Minerals has supported other opposition parties to the tune of about ZAR 3.5 million, with the DA receiving ZAR 2.115 million of this. In 2023, Motsepe also donated to the conservative and predominantly

54 E Matwadia, "Party Funding: DA Rakes in R15mn in Donations, ANC R10mn", *Mail & Guardian*, 9 September 2021, https://mg.co.za/politics/2021-09-09-party-funding-da-rakes-in-r15-million-in-donations-anc-r10-million/ (accessed 30 March 2023); Independent Electoral Commission, *Political Party Funding: Annual Report 2022*, (2022a) and (2022b), https://static.pmg.org.za/PPF_Annual_Report_2022Final.pdf (accessed 20 April 2023); Independent Electoral Commission, *IEC Published Declarations Report: Quarter 1 2022/2023*, https://results.elections.org.za/home/PartyFundingReports/5/1/5_1_Published_Declarations_Report.pdf (accessed 20 April 2023); HA Thuynsma, "Willing to be Transparent? Assessing Political Parties' Commitment Towards Regulating Party Aid in South Africa", Policy Studies Special Issue on Building Party Resilience: Improving Party Aid in An Age of Democratic Decline (forthcoming).

55 N Masungwini, "EFF Declares Donations for the First Time", *City Press*, 22 February 2022; Independent Electoral Commission, *ibid.*

56 Independent Electoral Commission, *ibid.*

Afrikaans party, Freedom Front Plus. President Ramaphosa and the businessman Cedric Muziwakhile Ntombela are also listed among the ANC's individual donors.[57]

Within the DA, however, questions about how individual campaigns are financed did not generate the same media attention – possibly because the party has traditionally raised far less money than its main rival. However, according to the IEC published quarterly reports, in 2021 the DA raised an impressive ZAR 15 million, outpacing the ANC which declared only ZAR 10 million in donations for that reporting cycle.[58] These reports have lifted the secrecy surrounding party financing, with the DA forced to declare another ZAR 15 million in donations from Mary Slack, daughter of the late mining mogul Harry Oppenheimer, Martin Moshal, the co-founder of Entrée Capital who also supports scholarships for students studying in Israel, South Africa, and the Ukraine, and the insurance company Fynbos Ekwiteit.[59] Michiel Le Roux, the founder of Capitec Bank, also donated more than ZAR 50 million prior to the 2024 election.[60]

Since 2021 the ANC has declared multimillion-rand donations from donors such as the Sandton-based business management holding company Chancellor House; investment house Botho-Botho Commercial Enterprise; mining company African Rainbow Minerals; residential construction consulting business NEP Consulting; Nonkwelo Investment Holdings; Majestic Silver Trading 40; and United Manganese of Kalahari.

Foreign governments and agencies were also not permitted to make direct donations to a political party except in cases where the funding is there to support training and policy development initiatives (any such funding must be declared). As a result, the DA declared donations from political foundations such as the Friedrich Naumann Foundation (which provided support through both cash and in-kind donations); the Danish Liberal Democracy Programme; and the Dutch-based Volkspartij Voor Vrijheid En Democratie (the latter two provided in-kind support).[61] In addition,

57 N Subramoney, "Party Funding: 'Broke" ANC Declares R22 Million as Cyril Digs into His Pockets", *The Citizen,* 19 November 2021, https://www.citizen.co.za/news/south-africa/politics/anc-r22-million-party-funding-second-quarter/ (accessed 20 April 2023); Independent Electoral Commission, *ibid.*

58 Matwadia, *supra* n. 54.

59 Independent Electoral Commission, *supra* n. 54.

60 R Davis, "The Big Eight Funders of South Africa's Major Political Parties", *Daily Maverick,* 10 September 2023.

61 Independent Electoral Commission, *supra* n. 54.

donations from corporates such as the environmentally responsible plastic packaging firm Polyoak Packaging and the media conglomerate Naspers were acknowledged. The party also received international funding from the former chief executive and treasurer of the British Conservative Party, Sir Michael Lawrence Davis (note that donations from foreign individuals to political parties are allowed under law but cannot exceed ZAR 5 million a year).[62]

4.2 Measuring the impact of courting private donors

The next element that parties needed to understand was the likely costs and benefits of courting private donors. Despite the ZAR 15 million donation restriction, billionaires such as the Oppenheimer family, Patrice Motsepe, and Martin Moshal have retained their influence on the fundraising strategies of political parties. The perception is that their contributions have shaped party dynamics, funding approaches, and policy priorities, with this often leading to concerns about the implications for democratic processes and governance.

The existing data suggests that parties continue to rely on a small number of wealthy donors. For instance, Le Roux, Motsepe, and Moshal, along with the Oppenheimer family, collectively contributed more than ZAR 150 million to various parties ahead of the 2024 election cycle, with this making up a significant portion of the parties' overall funding.[63] Such levels of dependency have encouraged parties to align their messaging and policy approaches with the interests of these donors in order to secure ongoing financial support.

For example, Motsepe's donations to parties ranging from the ANC, DA, Freedom Front, and EFF reflects a strategy of maintaining influence across the political spectrum.[64] By supporting various parties, Motsepe has sought to ensure that his commercial interests, particularly in mining and business, are represented regardless of which party, or coalition of parties, gets to be in power. In other democracies (such as the USA), such broad support

62 Ibid.

63 Davis, *supra* n. 60.

64 *Ibid*; J Felix, "Meet the 3 Biggest Funders Behind SA's Political Parties", *News24*, 27 July 2023, https://www.news24.com/news24/politics/parliament/meet-the-3-biggest-funders-behind-sas-political-parties-20230727 (accessed 1 June 2024).

has created a more fragmented policy landscape, with parties scrambling to attract key donor support and adopting very similar pro-business policies.[65] Donors expect their interests to be represented on party platforms and in legislative agendas, such that the Oppenheimers' support for economically conservative parties like the DA suggests a preference for the neoliberal policies that align with their business interests in mining and other sectors.[66]

As Davis reports, Le Roux is not only a close ally of the DA party leader, Hellen Zille, but in 2019 sat on the party's review panel alongside former party strategist Ryan Coetzee and the former party leader, Tony Leon. The panel, charged with investigating the party's dramatic decline, recommended removing then party leader Mmusi Maimane.[67] These strategic partnerships raise concerns about what has become known as "policy capture", where the interests of a few wealthy individuals overshadow the broader public interest.[68]

In another example, Martin Moshal and three members of the Oppenheimer family made multi-million rand donations to a number of newly formed opposition parties: ActionSA (led by former DA member and businessman Herman Mashaba); Mmusi Maimane's Build One South Africa; and Songezo Zibi's Rise Mzanzi. These parties all challenged the ANC's dominance but found themselves participating in coalition talks with the former liberation movement after no single party received a clear winning majority. In this case, it seems likely that the interests of their wealthy backers influenced the parties to set aside their opposition and join a strategic alliance with their former foes such as the IFP, Patriotic Alliance, ANC, and DA.

However, ActionSA also declared that funding came from the investment company AEEI Group. This is a subsidiary of Sekunjalo Investment Holdings, which was founded by the controversial "struggle doctor", Dr Iqbal Surve. For the more cynical analysts, this contribution is likely to have inspired the party's unexpected break with its coalition partners in local

---

65 Bailey, *supra* n. 2.

66 D Steyn, "How to See Where Political Parties Get Their Money", *GroundUp*, 4 August 2023, https://groundup.org.za/article/how-to-see-where-political-parties-get-their-money/ (accessed 14 August 2023); Felix, *supra* n. 64.

67 Maimane was subsequently removed, after which he formed his own party, Build One South Africa. Davis, *supra* n. 60.

68 OECD, Preventing Policy Capture: Integrity in Public Decision Making, Paris, OECD Public Governance Reviews (2017).

municipalities such as Tshwane shortly after the national and provincial polls.[69] Under a moneyball approach, the seeming ambiguity of these actions implies that one donor's money is more influential than another's.

The substantial financial backing of private donors also allowed parties to broaden their electoral strategies to boost their campaign advertising, outreach efforts, and mobilisation activities. Both the ANC and DA were able to strengthen their campaign infrastructure and increase their visibility via electronic billboards and increased campaign advertising on radio and television channels.[70] Although the PPFA requires parties to disclose donations above ZAR 100,000, there are ongoing debates about the adequacy of these regulations.

4.3 Engaging small donors

While major donors play a significant role in South African political funding, a moneyball approach encourages parties to also focus on small donors. In fact, careful scrutiny of the legislation reveals a very convenient loophole – while parties must record donations received from all sources, amounts below ZAR 100,000 must be regularly audited but do not have to be publicly disclosed.[71] For Butler, this means that parties have canvassed for small-scale or "low-dollar" donors while simultaneously recruiting members and collecting small membership fees to support their operations without being required to disclose their details or the specific amount of their donations.[72]

This strategy exploited a loophole in the PPFA which parties could use to help donors not keen to have their support publicly recognised and also to obscure the true extent of their party infrastructure. In theory,

69 N Njilo, "ActionSA About-Turn on Governance with Tshwane Mayoralty at Stake", *Daily Maverick*, 10 September 2024, https://www.dailymaverick.co.za/article/2024-09-10-actionsa-about-turn-on-governance-with-tshwane-mayoralty-at-stake/ (accessed 1 April 2023).

70 It is difficult to provide absolute amounts of expenditure for these activities, which were launched mostly after 10 May 2024 when the Electoral Matters Amendment Bill of 2024 was passed. Its provisions are discussed later in the chapter, but it effectively suspended all reporting regulations two weeks ahead of the election.

71 Political Party Funding Act 6 of 2018.

72 A Butler, "Most Party Funding Flies Below the Radar", *Business Day*, 17 May 2024, https://www.businesslive.co.za/bd/opinion/columnists/2024-05-17-anthony-butler-most-party-funding-flies-below-the-radar/#google_vignette (last accessed 21 November 2024).

this strategy is particularly useful for established parties and is a generally sound strategy for raising money as well as increasing voter support. But, for newly registered parties, such operations might be out of reach on account of their limited financial and institutional capacity. Furthermore, because these amounts fall below the reporting threshold, it is difficult to ascertain the extent to which parties mined small donors.

Nevertheless, by analysing data on grassroots contributions and the promotion of issues that are relevant to these donors, parties can develop strategies to diversify their funding sources. This not only helps in compliance with donation limits, but also enhances the party's appeal to the broader electorate.

4.4 Using key challenges to political-party advantage

There are a number of challenges that political parties use to their advantage. The first and foremost concern is the ability (and willingness) to comply with the PPFA. As Piper and Schrire point out, the IEC plays a fundamental role in upholding the transparency of political financing by ensuring that political parties comply with the Act and, therefore, is central in regaining the public's trust.[73] But technical and bureaucratic delays have impeded the IEC's ability to oversee a party's compliance with the PPFA. In 2023, the IEC's budget was targeted for a cut of ZAR 800 million over a three period (2023–2025), including a sum of ZAR 281 million to be cut in 2024. The IEC noted that its ability to recruit the staff necessary to effectively discharge its functions under the PPFA was adversely affected by these cuts.[74]

Calland and Graham also recognise the Act's uneven application, arguing that the PPFA's usefulness relies a great deal on political parties themselves and their commitment to adhere to the new standards.[75] Despite the capacity problems experienced by political parties, their books need

73 L Piper and R Schrire, "Transparency and the Effectiveness of the Independent Electoral Commission in Regulating Political Party Funding", 33 (2019) *South African Governance and Political Issues*, pp 113–131.

74 L Dentlinger, "IEC Warns Govt Budget Cuts Could Impact Meeting Amended Electoral Law Requirements", *EWN*, 28 February 2024, https://www.ewn.co.za/2024/02/28/iec-warns-govt-budget-cuts-could-impact-meeting-amended-electoral-law-requirements (accessed 1 March 2024).

75 R Calland and P Graham, "The Effects of the Political Party Funding Act on South African Politics", 25 (2018) *South African Journal of International Affairs*, pp 545–562.

to be regularly audited, with the results submitted to the IEC in the last six months of each financial year. The PPFA also makes provision for the Auditor-General, at his or her discretion, to conduct an additional audit.

In fact, the fine for non-compliance is so lenient that parties, especially the smaller ones, prefer to incur temporary censure rather than expend valuable resources on ensuring compliance. The PPFA requires political parties to submit reports to the IEC on a quarterly basis for monies received from both the MPF and private donors. In terms of enforcement, the IEC can apply to the Electoral Court for an order to compel compliance. Should the party refuse, directives can be issued that, variously, suspend payment of any monies to be allocated; force the party to pay monies that were irregularly accepted or spent by instituting a civil claim; offset the liability against the monies due to the party from the MPF; or impose a fine. The fines are disaggregated based on the offence –for receiving donations from sources that are disallowed or not disclosing donations received above the ZAR 100,000 threshold, parties can be fined ZAR 500,000 or 10 per cent of income (whichever is higher). Depending on the number of offences committed within a three-year period, that amount can increase to ZAR 1 million or 30 per cent of income (whichever is higher). Should the party not account for other income received from, say, membership fees, fines range from ZAR 40,000 to a maximum of ZAR 150,000 depending on the number of offences committed during a three- year period.[76]

Such sanctions have been instituted on very few occasions. The most recent was handed down on 10 May 2024 in the judgement delivered in *Electoral Commission of South Africa v African Independent Congress and others.*[77] Here, 486 political actors were found to be non-compliant with the PPFA's provisions and each fined between ZAR 10,000 and ZAR 40,000. As a result, there were calls to revise the reporting thresholds and the disclosure criteria to better balance the need for transparency and with protection of donor privacy.

For the PPFA to be effective, its provisions should be continually assessed and adapted to address emerging challenges and incorporate feedback from a range of stakeholders. According to a Human Sciences Research Council (HSRC) study, the public, a key stakeholder in the process,

76 Political Party Funding Act 6 of 2018.

77 *Electoral Commission of South Africa v African Independent Congress and others* (0011/23EC) [2024] ZAEC 11, Judgement, 10 May 2024, https://lawlibrary.org.za/akn/za/judgment/zaec/2024/11/eng@2024-05-10 (accessed 30 December 2024).

has mixed feelings about the PPFA.[78] Confronted with the fact that relatively few political parties complied with the disclosure requirements between 2021 and 2024, respondents claimed to appreciate the aims of the PPFA but were sceptical about whether political parties have the political will to comply and further questioned whether the IEC had the capacity to effectively enforce the legislation. Similar sentiments were echoed by the other stakeholders (namely, businesses, civil society organisations, scholars, and policy-makers) who were also surveyed.[79]

Nevertheless, there has been some response to the underlying issues. The amendment to the Executive Members' Ethics Act[80] (discussed above) was an attempt to monitor the ethical conduct of cabinet members, deputy ministers, and members of provincial executive councils and to curb rising campaign expenditure. The National Assembly's passing of the Electoral Matters Amendment Bill (EMAB)[81] on 7 May 2024 is, to some degree, another example. The EMAB amended the PPFA in line with the provisions of the Electoral Amendment Act that allowed independent candidates to contest the 2024 national and provincial elections.[82]

At the same time, the EMAB also heeded the ANC's calls (in its 2017 submission on the PPFA) for a higher threshold for disclosure, the raising of the amount of money a single donor can contribute per financial year, and removal of the ZAR 15 million cap on single donors. By removing the disclosure clause, the EMAB created a temporary lacuna in the law, one that will exist until the President establishes a new limit and threshold. The Act also amended the proportional MPF allocations to allow independent candidates to receive such funding, but rolled back the PPFA's allocation requirements and reverted to the levels seen under the 1997 Public Funding Act. In essence, the EMAB rendered the PPFA and its provisions meaningless, mere weeks before the 2024 national and provincial election. Political parties and the civil society organisation My Vote Counts have vowed to challenge the amendment.

---

78 HSRC, *supra* n. 24.

79 Ibid.

80 Executive Members' Ethics Act 82 of 1998.

81 Electoral Matters Amendment Act 14 of 2024 (Vol. 707, No. 50624, Cape Town, 7 May 2024), https://www.gov.za/sites/default/files/gcis_document/202405/50624gon4790electoralmattersamendmentact14of2024.pdf (accessed 2 June 2024).

82 Electoral Amendment Act 1 of 2023 (Vol. 694, No. 48432, Cape Town, 17 April 2023), https://www.gov.za/sites/default/files/gcis_document/202304/48432electoralamendmentact1of2023.pdf (accessed 2 June 2024).

Clearly, the effectiveness of these reforms depends on various factors: the ability of the IEC to enforce the relevant laws; how they are perceived by the public; and the extent to which political parties are willing to comply with the law.

5. Conclusion

This chapter has provided an analysis of the complex relationship between money and politics, doing so by drawing on publicly available information and exploring the potential costs and benefits of public and privately funded political campaigns. It acknowledges that while public financing does exist for political parties within South Africa, this funding is insufficient and its reporting requirements are too restrictive for parties to implement or the IEC to enforce. To supplement their resources, political parties have courted private donors to fund viable election campaigns and give citizens a greater choice at the ballot box. Donations from billionaires like Patrice Motsepe and Martin Moshal, whose financial contributions seem to shape policy priorities and party dynamics, often leading to concerns about the implications for democratic governance and public trust. The unequal distribution of wealth raises concerns that the wealthy may be able to exert disproportionate influence over the political process, potentially undermining the democratic ideal of political equality in which all citizens have an equal say.

This study has also shown that, prior to the enactment of the EMAB in 2024, business, civil society, and other likeminded stakeholders displayed some vigour and political will in complying with the legislation. Prominent decision-makers from political parties, parliamentary committees, civil society, and the broader public were all involved in the initial policy research discussions. The PPFA also includes a provision for the IEC to enforce the Act and stipulates specific reporting milestones and monetary sanctions for those found to be non-compliant. There is, too, a clear role for civil society to monitor and evaluate the PPFA's implementation and it is encouraged to provide recommendations for future amendments.

Unfortunately, there are also some drawbacks. First, the ANC-led government cut the IEC's budget by ZAR 281 million, effectively compromising the entity's ability to hire adequate levels of staffing for the monitoring and enforcement of the PPFA. Secondly, the EMAB's enactment completely suspended the necessary disclosure and donation limits needed to keep the system transparent and accountable. Enacting the EMAB illustrates just how powerfully political parties (and their donors) can influence the legislative process. In this instance the ANC used its parliamentary dominance to hurry the process through on the pretext of providing state funding for the new independent candidates. It is worth noting that the EMAB also reversed the PPFA's disclosure and reporting provisions.

Lastly, even before the EMAB was enacted, the public was largely cynical about the party-finance regulatory process. According to the previously mentioned HSRC study, the public viewed these reforms as inadequate or merely symbolic.[83] In the end, what started out as a commitment to create more transparency and greater accountability may in fact have highlighted the willingness, especially by political parties, to keep political funding in the shadows, and paradoxically increased levels of distrust among the electorate.

The enactment of the PPFA represents a significant stride towards enhancing transparency and reducing the influence of undisclosed donations. However, as the political landscape shifts, so too must the mechanisms that oversee party financing, ensuring that they keep pace with both internal dynamics and external pressures. Despite the necessary but lofty ideals, the effectiveness of such mechanisms hinges on the will of political parties to comply with them and the ability of the IEC to oversee compliance. But while these reforms of party-funding laws can potentially build public trust and reinvigorate the electorate, their ultimate success relies on the public's perception that the law is being followed.

As political parties navigate these challenges, the need for transparency and public responsiveness in party finance remains crucial to ensuring that the interests of a few do not overshadow the needs of the broader electorate.

References

Books, articles, chapters in books, and others

Bailey M, "The Two Sides of Money in Politics: A Synthesis and Framework", 3 (2004) *Election Law Journal*, pp 653–669

Booysen S, "Money, Politics and Power: Impacts of Party Financing in South Africa", 50 (2012) *Journal of Modern African Studies*, pp 221–248

Butler A (ed.), Paying for Politics: Party Funding and Political Change in South Africa and the Global South, Johannesburg, Jacana Media (2010)

83 HSRC, *supra* n. 24.

Butler A, "Most Party Funding Flies Below the Radar", *Business Day*, 17 May 2024, https://www.businesslive.co.za/bd/opinion/columnists/2024-05-17-anthony-butler-most-party-funding-flies-below-the-radar/#google_vignette (last accessed 21 November 2024)

Calland R and Graham P, "The Effects of The Political Party Funding Act on South African Politics", 25 (2018) *South African Journal of International Affairs*, pp 545–562

Corruption Watch, "Cleaning up Political Party Funding", *Corruption Watch*, 15 June 2016, https://www.corruptionwatch.org.za/cleaning-political-party-funding/ (accessed 12 December 2016)

Corruption Watch, "Political Parties: The Missing Link in Our Constitution?", *Corruption Watch*, 28 August 2015, https://www.corruptionwatch.org.za/political-parties-the-missing-link-in-our-constitution/ (accessed 12 December 2016)

Crepaz M and Arikan G, "The Effects of Transparency Regulation on Political Trust and Perceived Corruption: Evidence from A Survey Experiment", September (2003), *Regulation and Governance*

Davis R, "The Big Eight Funders of South Africa's Major Political Parties", *The Daily Maverick*, 10 September 2023, https://www.dailymaverick.co.za/article/2023-09-10-the-big-eight-funders-of-south-africas-major-political-parties/ (accessed 1 June 2024)

Dentlinger L, "IEC Warns Govt Budget Cuts Could Impact Meeting Amended Electoral Law Requirements", *EWN*, 28 February 2024, https://www.ewn.co.za/2024/02/28/iec-warns-govt-budget-cuts-could-impact-meeting-amended-electoral-law-requirements (accessed 1 March 2024)

Du Plessis, C, "Cyril Ramaphosa to Zondo Commission: My CR17 Campaign Did Not Cost a Billion Rand", *News24*, 29 April 2021, https://www.news24.com/news24/southafrica/news/cyril-ramaphosa-to-zondo-commission-my-cr17-campaign-did-not-cost-a-billion-rand-20210429 (accessed 1 April 2023)

Felix J, "Meet the 3 Biggest Funders Behind SA's Political Parties", *News24*, 27 July 2023, https://www.news24.com/news24/politics/parliament/meet-the-3-biggest-funders-behind-sas-political-parties-20230727 (accessed 1 June 2024)

Ferreira E, "National Assembly Passes Controversial Electoral Amendment Bill Amid Protests from Opposition Parties", *Mail & Guardian*, 20 October 2022, https://mg.co.za/politics/2022-10-20-national-assembly-passes-controversial-electoral-amendment-bill-amid-protests-from-opposition-parties/ (accessed 22 April 2023)

Gilbert MD and Aiken BF, "Disclosure and Corruption", 14 (2015) *Election Law Journal*, pp 148–164

Gilbert MD, "Disclosure, Credibility, and Speech", 27 (2012) *Journal of Law & Politics*, pp 627–683

Human Sciences Research Council (HSRC), *Assessing Progress After the First Year of Implementation of the Political Party Funding Act (PPFA) in South Africa*. Report prepared for the Electoral Commission of South Africa (IEC), Pretoria, HSRC (2023)

Independent Electoral Commission, *IEC Published Declarations Report: Quarter 1 2022/2023*, https://results.elections.org.za/home/PartyFundingReports/5/1/5_1_Published_Declarations_Report.pdf (accessed 20 April 2023)

Independent Electoral Commission, *Political Party Funding: Annual Report 2022*, https://static.pmg.org.za/PPF_Annual_Report_2022Final.pdf (accessed 20 April 2023)

Kotze D, "Political Party Funding in the 2004 Election", 3 (2004) *Journal of African Elections*, pp 27–46

Lewis M, *Moneyball: The Art of Winning an Unfair Game*, New York, WW Norton & Company (2004)

Makhanya M, "The Horse Has Bolted", *City Press*, 6 November 2022, https://www.news24.com/citypress/columnists/mondlimakhanya/mondli-makhanya-the-horse-has-bolted-20221106 (accessed 30 March 2023)

Maphunye K and Motubatse K, "Consequences of (Un)Regulated Party Funding in South Africa between 1994 and 2017", 15 (2019) *The Journal for Transdisciplinary Research in Southern Africa*, pp 1–10

Maphunye K, "Politics-Law Convergence or Divergence? 'Small' Political Parties, Realpolitik and South Africa's 20 Years of Democracy", 2 (2015) *Journal of Law Society and Development*, pp 66–92

Masungwini N, "EFF Declares Donations for the First Time", *City Press*, 22 February 2022, https://www.news24.com/citypress/politics/eff-declares-donations-for-the-first-time-20220222 (accessed 2 June 2023)

Matwadia E, "Party Funding: DA Rakes in R15mn in Donations, ANC R10m", *Mail & Guardian*, 9 September 2021, https://mg.co.za/politics/2021-09-09-party-funding-da-rakes-in-r15-million-in-donations-anc-r10-million/ (accessed 30 March 2023)

Milo D and Pillay L, "Donations to Political Party Candidates Must Now See the Light of Day After Successful Court Challenge by Amabhungane", *Daily Maverick*, 6 December 2021, https://www.dailymaverick.co.za/article/2021-12-06-donations-to-political-party-candidates-must-now-see-the-light-of-day-after-successful-court-challenge-by-amabhungane/ (accessed 30 March 2023)

Netshakhuma N, "The Implications of Political Party Funding Act, No. 6 of 2018 in South Africa on Records Management", 70 (2020) *Global Knowledge Memory and Communication*, pp 293–303

Njilo N, "ActionSA About-Turn on Governance with Tshwane Mayoralty at Stake", *Daily Maverick*, 10 September 2024, https://www.dailymaverick.co.za/article/2024-09-10-actionsa-about-turn-on-governance-with-tshwane-mayoralty-at-stake/ (accessed 1 April 2023)

Njilo N, "Zuma Rips into Ramaphosa's 'Vote-Buying' to Secure ANC Top Job'", *Daily Maverick*, 7 November 2022, https://www.dailymaverick.co.za/article/2022-11-07-zuma-accuses-ramaphosa-of-vote-buying-to-secure-anc-top-job/ (accessed 30 March 2023)

OECD, Preventing Policy Capture: Integrity in Public Decision Making, Paris, OECD Public Governance Reviews (2017)

Open Secrets, "Declassified: Apartheid Profits – Who Funded the National Party?", *News24*, 14 August 2017, https://www.news24.com/news24/declassified-apartheid-profits-who-funded-the-national-party-20170814 (accessed 1 May 2024)

Overton S, "The Donor Class: Campaign Finance, Democracy, and Participation", 153 (2004) *University of Pennsylvania Law Review*, pp 73–73

Patel L, Sadie Y, Bryer M, and de Klerk J, *Factors Determining Voter Choice between 2017 and 2021*, Johannesburg, Centre for Social Development in Africa, University of Johannesburg (2021)

Payne S, "ANC NEC Candidates Ordered to Divulge All Election Campaign Financial Details", *Daily Maverick*, 3 November 2022, https://www.dailymaverick.co.za/article/2022-11-03-anc-nec-candidates-ordered-to-divulge-all-election-campaign-financial-details/ (accessed 30 March 2023)

Pienaar G, "Addressing the Implications of Political Party Funding for Democratic Governance: A South African Case Study", 58 (2014) *Journal of African Law*, pp 259–287

Pinto-Duschinsky, M, "Financing Politics: A Global View", 13 (2002) *Journal of Democracy*, pp 69–86

Piper L and Schrire R, "Transparency and the Effectiveness of the Independent Electoral Commission in Regulating Political Party Funding", 33 (2019) *South African Governance and Political Issues*, pp 113–131

Power S, *Party Funding and Corruption*, Berlin, Springer Nature (2020)

Primo DM, "Information at the Margin: Campaign Finance Disclosure Laws, Ballot Issues, and Voter Knowledge", 12 (2013) *Election Law Journal*, pp 114–129

Rashkova E and Biezen I, "The Legal Regulation of Political Parties: Contesting or Promoting Legitimacy?", 35 (2014) *International Political Science Review*, pp 265–274

Robinson V and Brummer S, "SA Democracy Incorporated: Corporate Fronts and Political Party Funding", 129 (2006) *Institute for Security Studies Papers*, pp 1–129

Rowbottom J, "Corruption, Transparency, and Reputation: The Role of Publicity in Regulating Political Donations", 75 (2016) *Cambridge Law Journal*, pp 398–425

Steyn D, "How to See Where Political Parties Get Their Money", *GroundUp*, 4 August 2023, https://groundup.org.za/article/how-to-see-where-political-parties-get-their-money/ (accessed 14 August 2023)

Stoltz E, "'All Systems Go' for IEC's Political Party Funding Act", *Mail & Guardian*, 1 April 2021, https://mg.co.za/politics/2021-04-01-all-systems-go-for-iecs-political-party-funding-act/ (accessed 30 March 2023)

Subramoney N, "Party Funding: 'Broke' ANC Declares R22 Million as Cyril Digs into His Pockets", *The Citizen,* 19 November 2021, https://www.citizen.co.za/news/south-africa/politics/anc-r22-million-party-funding-second-quarter/ (accessed 20 April 2023)

Thomsen DM, "Competition in Congressional Elections: Money versus Votes", 117 (2022) *American Political Science Review*, pp 675–691

Thuynsma HA (ed.), Political Parties in South Africa: Do They Undermine or Underpin Democracy? Pretoria, Africa Institute of South Africa (2017)

Thuynsma HA, "Willing to be Transparent? Assessing Political Parties' Commitment Towards Regulating Party Aid in South Africa", Policy Studies Special Issue on Building Party Resilience: Improving Party Aid in An Age Of Democratic Decline (forthcoming)

Van Vuuren H, *Apartheid Guns and Money: A Tale of Profit*, Johannesburg, Jacana Media (2017)

Venter A, "The Need to Reform the Electoral System in South Africa", in HA Thuynsma (ed.), *Political Parties in South Africa: Do they Undermine or Underpin Democracy?* Pretoria, Africa Institute of South Africa (2017) pp 23–46

Zondo RM, *Judicial Commission of Inquiry into State Capture Report: Parts I–VI* (2022), https://www.statecapture.org.za/site/information/reports (accessed 23 April 2023)

Table of cases

Constitutional Court of South Africa, Amabhungane Centre for Investigative Journalism v President of the Republic of South Africa (CCT 385/21), Judgement, 20 September 2022

Constitutional Court of South Africa, *My Vote Counts NPC v Minister of Justice and Correctional Services and Others* (CCT249/17), ZACC 17, Judgement, 21 June 2018

Constitutional Court, One Movement South Africa NPC v President of the Republic of South Africa and Others (CCT 158/23), Judgement, 4 December 2023

Electoral Court of South Africa, *Electoral Commission of South Africa v African Independent Congress and others* (0011/23EC) [2024] ZAEC 11, Judgement, 10 May 2024

High Court of South Africa – Western Cape Division, Institute for Democracy in South Africa and Others v African National Congress and Others, Judgement, 20 April 2005

Table of legislation

Constitution of the Republic of South Africa 1996

Constitutional Matters Amendment Act 15 of 2005

Determination of Delegates (National Council of Provinces) Act of 1998

Electoral Amendment Act 1 of 2023

Electoral Commission Act 51 of 1996

Electoral Matters Amendment Act 14 of 2024

Executive Members' Ethics Act 82 of 1998

Political Party Funding Act 6 of 2018

Promotion of Access to Information Act 2 of 2000

Public Funding of Represented Political Parties Act 103 of 1997

Chapter 17 The Funding of Political Parties in Post-2018 Ethiopia: Implications for the Future of Democracy and Constitutionalism

Zelalem Degifie

1. Introduction

Ethiopia has experienced highly contested political reforms since the disintegration of the Ethiopian People's Revolutionary Democratic Front (EPRDF) in 2018. A reformist faction – led by Prime Minister Abiy Ahmed Ali – developed into the now incumbent Prosperity Party (PP).[1] The new government has launched several reform initiatives aimed at addressing legal and policy issues that are believed to have contributed to political discontent over the past three decades.[2] Reform has included the revision of various areas of law – among them political-party registration law, media law, and electoral law – and the reorganisation of the National Election Board of Ethiopia (NEBE). All of these have had implications for political-party financing.[3] Nevertheless, reform's effectiveness in promoting fair political competition and meaningful participation remains a matter of

1 ZA Ayele, "Constitutionalism and Electoral Authoritarianism in Ethiopia: From EPRDF to EPP", in CM Fombad and N Steytler (eds.), *Stellenbosch Handbooks in African Constitutional Law: Democracy, Elections, and Constitutionalism in Africa*, 1st ed, Oxford University Press (2021), pp 188–194. The EPRDF was a coalition of four political organisations: the Tigray People's Liberation Front, Oromo Democratic Party, Amhara Democratic Party, and Southern Ethiopian People's Democratic Movement. In addition, five partner parties – the Afar National Democratic Party, Somali Democratic Party, Benishangul Gumuz Democratic Party, Gambela Peoples' Unity Democratic Movement, and Harari National League – were aligned with it and implemented its policies.

2 G Assefa and SA Yeshanew, "Revamping the Electoral Laws of Ethiopia: Major Areas of Reform and Lessons Learned", in SA Yeshanew and AM Ibrahim (eds.), *Righting Human Rights through Legal Reform: Ethiopia's Contemporary Experience*, Vol. XII, Addis Ababa, Addis Ababa University, School of Law (2020), pp 277–308.

3 SA Yeshanew and AM Ibrahim, "Righting Human Rights through Legal Reform: The Ethiopian Experience from Past to Present", *ibid*, pp 1–15.

contention. Opposition parties demand further electoral reforms, including those regarding party finances.[4]

This chapter analyses the legislative framework for and practice of party financing in post-2018 Ethiopia.[5] To this end, the author conducted focus group discussions and interviews with political-party leaders, a civil society organisation (CSO), and an expert in the NEBE in order to gather information on the post-2018 political finance situation.[6] The chapter aims to examine the implications of post-2018 reform for the future of democracy and constitutionalism in Ethiopia.

The next section provides an overview of the theoretical framework for party financing, an account based largely on the author's work previously published.[7] In particular, it highlights the main issues concerning the funding of political parties, the standards and principles of party financing, and the sources of these standards.

In turn, the third section assesses Ethiopia's post-2018 legislative framework: it considers party-financing principles and standards in order to determine their effectiveness in supporting democracy. As context is always a crucial dimension in discussing political finance, this section describes the particular Ethiopian context in which the political and electoral processes under discussion are conducted. The fourth section examines the practice of political-party financing; the fifth delves into the implications of post-reform regulation for democracy and constitutionalism in Ethiopia. Finally, the chapter discusses the deficits of Ethiopia's party-finance system and proposes reforms for enhancing electoral competitiveness and transparency.

4 Political Parties' Joint Council, "Minutes of a Dialogue between Political Parties on Multiparty Democracy", Addis Ababa, Ethiopia, Inter-luxury Hotel, 5 June 2023.

5 This chapter provides an updated treatment of the author's previous work examining party-political financing, democracy, and constitutionalism in Ethiopia from 1991–2018 and published in the 2021 Stellenbosch Handbook in African Constitutional Law. See Z Degifie, "Party-Political Financing, Democracy, and Constitutionalism in Ethiopia", in Fombad and Steytler, *supra* n. 1, pp 293–327.

6 In August 2024, two focus group discussions were conducted with 13 political parties; interviews were also held with three party leaders, one leader of a civil society organisation, and one expert on the country's election board.

7 Degifie, *supra* n. 5.

2. Party-financing regulation in constitutional democracies

Political-party financing is vital to democracy, but no universally agreed standards for regulation exist.[8] However, the African Union's 2003 Convention on Preventing and Combating Corruption and the 2005 UN Convention against Corruption provide some guidance for the promotion of transparency in political finance.[9] This is supplemented by the work of several international organisations which call for standards of transparency, the regulation of private funds, expenditure limits, and public funding.[10] These statements all help to form a normative framework for political finance in the democratic process.[11]

Private funding sources include membership fees, fundraising activities, and donations.[12] Best practice suggests that party membership dues, local fundraising activities, and small, individual donations by party members and sympathisers are the sources of party financing most compatible with a democracy.[13] Private donations can threaten democracy by making national politics a "savings club" for wealthy individuals or organisations.[14] International standards and good practices in party finance suggest limitations on the private funding system through banning and capping rules. According-

8 European Commission for Democracy through Law (Venice Commission), *International Standards of Financing of Political Parties and Election Campaigns*, Conference Reports, Astana, Kazakhstan, 1 December 2008, pp 8–14.

9 African Union Convention on Preventing and Combating Corruption, adopted by the 2nd Ordinary Session of the Assembly of the Union, Maputo, 11 July 2003; Article 7(3), United Nations Convention Against Corruption. General Assembly Resolution 58/4, adopted 31 October 2003, entered into force 14 December 2005, 2349 UNTS. 41. See also M Őhman, "Africa", in E Falguera, et al. (eds.), *Funding of Political Parties and Election Campaigns: A Handbook on Political Finance*, Stockholm, Sweden International Institute for Democracy and Electoral Assistance (2014), pp 40–42.

10 These organisations include Transparency International, the International Foundation for Electoral Systems, the International Institute for Democracy and Electoral Assistance, the Organisation for Economic Co-Operation and Development, and the European Council.

11 Degifie, *supra* n. 5.

12 I van Biezen, *Financing Political Parties and Election Campaigns Guidelines*, Germany, Council of Europe Publishing (2003), pp 17–31.

13 Y Saffu, "The Funding of Political Parties and Election Campaigns in Africa", in R Austin and M Tjernstrom (eds.), *Funding of Political Parties and Election Campaigns: Handbook Series*, Stockholm, International IDEA (2003), p 22.

14 *Ibid*, p 24; A Butler, "Introduction: Money and Politics", in A Butler (ed.), *Paying for Politics: Party Funding and Political Change in South Africa and the Global South*, South Africa, Jacana Media and Konrad Adenauer Foundation (2010), pp 6–8.

ly, donation-banning rules restrict harmful income sources, minimise political influence and corruption, and set donor qualifications.[15] Donation caps set the maximum amount that eligible donors can contribute to political parties, limiting a donor's influence on the political process and reducing the flow of substantial donations into politics.[16]

Public funding helps to finance political parties from the state budget. It reduces the effect of financial inequality on the political process; it encourages good behaviour by making access conditional on compliance with reporting and auditing rules.[17] The principle of transparency requires financial information from political parties to be open to scrutiny through disclosure and reporting rules.[18] An independent and professional body is necessary to enforce transparency rules, and this should be supported by civil society and public media.[19] A well-designed legal framework for political-party financing is crucial, and needs to include general principles and norms that recognise the basic rights of political parties in the constitution.[20] The constitutionalisation of political parties ensures fair treatment of political parties, restricts majoritarian influence, and levels the political playing field.[21]

3. The design of the party-finance system in post-2018 Ethiopia

3.1 Background and context

The idea of multiparty democracy emerged in Ethiopia after the overthrow of the military regime by the EPRDF in 1991 and was supported by the

15 KH Nassmacher, "Introduction: Political Parties, Funding and Democracy", in *supra* n. 13, pp 42–43; Van Biezen, *supra* n. 12, pp 22–27.

16 *Ibid*, pp 42–43.

17 Saffu, *supra* n. 13, pp 25–28; Van Biezen, *supra* n. 12, pp 33–36.

18 Őhman, *supra* n. 9, pp 59–62.

19 H Zainulbhai, "Practical Solutions for Political Finance Enforcement", in M Őhman and H Zainulbhai (eds.), *Political Finance Regulation: The Global Experience*, USA, International Foundation for Electoral Systems (2009), pp 86–94.

20 S Choudhry et al., *Political Party Finance Regulation: Constitutional Reform After the Arab Spring*, Center for Constitutional Transitions and International IDEA (2014), pp 8–20.

21 CM Fombad, "Challenges to Constitutionalism and Constitutional Rights in Africa and the Enabling Role of Political Parties: Lessons and Perspectives from Southern Africa", 55 (2007) *The American Journal of Comparative Law*, pp 1–45.

promulgation of the 1995 Constitution.[22] Ethiopian politics since 1991 has seen the emergence of various political parties. These can be categorised as ethnic-based parties under the EPRDF; regional ethnic-based parties cooperating with the EPRDF; and multinational or ethnic-based opposition parties.[23] Teshome offers a further categorisation of opposition parties into loyal oppositions (legally registered and participating in elections) and phony oppositions (allegedly created or supported by the incumbent party).[24] He points out that the phony opposition parties secretly collaborate with the incumbent ruling party, and receive financial rewards for working to discredit the opposition camp.[25] All in all, the Ethiopian party system is nascent and marked by fragmentation, ethnic mobilisation, and polarisation.[26]

This is the general context in which national elections were held in 1995, 2000, 2005, 2010, and 2015. In each case, the ruling party (the EPRDF) claimed landslide victories.[27] Between 1995 and 2004, the freedom and financial capacity of opposition parties was limited, making it impossible for any of them to compete effectively with the EPRDF.[28] However, the 2005 election saw a significant increase in the competitiveness of opposition parties on account of the availability of funds from diaspora Ethiopians, local supporters, and international assistance provided by Western donors. As a result, the Coalition for Unity and Democracy (CUD) and United Ethiopian Democratic Forces (UEDF) secured more than 32 per cent of seats.[29]

---

22 K Berhanu, "Political Parties and Political Culture in Ethiopia", in MA Salih (ed.), *African Political Parties Evolution: Institutionalisation and Governance*, London, Pluto Press (2003), p 141.

23 K Berhanu, "Ethiopia: Beleaguered Opposition under a Dominant Party System", 23 (2009) *Politics*, pp 1–21.

24 W Teshome, "Ethiopian Opposition Political Parties and Rebel Fronts: Past and Present", 4 (2009) *International Journal of Human and Social Sciences*, pp 60–68.

25 *Ibid.*

26 M Gudina, "Party Politics, Political Polarisation and the Future of Ethiopian Democracy", Paper 108 (2007) *International Conference on African Development Archives*, pp 1–17; S Yusuf, *Drivers of Ethnic Conflict in Contemporary Ethiopia*, Monograph 202, Institute for Security Studies (2019), pp 5–10.

27 Ayele, *supra* n. 1.

28 *Ibid.*

29 *Ibid*; J Abbink, "Discomfiture of Democracy? The 2005 Election Crisis in Ethiopia and its Aftermath", 105 (2006) *African Affairs*, pp 173–198.

Following the 2005 election, the ruling party enacted various laws which abolished many party freedoms and income sources, leading to the EPRDF's 100 per cent and 99.6 per cent victories in the 2010 and 2015 national elections.[30] Thanks to the EPRDF's non-competitive elections and effective dominance, Ethiopia became a prime example of electoral authoritarianism in action.[31] The EPRDF's hegemony was reinforced by its abundance of financial resources and its control of state institutions.[32] Opposition parties, by contrast, struggled with fragmentation, financial constraints, and limited resources, with all of this making it difficult for them to challenge the EPRDF's electoral success.[33]

In 2018, Abiy Ahmed became the head of the EPRDF and Prime Minister, tabling various reform agendas and pledging to open the political space.[34] In November 2019, the EPRDF coalition was dissolved, and a new successor party, the PP, was established.[35] Despite some differences in ideology, outlook, and political discourse, the PP maintains significant continuity with the authoritarian characteristics of the EPRDF.[36] Indeed, some accuse it of being "EPRDF 2.0.".[37] As Lyons and Verjee assert, the ruling PP's authoritarian nature and its relationship to elections remain the same as that of the EPRDF.[38] As such, the 2021 elections in Ethiopia changed little concerning the ruling PP's hold on power. It won 95 per cent of the federal parliamentary seats where elections were held.[39]

---

30 K Tronvoll, "The Ethiopian 2010 Federal and National Elections: Re-Establishing the One-Party State", 110 (2011) *African Affairs*, pp 1–16; LR Arriola and T Lyons, "Ethiopia's 100% Elections", 27 (2016) *Journal of Democracy*, pp 76–88.

31 Ayele, *supra* n. 1.

32 *Ibid.*

33 *Ibid*; Degifie, *supra* n. 5.

34 International Crisis Group, "Keeping Ethiopia's Transition on the Rails", 283 (2019) *Africa Report*, pp 1–10.

35 SD Dibaba, "The Merger of Ethiopia People's Revolutionary Democratic Front (EPRDF) into Ethiopia Prosperity Party (EPP) and its Impact on the Constitution", 12 (2021) *International Journal of Scientific & Engineering Research*, pp 961-978.

36 T Lyons and A Verjee, "Asymmetric Electoral Authoritarianism? The Case of the 2021 Elections in Ethiopia", 49 (2022) *Review of African Political Economy*, pp 339–354.

37 *Ibid.*

38 *Ibid.*

39 The June 2021 elections were held for 436 seats (for the 547–seat parliament). Elections were not held for 111 constituencies, including 38 in Tigray due to security reasons. See the National Election Board of Ethiopia (NEBE), "6th National Elections Summary Report", https://nebe.org.et/en/electionresult#undefined (accessed 4 August 2024).

3.2 The legal framework

The Ethiopian Constitution acknowledges the freedom of association and election to public office, but it does not explicitly recognise political parties as distinct associations with unique rights and responsibilities in the democratic process.[40] The Constitution lacks specific provisions providing privileges and protections to political parties, including those related to party finance. All in all, political parties have yet to be constitutionalised in Ethiopia.

Ethiopia has no specific law for dealing with political-party financing. This is mainly regulated through political-party registration and electoral proclamations such as Proclamation No. 1162/2019, which has been the main law governing the field since 2019.[41] This law has been supplemented by a range of directives issued by the NEBE.[42] Other laws, including the National Electoral Board of Ethiopia Establishment Proclamation No. 1133/2019 and the Mass Media Proclamation No. 1238/2021, contain some provisions relating to party finance.[43] Consequently, the Ethiopian legislative framework for political-party finance is fragmented and dispersed among various legislative instruments.

Post-2018 electoral law reform aims to address the shortcomings of the previous legislation on elections and political-party regulation.[44] Proclamation No. 1162/2019 purports to introduce the significant changes that are necessary to institutionalise political parties and improve political partic-

40 Proclamation No. 1/1995, Federal Democratic Republic of Ethiopia (FDRE) Constitution, Federal Negarit Gazeta, 1st Year No. 1, Addis Ababa, 8 December 1994. Articles 31, 38, 54, 56, and 60(5) of the Constitution mention political parties without granting them special rights. For more, see G Hailu and T Alebachew, "The Quest for Constitutionalising Political Parties in Ethiopia", 2 (2019) *Journal of Citizenship and Morality*, pp 47–49.

41 Proclamation No. 1162/2019, the Ethiopian Electoral, Political Parties Registration and Election's Code of Conduct Proclamation, Federal Negarit Gazeta, 25th Year, No. 97, Addis Ababa, 16 October 2019. Proclamation No. 46/93 regulated it from 1991 to 2008; from 2008 to 2018, it was regulated by Proclamation No. 573/2008.

42 Directive No. 16/2021, A Directive for Providing Government Funding to Political Parties, NEBE, 25 March 2021, Addis Ababa.

43 Proclamation No. 1133/2019, National Electoral Board of Ethiopia Establishment Proclamation, Federal Negarit Gazeta, 25th Year, No. 71, 6 June 2019; Proclamation No. 1238/2021, Media Proclamation, Federal Negarit Gazeta, 27th Year, No. 22, Addis Ababa, Ethiopia, 5 April 2021.

44 Assefa and Yeshanew, *supra* n. 2.

ipation.[45] As Assef and Yeshanew claim, the legal reform debates, inter alia, focused on enhancing the political participation and inclusion of women and persons with disabilities (PWDs); regulating political-party finance; and addressing state funding issues for political parties.[46] In effect, Proclamation No. 1162/2019 introduces new criteria for state funding of political parties and stipulates the timing of public funding disbursements.[47] It also utilises party financing as an instrument to increase the political participation of women and PWDs. In addition, the law clearly outlines the prohibited income sources for political parties and the latter's auditing and reporting obligations.[48] Hence, the post-2018 framework addresses basic party-financing issues, including funding sources, private and public funding schemes, and transparency, but – as we shall see – it also has potentially negative effects on political competition and the political playing field.

3.2.1 Rules regulating private funding

The legal framework recognises private funding (from membership fees, local fundraising activities, and donations) as a legitimate income source for political parties.[49] Parties can collect money from their members and engage in public fundraising activities without requiring specific permission from federal, regional, or local authorities.[50] Additionally, the law sets conditions for the qualifications necessary for donors to be able to support political parties.[51] Only Ethiopian nationals are allowed to make donations.[52] Many diasporic Ethiopians, despite their Ethiopian origin, do not have rights to Ethiopian nationality.[53] Consequently, the nationality requirement restricts a significant portion of the Ethiopian diaspora com-

45 *Ibid.*
46 *Ibid.*
47 Ibid; Proclamation No. 1162/2019, articles 100–113.
48 *Ibid.*
49 Proclamation No. 1162/2019, Article 108.
50 The previous law required the government or regional state administration to grant permission to organise fundraising events. See Proclamation No. 573/2008, Article 51(2).
51 Proclamation No. 1162/2019, Article 109.
52 *Ibid*, Article 108(1)(b).
53 The FDRE diaspora policy defines the Ethiopian diaspora as comprising Ethiopians and those of Ethiopian origin who live outside of Ethiopia.

munity (foreign nationals of Ethiopian origin) from making financial and material contributions to political parties.

Likewise, the law allows only "companies controlled by Ethiopians" to make financial contributions to political parties.[54] While the previous law had focused on the nationality of the company, Proclamation No. 1162/2019 determines the eligibility of corporate donations according to the nationality of the shareholders. As a result, political parties can receive donations from non-Ethiopian companies controlled by Ethiopian nationals, but foreign-controlled companies incorporated under Ethiopian law may not provide money to political parties. Shareholder nationality matters more than company nationality in determining the eligibility of the donors. This approach is supposed to prevent foreign influence on national politics, and aligns with the ban on foreign sources of income for political parties.

Ethiopia's party-finance legal framework prohibits certain donation sources. These include foreign donations; organised interest associations (welfare, non-governmental, and religious organisations); prisoners serving sentences; individuals or groups planning to assume state power unconstitutionally; and designated terrorist organisations.[55] However, the scope of the illicit funding ban is, in some ways, narrow. It does not mention or indicate possible illegal funding sources such as organised crime, human trafficking, and money laundering.

The law also bans financial support given to political parties with corrupt motives, kickbacks, and *quid pro quo* donations.[56] The NEBE has broad discretion to determine the lawfulness of a specific donation in the light of this prohibition. However, its discretionary power is open to abuse,

---

54 Companies controlled by Ethiopians are not necessarily "Ethiopian companies", which was the term used in the previous political-party registration arrangement under Proclamation No. 573/2008. Companies may be considered Ethiopian if they are incorporated under Ethiopian laws, with defining features such as business registration, licensing, and a separate legal personality from their shareholders. Hence, the company's nationality is determined by its place of incorporation, not by its members or shareholders' nationality. As such, companies controlled by Ethiopians include Ethiopian companies as well as non-Ethiopian ones with Ethiopian shareholders. Political parties can receive donations from non-Ethiopian companies controlled by Ethiopian nationals. Political parties may not receive donations from companies that are incorporated under Ethiopian law (known as Ethiopian companies) but which are controlled by foreigners. Therefore, the nationality of the shareholders is the most significant factor, rather than the company's nationality determined by the place of incorporation.

55 Proclamation No. 1162/2019, Article 109(1)(a)–(h).

56 *Ibid.*

particularly with regard to the selective application of party-finance rules. Indeed, the NEBE is often accused of bias in favour of the ruling party.

To avoid abuse of state resources for partisan ends, the law also bans fully- or semi-government developmental organisations from supporting political parties.[57] Moreover, and finally, Proclamation No. 1162/2019 outlaws anonymous sources of funding.[58] As a result, only named and identifiable persons are allowed to make donations to political parties in Ethiopia. While this ban, bolstered by disclosure rules, could enhance transparency and the monitoring of political finance regulations, it poses serious risks to donors who choose to support opposition parties.[59] In view of that, the post-2018 framework sets ETB 5,000 (about USD 50) as a disclosure threshold, thus allowing political parties to avoid disclosing the identity of donors who make contributions below this threshold.[60]

Some of the bans and prohibitions target the potential funding sources of opposition political parties. Financial support from Ethiopians living abroad and anonymous donations have long been the main sources of income for opposition political parties.[61] Additionally, the identity disclosure requirement serves both symbolic and practical purposes in deterring potential local supporters of opposition parties from making financial contributions.[62] The ETB 5,000 disclosure threshold introduced by Proclamation No. 1162/2019 is too low to protect potential donors who might otherwise be able to make significant contributions to opposition parties.[63]

Proclamation No. 1162/2019 imposes a limit on the amount of the private contributions that parties can receive from donors. The NEBE has been tasked with determining the donation limit, but it has yet to set the ceiling for private donations.[64] As a result, political parties can receive unlimited sums from individuals and companies. The ruling party benefits from this, as it controls the state's political economy and bureaucracy, offering

57 *Ibid.*
58 *Ibid.*
59 Santucci J and Őhman M, "Practical Solutions for the Disclosure of Campaign and Political Party Finance", in *supra* n. 19, pp 35–40.
60 Proclamation No. 1162/2019, Article 111(2)b.
61 Two focus group discussions with 13 opposition parties' leaders (Addis Ababa, Ethiopia, the Hub Hotel, 20 August 2024); W Teshome, "Political Finance in Africa: Ethiopia as a Case Study", 4 (2009) *International Journal of Human and Social Science*, pp 1641–1649.
62 Two focus group discussions, *supra* n. 61; Political Parties' Joint Council, *supra* n. 4.
63 Proclamation No. 1162/2019, Article 111(2)b.
64 *Ibid*, Article 108(1)b.

significant incentives for private donors to support it over the opposition parties.[65] The absence of a donation ceiling heightens the financial disparity between the ruling PP and opposition parties, resulting in an uneven playing field for political competition.

3.2.2 Public funding for political parties

The Ethiopian legal framework provides for public funding of political parties, which is overseen by the NEBE.[66] This funding is intended for various purposes, including daily operations and election campaigns, as outlined in Proclamation No. 1162/2019 and Directive No. 16/2021.[67] The legal framework allows direct cash funding, enabling political parties to use the funds according to their priorities and thus enhancing their competitiveness.[68] It also recognises indirect funding methods, including income tax relief and free access to public facilities such as meeting halls and state-owned media, which Öhman argues may be more effective in ensuring equitable political competition.[69] As Öhman suggests, indirect funding reduces potential embezzlement and helps ensure that contributions are utilised for their intended purpose.[70] Free access to public media and spaces increases opposition parties' chances of reaching the electorate, particularly in a dominant-party system where direct funding per se might not guarantee media access.[71]

The annual public funding distribution is based on the proportionality principle, with several criteria taken into account: votes received in past

65 For instance, the ruling PP raised more than ETB 1.5 billion (USD 15 million) for the 2021 election at a fundraising event which was attended by the Prime Minister, cabinet members, regional state heads, and businesspersons and broadcast live on state-owned media. See International Republican Institute and National Democratic Institute, "Ethiopia June 21, 2021 National Elections Report", Ethiopia (2021), pp 15–16.

66 Proclamation No. 1162/2019, articles 100–103; Directive 16/2021, articles 9–10.

67 *Ibid.*

68 *Ibid*; M Öhman, "Practical Solutions for the Public Funding of Political Parties and Election Campaigns", in *supra* n. 19, pp 67–68.

69 Proclamation No. 1162/2019, articles 44–45, 77, 100(4); Directive No. 16/2021, articles 9, 20–22.

70 Öhman, *supra* n. 68, pp 67–68.

71 *Ibid*; International Republican Institute and National Democratic Institute, *supra* n. 65, p 18.

elections; matching funds generated from party members and supporters; and representation of women and persons with disabilities (PWDs) in membership, candidates, and leadership positions.[72] The public funding scheme does not impose specific eligibility criteria for parties to access annual funding, such as securing a minimum share of votes or a certain number of seats in an elected body.[73] Consequently, all registered parties can receive funding, provided they meet the conditions outlined in the distribution formula.

Moreover, Directive No. 16/2021 explains how the public funding distribution criteria are weighted and sets thresholds for each criterion. A party receiving five million votes gets ETB 0.5 for each vote; one with more than 5 million votes receives ETB 0.75 for each 5 million votes and ETB 0.5 for remaining votes above the cut-off point of million.[74] Under this criterion, in order to qualify for funding, parties must meet a threshold of 0.25 per cent or 0.5 per cent of valid votes cast for the federal legislature or state council (except for minority parties).[75] In addition, the matching fund scheme matches each ETB raised from private donations with ETB 0.3 up to ETB 50,000 (USD 500).[76] A further 25 per cent (for gender equality) and 7 per cent (for PWDs) of overall funds are also set aside.[77] While the directive sets the eligibility criteria for receiving gender-targeted public funding, stating that parties must have at least 5 per cent female membership to qualify, there is no specific eligibility condition for inclusion-targeted public funding.[78] All parties also receive funding in proportion to the extent of their inclusion of PWDs in their membership and leadership.

As Öhman suggests, public funding thresholds and criteria can shape party dynamics, in that they encourage the merging of smaller parties or promote political pluralism.[79] The appropriateness of the threshold is thus linked to the objectives of the system. A high threshold can encourage mergers, fostering institutionalisation and enhancing electoral competitiveness;[80] conversely, a low threshold promotes political pluralism, enabling

72 Proclamation No. 1162/2019, Article 100.
73 *Ibid.*
74 Directive No. 16/2021, Article 12.
75 Proclamation No. 1162/2019, Article 100(3); Directive No. 16/2021, Article 12(2).
76 Directive No. 16/2021, Article 13.
77 *Ibid*, articles 14–15.
78 *Ibid.*
79 Öhman, *supra* n. 68, pp 62–64.
80 *Ibid.*

smaller parties to participate in political discourse and increasing overall political engagement.[81] However, a shallow threshold may impede institutionalisation by encouraging fragmentation and the emergence of non-viable parties.[82] In this regard, Ethiopia's legal framework, which lacks a specific qualification to access public funds and sets the threshold at 0.25 per cent or 0.5 per cent of valid votes, allows many political parties, including small and minority groups, to access public funding, thereby tending to promote pluralism rather than competitiveness.

The post-2018 system of public funding also influences the behaviour of political parties regarding gender equality, political inclusion, and transparency.[83] The funding scheme encourages parties to prioritise gender equality and political inclusion, rewarding those who recruit and nominate more women and PWDs.[84] The NEBE examines each party's financial statements from the previous year, requiring audits and detailed reports on fund utilisation to approve financial support for the upcoming year, enhancing accountability.[85] The matching fund criteria incentivises parties to disclose contributions from private sources (improving overall transparency); this also encourages parties to maintain connections with their constituencies and minimises their reliance on state funding. However, the ETB 50,000 matching-funds ceiling is insufficient to prevent excessive matching of large financial contributions by larger parties, particularly the ruling party, thereby preserving their advantage over the smaller parties.[86]

Despite the proportional model intended by Proclamation No. 1162/2019 and Directive No. 16/2021, the NEBE has implemented a hybrid funding system. This allocates an equal portion of the annual funds to each of the registered parties.[87] The NEBE's allocation of funds does not, in practice, consider previous election votes or the matching fund criteria, a situation that could disproportionately benefit the ruling party over opposition par-

81 *Ibid.*

82 *Ibid.*

83 Proclamation No. 1162/2019, Article 100(2)(c)–(f); Directive No. 16/2021, articles 14–15.

84 NEBE, "The Annual Government Support Granted to Political Parties for the 2022 Budget Year", https://www.facebook.com/photo/?fbid=275164771387786&set=a.260907382813525 (accessed 3 August 2024).

85 Proclamation No. 1162/2019, Article 103(4).

86 Directive No. 16/2021, Article 13(2).

87 NEBE, "Updates on the Fund Distribution of Political Parties", https://nebe.org.et/en/node/534 (accessed 20 July 2024); NEBE, "The Annual Government Support Granted to Political Parties for the 2022 Budget Year".

ties.[88] This decision to modify the allocation formula, made in consultation with political parties, seeks to reduce the ruling party's financial advantages. However, its effectiveness in leveling the playing field remains limited. [89] In fact, the flat-rate support provided to all registered parties (lacking reasonable thresholds) often promotes the formation of small and frivolous parties.[90] The NEBE's decision to modify the formula set by Proclamation No. 1162/2019 and Directive No. 16/2021 is deemed to weaken the rule of law and raise legality concerns. This trend may also lead to the misuse of party-financing laws, potentially compromising electoral competition.

The legal framework, particularly Directive No. 16/2021, allows annual public funding to cover daily expenses and some electoral costs, but it lacks explicit provisions for election-specific public funding.[91] Proclamation No. 1162/2019, unlike prior legislation, does not explicitly address the distribution of public funding for election-specific purposes.[92] Directive No. 16/2021 recognises state funding for election campaigns specifically for the 2021 national elections, but not for future elections. [93] As a result, state support for election campaigns in Ethiopia lacks formal legislative recognition, leaving its distribution to the discretion of the incumbent government.

In the 2021 elections, election-specific state funding was distributed based on a hybrid model that combined the principles of equality and proportionality.[94] Directive No. 16/2021 mandates that election-related funds be disbursed to parties within 15 days of candidate registration.[95] However, some parties (particularly those with limited financial resources) criticised this timing, arguing that financial support should be provided prior to candidate registration to better support their electoral efforts.[96]

---

88 For instance, the incumbent's vote share in the 2010, 2015, and 2021 national elections was 94.6 per cent, 94.9 per cent, and 90 per cent, respectively. See B Yimenu, "Continuities and Changes in Electoral Authoritarianism: Evidence from Ethiopia", 2024 *Regional and Federal Studies*, pp 12–13.

89 *Ibid.*

90 Nassmacher, *supra* n. 13, pp 14–15.

91 Directive No. 16/2012, Article 10.

92 Proclamation No. 573/2008, Article 42(2).

93 Directive No. 16/2021, articles 17–19.

94 NEBE, "The State Support Allocated for Political Parties for the 2021 National Elections", https://nebe.org.et/en/node/534 (accessed 20 July 2024).

95 Directive No. 16/2021, Article 27(1).

96 B Abdu, "Elections 2021: Already Favoring the Ruling Party?", *The Reporter*, 31 March 2021, https://www.thereporterethiopia.com/ (accessed 3 August 2024).

3.2.3 Spending limits

Ethiopia's legal framework does not set a spending limit for political parties. This exacerbates the financial inequality which there already is between rich and poor parties, and contributes to the uneven playing field of political competition. Some opposition party leaders claim that the PP spent about ETB 2 billion (USD 20 million) on nationwide campaigning during the 2021 national election, a figure far in excess of what was available to them (the opposition).[97] The Ethiopian Citizens for Social Justice (ECSJ) party (the second-largest party in the country) was allocated just ETB 143 million (USD 1.4 million) for its campaigning for the 2021 election.[98]

The absence of a spending ceiling in political systems such as Ethiopia, where the ruling party enjoys better access than others to income sources and has all the advantages of incumbency, undermines the very purpose of public funding: to level the playing field for political contest. As Öhman opines, the financial gap between political parties will not be addressed by providing state funds to financially affluent and poor political parties alike.[99] It makes little sense to provide public funding without setting reasonable limits on private donations and on actual expenditure, particularly when the state funding scheme cannot bridge the massive differences in funding available to opposition parties as compared to the ruling PP.[100] The lack of a spending cap in Ethiopian politics exacerbates the unevenness of political competition.

3.2.4 Oversight, monitoring, and enforcement

The Ethiopian party-finance framework includes provisions on disclosure, reporting, monitoring, and enforcement.[101] Political parties have to disclose detailed financial information, submit annual audit reports, and maintain records.[102] They are also required to make separate deposits for public funding and make sure to provide members with access to their party's

97 Political Parties' Joint Council, *supra* n. 4.
98 Abdu, *supra* n. 94.
99 Őhman, "Getting the Political Finance System Right", in *supra* n. 9, pp 22–23.
100 *Ibid.*
101 Proclamation No. 1162/2019, articles 82–85, 104-107, 111–113.
102 *Ibid.*

income and expenditure accounts.[103] The NEBE oversees political-party financing and requires regular audit reports certified by external auditors.[104] The House of Peoples' Representatives (HOPR) and the Auditor-General also oversee the proper allocation and utilisation of public funding.[105]

However, despite these provisions, there are issues with the design and implementation of the transparency rules. For instance, the NEBE has not published the audit reports and financial information of political parties as demanded by law.[106] Nevertheless, the law does not require parties to disclose their incomes and expenditures to the general public. In practice, financial statements from the different parties are not accessible either through publication or from online platforms. This hinders public scrutiny of party finances. While the NEBE has the authority to enforce party-finance rules through various sanctions (funding cuts, returns of improperly utilised funds, official warnings, suspension from elections, forfeiture of unlawful assets, and criminal penalties), its real effectiveness in enforcing the transparency rules is questionable.[107]

4. Post-2018 party financing in practice: The trap of old problems?

4.1 Opposition parties' dependency syndrome

Opposition parties in Ethiopia struggle to secure funding for their everyday operations, as they do for election campaigns.[108] Most of them rely on public funding for their income, but this is often insufficient for carrying out political activities, especially during elections.[109] Some parties also rely on financial support from the diaspora community to cover most of their expenditure.[110] Opposition parties face challenges in generating revenue

103 *Ibid*, Article 112(3).

104 Proclamation No. 1133/2019, Article 7(4); Proclamation No. 1162/2019, articles 103, 113.

105 Proclamation No. 1162/2019, articles 82(6), 105(3), 107; Directive No. 16/2021, Article 27.

106 *Ibid*, Article 68(9).

107 *Ibid*, articles 98, 106, 110, 142 *cum* 148; Directive 16/2021, articles 25, 30, 31.

108 Two focus group discussions, *supra* n. 61; Political Parties' Joint Council, *supra* n. 4.

109 *Ibid*.

110 B Habtie, M Tsehaye, et al., "The Ethiopian Diaspora: Their Role in Nation Building and Political Reformation", 1 (2019) *Mekelle University Journal of Political Science and Strategic Studies*, pp 211–222; interview with Zebiba Ibrahim, former

from membership fees and private donations due to evident concerns about government harassment and repression among their supporters.[111] Business owners are hesitant to donate to opposition parties due to concerns about government retaliatory measures.[112] Some of these fears stem from the post-2005 retaliatory measures and the authoritarian experiences of 10 years of EPRDF rule.[113] The local population's poor economic condition worsens their lack of awareness about the importance of financial support for the opposition.[114]

All in all, Ethiopian opposition parties lack diverse sources of funding, creating a dependency syndrome on state funding and diaspora support. The dependency syndrome often undermines the autonomy of parties, making them vulnerable to influence by the diaspora or the government. The policies of some opposition parties are over-influenced by diaspora views, resulting in factionalisation.[115] Public-funding dependency, in turn, can all too easily result in the co-option of opposition parties, disconnecting them from voters and undermining the formation of the critical perspectives that are necessary to challenge the incumbent government.[116]

4.2 Electoral market bias and hyper-incumbency advantages

The factors above serve to create a substantial financial disparity between the opposition and the ruling party. The electoral marketplace in Ethiopia is biased towards the incumbent PP, which utilises the state administrative apparatus to deduct and collect membership fees from public servants.[117]

executive member and candidate of the Balderas for Genuine Democracy Party (Addis Ababa, Ethiopia, ZeHub Hotel, 20 August 2024).

111 Two focus group discussions, *supra* n. 61; Political Parties' Joint Council, *supra* n. 4.

112 *Ibid.*

113 Interview with Abdul-Qadir Adem, chairperson of the Freedom and Equality Party and ex-deputy chairperson of the Political Parties' Joint Council (Addis Ababa, Ethiopia, 3 August 2024).

114 *Ibid.*

115 Habtie, Tsehaye et al., *supra* n. 110.

116 T Gashaw, "In Ethiopian Politics, Some Parties are about Monetisation, Not Representation", *IPI Global Observatory*, 27 September 2024, https://theglobalobservatory.org/2024/09/in-ethiopian-politics-some-parties-are-about-monetization-not-representation/ (accessed 12 November 2024).

117 Two focus group discussions, *supra* n. 61; Political Parties' Joint Council, *supra* n. 4, p 21. See also W Teshome, "Prosperity 'Federalism'?", *The Awash Post*, 1 November

The PP also receives significant financial support from private sources, including businesspeople who are often linked to the ruling elite. They make their donations on the understanding that they will receive privileged access to land for investment and other benefits, such as government contracts.[118]

The Prime Minister's Office raises resources from private donors and overseas friends or governments for special tourism-related and urban mega-projects.[119] The *Gebeta Le'Hager* ("Dine for Ethiopia") initiative was launched in 2019 by the Prime Minister, and raised nearly ETB 4 billion (USD 40 million) from private donations.[120] Many state-owned and public enterprises (such as Ethiopian Airlines and Ethio-Telecom) have also contributed funds to the mega-projects initiated by the Prime Minister.[121] In addition, the Prime Minister has funded projects from his personal coffer, including a donation to the First Lady's Office for rural school construction in all regions, using the proceeds from sales of his book.[122] These self-funded and off-budget projects are often presented to the public as exemplifying

---

2020, https://www.awashpost.com/prosperity-federalism/ (accessed 10 November 2024).

118 For instance, the PP raised more than ETB 1.5 billion (USD 15 million) for the 2021 election at a fundraising event, while the ECSJ, Ethiopia's second-largest party, planned to hold fundraising events to secure ETB 140 million (USD 1.4 million). See International Republican Institute and National Democratic Institute, *supra* n. 65; "Ezema Set to Compete in 500 Districts of Ethiopia", *New Business*, 6 February 2021, https://newbusinessethiopia.com/politics/ezema-set-to-compete-in-500-districts-of-ethiopia/ (accessed 20 July 2024); T Gardner, *The Abiy Project God, Power and War in the New Ethiopia*, UK London, C Hurst & Co (2024), pp 208–209.

119 Gardner, *ibid* n. 118, pp 207–210. See B Terrefe, "Urban Layers of Political Rupture: The 'New' Politics of Addis Ababa's Megaprojects", 14(3) (2020) *Journal of Eastern African Studies*, pp 375–395.

120 "PM Abiy Ahmed Pledges Thorough Audit of Non-government-Funded Mega Projects amid Transparency Concerns", *Addis Standard*, 6 July 2023, https://addisstandard.com/?p=35966 (accessed 20 August 2024).

121 *Ibid.* For instance: Ethiopian Airlines (ETB 1.2 billion/USD 12 million); Commercial Bank of Ethiopia (ETB 1.2 billion/USD 12 million); Ethio-Telecom (ETB 1 billion/USD 10 million); Ethiopian Shipping & Logistics Services Enterprise (ETB 200 million/USD 2 million); Ethiopian Development Bank (ETB 150 million/USD 1.5 million); and Ethiopian Electric Power (ETB 100 million/USD 1 million).

122 Ethiopian News Agency (ENA), "Abiy Donates over 110 Million Birr Proceeds of Book for Building Schools", *ENA*, 7 August 2020, https://www.ena.et/web/eng/w/en_16188 (accessed 3 August 2024).

the success story of the PP, led by the Prime Minister, and can thus be regarded as covert private funding of the incumbent party.[123]

The ruling PP misuses government resources to gain financial advantage over the opposition by exploiting public resources (such as employees, office supplies, phones, vehicles, and daily allowance payments) to support its election campaigns.[124] Some opposition parties claim that the incumbency advantage is so deep that it is nearly impossible to distinguish between the government and the party.[125] The PP's significant private funding and hyper-incumbency advantages enable easy election victories, whereas the opposition faces severe limitations in terms of financial and human capital resources. The International Republican Institute and National Democratic Institute joint report on the 2021 election revealed that the PP-led government merged government activities with election campaigning by launching major infrastructure and investment projects during the campaign silence period.[126] During it, publicity was given to ruling-party government officials who either inaugurated or simply visited national projects such as airports, highways, and factory construction sites.[127] Such public events undermine the principles of fair campaigning and the notion of a level playing field.

---

123 In some African countries, many political activities are funded by party leaders themselves, which is considered self-funding in the party-financing literature. It is well regulated, for instance, in Mali, Algeria, and Liberia. See NA Check, et al., "The Integrity of Political Finance Systems in Africa: Tackling Political Corruption", International IDEA Policy Paper No. 20, Stockholm, International IDEA (2019), pp 15–16.

124 International Republican Institute and National Democratic Institute, *supra* n. 65; Political Parties' Joint Council, *supra* n. 4; H Bratt, *Uneven Playing Field: Understanding Abiy Ahmed Manipulation of Democracy in Ethiopia*, Uppsala University (2019/2020), pp 20–25.

125 "Abiy Ahmed's Prosperity Party Accused of Diverting Public Resources for Political Training", *Ethiopia Observer*, 16 September 2024, https://www.ethiopiaobserver.com/ (accessed 10 November 2024).

126 International Republican Institute and National Democratic Institute, *supra* n. 65. The Ethiopian Electoral Cycle Guidelines state that the silence period, which includes four days before election day, requires political parties and their supporters to stop their campaigns four days before voting day. This includes using the internet and social media and having in-person, door-to-door, or public political meetings. Also, mass media outlets are prohibited from interviewing political-party candidates during this period, and may only transmit information from the NEBE.

127 *Ibid.*

4.3 Inequitable public funding: Reinforcing dominance

The post-2018 public funding scheme did not significantly alter the financial position of opposition parties. The ruling PP remains the primary recipient of public funding for parties both annually and during elections. The NEBE distributed ETB 98 million to 51 political parties during the 2021 national election, with 25 per cent of this distributed on the principle of equality. The first payout was ETB 483,452 (USD 10,998) for parties participating in the election, followed by the second tranche of the remaining three-quarters, which was awarded to political parties at the rate of each registered candidate (ETB 2,643 or USD 60), each woman candidate (ETB 9,982 or USD 227), each PWD candidate (ETB 155,722 or USD 3,542), and each woman party leader (ETB 255,062 or USD 5,802).[128]

Table 1: Parties with significant shares of public funding in the 2021 elections

Name of party	No. of candidates	No. of women candidates	No. of PWD candidates	No. women in leadership	Share of public funds
PP	2,799	1,171	15	5	24%
ECSJ	1,540	183	22	6	12%
FEP	578	80	8	2	4.7%
Enat Party	605	58	4	1	3.6%
United Ethiopia Democratic Party	258	37	6	3	3.3.%
All Ethiopian Unity Organisation	466	38	3	1	2.9%
National Movement of Amhara (NaMA)	510	16	2	0	2.3%

Source: NEBE's Excel Sheet: State Support Allocated for 2021 National Elections

As Table 1 shows, the PP received about a quarter of state funding, but the benefit level has decreased in comparison to the 2015 election, when the then-ruling party, the EPRDF, took 50 per cent of public funds allocated for elections.[129] The seven parties listed in the table collectively received 52 per cent of total state support for the 2021 election, with the remaining 48 per cent distributed between 44 parties.[130] Five of these parties received the minimum ETB 483,452 (USD 10,998), distributed based on the equality

128 *Ibid*; NEBE, *supra* n. 94.

129 *Ibid*. See also Degifie, *supra* n. 5, p 348.

130 *Ibid*.

principle (though without nominating a single candidate).[131] In addition, the PP received the largest share of annual public funding allocated to political parties for their daily operations.[132]

Opposition parties have expressed concern about insufficient public funding and delayed disbursement. Most political parties struggle to pay the rent for their offices, while some claim that state support does not cover even half of their election expenditures.[133] The indirect public funding scheme does not explicitly cover free or subsidised access to state buildings or office spaces, and political parties cannot demand this as a right.[134] The NEBE's role is limited to writing recommendation letters to government agencies such as the Federal Housing Corporation, which results in selective office space allocation for political parties, with most opposition parties receiving little to no support.[135] However, the ruling PP frequently uses state-owned buildings for its own offices. The indirect public funding package lacks duty-free privileges for political parties, causing them to face higher taxes for vehicle imports.[136] As a result, most opposition parties have no vehicles with which to reach out to the electorate, and particularly so voters in rural areas.[137] This is not a problem for the ruling party, however, since it often misuses state resources to carry out both regular political activities as well as election campaigns.

The 2021 election demonstrates that the public funding system is insufficient for most political parties to challenge the ruling party effectively. State support for regular party operations and election purposes favours the PP, despite its being the least in need of additional funding. It contributes to the

131 *Ibid.*

132 The EPRDF received 70 per cent of the state support granted to political parties for their daily activities, while the PP's share is about 20 per cent. See NEBE, "The Annual Government Support Granted to Political Parties for the 2022 Budget Year", *supra* n. 87; Degifie, *supra* n. 5, p 348.

133 Political Parties' Joint Council, *supra* n. 4; Two focus group discussions, *supra* n. 61; Abdu, *supra* n. 96.

134 Proclamation No. 1162/2019, Article 45. They are entitled to claim access to public facilities only during the election period.

135 Political Parties' Joint Council, *supra* n. 4 Two focus group discussions, *supra* n.61; interview with Desta Tilahun, Leader of the Ethiopian People's Revolutionary Party and deputy chairperson of the Political Parties' Joint Council (Addis Ababa, Ethiopia, Inter-luxury Hotel, 15 August 2024); S Sahlu, "Political Parties' Concerns over Federal Housing Corporation's Unfair Office Building Allocation", *The Reporter*, 11 September 2024.

136 Proclamation No. 1162/2017, Article 77; Directive 16/2021, Article 22.

137 Political Parties' Joint Council, *supra* n. 4; interview with Tilahun, *supra* n. 135.

unevenness of the political playing field in Ethiopia, and helps to reinforce the dominance of the ruling party.

4.4 Culture of non-compliance

Few political parties adhere to transparency rules, particularly in financial reporting. The NEBE announced that several parties failed to submit the required financial reports for the 2020/21 fiscal year.[138] Parties have also been accused of providing inaccurate membership information, including the number of women and PWD members, and engaging in financial fraud such as unauthorised disbursements and unlawful withdrawals.[139]

These failures to adhere to transparency rules can be attributed to a lack of internal capacity; political unwillingness; and unrealistic party-finance rules. Many parties lack the necessary staff and resources to comply with financial transparency rules (such as reporting and auditing).[140] Political parties are also hesitant to disclose their financial affairs to the public due to frequent allegations of illicit funding, corruption, and embezzlement, and hence often keep their financial records from the public eye.[141] Moreover, the NEBE has been found to compromise the strict application of certain rules, considering them unrealistic in Ethiopia's political setting. The funding provision requiring parties to disclose their members' age, gender distribution, and place of residence is impracticable in Ethiopia: these demands could not be effectively enforced.[142] The ruling PP claims to have over 7 million members. The NEBE accused certain parties of exaggerating figures on women and PWDs, with some claiming up to 900,000 such members (most parties lack a complete membership list).[143] The NEBE's

138 NEBE, "Announcement on the Financial Support Granted for the 2020/21 Fiscal Year", 17 May 2022, https://nebe.org.et/en (accessed 4 August 2024).

139 S Mengesha, "Election Board Threatens Administrative Action over Exaggerated Party Membership Figures", *The Reporter*, 29 June 2024; S Sahlu, "Election Board Suspends 'One Ethiopia' Party over Financial Fraud Allegations", *The Reporter*, 13 March 2024.

140 Two focus group discussions, *supra* n. 61.

141 Most political-party official pages contain party programmes, election manifestos, and by-laws, but not financial statements.

142 Proclamation No. 1162/2019, Article 78.

143 Mengesha, *supra* n. 139; NEBE, "Announcement for Political Parties: 28 June 2024", https://nebe.org.et/en/announcments (accessed 3 August 2024).

questionable ability to verify the accuracy of party membership lists makes the disclosure requirement impractical.

Some political parties use online funding systems to collect income from the diaspora community, but the NEBE rarely checks the permissibility of the contributions.[144] The NEBE has dropped the 5 per cent eligibility threshold for receiving gender-targeted public funding on the grounds that most parties fail to meet it.[145] Alleging equity concerns, it also modified Proclamation No. 1162/2019's public funding distribution formula.[146] Despite their significance, especially for the opposition parties, disregarding clear laws often results in a culture of non-compliance. This undermines the rule of law and facilitates the selective application of party-financing rules based on favouritism.

All in all, the NEBE has not effectively enforced all political finance rules. This is likely due both to its limited capacity as well as to political reluctance.[147] Despite its power to impose sanctions, it has restricted its punitive interventions to further educating parties on transparency and compliance.[148] Only in some instances it has imposed sanctions on political parties for misuse of public funding by suspending, cancelling, or cutting such funds.[149] Since October 2024, the NEBE has suspended several political parties for non-compliance with audits, failure to provide financial support for female members, and failings in general assembly procedures.[150] It is noteworthy that the media and civil society organisations (CSOs) have not prioritised transparency and accountability in party financing as something requiring intervention;[151] indeed, CSOs working in the area of

144 Two focus group discussions, *supra* n. 61.

145 Directive No. 16/2021, Article 14(1). See NEBE, *supra* n. 94.

146 Compare Proclamation No. 1162/2019, Article 100 and Directive No. 16/2021, Article 11.

147 Anonymous phone interview with an expert in the NEBE (Addis Ababa, Ethiopia, 20 August 2024). When the NEBE doubts audit reports submitted by parties, it refers the matter to the general auditor for further examination.

148 *Ibid.*

149 Sahlu, *supra* n. 139; Anonymous phone interview, *supra* n. 147.

150 My Ethiopia, "NEBE Suspends Eleven Political Parties for Non-compliance", *My Ethiopia*, 22 October 2024, https://myethiopia.co.uk/nebe-suspends-eleven-political-parties-for-non-compliance/ (accessed 13 November 2024).

151 This is based on the author's two years of personal observation as a legal and policy advisor at the Ethiopian Civil Society Organizations Council, an umbrella organ representing more than 4,000 CSOs in Ethiopia.

elections often overlook it altogether.[152] As a result, the media and CSOs do not adequately support the NEBE's oversight role on political-party finance, which is there to ensure fair play, accountability, and transparency.

5. Post-2018 party financing: Implications for democracy and constitutionalism

5.1 The uneven political playing field

Democracy requires free, fair, and competitive elections; but it also requires a great deal more than just holding periodic elections.[153] The essence of democracy lies in the competitiveness of elections, with a reasonably level playing field between incumbents and opposition being an essential component of this.[154] Post-2018 private funding regulation targets the income sources of opposition parties; it avoids the necessary contribution and expenditure caps, and thereby tilts the playing field in favour of the ruling party. The public funding distribution formula favours the ruling PP, with this advantage multiplied by incumbency advantage, including considerable funding from the private sector. In all these ways, the financial inequality between the ruling and opposition parties is exacerbated. Manipulation of state resources and institutions by the PP constrains the activities of opposition parties and works to eliminate their chances of winning elections. Consequently, the fairness necessary for political competition in a multiparty democracy is undermined.

The 2021 national election demonstrates the ways in which lack of resources played a key role in hindering opposition parties. In comparison to the ruling party, the opposition parties are underfunded. As a result, they proved unable to effectively mobilise, organise, and educate the electorate and to publicly articulate their objectives and alternatives. Their campaigns were mostly limited to the capital and main urban areas; no opposition

152 Interview with Abera Haile Mariam, executive director of the Coalition of Ethiopian Civil Society Organizations for Elections (Addis Ababa, Ethiopia, Inter-Luxury Hotel, 15 August 2024).

153 L Diamond, *The End of the Third Wave and the Global Future of Democracy*, Political Science Series No. 45, Vienna, Austrian Institute for Advanced Studies (HIS) (1997), pp 2–20.

154 *Ibid*; CM Fombad, "Constitutional Reforms and Constitutionalism in Africa: Reflections on Some Current Challenges and Future Prospects", 59 (2011) *Buffalo Law Review*, pp 1020–1027.

party was able to put candidates forward in every corner of the country. Indeed, no opposition party, with the exception of the ECSJ, was able to nominate the minimum number of candidates required to form a government at the federal level.[155] The ruling party ran uncontested in 104 of the 170 constituencies for the HOPR in the Oromia region, with opposition boycotts citing harassment and intimidation.[156] Some parties have reported detention and intimidation of their candidates, leaders, and supporters across the country.[157]

Simply put, the legal framework for party financing, combined with its actual practice, does not create equal opportunities for all political parties to compete in elections. The overwhelming strength of the ruling party's finances means the electoral marketplace is far from being free and fair. In every corner of the country, the PP's electoral chances are significantly better than the opposition's whereas the opposition's chances of winning elections are just about non-existent. As a result, Ethiopian elections have become empty symbolic gestures with predictable outcomes, rather than genuinely democratic competitions which would have uncertain results.

5.2 Weak and frivolous political parties

The post-2018 party-finance system significantly affects not only the playing field but also the strength and viability of the political parties themselves. Genuine democracy requires strong, independent, active, and disciplined political parties.[158] The party-financing system in Ethiopia fails to adhere to the necessary principles of equity and transparency, resulting in the weakening and fragmentation of political parties. Underfunding prevents opposition parties from effectively conducting elections, hindering their capacity to mobilise the electorate and nominate candidates for all

155 The PP successfully registered candidates in all 673 constituencies, consequently fielding 2,432 candidates for all regional state councils and federal parliamentary seats.

156 International Republican Institute and National Democratic Institute, *supra* n. 65, pp 13–15.

157 *Ibid.*

158 S Stocker, et al., "The Missing Piece: Political Parties are Critical to Democracy in Africa", 2024, *Atlantic Council*, pp 1–5.

constituencies.[159] Political parties' rights and privileges are not constitutionally recognised and protected, making them susceptible to self-serving legislation and unfair resource allocation.

Party financing practices are often shrouded in secrecy, leaving even party members and supporters in the dark about the party's funding and expenditure.[160] This contributes significantly to corruption and finance-driven factionalism within opposition political parties, undermining their existence and functions, as well as public trust in them.[161] A prominent political leader holds that there are numerous "briefcase parties" run by political entrepreneurs for personal gains.[162] As a result, political parties all too easily become battlegrounds where factions and party leaders fight each for power and over resources.[163] The public funding system encourages the proliferation of small parties that participate only symbolically in elections and go into hibernation between them.[164] It contributes to the growth of weak and frivolous opposition political parties in ways that hinder democratic transition and consolidation.[165]

5.3 Dominant party with unchecked powers

The post-2018 Ethiopian party-financing framework and its application helps maintain the ruling party's financial dominance. It creates an uneven playing field and prevents fair political competition, as was evident in the 2021 electoral marketplace.[166] It creates the conditions for rule by a permanent dominant-party system. The new dominance of the PP, coupled with the non-constitutionalisation of political parties, ultimately undermines the state of constitutionalism in Ethiopia. As Charles Fombad rightly notes, this

159 Political Parties' Joint Council, *supra* n. 4; Abdu, *supra* n. 96; interview with Adem, *supra* n. 113.

160 Interview with Tilahun, *supra* n. 135.

161 The 2021 national election saw relatively competent parties such as the ECSJ, NaMA, and Balderas for Genuine Democracy, but, post-election, they faced internal crises and factionalism. See Lyons and Verjee, *supra* n. 36.

162 Interview with Tilahun, *supra* n. 135.

163 Anonymous phone interview, *supra* n. 148; Gashaw, *supra* n. 116.

164 As Tilahun opines, most political parties go into hibernation after elections, with only a few remaining active. Interview with Tilahun, *supra* n. 136; Gashaw, *supra* n. 116.

165 Gashaw, *supra* n. 116.

166 See NEBE, *supra* n. 39.

non-constitutionalisation creates the opportunity for incumbent majorities to effect legislation that serves their partisan ends and allows the incumbent party to arbitrarily determine the rules of the political game.[167]

The PP's political hegemony also has powerful effects on the proper functioning of such potential constraints on executive power as Parliament, an independent judiciary, and the usual mechanisms of horizontal accountability. Thus, for instance, the Prime Minister defends the lack of transparency around the Addis Ababa beautification mega-projects by claiming that, since they are funded by foreign partners and local fundraising events, Parliament has no mandate to scrutinise them.[168] At the same time, the ruling PP can designate political parties as terrorist organisations and ban them with little opposition from Parliament.[169]

Recently, for example, Parliament passed the revised immigration proclamation. This granted the Director General of the Office of Immigration and Citizenship Services the power to prevent individuals from leaving Ethiopia on the advice of the security services.[170] Previously, such power had been granted exclusively to the courts.[171] Despite claims about the need to enhance national security and administrative efficiency, the shift from judicial oversight to administrative authority raises major concerns about the potential abuse of power and erosion of judicial checks and balances involved.[172] The PP-dominated Parliament approved this legislation with no serious attention to the views of stakeholders, including numerous human

---

167 Fombad, *supra* n. 21.

168 Addis Standard, *supra* n. 120; Terrefe, *supra* n. 119.

169 For instance, in May 2021 the HOPR unanimously approved the Council of Ministers' recommendation to designate the Tigray People's Liberation Front (TPLF) a terrorist organisation, whereas it removed it from the list in March 2023 with a majority vote, 61 votes against, and five abstentions. See HOPR, "TPLF and 'Shene' Designated as Terrorists", *Parliamentary News*, May 6, 2021, Addis Ababa, https://www.hopr.gov.et/en/web/guest (accessed 4 November 2024).

170 Immigration and Citizenship Service Reestablishment Proclamation No. 1338/2024. The Bill was approved by Parliament in June 2024, but has not yet been published in the Negarit Gazeta.

171 Immigration Proclamation No. 354/2003, Federal Negarit Gazeta 9th Year No. 75, Addis Ababa, 3 July 2003, Article 7.

172 HOPR, "Explanatory Notes on the Immigration and Citizenship Services Reestablishment Draft Proclamation", May 2024, Addis Ababa, Ethiopia (archived at the HOPR).

rights defenders.[173] As noted, this law is open to abuse and potentially limits the activities of a range of democratic actors, including political parties.

6. Conclusion

Ethiopia's post-2018 party-finance regulations continue to create an uneven political landscape that favours the incumbent PP over opposition parties. The shortcomings in the design of party-financing rules, coupled with their misuse and manipulation in an undemocratic political setting, present obstacles to achieving competitive elections and ensuring equal opportunities for all political parties.

This chapter demonstrates that the legal framework governing party funding introduces bias into the electoral marketplace, making it difficult for opposition parties to secure the funding essential to their operations. Flawed regulations surrounding private donations discourage individuals and businesses from supporting these parties, while the ruling PP benefits from a diverse array of income sources, with no income or expenditure limits. The absence of these limits increases the financial disparity between the ruling PP and opposition parties, causing uneven political competition. It has also obscured the purpose of public funding, which above all is to level the political playing field for the purposes of political competition.

The chapter has also illustrated that, despite the 2018 reforms and the promise they held to promote fair competition and mitigate the dominance of the incumbent party, the political landscape remains largely unchanged in the post-2018 period. The PP continues to exhibit the same patterns of manipulation and dominance previously seen under the EPRDF, benefiting from a significant hyper-incumbency advantage and the misuse of state resources for partisan purposes. This environment severely distorts fair political competition. Furthermore, the existing party-finance system undermines the viability of political parties, leading to a proliferation of underfunded and frivolous opposition parties. The government's tactics of coercion and intimidation further constrain opposition parties' ability to garner support from private sources, resulting in an over-reliance on public funding and diaspora contributions, with these jeopardising their independence.

173 During the public hearing, some CSOs and human rights defenders expressed their concerns.

The chapter also underscores an alarming new trend in which political parties flout the transparency regulations, with this fostering an environment ripe for corruption and factionalism (driven by financial interests). This situation is exacerbated by NEBE's weak enforcement of transparency rules and the disengagement of CSOs in ensuring accountability in political party funding.

All in all, the political finance system in Ethiopia has undermined both democracy and constitutionalism by fostering an uneven political landscape that disadvantages opposition parties and skews the electoral marketplace in favour of the ruling PP. This dynamic considerably hampers electoral competitiveness and perpetuates a dominant-party system, posing serious challenges to the prospects for democratic transition and consolidation in Ethiopia.

This chapter therefore advocates for comprehensive reform of political-party financing to ensure a fair playing field and the proper institutionalisation of political parties. It suggests constitutionalising basic political-party rights; setting reasonable limits on private donation and expenditure; placing a reasonable threshold on the allocation of public funding; preventing the abuse of state resources; and enforcing transparency rules. It is essential to make political finance information accessible and to engage CSOs and the media to raise awareness and advocate for transparency and the fair funding of political parties. Overall, a democratic environment with respect for the rule of law is crucial if political parties are to be able to mobilise resources freely.

References

Books, articles, chapters in books, and others

"Abiy Ahmed's Prosperity Party Accused of Diverting Public Resources for Political Training", *Ethiopia Observer*, 16 September 2024, https://www.ethiopiaobserver.com/ (accessed 10 November 2024)

"Ezema Set to Compete in 500 Districts of Ethiopia", *New Business*, 6 February 2021, https://newbusinessethiopia.com/politics/ezema-set-to-compete-in-500-districts-of-ethiopia/ (accessed 20 July 2024)

"PM Abiy Ahmed Pledges thorough Audit of Non-government-Funded Mega Projects amid Transparency Concerns", *Addis Standard*, 6 July 2023, https://addisstandard.com/?p=35966 (accessed 20 August 2024)

Abbink J, "Discomfiture of Democracy? The 2005 Election Crisis in Ethiopia and its Aftermath", 105 (2006) *African Affairs*, pp 173–198

Abdu B, "Elections 2021: Already Favoring the Ruling Party?", *The Reporter*, 31 March 2021, https://www.thereporterethiopia.com/ (accessed 3 August 2024)

Arriola LR and Lyons T, "Ethiopia's 100% Elections", 17 (2016) *Journal of Democracy*, pp 76–88

Assefa G and Yeshanew SA, "Revamping the Electoral Laws of Ethiopia: Major Areas of Reform and Lessons Learned", in SA Yeshanew and AM Ibrahim (eds.), *Righting Human Rights through Legal Reform: Ethiopia's Contemporary Experience*, Vol. XII, Addis Ababa University, School of Law (2020), pp 277–308

Ayele ZA, "Constitutionalism and Electoral Authoritarianism in Ethiopia: From EPRDF to EPP", in CM Fombad and N Steytler (eds.), *Stellenbosch Handbook in African Constitutional Law: Democracy, Elections, and Constitutionalism in Africa*, 1st ed, Oxford University Press (2021), pp 188–194

Berhanu K, "Ethiopia: Beleaguered Opposition under a Dominant Party System", 13 (2009) *Politics*, pp 1–21

Berhanu K, "Political Parties and Political Culture in Ethiopia", in MA Salih (ed.), *African Political Parties: Evolution, Institutionalisation, and Governance*, London, Pluto Press (2003)

Bratt H, *Uneven Playing Field: Understanding Abiy Ahmed's Manipulation of Democracy in Ethiopia*, Uppsala University (2019/2020)

Butler A, "Introduction: Money and Politics", in A Butler (ed.), *Paying for Politics: Party Funding and Political Change in South Africa and the Global South*, South Africa, Jacana Media and Konrad Adenauer Foundation (2010), pp 6–8

Check NA, et al., "The Integrity of Political Finance Systems in Africa: Tackling Political Corruption", International IDEA Policy Paper No. 20, Stockholm, International IDEA (2019)

Choudhry S et al., *Political Party Finance Regulation: Constitutional Reform after the Arab Spring*, Center for Constitutional Transitions and International IDEA (2014)

Degifie Z, "Party-Political Financing, Democracy, and Constitutionalism in Ethiopia", in CM Fombad and N Steytler (eds.), *Stellenbosch Handbooks in African Constitutional Law: Democracy, Elections, and Constitutionalism in Africa*, 1st ed, UK, Oxford University Press, 2021, pp 293–327

Diamond L, *The End of the Third Wave and the Global Future of Democracy*, Political Science Series No. 45, Vienna, Austrian Institute for Advanced Studies (HIS) (1997)

Dibaba SD, "The Merger of Ethiopia People's Revolutionary Democratic Front (EPRDF) into Ethiopia Prosperity Party (EPP) and its Impact on the Constitution", 12 (2021) *International Journal of Scientific & Engineering Research*, pp 961–978

Ethiopian News Agency (ENA), "Abiy Donates over 110 Million Birr Proceeds of Book for Building Schools", *ENA*, 7 August 2020, https://www.ena.et/web/eng/w/en_16188 (accessed 3 August 2024)

European Commission for Democracy through Law, *International Standards of Financing of Political Parties and Election Campaigns*, Conference Reports, Astana, Kazakhstan, 1 December 2008

Fombad CM, "Challenges to Constitutionalism and Constitutional Rights in Africa and the Enabling Role of Political Parties: Lessons and Perspectives from Southern Africa", 55 (2007) The *American Journal of Comparative Law,* pp 1–45

Fombad CM, "Constitutional Reforms and Constitutionalism in Africa: Reflections on Some Current Challenges and Future Prospects", 59 (2011) *Buffalo Law Review,* pp 1020–1027

Gardner T, *The Abiy Project: God, Power and War in the New Ethiopia,* London, C Hurst & Co. (2024)

Gashaw T, "In Ethiopian Politics, Some Parties are about Monetization, Not Representation", *IPI Global Observatory*, 27 September 2024, https://theglobalobservatory.org/2024/09/in-ethiopian-politics-some-parties-are-about-monetization-not-representation/ (accessed 12 November 2024)

Gudina M, "Party Politics, Political Polarisation and the Future of Ethiopian Democracy", Paper 108 (2007) *International Conference on African Development Archives,* pp 1–17

Habtie B, Tsehaye M, et al., "The Ethiopian Diaspora: Their Role in Nation Building and Political Reformation", 1 (2019) *Mekelle University Journal of Political Science and Strategic Studies,* pp 211–222

Hailu G and Alebachew T, "The Quest for Constitutionalising Political Parties in Ethiopia", 2 (2019) *Journal of Citizenship and Morality*, pp 47–49

House of Peoples' Representatives, "Explanatory Notes on the Immigration and Citizenship Services Reestablishment Draft Proclamation", May 2024, Addis Ababa, Ethiopia (archived at the HOPR)

House of Peoples' Representatives, "TPLF and 'Shene' Designated as Terrorists", *Parliamentary News*, 6 May 2021, https://www.hopr.gov.et/en/web/guest (accessed 4 November 2024)

International Crisis Group, "Keeping Ethiopia's Transition on the Rails", 283 (2019) *Africa Report,* pp 1–10

International Republican Institute and National Democratic Institute, "Ethiopia June 21, 2021 National Elections Report", Ethiopia (2021), pp 15–16

Lyons T and Verjee A, "Asymmetric Electoral Authoritarianism? The Case of the 2021 Elections in Ethiopia", 49 (2022) *Review of African Political Economy*, pp 339–354

Mengesha S, "Election Board Threatens Administrative Action over Exaggerated Party Membership Figures", *The Reporter*, 29 June 2024

My Ethiopia, "NEBE suspends eleven political parties for non-compliance", *My Ethiopia*, 22 October 2024, https://myethiopia.co.uk/nebe-suspends-eleven-political-parties-for-non-compliance/ (accessed 13 November 2024)

Nassmacher KH, "Introduction: Political Parties, Funding and Democracy", in R Austin and M Tjernstrom (eds.), *Funding of Political Parties and Election Campaigns: Handbook Series*, Stockholm, Sweden, International IDEA (2003)

National Election Board of Ethiopia (NEBE), "6th National Elections Summary Report", https://nebe.org.et/en/electionresult#undefined (accessed 4 August 2024)

National Election Board of Ethiopia , "Announcement on the Financial Support Granted for the 2020/21 Fiscal Year", 17 May 2022, https://nebe.org.et/en (accessed 4 August 2024)

National Election Board of Ethiopia, "6th National Elections Summary Report", https://nebe.org.et/en/electionresult#undefined (accessed 4 August 2024)

National Election Board of Ethiopia, "Announcement for Political Parties", 28 June 2024, https://nebe.org.et/en/announcments (accessed 3 August 2024)

National Election Board of Ethiopia, "Announcement for Political Parties: 28 June 2024", https://nebe.org.et/en/announcments (accessed 3 August 2024)

National Election Board of Ethiopia, "The Annual Government Support Granted to Political Parties for the 2022 Budget Year", https://www.facebook.com/photo/?fbid=275164771387786&set=a.260907382813525 (accessed on 3 August 2024)

National Election Board of Ethiopia, "The State Support Allocated for Political Parties for the 2021 National Elections", https://nebe.org.et/en/node/534 (accessed 20 July 2024)

National Election Board of Ethiopia, "Updates on the Fund Distribution of Political Parties", https://nebe.org.et/en/node/534 (accessed 20 July 2024)

Őhman M, "Africa", in E Falguera, et al. (eds.), *Funding of Political Parties and Election Campaigns: A Handbook on Political Finance*, Stockholm, Sweden International Institute for Democracy and Electoral Assistance (2014), pp 40–42

Őhman M, "Getting the Political Finance System Right", in E Falguera et al (eds.), *Funding of Political Parties and Election Campaigns: A Handbook on Political Finance*, Stockholm, Sweden, International Institute for Democracy and Electoral Assistance (2014)

Öhman M, "Practical Solutions for the Public Funding of Political Parties and Election Campaigns", in M Őhman and H Zainulbhai (eds.), *Political Finance Regulation: The Global Experience, USA, International Foundation for Electoral Systems* (2009), pp 67–68

Political Parties' Joint Council, "Minutes of a Dialogue between Political Parties on Multiparty Democracy", Addis Ababa, Ethiopia, Inter-Luxury Hotel, 5 June 2023

Saffu Y, "The Funding of Political Parties and Election Campaigns in Africa", in R Austin and M Tjernstrom (eds.), *Funding of Political Parties and Election Campaigns: Handbook Series*, Stockholm, Sweden: International IDEA (2003)

Sahlu S, "Election Board Suspends 'One Ethiopia' Party over Financial Fraud Allegations", *The Reporter*, 13 March 2024

Sahlu S, "Political Parties' Concerns over Federal Housing Corporation's Unfair Office Building Allocation", *The Reporter*, 11 September 2024

Santucci J and Őhman M, "Practical Solutions for the Disclosure of Campaign and Political Party Finance", in M Őhman and H Zainulbhai (eds.), *Political Finance Regulation: The Global Experience*, USA, International Foundation for Electoral Systems (2009), pp 35–40

Stocker S, et al., "The Missing Piece: Political Parties are Critical to Democracy in Africa", 2024, *Atlantic Council*, pp 1–5

Terrefe B, "Urban Layers of Political Rupture: The 'New' Politics of Addis Ababa's Megaprojects", 14 (2020) *Journal of Eastern African Studies*, pp 375–395

Teshome W, "Ethiopian Opposition Political Parties and Rebel Fronts: Past and Present", 4 (2009) *International Journal of Human and Social Sciences*, pp 60–68

Teshome W, "Political Finance in Africa: Ethiopia as a Case Study", 4 (2009) *International Journal of Human and Social Science*, pp 1641–1649

Teshome W, "Prosperity 'Federalism'?", *The Awash Post*, 1 November 2020, https://www.awashpost.com/prosperity-federalism/ (accessed 10 November 2024)

Tronvoll K, "The Ethiopian 2010 Federal and National Elections: Re-Establishing the One-Party State", 110 (2011) *African Affairs*, pp 1–16

Van Biezen I, *Financing Political Parties and Election Campaigns: Guidelines*, Germany, Council of Europe Publishing (2003)

Yeshanew SA and Ibrahim AM, "Righting Human Rights through Legal Reform: The Ethiopian Experience from Past to Present", in SA Yeshanew and AM Ibrahim (eds.), *Righting Human Rights through Legal Reform: Ethiopia's Contemporary Experience*, Vol. XII, Addis Ababa University, School of Law (2020), pp 277–308

Yimenu B, "Continuities and Changes in Electoral Authoritarianism: Evidence from Ethiopia", 2024, *Regional & Federal Studies*, pp 12–13

Yusuf S, *Drivers of Ethnic Conflict in Contemporary Ethiopia*, Monograph 202, Institute for Security Studies (2019)

Zainulbhai H, "Practical Solutions for Political Finance Enforcement", in M Őhman and H Zainulbhai (eds.), *Political Finance Regulation: The Global Experience*, USA, International Foundation for Electoral Systems (2009), pp 86–94

Table of legislation

International instruments

Africa Union, African Union Convention on Preventing and Combating Corruption, Adopted by the 2nd Ordinary Session of the Assembly of the Union, Maputo, 11 July 2003

United Nations, United Nations Convention against Corruption: General Assembly Resolution 58/4, Adopted 31 October 2003, Entered into Force 14 December 2005, 2349 UNTS 41

National legislation

Directive No. 16/2021, A Directive for Providing Government Funding to Political Parties", NEBE, 25 March 2021, Addis Ababa

Immigration and Citizenship Service Reestablishment Proclamation No. 1338/2024

Immigration Proclamation No. 354/2003, Federal Negarit Gazeta 9th Year No. 75, Addis Ababa, 3 July 2003

Proclamation No. 1/1995, The Federal Democratic Republic of Ethiopia (FDRE) Constitution, Federal Negarit Gazeta, 1st Year No. 1, Addis Ababa, 8 December 1994

Proclamation No. 1133/2019, National Electoral Board of Ethiopia Establishment Proclamation, Federal Negarit Gazeta, 25tth Year, No. 71, 6 June 2019

Proclamation No. 1162/2019, The Ethiopian Electoral, Political Parties Registration and Election's Code of Conduct Proclamation, Federal Negarit Gazeta, 25th Year, No. 97, Addis Ababa, 16 October 2019

Proclamation No. 1238/2021, Media Proclamation, Federal Negarit Gazeta, 27th Year No. 22, Addis Ababa, Ethiopia, 5 April 2021

Proclamation No. 46/ 93, A Proclamation Providing for the Registration of Political Parties, The Transitional Government of Ethiopia (1993), Addis Ababa

Proclamation No. 573/ 2008, The Revised Political Parties Registration, Federal Negarit Gazeta, 14th Year No. 62, Addis Ababa, 24 September 2008

Conclusions

Chapter 18 Party Constitutionalisation and the State of Democracy in Sub-Saharan Africa: Key Findings and Possible Ways Forward

Johannes Socher and Charles M Fombad

1. Introduction

According to the 2024 Afrobarometer survey "Democracy at Risk – The People's Perspective", Africans continue to overwhelmingly reject one-party rule and prefer democracy to any other kind of government.[1] At the same time, less than half of Africans think their countries are democratic, and only slightly more than one-third of them are satisfied with the way democracy works in their countries.[2] As the case studies in this volume illustrate, this dissatisfaction is also a reflection of the way Africans experience multipartyism and how the latter is shaped by the constitutional and legal frameworks in which it operates.

A first general conclusion that can be drawn from this volume is that party constitutionalisation in sub-Saharan Africa is not influenced by colonial legacies to the same extent as are many other areas of African constitutional law. On the contrary, it may be said that across the anglophone, francophone, and lusophone divides, almost all sub-Saharan African countries follow a similar approach in that they understand the function of political parties in the constitutional system principally by combining elements of the "parties as public utilities" model with those of the "defending democracy" model, such that political parties are constitutionally designed as permanent organisations with public functions that go beyond those that are instrumental solely for holding elections.[3] Overall, we can therefore

1 Afrobarometer, "African Insights 2024: Democracy at Risk – The People's Perspective", *Afrobarometer* (2024), p 5, https://www.afrobarometer.org/wp-content/uploads/2024/05/Afrobarometer_FlagshipReport2024_English.pdf (accessed 27 March 2025).

2 *Ibid.*

3 The only exception is Mauritius, where the constitutional function of parties is limited to elections. On the different models, see J Socher, "Constitutionalisation of Political Parties: International Standards and the Experience of Continental Europe", in this volume.

agree with Sujit Choudhry that "it is preferrable to think about regulating political parties in *any* legal tradition".[4] At the same time, this does of course not mean that experiences of party constitutionalisation are not also shaped by specific regional contexts. In the case of sub-Saharan Africa, several key findings may be derived below (in section 2) from the preceding chapters in this volume. In view of these findings, we then make some concrete suggestions for possible ways forward (in section 3).

2. Key findings

A first key finding is that the constitutionalisation of political parties is the norm in sub-Saharan Africa. All 12 case-study countries in this volume have constitutionalised political parties in one way or another. An explicit commitment to multipartyism is sometimes additionally constitutionalised. Against the background of past one-party regimes in most countries, some constitutions also either prohibit the creation of a one-party state or guarantee the right *not* to join a political party. However, remnants of constitutionalised one-party rule still exist in some instances, as can be seen, for example, from the way in which the Ugandan constitution leaves a return to the "movement system" open as an abiding possibility.[5]

While references to political parties in constitutional provisions can be found across sub-Saharan Africa, such references vary significantly in their scope and depth. The constitution of Cameroon, for instance, merely recognises the right to form political parties but otherwise leaves the specification of the exact nature, scope and limits of that right to a political-party law – the effect of which was that, until the enactment of such a law in 1990, the lack of regulation amounted to an indirect party ban. The Ethiopian and Zimbabwean constitutions also refer to political parties only incidentally, while in Mauritius, party constitutionalisation is limited to stipulating registration requirements for the purpose of elections.

In most cases, however, dedicated chapters in the constitution regulate political parties to some extent and outline their main rights and obligations. Moreover, except for Zimbabwe, all of the cases studied in this volume make party status dependent on registration with the state. On

4 S Choudhry, "Constitutional Design and Political Parties", in VC Jackson and M Khosla (eds.), *Redefining Comparative Constitutional Law: Essays for Mark Tushnet*, Oxford, Oxford University Press (2025), pp 310–326, p 324.

5 See sections 69 and 70 of the Constitution of Uganda, 1995.

the one hand, requirements for registration may be necessary to avoid the fragmentation of the political landscape; on the other hand, the example of Rwanda shows that registration requirements and processes can also be used deliberately as a means to ensure that an opposition party is rendered entirely dependent on the goodwill of the authorities. Conversely, the case study on Zimbabwe demonstrates that a complete lack of a registration process for political parties can also work against opposition parties and lead ultimately to their (self-) destruction. With these general observations having been made, we now discuss a number of specific key findings.

2.1 Insufficient or inadequate constitutional power-sharing arrangements

Critically, constitutional power-sharing arrangements are insufficient or inadequate. As almost all of the case studies show, particularistic interests based on ethnicity, religion or region play a major role in party politics in sub-Saharan countries. The common constitutional response, namely to take an integrationist approach by prohibiting or ignoring these considerations, seems to have little or no effect. This is particularly evident if one considers the widespread constitutional prohibition of ethnicity-based political parties, a prohibition which is nonetheless almost never used as a justification for actual party bans, probably due to its perceived sensitivity.[6] Other measures aimed at fostering inter-ethnic cooperation – such as requiring parties to have a national presence or representatives of different regions in their governing bodies – seem to fare better, albeit that such requirements can also erect significant obstacles to the emergence of new political parties.

2.2 Absence of, or unclear and ineffective, requirements for intra-party democracy

Although a number of sub-Saharan African countries demand that political parties adhere to democratic principles or even explicitly require them to be internally democratic, what this means in concrete terms often remains

6 See J Socher and CM Fombad, "Prohibition of Ethnic Political Parties and Constitutionalism in Sub-Saharan Africa", in CM Fombad, N Steytler, and Y Fessha (eds.), *Ethnicity and Constitutionalism in Africa,* Oxford, Oxford University Press, forthcoming.

unclear. What *is* clear, though, is that even where such requirements exist, they do not prevent the widespread undemocratic practices that have been observed in almost all of the case studies in this volume. The most obvious illustration of this is that party leaders are frequently hand-picked in untransparent processes rather than elected by regular party members in a bottom-up process. Examples of such practices abound in the case studies, with some of them described in dramatic terms – parties in Senegal, for instance, are subject to "the iron law of oligarchy", those in Nigeria are under the power of "godfathers and party barons", and Kenya is fraught with "a cult of party leadership".

Undemocratic practices within political parties often result in internal conflict, which in turn can lead to fragmentation or defection of individual members.[7] To address this, some constitutions sanction defection. For example, in Nigeria, Members of Parliament lose their seats when migrating from one political party to another; however, an exception in the relevant law exists for cases where the defection is a result of a "division" within the party. As the Nigerian case study in this volume shows, this exception in the law is widely used by politicians as a loophole to avoid losing their seats in parliament.

2.3 Ineffective regulations for holding ruling parties accountable

Another key finding concerns the effectiveness of regulations designed to hold ruling parties accountable. Many case studies in this volume show that the use of state resources by ruling parties for their benefit is commonplace. The study on Liberia, for instance, details how civil servants campaign for the ruling party during working hours and how government buildings and vehicles are used for that purpose. In Rwanda, dedicated regulations exist to prevent the abuse of public resources for partisan purposes, but a lack of proper enforcement means that state resources can still be used indirectly to help the ruling party. In the chapter on Mozambique, the authors even speak of a "Frelimisation" of public institutions, one in which public entities are under the directorship of party affiliates and companies receive lucrative contracts with the state in exchange for party donations. In Uganda, the ruling party's use of state resources is exacerbated by extensive military

7 On this problem, see generally M Khosla and M Vaishnav, "Democracy and Defections", 22 (2024) *International Journal of Constitutional Law*, pp 400–430.

involvement in the country's economy and public service delivery, as well as by an increasing militarisation of public-security and law-enforcement functions that are normally executed by civilian authorities.

2.4 The increasing importance of regulating party agreements

Although alliances of multiple parties under an umbrella name are a well-known phenomenon in sub-Saharan Africa, the rise of coalition governments in many countries that have long been ruled by a single party has highlighted the increased importance of formally recognising and regulating such cooperation. In Kenya, an alliance of opposition parties was able to break the decades-long dominance of the Kenya African National Union, but the collapse of that alliance only three years later – as a result of a dispute over a legally non-binding memorandum of understanding – revealed a gap in the regulatory framework at the time. Consequently, a new party law with elaborate provisions on party coalitions was enacted.

While the detailed nature of Kenya's framework regulating coalitions is exceptional, some other countries at least provide for the possibility of multiple parties forming coalitions. Yet, as the example of Uganda shows, gaps in these frameworks can be used by ruling parties to co-opt smaller opponents: since Uganda's party law simply mentions "alliances" but does not say anything about their creation, their status, or the relationship between their constituent parties, this has created uncertainty as to whether the leader of the Democratic Party could indeed sign an agreement with the ruling party that was widely perceived as a "sell-out" of the country's oldest opposition party.

2.5 Limited recognition and weak protection of opposition parties

Another key finding relates to specific regulations addressed at opposition parties. As many examples in almost all of the case studies attest, the existing provisions in the constitutional and legal frameworks recognising and protecting political opposition are insufficient.[8] In particular, while many constitutional frameworks recognise the position of an opposition leader,

8 For a detailed comparative study building on the case studies of Kenya, Uganda and Zimbabwe in this volume, see J Socher, "Constitutionalisation of Political Parties, Multipartyism and Political Opposition in Anglophone Eastern Africa", 57 (2024) *Verfas-*

this seems to be largely symbolic and is generally limited to a parliamentary role.

An interesting exception is Senegal, where the position has recently been introduced and was given not to the leader of the party with the second-highest number of seats in parliament but to the candidate that comes second in the presidential election. The exact status, rights and duties of Senegal's opposition leader are however still unclear, as the relevant organic law has not yet been enacted. Uncertainty about the exact role and independence of the opposition leader seems to exist in other countries as well. In Mozambique, for example, the acceptance of the Renamo leader to take on the position and the privileges associated with it has raised suspicion about his independence from the ruling party.

If recognition of opposition parties is only limited, constitutional and legal frameworks aimed at protecting the members and supporters of these parties against intimidation, harassment and violence are either absent or not applied. As the different examples of "majoritarian abuse" in the case study on Senegal show, this observation is unfortunately applicable not only to authoritarian regimes such as Cameroon and Uganda, but also to the seemingly more democratic countries in sub-Saharan Africa.

2.6 Gaps in party-financing regulation and weak enforcement mechanisms

Although many constitutional systems in sub-Saharan Africa envisage laws dedicated to issues of party funding, their enactment is often still pending. The Electoral Code of Cameroon, for instance, envisages a special instrument regulating private party funding, but to date it has not been enacted. In Senegal, a recently introduced amendment to the constitution foresees the enactment of a dedicated party finance law but, again, no such law has been enacted so far. As the case studies on these and certain other countries in this volume show, the general lack of dedicated party financing laws points to significant gaps in the regulatory system. In Mozambique, for

sung und Recht in Übersee/World Comparative Law. On the potential for empowering African opposition parties more broadly, see also AK Abebe, "Tackling Winner-Takes-All Politics in Africa: Inclusive Governance through Constitutional Empowerment of Opposition Parties", in T Ginsburg, AZ Huw, and T Khaitan (eds.), *The Entrenchment of Democracy: The Comparative Constitutional Design of Elections, Parties and Voting*, Cambridge, Cambridge University Press (2024), pp 119–135.

example, private funding of political parties is not regulated at all, thereby leaving the door wide open for corruption.

In cases where private party funding is regulated, limitations are often placed on donations from abroad. This has led to criticism, especially in countries where there are no exceptions for support from the diaspora – a situation that arguably results in discrimination against citizens residing abroad . Some countries provide for other exceptions to the prohibition for party financing from abroad. In South Africa, the prohibition applies only to foreign governments and agencies, whereas foreign individuals are allowed to make donations up to a certain amount. Similarly, in Senegal in-kind contributions from abroad are exempt from the prohibition (making it easy to circumvent the latter).

When it comes to the availability of public funding, the case studies in this volume suggest that sub-Saharan Africa is roughly split in two halves. While Liberia, Mauritius, Mozambique, Nigeria, and Senegal do not provide public funds to political parties, public party funding is available in Cameroon, Ethiopia, Kenya, Rwanda, Senegal, South Africa, and Zimbabwe. Such funding is generally aimed at supporting the functioning of political parties and establishing a level playing field; nevertheless, the example of Rwanda shows that state funding of parties can also be used by the government to control the opposition. Moreover, an elaborate party funding system in Ethiopia seems not to have made any discernible difference in altering the imbalance between the ruling party and its much less powerful competitors.

Further gaps are observed in the regulation of party spending: in Ethiopia, for example, there are no spending limits at all. In many other countries, such limits do exist but the enforcement mechanisms are weak. In Mauritius, the legislation on party spending is outdated and no enforcement mechanism is in place to impose sanctions outside of election periods. In Nigeria, the sanction mechanism to enforce spending limits has not been able to curb the extreme monetisation of the country's party politics. In South Africa, the sanction mechanism for non-compliance is so lenient that parties often prefer not to comply rather than expend resources on ensuring compliance; in addition, sanctions have been applied in practice only on very few reported occasions.

2.7 Lack of independent oversight

While many sub-Saharan African countries have electoral management bodies (EMBs) or other fourth-branch institutions to oversee political parties, this is far from always being the case. In Cameroon, the Ministry of Territorial Administration is tasked with party oversight, thereby exposing opposition parties to the whims and caprices of the ruling party. Similarly, the Rwandan Governance Board is an executive-controlled entity and has been accused of arbitrarily denying registration to opposition parties. In Senegal, the opposition party PASTEF has been dissolved by the Ministry of the Interior.

Where party oversight bodies are indeed separate from the executive, their status, structures and governance are not always constitutionalised but left instead to statutory law, thus making them vulnerable to political interference. But even where this is the case, maintaining their independence from the executive is often challenging. In Nigeria, for example, the EMB's independent status is guaranteed in the constitution and its commissioners have to be non-partisan. However, as the Nigerian case study in the volume shows, this has not prevented questionable appointments. It is hence interesting to note the different approach taken in Mozambique, where the independence of the electoral commission is ensured not through non-partisanship but through equal representation of party members as commissioners.[9] A third approach is taken by Kenya, where the creation of a separate Office of the Registrar of Political Parties seems to have contributed to improving intra-party democracy and increasing the transparency of party financing.

At a more practical level, many case studies in this volume indicate that oversight bodies have insufficient capacities and resources to execute their conferred functions, making them vulnerable to corruption and compromising their independence and autonomy.

9 The African Court on Human and Peoples' Rights found that having representatives of political parties as commissioners is not necessarily a violation of the obligation to establish an independent and impartial electoral body. See *Suy Bi Gohore Emile & Others v Côte d'Ivoire*, Application No. 044/2019, Judgement, 15 July 2020. See also CM Fombad and J Socher, "African Regional Standards for Regulating Political Parties", in this volume.

2.8 Limited impact of international and regional standards and bodies

Finally, despite the existence of a broad range of international and regional standards and bodies relevant for the regulation of political parties, the case studies suggest that their impact at the domestic level is fairly limited. There are many reasons for this, and the chapter on regional standards identifies some of them. The African Charter on Democracy, Elections and Governance, the most relevant regional instrument for the regulation of political parties, has been ratified by less than three-quarters of African Union member states, and implementation by many state parties remains incomplete. At a sub-regional level, only the Economic Community of West African States (ECOWAS) and Southern African Development Community (SADC) have instruments in place that could influence the approach adopted by their member states to regulate political parties at the domestic level.

The case studies suggest, furthermore, that supranational enforcement of these standards plays only a marginal role. Regional courts became active merely in a few cases, and when they did, they normally did not interfere substantially. For example, in the case before the ECOWAS Court challenging the dissolution of the PASTEF party in Senegal, the court limited its analysis to simply recognising that, in terms of Senegalese law, the government has the authority to dissolve political parties by presidential decree.

3. Possible ways forward

Against the background of these findings, what are possible ways forward that could lead towards more robust constitutional and legal frameworks for regulating political parties in sub-Saharan Africa? In general, the widespread historical experience of one-party regimes and the continued existence of dominant parties in many of these countries arguably calls for constitutionalising an explicit commitment to multipartyism and entrenching at least the most basic principles of political-party regulation where this is not already the case. In addition, a number of specific suggestions can be made.

Firstly, new ways should be considered to channel ethnic considerations in African party politics. As some of the case studies also recommend, inspiration could be taken from Arend Lijphart's model of consociational democracy to better manage ethnic diversity with measures that integrate, and protect, particularistic interests in the foundations of the political system.[10] Lesser-known models to accommodate ethnic considerations such as the best-loser system in Mauritius could be studied in more detail to draw lessons for other political systems on the continent.

Secondly, considering the undemocratic processes and structures that are widespread among many African political parties, a strong argument can be made for the constitutionalisation of the requirement of internal political-party democracy, combined with strong oversight and enforcement mechanisms. Apart from drawing on the experiences of the few African countries that have constitutionally entrenched this requirement, one could also take inspiration from countries outside of Africa that have done so too. For example, the requirement is enshrined in the German Basic Law and has been further concretised in the country's Political Parties Act. While the details would have to be adapted to each country's realities, a parallel regulation could make use of the principles developed in German constitutional doctrine. The experience of Nigeria with the principle suggests, furthermore, that some kind of internal dispute resolution mechanism should be established to reduce the case-load of oversight bodies mandated to decide on internal party disputes.

Thirdly, although the example of Uganda shows that coalition agreements can be used to co-opt entire opposition parties, Kenya's positive experience with coalitions illustrates how they can also provide a tool for the opposition to overcome fragmentation and join forces against ruling parties. In order to avoid uncertainties over the status and contents of such agreements, these could be made legally binding, with the basic features and requirements outlined in the agreements. Moreover, the approach taken by Senegal in conferring the role of opposition leader to the presidential candidate with the second-highest votes is an interesting departure from the practice in other African countries and should be seriously considered as an alternative in countries with presidential systems. While awarding such a "consolation prize" might entail the risk of co-option by the ruling party, it has at least the potential to strengthen the significance of the position and would reflect the political reality that the most powerful opposition politicians in the presidential systems of sub-Saharan Africa do not compete for parliamentary seats but for the office of the president.

10 A Lijphart, *The Politics of Accommodation: Pluralism and Democracy in the Netherlands,* Berkeley, University of California Press (1968).

Fourth, the legal frameworks regulating party financing need to be improved. Limitations on funding from abroad often work disproportionally against opposition parties and should be reconsidered. Where state funding does not already exist, the provision of such funds could reduce the reliance of parties on private funding and engender a more level playing field. As suggested by international standards, reasonable limitations on campaign expenditure could also be introduced to ensure that the free choice of voters is not undermined or the democratic process distorted.[11] To improve oversight of political-party financing, independent supervisory bodies need to be established or, where they already exist, strengthened.

Fifth, the potential of regional and international standards could be leveraged more effectively. Initiatives such as the preparation of a study on the implementation of the Freedom of Association Guidelines by the African Commission on Human and Peoples' Rights are welcome developments, but further specific guidance on the regulation of political parties on issues such as party financing and oversight would be important steps towards strengthening the existing constitutional and legal frameworks.[12] Regional bodies, furthermore, could issue recommendations upon request on specific planned reforms touching on the constitutionalisation of political parties, such as the Venice Commission does for the member states of the Council of Europe. In addition, sub-regional and regional approaches to election observation could be developed and further harmonised, using the guidelines developed by SADC and other international and regional organisations as an inspiration. Provisions guaranteeing and protecting election observation by civil society organisations could enhance multipartyism and the integrity of election processes to rebuild trust among Africans in democracy.

---

11 See UN Human Rights Committee, General Comment No. 25: Article 25 (Participation in Public Affairs and the Right to Vote), 12 July 1996, CCPR/C/21/Rev.1/Add.7, paragraph 19.

12 African Commission on Human and Peoples' Rights, *Guidelines on Freedom of Association and Assembly in Africa*, May 2017. See Fombad and Socher *supra* n. 9.

References

Books, articles, chapters in books, and others

Abebe AK, "Tackling Winner-Takes-All Politics in Africa: Inclusive Governance through Constitutional Empowerment of Opposition Parties", in T Ginsburg, AZ Huw, and T Khaitan (eds.), *The Entrenchment of Democracy: The Comparative Constitutional Design of Elections, Parties and Voting*, Cambridge, Cambridge University Press (2024), pp 119–135

Afrobarometer, "African Insights 2024: Democracy at Risk – The People's Perspective", *Afrobarometer* (2024), https://www.afrobarometer.org/wp-content/uploads/2024/05/Afrobarometer_FlagshipReport2024_English.pdf (accessed 27 March 2025)

Choudhry S, "Constitutional Design and Political Parties", in VC Jackson and M Khosla (eds.), *Redefining Comparative Constitutional Law: Essays for Mark Tushnet*, Oxford, Oxford University Press (2025), pp 310–326

Khosla M and Vaishnav M, "Democracy and Defections", *International Journal of Constitutional Law* 22 (2024), pp 400–430

Lijphart A, *The Politics of Accommodation: Pluralism and Democracy in the Netherlands*, Berkeley, University of California Press (1968)

Socher J, "Constitutionalisation of Political Parties, Multipartyism and Political Opposition in Anglophone Eastern Africa", Verfassung und Recht in Übersee/World Comparative Law, forthcoming

Socher J and Fombad CM, "Prohibition of Ethnic Political Parties and Constitutionalism in Sub-Saharan Africa", in CM Fombad, N Steytler and Y Fessha (eds.), *Ethnicity and Constitutionalism in Africa,* Oxford, Oxford University Press, forthcoming

Table of cases

African Court on Human and Peoples' Rights, *Suy Bi Gohore Emile & Others v Côte d'Ivoire*, Application No. 044/2019, Judgement, 15 July 2020

Table of legislation

National legislation

Constitution of Uganda, 1995

Comments, guidance, and opinions by international bodies

African Commission on Human and Peoples' Rights, *Guidelines on Freedom of Association and Assembly in Africa*, May 2017

UN Human Rights Committee, General Comment No. 25: Article 25 (Participation in Public Affairs and the Right to Vote), 12 July 1996, CCPR/C/21/Rev.1/Add.7

Information on Contributors

Abdulrauf, Lukman, is Associate Professor of Law in the Department of Public Law at the University of Ilorin, Nigeria, and a Fellow of the Institute for International and Comparative Law at the University of Pretoria, South Africa. His teaching and research interests focus on constitutional law, with a particular emphasis on its intersection with the digital space.

Adalima, José, is Assistant Professor of Anthropology at Eduardo Mondlane University, Mozambique. His research focuses on large-scale investments in land, economic transformation, and democratisation.

Bwire, Buluma, holds a PhD in comparative constitutional law from the University of Nairobi, and has extensive practical knowledge and experience working, researching, publishing, and teaching on governance, anti-corruption, democracy, rule of law, and sexual and gender-based violence.

Cheng, Mai, is Professor of Law at East China University of Political Science and Law, China. One of his primary research areas is African constitutional law.

Degifie, Zelalem Eshetu, is Assistant Professor of Law at Wollo University, School of Law, Ethiopia. He holds an LLM in comparative public law and good governance and is currently pursuing his LLD at the University of Pretoria, South Africa. His research interests encompass constitutional amendment, political parties, civil-military relations and civil society organizations.

Diop, Abdou Khadre, is Associate Professor of Public Law at the Université Numérique Cheikh Hamidou Kane, Senegal. He also serves as President of the Senegalese Association of Constitutional Law (ASDC) and as Vice President for West Africa in the African Network of Constitutional Lawyers (ANCL).

Fombad, Charles Manga, is Professor of Law and Director of the Institute for International and Comparative Law in Africa (ICLA), Faculty of Law, University of Pretoria. In the course of a career that has spanned over 30 years he has more than 180 accredited outputs and has received several prizes for his research.

Gumbo, Bekezela, is a political scientist and African studies scholar. He has held academic positions in Canada, the United Kingdom, and Southern Africa, and his work explores institutional reform, political transitions, civic space, and inclusive governance in Africa. He holds a PhD in African studies from the University of the Free State, South Africa, and currently serves as a researcher and network facilitator for the EU-SEE (System for Enabling Environment for Civil Society) project, while also supporting evidence-based advocacy through his work with Hivos.

Nkuubi, James, is a scholar and activist specializing in constitutional and human rights law with an LLD focused on militarisation, peace, and sustainable development, complemented by a Master's in human rights and democratisation in Africa, from the Centre for Human Rights, University of Pretoria, South Africa. His work, both through academia and activism, concentrates on security sector reform, citizen resilience, and resistance to state-led militarisation across Africa. He has published extensively on militarisation, electoral security, and liberative politics. James actively engages in strategic activism and research to address militarism and militarisation's impact on democracy and human rights in Africa.

Nuvunga, Adriano, is Assistant Professor of Political Science at Eduardo Mondlane University, Mozambique, a prominent human rights advocate, and a leading voice in civil society across Africa.

Purmah, Neel Raamandarsingh, is Lecturer in Law at Middlesex University, Mauritius. His main areas of research include constitutional law and public international law.

Socher, Johannes, is a Senior Postdoctoral Fellow and former Walter Benjamin Fellow (DFG) at the Institute for International and Comparative Law in Africa (ICLA), Faculty of Law, University of Pretoria, South Africa. He is a member of the German government's expert roster for election observation missions and an executive member of the African Network of Constitutional Lawyers (ANCL), where he represents non-African members.

Thuynsma, Heather, is Senior Lecturer in the Department of Political Sciences at the University of Pretoria, South Africa. Her research interests have grown from her extensive experience of working with political parties on various campaigns in the United States and across the African continent.

Tichok, Ajereboh Jespa, is a PhD candidate in the Department of Public Law at the Faculty of Law and Political Science, University of Bamenda, Cameroon. He is a practicing lawyer and holds an LLM in International and Human Rights Law from the University of Notre Dame Law School, United States. Since 2007, he has served as an international election observer, electoral expert, and legal analyst with organisations such as the African Union, the Carter Center, and the National Democratic Institute for International Affairs (NDI).

Yeakula, Gerald Dan, is a candidate for the Doctor of Laws degree at the University of Pretoria, South Africa. He is Assistant Professor of Law at the Liberia School of Law and Program Manager at the Center for Transparency and Accountability in Liberia (CENTAL).

Ziso, Edson, teaches in the Department of Politics & International Relations, University of Adelaide, South Australia, where he is also a Visiting Research Fellow. He researches and writes on a wide-range of issues cutting across political economy, governance in the Global South, foreign policy, South-South and North-South relations, non-Western international relations and international public policy.

Index